Suicide: A Global Perspective

Edited By

Maurizio Pompili

Department of Neurosciences
Mental Health and Sensory Functions
Sapienza University of Rome
Italy

and

McLean Hospital
Harvard Medical School
USA

CONTENTS

FOREWORD

Suicide and non-lethal suicidal behaviors represent a global public health problem with estimates of around one-million suicides yearly and likely 20 to 25 million suicide attempts per year. Although controversial, if United States-based estimates of the number of people intimately and negatively impacted by suicide are extrapolated to the rest of the world, an additional six million people world-wide become suicide survivors on an annual basis. One suicide is a tragedy – one million suicides is a catastrophe that cannot be ignored!

To the extent that I can generalize from my experience as a suicidologist for over 20 years, and the concerted efforts of the World Health Organization, the International Association for Suicide Prevention, and the International Academy for Suicide Research notwithstanding, for most of us in the field, our efforts at understanding and preventing suicide and other suicide-related behaviors tend to be focused within national, regional, or local parameters. That is, although we may be rightfully channeling our research and prevention efforts to our particular cultural settings, doing so in the absence of a global perspective on suicidal behaviors represents a form of "tunnel vision" that many would agree parallels the psychological condition that brings most people to the brink of suicide. Thus, it is time to seriously move beyond our tendency towards "cultural encapsulation" to learn how suicide research, prevention and intervention perspectives outside of our national borders can provide a broader context to inform our local initiatives.

To that end, I am very pleased to be writing this foreword to Suicide: A Global Perspective edited by Dr. Maurizio Pompili. In this volume, Dr. Pompili has brought together a host of international experts in suicidology to provide a global context for understanding suicide and suicidal behavior. Chapters in this text will serve to increase our understanding of both the unique aspects of suicidal behavior between continents as well as highlight some of the important risk factors for suicide that are more common across continental, national, and cultural boarders. The chapters in this volume have provided an impetus for me to think outside my national and cultural milieu in my work as a suicidologist. I trust it will do the same for you as well.

James R. Rogers
Consortium for Leadership in Evaluation, Assessment and Research
411 Wolf Ledges Parkway, Suite 106
Akron, OH 44311
USA

PREFACE

This book is the result of contribution from scholars belonging to different fields that are all dedicated researchers in suicidology. More and more often we are faced with the fact that suicide is not properly prevented despite the enormous knowledge worldwide.

Suicide is the leading cause of death for people worldwide, and one of the three leading causes of death for young people under 25. Every year, approximately one million people die by suicide - one death every two minutes. The World Health Organization estimates that by the year 2020, this annual toll of suicide deaths will have risen to one and a half million, and suicide will represent 2.4% of the global burden of disease. Suicide deaths account for more than half of all violent deaths in the world - more than all deaths from wars and homicides combined.

Every year, many million more people make serious suicide attempts which, while they do not result in death, require medical treatment and mental health care, and reflect severe personal unhappiness or illness. Million more people - the family members and close friends of those who die by suicide — are bereaved and affected by suicide each year, with the impact of this loss often lasting for a lifetime.

Suicide exacts huge psychological and social costs, and the economic costs of suicide to society (lost productivity, health and social care costs) are estimated at many billions of dollars each year.

Because almost a quarter of suicides are of teenagers and young adults aged less than 25 years (250,000 suicides each year), suicide is a leading cause of premature death, accounting for more than 20 million years of healthy life lost.

There are substantial variations in suicide rates among different countries, and, to some extent, these differences reflect cultural differences to suicide. Cultural views and attitudes towards suicide influence both whether people will make suicide attempts and whether suicides will be reported accurately. Suicide rates, as reported to the World Health Organisation, are highest in Eastern European countries including Lithuania, Estonia, Belarus and the Russian Federation. These countries have suicide rates of the order of 45 to 75 per 100000.

Scholars worldwide have puzzled over what makes a person suicidal and what individuals who die by suicide have in their minds. Most often the focus is not on the motives for suicide, nor on the phenomenology of this rare act. It is rather on what is found from small cohorts of suicidal individuals. Each day, dozens of papers on suicide are added to the enormous literature related to this topic.

Models of suicide are less frequently encountered in the literature. It is difficult to produce a sound synthesis of a complex phenomenon, after which many in the scientific community comment that the model omits key features that are not easily identifiable. The lack of models that can actually help in the management of suicide is reflected by the fact that suicide rates have been only mildly changed by the tremendous efforts in this field.

Various models have been reported for suicide such as (1) the scientific view - suicide is caused by factors beyond the individual's control (the determinist view of suicide), (2) the "Cry for Help" - individuals who die by suicide do not want to die but are seeking help to reduce their distress, (3) suicide as sociogenic - social forces causes suicide (Durkheim's altruistic, egoistic, anomic and fatalistic suicide). More recently, a stress-diathesis model has been proposed in which the risk for suicidal acts is determined not merely by a psychiatric illness (the stressor) but also by a diathesis. This diathesis may be reflected in a tendency to experience more suicidal ideation and to be more impulsive and, therefore, to be more likely to act on suicidal feelings.

Many clinicians perform careful assessments for suicidal risk in their patients and assume that suitable treatments will resolve this risk. They rarely investigate suicidality in-depth in their patients. The key words here are from the Ancient Greek aphorism "Know yourself" that were inscribed in the pronaos (forecourt) of the Temple of Apollo at Delphi. There are myths and resistances that impair a proper understanding of suicidal people. Many believe that talking about suicide will reinforce the patient's suicidal ideation, others believe that, when patients talk about suicide, the risk of suicidal behaviour is low. ("Those who talk about it don't do it."). Myths and stigmatization should be replaced by a meaningful phenomenology of suicide that involves a true understanding of the suicidal individual's intimate world.

Increasing globalization, ease of international travel, and refugees and asylum seekers from war and disaster have swelled the number of immigrants worldwide. People who are alienated from their country and culture of origin are vulnerable to various stresses, mental health problems, loneliness and suicidal behaviour. Suicide prevention strategies, tailored to the specific needs of migrant groups, exist in many countries. These programs typically focus on understanding the specific cultural and religious attitudes to mental health and suicide of the migrant group, reasons for migration, and family and social structures. Interventions include educational and social programs designed to identify stresses, teach coping skills, promote use of preventative health practices, improve access to health services and encourage socialising. Suicide prevention programs for migrants may require involvement, championship or leadership from religious or community leaders to be successful.

During the last three decades we have learned a great deal about the causes of this complex behaviour. Suicide has biological, cultural, social and psychological risk factors. People from socially and economically disadvantaged backgrounds are at an increased risk of suicidal behaviour. Childhood adversity and trauma, and various life stresses as an adult influence risks of suicidal behaviour. Serious mental illnesses, most commonly depression, substance abuse, anxiety disorders and schizophrenia, are associated with an increased risk of suicide. Diminished social interaction increases suicide risk, particularly among adults and older adults.

Despite its often complex origins, suicide can be prevented. Communities and societies that are well integrated and cohesive have fewer suicides. Restricting access to methods of suicide (such as firearms or pesticides) reduces suicides. Careful media reporting of suicide prevents further suicides. Educating communities and health and social services professionals to better identify people at risk of suicide, encourages them to seek help, and providing them with adequate, sustained and professional care can reduce suicide amongst people with mental illness. Providing adequate support for people who are bereaved by suicide can reduce their risk of suicide.

Such an appraisal of phenomenology of suicide stresses the need to better understand the suicidal dimension as opposed to the psychiatric dimension and to avoid myths and stigmatization.

This book is an attempt to put together some of the knowledge on suicide and propose proper suicide prevention actions around the world. It presents the rare opportunity to get to know the phenomenon with a broad view of suicide in various continents. Controversial topics are also related to the suicide risk, which makes this volume an update resource for those who want a global perspective.

Maurizio Pompili

Sapienza University of Rome

Italy

INTRODUCTION

In the year 2000, approximately one million people died from suicide: a "global" mortality rate of 16 per 100,000, or one death every 40 seconds.

In the last 45 years suicide rates have increased by 60% worldwide. Suicide is now among the three leading causes of death among those aged 15-44 years (both sexes); these figures do not include suicide attempts up to 20 times more frequent than completed suicide. Suicide worldwide is estimated to represent 1.8% of the total global burden of disease in1998, and 2.4% in countries with market and former socialist economies in 2020. Although traditionally suicide rates have been highest among the male elderly, rates among young people have been increasing to such an extent that they are now the group at highest risk in a third of countries, in both developed and developing countries. Mental disorders (particularly depression and substance abuse) are associated with more than 90% of all cases of suicide; however, suicide results from many complex sociocultural factors and is more likely to occur particularly during periods of socioeconomic, family and individual crisis situations (*e.g.,* loss of a loved one, employment, honour).

The economic costs associated with completed and attempted suicide are estimated to be in the billions of dollars. One million lives lost each year are more than those lost from wars and murder annually in the world. It is three times the catastrophic loss of life in the tsunami disaster in Asia in 2005. Every day of the year, the number of suicides is equivalent to the number of lives lost in the attack on the World Trade Center Twin Towers on 9/11 in 2001.

Everyone should be aware of the warning signs for suicide: Someone threatening to hurt or kill him/herself, or taking of wanting to hurt or kill him/herself; someone looking for ways to kill him/herself by seeking access to firearms, available pills, or other means; someone talking or writing about death, dying or suicide, when these actions are out of the ordinary for the person. Also, high risk of suicide is generally associated with hopelessness; rage, uncontrolled anger, seeking revenge; acting reckless or engaging in risky activities, seemingly without thinking; feeling trapped – like there's no way out; increased alcohol or drug use; withdrawing from friends, family and society, anxiety, agitation, unable to sleep or sleeping all the time; dramatic mood changes; no reason for living; no sense of purpose in life.

Table 1: Understanding and helping the suicidal individual should be a task for all

Suicide Myths	How to Help the Suicidal Person	Warning Sights of Suicide
Myth: Suicidal people just want to die. **Fact**: Most of the time, suicidal people are torn between wanting to die and wanting to live. Most suicidal individuals don't want death; they just want to stoop the great psychological or emotional pain they are experiencing	-Listen; -Accept the person's feelings as they are; -Do not be afraid to talk about suicide directly -Ask them if they developed a plan of suicide;	-Expressing suicidal feelings or bringing up the topic of suicide; -Giving away prized possessions settling affairs, making out a will; -Signs of depression: loss of pleasure, sad mood, alterations in sleeping/eating patterns, feelings of hopelessness;
Myth: People who commit suicide do not warn others. **Fact**: Eight out of every 10 people who kill themselves give definite clues to their intentions. They leave numerous clues and warnings to others, although clues may be non-verbal of difficult to detect.	-Remove lethal means for suicide from person's home -Remind the person that depressed feelings do change with time; -Point out when death is chosen, it is irreversible;	-Change of behavior (poor work or school performance) -Risk-taking behaviors -Increased use of alcohol or drugs -Social isolation -Developing a specific plan for suicide
Myth: People who talk about suicide are only trying to get attention. They won't really do it. **Fact**: Few commit suicide without first letting someone know how they feel. Those who are considering suicide give clues and warnings as a cry for help. Over 70% who	-Express your concern for the person; -Develop a plan for help with the person; -Seek outside emergency	

do threaten to commit suicide either make an attempt or complete the act.	intervention at a hospital, mental health clinic or call a suicide prevention center	
Myth: Don't mention suicide to someone who's showing signs of depression. It will plant the idea in their minds and they will act on it. **Fact**: Many depressed people have already considered suicide as an option. Discussing it openly helps the suicidal person sort through the problems and generally provides a sense of relief and understanding.		

Suicide is preventable. Most suicidal individuals desperately want to live; they are just unable to see alternatives to their problems. Most suicidal individuals give definite warnings of their suicidal intentions, but others are either unaware of the significance of these warnings or do not know how to respond to them. Talking about suicide does not cause someone to be suicidal; on the contrary the individual feel relief and has the opportunity to experience an empathic contact.

Suicide profoundly affects individuals, families, workplaces, neighbourhoods and societies. The economic costs associated with suicide and self-inflicted injuries are estimated to be in the billions of dollars. Surviving family members not only suffer the trauma of losing a loved one to suicide, and may themselves be at higher risk for suicide and emotional problems.

Mental pain is the basic ingredient of suicide. Edwin Shneidman calls such pain "psychache" [1], meaning an ache in the psyche. Shneidman suggested that the key questions to ask a suicidal person are 'Where do you hurt?' and 'How may I help you?'. If the function of suicide is to put a stop to an unbearable flow of painful consciousness, then it follows that the clinician's main task is to mollify that pain. Shneidman (1) also pointed out that the main sources of psychological pain, such as shame, guilt, rage, loneliness, hopelessness and so forth, stem from frustrated or thwarted psychological needs. These psychological needs include the need for achievement, for affiliation, for autonomy, for counteraction, for exhibition, for nurturance, for order and for understanding. Shneidman [2], who is considered the father of suicidology, has proposed the following definition of suicide: 'Currently in the Western world, suicide is a conscious act of self-induced annihilation, best understood as a multidimensional malaise in a needful individual who defines an issue for which the suicide is perceived as the best solution'. Shneidman has also suggested that 'that suicide is best understood not so much as a movement toward death as it is a movement away from something and that something is always the same: intolerable emotion, unendurable pain, or unacceptable anguish.

Strategies involving restriction of access to common methods of suicide have proved to be effective in reducing suicide rates; however, there is a need to adopt multi-sectoral approaches involving other levels of intervention and activities, such as crisis centers. There is compelling evidence indicating that adequate prevention and treatment of depression, alcohol and substance abuse can reduce suicide rates. School-based interventions involving crisis management, self-esteem enhancement and the development of coping skills and healthy decision making have been demonstrated to reduce the risk of suicide among the youth. Worldwide, the prevention of suicide has not been adequately addressed due to basically a lack of awareness of suicide as a major problem and the taboo in many societies to discuss openly about it. In fact, only a few countries have included prevention of suicide among their priorities.

Reliability of suicide certification and reporting is an issue in great need of improvement. It is clear that suicide prevention requires intervention also from outside the health sector and calls for an innovative, comprehensive multi-sectoral approach, including both health and non-health sectors, *e.g.,* education, labour, police, justice, religion, law, politics, the media.

REFERENCES

[1] Shneidman ES. Suicide as psychache. A clinical approach to self-destructive behavior. Nortvale, Aronson, 1993.

[2] Shneidman ES. Definition of suicide. Northvale, Aronson; 1985.

List of Contributors

Antonella Spacca

Department of Neurosciences, Mental Health and Organs Functions, Suicide Prevention Center, Sant'Andrea Hospital, Sapienza University of Rome, Italy;

Antoon A. Leenaars

1500 Ouellette Avenue, Suite 203, Windsor, ON, Canada, N8X 1K7

Bijou Yang

Drexel University, Philadelphia, PA, USA

C.K. Law

Hong Kong Institute of Asia-Pacific Studies, The Chinese University of Hong Kong;

Candi M.C. Leung

Department of Psychology, The University of Hong Kong, Republic of China

Erminia Colucci

Centre for International Mental Health, School of Population Health, University of Melbourne, Level 5, 207 Bouverie St, Carlton (Melbourne, VIC), 3053, Australia

Ingo W. Nader

Department of Basic Psychological Research and Research Methods, School of Psychology, University of Vienna, Liebiggasse 5, A-1010 Vienna, Austria;

Cristina Di Vittorio

Department of Neurosciences Division of Psychiatry, University of Parma, Italy

Luigi Janiri

Department of Neurosciences, Day-Hospital of Psychiatry, Catholic University of the Sacred Heart, Rome, Italy

Mario Amore

Department of Neurosciences, Division of Psychiatry, University of Parma – Italy, Str. Del Quartiere, 2, IT-43100 Parma, Italy;

Nestor D. Kapusta

Department of Psychoanalysis and Psychotherapy, Medical University of Vienna, Währinger Gürtel 18-20, A-1090 Vienna, Austria;

Karolina Krysinska

Faculty of Psychology and Educational Sciences, KU Leuven, University of Leuven, Belgium;

Leonardo Tondo
Faculty of Psychology, University of Cagliari, Italy

Michele Raja
Private Practice, Via Prisciano 26, 00136 – Rome, Italy

Roger Pycha
Psychiatric Service, Brunico, Italy

Ross J. Baldessarini
Department of Psychiatry, Harvard Medical School; Psychopharmacology Program, McLean Division of Massachusetts General Hospital Boston, Massachusetts, USA

Thomas Stompe
Department of Psychiatry and Psychotherapy, Medical University of Vienna, Währinger Gürtel 18-20, A-1090 Vienna, Austria

Giancarlo Giupponi
Psychiatric Service, St. Maurizio Hospital, Via Böhler No. 4, 39100 Bolzano, Italy and

David Lester
The Richard Stockton College of New Jersey, USA

T. Maniam
Department of Psychiatry UKM Medical Centre, National University of Malaysia, Kuala Lumpur, Malaysia

Paul S.F. Yip
Department of Social Work and Social Administration, The University of Hong Kong and HKJC Centre for Suicide Research and Prevention, The University of Hong Kong

Gernot Sonneck
Ludwig Boltzmann Institute for Social Psychiatry, Lazarettgasse 14A-912, A-1090 Vienna, Austria

Maurizio Pompili
McLean Hospital - Harvard Medical School, MA, USA;

Karl Andriessen
Parenting and Special Education, Faculty of Psychology and Educational Sciences, University of Leuven, Belgium;

Jorge Forero Vargas
Professor of Psychiatry, Universidad El Bosque, Coordinator Suicide Prevention Presidential's Program, Latin American Psychiatry Association (Apal) Bogota, Colombia

Jorge Tellez-Vargas

Professor of Psychiatry, Universidad El Bosque, IASP Colombia National Representative, Associate Secretary Treasurer World Federation of Societies of Biological Psychiatry, Bogota, Colombia and

Elmar Etzersdorfer

Furtbach Hospital, Furtbachstraße 6, D-70178 Stuttgart, Germany;

Christine Tartaro

The Richard Stockton College of New Jersey, Pomona, NJ, USA

Denise Erbuto

Department of Neurosciences, Mental Health and Organs Functions, Suicide Prevention Center, Sant'Andrea Hospital, Sapienza University of Rome, Italy

Désirée Harnic

Department of Neurosciences, Day-Hospital of Psychiatry, Catholic University of the Sacred Heart, Rome, Italy

Gianluca Serafini

Department of Neurosciences, Mental Health and Organs Functions, Suicide Prevention Center, Sant'Andrea Hospital, Sapienza University of Rome, Italy

Kristina Ritter

Department of Psychiatry and Psychotherapy, Medical University of Vienna, Währinger Gürtel 18-20, A-1090 Vienna, Austria

Marco Innamorati

Department of Neurosciences, Division of Psychiatry, University of Parma – Italy, Str. Del Quartiere, 2, IT-43100 Parma, Italy and Department of Neurosciences, Mental Health and Sensory Functions, Suicide Prevention Center, Sant'Andrea Hospital, Sapienza University of Rome, Italy

Martin Voracek

Department of Basic Psychological Research and Research Methods, School of Psychology, University of Vienna, Liebiggasse 5, A-1010 Vienna, Austria

Michele Battuello

Department of Neurosciences, Mental Health and Organs Functions, Suicide Prevention Center, Sant'Andrea Hospital, Sapienza University of Rome, Italy

Paolo Girardi

Department of Neurosciences, Mental Health and Organs Functions, Suicide Prevention Center, Sant'Andrea Hospital, Sapienza University of Rome, Italy

Paolo Roma

Department of Neurosciences, Mental Health and Organs Functions, Suicide Prevention Center, Sant'Andrea Hospital, Sapienza University of Rome, Italy

Sara Martino

The Richard Stockton College of New Jersey, USA

Stefano Baratta

Department of Neurosciences, Division of Psychiatry, University of Parma – Italy, Str. Del Quartiere, 2, IT-43100 Parma, Italy

Stefano Ferracuti

Department of Neurosciences, Mental Health and Organs Functions, Suicide Prevention Center, Sant'Andrea Hospital, Sapienza University of Rome, Italy

Thomas Niederkrotenthaler

Department of General Practice and Family Medicine, Center for Public Health, Medical University of Vienna, Währingerstraße 13a, A-1090 Vienna, Austria and Department of Medical Psychology, Center for Public Health, Medical University of Vienna, Severingasse 9, A-1090 Vienna, Austria

CHAPTER 1

Assessment and Management of Suicide Risk

Maurizio Pompili[1,2,*], David Lester[3] and Paolo Girardi[1]

[1]*Department of Neurosciences, Mental Health and Organs Functions, Suicide Prevention Center, Sant'Andrea Hospital, Sapienza University of Rome, Italy;* [2]*McLean Hospital - Harvard Medical School, USA and* [3]*The Richard Stockton College of New Jersey, Pomona, NJ, USA*

Abstract: The assessment and management of suicide risk are probably the most difficult tasks that clinicians encounter during their professional careers despite the abundant literature and guidelines now available. Each health professional should be able to perform an assessment of suicide risk, although such assessments are usually performed by psychiatrists. During such assessments, clinicians may be helped by psychometric instruments despite the fact that such instruments are not in many cases entirely reliable. The management of suicide risk is an art that must be based on science. Clinicians should evaluate the role of pharmacotherapy, psychotherapy and hospitalization in the reduction of suicide risk, while maintaining high levels of empathy with the patient. At the present time, only lithium and clozapine have shown promise for reducing suicidality, more so than antidepressants. Education of psychotherapists and medical staff remains one of the priorities for better assessing and managing suicide risk.

Keywords: Suicide, assessment, prevention.

1. INTRODUCTION

The assessment and management of suicide risk is an art that health professionals, and in particular mental health professionals, should learn from the beginning of their training. Furthermore, recent campaigns from eminent institutions have emphasized the role of every citizen in understanding and helping the suicidal person [1]. Unfortunately, only rarely is suicide risk assessed properly, and many clinicians avoid asking clients whether they are feeling suicidal, mistakenly assuming that talking about suicide will evoke suicidal ideation, planning and actions. Simon [2] has recently investigated the concept of imminent suicide and noted that suicide risk varies from minute to minute, hour to hour and day to day. As a result of this, suicide assessment must be a continual process, not a single event.

The first psychological autopsy studies ever conducted produced clear evidence, that was in most instances confirmed by subsequent research, that two thirds of those who commit suicide communicate their suicidal intent in the weeks prior to their death, often to several different persons. Forty percent communicated their suicidal intent in very clear and specific terms. Half of the persons dying by suicide had never been in contact with a mental health professional in their lifetime, not even once. About 90% of suicides had received some kind of health care attention in the year prior to death, but this care was not provided by a mental health professional [3-5].

Many suicidal individuals want to live, but they are unable to see alternatives, an issue that should always be taken seriosuly when assessing their risk of suicide. Although, most suicidal individuals give definite warnings of their suicidal intentions, many people, including professionals, are either unaware of the significance of these warnings or do not know how to respond to them. Clinical assessment should be carried out when individuals threaten to hurt or kill themselves, talk of wanting to hurt or kill themselves, search for ways to kill themselves (by seeking access to firearms, pills, or other means) or when they are talking or writing about death, dying or suicide, since these actions are unusual actions for ordinary nonsuicidal individuals.

***Address correspondence to Maurizio Pompili:** Department of Neuroscience and Mental Health, Suicide Prevention Center, Sant'Andrea Hospital, Sapienza University of Rome, Italy; E-mail: maurizio.pompili@uniroma1.it

2. PSYCHIATRIC EXAMINATIONS

Although increased suicidal risk is not always associated with psychiatric disorder, a psychiatric examination is the most useful component for risk assessment. During the course of the examination, patients should be investigated for current and past psychiatric illnesses, a history of suicidal behavior, life events which have caused psychological pain, and their available coping skills. It is also important to investigate acute and chronic stressors and what support the individual can rely on. An in-depth analysis of present suicidal ideation, suicidal plan and possible methods to commit suicide should always be carried out. Questions regarding the following items should also be part of such examination: hopelessness, rage, uncontrolled anger, seeking revenge, acting recklessly or engaging in risky activities impulsively, feeling trapped as if there is no way out, increased alcohol or drug use, withdrawing from friends, family and society, anxiety, agitation, inability to sleep or sleeping all the time, dramatic mood changes, no reason for living and no sense of purpose in life.

3. ASSESSMENT TOOLS

The clinical utility of suicide assessment scales is limited due to the high false positive and false negative rates, and they may have low positive predictive value. Nevertheless, there is evidence to argue that they constitute an important tool for an accurate assessment of suicide risk. They may also help the clinician to introduce items related to suicide that are not otherwise part of the patient's clinical evaluation. We have provided a list of assessment tools that are routinely used in clinical setting (see Tables **1, 2, 3**).

Table 1: Scales for assessing suicide risk

Self-administered Scales	
-	Beck Hopelessness Scale [6]
-	Index of Potential Suicide [7]
-	Reasons for Living Inventory [8]
-	Rorschach Suicide Constellation [9]
-	Suicide Probability Scale [10]
-	Suicide risk Measure [11]
Clinican-administered Scales	
-	Clinical Instrument to Estimate Suicide Risk [12]
-	Instrument for the Evaluation of Suicide Potential [13]
-	Intent Scale [14]
-	Los Angeles Suicide Prevention Scale [15]
-	Neuropsychiatric Hospital Suicide Prediction Schedule [16, 17]
-	Scale for Assessing Suicide Risk [18]
-	Suicide Death Prediction Scale, Long and Short Form [19]
-	Short Risk Scale [20]
-	Suicide Intent Scale [21]
-	SAD PERSON [22]
-	Suicide Potential Scale [23]
-	Scale for Predicting Subsequent Suicidal Behavior [24]

Table 2: Management of suicide risk

1. Be aware. Learn the warning signs.
2. Get involved. Become available. Show interest and support.
3. Ask if he/she is thinking about suicide.

4. Be direct. Talk openly and freely about suicide.
5. Be willing to listen. Allow for expression of feelings. Accept the feelings.
6. Be non-judgmental. Don't debate whether suicide is right or wrong, or feelings are good or bad. Don't lecture on the value of life.
7. Don't dare him/her to do it.
8. Don't give advice by making decisions for someone else, or telling them to behave differently.
9. Don't ask 'why'. This encourages defensiveness.
10. Offer empathy, not sympathy.
11. Don't act shocked. This creates distance.
12. Don't be sworn to secrecy. Seek support.
13. Offer hope that alternatives are available; do not offer glib reassurance; it only proves you don't understand.
14. Take action! Remove means! Get help from individuals or agencies specializing in crisis intervention and suicide prevention.

Table 3: Assessment of suicide risk

-	Identify the multiple contributing factors
-	Conduct a thorough psychiatric examination, identifying risk factors and protective factors and distinguish risk factors which can be modified from those which cannot
-	Ask directly about suicide;
-	Determine level of suicide risk: low, moderate, high
-	Determine treatment setting and plan
-	Investigate past and present suicidal ideation, plans, behaviors, intent; methods; hopelessness, anhedonia, anxiety symptoms; reasons for living; associated substance use; homicidal ideation;
-	Warning signs: Expressing suicidal feelings or bringing up the topic of suicide; giving away prized possessions, settling affairs, making out a will; signs of depression: sad mood, alterations in sleeping/eating patterns; change of behavior (poor work or school performance); risk-taking behaviors; increased use of alcohol or drugs; losing interest in their personal appearance; social isolation; developing a specific plan for suicide;.

(Adapted from APA Guidelines [36] and Jacobs [37]).

Among the various scales, the Beck Hopelessness Scale (BHS) [6] has showed convincing evidence of its proprieties for the prediction of completed suicide. This is a 20-item scale for measuring the cognitive component of the syndrome of depression. The scale assesses three major aspects of hopelessness: feelings about the future, loss of motivation, and expectations. Responding to the 20 true or false items on the Beck Hopelessness Scale, individuals have to either endorse a pessimistic statement or deny an optimistic statement. Research consistently supports a positive relationship between BHS scores and measures of depression, suicidal intent, and current suicidal ideation. In addition, Beck *et al.* [25] carried out a prospective study of 1,958 outpatients and found that BHS scores were significantly related to subsequent completed suicide. A cut-off score of 9 or above identified 16 (94%) of the 17 patients who eventually committed suicide. The high-risk group identified by this cut-off score was 11 times more likely to commit suicide than the rest of the outpatients. The BHS may, therefore, be used as an indicator of suicide potential.

4. THE MANAGEMENT OF SUICIDAL RISK

The management of suicidal risk requires the mobilization of resources for the client. Too often the severity of suicidal crises is underestimated, and the management of the crises lacks precise tactics, proper decisions and step by step interventions.

Shneidman's conceptualization of suicide refers to unbearable mental pain, which he named psychache, and the need to stop such pain. Suicide occurs when the psychache is deemed by that person to be unbearable, and Shneidman suggested, therefore, that the key questions to ask a suicidal person are 'Where do you hurt?' and 'How may I help you?. If the function of suicide is to put a stop to an unbearable flow of painful consciousness, then it follows that the clinician's main task for the management of suicide risk is to mollify that pain.

The management of suicide risk can be performed through pharmacotherapy, psychotherapy and hospitalization. Family members should always be involved in this process, and often others besides mental health professionals are needed to assist the suicidal individual.

Suicidal Risk During Pharmacotherapy

Lithium in bipolar disorder and major affective disorders [26, 27] and clozapine in schizophrenia [28] are the chief drugs that have proved to be effective in the reduction of suicide risk. Antidepressants have been scrutinized extensively, but their role in the reduction of suicide risk remains doubtful [29]. One of the major issues when using antidepressants may be the emergence of suicidality as a result of a number of side effects such as akathisia, agitation, anxiety, irritable dysphoria and insomnia [30]. The identification of such symptoms should lead the psychiatrist to decrease the dose of antidepressant therapy and to opt for the introduction of an atypical antipsychotic, anticonvulsant or sedative. Lithium should be considered when appropriate, especially following inadequate antidepressant response.

Suicidal Risk During Psychotherapy

Hendin's [31] seminal paper on psychotherapy and suicide stressed that often the management of suicide risk is confused with psychotherapy. The recommendations mentioned above may not be first option for dealing with suicidal risk that occurs during psychotherapy. Encouraging suicidal patients to give up their intention to kill themselves for the sake of treatment, family or friends implies that they are simply living for the sake of others. They are likely to conclude that no effort is being made to understand the problems that are making them suicidal.

The proper management of suicide risk during psychotherapy requires skill and also awareness of the therapist's own reaction to suicidal patients. Therapists who are especially made anxious by the possibility that a patient can commit suicide are not in the best position to help that individual. Reviewing the cases of thirty individuals who committed suicide, Wheat [32] identified three factors involved in these suicides: 1) the refusal of the therapist to tolerate infantile dependency so that the therapist conveyed to the patient an expectation of mature behavior that exceeded the patient's capacity; 2) discouragement on the part of the therapist about the progress of treatment; 3) an event or environmental crisis of overwhelming importance to the patient unrecognized by the therapist or beyond the control of the therapeutic situation.

Suicidal Risk During Psychiatric Hospitalization

The suicide rate in psychiatric patients is higher than in the general population. Several studies have found that a high percentage of patients with schizophrenia who die from suicide were seen by an apparently unsuspecting clinician a few days just prior to death [33]. Most patients committing suicide have either fluctuating suicidal ideation or are continuously nonsuicidal, and both of these observations are consistent with the reports of inpatients committing suicide when they appeared to be improving. Goh, *et al.* [34] noted that a proximal factor for the suicide in several of these long-stay patients was the planning of their discharge, which led to the painful realization that they were losing the hospital and staff and/or that their family was not prepared to have them home.

Goh *et al.* [34] emphasized also the environmental impact of staff variables, such as low morale or the absence of key personnel, as well as the need for effective communication among relevant staff about patients judged as having an increased risk of suicide. Adverse circumstances such as single-occupancy rooms or the return to a family in which the patient's presence represents a severe emotional or financial strain, add to the risk of suicide risk [35]. Poor communication about the risk of suicide between medical and nursing staff, changes in staff, and ward layout have also been suggested as risk factors.

Suicide precautions must be carefully adhered to by staff, including constant observation while the patient remains acutely psychotic, especially during the first week of hospitalization. Lapses in observation should not be permitted while suicidal patients are in the bathroom or in their rooms.

Proper aftercare programs should always be tailored to the patient's need since there is a high risk of suicide after discharge.

ACKNOWLEDGEMENT

Some guidelines included in this chapter are based on the information to prevent suicide disseminated by the American Association of Suicidology.

REFERENCES

[1] Lester D. Why people kill themselves. Philadelphia, PA: The Charles Press Publishing, 1997.
[2] Simon RI. Imminent suicide: the illusion of short-term prediction. Suicide Life Threat Behav 2006; 36: 296-301.
[3] Robins E, Gassner S, Kayes J, Wilkinson RH Jr, Murphy, GE. The communication of suicidal intent: a study of 134 consecutive cases of successful (completed) suicide. Am J Psychiatry 1959; 115: 724-33.
[4] Dorpat TL, Ripley HS. A study of suicide in the Seattle area. Compr Psychiatry 1960; 1: 349-59.
[5] Barraclough B, Bunch J, Nelson B, Sainsbury PA. hundred cases of suicide: clinical aspects. Br J Psychiatry 1974; 125(0):355-73.
[6] Beck AT, Weissman A, Lester D, Trexler L. The measurement of pessimism: the hopelessness scale. J Consult Clin Psychol 1974a; 42: 861-5.
[7] Zung WWK. Index of Potential Suicide (IPS): a rating scale for suicide prevention. In: Beck AT, Resnik HLP, Lettieri JD, Bowie MD, Eds. The Prediction of suicide. Charles Press. 1974; pp. 222-249.
[8] Linehan MM, Goodstein JL, Nielsen SL, Chiles, J. Reasons for staying alive when you're thinking of killing yourself: the Reasons for Living Inventory. J Consult Clin Psychol 1983; 51: 276-86.
[9] Exner JE Jr, Wylie J. Some Rorschach data concerning suicide. J Pers Assess 1977; 41: 339-48.
[10] Cull JG, Gill WS. Suicide Probability Scale manual. Los Angeles, Western Psychological Services; 1988.
[11] Plutchik R, van Praag HM, Conte HR, Picard S. Correlates of suicide and violence risk 1: the suicide risk measure. Compr Psychiatry 1989; 30: 296-302.
[12] Motto JA, Heilbron DC, Juster RP. Development of a clinical instrument to estimate suicide risk. Am J Psychiatry 1985; 142: 680-6.
[13] Cohen E, Motto JA, Seiden RH. An instrument for evaluating suicide potential: a preliminary study. Am J Psychiatry 1966; 122: 886-91.
[14] Pierce DW. Suicidal intent in self-injury. Br J Psychiatry 1977; 130: 377-85.
[15] Beck AT, Resnik HLP, Lettieri JD, Eds. The Prediction of suicide. Bowie, MD: Charles Press, 1974b.
[16] Farberow NL, MacKinnon DR. A suicide prediction schedule for neuropsychiatric hospital patients. J Nerv Ment Dis 1974a; 158: 408-19.
[17] Farberow NL, MacKinnon DR. Prediction of suicide in neuropsychiatric hospital patients. In: Neuringer C, Ed. Psychological assessment of suicide risk. Springfield IL: Charles C. Thomas. 1974b; pp. 186-224.
[18] Tuckman J, Youngman WF. Assessment of suicide risk in attempted suicide. In: Resnik HL, Ed. Suicidal behavior: diagnosis and management. Boston, Little Brown. 1968; pp. 190-7.
[19] Lettieri DJ. Research issues in developing prediction scales. In: Neuringer C, Ed. Psychological assessment of suicide risk. Springfield IL: Charles C. Thomas. 1974; pp. 43-73.
[20] Pallis DJ, Barraclough BM, Levey AB, Jenkins JS, Sainsbury P. Estimating suicide risk among attempted suicides: I. The development of new clinical scales. Br J Psychiatry 1982; 141: 37-44.
[21] Beck AT, Schuyler D, Herman I. Development of suicidal intent scale. In: Beck AT, Resnik HLP, Lettieri JD, Eds. The Prediction of suicide. Bowie, MD: Charles Press. 1974c; pp 45-56.
[22] Patterson WM, Dohn HH, Bird J, Patterson GA. Evaluation of suicidal patients: the SAD PERSONS scale. Psychosomatics 1983; 24: 343-9.
[23] Dean RA, De Cook R, Maley RF, Miskimins W, Wilson LT. Prediction of suicide in a psychiatric hospital. J Clin Psychol 1982; 23: 296-301.
[24] Buglass D, Horton JA. Scale for predicting subsequent suicidal behaviour. Br J Psychiatry 1974; 124: 573-8.
[25] Beck AT, Brown G, Berchick RJ, Stewart BL, Steer RA. Relationship between hopelessness and ultimate suicide: A replication with psychiatric outpatients. Am J Psychiatry 1990; 147: 190–5.
[26] Baldessarini RJ, Tondo L, Davis P, Pompili M, Goodwin FK, Hennen J. Decreased risk of suicides and attempts during long-term lithium treatment: a meta-analytic review. Bipolar Disord 2006; 8: 625-39.
[27] Baldessarini RJ, Pompili M, Tondo L. Bipolar disorder. In: Simon RI, Hales RE, Eds. Textbook of suicide assessment and management. Washington, DC: American Psychiatric Publishing. 2006b; pp. 277-99.
[28] Hennen J, Baldessarini RJ. Suicidal risk during treatment with clozapine: a meta-analysis. Schizophr Res 2005; 73: 139-45.

[29] Baldessarini RJ, Pompili M, Tondo L. Suicidal risk in antidepressant drug trials. Arch Gen Psychiatry 2006c; 63: 246-8.

[30] Pompili M, Tondo L, Baldessarini RJ. Suicidal risk emerging during antidepressant treatment: Recognition and intervention. Clin Neuropsychiatry 2005a; 2: 66-72.

[31] Hendin H. Psychotherapy and suicide. Am J Psychother 1981; 35: 469-80.

[32] Wheat WD. Motivational aspects of suicide in patients during and after psychiatric treatment. South Med J 1960; 53: 273-8.

[33] Pompili M, Mancinelli I, Ruberto A, Kotzalidis GD, Girardi P, Tatarelli R. Where schizophrenic patients commit suicide A review of suicide among inpatients and former inpatients. Int J Psychiatr Med 2005b; 35: 171-90.

[34] Goh S, Salmons P, Whittington R. Hospital suicides: Are there preventable factors? Profile of the psychiatric hospital suicide. Br J Psychiatry 1989; 154: 247-9.

[35] Vaughn CE, Leff JP. The influence of family and social factors on the course of psychiatric illness. A comparison of schizophrenic and depressed neurotic patients. Br J Psychiatry 1976; 129: 125-37

[36] American Psychiatric Association. Practice guideline for the assessment and treatment of patients with suicidal behaviors. Am J Psychiatry (Suppl) 2003; 160: 1-97.

[37] Jacobs DG, Ed. The Harvard medical School Guide to suicide assessment and intervention. San Francisco, CA: Jossey-Bass, 1998.

CHAPTER 2

Culture and Suicide

David Lester*

The Richard Stockton College of New Jersey, USA

Abstract: The impact of culture of suicide, both at the aggregate level and the individual level, is discussed. The deleterious impact of a changing culture, especially for native and aboriginal groups, is noted, and the assumption of the cultural invariability of suicidal phenomena questioned. The implications of cultural differences for counseling the suicidal client are explored.

Keywords: Suicide, culture, prevention.

1. SOCIETAL AND CULTURAL SUICIDE RATES

It is an obvious fact that societal suicide rates differ widely. As shown in Table **1**, male suicide rates in 2000 ranged from 80.4 per 100, 000 per year in Lithuania to 0.1 in Egypt. For females, the suicide rates ranged from 16.9 in Lithuania to 0.0 in Egypt. Knowledge of worldwide trends in suicide are limited because many African, Middle East and Central and South American countries do not report their suicide rates to the World Health Organization, [1] although Jacob *et al.* [2] claim to have accurate suicide rates for 183 nations, ranging from Afghanistan to Zimbabwe.

Table 1: Suicide rates around the world for men and women for 2000

(From the World Health Organization, December 1, 2005, from www.who.int)		
	Male	**Female**
Albania	2.4	1.2
Argentina	12.3	2.9
Armenia	2.5	0.7
Australia	19.8	5.2
Austria	29.3	10.4
Azerbaijan	1.2	0.4
Belarus	63.6	9.5
Brazil	6.4	1.6
Bulgaria	25.2	9.1
Canada	18.4	5.2
Chile	16.8	2.7
Costa Rica	10.7	1.5
Croatia	32.9	10.3
Cuba	23.4	9.6
Czech Rep.	26.0	6.7
Ecuador	6.0	2.6
Egypt	0.1	0.0
Estonia	11.9	45.8
Finland	34.6	10.9
France	27.9	9.5
Germany	20.3	7.0
Georgia	4.8	1.2

***Address Correspondence to David Lester:** The Richard Stockton College of New Jersey, USA; E-mail: david.lester@stockton.edu

Maurizio Pompili (Ed)

Table 1: cont....

Greece	5.5	1.5
Hong Kong	16.1	10.1
Hungary	50.7	15.1
Ireland	20.3	4.3
Italy	10.9	3.5
Japan	35.2	13.4
Kazakhstan	51.7	9.7
Kuwait	1.6	1.6
Kyrgyzstan	17.2	3.9
Latvia	56.6	11.9
Lithuania	80.4	16.9
Macedonia	10.3	4.5
Mauritius	18.8	5.2
Mexico	6.0	1.1
Moldova	26.7	4.1
Netherlands	12.7	6.2
New Zealand	19.8	4.2
Norway	18.5	5.8
Panama	8.4	1.3
Paraguay	3.9	1.7
Poland	25.9	4.9
Portugal	8.5	2.0
Puerto Rico	15.2	1.4
Romania	21.2	4.5
Russia	70.6	11.9
Singapore	12.5	6.4
Slovakia	22.6	4.9
Slovenia	45.2	15.2
South Korea	18.8	8.3
Spain	13.1	4.0
Sweden	18.3	7.3
Switzerland	27.8	10.8
Thailand	13.5	3.7
Ukraine	52.1	10.0
United Kingdom	11.3	3.2
United States	17.1	4.0
Uruguay	29.0	5.5
Uzbekistan	11.8	3.8
Venezuela	8.8	1.5

For all the nations shown in Table **1**, the male suicide rate is higher than the female suicide rate. The lone exception is China where women have a higher suicide rate than men[1]. However, China documents suicide

[1] Phillips, Liu and Zhang [3] reported suicide rates of 33.6 per 100, 000 per year *versus* 24.2 for the 1990-1994 period for women and men, respectively.

fatalities for only a small percentage of the nation, and so the suicide rates are not accurate for the nation as a whole[2].

These differences in national suicide rates are large and generally stable over time. For example, in Table **2** the suicide rates for 16 nations in 1901, 1950 and 1990 are shown and, despite fluctuations, the rates in one year are positively associated with the rates in other years.

Table 2: Suicide rates in 1901, 1950 and 1990

	1901	1950	1990
Australia	11.9	9.3	12.9
Belgium	12.7	12.9	19.0
England/Wales	9.6	10.2	7.8
Finland	6.1	15.6	30.3
Germany	20.8	18.8*	17.5
Ireland	2.9	2.6	9.5
Italy	6.2	6.5	7.6
Netherlands	5.8	5.5	9.7
New Zealand	10.2	9.2	13.5
Norway	5.5	7.4	15.5
Portugal	4.3	10.1	8.8
Scotland	5.3	5.3	10.5
Spain	2.0	5.4	7.5
Sweden	13.1	14.9	17.2
Switzerland	22.4	23.5	21.9
United States	10.4	11.4	12.4

* This rate is for West Germany.

Sources: www.who.int/m/topics/whosis/en/index.html and WHO [1956].

Suicide rates also vary widely over the different geographic regions of a nation (for example, over American states and Canadian provinces, suicide rates increase toward the west [4]) and over the different social groups within a nation (for example, some groups of both native Americans and native Canadians have very high suicide rates [5]).

An obvious explanation of such variations in the aggregate suicide rate is that the reporting and counting of suicides in different nations and cultures differ greatly in accuracy [6]. Indeed, it has been easy to document serious official under-reporting of suicides, for example, in Newfoundland [7] and native Americans in Alaska [8].

Nevertheless, it is very unlikely that completely accurate reporting of suicides would eliminate the national and cultural differences. The suicide rates of immigrant groups both to the United States and to Australia are strongly associated with the suicide rates in the home nations from which they arrived [9, 10]. For example, the Irish had a relatively low suicide rate in 1959, 2.5 per 100, 000, while Irish immigrants to the United States in 1959, where they encountered the same medical examiners as other immigrant groups, also had the lowest suicide of all immigrants groups from European countries, only 9.8 [11].

The distribution of suicide rates by age varies with the level of economic development of the nation [12]. Male suicide rates increase with age in most nations of the world. For females, the distribution of suicide rates by age varies with the level of economic development of the nation. For the wealthy nations, such as

[2] Suicide rates for China in 2000 were not available from the World Health Organization.

the United States and Sweden, female suicide rates tend to peak in middle age. For poorer nations, such as Venezuela, suicide rates are higher for elderly women, while for the poorest nations, such as Thailand, the peak shifts to young women [12].

2. EXPLAINING NATIONAL DIFFERENCES IN SUICIDE

The association of sociodemographic and economic variables with national suicides has been best analyzed using factor analysis. Conklin and Simpson [13] identified two clusters of variables that appear to be associated with national suicide rates: one cluster had the highest loading from the Islam religion and the second cluster assessed economic development. Lower suicide rates were found for nations with less economic development and where Islam was the dominant religion.

In a similar study of cross-national suicide rates in 72 countries, Lester [14] identified thirteen independent orthogonal factors for the social variables, only one of which was associated with suicide rates. This factor was economic development, with high loadings from such social variables as low population growth and high gross domestic product per capita.

Physiological Differences

One possible explanation for differences in national suicide rates is that different nationalities differ in their physiology. For example, there are clear differences in the frequency of genes in the people from the different nations of Europe [15]. Thus, different nations and cultures may differ in their genetic structure. Current research on identical twins and adopted children has shown that psychiatric disorders have a strong genetic basis. These differences in inherited psychiatric disorders, particularly affective disorders, or in brain concentrations of serotonin, the neurotransmitter believed to be responsible for depression, may be responsible for the differences in the suicide rates of nations and cultures.

Lester [16] found that the suicide rates of nations were associated with the proportion of people with Types O, A, B and AB blood – the higher the proportion of people in the nation with Type O blood, the lower the suicide rate. Kondrichin and Lester [17] and Voracek *et al.* [18] have shown that the Finno-Ugrian gene may result in high suicide rates in nations with a high proportion of citizens with that ethnic background. However, few studies have explored the role of physiological differences in accounting for national differences in suicide rates.

Psychological/Psychiatric Differences

The major psychological factors found to be associated with suicidal behavior are depression, especially hopelessness, and psychological disturbance, such as neuroticism, anxiety, or emotional instability. Psychiatric disorder appears to increase the risk of suicide, with affective disorders and alcohol and drug abuse leading the list. Nations may differ in the prevalence of these conditions, and such differences could account for the differences in suicide rates. For example, nations certainly do differ in their consumption of alcohol [19], as well as depression [20].

Social Composition

Moksony [21] noted that one simple explanation of national differences in suicide rates is that the national populations differ in the proportion of those at risk for suicide. For example, typically in developed nations, suicide rates are highest among the elderly, especially elderly males. Therefore, nations with a higher proportion of elderly males will have a higher suicide rate.

Societal Differences

The most popular explanation of the variation in national suicide rates focuses on social variables. These social variables may be viewed in two ways: (1) as direct causal agents of the suicidal behavior, or (2) as indices of broad social characteristics which differ between nations.

Durkheim [22] hypothesized that the suicide rate is related to the level of social integration (the degree to which the people are bound together in social networks) and the level of social regulation (the degree to which people's desires and emotions are regulated by societal norms and customs). According to Durkheim, egoistic and anomic suicides result from too little social integration and social regulation, respectively, while altruistic and fatalistic suicides result from too much social integration and social regulation, respectively. Later sociologists have argued that altruistic and fatalistic suicide are rare in modern societies. Therefore, suicide rarely results from excessive social integration or regulation. As a result, suicide in modern societies seems to increase as social integration and regulation decrease [23].

Studies of samples of nations have found that suicide rates are associated with such variables as low church attendance, the amount of immigration and inter-regional migration, and divorce [24]. Some investigators view these associations as suggesting a positive relationship between broken relationships and suicidal behavior. For example, divorce may be associated with suicide at the societal level because divorced people have a higher suicide rate than those with other marital statuses.

A major issue here has been raised by Moksony and Taylor [21, 25] concerning whether specific social variables are directly related to social suicide rates or whether these specific social variables are measures of more basic, abstract and broad social characteristics which determine social suicide rates. Lester [26] proposed that the strong associations between social variables argues for the importance of basic broad social characteristics. For example, in the United States, interstate migration, divorce, church non-attendance and alcohol consumption all inter-correlate highly, supporting the importance of a social characteristic, perhaps best called social disorganization, as a determinant of societal suicide rates. In this case, regions of the world with high rates of divorce would have high rates of suicide for those in all marital statuses. This is found for the United States where states with higher divorce rates have higher suicide rates among the single, the married, the divorced and the widowed [27].

Predicting National Suicide Rates

Lester [28] entered percentage Type O blood type, alcohol consumption, percentage elderly, divorce rate and birth rate into a multiple regression for 17 industrialized nations. The multiple R was 0.85. He then used the regression equation to predict the suicide rate of seven other European nations, and the Spearman rank correlation was 0.89. However, using the regression equation to predict the suicide rates in seven non-European nations gave a rank correlation of zero! Thus, the predictors (and, therefore, the causes) of suicide rates in non-Western nations may be quite different from those for European nations.

There is clearly much more research needed to compare and contrast these competing explanations for differences in national suicide rates.

3. CULTURAL INFLUENCES ON THE MOTIVES FOR SUICIDAL BEHAVIOR

Suicidal behavior is differently determined and has different meanings in different cultures, as demonstrated by Hendin's [29] study of suicide in Scandinavian countries. In Denmark, Hendin noted that guilt arousal was the major disciplinary technique employed by Danish mothers to control aggression, resulting in strong dependency needs in their sons. This marked dependency was the root of depression and suicidality after adult experiences of loss or separation. Reunion fantasies with lost loved ones were common in those committing suicide.

In Sweden, a strong emphasis was placed by parents on performance and success, resulting in ambitious children for whom work was central to their lives. Suicide typically followed failure in performance and the resulting damage to the men's self-esteem.

At the time Hendin conducted his study in Norway, the suicide rate was much lower than that found for Denmark. Although Hendin found strong dependency among the sons on their mothers in both countries, Norwegian children were less passive and more aggressive than Danish children. Alcohol abuse was more common among the Norwegians, and Norwegian men were more open about their feelings - able to laugh at themselves and cry more openly. Norwegian boys strove to please their mothers by causing no trouble, and they did not worry unduly about failure, typically blaming others for their personal failures and retreating into alcohol abuse.

In her account of suicide among females in Papua-New Guinea, Counts [30] has illustrated the ways in which a culture can determine the meaning of the suicidal act. In Papua-New Guinea, female suicide is a culturally-recognized way of imposing social sanctions. Suicide also holds political implications for the surviving kin and for those held responsible for the events leading women to commit suicide. In one such instance, the suicide of a rejected fiancée led to sanctions being imposed on the family which had rejected her. Counts described this woman's suicide as a political act which symbolically transformed her from a position of powerlessness to one of power.

Cultures also differ in the degree in which suicide is condemned. It has been argued that one explanation for the low suicide rate in African-Americans is that suicide is a less acceptable behavior for African-Americans [31]. Murder rates are much higher in African-Americans, both as murderers and as victims, and a larger proportion of the murders involving African Americans are victim-precipitated, that is, the victim played some role, conscious or unconscious, in precipitating their own demise [32]. African-American culture appears to view a victim-precipitated murder as a more acceptable method of dying than suicide [33].

4. CHOICE OF METHOD FOR SUICIDE

The methods chosen for suicide differ between cultures. DeCatanzaro [34] documented culturally unique methods for suicide, such as hanging by tying a noose around one's neck and running to another part of the house in Tikopia. Suttee, which is suicide by burning on the husband's funeral pyre, is a popular form in India, while seppuku, which is ritual disembowelment, is popular in Japan. These well-known examples of cultural influences on suicide methods also have culturally determined motives (grief and shame, respectively).

Firearms are the most common method for suicide in the United States and Canada presently, while in Switzerland, whose residents typically own firearms as part of their participation in the civilian militia, hanging is the most common method for suicide. A method may come to symbolize the act of suicide, as in England earlier this century when "to take the pipe" meant to commit suicide by inhaling toxic domestic gas since the gas was brought into houses by means of pipes and this was the most common method for suicide. (After the 1960s, domestic gas became less toxic as a result of the switch from coal gas to natural gas). Burvill and his colleagues [35] found that immigrants to Australia shifted over time from using the most common methods of suicide in their home nations to those most common in Australia.

Research indicates that increased availability of a method for suicide is associated with an increase in its use for suicide [36]. For example, Killias, van Kesteren and Rindlisbacher [37] found that, in nations where a large proportion of the population owned guns, higher numbers of suicide were committed with guns. However, ownership of guns had no association with the total suicide rate. This suggests that, if guns are not freely available, people use guns less often for committing suicide but switch instead to other methods for suicide, such as poisons, hanging, stabbing, jumping and drowning.

Related to this is the recent proposal for preventing suicide by limiting access to lethal methods for suicide [36]. Kreitman [38] documented how detoxification of domestic gas in England and Wales led to a virtual elimination of domestic gas for suicide and a reduction in the overall suicide rate. Lester [39] studied this phenomenon in six other nations and found that detoxification of domestic gas reduced the use of domestic gas for suicide in all of the nations and, in those nations where suicide by domestic gas was more common, reduced the overall suicide rate as well.

5. SUICIDE IN ONE CULTURE: THE CHINESE

Studies by Lester [40, 41] on suicidal behavior in Chinese illustrates the role of culture, a culture of particular interest because the Chinese are native to many nations (such as mainland China and Hong Kong) and have emigrated in large numbers to nations such as America.

The suicide rates of Asian Americans are relatively low compared to whites in the United States. For example, in 1980, the suicide rates were 13.3 per 100, 000 per year for Native Americans, 13.2 for white Americans, 9.1 for Japanese Americans, 8.3 for Chinese Americans, 6.1 for African Americans and 3.5 for Filipino Americans [41].

Lester noted that the patterns of suicide also differed for these ethnic groups. The ratio of the male to female suicide rates was much larger for whites and African Americans than for Asian Americans for whom the suicide rates of men and women were more similar. In addition, suicide rates increased with age for Asian Americans, whereas the suicide rates peaked in young adulthood for African Americans and Native Americans. Asian Americans used hanging for suicide much more often than whites and African Americans, and they used firearms relatively less often.

Lester concluded that the epidemiology of suicide in Asian Americans in America showed similarities to the results of epidemiological studies of suicide in their home nations, indicating that cultural factors have an important influence on the circumstances of suicidal behavior.

Lester [40] then examined the epidemiology of suicide in Chinese in Hong Kong, Singapore, Taiwan, mainland China, and the United States as a whole. A couple of examples here will illustrate the results. The ratio of the male to female suicide rates in 1980 were 1.2 for Chinese Americans, 1.2 for Hong Kong residents, 1.2 for Taiwanese residents and 1.2 for Singapore Chinese, identical gender ratios. Suicide rates peaked in the elderly in all the nations: for those 65 and older in Chinese Americans, 75 and older in Hong Kong and Taiwan and 70 and older in Singapore Chinese [40].

However, the methods used for suicide did differ: jumping was more common in the Chinese in Singapore and Hong Kong, hanging in Chinese Americans and poisons in Taiwan, probably a result of the difference between the nations in the availability of methods for suicide [40]. Furthermore, the suicide rates differed: in 1980 the suicide rates were 13.5 in Singapore and Hong Kong Chinese, 10.0 in Taiwan and 8.3 for Chinese Americans.

Thus, the gender and age patterns in Chinese suicide seem to be affected strongly by culture, while the absolute suicide rates and methods used are affected by the nation in which the Chinese dwell.

6. CULTURE, LINGUISTICS AND SUICIDE

As Douglas [6] pointed out, a shared linguistic terminology for suicidal behavior is associated with shared meanings of the behavior, and there are also shared associated terms and phrases, such as despair, hopelessness, and "life isn't worth living". Douglas emphasized that these terms are not the phenomenon itself but rather are adopted by members of the culture (or subculture) to construct meanings for suicidal behavior. However, since the terms are rarely clearly defined or detailed and since there is often disagreement among commentators on their meaning, it follows that the meaning of suicide is ambiguous. Furthermore, since the terms are used to construct meanings for suicidal behavior, then estimates of the incidence and circumstances of suicidal behavior are in part a social construction.

For example, according to the Mohave, a Native American tribe in the southwest of the United States, a fetus which presents itself in the transverse position for birth, leading to its own death and that of its mother, is viewed as having intended to commit suicide and to murder its mother so that they can be together in the spirit world [43]. Medical examiners and coroners in the rest of the United States would not view such a still-born infant as a suicide.

Counts [44], who has studied the suicidal behavior of women in the Kaliai district of Papua New Guinea, noted that in the past elderly widows sometimes immolated themselves on their husband's funeral pyre. The German and Australian colonial governors considered this behavior to be a form of ritual murder rather than suicide, and they outlawed it. Counts, however, saw neither term (suicide or murder) as appropriate for this custom since it differed so much from what North Americans and Europeans regard as either suicide or murder. Neither term describes the behavior, the interpersonal relationships involved, or the attitudes toward the widow and those assisting in her death, nor do they predict how the community will respond to her death.

Recently, some scholars, especially in Europe, have expressed doubts that people engaging in nonfatal suicidal behavior have self-destruction as their aim, and they have moved to calling the behavior "self-poisoning" or "self-injury" [45]. The semantic implication is that nonfatal suicidal behavior is not "suicide". Since in most cultures women engage in more nonfatal suicidal actions than do men, this renaming of nonfatal suicidal behavior as self-injury makes "suicidal behavior" less common in women than it was hitherto.

Other suicidologists, on the other hand, include a wider range of behaviors under the rubric of "suicidal behavior". For example, Menninger [46] classified behaviors such as alcoholism, drug abuse and anorexia as chronic suicide since the individuals were shortening their lives by their behaviors. Menninger also classified such behaviors such as polysurgery, self-castration, and self-mutilation as focal suicide, in which the self-destructive impulse is focused on one part of the body. These behaviors are often gender-linked. For example, anorexia is more common in women whereas illicit drug abuse is more common in men. Canetto [47] has speculated that adolescents may respond differentially when under stress, with girls choosing nonfatal suicidal behavior more while boys choose drug abuse more. The use of Menninger's categories would change greatly the relative incidence of nonfatal suicidal behavior in women and men.

7. THE STUDY OF CULTURE CAN CHALLENGE MYTHS

Many theories of human behavior, including suicidal behavior, are based on physiological factors. Cultural anthropology helps challenge such theories by showing, for example, that behaviors which we consider gender-specific are not found in every culture. As we have noted above, in the United States and in European nations, nonfatal suicidal behavior appears to occur at a higher rate in women than in men; as a result it is has come to be viewed as a "feminine" behavior by the general public [48] and by suicidologists as well. Other cultures, however, provide examples where nonfatal suicidal behavior, often carried out in front of others, is more common in men rather than women. The Nahane (or Kaska), a Native Canadian tribe located in British Columbia and the Yukon, provide a good example of this:

> Observations and communications agree that attempted suicide by men is of frequent occurrence and very likely to appear during intoxication. There is a general pattern for such attempted self-destruction. In the two cases of the sort observed during field work, the weapon selected was a rifle. As he brandishes the weapon the would be suicide announces his intention in an emotional outburst. This becomes the signal for interference to block the deed. One or more men leap forward to wrest the gun from the intended suicide's possession and toss it out of sight. The would be victim is now usually emotionally overwhelmed by his behavior. This pattern is illustrated by Louis Maza's behavior during intoxication. Several times during the afternoon, Louis had manifested aggression toward himself, crying: "I don't care if I'm killed. I don't care my life". After several hours of such emotional outbursts interspersed with quarreling and aggression toward his companions, he seized his large caliber rifle and threatened to kill himself. Old Man threw himself on the gun and as the two men grappled for the weapon, Louis succeeded in firing one wild shot. John Kean and the ethnographer ran to the camp and together wrenched the gun from the drunken man. John fired the shells in the chamber and Old Man tossed the gun half-way down the cutbank. No punishment or other discrimination is reserved for attempted suicides. The individual is comforted and in the future, while intoxicated, he is watched lest he repeat the attempt [49].

Among the Washo, located in Nevada and California, nonfatal suicidal behavior seems to be equally common in men and women.

> In one case, a man had been having difficulty with his wife; she was interested in another man. The husband ate wild parsnip, but was saved. As a result his sons brought pressure on the wife and made her behave. The couple stayed together until the husband died.Pete also says that men attempt suicide more than women, who just leave home when interpersonal difficulties arise. The

destruction of the self is an ultimate, and the fact that men are more likely to invoke it than women indicates a lack of male authority in Washo culture [50].

The Washo man is described as lacking authority and lacking in self-confidence, perhaps because the Washo man has had more difficulty adapting to the changing culture than has the Washo woman. Interestingly, the explanation provided by these Western anthropologists for the occurrence of nonfatal suicidal behavior among Washo men may be generalizable to societies where nonfatal suicidal behavior is more common in women. It may be that nonfatal suicidal behavior is not simply a "feminine" behavior, but rather a behavior found more commonly in those who are oppressed in a society, perhaps because the oppressed have fewer options for expressing their discontent.

8. THE IMPACT OF CULTURE CONFLICT

An issue that has become important in recent years is the impact of the pervasive Western culture on the suicidal behavior of those living in less modern cultures. The high suicide rates in some native American and Canadian groups and in some Micronesian islands has made this an issue of grave concern rather than mere academic debate.

Cultures often come into conflict. For example, the conflict between the traditional Native American culture and the dominant American culture has often been viewed as providing a major role in precipitating Native American suicide. May and Dizmang [51] noted that there were three major sociological theories which have been proposed for explaining the Native American suicide rate. One theory focuses on social disorganization. The dominance of the Anglo-American culture has forced Native American culture to change and has eroded traditional cultural systems and values. This changes the level of social regulation and social integration, important causal factors for suicide in Durkheim's [22] theory of suicide.

A second theory focuses on cultural conflict itself. The pressure from the educational system and mass media on Native Americans, especially the youth, to acculturate, a pressure which is opposed by their elders, leads to great stress for the youths.

A third theory focuses on the breakdown of the family in Native American tribes. Parents are often unemployed, substance abusers and in trouble with the law, and divorce and desertion of the family by one or more parents is common.

Acculturation occurs when a culture encounters a dominant alternative culture. The resulting pressure from the dominant culture leads to a variety of changes in the non-dominant culture [52]: physical changes (such as type of housing, urbanization and increasing population density), biological changes (resulting from changing diet and exposure to new diseases), political changes (such as loss of autonomy for the non-dominant culture), economic changes (such as changes in type of employment), cultural changes (in language, religion, education and the arts), social relationships (both within the culture and between the two cultures), and psychological changes at the individual level (in behavior, values, attitudes and motives).

Berry noted that four possibilities are open to the non-dominant culture: integration -- maintaining relations with the dominant culture while maintaining cultural identity; assimilation -- maintaining relations with the dominant culture but not maintaining cultural identity; separation -- not maintaining relations with the dominant culture but maintaining cultural identity; and marginalization -- not maintaining relations with the dominant culture and not maintaining cultural identity.

It would be of great interest to categorize the different Native American tribes as to which strategy appears to have been chosen and to examine the different consequences for the society and for the individuals in the society.

Research on Acculturation

Supportive results for the influence of acculturation on suicide in Native Americans comes from Van Winkle and May [53] who examined suicide rates in three groups of Native Americans in New Mexico (the

Apache, Navajo and Pueblo) and attempted to account for the differences in terms of the degree of acculturation. Overall, the crude suicide rates were 43.3 per 100, 000 for the Apache, 27.8 for the Pueblo, and 12.0 for the Navajo.

The Jicarilla and Mescalero Apache of New Mexico were originally nomadic hunters and gatherers, organized into self-sufficient bands whose leaders held limited power. Their religion had no organized priesthood and was not a cohesive force in their lives. Individualism was a highly valued characteristic. Today they live in homes scattered about the reservation or in border towns. They raise livestock, cut timber or work in tribally-owned businesses. Formal tribal governments have been established, but religion remains unimportant. Individualism is still valued. However, the raiding parties which formerly provided a some degree of social integration have been eliminated. The Apache appear, therefore, to have few integrating forces in their culture, and Van Winkle and May saw their high suicide rate as a direct result of this lack of integration.

The Apache have been in close contact with whites. Their reservations are small and surrounded by white communities. Indeed many Apache live in mixed communities. Thus, the Apache have high acculturation in addition to their low social integration.

The Pueblo traditionally lived in compact towns and engaged in agriculture. Religion permeated their lives and was a strong integrating force. There was an organized priesthood and religious societies which took care of religious and civil matters. Individualism was discouraged and conformity valued. Thus, the Pueblo were the most integrated group, and Van Winkle and May found their intermediate suicide rate a puzzle. They tried to explain the Pueblo suicide rate using the role of acculturation. The Pueblo have had increasing contact with whites since 1959. Many of the Pueblos are near large cities such as Albuquerque and Santa Fe. Thus, they have high social integration and moderate but increasing acculturation. For the larger Pueblo tribes, Van Winkle and May compared the suicide rates of those tribes which had acculturated and those which had remained traditional and found a clear tendency for the acculturated and transitional tribes to have the higher suicide rates.

The Navajo, who have the lowest suicide rate, were nomadic hunters and gatherers who later settled down and turned to agriculture. They are organized into bands, but matrilineal clans exert a strong influence. Although religion is important in their lives, they have no organized priesthood. Individualism is valued but not as strongly as among the Apache. Thus, their social integration appears to be intermediate between that of the Apache and that of the Pueblo. However, the Navajo were the most geographically and socially isolated from whites of the three groups until the 1970s when mineral exploration increased on their reservations and some Navajo began to take wage-earning jobs.

Van Winkle and May's explanation of the suicide rates in the three groups can be summarized as follows:

	Social Integration	**Acculturation**	**Suicide Rate**
Apache	low	high	high
Pueblo	high	moderate	moderate
Navajo	moderate	low	low

It can be seen that acculturation performed better than social integration an as explanation of the differing suicide rates.

In contrast, however, Bagley [54] found in Alberta that it was those native Canadian reservations which were more isolated (and, incidentally, poorer) which had the higher suicide rates. In Taiwan also, Lee, Chang and Cheng [55] found that the less assimilated aboriginal groups had higher suicides rates than those groups which were more assimilated in the mainstream culture.

These studies indicate that when different cultures encounter each other, the problems of acculturation can result in stress and its consequences, including increased rates of suicidal behavior, especially in the less dominant cultural group. But acculturation may not always lead to an increased incidence of suicide (and other disturbed behaviors). In the future, anthropologists may be able to identify which cultural characteristics enable some cultures to acculturate with few social and personal problems while other cultures develop many problems.

9. THE ASSUMPTION OF CULTURAL INVARIABILITY

Investigators often assume that a research finding found in one culture will apply to other cultures. It is, therefore, important to replicate research findings in cultures other than the one in which the results were first obtained to check on this assumption. For example, at the sociological level, Lester and Yang [56] found that females in the labor force and the ratio of divorces to marriages predicted suicide rates in the United States and Australia from 1946 to 1984, but that the associations were in opposite directions for the two nations. While in the United States the ratio of divorces to marriages was positively associated with the suicide, the association was negative in Australia.

Stack [57] found that divorce had a deleterious effect on the suicide rate in Sweden and Denmark, but not in Japan. Stack offered four possible reasons; the divorce rate may be too low in Japan to affect the suicide rate, Japanese family support may be strong enough to counteract the loss of a spouse, ties between couples may be weak in Japan, and the cultural emphasis on conformity in Japan may suppress suicidal behavior.

At the individual level, Lester, Castromayor and Icli [58] found that an external locus of control was associated with a history of suicidal preoccupation in American, Philippine and Turkish students, but that the association was no longer found for American students once the level of depression was controlled.

In a comparison of depression and suicide in mainland China and the United States, Chiles *et al.* [59] found that suicidal intent was predicted better by depression for Chinese psychiatric patients and better by hopelessness for American psychiatric patients.

De Man and his associates [60] have published a number of studies of suicidal behavior in French-Canadians in order to explore the replicability of research findings originally identified for English-speaking cultures.

It is important, therefore, for researchers to identify which findings have cross-cultural generality (and to which cultures) and which are specific to one culture.

10. SUBCULTURES

Wolfgang and Ferracuti [61] examined the role that a subculture of violence plays in producing high murder and assault rates. For example, Gastil [62] argued that such a subculture of violence pervaded the southern portion of the United States, and Marks and Stokes [63] used this to account for the greater use of firearms for suicide in southern states as compared to the rest of America.

Platt [64] suggested that electoral wards in Edinburgh, Scotland differed in their rates of attempted suicide and had different norms for suicidal behavior, thereby differing in their subculture of suicide. Those living in wards with the highest rate had more intimate contact with suicidal individuals and had different values about life, such as having a greater expectation that married couples would quarrel and that men would fight in public. However, Platt was unable to find to his satisfaction that the wards differed in the proposed subculture of suicide.

11. SUICIDE AMONG INDIGENOUS PEOPLES

In some nations there has been a good deal of research on and speculation about suicidal behavior in indigenous peoples, sometimes called aborigines. A great deal of research has been conducted on Native

Americans in the United States, and some on aborigines in Australia and Taiwan and on the Inuit in Canada and Greenland.

What is noteworthy, however, is that many nations have indigenous peoples, yet we hear little about their suicidality and other self-destructive behaviors. For example, in Central and South America, almost every nation has an indigenous population: 71% in Bolivia, 66% in Guatemala, 47% in Peru, 38% in Ecuador, 14% in Mexico, 8% in Chile, 2% in Colombia, 1.5% in Paraguay, 1% in Venezuela, and 0.4% in Brazil [65]. In recent years, these indigenous peoples have become organized politically. They have begun to protest against the governments of their nations, often toppling governments (as in Bolivia and Ecuador).

Even in developed nations, the oldest inhabitants are often ignored. In suicide statistics from the United Kingdom, data from England and Wales are reported together. A recent report on suicide in Wales [66] was rejected by reviewers for the British Journal of Psychiatry as being of no interest![3] The United Kingdom has ethnic groups in Wales and the county of Cornwall who predate the Roman, Danish and French invaders and who have their own languages and ethnic identity. Yet their suicidal behavior has received no attention.

In Africa, the situation is odd in a different way. Setting aside the remnants of the European colonialists, all of the peoples there can be considered indigenous. Yet, when data on suicide are reported, they are reported for the artificial nations that the colonial rulers established with no regard for the tribal groups in each country. For example, suicide rates have been reported for Zimbabwe [67, 68], yet Zimbabwe has two major ethic groups, the Shona (the dominant ethnic group) and the Ndebele. It would make much more sense to explore and compare suicide in these two ethnic groups.

Some nations are only now beginning to organize their mortality-reporting procedures and structures. In many of these, it will be important to take into account the various indigenous groups in the country, such as China which has a multitude of ethnicities within its borders.

12. COMPARISONS OF INDIGENOUS PEOPLES WITHIN A NATION

In a couple of nations, it has been possible to compare different ethnic groups within a nation. Lester [5] reviewed all of the studies on Native American suicide and summarized the suicide rates by tribe and by era (see Table **3**). It can be seen that there was a slight tendency for the suicide rates to rise during the 20th Century and for the tribes to differ greatly in their suicide rate, ranging in the 1970s from 149 per 100, 000 per year in the Kwakiutl and 73 in the Sioux to 7 in the Pima and 9 in the Lumbee.

Table 3: Tribal suicide rates in America [3]

Tribe	1910's	1920's	1930's	1940's	1950's	1960's	1970's	1980's
Aleut							16	
Apache					26	18	40	
Blackfoot						125		
Cherokee							23	
Cheyenne	22	21	13	6	40	48		
Eskimo							42	
Kwakiutl						40	149	
Lumbee							9	
Navajo					8	13		
Ojibway					6		56	
Papago						100		
Pima						40	7	

[3] It is no wonder that there is a Welsh liberation movement.

Table 3: cont….

Pueblo					10	55		
Pueblo (Hopi)					8	13	30	17
Shoshoni							38	
Shoshoni-Bannock						98		
Shoshoni-Paiute					113			
Sioux							73	31
Tlingit							30	
Yaqui						30		

Cheng [69, 70] compared suicide in Taiwan in two aboriginal groups (the Atayal and the Ami) with suicide in the dominant Han Chinese. The Atayal had a suicide rate of 68.2 per 100, 000 per year, the Ami 15.6 and the Han Chinese 18.0. The suicides in all three groups had a similarly high incidence of psychiatric disorder, and the high suicide rate in the Atayal was attributed to their high rate of alcoholism and earlier onset of major depressive disorders.

We need many more studies comparing the different groups of indigenous peoples within a nation, not simply the crude suicide rates, but also the circumstances, motives and meanings of suicide in these different groups.

13. THE HUMAN RELATIONS AREA FILES

Anthropologists have typically studied historical societies or societies which have been relatively less influenced by modernization, often called preliterate, nonliterate or primitive societies, societies composed of whom we would now call indigenous peoples.

There is a superb source of data on indigenous peoples in the Human Relations Area Files (HRAF). The headquarters for this project are at Yale University, but microfiche copies of the results of the project are available at other major universities in the United States and around the world. The staff of the project have collected reports from visitors to these cultures as far back as they can and from all kinds of visitors (such as missionaries, colonial administrators and anthropologists). The content of the reports is coded for topic, and, for example, to see what has been written about suicide in these cultures, the code for suicide is ascertained from the codebook (it is 762), and then the section for 762 can be located for each culture in the HRAF. There are about 330 cultures represented in the HRAF. The files are now available on a CD-ROM, and there is a website for the HRAF (www.yale.edu/hraf/collections.htm).

The files are updated and enlarged continually. To give some examples of the source material, in 1994, the Ainu in Japan had 1, 573 text pages from 11 sources that had been coded, the Lapps in Finland 3, 284 text pages from 16 sources, the Yoruba in Nigeria 1, 637 text pages from 45 sources, and Delaware Indians in the United States 1, 733 text pages from 15 sources.

Several projects on suicide can be devised from the HRAF. First, some investigators have read the files on suicide for a sample of societies and tried to estimate the suicide rate for each society.

Masumura [71] had two judges rate 35 nations for the frequency of suicide by having them read the suicide entries in the HRAF, and his ratings are shown in Table **4** [71]. From this group of cultures, it would appear that, among Native American groups, the Kwakiutl have a relatively high suicide rate and the Pomo a relatively low suicide rate. In a research study on this sample, Masumura found that the estimated suicide rate was positively associated with a measure of social integration in opposition to a prediction from Durkheim's [22] classic sociological theory of suicide.

Table 4: Estimates of relative suicide rates for 35 non-literate societies by Masumura [71]

Group	Suicide Score (Range 2-8)
Ainu	6
Andamanese	2
Araucanians	5
Ashanti	6
Bakongo	6
Banks Islanders	7
Bushmen	6
Chippewa	7
Chukchee	8
Creek	6
Crow	6
Dahomeans	6
Fang	6
Hottentot	6
Iban	7
Iroquois	5
Jivaro	7
Kazak	6
Kutenai	4
Kwakiutl	8
Lango	8
Maori	8
Navajo	2
Norsemen	5
Omaha	4
Pomo	2
Rwala	7
Samoans	8
Sema Naga	6
Semang	2
Toda	6
Trobrianders	8
Tuareg	4
Vedda	4
Yahgan	2

Ember and Ember [72] drew attention to the fact that the materials on suicides in the HRAF come from very different time periods. Therefore, they urged that it was important to specify the year from which the data were derived. For example, they rated the Creek suicide rate as 1.74 (on a scale of 0-8) in 1800 and the Omaha as 1 in 1860.

Case Studies

On occasions, anthropologists who have studied particular cultures write specifically on suicide. For example, Bohannan [73] edited a book on suicide in Africa in which the contributors looked at suicidal behavior in several tribes from Uganda and Kenya.

Bohannan noted first that earlier investigators had differed greatly in whether they thought that suicide in primitive societies was rare [74] or common [75]. It is more reasonable to conclude that the range for the incidence of suicide in primitive societies may be as great as in modern societies [76]. Not only may the rate of suicide vary from one primitive society to another, but these differences may be stable even after emigration, forced as a result of slavery or free. For example, Bastide [77] noted that Mina, Dahomeans and Yoruba slaves in Brazil tended more often to assault and kill their slave owners, whereas Fulani slaves and those from Gabon and Mozambique tended more often to kill themselves.

As an anthropologist, Bohannan was not so much interested in the individual motives that people had for killing themselves in a society (he viewed what was in the mind of the suicide as unknowable), but rather he was interested in the causes ascribed to the suicide by members of the society. These popular ideas about suicide tell us something about the culture.

For example, Fallers and Fallers [78] examined suicide among the Busoga of southeastern Uganda. The Busoga view suicide as an irresponsible and foolish act, probably impulsive. Thus, suicide, like homicide, is an act which must be punished. The body of a suicide is burnt, along with the tree or hut from which the person hung himself, and buried in waste land or at a crossroads. For the period from 1952 to 1954, the official suicide rate for the society was 7.0 per 100, 000 per year, which the Fallers thought was a slight underestimate.

Taking one hundred cases of suicide, the Fallers found that 86 percent hung themselves, in most cases impulsively. Sixty-nine percent were men. The most common motive was disease (31%) followed by quarrels with spouse, lover or kinsman (23%). Quarrels with a spouse was present in 48 percent of the homicides and 21 percent of the suicides, suggesting that marriage was full of conflict. The patrilineal nature of the society means that spouses have divided loyalties. The wife, in particular, feels drawn back to her family, and wives who feel oppressed by their husbands (which is not uncommon) often flee back to their father. The Fallers noted that the breaking down of the cultural traditions in recent times had decreased the incidence of suicide and homicide, probably as a result of the weakening of intergenerational family ties, which in turn has reduced marital conflicts.

In commenting on this and other reports, Bohannan [73] noted that domestic institutions are responsible for the greatest number of the suicides. Women committed suicide as wives - they were unable to play the role of wife or mother because of husbands or fathers, co-wives or fate. Men, to a lesser extent, committed suicide as husbands, but impotence and loss of status played roles too. Suicide is consistently viewed as irresponsible and evil, and rituals involve destruction of the suicide's possessions and ritual cleaning. Bohannan felt that the suicide rates were moderate to low, though accurate estimates were mostly absent.

It should be noted that historical studies of indigenous peoples may become more important as indigenous peoples cross-marry with the dominant cultures. For example, at the present time in New Zealand, there are no "pure" Maoris. All surviving Maoris have at least one white ancestor.

Theories of Suicide

There has been one theory of suicide, proposed by Naroll [79-81] which was based on a study of these nonliterate societies and tested using data from the societies rather than data from modern nations, the basis for Durkheim's [22] theory of suicide. Naroll proposed that suicide occurred in those who were socially disoriented, that is, in those who lack or lose basic social ties. But since all of those who are in this condition do not commit suicide, there must also be a psychological factor involved, that is, the individual's reaction to thwarting disorientation contexts. Thwarting disorientation contexts are those in which the individual's social ties are broken or weakened and those in which another person thwarts the individual and prevents him or her from achieving desired and expected satisfactions or in which they experience frustration. This thwarting must be interpersonal and not impersonal. Storm damage to one's dwelling is not thwarting but, when another person sets fire to it and destroys it, it is thwarting. The widow is not thwarted, but the divorced spouse is thwarted. Under the conditions of thwarting disorientation, individuals are more prone to commit suicide in such a way that it comes to public notice, that is, protest suicide. Naroll felt that this theory, better than other theories, explained suicide committed by indigenous peoples [80].

Jeffreys [82] felt that Durkheim's [22] categories of suicide, based on the concepts of social integration and social regulation, were not sufficient to explain cases of suicide he found in African tribes. He described suicide committed in order to revenge oneself on those one is angry at - a type of suicide he called "Samsonic suicide" after the story of Samson in The Bible.

Revenge can be obtained in two ways. In some societies, the belief is that one's ghost can return and harm those at whom one is angry, as among the Herero of South West Africa [83]. Alternatively, the societal laws demand that those who provoked a suicide must pay some penalty, usually a fine, but in some societies death. The payment of a heavy fine by the person who provoked a suicide is customary, for example, among the Bavenda [84] and the Kassena [85].

Lester [86] noted that the Mohave have a clearly specified theory of suicide - namely that suicide in their people is increasingly due to a breakdown in ties to the community and tribe as a whole and to an increasing dependence on a primary relationship with a lover or spouse. Lester tested this hypothesis that suicide would be common in nations with higher levels of individualism, and the results confirmed this hypothesis.

It can be seen that examples of suicide behaviors, customs and attitudes in indigenous peoples can challenge traditional Western theories of suicide.

Comment

There has been a failure of suicidologists to study suicidal behavior in many indigenous peoples. On occasions they ignore indigenous peoples completely, such as the Welsh and Cornish peoples in the United Kingdom or the Basques in France and Spain. On other occasions, as in Africa, they study suicide in the artificially-created nations (created by the colonial rulers) rather than in the more meaningful ethnic groups. Occasionally, when suicide is studied in these nations, the investigators omit to mention the ethnic background of the people [87].

Second, this section has drawn attention to the Human Relations Area Files (HRAF) with its rich source of data on indigenous peoples, including suicide. Data from the HRAF were used to illustrate how suicide rates can be estimated and how the data can be used to test theories of suicide.

Finally, examples were given of theories of suicide which derive from studies of suicide in indigenous peoples rather than from studies of suicide in Western nations.

14. PSYCHOTHERAPEUTIC IMPLICATIONS

All of this scholarly discourse is important at the theoretical level, but it may be asked whether there are implications for counseling and psychotherapy. It is sometimes argued that only 'like' can counsel 'like', that is, that only homosexuals can counsel homosexuals, women counsel women, ex-addicts counsel addicts, and so on. Is the same true also for different cultures? The majority of counselors and psychotherapists deny this, claiming that a good counselor or psychotherapist can counsel any kind of patient. However, to counsel someone very different in background from oneself may require that the counselor learn about the background and culture from which the individual comes. Sue and Sue [88] have addressed the issues that psychotherapists of one culture must confront when counseling clients from different cultures, such as racism and cultural differences in verbal and nonverbal communication styles.

Zimmerman and Zayas [89] have illustrated this point in their discussion of treating the suicidal adolescent Hispanic female. They noted that, in New York City, the values of the adolescent latina often clash with those of her more traditional mother. Both mother and daughter experience problems in communication and a rupture in their relationship. Thus, the problem of acculturation exacerbates the normal adolescent turmoil. The latina's mother wants her daughter to succeed in this new culture, yet she also wants her daughter to maintain traditional cultural attitudes and roles. The adolescent latina feels overwhelmed by this conflict and, in extreme cases, makes a suicide attempt in an effort to reduce the tension felt in this conflict. After a suicide attempt, the psychotherapist must explain the conflict to the mother and daughter and help them find ways to re-establish mutual understanding and empathy.

It is possible, of course, that psychotherapists could identify the nature of the problems confronting suicidal people and their families each time they encounter such a family, but the psychotherapeutic process is facilitated if psychotherapists have some notion of the cultural issues which they are likely to encounter.

Sue and Sue [88] presented the case of Janet, a Chinese-American female college senior majoring in sociology, who came to the college counseling center complaining of depression, feelings of worthlessness and suicidal thoughts. She had difficulty identifying the causes of her depression, but she seemed quite hostile to the psychotherapist who was also Chinese-American.

Discussion of this revealed that Janet resented being seen by a Chinese psychotherapist, feeling that she had been assigned to one because of her own race. Janet disliked everything Chinese, including Chinese men whom she found sexually unattractive. She dated only white men, which had upset her parents. However, her last romance had broken up partly because her boyfriend's parents objected to him dating a Chinese woman.

Janet clearly had difficulties stemming from her continuing denial of her Chinese heritage. She was being forced to realize that she was Chinese for she was not fully accepted by white America. Initially she blamed the Chinese for her dilemma, but then she turned her hostility toward herself. Feeling alienated from her own culture and rejected by the white culture, she was experiencing an identity crisis with a resulting depression.

The psychotherapist in such a case must deal with cultural racism and its effects on minorities. Positive acculturation must be distinguished from rejection of one's own cultural values, as well as typical adolescent rebellion from one's parents. Psychotherapists can work with such a client more effectively if they are conversant with the cultural history and experiences of Asian-Americans.

Does Cultural Conflict Cause Suicide?

Although the problem of acculturation has been proposed as one of the major causes of depression and suicidal behavior among Native Americans, the majority of research reports on Native American individuals who attempt or complete suicide mention precipitating causes such as grief over loss and quarrels with relatives and friends. Rarely is cultural conflict listed among the precipitating causes. Of course, it may be that the problems of acculturation raise the stress level of individuals so much that stressors, which under ordinary circumstances would not precipitate suicide, now do so.

A few brief case histories have been published which do illustrate the problems of acculturation and culture conflict. For example, Berlin [90] described the case of a bright young Native American woman who completed undergraduate school and qualified as a teacher and who was admitted to graduate school. Her clan, however, told her that she was required to teach on the reservation. Her desire to go to graduate school was seen as striving to be better than her peers, and this was unacceptable and forbidden. The young women had a psychiatric breakdown and was hospitalized. In a similar situation, the tribe and another family could not decide whether to let a young woman go to graduate school for an MBA after she obtained her undergraduate degree and, during the long wait for a decision, she attempted suicide.

In this latter case, the young woman, whom Berlin called Josie, had alcoholic parents who frequently sent her and her brothers and sisters to live with relatives while they went on drinking sprees. A teacher realized Josie's potential and received permission for Josie to live with her. With this teacher's help, her academic performance improved, and she went to college. Josie now resented that her parents, who had neglected her, were involved in decisions about her life. The clan leadership and tribal council were relatively enlightened about the issues and eventually gave permission for Josie to attend graduate school. While at graduate school, Josie underwent psychotherapy to deal with her depression and anger and other personal problems. After graduation, she returned to the tribe to manage their business office, marrying a young man who had fought a similar battle in order to obtain an MSW degree.

Westermeyer [91] provided cases of Native Americans seen at the University of Minnesota Hospitals for whom trying to live in the mainstream American culture had presented problems. Westermeyer felt that identity problems were perhaps no more common in Native Americans than in whites, but that Native Americans did show a unique type of identity problem, namely, ambivalent or negative feelings about their ethnic identity. Westermeyer presented cases of urban Native Americans who illustrate this problem.

Five of the patients, ranging in age from 12 to 23, had identity crises - they experienced conflict about their Native American identity and about what being "Indian" meant. All were students and economically dependent upon others. For example, one young girl, who was seen after a suicide attempt, had her Indian mother die two years earlier. She then lived with her white father and six siblings for a year. The father had trouble supporting them and sent the children to live with their Indian maternal grandmother. The patient began to use drugs and had problems with her white teachers at school. Eventually a white welfare worker sent her to a white foster home, at which point she attempted suicide. In the hospital, she said, "I'm the only Indian here and I hate everybody like they hate me". She had a recurrent dream in which she gave birth to baby girl with blue eyes which she loved but which she also wanted to injure.

Five of the cases were judged to have a negative identity. These were older than the patients with identity crises, and all were male. They were estranged from their Indian family members, and they lived as lower class individuals on the periphery of the white society. One patient was admitted with hallucinations and paranoid delusions after a drinking binge. He had a record of multiple psychiatric admissions. Although he supported the idea of Indian activism, he felt estranged from Indians, had little respect for them and avoided them. He had joined a Jewish student activist group which he admired, and he wondered whether his Indian tribe might be a lost tribe of Israel. He identified himself as a Zionist.

CONCLUSIONS

There are large cultural differences in the incidence of suicidal behavior, and culture influences also the methods used for committing suicide and the reasons for doing so. Although these cultural differences may be a result of physiological differences between the members of the different cultures, the more plausible explanations involve psychological and social variables, such as the abuse of alcohol and the level of social integration and regulation. When competing cultures interact, there may be increased stress (and, as a result, an increase in suicidality) in the less dominant culture.

It should be noted also that, in societies which are culturally heterogeneous, such as the United States, Canada and Australia, it cannot be assumed that suicides from the different cultural groups are similar in rate, method, motive and precipitating factors. Those working to prevent suicide in such societies must take these cultural influences into account.

This chapter has attempted to raise and briefly discuss several of the issues involved in the interaction of culture and suicide. These issues should not be viewed as problems, but rather as opportunities to plan and execute innovative and exciting research and to work more effectively with suicidal clients from diverse cultures.

REFERENCES

[1] Lester D. Suicide and culture. World Cult Psychiatry Res Rev 2008; 3(2): 51-68.

[2] Jacob KS, Sharan P, Mirza I, *et al.* Mental health systems in countries. Lancet 2007; 370: 1061-77.

[3] Phillips MR, Liu H, Zhang Y. Suicide and social change in China. Cult Med Psychiatry 1999; 23: 25-50.

[4] Lester D. Variation in suicide and homicide rates by latitude and longitude in the US, Canada and Australia. Am J Psychiatry 1985; 142: 523-4.

[5] Lester D. Suicide in American Indians. Commack NY: Nova Science, 1997a.

[6] Douglas JD. The social meanings of suicide. Princeton. NJ: Princeton University, 1967.
[7] Malla A, Hoenig J. Differences in suicide rates. Can J Psychiatry 1983; 28: 291-3.
[8] Hlady WG, Middaugh JP. The underrecording of suicide in state and national records, Alaska, 1983-1984. Suicide Life-Threat Behav 1988; 18: 237-44.
[9] Sainsbury P, Barraclough BM. Differences in suicide rates. Nature 1968; 220: 1252.
[10] Lester D. Migration and suicide. Med J Aust. 1972; 1: 941-2.
[11] Dublin LI. Suicide. New York: Ronald, 1963.
[12] Girard C. Age, gender, and suicide. Am Soc Rev 1993; 58: 553-74.
[13] Conklin GH, Simpson ME. The family, socioeconomic development and suicide. J Com Fam Stud 1987; 18: 99-111.
[14] Lester D. Patterns of suicide and homicide in the world. Commack, NY: Nova Science, 1996.
[15] Menozzi P, Piazza A, Cavalli-Sforza L. Synthetic maps of human gene frequencies in Europeans. Science 1978; 201: 786-92.
[16] Lester D. National distribution of blood groups, personal violence (suicide and homicide), and national character. Pers Individ Dif 1987; 8: 575-6.
[17] Kondrichin SV, Lester D. Finno-Ugrians and homicide. Psychol Rep 2002; 90(3 Pt 2):1190.
[18] Voracek M, Loibl LM, Kandrychyn S. Testing the Finno-Ugrian suicide hypothesis. Percept Mot Skills 2007; 104: 985-94.
[19] Adrian M. International trends in alcohol production, trade and consumption, and their relationship to alcohol-related problems, 1970 to 1977. J Public Health Policy 1984; 5: 344-67.
[20] Weissman MM, Klerman GL. Sex differences and the epidemiology of depression. Arch Gen Psychiatry 1977; 34: 98-111.
[21] Moksony F. Ecological analysis of suicide. In: Lester D, Ed. Current concepts of suicide. Philadelphia: Charles. 1990; pp. 121-138.
[22] Durkheim E. Le suicide. Paris: Felix Alcan, 1897.
[23] Johnson BD. Durkheim's one cause of suicide. Am Soc Rev; 1965; 30: 875-86.
[24] Stack S. The effect of religious commitment on suicide. J Health Soc Behav 1983; 24: 362-74.
[25] Taylor S. Suicide, Durkheim, and sociology. In Lester D, Ed. Current concepts of suicide. Philadelphia: Charles, 1990; pp. 225-236.
[26] Lester D. Thinking about suicide. Hauppauge, NY: Nova Science, 2004.
[27] Lester D. Explaining the regional variation of suicide and homicide. Arch Suicide Res 1995a; 1: 159-74.
[28] Lester D. Predicting suicide in nations. Arch Suicide Res. 2005; 9: 219-23.
[29] Hendin H. Suicide and Scandinavia. New York: Grune & Stratton, 1964.
[30] Counts DA. Ambiguity in the interpretation of suicide. In: Lester D, Ed. Why women kill themselves. Springfield, IL: Charles Thomas.1988; pp. 87-109.
[31] Early KE. Religion and suicide in the African-American community. Westport, CT: Greenwood, 1992.
[32] Wolfgang ME. Victim-precipitated criminal homicide. J Crim Police Sci; 1957: 48: 1-11.
[33] Gibbs J. Conceptual, methodological, and sociocultural issues in black youth suicide. Suicide Life Threat Behav 1988;18: 73-89.
[34] DeCatanzaro D. Suicide and self-damaging behavior. New York: Academic Press, 1981.
[35] Burvill P, McCall M, Woodings T, Stenhouse N. Comparison of suicide rates and methods in English, Scots and Irish immigrants in Australia. Soc Sci Med 1983; 17: 705-8.
[36] Clarke RV, Lester D. Suicide: Closing the exits. New York: Springer-Verlag, 1989.
[37] Killias M, Kesteren J van, Rindlisbacher M. Guns, violent crime, and suicide in 21 countries. Can J Crim 2001; 43: 429-48.
[38] Kreitman N. The coal gas story. Br J Prevent Soc Med 1976; 30: 86-93.
[39] Lester D. Effects of the detoxification of domestic on suicide rates in six nations. Psychol Rep 1995b; 77: 294.
[40] Lester D. The epidemiology of suicide in Chinese populations in six regions of the world. Chin Ment Health J 1994a; 7: 21-4.
[41] Lester D. Differences in the epidemiology of suicide in Asian Americans by nation of origin. Omega 1994b; 29: 89-93.
[42] Lester D. Suicide by jumping in Singapore as a function of high-rise apartment availability. Percept Mot Skills 1994c; 79: 74.
[43] Devereux G. Mohave ethnopsychiatry. Washington, DC: Smithsonian Institution, 1961.
[44] Counts DA. Fighting back is not the way: Suicide and the women on Kaliai. Am Ethnol 1980; 7: 332-51.

[45] Ramon S. Attitudes of doctors and nurses to self-poisoning patients. Soc Sci Med 1980; 14A: 317-24.
[46] Menninger K. Man against himself. New York: Harcourt, Brace & World, 1938.
[47] Canetto SS. Gender roles, suicide attempts, and substance abuse. J Psychol 1991; 125: 605-20.
[48] Linehan M. Suicide and attempted suicide. Percept Mot Skills 1973; 37: 31-4.
[49] Honigmann JJ. Culture and ethos of Kaska society. New Haven, CT: Yale University Press, 1949.
[50] D'Azevedo WL, Freed SA, Freed RS, *et al.* The Washo Indians of California and Nevada. Salt Lake City, UT: University of Utah, 1963.
[51] May PA, Dizmang LH. Suicide and the American Indian. Psychiatr Annals 1974; 4(11): 22-8.
[52] Berry JW. Acculturation and adaptation. Arch Med Res. 1990; 49: 142-50.
[53] Van Winkle NW, May PA. Native American suicide in New Mexico, 1959-1979. Human Organization, 1986; 45: 296-309.
[54] Bagley, C. Poverty and suicide among native Canadians. Psychol Rep 1991; 69: 149-50.
[55] Lee CS, Chang JC, Cheng AT. A. Acculturation and suicide. Psychol Med 2002; 32: 133-41.
[56] Lester D, Yang B. The relationship between divorce, unemployment and female participation in the labor force and suicide rates in Australia and America. Aust New Zeal J Psychiatry 1991; 25: 519-23.
[57] Stack S. The effect of divorce of suicide in Japan. J Marriage Fam 1992; 54: 327-34.
[58] Lester D, Castromayor IJ, Icli T. Locus of control, depression, and suicidal ideation among American, Philippine and Turkish students. J Soc Psychol 1991; 131: 447-9.
[59] Chiles JA, Strosahl K, Ping ZY, *et al.* Depression, hopelessness and suicidal behavior in Chinese and American psychiatric patients. Am J Psychiatry 1989; 146: 339-44.
[60] De Man AF, Balkou S, Iglesias RI. A French-Canadian adaptation of the scale for suicide ideation. Can J Behav Sci 1987; 19: 50-5.
[61] Wolfgang ME, Ferracuti F. The subculture of violence. London, UK: Tavistock, 1967.
[62] Gastil R. Homicide and a regional culture of violence. Am Soc Rev 1971; 36: 412-27.
[63] Marks A, Stokes CS. Socialization, firearms and suicide. Soc Probl 1976; 23: 622-9.
[64] Platt SD. A subculture of parasuicide? Hum Relat 1985; 38: 257-97.
[65] (2/21/2004). A political awakening. The Economist 2004, 370(8363): 35-7.
[66] Lester D. Predicting the suicide rate in Wales. Psychol Rep 1994d; 75: 1054.
[67] Rittey DAW, Castle WM. Suicides in Rhodesia. Cent Afr J Med 1972; 18: 97-100.
[68] Lester D, Wilson C. Suicide in Zimbabwe. Cent Afr J Med 1988; 34: 147-9.
[69] Cheng ATA. Mental illness and suicide. Arch Gen Psychiatry 1995; 52: 594-603.
[70] Cheng ATA. Personality disorder and suicide. Br J Psychiatry1997; 170: 441-6.
[71] Masumura WT. Social integration and suicide. Behav Sci Res 1977; 12: 251-69.
[72] Ember CR, Ember R. Warfare, aggression, and resource problems. Behav Sci Res 1992; 26: 169-226.
[73] Bohannan P, Ed. African homicide and suicide. New York: Atheneum, 1967.
[74] Cavan RS. Suicide. Chicago: University of Chicago, 1928.
[75] Steinmetz SR. Suicide among primitive peoples. Am Anthropol 1894; 7: 53-60.
[76] Westermarck E. Suicide. Sociol Rev 1908 ; 1: 12-33.
[77] Bastide R. Le suicide du nègre brésilien. Cah Intern Sociologie 1952; 7(12): 79-90.
[78] Fallers LA, Fallers MC. Homicide and suicide in Busoga. In: Bohannan P, Ed. African homicide and suicide. New York: Atheneum. 1967; pp. 6593.
[79] Naroll R. Data quality control. New York: Free Press, 1962.
[80] Naroll R. Thwarting disorientation and suicide. Unpublished discussion paper, Northwestern University, 1963.
[81] Naroll R. Cultural determinants and the concept of the sick society. In: Plog SC, Edgerton RB, Eds. Changing perspectives in mental illness. New York: Holt, Rinehart & Winston. 1969; pp. 128-155.
[82] Jeffreys MDW. Samsonic suicide or suicide of revenge among Africans. Afr Stud 1952; 11(3): 118-22.
[83] Vedder H. The Herero. In: Hahn CHL, Ed. The native tribes of South West Africa. Cape Town: Cape Times. 1928; pp.153-211.
[84] Stayt HA. The Bavenda. Oxford: Oxford University Press, 1931.
[85] Cardinall AW. Natives of the northern territories of the Gold Coast. London: G. Routledge & Sons, 1920.
[86] Lester D. Note on a Mohave theory of suicide. Cross-Cult Res 1997b; 31: 268-72.
[87] Sefa-Dedeh A, Canetto SS. Women, family and suicidal behavior in Ghana. In: Gielen VP, Adler LL, Milgram NA, Eds. Psychology in international perspective. Amsterdam: Swets & Zeitlinger. 1992; pp. 299-309.
[88] Sue DW, Sue D. Counseling the culturally different. New York: Wiley, 1990.

[89] Zimmerman JK, Zayas L. Suicidal adolescent latinas. In: Canetto S, Lester D, Eds. Women and suicide. New York: Springer. 1995; pp. 120-132.

[90] Berlin IN. Psychopathology and its antecedents among American Indian adolescents. Adv Clin Child Psychol 1986; 9: 125-52.

[91] Westermeyer J. Ethnic identity problems among ten Indian psychiatric patients. Intern J Soc Psychiatry 1979; 25: 188-97.

CHAPTER 3

Economic Crises and Suicide

Marco Innamorati[1,*], Maurizio Pompili[1,2], David Lester[3], Bijou Yang[4], Mario Amore[5], Cristina Di Vittorio[5], Paolo Girardi[1]

[1]Department of Neurosciences, Mental Health and Sensory Functions, Suicide Prevention Center, Sant'Andrea Hospital, Sapienza University of Rome, Italy; [2]McLean Hospital - Harvard Medical School, MA, USA; [3]The Richard Stockton College of New Jersey, Pomona, NJ, USA; [4]Drexel University, Philadelphia, PA, USA and [5]Department of Neurosciences Division of Psychiatry, University of Parma, Italy

Abstract: As a result of the strong link between mental illness and suicide, the diagnosis and treatment of psychiatric disorders have been always considered a first-choice strategy in the prevention of suicide. However, prevention may take advantage from the study of other factors that may help to explain inequalities in the suicide rates between countries and fluctuations over time. The aim of the present chapter is to review empirical research which has investigated the impact of economic crises and recession on suicide. To this goal we performed careful MedLine and PsycINFO searches from 1980 to 2010. Our analysis of the literature indicates that there is no strong evidence that a recession in the economy is a causal factor for suicide.

Keywords: Suicide, economic crisis, risk factors.

1. INTRODUCTION

Several risk factors have been proposed to explain suicide, both at the group or societal level and at the individual level [1]. In 2002, the World Health Organization proposed an ecological model, which included individual, interpersonal, community and societal variables, to explain suicide [2]. At the individual level, several categories of risk factors have been proposed to explain suicide, such as demographic, clinical and socioeconomic variables. Psychiatric disorders, especially depressive disorders, have been thoroughly investigated and are considered to be the most common risk factors for suicide [3-6]. As a result of this strong link between mental illness and suicide, the diagnosis and treatment of psychiatric disorders have been always considered a first-choice strategy in the prevention of suicide. However, prevention may take advantage from the study of other factors that may help to explain inequalities in the suicide rates between countries and fluctuations over time. Social and economic factors may be useful in this task.

Emile Durkheim long ago theorized that variables at the societal (aggregate) level pertaining to the socioeconomic environment may be important determinants of suicide risk in emerging and high-income countries [7, 8]. Durkheim was not the first to point out the association between suicide and social and economic change. Falret back in 1822 contended that suicide rates tend to rise during periods of rapid social change and in times of economic depression [9]. However, Durkheim's seminal work on suicide has been the most influential in contemporary sociology [10, 11]. He proposed the abstract notions of social integration and social regulation in order to demonstrate the powerful social forces behind suicide. Durkheim contended that the greater the social integration and social regulation, the lower the suicide rate. He also added an economic dimension to the social framework of suicidal behavior. Economic booms and busts brought about less social integration and social regulation than did normal economic situations and the suicide rate rose accordingly during those times.

Besides Durkheim's theory, other sociological theories have been formulated to explain the link between economic cycles and suicide. Yang and Lester [12, 13] reviewed three distinctive sociological theories which

***Address correspondence to Marco Innamorati:** Department of Neurosciences, Mental Health and Sensory Functions, Suicide Prevention Center, Sant'Andrea Hospital, Sapienza University of Rome, Italy; E-mail: innamorati.marco@libero.it

Maurizio Pompili (Ed)

highlight the way in which the suicide rate of a society is influenced by its business cycle: (a) Durkheim's U-shaped theory; (b) Ginsberg's procyclical theory; and (3) Henry and Short's countercyclical theory.

According to Durkheim [7], a higher suicide rate is associated with a decline in social integration and social regulation. When the economy expands or contracts sharply, social integration and social regulation may weaken, and so the suicide rate rises. Ginsberg [14] argued that suicide arose from the dissatisfaction of individuals. Dissatisfaction itself was related directly to the discrepancy between the actual reward that individuals were receiving and their level of aspiration. Ginsberg assumed that the actual reward varies positively with the business cycle. When replacing the individual level of dissatisfaction, reward and aspiration with the average levels for the society, suicidal behavior at the societal level, may be seen as resulting from the discrepancy between aspirations and rewards. As the economy expands toward the peak of the business cycle, the prosperous economic environment pushes aspirations up at a rate faster than the rewards. The resulting growing disparity between aspirations and rewards triggers suicide. When the economy faces a recession, as it moves toward the trough of the business cycle, aspirations actually drop faster than rewards, thus shrinking the disparity between aspirations and rewards. As a result, the suicide rate will decline. Henry and Short [15] argued that the relationship between suicide and business cycle is countercyclical. Suicide rates tend to rise during times of economic busts and to fall during times of economic booms. Their theory is based on a frustration-aggression hypothesis which is grounded in five assumptions: (a) frustration often results in aggression; (b) business cycles affect the hierarchical rankings of persons by status; (c) frustrations are caused by a failure to maintain a constant or rising position in the status hierarchy relative to the status position of other groups; (d) high-status persons lose status relative to low status persons during business contractions, and they gain relative status during business expansions; and (e) suicide occurs mainly in high-status persons. During business contractions, some individuals of high economic status commit suicide due to their loss of status relative to low-status individuals, whereas during expansions, individuals of high status tend to gain relative status and so are less inclined to kill themselves.

As Yang [16] pointed out, all these theories imply a mediational model by which economic cycles affect suicide rates. In Durkheim's theory, the mediating variables are social integration and social regulation, in Ginsberg's theory, the mediating variable is aspiration level relative to actual rewards received and in Henry and Short's theory, the mediating factor is the relative status of social groups.

Yang [12] also proposed a real-income hypothesis of suicide which attempts to demonstrate that positive consequences can accompany economic development and growth. In this hypothesis, real income is used as a proxy for material well-being, since a higher level of real income is, presumably, associated with better facilities for ensuring the physical and mental health of the public. Three studies tested and confirmed the hypothesis [12, 16, 17]. The most recent study [16] used a cross-sectional study of 48 continental states of the United States in the census year 1990 to replicate the study conducted on the census year 1980 [18]. The results indicated that, for the total population, males and white males, the expansion of the economy was associated with the suicide rate in a counter-cyclical way; meaning that a more prosperous economy was linked with a lower suicide rate. In analyses regarding other groups, the impact of the economic environment was not significant.

Durkheim's, Ginsberg's and Henry and Short's theories propose different mechanisms between economic changes and suicide rates, and they hypothesize different relationships between economic cycles and suicide. Furthermore, not all these three theories hypothesize a direct link between recession in the country's economy and higher suicide rates. However, this link is indicated by several studies [19].

In recent years, most industrialized countries have experienced a profound recession in their economy. Therefore, it is important to better understand the link between suicide and economic crises and recessions. The aim of the present chapter is to review results from empirical research which has investigated the impact of economic crises and recessions on suicide rates.

2. METHOD

We performed careful MedLine and PsycINFO searches from 1980 to 2008. The following search terms were used: suicide (which comprises suicide, suicidal, suicidality, and other suicide-related terms), economic crisis OR economic recession. In addition, each category was cross-referenced with the others using the MeSH method (Medical Subjects Headings). Selection of papers suitable for this study allowed the inclusion only of those articles published in English peer-reviewed journals. Included were those studies that added an original contribution to the literature. A total of 110 articles were located through our search, and the most relevant articles were selected for this overview.

3. ECONOMIC RECESSIONS AND SUICIDE

Several studies have investigated the pro-cyclical *versus* the counter-cyclical nature of the link between economic crises and suicide. In a classic study, Brenner [19] restated old observations about economic cycles having an impact on health and mortality. In Brenner's view, economic instability and insecurity increased the likelihood of higher mortality rates. The increase in general mortality may be evident two and three years after the recession, while the increase in mortality by violent methods (suicide and homicide) would have shorter time lags after the economic recession. Following the research of Brenner [19], Ruhm [20], used 1972-1991 United States panel data to examine the relationship between economic conditions and health. He found robust and consistent evidence that the total mortality rate, age-specific mortality rates and most of the cause-specific death rates were pro-cyclically associated with economic crises. His finding that higher unemployment rates are associated with lower mortality, and *vice versa*, stands in contrast to Brenner's earlier work. Ruhm also found that, unlike other causes of mortality, suicide behaves counter-cyclically (increasing as economic growth falls). Suicides are predicted to rise 1.3% for each one percentage point increase in the state unemployment rate.

More recently, Neumayer [21], extending Ruhm's original analyses, analysed the effect of state unemployment and economic growth rates on mortality in the states of Germany over the period 1980-2000, both in a static and a dynamic econometric model. Controlling for state-specific effects, Neumayer found evidence that aggregate mortality rates for all age groups taken together, as well as for most of the specific age groups, were lower during economic recessions. Investigating specific causes of mortality, the results indicated that the unemployment rate was negatively associated with mortality from suicide for males, females and both sexes combined. A one percentage point increase in state unemployment rate caused a decrease in the suicide rate of 0.98% for males and 1.98% for females in the static econometric model. A one percentage point increase in state unemployment rate caused a 1.97% decrease in the female suicide rate in the dynamic short-run econometric model, and a 2.63% decrease in the female suicide rate in the dynamic long-run econometric model, but there was no significant change in the male suicide rate in these two models.

These studies, therefore, do not resolve the issue of the pro-cyclical *versus* counter-cyclical nature of the link between economic crises and suicide, nor whether this link really exists. However, one limit of Neumayer's study is that he did not study age bands separately, so that his results may mask different trends in the younger and older age bands. Consistent with this hypothesis are the results of Järventie and Kivelä [22] who investigated suicide mortality trends among the Finnish elderly population in 1960-1979. They reported that suicide rates remained unchanged among the elderly population between 1960 and 1979, and there were no peaks in the suicide rate which coincided with economic recessions. On the other hand, suicide mortality among the population aged 15-64 years increased in the years investigated.

All the analyses reviewed are limited to only single countries. Recently Stuckler *et al.* [23] investigated how economic changes have affected European Union mortality rates over the past three decades (1970-2007). They also examined associations between changes in employment and mortality and how these associations were modified by different types of government expenditures. The authors reported that a 1% increase in unemployment was associated with a 0.79% rise in suicide rates for those under the age of 65 years (95%CI 0.16-1.42). Furthermore, large rises in unemployment (>3% in a year) had a greater effect on suicide rates for those under the age of 65 years (4.45%; 95%CI: 0.65-8.24). However, across countries, the strength of the response of suicide rates to changes in unemployment varied substantially (from -0.13 in Sweden to +0.59 in Spain). Only two countries in the EU stood out as de-coupling economic crises from suicides: Finland between 1990 and 1993, when unemployment rates rose from 3.2% to 16.6% but suicide rates declined steadily, and Sweden between 1991 and 1992, when unemployment rates rose from 2.1% to 5.7% while suicide rates also declined.

Consistent with the hypothesis that the link between economic crises and suicide may be country-specific (and probably time-specific) are other studies from the European region. For example, La Harpe and Dozio [24] investigated cases of suicide in Geneva from 1991 to 1995. Their data showed a decrease in the suicide rate despite severe unemployment accompanying economic stagnation. Lucey *et al.* [25] examined the association between seven socioeconomic indicators (GDP, unemployment rate, female labor force participation rate, alcohol expenditures, marriage rate, percentage of births outside of marriage, and indictable crime rate) and total, male, and female rates of suicide and suicide plus undetermined deaths, in Ireland during the period 1968-2000. During the years investigated, there was a steady increase in the suicide rate in parallel with rapid social change. However, Lucey and colleagues found no evidence that trends in socioeconomic variables were the driving force behind the rising trends in the Irish suicide rate.

In Italy, two studies have produced somewhat contrasting results. Platt, Micciolo, and Tansella [26] assessed the relationship between suicide and unemployment during the period 1977-1987. They found that the annual rate of female unemployment was negatively correlated with the total female suicide rate but was unrelated to the suicide rate among the unemployed. While the unemployment rate was positively correlated over time with the male suicide rate, the change in the suicide rate across 18 geographic regions of Italy was unrelated to changes in the unemployment rate. Preti and Miotto [27] investigated suicide rates and economic cycles between 1982-1994. Over time, the suicide rates increased for both men and women, and the increase was greater among the unemployed than among the employed for both men and women. Each year, the suicide rate increased by 1.62 deaths per 100,000 among unemployed men and by 2.40 deaths per 100,000 among men in search of their first job, against only 0.19 for employed men. The increase was lower for unemployed women (0.26 and 0.51, respectively, for women seeking a new job and women seeking their first job), but still higher than among employed women who had an increase of only 0.04 deaths per 100,000.

The link between suicide and unemployment, an important feature of economic crises, is highlighted by other studies [28, 29], especially those investigating Northern European countries. For example, Hintikka, Saarinen, and Viinamaki [30] investigated whether there was an association between suicide mortality, growth and recession in the national economy, unemployment, divorce rates and mean alcohol consumption in Finland between 1985 and 1995. They reported that suicide mortality fell when the country experienced an economic recession. Age-adjusted suicide mortality in men and women increased by 20% and 22%, respectively, during the economic upswing from 1985 to 1990. During the economic recession (1990-1995), suicide mortality decreased by 13% and 4% respectively.

Lundin and Hemmingsson [31], commenting on the study by Stuckler *et al.*, suggested that the association between the experience of unemployment and the risk of suicide has often been viewed as causal and a result of economic problems and loss of social support among unemployed people. However, according to an alternative hypothesis, an association between unemployment and suicide may be a result of the fact that people with risk factors for suicide (*e.g.*, mental illness) are at higher risk of unemployment [9]. If this is the case, any association between unemployment and suicide would not affect the overall suicide rate. In support of this alternative hypothesis, the authors reported the results of a recent study in which they used prospective information about risk factors for suicide in a large cohort of middle-aged men during the Swedish recession of the 1990s [32]. Individuals with indicators of mental illness and other risk factors for suicide were more likely to become unemployed, and those who were unemployed had an increased relative risk of suicide compared with those still employed. However, at least two-thirds of the increased relative risk of suicide associated with becoming unemployed was explained by the higher prevalence of mental illness and the risk factors for mental illness.

Parallel to the results of that study are those studies investigating suicide attempts in Finland. For example, Ostamo and Lönnqvist [33] investigated rates of attempted suicide between 1989-1997 in Helsinki. These authors reported that Finland's severe economic recession of the 1990s, which led to very high unemployment rates in Helsinki, was not closely associated with attempted suicide rates.

When investigating the link between economic crises and suicide in recent years among European countries, the experience of Russia and other countries from the former Soviet Bloc are of great interest. These countries experienced major transitions in their socioeconomic structures and severe economic recessions after the fall of the Berlin wall in 1989. Russia underwent a transformational recession between 1989-1998, with the Russian economy losing 45% of its output. During these years, life expectancy dropped from 70 to 65 years. After a short-lived period of stabilization between 1995-98, the Russian economy underwent another economic crisis in August 1998 when the Russian currency lost over 60% of its value in several months, inflation spiraled out of control, and crime, suicide and mortality rates increased once more [34]. Economic growth and the gradual restoration of the government's ability to provide public goods led to improved social conditions. Suicide and mortality rates started to fall after 2002-2003. In response to this economic crisis, Gavrilova [35] reported an increase in the age-adjusted suicide mortality rate both in males and females - 1.6 times higher for males and 1.2 times higher for females in 1994 compared to 1990. Furthermore, the relative role of suicide in the recent rise of violent mortality was higher for males compared to females.

Rancans *et al.* [36] examined the dynamics of suicide rates in Latvia during the period 1980-1998, with special attention to major socioeconomic correlates influencing the dynamics of suicide rates. The authors reported that, during the stagnation period of 1970-1984, the total suicide rate was in the range of 28.0-34.3 per 100,000 inhabitants, after which a decline began in 1985, with the rate dropping to 23.1 in 1988. This coincided with perestroika and anti-alcohol campaigns initiated by Gorbachov. After this, a rapid increase in the suicide rate began in 1989, coinciding with the fall of the Berlin wall, and reached a peak of 42.5 per 100,000 in 1993, an 80% increase compared to the suicide rate for 1988. Finally, between 1993 and 1998, the suicide rate remained high, but with a steady decline, reaching a rate of 34.0 in 1998. When analyzing suicide rates separately by sex, between 1988 and 1993 the increase was almost entirely limited to Latvian men (from 35.0 suicides per 100,000 inhabitants in 1988 to 72.0 per 100,000 in 1993). Thereafter, suicide rates declined in both sexes by 20-40%. As for the gross domestic product (GDP), a steady increase began 1980 but was halted in 1990 when the GDP fell by 50% over the next 3 years. Then, a slow growth of GDP started in 1995 and reached 86.7% of the level of 1980 by 1998.

Rancans and colleagues argued that changes in GDP and the suicide rates over this period were clearly counter-cyclical — there was a simultaneous fall in GDP and a rise in suicide rates. Focusing on unemployment, the authors reported that, between 1992 (when official statistics for unemployment in Latvia started) and 1998, the unemployment rate increased steadily, reaching a maximum of 9.2% at the end of the period. Nevertheless, after a rapid increase of the suicide rate in 1991-1994, suicide rates declined in spite of a continuing increase in the unemployment rate.

Outside the European Region, Morrell *et al.* [37] conducted an ecological study investigating Australian annual age-adjusted male and female suicide rates and annual unemployment rates for the period 1907-1990. The results indicated a different impact of unemployment in men and women. While female suicide rates were generally stable throughout the period, those for males demonstrated sharp fluctuations, with the peaks coinciding with times of high unemployment. Furthermore, the association between suicide rates and unemployment was especially high for the period 1966-1990 in 15-24 year-old males.

In New Zealand, between 2001 and 2004, the Ministry of Health commissioned a set of five reports from the Wellington Medical School that examined a range of possible social explanations for the trends in New Zealand's suicide rates to 1999. The scope of the reports included a selective literature review of published studies examining a range of social factors for suicide, comparisons of suicide rates between Finland and New Zealand during economic recessions, and the correlation between suicide and socio-economic fluctuations in New Zealand over a 20-year period. A sixth report that draws conclusions from these five reports was released to coincide with the release of the Government's draft of an all-ages suicide prevention strategy.

Howden-Chapman *et al.* [38] examined institutional arrangements and policy conditions that may have contributed to the differences in suicide rates, particularly those of young men (aged 15 to 24), among New Zealand and Finland. New Zealand and Finland are both small, developed countries with governments that support redistributive welfare policies. A severe economic recession hit both countries in the late 1980s and early 1990s, but the New Zealand and Finnish governments reacted very differently. New Zealand's welfare state became less comprehensive and more of a liberal safety net model, while Finland largely maintained the comprehensive nature of the welfare state.

The authors used a shock model to test causation in suicide mortality. In this model, an environmental shock, such as an economic depression, affects the whole or part of the population during a definable period of time [39]. The fluctuations in economic output in Finland and New Zealand were used to test such a shock model by looking at the differential impact of recent recessions as part of a longer time-series over the post-war period, which included economic booms and periods of sustained growth. In line with the economic shock model, the model proposed by the authors was that a largely unavoidable global economic recession has a differential impact on a country's economy and society depending on the state of the economy and society when the recession hits and on the response of the national government.

Because the data sets of the two countries were not directly comparable, the authors ran separate analyses for each country. Furthermore, they tested three different models: the first one with the annual change in GDP as a predictor (and the time variable); the second model with the Gini coefficient as a predictor (and the time variable); and the third model with both the economic variables (and the time variable). All the models failed to find a statistically significant impact from the economic variables.

A second report indicated that rapidly rising levels of income inequality and unemployment in New Zealand between the late 1980s and early 1990s did in fact coincide with increasing youth suicide rates over that period, and coincided with falling suicide rates among people aged 45 years and older [40].

Finally, Collings, Atkinson, and Fawcett [41] investigated whether trends in suicide rates in New Zealand during the 1980s and 1990s were related to various social indicators such as age, gender, ethnic groups, and marital and socioeconomic status (household income, car access, highest educational qualification and labor-force status). Regarding trends over time in relation to unemployment, the suicide rate of 18-24 year-olds increased in all labor-force status groups (except unemployed 18–24-year-old males), and the most notable increases were among the employed. Among 25–44-year-old males, there was little change over time in suicide rates among the non-active, but a 73% increase among employed males (p for trend = 0.06). Finally, there were no clear trends in suicide rates by labor-force status among 45–64-year-olds, except among employed 45–64-year-old females whose suicide rate dropped by 50% over the period (p for trend = 0.04).

Finally, there was evidence that, over time, suicide trends varied by income. Among 25–44 and 45–64-year-olds, the association of low income with suicide risk increased over time. However, this increasing trend was largely removed in the multivariable analyses that controlled for marital status and socioeconomic factors.

In Asia several studies have investigated the impact of economic recessions on suicide trends in the last few decades [42-51]. For example, Chang *et al.* [42] investigated the impact of the Asian economic crisis (1997-1998) on suicide in six East Asian countries (Japan, Hong Kong, South Korea, Taiwan, Singapore and Thailand). During the years analysed, trends in GDP per capita showed an economic downturn in most East/Southeast Asian countries. Japan, Hong Kong, Korea, Singapore and Thailand were hit very hard, and they all experienced a sharp recession in 1998 (with negative GDP growth). During the same years, Taiwan experienced a slight slowing of economic growth. While GDP growth reversed or slowed, the unemployment rates rose and did not recover until 2006. Again in 2001, Taiwan and Singapore experienced another economic recession, with a slowing-down in GDP growth and a marked rise in unemployment.

The analyses indicated that the Asian economic crisis was associated with a rise in suicide rates in some, but not all, affected countries. In Japan, Hong Kong and Korea, there were 10,400 excess suicides in 1998 when compared to number of suicides in 1997. On the contrary, the recession did not appear to affect suicide rates in Taiwan and Singapore, where the economic crisis had a smaller impact on GDP and unemployment. The rise in the suicide rate appeared to be more prominent in men, especially working-age men (15-64 year olds). The increase in male suicide rates in Japan, Hong Kong and Korea appeared to remain about the same after controlling for changes in divorce and marriage rates. However, when further controlling for unemployment, the differences did not change much in Japan, but the association was eliminated in Hong Kong and Korea, suggesting that some of the impact of the crisis on male suicides was attributable to rises in unemployment in the latter two countries.

Results in females were similar too, but less striking than, those in males. Female suicide rates in Japan during the crisis period were higher than those in the rest of the study period, but the differences were less evident in Korea and absent in Hong Kong. As in men, the differences remained the same in Japan but diminished in Korea when controlling for changes in the unemployment rates. There is little evidence for a difference in female suicide rates between the crisis and the non-crisis periods in Taiwan and Singapore except for weak evidence of higher rates in Singapore in 1998 than those in the rest of study period.

More recently, Kwon *et al.* [52] investigated trends in both absolute and proportional suicide rates over the period of Korean economic development, crisis and recovery (1986-2005). The analyses indicated that the economic crisis before and after 1997/1998 appeared to result in a sudden increase in suicide rates in the short term, and the suicide rate showed a continuous increase until 2005. In both men and women, the proportional increases in suicide rates were more prominent among the younger age group (under the age of 45), despite the absolute increase being larger in the older group. There were conflicting patterns of correspondence between macro-social indicators and suicide rates. For example, per capita gross national income trends had two distinct components: a long-term increase and a short-term drop around 1998, which were in opposite directions. In contrast, suicide rates showed a steady increasing trend.

4. DISCUSSION

The aim of the present chapter was to review empirical research investigating the impact of economic crises and recessions on suicide. The review of the literature indicated mixed results. Several studies failed to produce evidence for a strong link between changes in GDP or unemployment and suicide rates.

This analysis of the literature seems to indicate that economic recessions do not directly influence the suicide rate of individuals. The link between economic crises, unemployment growth, and suicide is probably mediated by other social variables. For example, the study of Gunnell *et al.* [53], which investigated possible causes of the different suicide trends in younger people and in older people in England and Wales between 1950 and 1998, is in line with this hypothesis. Gunnell's statistical analyses indicated that factors most consistently associated with the rise in young male suicide were increases in divorce, declines in marriage and increases in income inequality (as measured by the Gini Index), whereas these changes had little impact on suicide in young females. In older people, declines in suicide were associated with increases in GDP, the size of the female workforce, marriage and the prescribing of antidepressants.

One factor that may mediate the impact of economic crisis on individual health is the public health policies adopted by governments. A recent paper [54], which investigated suicide rates in elderly people in the former European Community and their association with macro-socioeconomic variables, indicated that public health policies (relevant to total health expenditures, WHO estimates of public expenditures on health, WHO estimates of public expenditures on health as percentage of total government expenditures, acute care hospital beds per 100,000, and general practitioners per 100,000 population) are all associated with changes in suicide rates. All of these indices, except the number of acute care hospital beds, were negatively associated with suicide rates in the European Community. Surprisingly, when the number of acute care hospital beds increases, suicide rates increase in the elderly. Two factors were the strongest predictors of suicide mortality: public expenditures on health as a percentage of total government expenditures and acute care hospital beds per 100,000.

As Chatterjee [55] has argued, the situation may be particularly problematic in emerging countries where economic crises followed years of economic success which raised people's expectations enormously, and where improvements in the public health system did not follow the economic boom of the last decade. For example, the author reported that, in India, a country of over a billion people, there are only around 3,500 psychiatrists, mostly located in urban areas, whereas 75% of the population is located in rural areas.

Another possible factor mediating the link between economic crises and suicide rates may be changing habits in alcohol consumption [23, 56-58]. Support for the effect of alcohol consumption on suicide derive from several longitudinal and cross-sectional aggregate-level studies which have reported a significant and positive association between alcohol consumption and suicide [59-61], although studies from various countries indicate that this association varies with age [62], gender [63] and country [64]. Razvodovsky [65], analyzing vodka sales in Russia, reported that the coincident trends between the level of vodka sales and suicide rates in this period indicate that a restriction of vodka availability can be considered to be an effective measure for suicide prevention in countries where rates of both vodka consumption and suicide are high. His time-series analysis suggests a positive relationship between the level of vodka sales per capita and suicide rates, both with no time lag and with first-order lags.

In conclusion, there is no convincing evidence that recessions in the economy or increases in unemployment rates are causal factor for increases in suicide rates. However, policy makers should continue to evaluate how economic recessions impact welfare and public-health policies, which in turn impact those who have an individual diathesis for suicide (such as a severe mental illness). They also should plan national policies regarding the availability of alcohol beverages for populations at risk such as adolescents and young adults who, in times of economic recession, are those who have the greater possibility of losing their job or waiting a long time to find their first job. In this situation, alcohol use may be a culturally accepted strategy to cope with hopelessness and depression.

REFERENCES

[1] Lester D, Yang BJ. Microsocionomics *versus* macrosocionomics as a model for examining suicide. Psychol Rep 1991; 69: 735-38.
[2] World Health Organization. World report on violence and health. Geneva: World Health Organization, 2002.
[3] Conwell Y, Duberstein PR, Caine ED. Risk factors for suicide in later life. Biol Psychiatry 2002; 52: 193-204.
[4] Haw C, Hawton K, Houston K, Townsend E. Psychiatric and personality disorders in deliberate self-harm patients. Br J Psychiatry 2001; 178: 48-54.
[5] Henriques GR, Brown GK, Berk MS, Beck AT. Marked increases in psychopathology found in a 30-year cohort comparison of suicide attempters. Psychol Med 2004; 34: 833-41.
[6] Suominen KH, Henriksson M, Suokas J, Isometsa E, Ostamo A, Lonnqvist J. Mental disorders and comorbidity in attempted suicide. Acta Psychiatr Scand 1996; 94: 234-40.
[7] Durkheim E. Le suicide. Paris: Felix Alcan, 1897.
[8] Berkman LF, Glass T, Brissette I, Seeman TE. From social integration to health: Durkheim in the new millennium. Soc Sci Med 2000; 51: 843-57.
[9] Platt S. Unemployment and suicidal behavior: a review of the literature. Soc Sci Med 1984; 19: 93-115.
[10] Taylor SH. Durkheim and the study of suicide. London: Macmillan, 1982.
[11] Taylor SH. Suicide and social theory. In: Lester D, Ed. Emile Durkheim: Le suicide 100 years later. Philadelphia: Charles Press. 1994; pp. 1-10.
[12] Yang BJ. A real income hypothesis of suicide. Annual meeting of the Eastern Economic Association; 1989 March; Baltimore. 1989.
[13] Lester D, Yang BJ. The economy and suicide: economic perspectives on suicide. Commack: Nova Science, 1997.
[14] Ginsberg RB. Anomie and aspirations. Dissertation Abstracts 1966; 27A: 3945-6.
[15] Henry AF, Short JF. Suicide and homicide. New York: Free Press, 1954.
[16] Lester BY. Learnings from Durkheim and beyond: the economy and suicide. Suicide Life Threat Behav 2001; 31: 15-31.
[17] Yang BJ. The economy and suicide: A time-series study of the U.S.A. Am J Econ Soc 1992; 52: 87-99.
[18] Yang BJ, Lester D. Is there a natural suicide rate for a society? Psychol Rep 1991; 68: 322.

[19] Brenner MH. Mortality and the national economy. A review, and the experience of England and Wales, 1936--76. Lancet 1979; 2: 568-73.
[20] Ruhm C. Are Recessions Good For Your Health? Quarterly Journal of Economics 2000; 115: 617-650.
[21] Neumayer E. Recessions lower (some) mortality rates: evidence from Germany. Soc Sci Med 2004; 58: 1037-47.
[22] Jarventie I, Kivela SL. Suicide mortality among the elderly Finnish population 1960-1979. Public Health 1986; 100: 373-84.
[23] Stuckler D, Basu S, Suhrcke M, Coutts A, McKee M. The public health effect of economic crises and alternative policy responses in Europe: an empirical analysis. Lancet 2009; 374: 315-23.
[24] La Harpe R, Dozio A. [Economic crisis and suicide in Geneva: 1991-1995]. Arch Kriminol 1998; 202: 69-74.
[25] Lucey S, Corcoran P, Keeley HS, Brophy J, Arensman E, Perry IJ. Socioeconomic change and suicide: a time-series study from the Republic of Ireland. Crisis 2005; 26: 90-4.
[26] Platt S, Micciolo R, Tansella M. Suicide and unemployment in Italy: description, analysis and interpretation of recent trends. Soc Sci Med 1992; 34: 1191-201.
[27] Preti A, Miotto P. Suicide and unemployment in Italy, 1982-1994. J Epidemiol Community Health 1999; 53: 694-701.
[28] Crombie IK. Can changes in the unemployment rates explain the recent changes in suicide rates in developed countries? Int J Epidemiol 1990; 19: 412-6.
[29] Gunnell D, Lopatatzidis A, Dorling D, Wehner H, Southall H, Frankel S. Suicide and unemployment in young people. Analysis of trends in England and Wales, 1921-1995. Br J Psychiatry 1999; 175: 263-70.
[30] Hintikka J, Saarinen PI, Viinamaki H. Suicide mortality in Finland during an economic cycle, 1985-1995. Scand J Public Health 1999; 27: 85-8.
[31] Lundin A, Hemmingsson T. Unemployment and suicide. Lancet 2009; 374: 270-1.
[32] Lundin A, Lundberg I, Hallsten L, Ottosson J, Hemmingsson T. Unemployment and mortality--a longitudinal prospective study on selection and causation in 49321 Swedish middle-aged men. J Epidemiol Community Health; 64: 22-8.
[33] Ostamo A, Lonnqvist J. Attempted suicide rates and trends during a period of severe economic recession in Helsinki, 1989-1997. Soc Psychiatry Psychiatr Epidemiol 2001; 36: 354-60.
[34] Popov V. After 10 years of growth, the Russian economy may be losing steam. Russian Analytical Digest 2008; 48/08: 2-23.
[35] Gavrilova NS, Semyonova VG, Evdokushkina GN, Gavrilov LA. The response of violent mortality to economic crisis in Russia. Pop Res Policy Rev 2000; 19: 397-419.
[36] Rancans E, Salander Renberg E, Jacobsson L. Major demographic, social and economic factors associated to suicide rates in Latvia 1980-98. Acta Psychiatr Scand 2001; 103: 275-81.
[37] Morrell S, Taylor R, Quine S, Kerr C. Suicide and unemployment in Australia 1907-1990. Soc Sci Med 1993; 36: 749-56.
[38] Howden-Chapman P, Hales S, Chapman R, Keskimäki I. The Impact of Economic Recession on Youth Suicide: a comparison of New Zealand and Finland. Wellington: Ministry of Health, 2005.
[39] Foster A. Are cohort mortality rates autocorrelated? Demography 1991; 28: 619-637.
[40] Ferguson S, Blakely T, Allan B, Collings S. Suicide Rates in New Zealand: exploring associations with social and economic factors. Wellington: Ministry of Health, 2005.
[41] Collings S, Atkinson J, Fawcett J. Suicide Trends and Social Factors New Zealand 1981-1999: analyses from the New Zealand census- mortality Study. Wellington: Ministry of Health, 2005.
[42] Chang SS, Gunnell D, Sterne JA, Lu TH, Cheng AT. Was the economic crisis 1997-1998 responsible for rising suicide rates in East/Southeast Asia? A time-trend analysis for Japan, Hong Kong, South Korea, Taiwan, Singapore and Thailand. Soc Sci Med 2009.
[43] Khang YH, Lynch JW, Kaplan GA. Impact of economic crisis on cause-specific mortality in South Korea. Int J Epidemiol 2005; 34: 1291-301.
[44] Kim H, Song YJ, Yi JJ, Chung WJ, Nam CM. Changes in mortality after the recent economic crisis in South Korea. Ann Epidemiol 2004; 14: 442-6.
[45] Lotrakul M. Suicide in Thailand during the period 1998-2003. Psychiatry Clin Neurosci 2006; 60: 90-5.
[46] Chuang HL, Huang WC. A re-examination of the suicide rates in Taiwan. Soc Indic Res 2007; 83: 465-85.
[47] Inoue K, Tanii H, Abe S, *et al.* The report in the correlation between the factor of unemployment and suicide in Japan. Am J Forensic Med Pathol 2008; 29: 202-3.
[48] Loh M, Tan CH, Sim K, *et al.* Epidemiology of completed suicides in Singapore for 2001 and 2002. Crisis 2007; 28: 148-55.

[49] Park JS, Lee JY, Kim SD. [A study of the effects of the economic growth rate and unemployment rate to the suicide rate in Korea]. Korean J Prev Med 2003; 36: 85-91.

[50] Yamasaki A, Sakai R, Shirakawa T. Low income, unemployment, and suicide mortality rates for middle-age persons in Japan. Psychol Rep 2005; 96: 337-48.

[51] Watts J. Suicide rate rises as South Korea's economy falters. Lancet 1998; 352: 1365.

[52] Kwon JW, Chun H, Cho SI. A closer look at the increase in suicide rates in South Korea from 1986-2005. BMC Public Health 2009; 9: 72.

[53] Gunnell D, Middleton N, Whitley E, Dorling D, Frankel S. Why are suicide rates rising in young men but falling in the elderly?-- a time-series analysis of trends in England and Wales 1950-1998. Soc Sci Med 2003; 57: 595-611.

[54] Innamorati M, Tamburello A, Lester D, *et al.* Inequalities in suicide rates in the european union's elderly: trends and impact of macro-socioeconomic factors between 1980 and 2006. Can J Psychiatry. In press.

[55] Chatterjee P. Economic crisis highlights mental health issues in India. Lancet 2009; 373: 1160-1.

[56] Makela P, Valkonen T, Martelin T. Contribution of deaths related to alcohol use to socioeconomic variation in mortality: register based follow up study. BMJ 1997; 315: 211-6.

[57] Razvodovsky YE. Alcohol psychoses and all-cause mortality in Belarus. Adicciones 2008; 20: 395-405.

[58] Brenner MH. Relation of economic change to Swedish health and social well-being, 1950-1980. Soc Sci Med 1987; 25: 183-95.

[59] Caces F, Harford T. Time series analysis of alcohol consumption and suicide mortality in the United States, 1934-1987. J Stud Alcohol 1998; 59: 455-61.

[60] Pridemore WA, Chamlin MB. A time-series analysis of the impact of heavy drinking on homicide and suicide mortality in Russia, 1956-2002. Addiction 2006; 101: 1719-29.

[61] Razvodovsky YE. Suicide and alcohol psychoses in Belarus 1970-2005. Crisis 2007; 28: 61-6.

[62] Makela P. Alcohol consumption and suicide mortality by age among Finnish men, 1950-1991. Addiction 1996; 91: 101-12.

[63] Lester D. Alcoholism and drug abuse. In: Maris RW, Berman AL, Maltsberger JT, Yufit RI, Eds. Assessment and prediction of suicide. New York, Guilford Press. 1992; pp. 321-6.

[64] Lester D. The association between alcohol consumption and suicide and homicide rates: a study of 13 nations. Alcohol Alcohol 1995; 30: 465-8.

[65] Razvodovsky YE. Beverage-specific alcohol sale and suicide in Russia. Crisis 2009; 30: 186-91.

CHAPTER 4

Suicide and Alcohol Abuse

Marco Innamorati[1,*], Maurizio Pompili[1,2], Gianluca Serafini[1], Luigi Janiri[3], Désirée Harnic[3], Denise Erbuto[1] and David Lester[4]

[1]Department of Neurosciences, Mental Health and Organs Functions, Suicide Prevention Center, Sant'Andrea Hospital, Sapienza University of Rome, Italy; [2]McLean Hospital - Harvard Medical School, USA; [3]Department of Neurosciences, Day-Hospital of Psychiatry, Catholic University of the Sacred Heart, Rome, Italy and [4]The Richard Stockton College of New Jersey, USA

Abstract: Suicide is an escalating public health problem, and alcohol use has consistently been implicated in the precipitation of suicidal behavior. We reviewed evidence for the relationship between alcohol use and suicide through a search of MedLine and PsychInfo electronic databases. The results of our review indicate a clear link between alcohol use disorders and suicide but, to date, the causal nature of this relationship is speculative. The solution may be in research investigating the possible biological, social and psychological variables that mediate this link.

Keywords: Alcohol abuse, suicidal behaviour, psychiatric disorders.

1. INTRODUCTION

Within the European Region, the ESEMeD/MHEDEA 2000 Investigators Scientific Committee [1] examined the 12-month and lifetime prevalence rates of mood, anxiety and alcohol disorders in six European countries (Belgium, France, Germany, Italy, the Netherlands, and Spain), in over 21,000 adults. The investigators reported a lifetime prevalence of 5.2% (95%CI: 4.8-5.6) for any alcohol disorder, higher in males (9.3% [95%CI: 8.5-10.1]) than in females (1.4% [95%CI: 1.1-1.7]). In Italy, Piccinelli *et al.* [2] reported a 12-month prevalence of 1.3% for alcohol dependence and 5.6% for harmful use. More recently, also in Italy, Faravelli *et al.* [3] reported a lifetime prevalence for alcohol dependence of 0.8% in males and 0.5% in females (0.3% *vs.* 0.2% for 12-month prevalence; 0.2% *vs.* 0.2% for 1-month prevalence in males and females, respectively). In the United States, recent findings from the National Epidemiological Survey on Alcohol and Related Conditions (NESARC) [4] indicate that the 12-month prevalence of DSM-IV-TR alcohol dependence in the adult population is 3.8% and that of alcohol abuse 4.7% [5]. This means that, every year, 8.5% of the adult United States population has an alcohol use disorder [5].

These rates are alarming because the consumption of alcoholic beverages is estimated to be responsible for some 9% of the total disease burden worldwide [6]. The existence of a possible link between alcohol use and suicide has been known since the time of Kraepelin [7]. This link has been supported more convincingly since the mid-1960s [8-10] and confirmed in recent years [11-14]. Several studies have documented a link between alcohol use and suicidal ideation and attempted suicide [15], two strong precursors of completed suicide. Crombie *et al.* [16] found that alcohol consumption is a common precursor to suicide, suggesting that alcohol may play an important role in the events leading to suicide in individuals with no previous psychiatric history. Retrospective post-mortem studies report that between 34% and 56% of suicides meet the criteria for alcohol use disorder [17-21]. A meta-analytic study by Harris and Barraclough [22] indicated a positive association between alcohol use disorders and suicide.

These studies indicate that alcohol use disorders and suicide, two major public health problems, with a tragic impact on society, are linked. However, it is difficult to establish the nature of this relationship. The goal of this chapter is to provide a broad overview of the link between alcohol use and suicide, focusing on the nature of this relationship.

***Address correspondence to Marco Innamorati:** Department of Neurosciences, Mental Health and Organs Functions, Suicide Prevention Center, Sant'Andrea Hospital, Sapienza University of Rome, Italy; E-mail: innamorati.marco@libero.it

Maurizio Pompili (Ed)

2. METHOD

We performed a MedLine and PsychInfo search for articles from 1991 to 2010. We used the following search strategy: (suicide OR suicide attempt OR suicide ideation) AND (epidemiology OR rates OR trends OR incidence) AND (alcohol use OR alcohol intoxication OR alcohol drinking OR alcoholism OR alcohol use disorder OR alcohol dependence). Each category was cross-referenced with the others using the MeSH method (Medical Subjects Headings). Selection of papers suitable for this study allowed the inclusion only of those articles published in English peer-reviewed journals. Duplicate articles were removed, and those abstracts that did not explicitly mention suicide and alcohol use and articles that did not provide levels/measures of alcohol use specifically for suicides were excluded.

3. ALCOHOL AND COMPLETED SUICIDE

Several studies have found an excess of suicide among alcoholics [23-30]. For example, Beck and Steer [31] and Beck *et al.* [32] found that alcoholism was the strongest single predictor of subsequent completed suicide in a sample of patients who attempted suicide. Studies of samples of completed suicides indicate that alcoholics account for between 20% and 40% of all suicides [33]. Follow-up studies suggest that alcoholics may be between 60 and 120 times more likely to complete suicide than those free from psychiatric illness [13].

Post-mortem investigations have revealed that alcohol was in the blood of 45% of Swedish [34], 36-40% of Finnish [35, 36], 35-48% of Estonian [37], 28-29% of American [38, 39] and 20% of Dutch [40] suicides. Psychological autopsy studies have confirmed the association between alcohol use and suicide [41], despite often combining alcohol with other drugs because of sample size limitations [42]. In spite of their limited statistical power, psychological autopsy studies in different nations over different decades have consistently documented that mood and substance use disorders, particularly alcoholism, are the most prevalent disorders in suicides [17, 43-45]. Psychological autopsy, follow-up, and case-control studies [22, 46, 47] all indicate that alcohol and other drug-related disorders are risk factors for suicide [18, 21, 42, 48, 49].

In 1997, Harris and Barraclough, in their unusually comprehensive meta-analysis, analysed thirty-two papers related to alcohol dependence and abuse, comprising a population of over 45,000 individuals [22]. They found that, combining the studies, the suicide risk was almost six times that expected, but with variation of 1-60 times. Specifically, they found that the suicide risk for females was very much greater than for males, about 20 times that expected compared with four times for males. Suicide risk among alcohol-dependent individuals has been estimated to be 7% (comparable with 6% for mood disorders; [50]). Of 40,000 Norwegian conscripts followed prospectively over 40 years, the probability of suicide was 4.76% (relative risk= +6.9) among those classified as alcohol abusers compared with 0.63% for non-drinkers [51]. Similar findings have been made worldwide [52]. Murphy *et al.* studied 50 suicides and found that an alcohol use disorder was the primary diagnosis in 23% of the suicides and a co-occurring diagnosis in 37% [53]. Conwell *et al.* performed a study in New York City and reported that alcohol misuse was present in the history of 56% of individuals who completed suicide [17].

Reviewing the literature for the period 1991-2001, Cherpitel, Borges, and Wilcox [54] found a wide range of alcohol-positive cases for both completed suicide (10-69%) and attempted suicides (10-73%). Several case-control studies at the individual level have shown a high prevalence of alcohol abuse and dependence among suicides [55, 56]. Kolves *et al.* [55], in a psychological autopsy study, reported that 68% of males and 29% of females who committed suicide met the criteria for alcohol abuse or dependence.

4. NATURALISTIC STUDIES

The association between alcohol use and suicide has also been documented using aggregate studies of alcohol consumption in various countries [57-61]. This association varies with age [62], gender [63] and country [58]. Results from time-series analyses on aggregate level data from several European countries indicate a stronger effect of alcohol consumption on suicide in low consumption countries than in high consumption countries [64-68].

For example, Norstrom [69] reported that the estimated effect was stronger in Sweden (13% per litre) than in France (3% per litre). Ramstedt [67] studied the association for the period 1950-1995 in 14 European Union countries and found that an increase in drinking had a larger impact on suicide in northern Europe (8.6% per litre for men and 11.4% for women) than in mid-Europe and southern Europe (0.6% per men and 0.5% per women). If these data were to be confirmed, there is support for the hypothesis that the effect of alcohol on suicide rates is stronger in the northern European countries characterized by a low per capita consumption, with the bulk of consumption concentrated on a few occasions (binge-drinking pattern), or so-called "dry" drinking cultures, than in the southern European wine countries with a high average consumption that is more evenly distributed throughout the week, or so-called "wet" drinking cultures [70].

Razvodovsky [70] analyzed vodka sales in Russia. He reported that the coinciding trends between the level of vodka sales and suicide rates indicated that a restriction of vodka availability might be an effective measure for suicide prevention in countries where rates of both vodka consumption and suicide are high. His time-series analysis suggests a positive relationship between the level of vodka sales per capita and suicide rates with no time lag and with a first-degree lag. As a matter of fact, the association between the two time-trends may indicate that binge-drinking of strong spirits is a risk factor for autodestructive behavior. It is important to point out that the size of the bivariate association between the level of vodka sales and suicide rates was substantially greater for men than for women.

5. ALCOHOL, ATTEMPTED SUICIDE AND SUICIDAL IDEATION

The National Comorbidity Survey (NCS), focusing on adolescents, reported a significant association between alcohol-related disorders and suicide attempts [71]. Swahn *et al.* [72] examined the associations between early alcohol use and suicide attempts, while controlling for demographic characteristics, alcohol-related beliefs and norms (*e.g.*, believing that alcohol causes harm to health or that adults or friends disapprove of alcohol use) and potential confounders, in students in grades 6, 8, 10 and 12. The authors reported that pre-teen alcohol use initiation was associated with suicide attempts (adjusted OR = 1.51; 95%CI = 1.38-1.66) relative to not drinking, with similar associations for boys (adjusted OR = 1.72; 95%CI = 1.52-1.94) and girls (adjusted OR = 1.26; 95%CI = 1.08-1.45).

Kim *et al.* [73] examined the association between early initiation of problem behaviors (alcohol drinking, cigarette smoking and sexual intercourse) and suicidal behaviors (suicidal ideation and suicide attempts) among a nationally representative sample of middle and high school Korean students (32,417 males and 31,467 females) in grades seven through twelve. The analyses indicated that both male and female pre-teen early initiators of each problem behavior were at greater risk for suicidal behaviors than non-initiators, even after controlling for covariates. Among males, 23.4% of pre-teen alcohol drinking initiators reported suicidal ideation *vs.* 19.9% and 13.4% respectively of teen initiators and non-initiators. Among females, the respective percentages were 37.0%, 29.1%, and 20.1% respectively. For suicide attempts, the percentages were 6.4%, 4.2%, and 2.7% in males, and 10.2%, 5.8%, and 3.3% in females.

Innamorati *et al.* [74] explored recreational drug use patterns and suicidality among a sample of 340 Italian young adults. Alcohol misuse, as measured by the Michigan Alcohol Screening Test (MAST), was significantly associated with reasons for living ($r=-0.18$; $p<0.01$), hopelessness ($r=0.23$; $p<0.01$), and depression (as measured by the Zung depression scale; $r=0.26$; $p<0.01$), although the effect sizes were weak.

In clinical samples, about 40% of all patients seeking treatment for alcohol dependence report at least one suicide attempt at some point in their lives [75-77]. Chavira *et al.* [78] investigated suicidal ideation and behaviours among youths recruited from five public sectors of care (child welfare, juvenile justice, special education, alcohol and drug, and county mental health services). The authors reported that 41.5% of individuals from alcohol and drug services had thought about death in the past year, 4.2% had talked about killing themselves in the last year, and 20.2% had attempted suicide at last once in their lifetime. However when analyzing predictors of suicidal behaviour using longitudinal data (in a 2-year follow-up), the effect of alcohol use disorder did not reach statistical significance (OR=1.60; p=0.06).

Yaldizli *et al.* [79], investigating risk factors for attempted suicide in patients with a history of alcohol dependence or abuse and depressive symptoms, reported that 35.6% of 292 patients attempted suicide at least once in their lifetime.

Robinson *et al.* [80] examining the prevalence of and risk factors for suicide attempt in a cohort of patients with first-episode psychosis over a 7.4 year follow-up period, reported that a history of problem alcohol use increased the risk of multiple suicide attempts (OR=4.43; 95% CI = 1.05-18.7; $p<0.05$).

Although these studies indicate an association between alcohol use disorders and suicide attempts, some studies have reported contrasting results. For example, an Italian study, carried-out in the context of the European Study of the Epidemiology of Mental Health Disorders, a part of the WHO World Mental Health Survey Initiative, showed that suicidal thinking and planning are increased by having an alcohol-related disorder, but that this increase was not paralleled by an increase in suicide attempts [81].

6. SUICIDE AND ALCOHOL ABUSE IN ADOLESCENTS

Suicide among adolescents constitutes 6% of all suicides and is the second or third leading cause of death in adolescents. According to data from the Youth Risk Behavior Surveillance study [82], 16.9% of high school students had seriously considered attempting suicide, 11.3% had made a suicide plan, and 8.4% had actually attempted suicide in 2005. These figures changed slightly in the 2007 report [83]. Serious consideration of attempting suicide fell to 14.5%, making a suicide plan rose to 13%, and the actual suicide attempt rate fell to 6.9%. Whether these small changes are due to the enforcement of preventive programs is hard to say at present. The changes appear to follow a decreasing trend [83]. Interestingly, a similarly steadily decreasing pattern is shown for alcohol consumption in youths, although of a lesser degree, going from 82% lifetime alcohol use in 1991 to 75% in 2007 [83]. Alcohol use in youths was associated with increased mortality and an increased death rate from vehicle accidents when driving while drunk [95], and this behaviour might constitute in some cases unconsciously motivated (or subintentioned) suicide attempts. According to Petersen [84], 20% of youths between 14 and 19 years of age have had thoughts about their own death, and 40% of youths who do not succeed in their first suicide attempt repeat the attempt. The rates of attempted suicide range from about 5 cases per 100,000 per year in 10-12 year-olds, 6 for 20-24 year-olds, to 15 for those over the age of 65.

Singh *et al.* [85] reviewed autopsy and field reports for all paediatric suicide cases referred to the New Mexico Office of the Medical Examiner from 1979 to 2005. The age-adjusted suicide rate was 4.8 per 100,000 per year. Seventy-six percent of the suicides occurred in the victim's home or yard. Shooting was the most common method overall (58%), followed by hanging (30%). In 26% of the cases, alcohol or other drugs were detected post-mortem. The results of toxicology testing were more often positive in decedents over the age of 15, and rare in suicides younger than 15. Males were 2.7 times more likely to have an alcohol use disorder than were females. Those who shot themselves were 2.4 times more likely to have an alcohol use disorder than those who hanged themselves or used other methods. Boys were more often intoxicated at the time of suicide than were girls. However, although alcohol or illicit drug use is frequently cited as a risk factor for suicide, the authors reported a low prevalence of intoxication, again suggesting that suicide is not simply (or not often) the result of an impulse. Therefore, the use of suicide as a way of solving a chronic problem, rather than an impulsive response to stress, means that prevention programs based on impulse control, such as crisis intervention, will be less effective in this population. However, impulse reduction may reduce self-damaging acts and, therefore, contribute to a reduction in self-inflicted mortality, be it suicidal in nature or not.

Although the age-adjusted suicide rate was higher in New Mexico than nationally, the trends in the overall population remained similar. In a recent case-control study on the utilization of healthcare services prior to suicide (across different time periods), among children and adolescents aged 11 to 18 years in the Province of Quebec, Canada, Renaud and colleagues [86] investigated the utilization of services (*i.e.*, contact with general practitioners, mental health professionals, psychiatrists and/or youth protection groups) at different time periods in 55 child and adolescent suicides and 54 matched community controls using proxy-based interviews and questionnaires. More than 90% of the child and adolescent suicides, suffered from a mental disorder, and a significant proportion of them were left without appropriate healthcare support (including psychiatric consultations) in the period preceding their suicide. Furthermore, 20% of the suicides and no control subjects had made prior suicide attempts. More specifically, over two-thirds of the suicides had no treatment contact within the month prior to the suicidal action, while only 12.7% of them were in contact with psychiatric services during that same period. Females seemed to have more psychiatric and mental health service contacts in the most recent month, and those adolescents with depressive and anxious disorders had received more psychiatric and general mental health services in the past year. Past-month hospitalisation was more often associated with alcohol abuse and psychosis. The authors highlighted the need for an overall increase in the rates of healthcare services delivered to young people at risk for suicide, as well as better training of health professionals in detecting and treating adolescent psychopathology. In this population of adolescents referred to healthcare services, at least a quarter of the suicides abused drugs and/or alcohol.

More worrying data comes from research reported by the CDC (Centers for Disease Control and Prevention) [87] indicating that 25.6% of high school students had drunk their first alcoholic drink by age 13, and 25.5% admitted having drunk five or more alcoholic drinks in a row within the last two weeks. Translated, this mean that one out of four youths regularly engages in binge drinking and that about the same proportion had started taking alcohol early in their life, when their brain was still maturating. Among people with depression, those who consumed substances or alcohol have a higher probability of attempting suicide as compared with depressed individuals who did not [88].

Many factors associated with suicide in adults are also present in younger people. Family transmission of suicide risk is important, especially when suicidal behaviour has occurred on the maternal side [89]. Most young people who die by suicide have psychiatric disorders. Affective disorders, substance-related disorders and disruptive behaviour disorders are the most frequent [90]. Other important contributing factors include previous suicide attempts, family disruption and discord, recent losses, physical and sexual abuse, homelessness, and a homosexual or bisexual gender orientation [90, 91]. Media influences are important in young people [92], and some suicides occur in clusters, indicating a role for the "Werther effect" in adolescent suicide [93].

In light of the above evidence, it is difficult to attribute a role for alcohol in adolescent suicide. Patterns of alcohol consumption by youngsters in Western countries are changing, and singling out its role in suicide becomes an increasingly harder task since alcohol use is increasing, as far as absolute numbers are concerned, while suicide changes very little in numerical terms. However, drinking alcohol has been used in human societies in ritualistic contexts and has a symbolic value, and it has maintained this role even when the formal framework has changed. Its anxiolytic properties help people in personal and social contexts in which they are confronted with difficulties. Alcohol becomes a way of facilitating communication with others and adapting to the environment. Suicide is also both a social and a personal act, as is social alcohol drinking, and is related to conditions that render life difficult. It is possible that when one decides to commit suicide, he or she may select one of the options available to make the act more socially and personally acceptable, and one of these may be alcohol. In doing so, the person communicates to others and adapts to his/her environment. The results of research do not support the hypothesis that, when youths get drunk, this in itself leads to those youths deciding to commit suicide.

7. SUICIDAL BEHAVIOUR AND ALCOHOL ABUSE IN ELDERLY PEOPLE

In almost all industrialised countries, the highest suicide rate is found among men aged 75 years and older [94]. Whereas suicidal behaviour in youths is often impulsive and communicative, in older people it is often long-planned and involves highly lethal methods. Its lethality increases also as a result of the structural frailty and social isolation that are often present in the elderly. Alcohol misuse is an important risk factor for suicide in elderly people [95]. Psychiatric disorders, especially depression, are common in those who commit suicide in Western [95], as well as in Eastern countries [96]. Depression, on the other hand, is frequently comorbid with alcohol abuse/dependence in the aged [97-99].

In later life, in both sexes, major depression is the most common diagnosis both in those who attempt suicide and those who complete suicide. In contrast to other age groups, comorbidity with substance abuse and personality disorders is less frequent [94]. Cognitive rigidity and obsessional traits seem to influence the risk of suicide in the elderly [100, 101], probably because these traits undermine the ability of the elderly to cope with the challenges of ageing, which often calls for substantial adaptations. Physical illness [102], bereavement and loss of independence [103] are also important factors. Physical illnesses play an important role in the suicidal behaviour of the elderly. Depression and physical illness are frequently comorbid. In many cases, the physical illness itself, and medications adopted to treat it, may cause depressive symptoms. About 2-4% of terminally-ill elderly patients commit suicide. Complicated or traumatic grief, anxiety, unremitting hopelessness after recovery from a depressive episode, and a history of previous suicide attempts are risk factors for attempted and completed suicide. Overt suicidal behaviour and indirect self-destructive behaviours, which often lead to premature death, are common, especially in residents of nursing homes where more immediate means to commit suicide are restricted.

The alcohol-suicide-psychiatric disorder/psychological distress link in the elderly may differ from the link in those of other ages. In the elderly, the highest incidence of suicide ideation is found among the lower age ranges, and at-risk alcohol use appears to be less accompanied by such ideation as compared to the psychiatric disorders, such as depressive and anxiety disorders [104], whereas in young people, suicidal ideation is associated with both depression and alcohol abuse [105].

8. SUICIDAL BEHAVIOUR AND ALCOHOL ABUSE IN AFFECTIVE BONDS AND SOCIAL RELATIONSHIPS

Alcohol use disorder has an enormous impact on relationships, generating ambivalence and anger. These effects are even stronger in the face of suicidal behaviour. According to Wasserman [106], many suicidal persons with alcohol dependence have borderline personality disorder. They have contradictory affective reactions and are often confused as to whether others love or hate them and whether they love or hate others. They have difficulty in distinguishing between the good and evil impulses in themselves and other people. Copello *et al.* [107], after reviewing the literature, concluded that people with drug and alcohol use disorders often behave in ways destructive to family life and relationships with relatives.

Velleman and Templeton [108] noted that family members (children, partners, siblings, parents, and other close relatives) are often affected by this. Wolk-Wasserman [109] found that suicidal, substance-abusing patients commonly break-off relations with a significant other before committing suicide and increase their suicidal communications during the break-off period. Marshal [110] tested two competing hypotheses relating alcohol use disorder and marital functioning: (1) that alcoholism disrupts and ends marriage, and (2) that alcohol use disorder is secondary to marital dysfunction and tends to stabilize marriage and perhaps prevent its dissolution. His results found no support for the latter hypothesis, supporting the hypothesis that alcohol use is maladaptive and is associated with dissatisfaction, negative marital interaction patterns and higher levels of marital violence.

Wolk-Wasserman [109] found that the suicidal hints or threats were usually not taken seriously by the partners of those with alcohol dependence, even when suicide had been attempted previously. Parents of substance-abusing suicide attempters fear that their children will commit suicide, which makes them desperate [109]. They often accused their partners of causing their children's troubles and reproached social service and psychiatric authorities for failing to look after them properly.

Velleman and Templeton [108] described the impact of parental substance use disorder on adolescents and young adults. They concluded that the offspring of persons with alcohol dependence are particularly likely to report being detached, switching-off, avoiding the drinking parent and blaming themselves. Offspring described a variety of ways of escaping childhood adversity, such as leaving home significantly earlier than others.

The spouses of suicides who misused alcohol were significantly more likely to react with anger than the spouses of those who did not. The children of parents with alcohol use disorder who completed suicide were less likely to feel guilty or abandoned than the children of non-alcohol-related suicide in parents. Alcohol use disorder before suicide changes the affective responses in the spouses and children who are left behind. Survivor reactions to suicide are strongly influenced by the nature of the relationship between survivors and the suicide. Bereavement counsellors should be alert for complex grief and mourning responses among this group of suicide survivors.

Emotional reactions in survivors differ, with spouses and parents significantly more affected than adult children [111]. Parents showed more sorrow, depression, feeling of powerlessness and guilt, while spouses felt more abandoned and angry [111]. Their anger is directed to the lost person significantly more than that of spouses whose suicidal partner had no alcohol problems [112]. Alcoholism in any close relationship causes tension and conflicts and complicates bereavement.

Further research is needed to address the impact of the quality of the relationship, emotional attachment, age (of the survivor and the suicide) and other factors on bereavement.

9. DISCUSSION AND CONCLUSIONS

The above research indicates a relationship between alcohol use and suicidal behaviour. However, it is difficult to be sure whether this link is causal and what is the direction of the relationship. For example, most researchers who have investigated this relationship hypothesize that alcohol use may be a risk factor for subsequent suicide behaviour, and it has been suggested that alcohol may influence an individual's decision to complete suicide, but few studies have investigated this possibility [113].

Most of the literature on the topic is correlational, and any causal conclusion is arbitrary and dangerous. In fact causality is a complex problem in the behavioural sciences [114]. Lipsey *et al.* [115], reviewing literature regarding alcoholism and violence, drew three general conclusions:

1. The research investigating the causal role of alcohol consumption in violent behaviour is very unsatisfactory. As a result, the causal issue is still “cloudy and uncertain” (p. 277).

2. Despite the problems in the research, none of the relevant bodies of research yield a consistently negative or null result on the causal question. Each provides substantial evidence of an alcohol-violence association that is consistent with a causal interpretation.

3. While the causal question may not be solved, it is apparent that there is a main effect of alcohol on violence. If alcohol has any causal effect on violence, it is true only in some people and/or some circumstances.

We think that these general conclusions of Lipsey *et al.* may be extended also to the question of the causal role of alcohol use and suicide. Alcohol use is neither a necessary nor sufficient condition for suicide, but it may be regarded as a contributing factor. Furthermore, an inverse causal relationship (that suicidality may be a causal factor in alcohol use) has not been excluded. For example, Light *et al.* [116] investigated the link between alcohol use and suicidality with data from a longitudinal survey of junior and senior high school students from a suburban community in northern California. The results of the study indicate a possible causal relationship from alcohol problems to suicidality for adolescent males and a causal relationship from suicidality to alcohol problems for adolescent females. However, the results of Light and colleagues are limited by several factors. First of all, few, if any, of the young people in this study were problem drinkers or dependent on alcohol, and all of them were relatively early in their drinking careers. Second, suicide behaviour was a rare event in this sample of adolescents. Third, the study was only observational, and the causal relationship may not be justified. The same drawbacks are evident in a more recent study. In this study, Swahn *et al.* [117] examined the cross-sectional associations between preteen alcohol use initiation and subsequent suicide ideation and attempts for boys and girls in the 2005 national Youth Risk Behavior Survey, which includes a representative sample of over 13,000 high-school students in grades 9-12 in the United States. The authors concluded that pre-teen alcohol use initiation was significantly associated with suicidal ideation (adjusted OR= 1.89) and suicide attempts (adjusted OR=2.71) relative to non-drinkers. However, in the final multivariate model, an increased likelihood of suicide ideation and suicide attempts were also significantly associated with sadness, sexual assault, fighting, weapon carrying, and attending 9th grade (for suicide attempts only). A negative association between suicide ideation and students who were white or classified ethnically as "other" was also noted. Similar results were obtained from analyses comparing those reporting teen alcohol use initiation with non-drinkers and pre-teen alcohol use initiation. Different conclusions were drawn by Chatterji *et al.* [71]. These authors used data from the 1991, 1993, 1995, 1997 and 1999 Youth Risk Behavior Survey samples, and a new estimation strategy proposed to address the issue of causal relationship between alcohol use and suicide. This study suggested that a causal relationship between binge drinking and suicide attempts is very unlikely, although a causal relationship between clinically defined alcohol use disorders and suicide attempts among female adolescents may exist.

A failure to prove a clear causative relationship leaves the alternative as a possibility, that is, the hypothesis that mediating variables play a role in the association between alcohol use and suicide, such as mood disorders and impulsivity. For example, impulsive suicide attempts are common in patients with an alcohol use disorder [118, 119], and an interaction has been found among alcohol use, impulsiveness and suicide risk [12, 119]. Among alcoholics, the lifetime risk of suicide is about 10-15%, and the majority of suicide attempts occur in a context of impulsiveness and alcohol abuse. Wojnar *et al.* [120] investigated the correlates of impulsive and non-impulsive suicide attempts in 154 hospitalised patients with alcohol dependence. Lifetime suicide attempts were reported by 43% of the patients, 62% of whom scored high on impulsiveness. The only significant factor that distinguished patients making impulsive suicide attempts from patients making non-impulsive suicide attempts and patients with no suicide attempt was a higher level of behavioural impulsivity.

Simon *et al.* [121] found that individuals who made impulsive suicide attempts reported higher rates of aggressive behaviour than those who made non-impulsive suicide attempts. They hypothesised that poor behavioural control, largely dependent on factors such as alcohol abuse, was an important indicator of risk for impulsive suicide attempts. Alcohol intake may result in a lack of behavioural inhibition and other aspects of impulsiveness, such as poor thinking and planning, as well as impaired attention. However, despite higher rates of impulsive attempts and a higher level of lethality in patients with alcohol use disorders, the use of alcohol at the time of attempt did not differ significantly between impulsive and non-impulsive attempters [121-123].

Depression and/or alcoholism were comorbid in one study in 85% of 100 cases of completed suicide [43], and this finding has been replicated more recently [17, 124]. Cornelius *et al.* [125] stated that "patients who have alcohol dependence should be assessed for suicidal ideation whenever they exhibit significant level of other depressive symptoms, whenever they have a relapse of alcohol or drug use and whenever they have experienced a recent interpersonal loss or a loss of housing or employment. Alcoholic patients with any depressive symptoms should be questioned carefully about symptoms that would define a major depressive disorder, because the presence of that comorbid disorder would be associated with a significantly increased risk for suicide".

Bipolar disorder (BD) is strongly associated with high rates of attempted and completed suicide. Alcoholism was associated with an increased rate of attempted suicide in 96 adult patients with BD-I, but not in 42 patients with BD-II, with or without a comorbid substance use disorder [126]. Earlier BD onset increased the likelihood of an association between alcohol use disorder and suicide attempts. The higher rate of attempted suicide associated with other drug use disorders appeared to be the result of higher impulsiveness, hostility and aggression. Co-occurrence of alcohol and drug use disorders increased the size of the association - 97% of patients with BD-I and comorbid drug and alcohol use disorders had made a suicide attempt [126]. In another study, 99 of 239 patients with BD had a history of suicide attempts (41.4%). Of those positive for a history of suicide, only three were diagnosed with BD-II (3.03%) [127]. In this sample, borderline personality disorder and alcoholism were associated with past violent suicide attempts.

Alcohol use disorders and suicide may also share common pathophysiology. For example, reduced serotonin function has been identified in suicides and possibly in serious suicide attempters (see [128] for a review) and alcohol dependence patients [129]. Serotonin depletion was also found in individuals displaying aggressive and impulsive behaviour [128] and was a predictor of both early-onset alcohol use disorders [130] and suicide attempts among alcoholics [131, 132]. Koob and LeMoal [133] suggested that the changes in hedonic tone that accompany substance use are central aspects of the addictive process, and the maintenance of substance use in the dependent person, is driven by attempts to regulate the affective disturbance that results from substance use. Ethanol has been shown to potentiate 5-HT3 receptor function acutely and to modulate 5-HT3-augmented mesolimbic dopaminergic function chronically, but also to regulate alcohol drinking and its reinforcing properties at the ventral tegmental area level [134, 135]. However, 5-HT3 receptors were not found to be altered post-mortem in suicides [136]. An association between suicide attempts, impulsiveness, alcohol dependence and serotonin neurotransmission deficiency has been proposed [137-140], but the possibility that impulsive suicide attempts may reflect mood disturbance-related low serotonin activity in alcohol-dependent individuals is currently only speculative. So far, research is highly suggestive, but not conclusive, and a direct relationship between alcoholism, suicidal behaviour and specific changes in cerebral areas is not easily traceable.

Other possible mediators in the relationship between alcohol use and suicide have been proposed. For example, a state of intoxication may trigger self-inflicted injuries, not only by increasing impulsivity, but also by promoting depressive thoughts and feelings of hopelessness, while simultaneously removing inhibiting barriers to hurting oneself [141]. Indirect mechanisms, including alcohol consumption as a form of self-medication for depression, or alcohol use as a marker for other high-risk behaviours, may also be relevant. Additionally, cognitive constriction (narrowed attention which reduces perceived potential solutions to a dichotomy - finding an immediate solution or committing suicide) is frequently observed prior to a suicide attempt [142]. Alcohol produces cognitive constriction through alcohol myopia [143], and this process has been confirmed by research showing that inhibition conflict (weighing pros and cons and identifying alternative solutions) mediates the relation between intoxication and social behaviour [144].

Once a decision has been made to attempt suicide, alcohol use may serve several functions. Alcohol expectancies play an important role in determining alcohol use and behaviour [145] and, consequently, it is reasonable to hypothesize that suicide-related alcohol expectancies relevant to gaining courage, numbing fears or anesthetizing the pain of dying may lead to the incorporation of alcohol use into a suicide plan. Alcohol may also serve as a "means to an end" as the suicide method itself [146-148].

There is a vulnerability to the neurotoxic effects of alcohol, and adolescent substance use has adverse consequences on brain development and executive functioning [149]. Some mood disorders may be alcohol induced (and remit after a period of abstinence) [150], and alcohol withdrawal is often associated with affective disturbance [151].

Sociological interpretations include the hypothesis that acute alcohol use leads to increased social deterioration and anomie [141], unemployment, debts, and social isolation [152-154]. Biological interpretations of the association include impaired physical and mental functioning [155] and interactions with other psychotropic drugs [156]. Disinhibition, in which alcohol acts to remove psychological and even physiological barriers to self-harm, has also been proposed as a relevant factor [157].

Hufford [158] summarised four psychological pathways for the proposed relationship between acute alcohol use and suicidal behaviour: (1) increasing psychological distress, including hopelessness, loneliness and depression; (2) enhancing or facilitating aggressive behaviour, including self-aggression; (3) changing an individual's expectations and helping to propel suicidal ideation into action; and (4) constricting attention and inhibiting effective coping strategies that would facilitate avoiding suicidal behaviour.

In conclusion, the research examined indicates a clear link between alcohol use and suicide, but the causal nature of this relationship remains speculative. The solution may be in research investigating possible biological, social and psychological variables mediating this link.

However, at a clinical level we may see that the relationship between alcohol/drug use and the degree of suicidality in acute psychiatric patients is strong [159]. Among these patients, the most severely suicidal have a high rate of alcohol abuse/dependence (56%). Furthermore, in 40% of these patients, substance-alcohol use preceded and/or caused the hospitalisation. One factor underlying the association between substance use disorder and suicide attempts may be the severity of illness. Subjects with a more severe form of mental illness may be more likely to both attempt suicide and use substances to self-medicate. Thus, psychosocial intervention addressing common underlying factors such as deficits in coping strategies and problem-solving skills, low social competence, and poor family and community support, may lower the risk both of suicide behaviour and alcohol use disorders.

Furthermore, in view of the strong link between alcoholism and psychopathology, alcohol prevention programs may positively impact public mental health and help reduce suicide risk indirectly.

REFERENCES

[1] Alonso J, Angermeyer MC, Bernert S, *et al.* Prevalence of mental disorders in Europe: results from the European Study of the Epidemiology of Mental Disorders (ESEMeD) project. Acta Psychiatr Scand Suppl 2004: 21-7.

[2] Piccinelli M, Pini S, Bonizzato P, *et al.* Results from the Verona Centre. In: Ustun TB, Sartorius N, Eds. Mental illness in general health care: an international study. Chichester, John Wiley and Sons Ltd. 1995; pp. 301-22.

[3] Faravelli C, Abrardi L, Bartolozzi D, *et al.* The Sesto Fiorentino study: point and one-year prevalences of psychiatric disorders in an Italian community sample using clinical interviewers. Psychother Psychosom 2004; 73: 226-34.

[4] Dawson DA, Grant BF, Stinson FS, Chou PS, Huang B, Ruan WJ. Recovery from DSM-IV alcohol dependence: United States, 2001-2002. Addiction 2005; 100: 281-92.

[5] Grant BF, Dawson DA, Stinson FS, Chou SP, Dufour MC, Pickering RP. The 12-month prevalence and trends in DSM-IV alcohol abuse and dependence: United States, 1991-1992 and 2001-2002. Drug Alcohol Depend 2004; 74: 223-34.

[6] Rehn N, Room R, Edwards G. Alcohol in the European Region - consumption, harm and policies. Copenhagen: World Health Organization Regional Office for Europe, 2001.

[7] Kraepelin E. Psychiatrie. Ein Lehrbuch für Studirende und Aerzte, 6. vollständig umgearbeitete Auflage. Zweiter Band, Klinische Psychiatrie. Leipzig: Verlag von Johann Ambrosius Barth, 1899.

[8] Reimer F. Alkohol und Selbstmord bei Seeleuten (Alcoholism and suicide in sailors). Offentl Gesundheitsdienst 1964; 26: 423-6.

[9] Stenback A, Achte KA, Rimon RH. Physical disease, hypochondria, and alcohol addiction in suicides committed by mental hospital patients. Br J Psychiatry 1965; 111: 933-7.

[10] James IP. Blood alcohol levels following successful suicide. Q J Stud Alcohol 1966; 27: 23-9.

[11] Bernal M, Haro JM, Bernert S, *et al.* Risk factors for suicidality in Europe: results from the ESEMED study. J Affect Disord 2007; 101: 27-34.

[12] Conner KR, Duberstein PR. Predisposing and precipitating factors for suicide among alcoholics: empirical review and conceptual integration. Alcohol Clin Exp Res 2004; 28: 6S-17S.

[13] Murphy GE, Wetzel RD. The lifetime risk of suicide in alcoholism. Arch Gen Psychiatry 1990; 47: 383-92.

[14] Roy A, Linnoila M. Alcoholism and suicide. Suicide Life Threat Behav 1986; 16: 244-73.

[15] Flensborg-Madsen T, Knop J, Mortensen EL, Becker U, Sher L, Gronbaek M. Alcohol use disorders increase the risk of completed suicide--irrespective of other psychiatric disorders. A longitudinal cohort study. Psychiatry Res 2009; 167: 123-30.

[16] Crombie IK, Pounder DJ, Dick PH. Who takes alcohol prior to suicide? J Clin Forensic Med 1998; 5: 65-8.

[17] Conwell Y, Duberstein PR, Cox C, Herrmann JH, Forbes NT, Caine Ed. Relationships of age and axis I diagnoses in victims of completed suicide: a psychological autopsy study. Am J Psychiatry 1996; 153: 1001-8.

[18] Foster T, Gillespie K, McClelland R, Patterson C. Risk factors for suicide independent of DSM-III-R Axis I disorder. Case-control psychological autopsy study in Northern Ireland. Br J Psychiatry 1999; 175: 175-9.

[19] Henriksson MM, Aro HM, Marttunen MJ, *et al.* Mental disorders and comorbidity in suicide. Am J Psychiatry 1993; 150: 935-40.

[20] Rich CL, Fowler RC, Fogarty LA, Young D. San Diego Suicide Study. III. Relationships between diagnoses and stressors. Arch Gen Psychiatry 1988; 45: 589-92.

[21] Vijayakumar L, Rajkumar S. Are risk factors for suicide universal? A case-control study in India. Acta Psychiatr Scand 1999; 99: 407-11.
[22] Harris EC, Barraclough B. Suicide as an outcome for mental disorders. A meta-analysis. Br J Psychiatry 1997; 170: 205-28.
[23] Wilhelmsen L, Elmfeldt D, Wedel H. Cause of death in relation to social and alcoholic problems among Swedish men aged 35-44 years. Acta Med Scand 1983; 213: 263-8.
[24] Knop J, Fischer A. Duodenal ulcer, suicide, psychopathology and alcoholism. Acta Psychiatr Scand 1981; 63: 346-55.
[25] Fawcett J, Scheftner W, Clark D, Hedeker D, Gibbons R, Coryell W. Clinical predictors of suicide in patients with major affective disorders: a controlled prospective study. Am J Psychiatry 1987; 144: 35-40.
[26] Agren G, Jakobsson SW. Validation of diagnoses on death certificates for male alcoholics in Stockholm. Forensic Sci Int 1987; 33: 231-41.
[27] Barr HL, Antes D, Ottenberg DJ, Rosen A. Mortality of treated alcoholics and drug addicts: the benefits of abstinence. J Stud Alcohol 1984; 45: 440-52.
[28] Berglund M, Tunving K. Assaultive alcoholics 20 years later. Acta Psychiatr Scand 1985; 71: 141-7.
[29] Lindberg S, Agren G. Mortality among male and female hospitalized alcoholics in Stockholm 1962-1983. Br J Addict 1988; 83: 1193-200.
[30] Ohara K, Suzuki Y, Sugita T, *et al.* Mortality among alcoholics discharged from a Japanese hospital. Br J Addict 1989; 84: 287-91.
[31] Beck AT, Steer RA. Clinical predictors of eventual suicide: a 5- to 10-year prospective study of suicide attempters. J Affect Disord 1989; 17: 203-9.
[32] Beck AT, Steer RA, Trexler LD. Alcohol abuse and eventual suicide: a 5- to 10-year prospective study of alcohol-abusing suicide attempters. J Stud Alcohol 1989; 50: 202-9.
[33] Duffy J, Kreitman N. Risk factors for suicide and undetermined death among in-patient alcoholics in Scotland. Addiction 1993; 88: 757-66.
[34] Ferrada-Noli M, Ormstad K, Asberg M. Pathoanatomic findings and blood alcohol analysis at autopsy (BAC) in forensic diagnoses of undetermined suicide. A cross-cultural study. Forensic Sci Int 1996; 78: 157-63.
[35] Ohberg A, Vuori E, Ojanpera I, Lonngvist J. Alcohol and drugs in suicides. Br J Psychiatry 1996; 169: 75-80.
[36] Pirkola S, Isometsa E, Lonnqvist J. Do means matter? Differences in characteristics of Finnish suicide completers using different methods. J Nerv Ment Dis 2003; 191: 745-50.
[37] Varnik A, Kolves K, Vali M, Tooding LM, Wasserman D. Do alcohol restrictions reduce suicide mortality? Addiction 2007; 102: 251-6.
[38] Mendelson WB, Rich CL. Sedatives and suicide: the San Diego study. Acta Psychiatr Scand 1993; 88: 337-41.
[39] Garlow SJ. Age, gender, and ethnicity differences in patterns of cocaine and ethanol use preceding suicide. Am J Psychiatry 2002; 159: 615-9.
[40] Hansen AC, Kristensen IB, Dragsholt C, Hansen JP. [Alcohol, drugs and narcotics in suicides in the Aarhus police district]. Ugeskr Laeger 1995; 157: 1524-7.
[41] Cavanagh JT, Carson AJ, Sharpe M, Lawrie SM. Psychological autopsy studies of suicide: a systematic review. Psychol Med 2003; 33: 395-405.
[42] Lesage AD, Boyer R, Grunberg F, *et al.* Suicide and mental disorders: a case-control study of young men. Am J Psychiatry 1994; 151: 1063-8.
[43] Barraclough B, Bunch J, Nelson B, Sainsbury P. A hundred cases of suicide: clinical aspects. Br J Psychiatry 1974; 125: 355-73.
[44] Rich CL, Ricketts JE, Fowler RC, Young D. Some differences between men and women who commit suicide. Am J Psychiatry 1988; 145: 718-22.
[45] Duberstein PR, Conwell Y, Caine ED. Age differences in the personality characteristics of suicide completers: preliminary findings from a psychological autopsy study. Psychiatry 1994; 57: 213-24.
[46] Hiroeh U, Appleby L, Mortensen PB, Dunn G. Death by homicide, suicide, and other unnatural causes in people with mental illness: a population-based study. Lancet 2001; 358: 2110-2.
[47] Wilcox HC, Conner KR, Caine ED. Association of alcohol and drug use disorders and completed suicide: an empirical review of cohort studies. Drug Alcohol Depend 2004; 76 (Suppl): S11-19.
[48] Cheng AT. Mental illness and suicide. A case-control study in east Taiwan. Arch Gen Psychiatry 1995; 52: 594-603.
[49] Waern M. Alcohol dependence and misuse in elderly suicides. Alcohol Alcohol 2003; 38: 249-54.

[50] Inskip HM, Harris EC, Barraclough B. Lifetime risk of suicide for affective disorder, alcoholism and schizophrenia. Br J Psychiatry 1998; 172: 35-7.
[51] Rossow I, Amundsen A. Alcohol abuse and suicide: a 40-year prospective study of Norwegian conscripts. Addiction 1995; 90: 685-91.
[52] Foster T. Dying for a drink. Global suicide prevention should focus more on alcohol use disorders. BMJ 2001; 323: 817-8.
[53] Murphy GE, Wetzel RD, Robins E, McEvoy L. Multiple risk factors predict suicide in alcoholism. Arch Gen Psychiatry 1992; 49: 459-63.
[54] Cherpitel CJ, Borges GL, Wilcox HC. Acute alcohol use and suicidal behavior: a review of the literature. Alcohol Clin Exp Res 2004; 28: 18S-28S.
[55] Kolves K, Varnik A, Tooding LM, Wasserman D. The role of alcohol in suicide: a case-control psychological autopsy study. Psychol Med 2006; 36: 923-30.
[56] Pirkola SP, Isometsa ET, Heikkinen ME, Lonnqvist JK. Suicides of alcohol misusers and non-misusers in a nationwide population. Alcohol Alcohol 2000; 35: 70-5.
[57] Gruenewald PJ, Ponicki WR, Mitchell PR. Suicide rates and alcohol consumption in the United States, 1970-89. Addiction 1995; 90: 1063-75.
[58] Lester D. The association between alcohol consumption and suicide and homicide rates: a study of 13 nations. Alcohol Alcohol 1995; 30: 465-68.
[59] Caces F, Harford T. Time series analysis of alcohol consumption and suicide mortality in the United States, 1934-1987. J Stud Alcohol 1998; 59: 455-61.
[60] Pridemore WA, Chamlin MB. A time-series analysis of the impact of heavy drinking on homicide and suicide mortality in Russia, 1956-2002. Addiction 2006; 101: 1719-29.
[61] Razvodovsky YE. Suicide and alcohol psychoses in Belarus 1970-2005. Crisis 2007; 28: 61-6.
[62] Makela P. Alcohol consumption and suicide mortality by age among Finnish men, 1950-1991. Addiction 1996; 91: 101-12.
[63] Lester D. Alcoholism and drug abuse. In: Maris RW, Berman AL, Maltsberger JT, Yufit RI, Eds. Assessment and prediction of suicide. New York, Guilford Press. 1992; pp. 321-6.
[64] Norstrom T. Alcohol and suicide in Scandinavia. Br J Addict 1988; 83: 553-9.
[65] Skog OJ. Alcohol and suicide in Denmark 1911-24--experiences from a 'natural experiment'. Addiction 1993; 88: 1189-93.
[66] Rossow I. Suicide, alcohol, and divorce; aspects of gender and family integration. Addiction 1993; 88: 1659-65.
[67] Ramstedt M. Alcohol and suicide in 14 European countries. Addiction 2001; 96 (Suppl) 1: S59-75.
[68] Norstrom T, Ramstedt M. Mortality and population drinking: a review of the literature. Drug Alcohol Rev 2005; 24: 537-47.
[69] Norstrom T. Alcohol and suicide: a comparative analysis of France and Sweden. Addiction 1995; 90: 1463-9.
[70] Razvodovsky YE. Beverage-specific alcohol sale and suicide in Russia. Crisis 2009; 30: 186-91.
[71] Chatterji P, Dave D, Kaestner R, Markowitz S. Alcohol abuse and suicide attempts among youth. Econ Hum Biol 2004; 2: 159-80.
[72] Swahn MH, Bossarte RM, Ashby JS, Meyers J. Pre-teen alcohol use initiation and suicide attempts among middle and high school students: findings from the 2006 Georgia Student Health Survey. Addict Behav 2010; 35: 452-8.
[73] Kim DS, Kim HS. Early initiation of alcohol drinking, cigarette smoking, and sexual intercourse linked to suicidal ideation and attempts: findings from the 2006 Korean Youth Risk Behavior Survey. Yonsei Med J 2010; 51: 18-26.
[74] Innamorati M, Pompili M, Lester D, Tatarelli R, Girardi P. Recreational drug use and suicidality among Italian young adults. J Addict Dis 2008; 27: 51-9.
[75] Anderson BA, Howard MO, Walker RD, Suchinsky RT. Characteristics of substance-abusing veterans attempting suicide: a national study. Psychol Rep 1995; 77: 1231-42.
[76] Koller G, Preuss UW, Bottlender M, Wenzel K, Soyka M. Impulsivity and aggression as predictors of suicide attempts in alcoholics. Eur Arch Psychiatry Clin Neurosci 2002; 252: 155-60.
[77] Roy A. Distal risk factors for suicidal behavior in alcoholics: replications and new findings. J Affect Disord 2003; 77: 267-71.
[78] Chavira DA, Accurso EC, Garland AF, Hough R. Suicidal Behaviour Among Youth in Five Public Sectors of Care. Child Adolesc Ment Health; 15: 44-51.
[79] Yaldizli O, Kuhl HC, Graf M, Wiesbeck GA, Wurst FM. Risk factors for suicide attempts in patients with alcohol dependence or abuse and a history of depressive symptoms: a subgroup analysis from the WHO/ISBRA study. Drug Alcohol Rev 2010; 29: 64-74.

[80] Robinson J, Harris MG, Harrigan SM, *et al.* Suicide attempt in first-episode psychosis: a 7.4 year follow-up study. Schizophr Res 2010; 116: 1-8.

[81] Scocco P, de Girolamo G, Vilagut G, Alonso J. Prevalence of suicide ideation, plans, and attempts and related risk factors in Italy: results from the European Study on the Epidemiology of Mental Disorders--World Mental Health study. Compr Psychiatry 2008; 49: 13-21.

[82] Alireza Ayatollahi S, Mohammadpoorasl A, Rajaeifard A. Predicting the stages of smoking acquisition in the male students of Shiraz's high schools, 2003. Nicotine Tob Res 2005; 7: 845-51.

[83] Eaton DK, Kann L, Kinchen S, *et al.* Youth risk behavior surveillance--United States, 2007. MMWR Surveill Summ 2008; 57: 1-131.

[84] Petersen PE. The World Oral Health Report 2003: continuous improvement of oral health in the 21st century--the approach of the WHO Global Oral Health Program. Community Dent Oral Epidemiol 2003; 31 (Suppl) 1: 3-23.

[85] Singh VD, Lathrop SL. Youth suicide in New Mexico: a 26-year retrospective review. J Forensic Sci 2008; 53: 703-8.

[86] Renaud J, Berlim MT, Seguin M, McGirr A, Tousignant M, Turecki G. Recent and lifetime utilization of health care services by children and adolescent suicide victims: a case-control study. J Affect Disord 2009; 117: 168-73.

[87] Alcohol use among women of childbearing age--United States, 1991-1999. MMWR Morb Mortal Wkly Rep 2002; 51: 273-6.

[88] Glowinski AL, Bucholz KK, Nelson EC, *et al.* Suicide attempts in an adolescent female twin sample. J Am Acad Child Adolesc Psychiatry 2001; 40: 1300-7.

[89] Agerbo E, Nordentoft M, Mortensen PB. Familial, psychiatric, and socioeconomic risk factors for suicide in young people: nested case-control study. BMJ 2002; 325: 74.

[90] Bridge JA, Goldstein TR, Brent DA. Adolescent suicide and suicidal behavior. J Child Psychol Psychiatry 2006; 47: 372-94.

[91] Spirito A, Esposito Smythers C. Attempted and completed suicide in adolescence. Ann Rev Clin Psychol 2006; 2: 237-66.

[92] Gould MS, Shaffer D. The impact of suicide in television movies. Evidence of imitation. N Engl J Med 1986; 315: 690-4.

[93] Gould MS, Wallenstein S, Kleinman M. Time-space clustering of teenage suicide. Am J Epidemiol 1990; 131: 71-8.

[94] Szanto K, Gildengers A, Mulsant BH, Brown G, Alexopoulos GS, Reynolds CF, 3rd. Identification of suicidal ideation and prevention of suicidal behaviour in the elderly. Drugs Aging 2002; 19: 11-24.

[95] Conwell Y, Duberstein P. Suicide in older adults: determinants of risk and opportunities for prevention. In: Hawton K, Ed. Prevention and treatment of suicidal behaviour. New York, Oxford University Press. 2005; pp. 221-37.

[96] Chiu HF, Yip PS, Chi I, *et al.* Elderly suicide in Hong Kong--a case-controlled psychological autopsy study. Acta Psychiatr Scand 2004; 109: 299-305.

[97] Grant BF, Harford TC. Comorbidity between DSM-IV alcohol use disorders and major depression: results of a national survey. Drug Alcohol Depend 1995; 39: 197-206.

[98] Burns L, Teesson M. Alcohol use disorders comorbid with anxiety, depression and drug use disorders. Findings from the Australian National Survey of Mental Health and Well Being. Drug Alcohol Depend 2002; 68: 299-307.

[99] Wang J, El-Guebaly N. Sociodemographic factors associated with comorbid major depressive episodes and alcohol dependence in the general population. Can J Psychiatry 2004; 49: 37-44.

[100] Duberstein PR. Openness to experience and completed suicide across the second half of life. Int Psychogeriatr 1995; 7: 183-98.

[101] Harwood D, Hawton K, Hope T, Jacoby R. Psychiatric disorder and personality factors associated with suicide in older people: a descriptive and case-control study. Int J Geriatr Psychiatry 2001; 16: 155-65.

[102] Waern M, Rubenowitz E, Runeson B, Skoog I, Wilhelmson K, Allebeck P. Burden of illness and suicide in elderly people: case-control study. BMJ 2002; 324: 1355.

[103] Harwood DM, Hawton K, Hope T, Harriss L, Jacoby R. Life problems and physical illness as risk factors for suicide in older people: a descriptive and case-control study. Psychol Med 2006; 36: 1265-74.

[104] Bartels SJ, Coakley E, Oxman TE, *et al.* Suicidal and death ideation in older primary care patients with depression, anxiety, and at-risk alcohol use. Am J Geriatr Psychiatry 2002; 10: 417-27.

[105] Curran TA, Gawley E, Casey P, Gill M, Crumlish N. Depression, suicidality and alcohol abuse among medical and business students. Ir Med J 2009; 102: 249-52.

[106] Wasserman D. Alcohol and suicidal behaviour. Nord J Psychiatry 1993; 47: 265-71.

[107] Copello AG, Velleman RD, Templeton LJ. Family interventions in the treatment of alcohol and drug problems. Drug Alcohol Rev 2005; 24: 369-85.
[108] Velleman R, Templeton L. Alcohol, drugs and the family: results from a long-running research program within the UK. Eur Addict Res 2003; 9: 103-12.
[109] Wolk-Wasserman D. Suicidal communication of persons attempting suicide and responses of significant others. Acta Psychiatr Scand 1986; 73: 481-99.
[110] Marshal MP. For better or for worse? The effects of alcohol use on marital functioning. Clin Psychol Rev 2003; 23: 959-97.
[111] Tall K, Kolves K, Sisask M, Varnik A. Do survivors respond differently when alcohol abuse complicates suicide? Findings from the psychological autopsy study in Estonia. Drug Alcohol Depend 2008; 95: 129-33.
[112] Worden JW. Grief counselling and grief therapy: a handbook for the mental health practitioner. Hove: New York, 2001.
[113] Hayward L, Zubrick SR, Silburn S. Blood alcohol levels in suicide cases. J Epidemiol Community Health 1992; 46: 256-60.
[114] Mackie JL. Causes and conditions. Am Philosoph Q 1965; 2: 245-64.
[115] Lipsey MW, Wilson DB, Cohen MA, Derzon JH. Is there a causal relationship between alcohol use and violence? A synthesis of evidence. In: Galanter M, Begleiter H, Eds. Alcohol and violence: epidemiology, neurobiology, psychology, family issues. New York, Plenum Press. 1997; pp. 245-82.
[116] Light JM, Grube JW, Madden PA, Gover J. Adolescent alcohol use and suicidal ideation: a nonrecursive model. Addict Behav 2003; 28: 705-24.
[117] Swahn MH, Bossarte RM. Gender, early alcohol use, and suicide ideation and attempts: findings from the 2005 youth risk behavior survey. J Adolesc Health 2007; 41: 175-81.
[118] Ikeda RM, Kresnow MJ, Mercy JA, *et al.* Medical conditions and nearly lethal suicide attempts. Suicide Life Threat Behav 2001; 32: 60-7.
[119] Conner KR. A call for research on planned *vs.* unplanned suicidal behavior. Suicide Life Threat Behav 2004; 34: 89-98.
[120] Wojnar M, Ilgen MA, Czyz E, *et al.* Impulsive and non-impulsive suicide attempts in patients treated for alcohol dependence. J Affect Disord 2009; 115: 131-9.
[121] Simon OR, Swann AC, Powell KE, Potter LB, Kresnow MJ, O'Carroll PW. Characteristics of impulsive suicide attempts and attempters. Suicide Life Threat Behav 2001; 32: 49-59.
[122] Conner KR, Hesselbrock VM, Schuckit MA, *et al.* Precontemplated and impulsive suicide attempts among individuals with alcohol dependence. J Stud Alcohol 2006; 67: 95-101.
[123] Williams RL, Gutsch KU, Kazelskis R, Verstegen JP, Scanlon J. An investigation of relationships between level of alcohol use impairment and personality characteristics. Addict Behav 1980; 5: 107-12.
[124] Beautrais AL, Joyce PR, Mulder RT, Fergusson DM, Deavoll BJ, Nightingale SK. Prevalence and comorbidity of mental disorders in persons making serious suicide attempts: a case-control study. Am J Psychiatry 1996; 153: 1009-14.
[125] Cornelius JR, Clark DB, Salloum IM, Bukstein OG, Kelly TM. Interventions in suicidal alcoholics. Alcohol Clin Exp Res 2004; 28: 89S-96S.
[126] Sublette ME, Carballo JJ, Moreno C, *et al.* Substance use disorders and suicide attempts in bipolar subtypes. J Psychiatr Res 2009; 43: 230-8.
[127] Neves FS, Malloy-Diniz LF, Correa H. Suicidal behavior in bipolar disorder: what is the influence of psychiatric comorbidities? J Clin Psychiatry 2009; 70: 13-18.
[128] Kamali M, Oquendo MA, Mann JJ. Understanding the neurobiology of suicidal behavior. Depress Anxiety 2001; 14: 164-76.
[129] Sher L. Alcoholism and suicidal behavior: a clinical overview. Acta Psychiatr Scand 2006; 113: 13-22.
[130] Clark DB, Parker AM, Lynch KG. Psychopathology and substance-related problems during early adolescence: a survival analysis. J Clin Child Psychol 1999; 28: 333-41.
[131] Bergman B, Brismar B. Characteristics of violent alcoholics. Alcohol Alcohol 1994; 29: 451-7.
[132] Suominen K, Isometsa E, Henriksson M, Ostamo A, Lonnqvist J. Hopelessness, impulsiveness and intent among suicide attempters with major depression, alcohol dependence, or both. Acta Psychiatr Scand 1997; 96: 142-9.
[133] Koob GF, Le Moal M. Drug abuse: hedonic homeostatic dysregulation. Science 1997; 278: 52-8.
[134] McBride WJ, Lovinger DM, Machu T, *et al.* Serotonin-3 receptors in the actions of alcohol, alcohol reinforcement, and alcoholism. Alcohol Clin Exp Res 2004; 28: 257-67.

[135] Lovinger DM. 5-HT3 receptors and the neural actions of alcohols: an increasingly exciting topic. Neurochem Int 1999; 35: 125-30.
[136] Mann JJ, Arango V, Henteleff RA, Lagattuta TF, Wong DT. Serotonin 5-HT3 receptor binding kinetics in the cortex of suicide victims are normal. J Neural Transm 1996; 103: 165-71.
[137] Evenden J. Impulsivity: a discussion of clinical and experimental findings. J Psychopharmacol 1999; 13: 180-92.
[138] Gorwood P. Biological markers for suicidal behavior in alcohol dependence. Eur Psychiatry 2001; 16: 410-7.
[139] Joiner TE, Jr., Johnson F, Soderstrom K. Association between serotonin transporter gene polymorphism and family history of attempted and completed suicide. Suicide Life Threat Behav 2002; 32: 329-32.
[140] Mann JJ, Brent DA, Arango V. The neurobiology and genetics of suicide and attempted suicide: a focus on the serotonergic system. Neuropsychopharmacology 2001; 24: 467-77.
[141] Skog OJ. Alcohol and suicide-Durkheim revisited. Acta Sociol 1991; 34: 193-206.
[142] Shneidman ES. Definition of suicide. Northvale: Aronson, 1985.
[143] Steele CM, Josephs RA. Alcohol myopia. Its prized and dangerous effects. Am Psychol 1990; 45: 921-3.
[144] Steele CM, Southwick L. Alcohol and social behavior I: The psychology of drunken excess. J Pers Soc Psychol 1985; 48: 18-34.
[145] Goldman MS, Del Boca FK, Darkes J. Alcohol expectancy theory: the application of cognitive neuroscience. In: Leonard KE, Ed. Psychological theories of drinking and alcoholism. 2nd ed. New York, Guilford Press. 1999; pp. 203–46.
[146] Garfinkel BD, Froese A, Hood J. Suicide attempts in children and adolescents. Am J Psychiatry 1982; 139: 1257-61.
[147] Krajnc MS, Schmidt I, Gergoric A, Dogsa I. Suicide attempts in Slovenian juveniles, 1978-1994. Nord J Psychiatry 1998; 52: 487-92.
[148] Withers LE, Kaplan DW. Adolescents who attempt suicide: A retrospective clinical chart review of hospitalized patients. Prof Psychol Res Pr 1987; 18: 391-3.
[149] Crews FT, Braun CJ, Hoplight B, Switzer RC, 3rd, Knapp DJ. Binge ethanol consumption causes differential brain damage in young adolescent rats compared with adult rats. Alcohol Clin Exp Res 2000; 24: 1712-23.
[150] Widiger TA, Frances AJ, Pincus HA, First MB, Ross R, Davis W. DSM-IV sourcebook. Washington, DC: American Psychiatric Publishing, 1994.
[151] Sher KJ, Grekin ER. Alcohol and affect regulation. In: Gross J, Ed. Handbook of emotion regulation. New York, Guilford. 2007; pp. 560–580.
[152] Magne Ingvar U, Ojehagen A, Traskman Bendz L. Suicide attempters with and without reported overconsumption of alcohol and tranquillizers. Nord J Psychiatry 1997; 51: 415-21.
[153] Merrill J, Milner G, Owens J, Vale A. Alcohol and attempted suicide. Br J Addict 1992; 87: 83-9.
[154] Platt S, Robinson A. Parasuicide and alcohol: a 20 year survey of admissions to a regional poisoning treatment centre. Int J Soc Psychiatry 1991; 37: 159-72.
[155] Field CA, Claassen CA, O'Keefe G. Association of alcohol use and other high-risk behaviors among trauma patients. J Trauma 2001; 50: 13-9.
[156] Suokas J, Lonnqvist J. Suicide attempts in which alcohol is involved: a special group in general hospital emergency rooms. Acta Psychiatr Scand 1995; 91: 36-40.
[157] Kresnow M, Powell KE, Webb KB, *et al.* Assigning time-linked exposure status to controls in unmatched case-control studies: alcohol use and nearly lethal suicide attempts. Stat Med 2001; 20: 1479-85.
[158] Hufford MR. Alcohol and suicidal behavior. Clin Psychol Rev 2001; 21: 797-811.
[159] Ries RK, Yuodelis-Flores C, Roy-Byrne PP, Nilssen O, Russo J. Addiction and suicidal behavior in acute psychiatric inpatients. Compr Psychiatry 2009; 50: 93-9.

CHAPTER 5

Ethnic Aspects Involved in Suicide

Giancarlo Giupponi[1,*] and Roger Pycha[2]

[1]Psychiatric Service, St. Maurizio Hospital, Via Böhler No. 4, 39100 Bolzano, Italy and [2]Psychiatric Service, Brunico, Italy

Abstract: The phenomenon of suicide has been present throughout human history. It can be identified throughout the world as a consequence of factors pertaining to health, culture, and history. Cultural, ethnic and sociological aspects have been clarified by means of studies examining gender and age difference. In an ever more globalised world, migration and the formation of ethnic minorities within host countries, in conjunction with distinct socio-cultural features leads to new challenges regarding suicidal tendency. It is evident from past studies that the data that we have originates in various countries and when we refer to factors such as risk or protection in minorities we are referring to minorities which are not part of or related to our own cultural circle or our own country. The origin of data can limit the usefulness of our work. We can access limited scientific resources but are confronted with various methodological difficulties. The definition of minority, race and immigrant alone varies from country to country. Interaction between minority and host country, social integration and circumstance vary considerably. Despite these limitations chapter sets out to examine the ethnic aspect of suicide and provide an overall view however fragmented it may be.

Keywords: Suicide, ethnic aspects, minority.

1. INTRODUCTION

Suicide constitutes a worldwide cultural, historical and health oriented phenomena. It snuffs out life and shatters the lives of the ones left behind. Throughout history philosophers, theologians, sociologists and psychologists have all developed explanations to hold true for various cultural concepts of suicide. Medicine and psychiatry have neglected this concept, as if it were not part of their daily work, for far too long.

According to psychological autopsies, 90% of suicide victims show a psychiatric and 30-88% an affective disturbance [1] 58,000 people die every year in Europe as a result of suicide and 10 European countries report a suicide rate of 27 (people per 100,000 inhabitants per year) and higher. The world wide suicide rate is 0.6%. Suicide is the ninth most common cause of death [2] and in the 15-44 age groups the third most common. 10 to 18 percent of the adult world population admits to having had suicidal ideas and 3.5% have attempted suicide at least once in their lives [3, 4].

Patients with no psychiatric diagnoses develop a lifetime prevalence of 52% for death wishes and suicidal fantasies, on the other hand, a large proportion of psychiatric patients never develop suicidal thoughts [5]. For some time now, the World Health Organisation (WHO), as well as smaller organizations, has attempted to address this problem and continue their prevention campaigns [6].

Despite the development and availability of psychiatric treatment facilities it has not been possible to reduce global suicide rates. This could be attributed to a shortage of treatment, since a large number of suicide victims were never referred to a specialist [7].

83% of suicide patients had contact with a doctor; 66% of them even within a month before the attempt. Professionals can however rely on effective treatments for suicide prevention: pharmaceutical therapies have achieved positive results with the use of lithium and clozapine [8-10]. Specific psychotherapies have worked

***Address correspondence to Giancarlo Giupponi:** Psychiatric Service, St Maurizio Hospital, *Via* Böhler No. 4, 39100 Bolzano, Italy. Phone: +39 0471 305811 Fax: +39 0471 305829. E-mail: giancarlo.giupponi@asbz.it

Maurizio Pompili (Ed)

well, however evaluation of their effectiveness has only been carried out using small sample groups [11].

The prospect of a universal procedure for the prevention of suicide does not appear to be very promising due to differing health systems and the frequency and manifestations of suicidal behavior in individual countries.

Risk factors exist in every country, the name of a mental health problem may vary from country to country, from culture to culture, but similar psychopathological frameworks (with their depressive symptoms, psychotics). are always present [12].

Despite differing aetiology, psychological theories of suicide from Freud to Shneidman, independent of external influences, suggest similar internal dynamics of the suicidal mind for people throughout the world. This is the case although a confirmed mental illness represents a risk factor but does not seem to be (at least in most cases) sufficient cause for suicidal behavior. Suicide risk is not constant within a given population and varies significantly between different ethnic groups (African-Americans, Asians, Indians, *etc.*). These differences are due to a combination of protective and risk factors which are perceived differently in different geographical and cultural conditions [13].

Life events and their importance in relation to suicidal behavior vary considerably within a population. A twenty year old girl, who takes her own life in Italy, usually has other motives than those of a similarly aged girl in India. It is therefore of vital importance to pay attention to the great differences between cultures and question to what extent general knowledge with regard to suicide is transferable, or to what extent cultural aspects play a key role.

Further, it is important to consider how knowledge of risk factors and protective factors are applied in various populations with particular reference to ethnic minorities. This is possible, but it is not empirically tested.

Factors which may contribute to the geographic variations in suicidal risk;

- Socio-cultural and historical factors (*e.g.,* countries with similar characteristics and history have a similar risk)
- Differences in factors in society (*e.g.,* cultural and religious inclination for suicide, suicide is more frequent where it is less stigmatized, it is lower where it is stigmatized; legal and religious sanctions against suicide are important)
- A dominant religion and strong religious faith (Islamic countries have a lower suicide rate)
- Varying prevalence of psychiatric disorders (*e.g.,* alcoholism in Baltic countries, depression in Russia)
- Varying levels of risk as well as protective factors (*e.g.,* campaigns against alcohol and drugs; divorce, unemployment, family cohesion)
- Differing levels of access to implements and methods of suicide (*e.g.,* access to pesticides in the rural areas of China and India, weapons in El Salvador), and the availability of more or less lethal suicide methods.
- Differences in the availability of psychiatric care.
- Media coverage of suicides (*e.g.,* suicide rates increase with increasing media coverage of events)
- Genetic differences in population [14].

2. ETHNICITY AND SUICIDAL BEHAVIOR

The significance of cultural influences can always be made clear in investigations by reference to gender and age differences. Cultural and social issues affect the classification of a death or a suspicious death as suicide [15, 16]. This includes the style of reporting used by the media, reactions to political and economic changes *etc.*

At the end of the 19th century the well-known sociologist E. Durkheim [17] emphasized how society and culture influence the risk of suicide.

In an increasingly globalized world in which migration leads to the formation of ethnic minorities, there are specific socio-cultural peculiarities associated with suicidal tendency which form a new challenge for all of us. We can only rely on a relatively small amount of scientific experience and are challenged by various difficulties in methodology. Even the definition of the terms; minority, race and immigrant varies from country to country. Interaction between minority and host country, social integration and specific circumstances vary considerably.

Members of an ethnic minority who seek help from a health service should be considered as being at risk [18] because;

- they have a higher risk of suffering from psychological distress and/or difficulties
- despite mental disorders they have a higher risk of remaining untreated
- they often demonstrate a low rate of compliancy and/or satisfaction in their relationship with the health services

Conflicts with services and lack of compliance are major risk factors in explaining the suicidal behavior of people with mental disorders.

A review of the general hypothesis that ethnic minorities adapt over time and therefore their risk of suicide is reduced shows varying results. [19].

African-Americans demonstrate a low suicide risk whereas Indians are at ever increasing risk.

Longitudinal studies have shown the variations in suicide rates among various ethnic groups have decreased during the past 20 years [20]. Hispanic and African-American youths demonstrate that they are becoming more similar to European adolescents [21].

The large differences in suicide rates detected on the basis of gender have remained persistent.

The stigma of suicide has clear implications for the suicide candidate and his family. Paradoxically, it may protect from suicide, but hinder or impede cries for help. Cultural and societal attitudes towards suicide is therefore of great importance. The social environment modifies the influence of risk factors.

The predominant religion determines religious attitudes and therefore experience of depression and suicidal tendency [22, 23].

Unemployment is associated with a lower risk of suicide where collective unemployment is usual [24]. The risk of suicide in conjunction with alcohol consumption is low where alcohol consumption is socially sanctioned [25]. Personal relative economic impoverishment (*e.g.*, in comparison with neighbours) has a higher influence on suicide risk than general social deprivation. Exclusion and stigmatization may increase the risk [26]. The risk of suicide is higher for members of ethnic minorities which are widely scattered [27]. The study "Ethnic Density and Psychiatric Hospitalization: Hazards of Minority Status" has found that ethnic groups in New York City reported a high rate of psychiatric hospitalization for those individuals who live in geographical areas where their ethnic group is in minority. A proportionally low ethnic minority in a region can increase suicide rate, sometimes determined by an increase in the rate of mental disorder among these populations [28].

In a study of depression among single mothers, the density/concentration of ethnic minorities could be detected as a significant predictor variable. A relative shortage of supporters in similar social situations, the perception of a greater social hostility, could explain the greater incidence of depression in this group [29].

Other possible links between ethnic group and suicide have been established. Some studies show an increased risk and selective choice of suicide method among ethnic minorities. Influential factors which are discussed in connection with the study of the increased risk of suicide;

- Every circumstance which leads to situations in which the individual no longer experiences belonging to traditional or alternative cultures.

- Development and change of own cultural identity.

- Problems with acculturation, generation conflicts, increasing shortage of social norms, helplessness and decreasing collectivism may lead to increased insecurity and depression.

- Anomie (a concept first developed by Durkheim - social disintegration affecting tribal peoples under colonization) may contribute to alienation.

- Excessive adjustment of ethnic minorities may increase the risk of suicide, while group cohesion serves as a protective factor [30].

3. OBJECTIVES AND METHODOLOGY OF MEDICAL RESEARCH

The object of our article is to examine the ethnic aspect of suicide more deeply. We referred to the literature from 1966 to May 2009 with PubMed using the key words: suicide AND ethnic, AND minority; finding 72 items. These articles are complemented by other integrated studies. In these studies it is clear that the data available originates in various countries. When we talk about risk factors or protective factors we often refer to certain minorities which are not present in our own country. Based on the following table (Tables **1** and **2**) we can see that the majority of publications come from the USA or the UK. The risk or protective factors relate to specific minority groups (Latino, African American in USA, Indian, Asian, and Afro-Caribbean in the UK). The origin of the study may limit the usability of the data in our work.

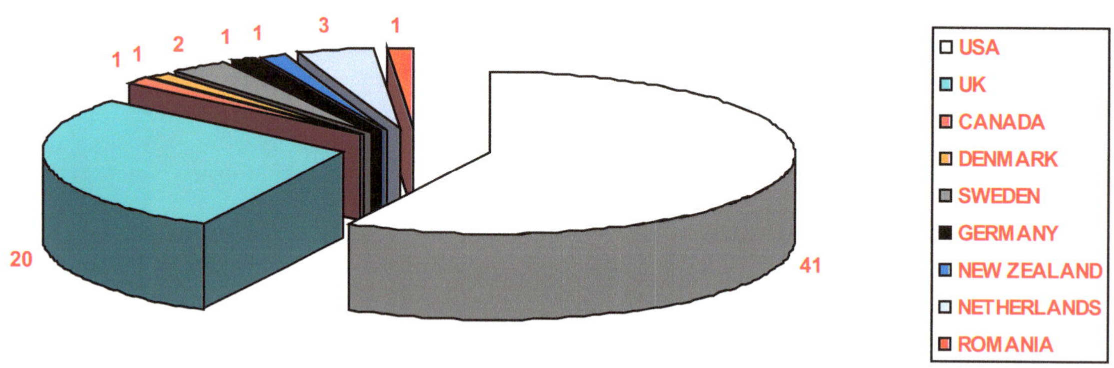

Figure 1: Percentage of publications.

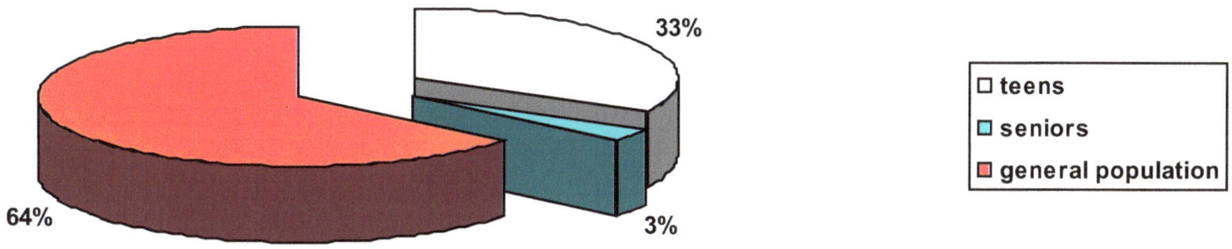

Figure 2: Percentage of publications and age.

Unfortunately, the majority of publications on suicide come from very few countries. This is a well known fact. It should also be taken into consideration that the number of cases analyzed (cases of suicide by a mental disorder) in the world until 2003 amounted to just over 15,000 cases of which 80% were from Europe. (Table **3**) shows this aspect clearly [31].

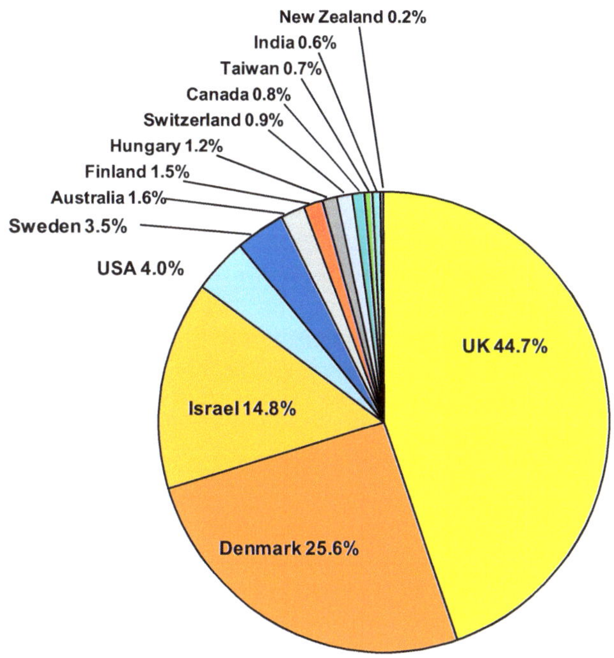

Figure 3: Percentage of analysed suicide in different cautries.

4. STUDY RESULTS AND DISCUSSION

The British study shows some important variations within the ethnic minority population. In Britain, ethnic minorities compose 9% of the population, but are 21% of the psychiatric population.

Suicide among members of ethnic minorities appears to be underestimated. British coroners appear to assess suspicious Asian and Afro Caribbean deaths as suicide less frequently than do in the case of white immigrants [32, 33]. Research lasting 4 years shows over 282 suicidal patients belonging to ethnic minorities had contact with help services in the 12 months before the suicide attempt (approximately 70 suicides per year). Caucasian suicide was associated with; violent methods, schizophrenia, unemployment, violence, non-compliance. 50 percent of the cases had SA. Among the group of African-Caribbean origin,

74% were schizophrenics and 85% were unemployed (different risk factors than the general population). The African had the highest suicide rate during hospitalization. Among the Asian group, members showed a correlation with an affective disorder, 20% lived alone, 50% were married, and a history of drugs or alcohol was unusual. A low compliance to treatment was shared with African minority members. The study emphasizes, similar to other studies [34, 35], that suicide was common among Asian women. Raleigh had already shown a low risk of suicide in men born in Bangladesh, Sri Lankan and Pakistan, but an increased risk in young men of Indian and east African origin. Women of African and East Indian origin had a 2-3 times greater risk between the age of 15-34 years [36].

Similarly, a study by Bhui *et al.* compares the risk of suicide (clinical symptoms, perception preventability of suicide) among people of 4 ethnic groups (the Caribbean, Africans, Asians and Caucasians) after (or within) 12 months of discharge from their department from 1996 to 2001 in Wales and England. Clear sociodemographic differences were observed between the 4 groups: ethnic minority suicide was higher among younger people, and it was more closely related to unemployment. Schizophrenia was the most common diagnosis among people of African origin where high rates of hallucinations and SA but low percentages of other indicators were observed. Depression and suicidal thoughts were reported less in these groups. Among Asians a high percentage of hopelessness, psychotic symptoms and depression, but lower levels of suicidal conception were reported (compared with Caucasions). Psychotic symptoms were more frequently present among ethnic minorities who then committed suicide, and the perceived preventability was highest among people of Afro Caribbean origin (therefore it is suggested to deeper than psychosis). Particularly at risk are men of colour and African Caribbean origin between the ages of 13-24 ; among Asian women and of African or Caribbean origin the risk was greatest between 25-39 years [37]. Unemployment as a particular risk factor among those who belong to ethnic minorities with schizophrenia also appears in other studies. [38].

With regards to suicide attempts, women of Asian origin have a three times greater risk than Caucasian women [39]. Indian women seem to have a 2.6 times higher risk than whites. Among Indian women born in Britain the risk is 7.8 times higher than for white women. The risk of SA was 9 times higher among unemployed whites and 3 times higher among unemployed ethnic minorities (suggesting that this association changes the risk of suicide). Unemployment appears to be a higher stress factor in some groups than in others.

The number of cases in the study is small, the over-representation of Indians compared to people of Afro-Caribbean origin shows how SA is more frequent in this group (although stigma before suicide may lead to an underestimation of the real risk of SA among people of Afro-Caribbean origin) [39].

Life events as a cause, especially related to personal relationships; psychiatric diseases seem to be a minor risk factor for women of south Asian origins [40, 41]. Crawford *et al.* examined 6 ethnic groups within 4,000 patients. With the exception of Irish men, suicidal conception appears to be less common among men than women in ethnic minorities. The life-time risk of SA was 3%; lowest among men of from ethnic minorities and highest among Indian and Pakistani women (compared to white English and Irish women). The risk factors in ethnic minorities were similar to those observed in samples of whites [42]. The risk is strongly linked to symptoms of a mental disorder and less to factors of acculturation [43].

There are significant variations in help-seeking behavior. 2/3 of whites seek help after SA in comparison with only 1/3 of black people of Caribbean origin and it is not clear whether this lack of demand for help is linked to the fact that it not considered to be a significant or excessive stigma. The lower suicidal conception and the lower risk of SA in the minority, especially in men can perhaps explain the lower risk of suicide in minority groups. The low level of suicidal conception in minority groups appears to be contrary only to the high risk of suicide in Indian, Pakistani and Bangladeshi women. There does not appear to be a high risk of suicide among immigrant children [43].

A systematic study of SA in Asian minorities, Caribbean blacks and whites in Britain (a meta-analysis is not possible due to methodological problems) shows how cultural issues may influence the risk and methods related to SA. For the future a clearer definition of "ethnic group" is recommended, as well as follow up studies.

Factors that increase the risk of mental illness such as social exclusion, unemployment, financial problems are more common in ethnic minorities.

In summary, in addition to giving a rating, the studies reviewed, detect a demographic and cultural risk: Asian women under 35 are more at risk than those over 35 years, the Caribbean population under 35 is also subject to a high risk of suicide. The method most commonly used is poisoning. "Cultural conflict" is suggested as a possible cause although the exact meaning of the term is not explained [44].

Gilmer *et al.* highlights the differences in risk factors for mental illness before and after migration, to which some groups of immigrants may be more sensitive. Chronic episodes of depression were associated with more disadvantaged socio-economic situations as well as the social status of racial and ethnic minorities [45].

The Irish, a large ethnic minority in England, have a high risk of mental illness (except for psychosis, which is more frequent in members of the Afro-Caribbean community). The risk of hospitalization for depression in men is 3 times higher than in other white men and 2 and a half times higher than the risk for women. Possible reasons include; social selection, low class, culture, identity and racism, material deprivation and alcohol. As well as the manner of immigration (*e.g.,* an unplanned immigration) negative experiences (childhood trauma *etc.*), positive experiences (employment, social support *etc.*) and the post immigration situation can contribute to and affect suicide risk. Irish people with depression are at risk of social and medical problems as well as alcohol misuse. This underlines the importance of immediate preventive measures after immigration [46].

North America's data appears to be similar to the UK's. In Canada, the Francophone and Aboriginal groups seem to have the highest rates of suicide risk. The risk of suicide among Aboriginal people is double that of the general population (20 suicides per 100,000 in the North West Territories, Nunavut recorded 80 suicides per 100,000 in comparison to the 11.5 recorded in the general Canadian population), followed by non-Aboriginal people and the Francophone population. Clarke D E *et al.* have analyzed a sample of about 60,000 different models (pathway) of suicide in different ethnic groups by comparing the socio-economic status, the sense of community and the state of mental health. Among the ethnic groups different routes of suicide risk that could mean high risk even in ethnic groups normally at low risk were observed. For example, abuse and alcohol dependence (major risk factor) had a different effect on different ethnic groups [47]. Among the population of Hispanic origin and African Americans suffering from alcoholism in the United States, life events were more significant in causing addiction in the early years of their dependency before their death [48]. Therefore, prevention and treatment require differentiated adjustment applicable for various ethnic groups [47].

Becker *et al.* have examined the data for murders and suicides that occurred in New Mexico between 1958 and 1987 where death due to a violent cause, (whether murder or suicide) was a major problem for public health. (New Mexico was the state with the highest rate of violent death in the United States and disproportionately affected males belonging to minorities). This state consisted of three main ethnic groups: Hispanics, Native Americans and white non-Hispanics. What emerged was that the suicide rate for males in every ethnic group was higher than that found in females. Native American women also had a lower suicide rate than the other ethnic groups.

It is also noteworthy that Natives and Hispanics are the two social groups most at risk for suicide, and that this has been increasing in recent years; especially among the young. Native American women on the other hand have the highest homicide rate among all ethnic groups. The data shows that suicide is a significant problem and a major cause of death in New Mexico, especially among Native Americans (followed by non-Hispanics and Hispanics). Moreover, the rates of suicide note an increase in the male population and a decrease in age while performing these actions [49].

Epidemiological data of the United States reported a decrease in suicides among youths aged 15 to 19 years but unfortunately there was an increase in suicides among children belonging to certain ethnic minorities [50]. An exponent, The American Association of Suicidology, concludes that the suicide rate is disproportionally high among teenage Natives and Eskimos [51].

The rate of suicide among young African-Americans more than doubled between 1980 and 1995, with a percentage of 126% in the age group between 15-19, and 223% among those aged 10-14, compared to the so-called white American population. This increase appeared greater in Afro Americans males than in females. With often more than double the national rate [52], it is hypothesized that the increased risk of suicide is due to a decline of cultural traditions such as the extended family and spirituality (strong among people of colour), in contrast to the adoption of other models, solving problems through suicide [53].

An increasing prevalence of suicidal behaviors among young Latin Americans and Afro Americans is revealed by the Surgeon Generals Call to Action to Prevent Suicide and Behavior CDC's Youth Risk Surveillance System. Suicide is the cause of 11.7% of all deaths among those of 10 - 24 years of age in the United States [54].

In 1996, the Department of Health and Human Services noted that suicide is the third leading cause of death among young Hispanics between 10-24 years of age. (Suicide is the third leading cause of death among young Latinos aged between 10 and 24 years of age [55]. The Centre for Disease Control and Prevention (CDC) analyzed mortality data from 1997-2001 (8.744 Hispanics, among which 85% were males), finding that among those Hispanic suicides, most of them are young, males, and that the suicidal act is by means of a firearm. The age of suicide victims in about 50% of the cases was between 10-34 years. Despite this, a very high rate among people over 85 years, followed by those between 80-84 and 75-79 years is noticed (36.54% against 31.55% and 21.69% respectively). As for the female population, the age group most at risk is between 50-54 years, followed by 45-49 and between 15-19 years (3.12% against 2.52 and 2.36%, respectively). Among all sub-ethnic groups, the highest risk suicide group is in Mexico (56%). From the above data we can see that the suicide rate is higher among older males, which does not however mean that young Hispanics are subject to an equally elevated risk. Mental illness, substance abuse, accumulated stress, family problems and low socioeconomic level may all contribute to increased risk of suicidal behavior [55].

Suicidal behavior risk in young Latinos is just as high as other ethnic groups [56]. Latinos also have less access to mental health services than whites and are less likely to receive the necessary treatment.

This tendency in young Latin Americans can not be observed among African Americans, the YRBSS (Youth Risk Surveillance System Behavior) identified that during 1999 the percentage of attempted suicides among this minority had reached 12.8% compared to 7:30 % of white Americans [52].

Robert *et al.* analyzed 4186 multi ethnic students from different schools in Houston from 10 to 17 years of age (1994). The results show how females are more susceptible during their life to consider suicide attempts, whereas males appear to be those who implement these ideas better. The Mexican Americans, Pakistani Americans, and Vietnamese Americans present greater ideation, plans and suicide attempts compared to other ethnicities. It is also known that females, older adolescents, (around 17 years of age) and groups at a lower socioeconomic level are more susceptible to suicidal behavior, but it also highlights the high risks faced by young Hispanics, especially Americanized Mexicans [57].

Zayas *et al.* emphasize the cultural differences between girls and families of Spanish origin. The difficulties of acculturation are additional stress factors for these family members. Family therapy would be useful to limit this risk of SA [58].

O'Donnell L *et al.* examine the prevalence and predictor factors pertaining to suicide; 879 adolescents recruited from three different high schools in Brooklyn (New York). Each of these schools is located in an area of the city considered to be poor and with a high risk of violence and disease. 69% of the test subjects were African American while 16% were Latin American and the remaining 15% were mixed or of other ethnicity. Among all subjects 15% had seriously considered suicide in past years, 13% had devised a plan and 11% attempted suicide once while 4% had tried several times. The girls had ideation and suicide attempts, in light of insufficient intimate relationships, promiscuity and depressions. Resilience factors found were marginally the family unit and religiousness; while the family composition was not affected significantly (although the family constellation and its atmosphere could be of importance). Coping style, support of peers and the social return were not significantly associated with ideation and suicide attempts. Ethnic identity did not appear to be a significantly related factor as the resilient factor (especially in environments where racial discrimination is still high). Based on this consideration, the district would be more protective or at the same time riskier than ethnic identity.

A high level of access to firearms (Brooklyn is known for violence, substance use, unprotected sex, HIV) results in a strong relationship between this method and the rate of suicides [59].

Roberts *et al.* note lower depression and suicidal ideation among youths who speak English, suggesting that the process of acculturation may play a role. Young Mexican-Americans appear to have a higher risk of suicidal ideation than those of English origin. Moreover, it seems that most young people who are lonely, have a higher risk of depression and suicidal ideation [60].

Depression is the major factor in attempted suicide and is associated with disturbances in social functioning, family and school. People belonging to different ethnic and cultural groups with the same diagnosis of major depressive disorder display some differences (often somatic problems). People belonging to minority ethnic groups could be less adhering to standard criteria and more sceptical in respect to other prognosis. These minorities often respond differently than whites to medical care given.

Beyond the issues relating to access to medical care by these minorities, it was noticed that special attention should be paid to the choices and dosages of medicines available to subjects of different origins (African-American population in the response to SSRIs were less effective than tricyclic drugs, when compared to the white population) [61]. Sen *et al.* 9000 analyzes adolescents enrolled between 6 and 10 grade (non-Hispanic blacks, Hispanics, Asians and non-Hispanic whites). Female adolescents are more likely to suffer from depression (depressed mood), although males ask for help less frequently than females. All ethnic minorities suffer more from depression than non-Hispanic white counterparts, even though the risk of self harm in African Americans is lower. Moreover, African Americans and Asians are not subject to call for help, especially when it comes to males with particularly acute problems. Males less than females tend to ask for help if needed. Furthermore, data shows that the majority of both males and females with depression, or risk of harming themselves, tend not to ask for help from anyone. A lack of requests for aid is based on the degree of stigma that is associated with mental illness within a given culture [62].

Studies in Scandinavian countries reported that belonging to an ethnic minority can influence the risk of suicide. Johansson LM, *et al.* analyze the influence of ethnicity, age, gender, social status (marital status) and given immigration in Sweden for the risk of suicide. Analyzed is a population of individuals over the age of 15 (N = 6,725,274, from the Swedish census of 1985 and is based on individual data). Suicide and undetermined death are analyzed in the follow-up period 1986-1989. The ethnicity defined from being born abroad was a risk factor for suicide in men and women with ratios of 1.21 (1.11-1.31) and 1.36 (1.21-1.53), respectively, and with controlled age and family status (marital status). Not being married was a risk factor in both men and women with ratios from 1.26 to 5:55 in different age groups.

A high risk for suicide in Sweden, according to age, was determined for males born in Russia and in Finland the risk was higher than in their countries of birth. Women born in Hungary, Russia, Finland and Poland had a higher risk of committing suicide in Sweden than in their country of birth. Also being male, aged 45-54, 75 or older and born in Finland or eastern European countries, significantly increased the risk of suicide. The same increased risk appeared in immigrants in Sweden (in 1967 or before) who were born in Finland, Eastern Europe or outside Europe. This result is important for prevention and planning of psychiatric cures [63]. This data was confirmed by other studies, the risk is high even among immigrants who do not differ phenotypically and culturally from the general population [64].

Another study [65] shows how the second generation of immigrants tends to have a greater risk than the first. Hjern A *et al.* analyzed suicide records of a population of 2.7 million residents between the ages of 10-68 years.

The minority of Finnish origin had a particularly high risk in the first and second generation. The risk in the minority of the Middle Easterners was the lowest. The inter-country adoptees had very high odds for suicide death (adjusted OR: 5.0, 95% CI 3.5-7.0) [65]. Similar findings have been highlighted by Bille Brahe (an increased risk among second-generation immigrant women whose parents were from the 3rd world countries) [66]. V. Sundaram found a significant risk in women born abroad but low risk in men when compared Danes. The study confirmed three differences: 1. differences between foreign-born and born in Denmark and the general population. 2. The risk of suicide was not uniform among the foreign groups. 3. There are differences in kind between Danish and foreign groups. The risk was particularly high among immigrants from the north (which are most similar) and lowest among those born in Asia (with gender differences in suicide risks) [67].

Unfortunately, studies in German speaking countries are scarce. Again, social fragmentation seems to be a major risk factor. This is expressed in common values and loss of meaning (anomie), or lack of social support to immigrants. In Germany the male-female suicide ratio is 2.8. The risk of suicide increases with age.

Among immigrant women the risk of suicide is high when compared to women from the host country. Two risk factors seem to play a special role; 1 problems of acculturation 2 poor access to health services. The risk of suicide in migrants increases with increased length of hospitalization in psychiatry and in the following generations (second, third degeneration) becoming similar to the relationship between hospitalization and suicide in the host country population [68]. The children of migrants are a high risk group. Girls and young women in the Mediterranean area are frequently hospitalized for SA [69], although other data obtained on the population of Greek origin indicate that the risk is low [70].

Razume O. &, Zeeb H. analyze suicide mortality among male and female Turks in Germany. The study examines data on suicide between 1980 and 97 in the old West German states. 1,186 Turks and 143,318 Germans under the age of 65 years were analyzed. The suicide rate in Turkey is very low (3.4), suicide attempts, however, are frequent (124 per 100,000 inhabitants per year) [71].

Death by suicide is highest in the age group 18-29 in men as well as women. In women aged 30 and above the rate seems to decrease with age. Suicide rates are significantly higher for men than for women, with the exception of the age group 10 to 17 years. Turkish girls and young women have a higher suicide mortality rates than boys and young men. Compared to the German population, the suicide rates of the Turkish population are significantly lower. In 1998, a slightly higher proportion of death by firearms in German compared to non-German men (10.1% *vs.* 6.9%) was noted. Low percentage of drug poisoning in non-German to German women (13.5% *vs.* 19.1%) was noted. Compared with mortality in Turkey, the rate of suicide among male and female Turks in Germany was similar. The low suicide mortality rate in Turkey is interpreted by Sayil with religious prohibitions of suicide and a highly developed social coherence. [71]. Turkish girls and young women have a higher risk of suicide than their equal aged German peers and than Turkish boys and young men in Germany. 74 cases compared with 1,181 in total are considered. The high risk among girls and young women can not be explained. However, especially for young women, the tension between traditional roles and expectations of modern life is of great significance. Future studies must clarify whether suicides are associated with events such a family crisis situations or cultural conflicts. The risk does not appear to bind itself to a high presence of psychiatric illness (such as studies on Indian women in England). The ethnic Indian young women were disproportionately at risk if they were married. Among the Turkish men, the age group 18 to 29 years is at highest risk, unlike in German men, whose suicide risk increases greatly with age. The pattern among Turkish men in Germany is more similar to the English and Welsh. In England and Wales, a rise in suicide rates in the age group 25-34 years up to the level of the older men was also observed to coincide with rising unemployment and growing drug use [72].Unemployment among Turks is much higher than among the general population (risk factor for the Turks) [73]. Non-psychiatric patients and immigrants in different studies appear to have a greater likelihood of SA [74-77].

In adult psychiatry, Häfner [78] and Benkert [79] describe a low risk of suicide among migrants compared to German patients. It is possible that immigrants are lack treatment with outpatient medications (lithium, *etc.*) but also lack psychotherapy which could be influential in these results. [80, 81].

Grube M analyzes whether there are differences regarding the rate of suicide attempts between the Germans and migrants in psychiatric hospitalization. Correlation between ethnicity, suicide attempt, suicidal ideas and self-injury at admission were examined. 494 patients were studied at admission of which 111 were immigrants. 32% of Turkish origin, 10.9% ex-Yugoslavia, 8.5% Italian, Other reported results; The ultrasound diagnosis of depression, 14%, 31% schizophrenia, 37% addiction, 9.5% organic 7.5% St. Neurotic and Personality - Disturbances. Suicide attempts were present between 15,3% of the immigrant population and 8,9% of the German population.

Immigrant status increases the risk of suicide attempt by about a factor of 1.8 and immigrant status, low age (> 45), female gender increases the risk of suicide attempt by a factor of 3.02. Verbal Suicide remarks are noted in 21.9% of Germans and 24.5% of immigrants, self-harm acts are present in 5% of Germans and 1.8% of immigrants. In 70.6% of the immigrants who have committed a suicidal act, a trans-cultural conflict was to blame, in immigrants without suicidal acts 38.3%. Especially in young women, cultural tension between traditional roles and expectations of modern life are present. The suicide method among immigrants is 'soft' compared to the Germans. There are no differences in drugs treatment between immigrants and Germans is noted despite more frequent suicide attempts among immigrants and a higher risk of suicide for the Germans. Suicide attempts by immigrants are associated with a higher form illness [82].

Deisenhammer *et al.* highlighted clear differences in suicide risks in different ethnic groups in South Tyrol. In a 1996 published study he examined 676 suicide cases with the question of whether ethnicity was associated with varying suicide occurrence. The author found the average suicide rate of 11.8 (with rates of 18.0 for men and 5.7 for women). Men from German communities had a suicide rate of 21.7, Ladins 22.4, and Italians 15.1. Women from German communities had a suicide rate of 6, Ladins of 7.9, and Italians 5.5. Of the 116 municipalities examined, 102 demonstrated a German-speaking majority, 5 an Italian-speaking majority and 8 a Ladin-speaking majority. In his conclusions, the author notes that in South Tyrol, the suicide occurrence is influenced by the language group: the German men showed a significantly higher risk of suicide than the Italians. Also cross-gender differences between the language groups were identified. The differences were interpreted as impact of social and cultural factors [83].

Pycha *et al.* intensified the research to see if there were any differences between the rates and characteristics of suicide by ethnicity and gender in South Tirol, Italy. Psychological autopsy interviews were conducted for suicides between 1997 and January 2006. From 1997 to 2002, 332 suicides were reported (205 were expected to die, when estimating South Tyrolean suicide cases against Italian suicide rates (χ^2 =29.55; p=.000). Interviews indicated that Ladins had the highest average prevalence rate (16.90 suicides per 100,000 inhabitants per year *vs.* 11.81 and 6.90 suicides per 100,000 inhabitants per year respectively for Germans and Italians). There were differences between ethnicity and gender. Multivariate models indicated that German suicides were less likely to be divorced (OR=.43; 95% CI: .20/.91), and were more likely to have less education (OR=4.76; 95% CI: 2.47/9.16) and a history of suicide among family members (OR=7.77; 95% CI: 1.75/34.48) than were Italians. Ladins were more likely to have less education (OR=9.94; 95% CI: 2.51/39.35) and were less likely to be divorced (OR=.17; 95% CI: .03/.87) than were Italians. Men were less likely to have attempted suicide more than once (OR=.31; 95% CI: .11/.91), have received psychiatric treatment (OR=.43; 95% CI: .20/.91), or be older (OR=.97; 95% CI: .95/1.00) than were women. Men were more likely to be employed (OR=3.98; 95% CI: 1.75/9.05) or retired (OR=14.40; 95% CI: 4.55/45.56) and have comorbid alcohol abuse (OR=9.71; 95% CI: 2.96/31.91). The study indicated that suicide is an alarming health and social problem in South Tyrol and may require various means of preventive intervention for men and women of varying ethnicities [84].

Giupponi *et al.* seeks to expand on asocial aspects associated with suicide in South Tyrol. He examines whether socioeconomics risk factors and depressive symptoms are associated with suicide in men with alcohol use disorders in this region of Italy. He hypothesized that socioeconomic inequalities interact with greater psychopathology in men with alcohol use disorders who commit suicide and found a positive association between unstable work positions and low educational attainment and alcohol use disorders in individuals who committed suicide. The results of the study point to the need for careful assessment of subsyndromal depression in individuals with alcohol use disorders, especially when abuse is associated with socioeconomic risk factors, such as lower educational attainment and unemployment or employment instability [85].

In the study of suicide a worldwide comparison of religious belief (ideologies) and behavior is even more impressive than the study of minorities. In general it can be assumed that a very high level of religiousness in everyday life serves as a protective device and a factor which can prevent suicide. Deep faith seems to play a more prominent role when exercised in religious practices and these, in turn, contribute more than mere membership of a religious group. In closed religious communities, social factors such as high cohesion and solidarity come into play. The religious group corresponds to a form of an extended family. In addition the , Judaic, Christian and Islamic faiths propagate that life is a commodity borrowed from God, over which the individual has no control, [86] killing, and above all, suicide is to be avoided at all cost [87]. In investigating the suicide rates of 71 countries, a negative correlation with regard to the percentage of Muslim population was discovered [88]. In Canada, a 10 percent increase in non-religious census declarations showed a 3.2 percent increase in suicides [89].

In a survey of 28,000 people in 19 Western countries, religious belief and suicide risk correlated negatively, however, personal tolerance toward suicide and suicide rates was positive [90].

The suicide rates in countries with a higher percentage of believers were generally lower than those of countries with a lower percentage of believers. This is reflected at an individual and at a national level.

Religiousness is also a protective factor against suicide attempts in patients suffering from depression, whereby no single religion seems to offer advantages. The authors conclude that religion in general and kinship in particular foster and strengthen the sense of responsibility towards family members. These circumstances appear to make a suicide attempt less likely [91]. Fear, damnation and/or the vengeance of God is seen as a relevant conviction similar to fact that trust in God serves as a help and comfort. A God experienced as a punisher on the other hand, can act as an amplifier increasing fear of failure and thus encourage both depression and suicidal behavior indirectly - however rigorous scientific data is missing for this hypothesis [92].

China is a good example of the effect of the historical philosophical attitudes of Confucianism and Taoism to committing suicide despite a desired paradigm shift from the Maoist Cultural Revolution. Confucius himself described suicide as a possible way out in several stories; but not be the best solution to save a person's integrity or virtue. Teachers and Taoist parables also conclude that this attitude to suicide is largely acceptable, but usually originates in a narrow, extreme imprisonment in secular concerns. Even Mao Zedong as a young man gave his opinion in at least 9 contributions to the suicide of a newly married young woman's position. He interpreted her suicide as resistance against the traditionalist family and marriage system. Thus, although she had defended her freedom and personality, she had not chosen the best route. This was the social revolution [93].

The Buddhist tradition forbids the killing of humans or animals. Nevertheless, the Buddha himself took an almost neutral attitude towards suicide, and described it as a possible situational self-sacrifice [94]. Furthermore, Buddhism does not see death as a problem rather as a life event or a serious transformation. Only the fear of death is a problem, which is put into perspective only by the belief in a good or bad rebirth. A study of suicide rates of Asian countries where Buddhism is widespread, however, results in these countries having consistently high rates, but no correlation with the percentage of the Buddhist population. The socio-economic circumstance, whether it concerns developing, emerging or highly developed countries, seems to have no significant impact on the suicide rate [95].

The Hindus allow their followers to choose a temple and worship different gods. Only the priests belong to a particular temple. In this way death is only transition, a reincarnation takes place, which is an upward or downward development. Hindus attach great importance to a good death and suicide is ambivalent. The Upanishads banned suicide; while the ethical writings of Dharmashastra around 800 BC condemned suicide in general, permitted it in special situations such as an incurable disease, or as penance for murder or incest. The religiously motivated termination of life in old age due to starvation in sacred places is considered to be "a good death". "Sati" after all (the suicide of a woman after the death of her husband, or of subjects after the death of a prince), was seen as a sign of special love and devotion. In the light of the fact that widows in the caste system had almost no social rights, this suicidal act can be partly classified socially [96].

The frequent suicides of young women in India are very likely due to this self sacrificial tendency and arranged marriages in the strict caste system, which are refused by the brides affected.

Despite the various ways to justify and commit suicide in Hinduism, the suicide rate of very old Hindus is low. Hindus over 60 years of age enter the 4th Life Stage, one characterized through increasing distance from worldly pleasures, and an increase of meditation and modest lifestyle. Thus, the elderly are highly revered, taken care of and supported. Especially their sons are encouraged to take care of them. This ensures that marginalisation of the older population is virtually non-existent. Even a strong belief in reincarnation eviscerates suicide - a rather serene acceptance of the strokes of fate is in demanded [97].

Shinto is the main religion in Japan. It is constitutes worship at some 80,000 shrines, symbols of nature deities, which are embedded in the landscape. The Shinto culture knows no commandments or scriptures, but rather places of spiritual force in nature [98]. It allows reasonable suicides arising from patriotic, romantic, desperate and philosophical reasoning. Above all, the self-sacrifice for the benefit of an individual community or to atone for a malicious act for the community is highly regarded. The tradition of family suicides or suicides of several family members together still exists, making modern Japan a country of very high suicide rates (35.6 for men and at least 12.8 for women in 2007). The strong collectivization seems to contribute to suicide, which is primarily an individual phenomenon in virtually every other culture. [99]. In addition, mental disorders and their institutions are highly stigmatised in modern Japan. The stigma of seeking help outside the family makes it difficult [100].

While suicide victims are often described as brave or pathetic, survivors of suicide attempts and their families are faced with strong shame and rejection [101].

CONCLUSIONS

The risk of suicide attempt and suicide varies considerably worldwide. Upon close examination of the studies presented in the literature, it is clear that in multicultural countries prevention strategies should take into account changes in risks in minorities. These are differently exposed to known risk factors; socio-economic, the risk of social exclusion and poor access to healthcare systems. Commonly accepted risk factors are different in ethnic minorities. One case of varying risk which is often cited is "cultural conflict" (or stress of acculturation [75, 76]) although it is difficult to explain what this means. Therefore, it is important that preventive measures are applicable to these subcultures and that services are accepted by patients and *vice versa.*

The degree of belonging of a given ethnic group varies. The degree modifies the risk associated with ethnicity and varies the danger of suicidal behavior. It is important to disentangle the effect of exposure on the degree of risk exposure. Ethnicity may often be a confounding factor rather than a risk factor [27]. Especially in youth the formation of strong ethnic identity is a preventative factor against suicide and risk behavior. A positive attitude in-group encourages; high self-esteem, lower stress, a decrease in suicidal behavior and reduces the risk of depression. If the youth has a good sense of roots he will, most probably, feel less lonely and isolated in dealing with problems.

Another factor is a discriminatory style of coping. A person facing many obstacles and changes in life can be subject to an (especially youth) increased level of stress. Passive coping style is often associated with depression and suicidal behavior that is often prevalent in people at lower socioeconomic levels. Minorities often have a strong sense of survival through the activation of a range of coping strategies to deal with the situational (environmental) stress.

Religion is another significant factor; strong religious beliefs can play a role in the decrease of suicide risk. Religion can consider suicide as a sinful act and encourage antithetical behavior such as optimism and resilience. It is to be noted that certain groups, where a high level of religious participation is identified, are less tolerant towards suicide than others.

Gender is a major risk factor; in many groups, women attempt suicide at a frequency equal to twice that of the male population, while the actual suicide rate present in males is four times that of females. Furthermore, it has been found that among young gay men, lesbians and bisexuals the risk of suicidal ideation and attempted suicide is much higher than among the heterosexual population. Other factors include a history of depression, low levels of attachment to family and school and limited social input.

In summary: The current state of knowledge on ethnic issues is very fragmented and difficult to summarize. The studies have several critical points;

Ethnic minorities, immigrants and their situation have changed in the last ten years. The reasons for emigration, adaptation, integration and acculturation vary from group to group. The characterisation of specific factors in immigration shows that; change of place, trauma, isolation, and inability/motivation to fit into a new cultural tradition, language barriers *etc.* as being factors which contribute to the development of depressive moods, and prevent individuals from seeking help.

Different frequencies of mental disorders, especially depressive manifestations (different psychopathology and treatment) exist within the various groups. Eligibility for services which are part of treatment (accessibility, barriers) is not taken into consideration.

Scientific investigations are implicitly influenced by the culture of the dominant group. For example, the mistrust of some ethnic groups; Indians mistrust of health services, the importance of mediators and the significance of discrimination (Racism, segregation). Poverty among ethnic minorities is frequent. The variables; minorities mixed with socio-economic factors and limited economic opportunities, the stigma of suicide have an impact on the suicide and his family. It is important to collect and evaluate how society and subcultures rate suicide. The paradox: stigma protects from the suicidal act, however, complicates the cry for help and social support.

There are clear differences in suicide risk in elderly populations within different ethnic groups. Life expectancy, which differs between ethnic minorities, changes the risk of suicide. There are few studies of the suicidal behavior of older people in ethnic minorities.

REFERENCES

[1] Lönnqvist JK, Koskenvuo M. Mortality in depressive disorders: a 3-year prospective follow-up in Finland. In: Helgason T, Darragh PM, Eds. Depressive illness: Prediction, course and outcome. Springer: Berlin. 1988; pp. 126-30.

[2] Kessler RC, Berglund P, Borges G, Nock M, Wang PS. Trends in suicide ideation, plans, gestures, and attempts in the United States, 1990-1992 to 2001-2003. JAMA 2005;293(20): 2487-95.

[3] Kessler RC, Borges G, Walters EE. Prevalence of and risk factors for lifetime suicide attempts in the National Comorbidity Survey. Arch Gen Psychiatry 1999;56(7):617-26.

[4] Szádóczky E, Vitrai J, Rihmer Z, Füredi J. Suicide attempts in the Hungarian adult population. Their relation with DIS/DSM-III-R affective and anxiety disorders. Eur Psychiatry 2000;15(6):343-7.

[5] Renberg ES. Self-reported life-weariness, death-wishes, suicidal ideation, suicidal plans and suicide attempts in general population surveys in the north of Sweden 1986 and 1996. Soc Psychiatry Psychiatr Epidemiol 2001;36(9):429-36.
[6] W.H.O. SuPRE (Suicide Prevention). Available from: http://www.who.int/mental_health/prevention/suicide.
[7] Garlow SJ, Purselle D, Heninger M. Ethnic differences in patterns of suicide across the life cycle. Am J Psychiatry 2005;162(2):319-23.
[8] Thies-Flechtner K, Müller-Oerlinghausen B, Seibert W, Walther A, Greil W. Effect of prophylactic treatment on suicide risk in patients with major affective disorders. Data from a randomized prospective trial. Pharmacopsychiatry 1996;29(3):103-7.
[9] Glick ID, Zaninelli R, Hsu C, *et al.* Patterns of concomitant psychotropic medication use during a 2-year study comparing clozapine and olanzapine for the prevention of suicidal behavior. J Clin Psychiatry 2004;65(5):679-85.
[10] Meltzer HY, Alphs L, Green AI, *et al.* Clozapine treatment for suicidality in schizophrenia: International Suicide Prevention Trial (InterSePT). International Suicide Prevention Trial Study Group.Arch Gen Psychiatry 2003;60(1):82-91.
[11] Shearin EN, Linehan MM. Dialectical behavior therapy for borderline personality disorder: theoretical and empirical foundations. Acta Psychiatr Scand 1994;379 (Suppl):61-8.
[12] Mishara BL.Cultural specificity and universality of suicide: challenges for the International Association for Suicide Prevention. Crisis 2006;27(1):1-3.
[13] Garlow SJ, Purselle D, Heninger M. Ethnic differences in patterns of suicide across the life cycle. Am J Psychiatry 2005;162(2):319-23.
[14] Gunnel D. Time trends and geographic differences in suicide: implication for the prevention.In: Hawton K, Ed. Prevention and treatment of suicidal behavior. Oxford: Oxford University Press. 2005; pp. 29-52.
[15] Ji LJ, Nisbett RE, Su Y. Culture, change, and prediction. Psychol Sci. 2001;12(6):450-6.
[16] Makinen IH. Eastern European transitino and suicide mortalità. Soc Sci Med. 2000; 51: 1405-20.
[17] Durkheim E. Il suicidio. Milano: BUR, 2003; pp. 168.
[18] De Hert M, McKenzie K, Peuskens J. Risk factors for suicide in young people suffering from schizophrenia: a long-term follow-up study. Schizophr Res. 2001;47(2-3):127-34.
[19] McKenzie K, Serfaty M, Crawford M. Suicide in ethnic minority groups. Br J Psychiatry 2003; 183: 100-1.
[20] Mohler B, Earls F. Trends in adolescent suicide: misclassification bias? Am J Public Health 2001;91(1):150-3.
[21] Centers for Disease Control and Prevention (CDC). Suicide among Hispanics--United States, 1997-2001. MMWR Morb Mortal Wkly Rep 2004;53(22):478-81.
[22] Brown GW, Prudo R. Psychiatric disorder in a rural and an urban population. Etiology of depression. Psychol Med 1981; 11: 581-99.
[23] Neeleman J, Halpern D, Leon D, Lewis G. Tolerance of suicide, religion and suicide rates: an ecological and individual study in 19 Western countries. Psychol Med. 1997;27(5):1165-71.
[24] Platt S, Kreitman N. Trends in parasuicide and unemployment among men in Edimburgh, 1968-82. BMJ 1984; 289:1029-32.
[25] Skog OJ. The collectivity of drinking cultures: a theory of distribution of alcohol consumption. Br J Addiction 1985; 80:83-99.
[26] Wilkinson RG. Incombe distribution and life expectancy. BMJ 1992; 304:165-8.
[27] Neeleman J, Wilson-Jones C, Wessely S. Ethnic density and deliberate self harm; a small area study in south east London. J Epidemiol Community Health. 2001;55(2):85-90.
[28] Lester D. Regional suicide rates and the hazards of minority status. Am J Psychiatry. 1980;137(11):1469-70.
[29] Driessen G, Gunther N, Van Os J. Shared social environment and psychiatric disorder: a multilevel analysis of individual and ecological effects. Soc Psychiatry Psychiatr Epidemiol 1998;33(12):606-12.
[30] Trovato F. Suicide and ethnic factors in Canada. Int J Soc Psychiatry 1986;32(3):55-64.
[31] Bertolote JM, Fleischmann A, De Leo D, Wasserman D. Psychiatric diagnoses and suicide: revisiting the evidence. Crisis 2004;25(4):147-55.
[32] Neeleman J, Mak V, Wessely S. Br J Psychiatry 1997; 171:463-7.
[33] Hunt IM, Robinson J, Bickley H, *et al.* Suicides in ethnic minorities within 12 months of contact with mental health services. National clinical survey. Br J Psychiatry 2003;183:155-60.
[34] Soni Raleigh V, Balarajan R. Suicide and self-burning among Indians and West Indians in England and Wales. Br J Psychiatry 1992;161:365-8.
[35] Prosser D. Suicides by burning in England and Wales. Br J Psychiatry 1996;168(2):175-82.

[36] Raleigh *VS*. Suicide patterns and trends in people of Indian subcontinent and Caribbean origin in England and Wales.Ethn Health 1996;1(1):55-63.

[37] Bhui KS, McKenzie K. Rates and risk factors by ethnic group for suicides within a year of contact with mental health services in England and Wales. Psychiatr Serv 2008;59(4):414-20.

[38] Hunt IM, Kapur N, Windfuhr K, *et al.* Suicide in schizophrenia: findings from a national clinical survey. J Psychiatr Pract 2006;12(3):139-47.

[39] Neeleman J, Jones P, Van Os J, Murray RM. Parasuicide in Camberwell-ethnic differences. Soc Psychiatry Psychiatr Epidemiol 1996;31(5):284-7.

[40] Bhugra D, Desai M, Baldwin DS. Attempted suicide in west London, I. Rates across ethnic communities. Psychol Med 1999;29(5):1125-30.

[41] Crawford MJ, Nur U, McKenzie K, Tyrer P. Suicidal ideation and suicide attempts among ethnic minority groups in England: results of a national household survey. Psychol Med 2005; 35(9): 1369-77.

[42] Weissman MM, Bland RC, Canino GJ, *et al.* Prevalence of suicide ideation and suicide attempts in nine countries. Psychol Med 1999;29(1):9-17.

[43] Crawford MJ, Nur U, McKenzie K, Tyrer P. Suicidal ideation and suicide attempts among ethnic minority groups in England: results of a national household survey. Psychol Med 2005;35(9):1369-77.

[44] Bhui K, McKenzie K, Rasul F. Rates, risk factors & methods of self harm among minority ethnic groups in the UK: a systematic review.BMC Public Health 2007 Nov 19;7:336.

[45] Gilmer WS, Trivedi MH, Rush AJ, *et al.* Factors associated with chronic depressive episodes: a preliminary report from the STAR-D project. Acta Psychiatr Scand 2005;112(6):425-33.

[46] Ryan L, Leavey G, Golden A, Blizard R, King M. Depression in Irish migrants living in London: case-control study. Br J Psychiatry 2006;188:560-6.

[47] Clarke DE, Colantonio A, Rhodes AE, Escobar M. Pathways to suicidality across ethnic groups in Canadian adults: the possible role of social stress.Psychol Med 2008;38(3):419-31.

[48] Costello RM. Long-term mortality from alcoholism: a descriptive analysis. J Stud Alcohol 2006;67(5):694-9.

[49] Becker TM, Samet JM, Wiggins CL, Key CR. Violent death in West: Suicide and Homicide in New Mexico, 1958-1987. Suicide Life Threaten Behav 1997; 20 (4): 324-34.

[50] Gutierrez PM, Muehlenkamp JJ, Konick LC, Osman A. What role does race play in adolescent suicidal ideation? Arch Suicide Res 2005;9(2):177-92.

[51] McKeon R. Suicidal Behavior. Cambridge MA, Göttingen Germany: Hogrefe & Huber Publishers, 2009; pp.12.

[52] O'Donnell L, O'Donnell C, Wardlaw DM, Stueve A. Risk and resiliency factors influencing suicidality among urban African American and Latino youth. Am J Community Psychol 2004;33(1-2):37-49.

[53] Walker RL. Acculturation and acculturative stress as indicators for suicide risk among African Americans. Am J Orthopsychiatry 2007;77(3):386-91.

[54] Grunbaum JA, Kann L, Kinchen S, *et al.* Youth risk behavior surveillance--United States, 2003.

[55] Centers for Disease Control and Prevention (CDC). Suicide among Hispanics--United States, 1997-2001. MMWR Morb Mortal Wkly Rep 2004; 53(22):478-81.

[56] Canino G, Roberts RE. Suicidal behavior among Latino youth. Suicide Life Threat Behav 2001;31 (Suppl):122-31.

[57] Roberts RE, Chen YR, Roberts CR. Ethnocultural differences in prevalence of adolescent suicidal behaviors. Suicide Life Threat Behav 1997;27(2):208-17.

[58] Zayas LH, Pilat AM. Suicidal behavior inLatinas: explanatory cultural factors and implications for intervention. Suicide Life Threat Behav 2008;38(3):334-42.

[59] O'Donnell L, O'Donnell C, Wardlaw DM, Stueve A. Risk and resiliency factors influencing suicidality among urban African American and Latino youth. Am J Community Psychol 2004;33(1-2):37-49.

[60] Roberts RE, Chen YW. Depressive symptoms and suicidal ideation among Mexican-origin and Anglo adolescents. J Am Acad Child Adolesc Psychiatry. 1995;34(1):81-90.

[61] Harris PA. The impact of age, gender, race, and ethnicity on the diagnosis and treatment of depression. J Manag Care Pharm 2004;10(2 Suppl):S2-7.

[62] Sen, B. Adolescent propensity for Depression Mood and Help Seeking: Race and Gender Differences. J Ment Health Policy Econ 2004; 7:133-145.

[63] Johansson LM, Sundquist J, Johansson SE, Bergman B, Qvist J, Träskman-Bendz L. Suicide among foreign-born minorities and Native Swedes: an epidemiological follow-up study of a defined population. Soc Sci Med 1997;44(2):181-187

[64] Sundaram V, Qin P, Zøllner L. Suicide risk among persons with foreign background in Denmark. Suicide Life Threat Behav 2006;36(4):481-9.

[65] Hjern A, Allebeck P. Suicide in first- and second-generation immigrants in Sweden: a comparative study. Soc Psychiatry Psychiatr Epidemiol 2002;37(9):423-9.

[66] Hjelmeland H, Nordvik H, Bille-Brahe U, *et al.* A cross-cultural study of suicide intent in parasuicide patients. Suicide Life Threat Behav 2000;30(4): 295-303.

[67] Sundaram V, Qin P, Zøllner L. Suicide risk among persons with foreign background in Denmark. Suicide Life Threat Behav 2006;36(4):481-9.

[68] Schmidtke A, Bille-Brahe U, DeLeo D, *et al.* Attempted suicide in Europe: rates, trends and sociodemographic characteristics of suicide attempters during the period 1989-1992. Results of the WHO/EURO Multicentre Study on Parasuicide. Acta Psychiatr Scand 1996;93(5):327-38.

[69] Storch G, Poustka F. Mental disorders in hospitalized children of migrant families from the Mediterranean. Prax Kinderpsychol Kinderpsychiatr 2000;49(3):199-208.

[70] Fichter MM, Elton M, Diallina M, Koptagel-Ilal G, Fthenakis WE, Weyerer S. Mental illness in Greek and Turkish adolescents. Eur Arch Psychiatry Neurol Sci. 1988;237(3):125-134.

[71] Sayl I. Review of suicide studies in Turkey. Crisis 1997;18:496-506.

[72] Lewis G, Sloggett A. Suicide, deprivation, and unemployment: record linkage study. BMJ 1998;317(7168):1283-6.

[73] Razum O, Zeeb H. Suicide mortality among Turks in Germany Nervenarzt. 2004;75(11):1092-8.

[74] Hovey JD. Acculturative stress, depression and social ideationin Mexican immgrants. Cultur Divers Ethnic Minor Psychol 2000; 6:134-51.

[75] Hovey JD. Acculturative stress, depression and social ideationin among Central American immigrants. Suicide Life Threaten Behav 2000; 30:125-39.

[76] Hovey JD, King CA. Acculturative stress,depression and suicidal ideation among immigrant and secon-generation Latino adolescents. J Am Acad Child Adolesc Psychiatr 1996;35:1183-92.

[77] Sher L. On the role of neurobiological and genetic factors in the etiology and pathogenesis of suicidal behavior among immigrants. Med Hypotheses 1999; 53;110-1.

[78] Häfner H. Psychiatric morbidity among immigrant workers in Mannheim. Nervenarzt 1980;51(11):672-83.

[79] Benkert H, Floru L, Freistein H. Mental disorders in foreign workers hospitalized residential treatment in a psychiatric clinic Nervenarzt 1974;45(2):76-87.

[80] Carlsten A, Waern M, Ekedahl A, Ranstam J. Antidepressant medication and suicide in Sweden.Pharmacoepidemiol Drug Saf 2001;10(6):525-530.

[81] Tondo L, Hennen J, Baldessarini RJ. Lower suicide risk with long-term lithium treatment in major affective illness: a meta-analysis. Acta Psychiatr Scand 2001;104(3):163-72.

[82] Grube M. Nonfatal suicidal acts in a group of psychiatric inpatients. Situation of Mediterranean immigrants. Nervenarzt 2004;75(7):681-7.

[83] Deisenhammer EA, Haring C, Kemmler G, Pycha R, Hinterhuber H. Suicide in south Tyrol 1980-1992: influence of affiliation to different language groups. Eur Arch Psychiatry Clin Neurosci 1996;246:273-8.Pycha R, Pompili M, Innamorati M, *et al.* Sex and ethnic differences among South Tirolean suicides: a psychological autopsy study. Eur Psychiatry 2009;24(1):47-56.

[85] Giupponi G, Bizzarri J, Pycha R, *et al.* Socioeconomic risk factors and depressive symptoms in alcohol use disorders among male suicides in South Tirol. Drug and Alcohol Dependence J Addict Dis 2010;29(4):466-74.

[86] Murthy RS. Approaches to suicide prevention in Asia and the Far East. In: Hawton K, van Heeringen K, Eds. The International Handbook of Suicide and Attempted Suicide. Chichester: John Wiley. 2000; pp. 631-43.

[87] Koch HJ. Suicides and suicide ideation in the Bible: An empirical survey. Acta Psych Scand 2005;112:167-72.

[88] Simpson ME, Conklin GH. Socio-economic development, suicide and religion: a test of Durkheim's theory of religion and suicide. Social Forces 1989; 67: 945-64.

[89] Stack S. Sociological research into suicide. In: Lester D, edotor. Suicide Prevention. Resources for the Millennium. Philadelphia: Brunner and Routledge. 2001; pp. 17-30.

[90] Neeleman J, Lewis G, Suicide, religion and socioeconomic conditions. An ecological study in 26 countries, 1990. J Epidemiol Commun Health 1999; 53: 204-10.

[91] Dervic K, Oquendo MA, Grunebaum MF. Religious affiliation and suicide attempt. Am J Psychiat 2004; 161: 2303-08.

[92] Van Praag HM. The role of religion in suicide prevention. In: Wasserman D, Wasserman C, Eds. Suicidology and Suicide Prevention. Oxford: Oxford University Press. 2009; pp. 7-12.

[93] Mao Zedong. The question of love - young people and old people. In: Shram S, Ed. Maos Road to Power, 1. New York: Sharpe, Armonk. 1992.

[94] Keown D, Buddhism and suicide: The case of Channa. J Buddhist Ethics 1996; 3: 31

[95] Hendin H, Vijayakumar L, Bertolote JM. Epidemiology of Suicide in Asia. In: Hendin H, Phillips M, Vijayakumar L, Eds. Suicide and Suicide Prevention in Asia. Geneva: WHO Press. 2008; pp. 7-18.

[96] Vijayakumar L. Altruisitic suicide in India. Arch Suicide Res 2004; 8:73-80.

[97] Vijayakumar L. Hindu religion and suicide in India. In: Wasserman D, Wasserman C, Eds. Suicidology and Suicide Prevention, Oxford: Oxford University Press. 2009; pp. 19-26.

[98] Kaneko Y, Yamasaki A, Arai K. The Shinto religion and suicide in Japan. In: Wasserman D, Wasserman C, Eds. Oxford Textbook of Suicidology and Suicide Prevention. Oxford: Oxford University Press. 2009; pp. 37.

[99] Ueno K. Suicide as Japan's major export? A note on Japanese suicide culture. Revista Espaco Academico. 2005; 44: 1.

[100] Griffiths KM, Nakane Y, Christensen H, Yoshioka K, Jorm AF, Nakane H. Stigma in response to mental disorders: a comparison of Australia and Japan. BMC Psychiatry 2006;6:21.

[101] Young J. Morals, suicide, and psychiatry: a view from Japan. Bioethics 2002;16:412-24

CHAPTER 6

Spirituality, Religion and Suicide

Erminia Colucci*

Centre for International Mental Health, School of Population Health, University of Melbourne, Level 5, 207 Bouverie St, Carlton (Melbourne, VIC), 3053, Australia

Abstract: Parallel to the growing interest in spiritual life in mainstream culture, in Western culture there has been an increasing distinction between religion and spirituality. This article defines the concept of spirituality and its constitutive elements and presents evidence from the literature to show that, in spite of its importance for mental health patients and suicidal people, it is still an overlooked area in Suicidology. Not only are there relatively few studies addressing this topic, but 'religion/spirituality' is usually just one of a series of variables, generally measured with a single question (mainly inquiring about church attendance/affiliation). Furthermore, studies on non-religious forms of spirituality are rare. Attention is also given to meaning and purpose in life, a central aspect of spirituality that has been generally neglected in suicide research. Some examples of instrument to measure spiritual constructs are provided, with a particular focus on meaning/purpose in life. The paper concludes with suggestions for future research and stressing the importance of considering spirituality in the clinical assessment and treatment of suicidal behavior.

Keywords: Spirituality, religion, religiousness, culture, cross-cultural, meaning and purpose in life, suicide, self-harm, mental health, wellbeing.

"As you ought not to attempt to cure the eyes without the head,
or the head without the body,
so neither ought you to attempt to cure the body without the soul...
for the part can never be well unless the whole is well...
And therefore, if the head and body are to be well,
you must begin by curing the soul; that is the first thing."
(Plato, 380 B.C.)

1. INTRODUCTION

In pre-modern times, concerns related to illness and healing were often encompassed within the wider domain of a religious worldview and, in many cultures, healing was a sacred art [1]. Today, (Western) Medicine, including Psychiatry, and in general Psychology, are secular disciplines. But, as observed by D'Souza [2], in many parts of the world a holistic view of human being has survived. This is seen, for instance, in Chinese and Indian Medicine, in the healing arts of American Indians and among Indigenous Australian peoples.

However, as Swinton [3] points out in his "*Spirituality and mental health care. Rediscovering a 'forgotten' dimension*", albeit the idea of spirituality appears to belong to a surpassed era, in fact, the latter part of the twentieth century has seen a noticeable rise in interest in spirituality within the Western world[1]. But, as Swinton [3] clarifies later, this does not refer to institutionalized religions, which are becoming less popular: "whilst people may be becoming less *religious* (Italic in the original), it would be a mistake to assume from that that they are necessarily becoming less *spiritual* (idem)", (p. 11).

The growing positive connotation of spirituality, which contrasts the negative connotation of religiousness, has been pointed out also by Turner, Lukoff, Barnhouse and Lu (1995, cited in [4])[2]. The distinction

***Address Correspondence to Erminia Colucci:** Centre for International Mental Health, School of Population Health, University of Melbourne, Level 5, 207 Bouverie St, Carlton (Melbourne, VIC), 3053, Australia; E-mails: ecolucci@unimelb.edu.au or fera_76@hotmail.com

[1] For a further discussion of the distinction between religion and spirituality, and the change in the manifestation of religion in the West, see Dein [4].

[2] Hill and Pargament [24] warn on the several dangers of this kind of bifurcation of religion and spirituality and observe that the sacred, in its various conceptualizations, represents the common denominator of religious and spiritual life.

between religion and spirituality has gained greater prominence since the1960s [4] and, nowadays, there seems to be general agreement (*e.g.,* [5-12]) about the necessity to differentiate between these two concepts. Despite Ramsey and Blieszner's [13] radical opinion that we should substitute the word "religion" with the word "spirituality", it is necessary to maintain both words, keeping in mind that religion and spirituality do not necessarily overlap for everyone and individuals may be spiritual without being religious (unreligious spirituality) and religious without being spiritual (unspiritual religiosity). In fact, Oldnall [11] affirms that the concept of spirituality may exist in every human being, but may consist of either a religious (for example, Judeo-Christianity) or a secular dimension (atheism or humanistic views) or a combination of the two (agnosticism). Burkhardt [6], as well, distinguishes between the two concepts, stating that spirituality is the essence of one's human nature, whether or not it is expressed through religious beliefs or practices. Zinnbauer, Pargament, Cole, Rye and Butter (1997, cited in [4]) suggest that religiousness has increasingly become described as "narrow and institutional", whereas spirituality has increasingly been specified as "personal and subjective". Lerner (1994, cited in [8]) states that spirituality is the source dimension behind every religion and should be considered closer to the source dimension than religion that, in his opinion, has moved far from the experience of the spirit and primarily serves moral and social purposes. Consequently, religion-defined more narrowly as a formal, ritualized and institutionalized system of beliefs-should not be treated as synonymous of spirituality but, eventually, as one form of spirituality (or the most common cultural representation of spirituality, in Eckersley's words [97]).

After a brief discussion on the definition of spirituality, this chapter will present evidence from the literature that, in spite of the importance spirituality might have for mental health patients and suicidal people, it is still an overlooked area in Suicidology. Attention will also be given to a central aspect of spirituality that has, with few exceptions, been neglected in suicide research, *i.e.,* meaning and purpose in life. Findings from a cross-cultural study in Italy, India and Australia will support the critical role of investigating people's beliefs on afterlife. Suggestions for future research are offered in the closing section.

2. DEFINITION OF SPIRITUALITY

Although generally speaking spirituality is meant as a broad and inclusive term that refers to the non-material aspects of human being, Burkhardt's review [6] reveals that the concept of spirituality is used in different ways by different authors. Dein [4] agrees that there is little consensus about what the word means. Aldridge [8] lists 24 definitions that have been proposed for spirituality, organizing them in four tables. For example, he cites Muldoon and King's (1995, [8]) description of spirituality as "the experiential integration of one's life in term of one's ultimate values and meanings" (p. 27) and Reed's (1987, in [8]) definition as "personal views and behaviors that express a sense of relatedness to a transcendent dimension or to something greater than the self" (p. 28). The Oxford English Dictionary (cited in [14]) offers 10 pages of reference material on the concept of spirituality! The Mental Health Foundation report [15] observes how "spirituality is a word used in an abundance of contexts that means different things for different people at different times in different cultures" (p. 6). An exemplification of what stated in the report is represented by a recent exploratory study on the conceptualization of spirituality among Japanese youths [16].

Miller and Thorsen [14] note that spirituality as a term tends to elude tight operational definition and argue that "it often seems easier to point to what spirituality is not (*i.e.,* something material) than to what it is" (p. 27). Cohen, Wheeler and Scheier [17] use a beautiful analogy to describe this: "What is spirituality? Defining spirituality is a bit like trying to describe the smell of a rose. It feels elusive because it inspired different things to different people. It can involve religion, cultural practices, beliefs, philosophies of life, or simply put 'our ultimate concerns' (p. 7).

Albeit there is not a common and shared definition that can completely encapsulate what is meant by spirituality (or "soul[3]"), some elements are shared among different definitions, seeming to denote central

---

[3] In this regard, Hillman [101] observes that "the soul is a deliberately ambiguous concept resisting all definition in the same manner as do all ultimate symbols which provide the root metaphors for the systems of human thought" (p. 46).

components: faith/beliefs, values, sense of meaning and purpose in life, transcendence beyond the present context of reality or to something greater than the self, and sense of connectedness (with the Universe, Higher power, deity, community and/or nature).

As observed by Dein [4], there are several ways to attain a spiritual experience. These are highly culturally variable, ranging from meditation, prayer and the use of mantra, to art, literature and poetry[4]. The author also lists enjoyment of nature, being valued and opportunities to derive meaning from experiences as activities facilitating spiritual growth. Some of these individual and collective techniques are presented in Bartocci [18].

The photos in the next pages illustrate different ways in which people might experience their spirituality and religiosity (photos by Erminia Colucci, copyright E. Colucci, 2009). Other photos and a short-documentary can be viewed in the website: ermiphotoniac.weebly.com

Photo 1 Aarti (fire ceremony) on the Ganges

Photo 2 An ascetic in a yoga posture (India)

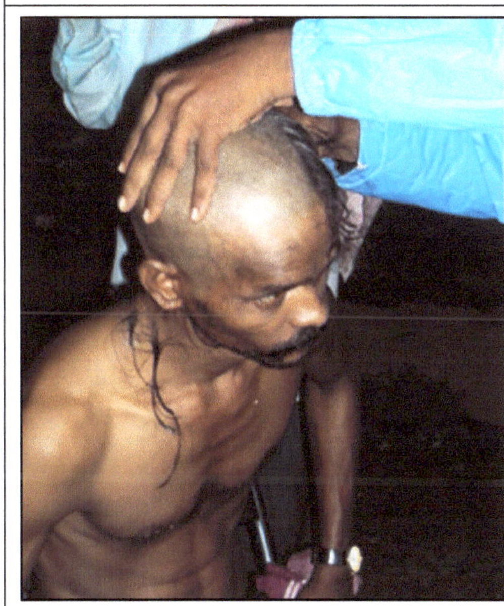

Photo 3 Hair offering at a Hindu temple (India)

Photo 4 Procession for Our Lady of Sorrows (South Italy)

[4] Dyson, Cobb and Forman [56] argue that whilst experience suggests that many hold a view that art forms provide an expression of spirituality, there is a paucity of literature in support of this view, indicating an area of study that needs exploration.

Photo 5 Feeling in connection with the environment (Lorne, Australia)

Photo 6 "Drawing the fortune" in a shrine during a Japanese New Year ritual

Before going to discuss the neglect and, at the opposite, the importance of spirituality in mental health and Suicidology, it is worth to note that culture does not only influence the forms of spirituality but that the degree of distinction between spirituality and religion, as observed by Miller and Thorsen [14] also varies between cultures[5].

3. NEGLECT OF SPIRITUALITY IN MENTAL HEALTH AND SUICIDOLOGY

"To date Psychiatry has excluded spirituality apart from seeing it as a form of pathology or pathological response" ([4], p. 538). Confirming this impression, in a review of research on religion in four major psychiatric journals from 1991 to 1995, Weaver and collaborators (1998, [3]) noted that only 1.2% of the 2766 quantitative research articles reviewed contained a religious/spiritual variable. A slightly better result was found in a review of quantitative research studies published between 1992 and 1996 in five adolescent journals [19], 11.8% of which reported a measure of religion. This result was interpreted by the authors as showing more sensitivity to religious factors in adolescence-related journals compared to psychological and psychiatric journals. The scarce importance given to spirituality/religion in research is reflected in clinical practice. Conway (1989, [12]) criticizes the ignoring of patients' spiritual concerns: "if we are to truly understand, study, and help people change, we must address issues that influence people's lives" (p. 132). Swinton's [3] observes that while some psychiatrists take issues of spirituality seriously, on the whole they have tended not to acknowledge that spirituality (and, in this case, with the term spirituality I mean a non-theological cultural factor and/or a extramundane psychological dynamic) may have a contribution to make to the process of mental health care. This, in my view, includes also the possibility that, in fact, spiritual/religious concerns or beliefs might play a negative role in the healing process.

The lack of consideration of religion and spirituality is particularly pronounced in Suicidology. In Kehoe and Gutheil's evaluation of suicide assessment instruments [20], the authors note that, although the psychiatric literature suggests that religion and spirituality are significant and meaningful forces in suicidal patients, the number of religious items included on assessment scales approaches zero. The authors criticize designers of suicide scales, which appear to seek factors that may help to identify people at risk of suicide but ignore the possible impact of what "a person, on the brink of life itself, believes about life and about life after death" (p. 368). In this regard, relevant is the contribution of Webb, who reports [21] that, during his own struggle with persistent suicidality, he found few health workers with whom he could discuss spiritual matters. He criticizes that: "spirituality, which was so central in my own recovery, was not only absent but was deliberately denied and excluded by Suicidology" (p. 2). To prove the exclusion of this spirituality

---

[5] Probably one of the reasons why the great majority of research to date has focused on religion is because, as reported by these authors, most research has been done in United States, a very religious country.

from Suicidology (or "flatland Suicidology" as he refers to it), Webb observes the lack of references to this topic (a part from the preface) in one of the major textbooks of the discipline[6].

So…why something that seems so central in many people's lives and their recovery from difficult times cannot penetrate inside Suicidology and, more in general, is overlooked by mental health sciences?

Among possible reasons for the neglect of the study of spirituality, there is the difficulty of researching a somewhat vague and abstract concept. Ellison [22] indicates that terms such as 'spirituality' and 'well-being' have subjective meanings that are impossible to operationalize, and it is for this reason that psychologists –in contrast to sociologists-have ignored the spiritual dimension of human welfare. That spirituality does not lend itself to measurement in a natural science sense has been postulated by Oldnall [11] as a reason for the omission of spiritual needs in nursing practice and by Burkhardt [6] as a reason for the limited research in the same area.

In a similar way, Bhugra and Osbourne [23] believe that seeing religion as primitive, untestable, unverifiable and unscientific is a key factor in why psychiatrists ignore it. Hill and Pargament [24] also attribute part of the reason for the religion/spirituality gap in health research to the wrong assumption that these issues fall outside the scope of scientific study.

Swinton [3], at the opposite, argues that spirituality can be studied in a scientific way, although our understandings of science may have to alter to accommodate for the new perspectives that spirituality brings to it. He criticizes the reductionist traditional scientific attempt to quantify spirituality, stating:

"Spirituality relates to such things as love, hope, meaning, purpose-things which cannot be fully captured by the traditional methodologies of science. Thus (...) there is a need to develop complementary methodologies and ways of exploring the spiritual dimension that can dig into the hidden depths of human emotion and experience and reveal aspects and perspectives that are unavailable to other ways of doing research" (p. 93)[7].

The author lists other reasons why mental health professionals are wary and skeptical about spirituality:

- the impact of Psychoanalysis and other therapeutic theories negative view of religion;
- lack of personal interest in spirituality/religion;
- professional pride and research credibility;
- fear of incompetence;
- lack of time;
- fear of imposing personal beliefs on the client;
- and fear of intruding on a patient's privacy.

It is also possible that psychologists and psychiatrists are less likely to have religious involvement or clinical training in religious issues than other mental health specialists (Sansone *et al.*, 1990, cited in [19, 25]). The lack of personal interest in spirituality and religion as linked to their neglect is supported by Baetz, Larson, Marcoux, Jokic and Bowen [26] who showed that, if the carer has personal interest in religion, they will more likely consider this construct during the therapy. The psychiatrists interviewed were all members of the Christian Medical and Dental Society (CMDS) and 80% of them declared that they often or always inquired about their patient's religious beliefs. Two thirds of them felt they were

[6] The author, however, notes that religion is sometimes discussed in Suicidology as a protective factor against suicide but comments that the emphasis is on religious taboos against suicide and the benefits of being a member of a church community whereas "spiritual needs and values as core human needs get little mention" ([69], p. 5).

[7] The author, and I agree with him, identifies these methodologies capable of capturing the deep dimensions of human being, such as spirituality, with Constructivism and Hermeneutic-Phenomenological approaches.

satisfactorily able to integrate spiritual issues into their practice if they chose to do so. In another study [27] physicians who had strong religious beliefs (and thosee who were Protestants) were more likely to discuss religious beliefs with patients. However, it must be noted that although most physicians had strong religious beliefs, only one third felt that they should ask their patients about faith-healing experiences. Moreover, Koenig and collaborators' finding (1991, cited in [24]) that mental health professionals seek out referrals from religious groups, but rarely make referrals to clergy or other religious leaders is of dubious interpretation. Is it for the professional pride mentioned above by Swinton or rather for a sense of self-sufficiency or both?

Basically, a definitive answer awaits further research that addresses the question "why patients' religious and spiritual dimensions are neglected by psychiatrists?" [20].

Colucci and Martin [28] have reviewed studies that have examined the variables of religion and spirituality in the context of suicidal behavior. As the authors point out, not only has spirituality been overlooked by suicidologists, but the studies have typically been restricted to the analysis of the relationship between religiosity (often operationalized as church affiliation or attendance) and suicidal ideation/attitude or suicide mortality statistics. Very rarely have researchers addressed non-religious form of spirituality or used a qualitative methodology. If the picture emerging from this summary is unsatisfactory, it becomes even more disappointing when we note that the findings about the influence of religion on suicide are inconsistent and ambiguous.

The authors recommend methods for future research to enhance the quality and utility of studies in this area, and to shed light on spirituality, the importance of which is discussed in the following paragraph.

> *There are more things in heaven and earth, Horatio, than are dreamt of in your philosophy*
>
> (Shakespeare, From Hamlet, Prince of Denmark, 1601, Act I: Scene 5)

4. IMPORTANCE OF SPIRITUALITY FOR MENTAL HEALTH AND SUICIDE PREVENTION

The impact of Eastern spiritual thought, the emergence of New Age philosophies and the popularity of alternative health practices have all called for a more holistic understanding of health related issues [2]. Over recent decades, professionals in several sectors of health have suggested to give more importance to spirituality in the healing process and health models [2, 13, 29-33] and mainstream medical journals have acknowledged the area of spirituality [4]. The change, however, seems to be more rhetoric than the reality of practice. For instance, in the area of general health, although physicians seldom question patients about their religious beliefs, patients express a desire for physicians to consider their spiritual needs [34]. The Mental Health Foundation report [15] underlines that some find that their religious/spiritual beliefs are not understood or explored within mental health services: "For many, clinicians either ignore an individual's spiritual life completely or treat their spiritual experience as nothing more than manifestations of psychopathology"[8] (p. 3). To this I add that another risk is that even clinicians who do not neglect their patients' spiritual needs might have a limited perspective on this matter and identify spirituality with religion. Thus, people whose spirituality has a non-religious expression might be offered even less opportunities of sharing their spiritual beliefs and/or concerns.

In the Fetzer Institute report [9] are listed various ways in which religiousness and spirituality may be connected to health outcomes:

- religiousness/spirituality provides supportive, integrative communities for their members;
- offers members a complex set of beliefs about God, ethics, human relationships, life and death, which are beneficial to health;

---

[8] For a discussion about the pathologization and normalization of spiritual states and the cross-culturally common presence of mystical states see Bartocci and Dein [95].

- may protect against disease, indirectly promoting healthy lifestyles (*e.g.,* healthy diets or prohibition to smoke and use drugs) and
- certain religious/spiritual practices affect physiological mechanisms and elicit relaxation responses.

Religion also helps patients to cope better with their illness: the majority of 850 studies on religion and mental health reviewed by Koenig [30] reported that religious people experience better mental health and adapt more successfully to stress.

In Sullivan's study, [12] half of the mental health services consumers indicated spiritual beliefs and practices as central to their successful struggle with severe mental illness. The author then speculates that the results can reflect the role of spirituality as a coping strategy, a source of social support and a system of meanings. Coping styles was one of the mechanisms though which potential benefits of spirituality on mental health may occur listed in the Mental Health Foundation report [15]. The others are: locus of control, social support and social networks, physiological mechanisms, and architecture and the built environment (including nature, art and music).

However, it must be considered that an interest in religious issues may be not shared by every patient and it is likely to be higher in more religious patients. In fact, in Exline, Yali and Sanderson's [35] investigation of the role of religious strain in depression and suicidality, the authors found that religiosity was positively associated with interest in addressing religious issues during treatment with a clinical sample of persons seeking psychotherapy. On the other hand, religion can be of such importance that some persons with mental health disorders frequently, and sometimes only, seek help from the clergy (Larson *et al.*, 1988, cited in [26]). The authors speculate that one of the possible reasons is people's fear of having their own spiritual needs and their faith overlooked or misinterpreted. This fear precludes those people from getting medical or psychological help, and the only way to improve access would be a change in the neglect and skepticism towards spiritual issues by mental health professionals. In particular, there is the risk that "non-religiously spiritual" people are left unable to find an outlet to express any kind of extramundane beliefs and concerns (*i.e.*, mental health professional are not interest in the topic and priests might try to indoctrinate them). As Koenig [30] notes in discussing the danger of not considering one of the three dimensions of the person (physical, emotional and spiritual): "for many patients, spirituality is an important part of the wholeness, and when addressing psychosocial aspects in medicine, that part of their personhood cannot be ignored" (p. 1708). This may be more important for psychiatric patients, as evidenced by Swinton [3]: "While spirituality remains a peripheral issue for many mental health professionals, it is in fact of central importance to many people who are struggling with the pain and confusion of mental health problem" (p. 7).

Religion and spirituality not only influence mental health and beliefs about mental illness but treatment can be affected as well [23, 36]. For instance, some religious groups will refuse to take capsules made from gelatin. Bhugra and Osbourne [23] recommend that the role of religion/spirituality "in individual's cultural identity must be taken into account when ascertaining mental state and formulating management strategies" (p. 6)". Shafranske and Malony (1996, cited in [37]) suggest that religion/spirituality needs to be considered like any other client cultural characteristic and mental health professionals have an ethical obligation to consider spirituality a part of a standard assessment.

In spite of the awareness of the role of the spiritual dimension in mental health and illness, only relatively few studies have investigated the role of spirituality in psychiatric patients. These studies reveal that religion/spirituality is important in dealing with mental illness (*e.g.,* 2; Sullivan, 1993 cited in [3, 38]) and, in patients' opinions, should be taken into account by a therapist. In D'Souza's study [2], for example, 79% of psychiatric patients rated spirituality as very important and 82% thought their therapists should be aware of their spiritual beliefs and needs, whereas 69% of them reported that those spiritual needs should be considered by the therapist in treating their psychological illness. Two-third of patients also believed that spirituality helped them to cope with psychological pain. On the other side, 16% of studies reviewed by Larson and colleagues [39] evidenced some negative associations between mental health and religion. A review by Gartner, Larson and Allen [40] suggests that both low and high levels of religiosity can be associated with psychopathology. More specifically, low levels of religiosity are associated with disorders related to under control of impulses, whereas high levels are more often related to disorders of over control.

The role of concerns about religion/spirituality as a possible font of distress and focal point for personal strain and conflict has been underlined also by Exline, Yali and Sanderson [35] and Johnson and Hayes [37]. Payne, Bergin, Bielema and Jenkins [41], in their review on religion and mental health, conclude that "religion as prevention" is a concept based on an illusion that one religion is as good as another, whereas some ways of being religious (*e.g.,* intrinsically instead of extrinsically) are healthier than other ways. In particular, spiritual beliefs which involve oppressive images of God, or which engender inappropriate guilt and increase anxiety, may be detrimental to mental health [3] and may put the person at risk of suicide. A similar case is made in the Mental Health Foundation report [15] where the author states that some expression of spirituality are more effective than others in promoting mental health and enabling people to cope when their mental health deteriorates.

The argument about a negative impact of religion on mental health needs further investigation, looking both at those religions that, throughout history, have not only sanctioned, but institutionalized suicide, such as Brahmanism, Buddhism and Shinto, the state religion of Japan [42] and, on the other hand, religions that traditionally have forbidden suicide, like Catholicism, Judaism and Islam (see [28]).

Thakker, Durrant, Schumaker, Nathawat and Palsane [43] found no meaningful relationship between religiosity and psychological well-being in a sample of university students from India. However, the authors attribute this finding to the pervasiveness of religious beliefs in India, with positive effects that permeate the culture as a whole. The same point is discussed in Dein's cultural analysis of spirituality [4], where he supports the idea that it may be senseless to distinguish between culture and religion in many parts of the world. Senseless or not, it is certain that religion, as the title of the paper by Tarakeshwar, Stanton and Pargament [85] says, is an overlooked dimension in Cross-Cultural Psychology as well as Trans/Cross-Cultural Psychiatry. Their article opens with: "Religion is inextricably woven into the cloth of cultural life" (p. 377). From this starting point the authors pass through the criticism of the existing cross-cultural research for the limited attention paid to religion and spirituality, list four reasons why religion (and, I add, spirituality) should be fully integrated into cross-cultural research and highlight how religion exercises its own impact on the beliefs and practices of cultures and how, in turn, cultural norms, behaviors and changes shape the manifestation of religion in different countries. Also Thakker and colleagues [43] are critical of the literature for the absence of cross-cultural investigations of the relationship between religion and mental health and the fact that the few studies done have been mainly conducted on western populations.

People's choice to live or to die is highly related to aspects of their spiritual life [5]. Religion and spirituality may influence the attitudes and beliefs people have toward experience of distress and illness, may be a means for coping with mental health problems, may enhance psychiatric patient's sense of social belonging and integration, may be part of people's explanatory model of their life's experiences, may ameliorate the relationship with mental health professionals and enhance the trust and access to mental health services. Furthermore, spiritual beliefs and values are part of the patient's cultural background and their consideration in mental health may help to pursue the important aim of offering culturally-sensitive prevention/intervention strategies. For all these reasons, it is expected (and hoped) that more professionals in general health and in mental health will be able to make an in-depth diagnostic assessment of what kind of spirituality the patient is "imbued with" so to address this aspect when treating their patients. This hope is based on the observation that, even though religious/spiritual issues (as recognized by scholars such as, to cite a few, [5, 20, 44]) have been generally overlooked in Suicidology, in recent years there has been a growing interest in the role religion and spirituality may play in reducing self-harm and suicidal behavior (Resnick *et al.*, 1997 cited in [45]).

The review by Colucci and Martin [28] analyses the role that religion and spirituality may play at each step along the suicidal path, reporting on research that has considered the relationship between spirituality/religion and suicidal ideation, suicidal attempt and death by suicide. Below, I summaries the main findings from the cited literature review but readers are referred to Colucci and Martin [28] for the complete review[9].

---

[9] Inconsistent findings are present in the literature investigating the spiritual/religious variables and suicide [28]. A possible reason for the disparity in results is the plethora of indicators used to study the impact of religion on suicidal behavior. Another issue that must be taken into consideration is that the impact of religion/spirituality changes in different cultural and socio-political contexts and during historical periods.

5. SPIRITUALITY IN THOUGHTS: SUICIDAL IDEATION AND ATTITUDES

Overall, studies have shown that religious factors are associated with lower suicidal ideation/plan and with more negative attitudes towards suicide. For instance, in the study I will mention later on [46], I showed that Indian students who defined themselves as religious/spiritual reported lower suicidal ideation compared to those who were non-religious/spiritual. Furthermore, participants' specific religious preference was associated with presence of suicidal thoughts. There was an association also between students' self-reported religiosity/spirituality and attitudes towards youth suicide as measured by the 21-items Attitude towards Youth Suicide scale (AtYS; [46]). In particular, whilst there were no statistically significant differences in India between religious/spiritual and non-religious/spiritual students, in Italy religious/spiritual students believed more that suicide is preventable and agreed less that it is acceptable. In Australia, religious/spiritual students manifested more negative attitudes and less acceptability. Scores on the subscales were also analyzed looking at the specific religious affiliations, which significantly impacted the scores on each of the four attitudes subscales. However, other scholars have shown that religiosity is only weakly associated [47] or not associated (*e.g.*, [48, 49]) with suicidal ideation. On the other hand, participants with distress and strain related to religious or spiritual concerns reported more suicidal ideation [35, 37]. In the former study, that was the belief of having committed a sin too big to be forgiven that associated with suicidal thoughts. An observation from this first part of the review [28] was that research has rarely focused on non-religious forms of spirituality and meaning in life or has put religion/spirituality in relation to the ethno-cultural context.

6. SPIRITUALITY IN NON-LETHAL SUICIDAL BEHAVIOR

First of all, of the three, this was the part of the suicide path least investigated by scholars. Although a few studies have shown that religious/spiritual persons have lower rates of suicide attempts, a few others did not find any association between religiosity and suicidal behavior. For instance, whilst in Italy and Australia a similar percentage of religious/spiritual and non-religious/spiritual students attempted suicide, Indian students who recognized themselves as non-religious/spiritual attempted suicide more often than religious/spiritual participants; the specific religion was also associated with suicide attempts [46]. At the opposite, Loewenthal *et al.* [49] found no association between participants' religiosity and suicide attempts. On the other side, a couple of studies suggested that in some circumstances religion might be a risk factor for such behavior (*e.g.*, [50]).

It is important to note that research suggested that only some aspects of religiosity (*e.g.*, importance of religion) or some spiritual variables (*e.g.*, sense of connectedness or coherence) might be associated with suicidal behavior [28].

7. SPIRITUALITY IN LETHAL SUICIDAL BEHAVIOR

The majority of research on lethal suicidal behavior has focused on mortality statistics and indicated that variables such as religious affiliation and church attendance offer some protection against suicide. Breault and Barkey [51] not only found an association between religious integration (as measured by religious book and newspapers production), but that this relationship was exponential: past a certain point or threshold, even a small decrease in integration was associated with a sharp increase in suicide rates.

However, some studies have shown that the association between religion and suicide is mediated or influenced by other variables underlining an overall weak association between religion and suicide, for instance, level of urbanization [52], whereas others have reported an overall absence of a significant association (*e.g.*, [53]).

The epidemiological data have been questioned and Sorri, Henriksson and Lonnqvist's study [54] showed that in some cases religiosity can support a suicidal decision. Also in this 'path section', research on non-religious spirituality is scarce. Important spiritual elements (*e.g.,* meaning and purpose) have been extensively and unreasonably neglected. Meaning in life is the subject of the next subchapter.

> *"He who has a way to live for can bear almost anything".*
>
> (Nietzsche, 1888)

8. MEANING IN LIFE

A particular aspect of spirituality that has not received yet the attention that, in my opinion, it deserves is the search for "meaning in life". Meaning or a sense of life's purpose has been proposed as a primary component of a definition of spirituality by several authors (*e.g.*, [15, 23, 55-58]). Doyle (1992, cited in [8]) states that spirituality, in essence, means "searching for existential meaning". Tacey [68] emphasizes that the soul is not nourished by social status or financial success, but only by meaning, value and purpose and that, the soul requires meaning that comes from connection to transcendent values. Swinton, [3] affirms that "It is the meaning and purpose that a person has discovered within their life which gives them the strength to find meaning and purpose within their suffering" (p. 58). In fact, individuals who experience a deeper and broader sense of meaning and purpose enjoy greater life satisfaction, higher levels of psychological and physical well-being, and positive mental health [59] whereas, in Petersen and Roy's opinion [60], people whose lives lack meaning and purpose, experience feeling of emptiness or a lack of direction, have difficulty making sense out of their existence and question the significance of being who or what they are. Antonovsky recognizes meaningfulness as the most important component of the Sense of Coherence (SOC) and concludes that high level of meaningfulness motivates individuals to search for order and to make sense of their environment, as well as kinaesthetically transform their coping resources (1990, cited in [61]). Personal meaning has three components: cognitive, affective, and motivational [62]. The cognitive system consists of beliefs, expectations and schemas, individually constructed and culturally based, whereas the affective component is defined as feelings of satisfaction and fulfillment. In terms of the motivational component, personal meaning is the pursuit of activities and life goals considered by the individual to be valuable and worthwhile. Different authors have underlined different aspects of this construct. For example, Thompson and Janigian [63] identify purpose and order as the two components of the "search for meaning". In their own words: "An event is meaningful when we understand how it follows in an orderly fashion from our views and beliefs and when it has a purpose whose value we recognize" (p. 263). The sense of commitment is a central part of meaning-making as well, as showed by Kosaba and colleagues (1979, 1982 cited in [63]) who found that stress resistant people are distinguished by the sense of commitment in their lives. "Hardy" people tend to have a strong sense of purpose: not only they have goals in their lives but a strong sense that those goals are important, of value, and they are actively involved in attaining them. Depression, in this view, results from the perception that important goals no longer appear to be achievable [63] or, in my experience, that they are no longer important or meaningful. A number of studies have found significant relationships between the sense of meaning in life and indices of health, particularly mental health [9]. Personal meaning plays both a health-protecting and a health-enhancing role and the mechanism underlying this effect is, in Reker's opinion [59], through cognitive restructuring or, more explicitly, through restructuring, redefining or re-evaluating stressful situations in order to reduce their negative impact. Some research shows that life meanings may be more influential in psychological wellbeing than religion *per se*. Two studies by Chamberlin and Zika (1992, cited in [43]) highlighted that, although religiosity and life satisfaction correlated, when life meaning was factored in, religiosity contributed little to life satisfaction. This result suggests that life meaning may mediate the relationship between religiosity and well-being.

Personal meaning has been a core concept for several phenomenological philosophers and existential scholars[10]. The most notable and influential is Victor Frankl, a psychiatrist survivor of a Nazi concentration camp in Germany. Frankl [64] suggested that the primary motivating factor of mental health is the human quest for meaning and purpose, which belongs to the *noetic* dimension of human beings. This concept was so important to him that he developed a therapeutic approach-*Logotherapy*-which focuses on meaning in life. Human survival depends on finding and preserving meaning and on filling the "existential vacuum", "a feeling of aimlessness and emptiness" [65]. Man is characterized by his reaching out for meaning and purpose in life. The lack of meaning, in Frankl's view, is experienced by the individual as a sense of complete emptiness, and an absence of purpose for continuing to live. Suicide, then, may seem a viable solution to relieve this distressing state of being [66]. A similar concept is affirmed by Fitzpatrick (1983,

---

[10] For a critical review of theories that have postulated that existential issues of meaning in life, meaningless, and emptiness are at the heart of the suicide, an excellent reading is Orbach's [102].

cited in [67]), Marsella [31] and Tacey [68][11]. The former asserts that those who have no meaning attached to life do not continue to live. Marsella [31] states the centrality of meaning along life's journey, the absence of which causes despair, alienation and suicide. Marsella declares: "It seems to me that many discomforts, disorders, and diseases of our time are related to an absence of meaning-seeking and meaning-making" [31], (p. 49). Tacey [68] criticizes our "rational" society for ignoring the soul[12]-"the unattended soul"-and states that this hollowness may express itself as despair, chronic anxiety, deep uncertainty, various kinds of addictions, or suicidal feelings. He states: "Spirit is seen as too abstract for science to be bothered with, and yet this is an illusion: nothing is more concrete than a reality that bestows purpose and value to life" (p. 109). Tacey [68] also sees the archetypical background of youth's self-mutilations in the initiation rituals: there is a desire to mark the body, to announce that one has been touched by something decisive, to mark their passage from one state to another. Moreover, Webb [69], from his "first-hand" experience, argues that hopelessness is the main indicator of suicidality and that hopelessness arises from an absence of meaning or purpose in life.

For Frankl [65] meanings are both relative and subjective: meaning differs from man to man and day by day. Consequently, there is no universal meaning of life although some meanings are shared by human beings throughout society and history (meanings which, in Frankl's theory, are understood as values). Frankl concluded that there are three types of values whereby an individual can discover meaning: creative (based on what the person gives to the world, such as achievements and good deeds), experiential (what the person receives from the world), and attitudinal (realized by adopting the right attitude towards situations). Later research by Reker and Wong (1988, cited in [58]) and Ebersole [70] examined the central source of meanings for people and found as representative sources: leisure activities and hobbies; relationships; personal achievement and growth; religious/spiritual and social/political values and beliefs; social and political activism and service; traditions and culture; creative work; life work; materialistic and basic needs.

Although it appears obvious that at least a number of suicides are an expression of absence of meaning in life or "attempts to escape from an existential vacuum" [62], (p. 413), studies into this aspect of suicide are very rare ([66, 67, 71-73] are some of the few exceptions). Moore [67] finding no study in the elderly examining suicide and meaning of life, interviewed elderly psychiatric inpatients with suicidal ideation, who revealed feelings of worthless and absence of connectedness with others. "Emptiness" appeared to make a unique contribution to the differentiation of suicidal and no suicidal groups beyond the contribution of depression, hopelessness and anxiety [73]. Harlow and collaborators [71] tested the theory that lack of purpose in life is an essential mediating factor in the relationship between depression and suicidal ideation, but the theory was confirmed only for young males. In a sample of college students, Lester and Badro [72] found that while depression scores were significant predictors of only current suicidal preoccupation, Purpose-in-Life scores were significant predictors of current suicidal ideation as well as a history of previous ideation and threats (see [74] for a description of instruments to assess a person's religiosity/spirituality[13]). Edwards and Holden [66] examined the relationship between coping strategies and purpose in life with suicidal manifestations in undergraduate Canadian students. Purpose in life correlated negatively with both suicidal ideation and likelihood of future suicidal behavior. The authors

---

[11] A different view on this is offered by Orbach [102], who argues that "it is not the lack of meaning that brings about suicidal behavior, but that mental pain is the emotional state that produces both lack of meaning as well as suicidal behavior" (p. 296). He highlights the role that unfulfilled needs have in this process. I believe that the lack of meaning might produce mental pain and suffering as well but I support the view that the link between needs, mental pain and meanings might be more complicated that what existential theory seem to suggest.

[12] The author also points out that the soul has been traditionally the province of the religions but in our increasingly secular society, the authority of religion has been reduced. He criticizes Western religion for not having been alert to the complexity of the inner life (emphasizing "belief" rather than interiority) and attributes to this youth's turn towards Indigenous religions or Buddhism. Webb [69] also argues that spiritual growth is difficult in a society that is largely in denial of spirituality as a core human need.

[13] For a wider list of instruments, see the book "Measure of Religiosity" by Hill and Hood [103], which classifies more than one hundred scales on religious development, beliefs, values, attitudes, attribution, orientation, practices, coping and problem-solving, commitment and fundamentalism. Scales on spirituality, mysticism, God concept, views of death/afterlife, forgiveness and others are represented in the book as well.

concluded that suicide prediction, prevention and intervention strategies may be enhanced if they address life meaning. Wong [62] reported that evidence suggests that promotion of personal meaning may be effective in addressing social problems, such as drug addiction, alcoholism and suicide. Although not focused on meanings, Foster's [75] examination of suicide notes pointed out the presence in "hopelessness/nothing to live for" amongst the most common themes, especially in suicides with major unipolar depression. Similarly, in Rogers, Bromley, McNally and Lester's [76] content analysis of suicide notes, spiritual motivation was present in 25% of the notes (particularly in younger writers) and many of these had a more existential component of loss of meaning and purpose in life than a specific reference to more traditional conceptualization of spirituality. Lester [77] offers a different perspective in regard to the role of meaning in suicidal behavior stating that, for some suicidal individuals, suicide is a search for spirituality, for God, for the meaning of life and for rebirth. This outlook on suicide has been criticized by Fournier [78]. On the side of survivors, the study of Currier, Holland and Neimeyer [79] on violent loss (including suicide) found that the failure to find meaning in a loss is a crucial pathway to complicated grief. The authors also suggest that religion and spirituality might influence such sense-making.

Sense of meaningfulness can be increased through therapy. Wong [62], for example, proposed a culturally-appropriate meaning-centered counseling, a hybrid between existential-humanistic Psychology and cognitive-behavioral therapy, growth-oriented instead of problem-focused.

D'Souza and Rodrigo [80] developed the *Spiritually-augmented Cognitive Behavior therapy* which includes techniques to find meaning and purpose (*i.e.,* meaning of the situation and global meaning).

As noted before, Frankl suggested three approaches for increasing meaning: "giving to the world", "taking from the world" and through the attitude toward inevitable suffering. In the Sappington, Bryant and Oden's study [81] of Frankl's hypothesis, students scoring low on purpose in life were randomly assigned to two treatments: the first aimed to increase meaning through helping others (the "giving to the world" approach) and the second through increasing enjoyment and appreciation (*i.e.,* "taking from the world"). Both experimental groups increased their purpose in life significantly more than the control group. Is it therefore possible to treat suicidal patients to make their lives more meaningful, helping them to find purpose in their lives? This study would suggest so but, incomprehensibly, at the moment there are too few studies to be able to answer this question.

The reasons why meaning in life has been neglected in this area of research and, more broadly [82], why the connections between goals, purpose and meanings with health and well-being are largely unexplored, are similar to those discussed earlier for, more in general, spirituality: the absence of a shared definition of the construct, the uncertainty about what is meant by 'meaning' and difficulty in operationalizing and quantitatively researching the concept. Wong [62] points out that it is a common viewpoint that questions about meaning and purpose are too subjective and philosophical to be answered scientifically. Ebersole [70] suggests as well that this concept of meaning apparently lacks demonstrated practical value. Despite this, he proposes some applications of meaning and strongly recommends doing more research in the area. In recent years, issues related to meaning and purpose is receiving increasing attention by researchers [62] but this does not seem to be happening in Suicidology. My hope is that other scholars will share my feeling that more research in this important direction is needed and the number of publications on this topic will see an increase in the near future. Part of this research should, in my opinion, embrace Antonovsky's (1987, cited in [61]) critique of the "disease model" so prevalent in Psychiatry and Psychology, and should address what keeps people alive, even when life has been particularly difficult for them. In this way, attention might shift from suicide prevention to the more promising sector of life promotion.

9. THE CULTURAL MEANINGS OF SUICIDE: FINDINGS ON SPIRITUALITY FROM A CROSS-CULTURAL COMPARISON AMONG YOUNG ITALIANS, INDIANS AND AUSTRALIANS

Besides "meanings" as a component of spirituality, "understanding" the cultural meanings (*i.e.,* representations, views, values and belief systems and so on) of suicide is my main other area of research. These two kinds of "meanings", to date, shared a common destiny: despite the number of scholars who have underlined the relevance of what suicide means to people belonging to different socio-cultural backgrounds, the study of meaning is another unjustifiably missing area in suicide research and prevention. Trying to amplify this field of knowledge, I explored the cultural meanings of youth suicide among university students of 18–24 years of age in three different countries: Italy, India and Australia. Data was collected through a multi-method approach, using a questionnaire titled 'Exploring the Meaning of Suicide' [46], which included structured and semi-structured questions (such as case scenarios, word association, attitude scale, open ended questions) and tape-recorded focus groups. The open-ended section of the questionnaire was composed of various parts investigating participants' mental associations with the word 'suicide' and interpretations of both this word and 'attempted suicide', feelings about death, gender-related issues, stereotypes of the 'kind of' youth who attempt suicide or kill themselves, reasons for living and suicide prevention strategies. The focus group questions were similar to the open-ended questions included in the questionnaire, and the aim of the focus groups was to go into those issues in more depth (research methods are partially described in [83, 84]).

Almost 700 students across countries took part at the first phase of the study (*i.e.*, survey) and 96 participated in the following focus groups (two sessions for each group for a total of 24 sessions).

The comparisons highlighted differences and similarities across cultures in meanings and social representations of suicide. Spirituality is concerned with how we experience the world, how we live and act in the world and how we make sense of it in an ongoing (and not static) process. Therefore, spiritual/religious beliefs cannot be differentiated from other cultural beliefs, given that they shape and impact each other, as observed also by Tarakeshwar and colleagues [85][14] and discussed–together with other cultural aspects of suicide–in Colucci [29]. Thus, as part of the understanding the cultural aspects of suicide, I also investigated participants' spiritual beliefs. In this section, I will report a few findings pertaining participants' spiritual beliefs. The rest of the study is currently under preparation for a co-edited book.

One of the questions in the survey asked if, at the present time, the participants would define themselves as being religious/spiritual persons and, if so, to indicate their religious affiliation. Most Indian participants identified with being religious/spiritual, followed by Italians, whereas Australians were the least religious/spiritual. Participants from the three countries reported different religious affiliations. The great majority of the Italian religious/spiritual participants reported to be Catholic. In India more than half of those who were religious/spiritual were Hindus, followed by Catholics. In Australia the religious/spiritual sample was divided mostly between Christians (non-Catholic) and Catholics[15].

Participants' spiritual/religious beliefs assessed in the survey have been analyzed in relation to their reported suicidal ideation and behavior. In this regard, while participants from Italy and Australia did not show any statistically significant difference on the basis of their religiosity/spirituality, Indians participants who were not religious/spiritual reported more suicidal ideation and attempts and higher scores on the suicide risk scale than religious/spiritual participants did. These data can be interpreted in various ways. For example, if being religious/spiritual acts as a deterrent against suicidal behavior (see [28] for a review), lack of religious/spiritual beliefs may have deprived those participants from this protection. On the other hand, participants who reported being non-religious/spiritual, may be less traditional, embracing modern values and beliefs and refusing traditions like religious rituals and celebrations. It might be that those more "anti-traditionalist" participants may be less accepted by their more "traditionalist" peers and family members and thus be less socially integrated and connected. Therefore, they may be more exposed to suicidal ideation and behavior [86]. Furthermore, the lack of statistically significant difference among religious/spiritual and non-religious/spiritual Italians might be interpreted as a decrease of the importance of religion in the life of young Italians parallel to a growing atheism. Alternatively, it might also be that

---

[14] The authors cited a work from Roccas and Schwartz (1997, cited in [85]) which found that there were stronger correlations between religiosity and values in countries, such as Italy, Spain and Portugal, that had more cordial church-state relations.

[15] Although the great majority of participants in India and, less, in Italy reported being religious or spiritual, it is important to note that the general belief that Italians and Indians are religious countries might not be fully true considering that almost a fifth of Indians and a third of Italians indicated being not religious/spiritual. In Australia almost half of the sample reported not being religious/spiritual.

because Catholicism is the most common religion amongst Italians (in fact 4/5 of the religious/spiritual participants identified themselves as Catholics), those aspects of Catholicism that Durkheim [87] underlined as being protective against suicide, could be part of the Italian culture as a whole, independently of what participants state their religious beliefs are[16]. Whitla [88] found that Italian youth (compared to Australians) placed a higher importance on religion. This finding was striking for the author because almost half of the sample reported that they attend a place of worship six or less times annually. The outcome may indicate that the importance of religion in the family might be better represented, for instance, in the presence of religious values in the family's daily life rather than in church attendance or affiliation.

A few other studies addressed the topic of youth suicide and religion/spirituality in the same countries. A study on Italian high school participants [89] showed that many more youth who declared to be non-believers had suicidal thoughts compared to the (mainly Catholics) believers. In Colucci [90], I found that, of the youth 15-24 years old who accessed the Padua Hospital Emergency Department following a suicide attempt during the years 1989-1999, 90% indicated that they were Catholics. However, a deeper analysis of the religious behavior revealed that only 35.1% of the Catholic attempters indicated to be believers and 18.4% that they were also practicing their religious belief.

In the study by Schweitzer, Klayich and McLean [91], Australian participants with no religion were at higher risk for suicide attempts than those affiliated with major religions. This result diverges from what I found in the current study, but the questions were different (in my study the first question asked if the person was spiritual or religious, and not just religious, and a second question differentiated participants' answers into more specific categories).

The link between religious beliefs and/or affiliation and suicide is complex. This is demonstrated by the observation that the same religious affiliation might have a different relationship with suicidal behavior in different countries (*e.g.,* in this study non-Catholic Christians had higher suicide risk scores in Italy and in Australia than in India) and that, although being religious/spiritual might protect people from suicidal ideation and behavior (*e.g.,* for the overall religious/spiritual Indians), being affiliated with a minority religion (which may also not be really well-accepted) might expose people to a greater risk of suicide, as was the case for Muslims in the Indian sample. This point is partially confirmed by the work of Pescosolido and Giorgianna [92] and Pescosolido [93] who contended that the influence of religion on suicide may be modeled within social and geographical context and that a religious denomination offers most protection at its "historical hub". In the study cited above [91], Australian participants with higher suicide attempts were those affiliated with religions other than Catholic and Protestant (*i.e.*, the two main religions in this country).

The question is further complicated when trying to relate people's religious affiliation and spiritual beliefs to religious and spiritual beliefs towards suicide. The attitudes of religions towards suicide change from one religion to another and in the same religion over time. As observed by Colucci and Martin [28], for instance, the Judeo-Christian religion has always had an ambivalent attitude. In fact, up to nine references to suicide can be found in the Old Testament and at least one in the New Testament but these cases, as Barraclough commented (1992, in [28]) were reported in a non-judgmental way. It was only since St. Augustine's condemnation that the official disapproval by the Catholic Church began to spread and increase. However, since the end of last century, as observed by Stein (1971, in [28]), the Church leans heavily toward a contextual or a situational ethic on the judgment of suicide. Also Hindu scriptures appear relatively ambivalent towards suicide and in some circumstances Hinduism has in some way encouraged suicide (*e.g.,* suttee)[17].

---

[16] The hypothesis of the "pervasiveness" of Catholicism (and Hinduism) is further indicated in the next subchapter. This pervasiveness probably interests Indians as well but the difference might be that being non-religious/spiritual has a greater negative impact in India (thus the report of more suicidal ideation and attempts and higher scores on the suicide risk scale among those Indian participants), a somehow more traditionalist (and coercive) society than Italy.

[17] See Leach [94] for a description of main religions' views on afterlife and suicide.

Religion and anthropology scholars have argued that views of an afterlife determine an individual or society's views of suicide [94]. To investigate this issue, I asked participants in the focus groups if they believed in "afterlife" and, later, what they believed happens in afterlife to young people who kill themselves and those who die in other ways. Following, I will present these data in details, also providing extracts from the focus groups to "hear" participants' own voices.

Spiritual Beliefs on the Afterlife

Italy: When asked if they believed there was some kind of life after death, only a few Italian participants reported a religious concept of an afterlife (usually Catholic)[18]. The majority of participants had a non-structured spiritual belief that there might be something after death but they did not know what this might be. Some participants identified this "something" as a sort of energy that remains after death or believed that people remain as loved ones' memories. Few other participants stated that they did not believe or did not have an opinion.

Some participants affirmed that, although rationally they might think that there is nothing after death, believing in something-even if vaguely-helps to live, to overcome life problems and to bear the death of close ones. These participants felt that it is too unbearable and sad to think that everything finishes with death. For instance (IT1F:50)[19]: "*(...) I have also thought that maybe it is more a need of believing that there is something after this life and I also thought that this [belief] makes me feel good and the belief of an afterlife makes me live this life in a different way than I would if I thought it did not exist".*

Similar thoughts were expressed in other groups and in one of them some participants suggested an opposite opinion, *i.e.,* the negative effect of religion, which becomes an "excuse to do nothing in this life". The following extract (IT3Mix:160-176) exemplifies these different views:

> *M1: I was saying that I think there is the need to believe in a life after death (...). I believe that also those [people] who do not believe should, I mean, have this push to believe in something after death (...) otherwise you'll say "tomorrow I'll die so I'll do nothing".*
>
> *F1: For me it is the opposite.*
>
> *Mod: She thinks the opposite...*
>
> *F1: Meaning that, however, if you know (...) that at a certain point your life will finish and that you don't have any other chance to restart from the beginning, you enjoy every instant you have and try to do it at the best you can...in my opinion, of course (...)*
>
> *M2: (...) In my opinion, I believe it would be easier to think that there is no deity, because you'll say "all right, I've nothing to do with anyone after [death], so I can behave how I think and please", whereas religions teach that if you behave evilly... I mean, I don't believe any religion says that you'll end up nicely (....) so in my opinion it [religion] may exist, I mean, exist more as a push to succeed in life more than anything else, rather than to limit.*
>
> *Mod: To the contrary, M3 [said before that he] believes the opposite?!*
>
> *M3: Yes!*

India: Indian participants showed conflicting beliefs about the existence of an afterlife. Approximately half of the sample reported a religious belief of an afterlife, usually Hindu and, less often, Christian. The latter

---

[18] One participant defined himself as being "partially" Catholic, because he did not believe in every aspect of Catholicism. He justified this statement by saying that his (partial) religious belief was due to the fact that Catholicism is part of the Italian culture and therefore his beliefs on afterlife were influenced by this religion.

[19] The code before the extracts (*e.g.,* IT1F:50-58) indicates the group (IT1F is Italian group 1, only female participants) and line(s) of the transcripts (*i.e.,* from line 50 to line 58). In each extract, participants are indicated by their sex and a number (*e.g.,* M1 means male number 1) so that it is possible to follow what each person stated. What I said, as the moderator of the focus group sessions, is indicated by the label "Mod".

generally believed that after death the person goes to Heaven if they have done good on earth, or to Hell if they have done bad. The Hindu beliefs were more ambiguous, with some participants believing that the soul goes to Heaven or Hell and then is reborn and others saying that the soul continues to be reborn until it does not do anything bad and is purified and, only then, the soul goes to Heaven. Some participants specified that these beliefs in reincarnation apply only to natural deaths whereas, for the other kind of deaths (including suicide), the soul roams the earth (this view will be discussed in the next paragraph). Some participants reported some cultural beliefs about the afterlife but then dissociated their personal beliefs from these, or gave their own personal re-interpretation. For example, one participant stated that, considering his Hindu background together with the scientific knowledge that when a dead body is burned it becomes carbon, he believed that people will be somehow reborn: as living creatures, stars, stones, or something else. Another participant showed interfaith beliefs, stating that he was Christian but he believed in Hindu mythology as well. In a group, participants pointed out how religious beliefs are forced upon them by parents and how they might follow these beliefs for the family but they, personally, might not believe in an afterlife.

The other half of the group generally believed that there is no life after death. Those few participants who believed that something remains, indicated that people remain as memories or through a transformation of energy in some form. A few participants specified that they did not believe in afterlife because no one knows what will happen after death, and a few others believed that Heaven and Hell are present in daily life. One participant had a spiritual belief of the existence of a not-defined "higher power".

The next extract (IN2Mix:33-63) exemplifies the variety of views expressed by Indians described above (*i.e.*, religious beliefs *vs.* lack of beliefs in afterlife):

> *M1: According to me, I don't believe in eternal life, only the body is there, like that.*
>
> *Mod: So there's no life after death?*
>
> *M2: After death most of us get to know what life means, but by that time we are dead. So people who do good things go to heaven, others go to hell and take the punishment. So we believe that wherever we are on earth, we should do something good so that we don't have to take the punishment.*
>
> *F1: I too don't believe in such things. We follow the tradition; even after death, in Kerala we have a thing called (unintelligible word) in which every year we give something as offering. So even though we do not believe in such things, we accept it for our parents (...)*
>
> *F2: I think there is life after death. It is told we do come down again in different forms. In Indian mythology they believe that if you don't do right things on earth, then next birth you take the form of an animal, or something else because humans are supposed to be the highest form. If you do good, then you get form of a human being. That's why people give charities when they are in their deathbeds and all and they give lots of money and all so they don't get to hell and they come down like human beings.*
>
> *M3: I don't believe ma'am in life after death. Because, what's going to happen tomorrow, nobody knows.*
>
> *Mod: What do other people think,[about] if there is life after death?*
>
> *M4: According to the Hindu culture, life after death is possible. In Hindu culture, if a man does not fulfill his worldly pleasures then his soul will not go to moksha[20]. If a man fulfils all his worldly pleasures, he'll go to the moksha.*
>
> *F3: Even I don't believe because after death we don't know.*
>
> *M4: I don't believe. After death the person doesn't know where he went, that's what I believe. Our culture believes that after, that after death there is a life, but there's no proof.*

[20] Hinduism and Jainism believe in a transcendental state arrived at by being set free from the cycle of reincarnation.

> *Mod: What about your beliefs?*
>
> *F5: It's forced on us. It's our parents who say something like that. We have to do something for our parents*
>
> *F2: What I think it's forced on us. Our parents think and it's not like we have a belief, like that. It's mostly forced on us. In Kerala, our parents will have to do something for our grandparents. They think that if we don't do that sort of thing we won't get moksha. So it's being forced on us. It's made compulsory.*

Australia: When asked about their spiritual beliefs on the afterlife, many Australian participants reported believing in the existence of a soul or "something" (*e.g.*, memory, "general consciousness") but, whilst some of them believed that this not described "something" has a life after death, others did not know if there is any afterlife. A few other participants dismissed the possibility that there is any soul and/or afterlife and one of them (*i.e.*, M3 in the extract below) argued that believing in an afterlife has a negative impact in the way people live and suggested focusing more on the present life rather than on the after life.

Of the participants who did not believe in an afterlife or stated not to know, some commented that it would anyway be nice to think that there is something after death, and one of them hypothesized that there must be something if so many people believe in it.

A few participants reported having been brought up in a religious way (Catholic or Christian). Some of these participants had a (non-religious) spiritual belief in "something" in the afterlife, as indicated above. A few others identified partially-or not strongly-with the family's religious belief, whereas only a small number of participants identified themselves as being Catholic or Christian.

One of the participants who rejected the family's religious beliefs and reported instead having a "spiritual belief", attributed this rejection to a rebellion to the way he was brought up ("hard in Catholicism"). In his words (AU4M:35/59): *"I'm starting to get a lot more spiritual, but yeah, not religious (...) I think it's a bit more rebellious as well, ...rebellious that I've been brought up this way [hard in Catholicism], yeah and then I've sort of tried to, I don't know, to have my own thoughts, and I think it has just led on that way".* A participant, later in the discussion, hypothesized the existence of a non-specified reincarnation (see next section).

The following extract exemplifies the spectrum of views that Australian participants had on an afterlife (AU2Mix:40-64):

> *F1: Eh...I think...I think once you are dead you are dead [laugh], I don't believe in any soul in after life or anything like that*
>
> *M1: I do, I think there is life after death, I believe in souls and journey of the soul, after you die*
>
> *Mod: But which kind belief, what are your beliefs in after death?*
>
> *M1: Ok, you live your life, and the way you live your life, at the end, kind of determines where I guess the next step of your soul is going to go. I'm very kind of Christian belief, I am not saying that I am a crazy Christian guy, but I just think that's the case.*
>
> *F2: I've sort of been brought up Catholic and it's sort of the same way, like, I sort of can't help not believing that there's not anything, it's crazy to think that I'm dead and I'm gone, but I still don't know where I stand with the whole "God is going to take us in some places and if we do bad things we're going to hell", like, I don't know where I stand on that yet, it's just, yeah, seems too much like a crutch for humankind, this whole God figure, but then again I believe in the afterlife so it's sort of the same. (...)*
>
> *M2: I am sort of the same, as F2, I believe that there is some sort of afterlife although as to what that is I'm not really too sure, I haven't made up my mind about beliefs really*
>
> *F3: I am pretty much the same, I definitely believe in an afterlife, but whether or not that's a religious thing, I'm a bit undecided*

F4: I was raised as Catholic too and there is always...there is this belief that there is, there is something there, but it is almost...even if you sit there and go against the Church and think "No, I don't believe in it anymore" then you think: " Oh! I am going to get in trouble now! [laugh]; there is still something there, I don't know what, but I think there is something.

M3: Ok! I don't believe in an afterlife or it's not something that really concerns me, I think this life is enough, like because just guessing whether there is an afterlife or not negatively impact on the way we live this life, we should be more focused on going on with this life, it's the only life we seem to have, so...

Beliefs on the Afterlife of Youths Who Suicide

A question investigated if, in participants' opinion, whatever they believed about the afterlife would be the same for a young person who killed him/herself.

Italy: Overall, Italian participants agreed that there is no difference in what happens in the afterlife-if an afterlife does exist-between youth who died by suicide compared to those who died by other deaths, for instance (IT4M:252): *"The outcome is the same: you are not anymore in this worldly life; however, if there is an afterlife, it is the same for everyone".* Participants thought that the afterlife would be the same for everyone and, as some participants stated, if there is any difference, it would be based on the way people lived their whole life rather than on the way they died. For instance (IT1F:167): *I think that it is not much the act of suicide per se that changes what it will be like after [death] (...). I mean, it is independent from the act of suicide, i.e., in my opinion if a person behaved well before and then kills himself, what will happen after won't change but if someone behaved badly all his life, he did evil and at the end he kills himself, I cannot consider him in the same way as someone else who suffered all life and then kills himself. So basically, in my opinion, it is not much the act of killing oneself that changes things, [rather] it is the way a person acted earlier on [in life].*

For a small number of participants the only difference between youth who killed themselves and those who did not are the memories they leave: a participant stated that they will be kept as a different memory or no one will have any memory because the person did not have any close one and therefore he/she will be forgotten. Another difference mentioned by a few other participants was that people who suicide do not think about the afterlife because, whatever this might be, for them it would anyway be better than the present (IT2Mix:143-149):

F1: I believe he/she does not neither have these problems. The only thing [that matter to him/her] is ending their life, what happens after is not his/her problem. His/her problem is to cease what is happening now (...). However, I believe one who kills him/herself might believe that there is something after.

F2: I believe that above all he cannot think that there is anything worse then what he is living, I agree [with F1].

A participant believed that people who die by suicide receive some kind of compensation after death for all the sufferings they had during life. The few Catholic participants in the group did not, generally, endorse the religious belief that who a suicide goes to Hell, and one participant believed that the soul of these people goes to Purgatory "to understand".

Some of the participants who had no opinion on the afterlife repeated that they did not know what might happen to anybody.

India: Also in this question Indian participants were divided into two main groups: those (slightly more) who thought that youth who kill themselves receive some sort of punishment and those who believed that there is no difference. Participants who believed in some punishment, often attributed this to the belief that God gives life and only he has the right to take it. Some of the participants who believed that there are differences had a Christian belief that people who suicide goes to Hell. The rest of them had Hindu beliefs, which were expressed in various forms: participants mainly stated that, if the person died by natural death, they are reborn whereas if they died by suicide –therefore, before the predefined time–they do not go to Hell or Heaven nor they are reborn, but the soul roams the earth. Some of these participants described the "roaming" as a kind of moment of reflection: people who killed themselves roam around earth until they realize that they have done something wrong by killing themselves and they are reborn. Some participants did not mention the roaming of the soul and believed that the person must be reborn over and over again, until the soul is purified and then it goes to Heaven. One participant believed that people who kill themselves take rebirth in the same family to complete what they had left undone. Basically, besides the specific beliefs (*i.e.,* Hell, roaming around earth or rebirth), slightly more than half of the participants believed that the afterlife of youth who kill themselves will be different from that of youth who die by natural death.

Those participants who denied the existence of any difference usually related this to their belief that there is no soul or afterlife and that "death is death". A small number of the participants who believed in afterlife thought that the souls of youth who died by suicide would go to God anyway.

It is worth noting that few participants who, in the previous question, denied the existence of an afterlife, in the question related to suicide believed that suicide is punished. In my view, this might be interpreted as an attempt to look more "modern" or rebellious in the first question by denying their religious beliefs (if this was the case, in the previous question a greater part of Indian participants should be considered as having religious beliefs) or these participants might really not believe in an afterlife but they believed anyway in the "punishment" of suicidal people. On one occasion, I asked this question trying to understand the reason for this change of perspective, but participants did not appear to see this as a conflict of beliefs.

A few participants reported being not sure about whether there is any difference in the afterlife for youth who kill themselves. In some instances, there were discussions between participants with opposite views, usually about the punishment of suicidal people and if God has the right to, or should, punish them. Next extract is a selection of a mixture of beliefs about what happens after death to youth who kill themselves (IN5M:46-118):

> *M1: They have better life before committing suicide. Once you think about committing suicide for what purpose? You have to think, why did God send us to earth? So many things we have to do on earth, so we should not commit suicide, we have to make our soul like a star.*
>
> *Mod: But what will happen to this soul after death?*
>
> *M1 (...) When the soul does good things without any bad thing, your soul should be purified. If you do bad things your soul has to be reborn.*
>
> *M2: We have to be reborn. Until you purify your soul you have to rebirth again and again, until you finish that off [Mod: So what will happen if a person commits suicide?]He will again reborn.*
>
> *Mod: So does it mean that he has done a bad thing [as stated by M1], that's why he has to reborn?*
>
> *M2: Yes, he has done a bad thing so he will be reborn. If he had done good things he will go to Heaven. When God wants, he will go to heaven. (...)*
>
> *M3: After suicide, he dies, that's it! (...)*
>
> *M4: In my family, it is our culture, if a person suicides he has to take rebirth in the same family again. He has to do what he has left undone. In the next birth he has to complete that [Mod: So he will have rebirth!] I'm drawing the line, this is not what I personally believe, it is my culture.[I think that] if a person dies by a normal death or by suicide, he will be buried or burnt, he will change into another form. For a few hundred years he will be carbon, then he will*

become a plant or tree. He has to take rebirth, everybody has to take rebirth but it doesn't have to be a living object. (...)

Mod: And you, what do you think?

M5: In my opinion, personally, they don't get the next birth because they don't complete their course, so God gives them relax.[Mod: Which kind of relax?]

M1: He won't be getting that rebirth again. God almighty will be putting them one day anywhere in the universe, any form, any shape. Could be that God is giving them relaxation for the time being and then the souls will be put back into some shape.

M2: God will give some punishment for committing suicide.

Mod: So is not very relaxed! (laughs)

M2: No, as a punishment. They will be roaming around. (...)

M6: Our life is from God. God has sent us on a mission.(...) He [person who suicides] will go to hell.

Some participants made comments on the effects of religious beliefs on suicide risk. In few instances, beliefs in an afterlife were seen as a deterrent against suicide: a participant reported that, when she felt depressed, she could not think about suicide because she would be punished and would go to Hell if she killed herself and another, later in the interview, stated that she would not kill herself because she would not get a funeral and the burial will not be in the family place, but in the common place. One participant believed that the fear of the unknown in afterlife would stop her but another argued that the unknown might be in some way more "appealing" than life for a suicidal person. Also another participant discarded the importance of beliefs in an afterlife for a suicidal person stating that, when something bad happens, the person stops believing in God. The next extract shows some of these beliefs (IN3F:288-296):

F1: 'Cause of the unknown, what will happen to us after we die, that will be [to stop me from killing myself].

Mod: So because you don't know what will happen after you die.

F2: You know! If we do well we go to heaven. You go to hell if you kill yourself. Killing yourself is forbidden by almost every religion. The prospect of the unknown, I mean, that wouldn't bother me very much. If you place yourself in the position to kill yourself, the unknown is probably an adventure. I mean, if your life is already awful.(...) what you don't know can't hurt you.

A participant expressed the belief that people suicide because they cannot fulfill an ambition, and after death the soul goes to another body and they can achieve what they wanted. This might suggest the existence of the belief among some youth that suicide offers another chance to live a more fulfilling life.

Australia: The majority of participants believed that there are no differences in what happens in the afterlife between young people who kill themselves and those who die by other means and that, whatever happens, if anything at all, is the same for everyone. A few participants also believed that, even if there was a difference, this would be based on the way the person has behaved and has treated people during his/her life rather than on the way they died. One participant reported that the loss of a friend through suicide brought her to this kind of belief, as shown in the example (AU2Mix:68-74):

F1: I used to...ehm...get really confused by that [afterlife for youth who suicide] because when I was 16 a friend of mine killed himself and I had, I was brought up Catholic and it was a big sin and my big thing was: "Gosh! What about if he's stuck in Hell right now because... just because he was sad and he did not want to be here anymore" and that really, it screwed with my head a bit and then I thought "No, that's stupid...I do not like the idea of any God that would do that sort of thing, and if you did ok and there was one act on one day that possibly they shouldn't have done but they shouldn't be judged on that for the whole afterlife

> *F2: I feel the same way as that and I don't understand how a God who loves everybody, a God who loves everybody can say: "No, I don't like you, I don't like you and you're all going to Hell because you didn't do the right thing" like, that's not a God who loves everybody yeah and... I don't understand*
>
> *Mod: So you do not understand but you think this may happen?*
>
> *F2: I don't anymore; I did think that when I was younger, I don't think of that now.*

Some other participants shared this latter disbelief in punishments, or rejected religious views on suicide and believed that everyone will be forgiven or redeemed. This belief was supported by one participant who added that suicide, besides being redeemed as any "evil" act, can even be an experience from which to learn for the next life (AU2Mix:104/114m): *"It seems likely that every action has a reaction, there's always a consequence of the action but I wouldn't say the consequence to a suicide is necessarily a bad consequence like going to Hell, it could be an incredible learning experience...you make mistakes during your life and you learn from them, I can't see why suicide will regress your soul after death (...) I think there's always redemption after an evil act; even somebody who's murdered a whole bunch of people can turn around and never redo what they did of course but steer them towards a more productive path".*

Conversely, in one group those participants who reported having a Christian belief commented that, if in religious books it was written that people who suicide go to Hell, less people would suicide, but later they argued that this would affect only people who are religious. They believed that the afterlife should depend on how people lived their lives.

One of the participants, who believed that there is no difference in the afterlife, commented that it would be nice to think that there was a difference "to make people work towards having a good life". Another participant thought that the age of death is predetermined, thus how a person dies does not matter because the person would have died anyway.

In some groups participants discussed that people who kill themselves want to escape this life for something better, or simply want to get out of this life so, whatever happens in the afterlife, it does not matter to them, because anything is a better option than living, for instance (AU3Mix:64-88):

> *F1: I think that, in any case, either dying of natural causes or dying by taking your own life, it's...um... it's the same sort of thing that happens [in afterlife] but it's, for people who commit suicide, it's something of a relief. Like, 'cause to commit suicide you have to have a fairly troubled soul and a fairly difficult existence and... um for people who sort of go through with that, with that act, then um where the soul goes is a better place than their sort of...then their life and I suppose what the large part of the motivation could be to commit suicide is that there's a sort of relief for the soul (...) is like calming for the soul (...)*
>
> *F2: Yeah, well, I don't know, I think what I said maybe sounded like I was saying people die so that they can get to a better place, like they intentionally kill themselves so that they can get to a better place, but I think in death people are often scared of it because there is some uncertainty, like, who knows if there is going to be a better place or a lack of what's already there or um you know it could even be somewhere worse, it's just uncertain and that's why people are sort of fearful of it [death]. But as with someone who O.D.s [overdoses] or something like that then if they are already depressed then their soul or their spirit is quite um, you know, troubled, it's in a state of um, you know, it's not at ease with its self that sort of thing. (...) It [death] is just an ending of trouble.*
>
> *Mod: Hmm all right! Anything else?*
>
> *M1: Ah, I just thought of something, sorry [laughs] (...), taking the point of view of maybe someone who is contemplating suicide um, they're not; they might not even be obsessed with the thought of the afterlife. It's just more about getting out of this life; it's not really thinking about the soul as such. The soul really isn't important, it's just, I think, it's more of a focus on the here*

> *and now and not so much of what is um eternal, so to speak. Um and maybe the soul...certainly to the person committing suicide, the soul might be completely irrelevant. [F1: Yeah. Even if..] Not necessarily a thought that comes to mind.*
>
> *F1: Even if the soul may go to a better place um as a person experiencing a life, you may not remember where the soul goes after, like you may not... upon death, your soul may go on but you won't be there experiencing it because you'll be dead, so um it doesn't really matter what goes on after. Its funny speaking so candidly about death [laughs]. Um so after you die, then, you're not there experiencing it so it doesn't matter what happens after. It's just um... yeah, like you were saying, what happens to the soul eternally isn't incredible relevant to a person who's contemplating suicide. So yeah, [F2: Yeah] possibly, unless they are religious fanatics or something like that...[laughs].*

In some instances, participants pointed out that in certain cases suicide might actually be due to religious reasons, such as it is for suicide-bombers or for some people who have the feeling that God has rejected them or that they have failed God.

In summary, the majority of Italian and, although fewer, Australian participants had a (non-structured) spiritual belief that there might be "something" after death but they reported not knowing what this might be. Some other Australian and fewer Italian participants indicated that they did not believe or did not still have an opinion about any kind of existence after death. Only a few Italian and slightly fewer Australian participants reported a religious concept of the afterlife, usually Catholic in the former and also Christian in the latter. Approximately half of the Indian sample reported religious beliefs on the afterlife, usually Hindu and, less often, Christian/Catholic. The other half of the sample generally did not believe in the afterlife, except for those few participants who believed that "something" remains after death.

In regard to the afterlife of youths who die by suicide and those who do not, the majority of Italian and Australian participants believed that there were no differences between the two and that whatever happens in afterlife was the same for everyone. Some participants, slightly more in Italy, believed that if there is any difference, this is based on the way the person lived their whole life rather than the way he/she died. Few others restated their lack of belief in an afterlife or that they did not know what might happen in the afterlife of anybody. Indian participants were divided into two main groups on this question: those (slightly more) who thought that youth who killed themselves have some sort of punishment (referring to Hindu or Christian beliefs) and others who believed that there was no difference. These latter usually thought that there was no soul or afterlife whereas few of them believed that the souls of youth who died by suicide would go to God anyway.

It is worth to note that, across countries, a minority of participants argued that people who kill themselves are not concerned about the afterlife but on ending their current life and troubles.

Apart from the discussions prompted by these two focus group questions, spiritual/religious concepts emerged also in other parts of the study. For instance, these where cited when discussing about reasons why participants would not suicide even if they encountered difficulties in their lives (*i.e.*, possible youth suicide deterrents). A few Italian participants cited religious concepts as protective against suicide, as a general faith or referring to God. Indians often cited religious concepts, usually expressed as the belief that life is God's and God has a plan for each person. This last concept could be linked to another theme that, with one exception in Italy, was mentioned only in India that is that we all have a destiny, a plan to fulfill. Religious beliefs were often cited also by Australians. In India God was mentioned more often as a deterrent than in Italy and Australia. Projects and things, such as hobbies, which give meaning to life were mentioned in each country among suicide deterrents, although more by Italian and Australian participants than Indians.

Finally, when asked whom they would talk to if they were considering killing themselves, whilst few Italians and Australians reported that they would talk to a priest or spiritual guide, more Indians stated that they would talk directly to God.

These study findings certainly raise more questions than answers. On the other hand, they show how the relationship between religion/spirituality and suicide is complex and needs greater attention and more in depth research, as argued in Colucci [29]. A follow-up study, where I explored the relationship between spiritual wellbeing and suicide with young college students attending a "spiritually-oriented" University/Ashram in India, is currently under submission and will shed more light on these important issues. For instance, the participants in this study indicated that their spiritual and religious beliefs are of great help to overcome their life's difficulties. When asked to give some examples of such help, they stated that these provide coping strategies (including religious and spiritual practices), give strength, stimulate positive feelings (*e.g.,* calm, peace, patience, determination), help to find meanings and provide with social support. Focus groups allowed for a more in depth exploration of how their spiritual/religious beliefs provide such help. Meaningful data on what is about religion/spirituality to protect some people from suicidal behavior (at least in a specific point in time), what might increase the risk and in which ways these protective/risk factors play a role are necessary if we want to improve our understanding of this important topic.

10. FUTURE DIRECTION

Birnbaum and Birnbaum [5] speculate that one of the reasons for the dearth of writing on the topic of spirituality and suicide may be related to the view that spirituality is necessarily and directly linked to religion. Miller and Thoresen [14] observe that, with rare exceptions, the available literature has measured religious rather than spiritual variables. The same criticism was made in the review by Colucci and Martin [28]. Also the Mental Health Foundation report [15] points out that, whilst there is recognition that there are differences between religion and spirituality, much of the research uses measures of religious practice as a proxy. But, as Swinton [3] affirms, the significant thing to bear in mind is that spirituality may well be significant to many people with mental health problems, even though they may not express an interest in or adherence to an established religious tradition. For instance, Webb [69] admits that a faith-based religious spirituality was not going to work for someone with a rationalistic and atheistic upbringing like his but that this form of sacred relationship with a religious God has been the key to the recovery of other suicidal patients.

Therefore, research should attempt to discover those aspects of life that give meaning to individuals that are beyond the traditional parameters of religion [15]. Consequently, the first suggestion for future direction in research is to focalize on the broader concept of spirituality. Research should address the personal and cultural ways of experiencing and expressing spirituality, such as art forms, meditation, spiritual rituals (for examples, pragya, of fire ceremony, in India) and mystical experiences. Researches should also address the knowledge of the biopsychocultural roots of that experience generally named religious experience [95]. There is sometimes the feeling that the current "scientific" understanding of suicide lacks highly relevant information on the lives, experiences and beliefs of suicidal individuals and this is, in Birnbaum and Birnbaum's [5] opinion, simply because it is not amenable to traditional, rational quantitative approaches.

One of the limits shown by quantitative studies of religion is that usually they are reductionist, simplistic and treat religion and spirituality as if they are unidimensional constructs, often assuming that these can be adequately measured by a single variable. In fact, one of the most frequent measures of religiosity consists in a question on church attendance, which may not be a reliable measure because of the complexity of this kind of constructs [96], (see [74] and [28] for a discussion on "measuring" spirituality). In the cross-cultural journals reviewed by Tarakeshwar *et al.* [85], the authors criticize that the religious dimension was assessed through a few global indicators (such as church affiliation, church attendance and prayer), which do not reflect the multidimensional nature of religion. One reason for the use of brief (generally single-item) indices is that, as also underlined by Hill and Pargament [24], religion and spirituality have often been included only as add-on variables in the context of other research agendas. Miller and Thoresen [14] are critical of operational definitions of spirituality that do not consider that spirituality, first of all, is not dichotomous (*i.e.,* it is not an attribute that is either present or absent in an individual) and cannot be defined as a single linear dimension (*e.g.*, something than one has more or less of). The Mental Health Foundation report [15] also indicates that one of the key shortcomings in mental health research is that: "(…) it relies exclusively on quantitative measures, which may not fully access the meaning spiritual activity has for the individual. Quantitative research tends to try and isolate the impact of one activity (*e.g.,* church attendance) upon another (*e.g.,* level of depression), which may not always capture the rich and complex interactions of other factors on any association found (p. 25)".

Swinton [3] is also very critical of the use of quantitative methods to study religion and spirituality and similarly points out:

"While they may be able to measure the frequency of an action or the commonality of proclaimed beliefs, they fail to take cognizance of the *meaning* (Italic in the original) that such thing have for people...To understand the possible benefits or otherwise of religion for a person's mental health, it is necessary to know what their religion means to them as individuals, how this is worked out in their lives and the ways they use it to understand and come to terms with their life experience" (p. 35).

Burkhardt [6] supports the opinion that spirituality lends itself more to qualitative measures, where subjectivity of response is valued. Qualitative research, I add, is the only way to access the deep and personal meanings (*i.e.*, the "what is it like?", "what does it mean to you?", "what is it about spirituality that…?" kind of questions), therefore, it is necessary to increase the use of qualitative methodology in the current research. More specifically, Daaleman, Cobb and Frey [55] found focus group discussions a well-suited method to investigate patient-reported spirituality. As suggested in the Mental Health Foundation report [15], to gain a fuller understanding of the link between spirituality and mental health/illness, researchers need to use a combination of methodologies that allow the complexities of the field to be explored. More in general, researchers (in this field as in any other) should ensure that the methodology and the methods employed are the most appropriate to answer the questions being addressed (*i.e.,* the method should reflect the same epistemology and "level of reality" of the research aims). Another limitation of research in this field underlined in the Mental Health Foundation report [15] is that the literature focuses on the effects of spirituality on mental health problems whereas few studies address the mechanism though which spirituality may promote good mental health and wellbeing in populations without those problems. From what written until now is evident that more and better research is needed in this direction.

A fundamental aspect of spirituality, meaning in life, needs to be addressed in more research on suicidal people (and not only) and more research is required to define which aspects of religiosity and spirituality are protective against suicide, because religious affiliation or simply attending church are not "necessary and sufficient" conditions to prevent suicidal behavior. In this regard, Whalley [42] sarcastically notes that "unless the suicides represent an entirely separate subgroup within the population, a great many of the people who killed themselves must have been active church members and most would at least have professed to believe in God" (p. 91). This supposition finds some support in Sorri and collaborators' study [54] where overt active religiosity was identified in a fifth of Finnish who killed themselves. This kind of evidence might confirm Allport's assertion (1950, in [24]) that it might be more important to ask "how" a person is religious rather than "whether" a person is religious. It would also be valuable to explore the meanings that people from diverse cultural groups, socio-economic background and life experiences attribute to religiousness and spirituality. There have been plenty of "professional" definitions of religion and spirituality but very little attention has been paid to the ways lay people define and interpret these terms [4]. Bearing in mind that differences in religious and spiritual beliefs, practices and affiliations are interwoven into other cultural features, as argued by Hill and Pargament [24], I strongly believe that it is of paramount importance that measures of religion/spirituality reflect greater sensitivity towards ethnocultural issues. For instance, as suggested by Miller and Thoresen [14], it must be considered that the magnitude and direction of the effect of spirituality/religiousness on health, may vary widely across ethnic groups that differ with regard to the cultural centrality of religion (and, I add, the spiritual dimension). The need to examine the ways in which culture influences religion's expression of the spiritual has been underlined by Eckersley [97] as well. Until this does not happen, we risk asking the wrong questions to our clients and research participants and offering them the wrong "solutions"/interpretations. And, above all, we need to learn to listen 'for understanding'.

Larson and Larson [38] also recommend more studies addressing religion/spirituality not only to understand better its importance as a coping strategy for mental health patients, but to clarify as well its less frequently found but clinically important harmful use [see 28]. I agree that the circumstances where spiritual/religious concerns (or beliefs) have a negative impact on mental health should also be explored (in the clinical and research settings).

In my opinion, it is also crucial to introduce spirituality routinely into prevention and intervention plans, given the importance it has for many people with (or without) mental health problems and, as recommended also by Miller and Thoresen [14], increase research on spiritually/religiously-based interventions. The importance of the spiritual dimension in healing for the suicide bereaved or survivors is another underestimated topic that needs greater investigation and understanding [98].

As D'Souza [2] points out: "Spiritual issues encompass what is most meaningful and central in human existence. In time of crisis, illness and transition, spiritual issues are likely to come to the fore of human awareness for both patients and professionals. (...) All health care professionals need to include the spiritual dimension in assessment and treatment of patients" (p. 46). And this may be particularly important in suicidal patients, where topics of meanings and purpose in life, sense of connection and coherence, systems of values and beliefs are all often central issues in their suffering.

CONCLUSIONS

In the "spirituality revolution" that is taking place during the post-modern era in Western societies, also found in Eastern countries [99], any branch dealing with mental health (Suicidololy included) is called to recognize people's quest for meaning, that search for the sacred, for something higher; that request to fill that spiritual vacuum left by the "illuministic" and secular society. Spiritual and religious concerns and needs must be examined further and more in depth in suicide research in order to understand their role as protective and/or risk factors for suicidal behavior, and to make use of the potential of spirituality/religiosity in suicide prevention strategies. Two factors raise my hopes that these aims may be reached in the near future. First of all, Dein [4] reports an increasing interest in religion among psychiatrists and psychologist (which I expect will soon spread also to non-religious/theological spirituality). Secondly, the fact that "religious and spiritual problem" has been added as an Axis I category in DSM-IV under "Other conditions that may be a focus of clinical attention", shows that clinicians are more aware of the frequent occurrence of religious and spiritual issues in the clinical practice[21]. It also acknowledges the importance of religion and spirituality in patient's lives [4]. The next move should be to ensure we do not pathologize religiosity and spirituality and only pay attention to these constructs when they became part of a psychiatric problem. It would be preferable to add religiosity and spirituality to a routine assessment, and to explore them in therapy with clients, particularly those for whom meaning of life and death are at the core of their suffering, as it is the case for many suicidal people.

Webb [69] argues that "suicidology cannot continue to turn a blind eye to the central role that spirituality often plays in the experience of and recovery from suicidality" (p. 5). I believe that some small steps have been made and that contributions like his, this manuscript and others' can help to remind Suicidologists, other scholars, professionals in mental health and policy makers that there is more than body and mind in everyone of us and that that "more" needs to be heard, nurtured and (re)considered in research, clinical practice and daily life.

The refuge in the transcendence, in the Nirvana,

in the marketing of the suspended states of conscience,

the dynamic of letting oneself disappear in the imagination in order to survive,

are ways to find a worldly niche of salvation from suffering the facts of the world.

[100]

---

[21] This is also probably due to the fact that, as reported by the Mental Health Foundation [15], service users, survivors and carers are adding their voices to the argument that mental health and spirituality are intrinsically linked.

ACKNOWLEDGEMENTS

I would like to thank Ass/Prof. David Tacey (La Trobe University, Melbourne) and Dr David Webb for references and discussions on post-modern spirituality, and Prof. Goffredo Bartocci (World Association of Cultural Psychiatry) and Dr. Simon Dein (UCL) for having stimulated and kept alive my interest in this area. My gratitude goes also to Ass/Prof. Harry Minas and Dr. Manjula O'Connor, (Centre for International Mental Health, The University of Melbourne) as well as Prof. Graham Martin (The University of Queensland) for having supported my passion for the study of spirituality and suicide.

Sections of this chapter are from Colucci, E. [74], Recognizing spirituality in the assessment and prevention of suicidal behavior. World Cultural Psychiatry Research Review (WCPRR), Special issue: Suicide and Culture, Vol. 3 (2); pp. 77-95, (http://www.wcprr.org/index-03_02.htm). Permission of reproduction granted by the editor.

REFERENCES

[1] Bathgate D. Psychiatry, religion and cognitive science. Aust N Z J Psychiatry 2003; 37:277-85.

[2] D'Souza R. Do patients expect psychiatrists to be interested in spiritual issues? Australas Psychiatry 2002 10:44-7.

[3] Swinton J. Spirituality and mental health care: Rediscovering a 'forgotten' dimension. London: J Kingsley Publishers, 2001.

[4] Dein S. Spirituality, psychiatry and participation: A cultural analysis. Transcult Psychiatry 2005; 42: 526-44.

[5] Birnbaum L, Birnbaum A. In search of inner wisdom: Guided mindfulness meditation in the context of suicide. ScientificWorldJournal 2004; 4:216-27.

[6] Burkhardt MA. Spirituality: An analysis of the concept. Holist Nurs Pract 1989; 3:69-77.

[7] Doka KJ, Morgan JD. Death and spirituality. Amityville, New York: Baywood Pub Co, 1993.

[8] Aldridge D. Spirituality, healing and medicine. London: Jessica Kingsley Publishers, 2000.

[9] Fetzer Institute/National Institute on Aging Working Group. Multidimensional measurement of religiousness/spirituality for use in health research [Retrieved 29 July 2003. Available from: http://www.fetzer.org/Resources/resources_ multidimens. htm], 1999.

[10] Hay MW. Principles in building spiritual assessment tools. Am J Hosp Care 1989; 6:25-31.

[11] Oldnall A. A critical analysis of nursing: Meeting the spiritual needs of patients. J Adv Nurs 1996; 23:138-44.

[12] Sullivan WP. "It helps me to be a whole person": The role of spirituality among the mentally challenged. Psychosoc Rehab J 1993; 16:125-34.

[13] Ramsey JL, Blieszner R. Transcending a lifetime of losses: The importance of spirituality in old age. In Harvey JH, Miller ED, Eds. Loss and trauma: General and close relationship perspectives. New York, US: Brunner-Routledge, 2000; pp. 225-36.

[14] Miller WR, Thoresen CE. Spirituality, religion, and health: An emerging research field. Am Psychol 2003; 58:24-35.

[15] Mental Health Foundation (MHF). The impact of spirituality on mental health. London: MHF, 2006.

[16] Colucci E, Watanabe N (submitted). The conceptualization of spirituality in Japan: An exploratory study using drawings.

[17] Cohen C, Wheeler S, Scheier D. Walking a fine line: Physician inquiries into patients'religious and spiritual beliefs. Hastings Centre Rep 2001; 31:29-9.

[18] Bartocci G. Transcendence techniques and psychobiological mechanisms underlying religious experience. Ment Health Relig Cult 2004; 7:171-81.

[19] Weaver AJ, Samford JA, Morgan VJ, Lichton AI, Larson DB, Garbarino J. Research on religious variables in five major adolescent research journals: 1992 to 1996. J Nerv Ment Dis 2000; 188:36-44.

[20] Kehoe NC, Gutheil TG. Neglect of religious issues in scale-based assessment of suicidal patients. Hosp Community Psychiatry 1994; 45:366-9.

[21] Webb D. Bridging the spirituality gap. Aust J Adv Ment Health 2005; 4:1-9.

[22] Ellison CW. Spiritual well-being: Conceptualization and measurement. J Psychol Theol 1983; 11(4):330-40.

[23] Bhugra D. Osbourne TR. Spirituality and Psychiatry. Indian J Psychiatry 2004; 46:5-6.

[24] Hill PC, Pargament KI. Advances in the conceptualization and measurement of religion and spirituality: Implications for physical and mental health research. Am Psychol 2003; 58:64-74.

[25] Shafranske EP, Malony HN. Clinical psychologists' religious and spiritual orientations and their practice of psychotherapy. Psychotherapy: Theory, Research, Practice, Training 1990; 27:72-8.
[26] Baetz M, Larson DB, Marcoux G, *et al.* Religious psychiatry: The Canadian experience. J Nerv Ment Dis 2002; 190(8):557-9.
[27] King DE, Sobal J, Haggerty J 3rd, *et al.* Experiences and attitudes about faith healing among family physicians. J Fam Pract 1992; 35:158-62.
[28] Colucci E, Martin G. Religion and spirituality along the suicidal path. Suicide Life Threat Behav 2008; 38(2):229-44.
[29] Colucci E. Cultural issues in suicide risk assessment. In: Kumar U, Mandal MK, Eds. Suicidal behavior: Assessment of people-at-risk. New Delhi: SAGE. 2009; pp. 107-35.
[30] Koenig HG. Religion, spirituality, and medicine: Application to clinical practice. JAMA 2000; 284:1708.
[31] Marsella AJ. In search of meaning. Some thoughts on belief, doubt, and wellbeing. Int J Transpersonal Stud 1999; 18:41-52.
[32] Oldnall AS. On the absence of spirituality in nursing theories and models. J Adv Nurs 1995 21:417-418.
[33] Underwood LG, Teresi JA. The Daily Spiritual Experience Scale: Development, theoretical description, reliability, exploratory factor analysis, and preliminary construct validity using health-related data. Ann Behav Med 2002; 24:22-33.
[34] King, DE, Bushwick B. Beliefs and attitudes of hospital inpatients about faith healing and prayer. J Fam Pract 1994; 39(4):349-52.
[35] Exline JJ, Yali AM, Sanderson WC. Guilt, discord, and alienation: The role of religious strain in depression and suicidality. J Clin Psychol 2000; 56:1481-96.
[36] Chiu L, Ganesan S, Clark N *et al.* Spirituality and treatment choices by South and East Asian women with serious mental illness. Transcult Psychiatry 2005; 42:630-56.
[37] Johnson CV, Hayes JA. Troubled spirits: Prevalence and predictors of religious and spiritual concerns among university students and counseling center clients. J Couns Psychol 2003 50:409-19.
[38] Larson DB, Larson SS. Spirituality's potential relevance to physical and emotional health: A brief review of quantitative research. J Psychol Theol 2003 31:37-51.
[39] Larson DB, Sherrill KA, Lyons JS, *et al.* Associations between dimensions of religious commitment and mental health reported in the American Journal of Psychiatry and Archives of General Psychiatry: 1978-1989. Am J Psychiatry 1992; 149:557-9.
[40] Gartner J, Larson DB, Allen GD. Religious commitment and mental health: A review of the empirical literature. J Psychol Theol 1991;19:6-25.
[41] Payne IR, Bergin AE, Bielema KA, *et al.* Review of religion and mental health: Prevention and the enhancement of psychosocial functioning. Prev Hum Serv 1991; 9:11-40.
[42] Whalley EA. Religion and suicide. Rev Relig Res 1964; 5:91-110.
[43] Thakker J, Durrant R, Schumaker JF, *et al.* Religiosity and mental health among Indian university students. Indian J Clin Psychol 1999; 26(1):35-40.
[44] Greening L, Stoppelbein L. Religiosity, attributional style, and social support as psychosocial buffers for African American and White adolescents' perceived risk for suicide. Suicide Life Threat Behav 2002; 32:404-17.
[45] Nonnemaker JM, McNeely CA, Blum RW. Public and private domains of religiosity and adolescent health risk behaviors: Evidence from the national longitudinal study of adolescent health. Soc Sci Med 2003; 57:2049-54.
[46] Colucci E. The cultural meaning of suicide: A comparison between Italian, Indian and Australian students. Unpublished doctoral dissertation. Australia: The University of Queensland, 2008.
[47] Lester D, Francis LJ. Is religiosity related to suicidal ideation after personality and mood are taken into account? Pers Individ Dif 1993; 15:591-2.
[48] Dervic K, Oquendo M, Grunebaum MF, *et al.* Religious affiliation and suicide attempt. Am J Psychiatry 2004; 161:2303-8.
[49] Loewenthal KM, MacLeod AK, Cook S, *et al.* The suicide beliefs of Jews and Protestants in the UK: How do they differ? Isr J Psychiatry Relat Sci 2003; 40:174-81.
[50] Grossoehme DH, Springer LS. Images of God used by self-injurious burn patients. Burns 1999; 25:443-8.
[51] Breault KD, Barkey K. A comparative analysis of Durkheim's theory of egoistic suicide. Sociol Q 1982; 23:321-31.
[52] Faupel CE, Kowalski GS, Starr PD. Sociology's one law: Religion and suicide in the urban context. J Sci Study Relig 1987; 26:523-34.
[53] Wasserman I, Stack S. The effect of religion on suicide: An analysis of cultural context. Omega (Westport) 1993; 27:295-305.

[54] Sorri H, Henriksson M, Lonnqvist J. Religiosity and suicide: Findings from a nationwide psychological autopsy study. Crisis 1996; 17:123-7.

[55] Daaleman TP, Cobb AK, Frey BB. Spirituality and well-being: An exploratory study of the patient perspective. Soc Sci Med 2001; 53:1503-11.

[56] Dyson J, Cobb M, Forman D. The meaning of spirituality: A literature review. J Adv Nurs 1997; 26:1183-8.

[57] Garroutte EM, Goldberg J, Beals J, Herrell R, Manson SM. Spirituality and attempted suicide among American Indians. Soc Sci Med 2003; 56:1571-9.

[58] Wong PT. Spirituality, meaning, and successful aging. In: Wong PT, Prem SF, Eds. The human quest for meaning. A handbook of psychological research and clinical applications. Mahwah, NJ, USA: Lawrence Erlbaum Associates. 1998; pp. 359-94.

[59] Reker GT. Logotheory and logotherapy: Challenges, opportunities, and some empirical findings. International Forum for Logotherapy 1994; 17(1):47-55.

[60] Petersen LR, Roy A. Religiosity, anxiety, and meaning and purpose: Religion's consequences for psychological wellbeing. Rev Relig Res 1985; 27:49-62.

[61] Korotkov D. The sense of coherence: Making sense out of chaos. In: Wong PT, Prem SF, Eds. The human quest for meaning. A handbook of psychological research and clinical applications. Mahwah, New Jersey: Lawrence Erlbaum Associates. 1998; pp. 51-70.

[62] Wong PT. Meaning-centered counseling. In: Wong PT, Prem SF, Eds. The human quest for meaning. A handbook of psychological research and clinical applications. Mahwah, NJ, USA: Lawrence Erlbaum Associates. 1998b; pp. 395-435.

[63] Thompson SC, Janigian AS. Life schemes: A framework for understanding the search for meaning. J Soc Clin Psychol 1988; 7:260-80.

[64] Frankl VE. Man's search for meaning: An introduction to logotherapy. Oxford, England: Washington Square Press, 1963.

[65] Frankl VE. What is meant by meaning? J Existent 1966; 7:21-8.

[66] Edwards MJ, Holden RR. Coping, meaning in life, and suicidal manifestations: Examining gender differences. J Clin Psychol 2001; 57:1517-34.

[67] Moore SL. A phenomenological study of meaning in life in suicidal older adults. Arch Psychiatr Nurs 1997 11:29-36.

[68] Tacey D. Spiritual perspectives on suicidal impulses in young adults. In: Cox RH, Ervin-Cox B, Hoffman L, Eds. Spirituality and psychological health. Colorado Springs, CO, US: Colorado School of Psychology Press. 2005; pp. 107-28.

[69] Webb D. Self, soul and spirit-Suicidology's blind spots? New Paradigm 2003; 4:23.

[70] Ebersole P. Types and depth of written life meanings. In: Wong PT, Prem SF, Eds. The human quest for meaning. A handbook of psychological research and clinical applications. Mahwah, New Jersey, USA: Lawrence Erlbaum Associates. 1998; pp. 237-59.

[71] Harlow LL, Newcomb MD, Bentler PM. Depression, self-derogation, substance use, and suicide ideation: Lack of purpose in life as a mediational factor. J Clin Psychol 1986; 42:5-21.

[72] Lester D, Badro S. Depression, suicidal preoccupation and purpose in life in a subclinical population. Pers Individ Dif 1992; 13:75-6.

[73] Orbach I, Mikulincer M, Gilboa-Schechtman E, *et al.* Mental pain and its relationship to suicidality and life meaning. Suicide Life Threat Behav 2003; 33:231-41

[74] Colucci E. Recognizing spirituality in the assessment and prevention of suicidal behavior. WCPRR. Special issue: Suicide and Culture 2008b 3(2):77-95.

[75] Foster T. Suicide note themes and suicide prevention. Int J Psychiatry Med 2003; 33:323-31.

[76] Rogers JM, Bromley JK, McNally CJ, *et al.* Content analysis of suicide notes as a test of the motivational component of the Existential-Constructivist model of suicide. J Couns Dev 2007; 85:182-8.

[77] Lester D. Suicide as a search for spirituality. Am J Pastor Counsel 1998; 1:41-7.

[78] Fournier RR. Spirituality as a resource for suicide prevention: A response to a fellow suicidologist. Am J Pastor Counsel 1999; 2:49-74.

[79] Currier JM, Holland JM, Neimeyer RA. Sense-Making, Grief, and the Experience of Violent Loss: Toward a Mediational Model. Death Stud 2006; 30:403-28.

[80] D'Souza RF, Rodrigo A. Spiritually-augmented cognitive behavioral therapy. Australas Psychiatry 2004;12:148-52.

[81] Sappington AA, Bryant J, Oden C. An experimental investigation of Victor Frankl's theory of meaningfulness in life. The International Forum for Logotherapy 1990; 13:125-30.

[82] Ryff CD, Singer B. The role of purpose in life and personal growth in positive human health. In: Wong PT, Prem SF, Eds. The human quest for meaning. A handbook of psychological research and clinical applications. Mahwah, NJ, USA: Lawrence Erlbaum Associates. 1998; pp. 213-235.
[83] Colucci E. "Focus groups can be fun": The use of activity-oriented questions in focus group discussions. Qualitat Health J 2007; 17(10):1422–33.
[84] Colucci E. On the use of focus groups in cross-cultural research. In: Liamputtong P Ed. Doing cross-cultural research: Ethical and methodological considerations. Dordrecht, The Netherlands: Springer. 2008; pp. 233-52.
[85] Tarakeshwar N, Stanton J, Pargament KI. Religion: An overlooked dimension in cross-cultural psychology. J Cross Cult Psychol 2003; 34(4):377-94.
[86] Colucci E, Martin G. Ethnocultural aspects of suicide in young people: A systematic literature review. Part 2: Risk factors, precipitating agents, and attitudes toward suicide. Suicide Life Threat Behav 2007; 37(2):222-37.
[87] Durkheim E. Il suicidio, Studio Italiano di Suicidologia (Scramaglia R, Trans.). Milan: BUR, 1997/1897.
[88] Whitla MME. Brief candles: Youth suicide in Australia and Italy. Unpublished PhD Thesis. Melbourne, Australia: The University of Melbourne, 2005.
[89] Calandra C, Gambitta C, Paci C, *et al.* L'influenza della religione cattolica sull'ideazione suicidaria degli adolescenti. Giornale Italiano di Suicidologia, 1993; (suppl 1): 115-20.
[90] Colucci E. Comportamento suicidario in adolescenza: Risultati del monitoraggio del WHO Collaborative Centre for Training and Research in Suicide Prevention di Padova; 1989-1999 [Suicidal behavior in adolescence: Monitoring results of the WHO Collaborative Centre for Training and Research in Suicide Prevention of Padua; 1989-1999]. Unpublished Honours Thesis. Padua, Italy: University of Padua, 2000.
[91] Schweitzer R, Klayich M, McLean J. Suicidal ideation and behaviors among university students in Australia. Aust N Z J Psychiatry 1995; 29:473-9.
[92] Pescosolido BA, Georgianna S. Durkheim, suicide, and religion: Toward a network theory of suicide. Am Soc Rev 1989; 54:33-8.
[93] Pescosolido BA. The social context of religious integration and suicide: Pursuing the network explanation. Sociol Q 1990; 31: 337-57.
[94] Leach MM, Cultural diversity and suicide. Binghamton, NY: The Haworth Press, 2006.
[95] Bartocci G, Dein S. Detachment: Gateway to the world of spirituality. Transcult Psychiatry 2005; 42:545-69.
[96] Hunsberger B. Religion, age, life satisfaction, and perceived sources of religiousness: A study of older persons. J Gerontol 1985; 40:615-20.
[97] Eckerseley R. Culture, Spirituality, religion and health: looking at the big picture. MJA 2007; 186:54-6.
[98] Gee T. Honouring the Spiritual Dimension for Survivors: The Development of a Hocokah or Healing Circle. Unpublished paper. International Association for Suicide Prevention. Uruguay, 2009.
[99] Tacey D. Rising waters of the spirit. The view from secular society. Studies in Spirituality 2003; 13:11-30.
[100] Bartocci G, Eligi A. L'antinomie entre thaumaturgie religieuse et thérapies médicales: le cas « Catholicisme et Psychiatrie » en Italie. L'Evolution Psichiatrique 2008; 73:53-67.
[101] Hillman J. Suicide and the soul. II ed. Dallas, Texas: Spring Publications, 1976.
[102] Orbach I. Existentialism and suicide. In: Tomer A, Eltason GT, Wong PTP, Eds. Existentialism and spiritual issues in death attitudes. Mahwah, NJ, USA: Lawrence Erlbaum Associates. 2007.
[103] Hill PC, Hood RW, Eds. Measures of religiosity. Birmingham, Alabama: Religious Education Press, 1999.

CHAPTER 7

Risk Factors for Suicide in Prisons

Maurizio Pompili[1,2,*], David Lester[3], Paolo Girardi[1] and Christine Tartaro[3]

[1]Department of Neurosciences, Mental Health and Sensory Functions, Suicide Prevention Center, Sant'Andrea Hospital, Sapienza University of Rome, Italy; [2]McLean Hospital - Harvard Medical School, USA and [3]The Richard Stockton College of New Jersey, Pomona, NJ, USA

Abstract: The present chapter reviews research on suicide in prisons and jails. The characteristics of prisoners committing suicide are described, the role of screening discussed, and the need for adequate training and standards for care to be implemented noted.

Keywords: Suicide, prisons, jails, screening, assessment, standards of care.

1. INTRODUCTION

Recent years have seen a surge of interest and concern about the deaths from suicide of those incarcerated in jails and prisons, a concern prompted in part by the lawsuits brought and won by relatives of defendants and convicts who have committed suicide while in custody. Despite this concern, suicide rates have not fallen appreciably among prisoners. Indeed, the suicide rate rose in British prisons from 74 per 100,000 per year in 1988 to 126 in 1998 [1] and has continued to rise since then [2].

Preventing suicide in jails and prisons requires a multifaceted approach involving establishing institutional policies and procedures, staff training, screening of prisoners, providing a safe environment free from ways of committing suicide, adequate supervision while prisoners are on suicide watch, and the availability of trained staff to assess the suicide risk of prisoners and provide adequate treatment. The present chapter will focus on screening and assessment.

2. WHO ARE THE PRISONERS?

The inmates of prisons, jails and police lock-ups are those individuals in society whose lives are in disarray. They frequently have psychiatric disorders, a history of drug and alcohol abuse, and medical conditions such as AIDS, all risk factors for suicide [3]. Marcus and Alcabes [4] found that 52% of jail suicides in their American city had a major psychiatric disorder, 73% were referred for a psychiatric evaluation while in jail, and 62% had prior suicidal behavior. In Canadian federal penitentiaries, Green, *et al.* [5] found that 44% of the suicides had previous psychiatric hospitalizations, 74% prior suicide attempts (of which half took place in prison), two-thirds had abused alcohol and 54% had abused drugs.

The risk of suicide in custody is made even greater by the impact of imprisonment itself. Entering custody often causes feelings of despair and frustration [6], and many inmates are under the influence of alcohol and drugs at the time of arrest and so must undergo withdrawal. Offenders lose contact with family and friends, face the loss of their jobs and a possible long-term incarceration, and may feel that they have lost control over their lives. Imprisonment may also mean the daily threat of assault and rape by other inmates, brutality at the hands of the guards, and emotional and intellectual deterioration resulting from incarceration in a stimulus-impoverished environment.

3. THE INCIDENCE OF SUICIDE

Suicide rates in custody are often high. Scotland reported a suicide rate of 129 in 1992-1993 [7], Greece a

***Address correspondence to Maurizio Pompili:** Department of Neurosciences, Mental Health and Sensory Functions, Suicide Prevention Center, Sant'Andrea Hospital, Sapienza University of Rome, Italy; E-mail: maurizio.pompili@uniroma1.it

Maurizio Pompili (Ed)

rate of 112 per 100,000 in 1977-1996 [8], Italy a rate of 112 in 1997 [9], and Canada a rate of 87 in 1971-1995 [10]. The average suicide rate for sentenced offenders in Austria between 1975 and 1997 was 81 per 100,000 inmates, and the average rate for prisoners on remand was 236 [11]. Rates in the general population rarely reach these levels.

Researchers have identified particular institutional settings that result in high suicide rates. Lester and Tartaro [12] calculated a suicide rate of 113 on the death rows in the United States from 1976 to 1999. A high suicide rate of 232 per 100,000 residents has been reported at an American state institution for the criminally insane [13]. Flaherty [14] found that juveniles had a suicide rate of 1,578 when placed in adult lock-ups (in police stations), 641 when placed in adult jails, but only 34 when placed in juvenile detention centers. Clearly juveniles should not be placed in custody in adult facilities.

4. WHO COMMITS SUICIDE?

Many investigators have described small samples of inmates who have committed suicide. For example, the typical suicide in American police lock-ups and jails occurs soon after booking (within the first three hours) and uses hanging in a poorly-supervised, isolation cell. The victim is usually a white male, under the age of 22, arrested for a relatively minor offense, often intoxicated, belligerent and confrontational, with no criminal record [15].

The profile for sentenced prisoners is less well-described and varies somewhat from prison to prison. In a study of the Maryland state prison system, the typical suicide victim was black, aged 25-34, sentenced for crimes against people, sentenced to more than eight years, in a maximum security institution, after serving about four years [16]. All of these prisoners had been tried, convicted and sentenced. On the other hand, in England, Shaw, *et al.* [17] reported that the modal suicide was male, white, and single, in for theft/burglary/robbery and on remand. Fifty-seven percent showed psychiatric symptoms on admission.

Descriptions of the modal or average prisoner suicide are not helpful, since the profile often resembles the modal prisoner, suicidal or not. What are required are comparisons of those inmates who commit suicide with those who do not. For example, Winter [18] found that the inmate suicide in an American jail in the Midwest was more often white, male, with prior drug use, alcohol abuse and suicide attempts, receiving psychiatric treatment, and in jail for a violent charge against others as compared to inmates who did not kill themselves.

Dissemination of the profile of the typical suicidal inmate to correctional staff and administrators sometimes leads them to assume, for example, that only single white males in their early twenties, in the first few hours of incarceration in a jail after committing a minor offense are at risk for suicide. Thus, they ignore other inmates at risk for suicide. Profiles are merely guidelines; exceptions often occur. A focus on circumstances that bring about the onset of a suicidal crisis can also be useful. For example, Blaauw, Winkel, and Kerkhof [19] found a significant relationship between being a victim of bullying while incarcerated and suicide risk. Other stressful situations include problems with other inmates, problems with staff, receipt of bad news from home, or receipt of bad news from a lawyer or judge.

5. HOW, WHEN AND WHERE INMATES COMMIT SUICIDE

In police lock-ups and jails, suicide frequently occurs shortly after initial incarceration, and hanging (a generic term for hanging, suffocation, self-suspension and strangulation) is the primary method for suicide available. Over 90% of inmates in jails who commit suicide use hanging [20]. Suicides in police lock-ups tend to involve the victim's clothing, while those in jails tend to use their bedding. Suicidal inmates in prison have the opportunity to accumulate more possessions, and cutting and jumping are more common as method for suicide than in jails, but hanging is again used most often for fatal suicidal acts [20].

In jails, it has been reported that 27% of suicides occur within three hours after admission, and over 50% within the first 24 hours [21]. In prisons, the time-frame is quite different. White and Schimmel [22] found that the average time between admission after sentencing and suicide was about five years. The most common stressors precipitating the suicides were marital or relationship problems, such as the spouse divorcing the inmate, and also concerns about personal safety in the prison.

A common method for dealing with suicidal inmates is to isolate them in a safe cell. However, isolating inmates also means that there is no cellmate to notice and halt any suicide attempts, and it may increase the inmate's sense of despair [23]. Over two-thirds of incarcerated suicide victims kill themselves while they are housed by themselves [20].

6. SCREENING FOR THE SUICIDAL INMATE

As mentioned above, each country or region (and even each institution) should develop a profile of the inmate suicide based on a comparison of those who have completed suicide in the institution(s) compared to those who did not. This will provide some simple demographic and background factors that predict suicide in those institutions. In addition, it is generally found that the psychological and psychiatric predictors of suicide in the general population are applicable to inmates, including depression, hopelessness, stressful life events and past suicidal behavior.

For new inmates to a facility, especially to police lock-ups and jails, an interview should inquire about the inmate's emotional state and include questions about depression and suicidality [24]. Questioning about drug and alcohol use, psychiatric symptoms, both past and present, and any history of psychiatric treatment or drug rehabilitation should also be mandatory. Checking for scars on wrists and the neck (evidence of past suicide attempts) is also a good idea. Hayes [25] listed some of the standard cues known to suicidologists that suggest an increased risk of suicide: changes in appetite, lethargy, expression of strong guilt over the offenses, severe agitation or aggressiveness, changes in mood or behavior, giving away possessions, having unrealistic expectations about the future, and increased difficulty in relating to others. Suicide screeners and other jail staff members should consider these cues to be warning signs of a potential suicide attempt. Excellent examples of screening instruments, together with data on their efficacy, can be found in McCleave and Latham [26] and Blaauw, Kerkhof, Winkel and Sheridan [27] (who identified 95% of the suicides in Dutch prisons retrospectively using their instrument). As experience with the instruments used to assess suicidality is accumulated, institutions can begin to computerize the data and explore the usefulness of particular measures for their institution with its unique population of inmates.

It is critical that such an evaluation is conducted before the inmate is placed in a cell - on intake, booking or admission. Cases of suicide have been reported where the inmate was placed in a cell, and the evaluation scheduled to be conducted later. Evaluation of every inmate should also take place on a regular schedule and at times of acute stress (such as a return from a court appearance or bad news from home). Furthermore, when an inmate is transferred from one institution to another, the prior institutional staff should be asked about the inmate's emotional state, behavior and suicidality in the former institution.

Good evaluation requires good communication between the staff members conducting the evaluation and the inmate. Thus, the officers in charge of maintaining discipline may not always be the best people to conduct evaluations. Nevertheless, they are the staff members who have the most contact with inmates. The custodial staff can be trained to recognize the clues of impending suicidal behavior, such as the kinds of suicidal communications that potential suicides make. For example, the potential suicide may not simply communicate an intention to kill himself, but merely express hopelessness about the future or give away possessions. Thus, all of the staff members involved with the inmates must be trained in suicide prevention and become convinced of the necessity of passing on information about suicidal cues to other staff members. It is also important that screening take into account cultural differences. For example, Native Americans are less open than other inmates, especially if the interviewer is in uniform, white and a stranger, if the process is rushed and not in a private setting, and if the questions are intrusive [28].

Even if reliable and valid screening instruments are used to evaluate suicide potential, and even if a statistically sound profile of the suicidal inmate is developed for the correctional facility, there will always be false negatives, that is, suicidal inmates who are not identified. More problematic for the staff is that there will also be a large number of false positives, that is, inmates who are judged to be suicidal but who are not. This is unavoidable, but it is no excuse for not screening for suicidal risk. What is unacceptable is failure to adequately screen. Dooley [29] found that 39% of suicide in English prisons had received a psychiatric review in the prior week, while Joukamaa [30] found that 51% of suicides in Finnish prisons had visited the prison doctor in the prior week. Clearly, there were opportunities to screen and assess these individuals.

7. STANDARDS

Several organizations, including the American Medical Association, the National Commission on Accreditation for Law Enforcement, the American Correctional Association (ACA), and the National Commission on Correctional Health Case (NCCHC) have proposed standards relating to the emergency response to suicide attempts in correctional institutions. The NCCHC has the most comprehensive set of standards pertaining to inmate suicide [31]. The standards address staff training, intake screening/assessment, and housing, levels of supervision, intervention and administrative review. While correctional standards are not legally binding, American courts have ruled that the standards serve as guidelines in assessing what is reasonable conduct on the part of corrections agencies.

CONCLUSIONS

Although several commentators on suicide prevention in jails and prisons are skeptical about suicide risk assessment [32], and although research on the problem is typically at a very rudimentary level, it would be foolish to eschew some strategies as ineffective before they have been adequately tested. Researchers need to become more involved with custodial institutions in order to improve the adequacy of suicide risk assessment and to evaluate its effectiveness.

Policy makers also need to address several important issues. As more and more psychiatrically disturbed individuals are admitted to jails and prisons in some countries, as a result of the trends toward de-institutionalizing psychiatric patients and the greater availability of psychiatric medications which permit psychiatric patients to be released into the community, more and more prisoners are going to be psychiatrically disturbed and, therefore, suicidal. The presence of drug and alcohol addicted prisoners also increases the likelihood of suicidal inmates. Keeping inmates in prison is expensive, and policy makers should consider alternatives to incarceration for some offenders (such as sentencing offenders to drug treatment instead of jail and providing psychiatric care in halfway houses for some non-dangerous offenders).

REFERENCES

[1] Ashraf H. Suicides in the UK prisons increase sin the past 10 years. Lancet 1999;354: 404.

[2] Fazel S, Benning R, Danes, J. Suicide in male prisoners in England Wales, 1978-2003. Lancet 2005;366: 1301-1302.

[3] Lester, D. Why people kill themselves, 4th Edition. Springfield, IL: Charles Thomas; 2000.

[4] Marcus P, Alcabes P. Characteristics of suicides by inmates in an urban jail. Hosp Community Psychiatry 1993; 44: 256-261.

[5] Green C, Andre G, Kendall K, Looman T, Polvi N. A study of 133 suicides among Canadian federal prisoners. Forum on Corrections research, 1992; 4: 17-19.

[6] Hayes LM, Rowan JR. National study of jail suicides. Alexandria, VA: National Center on Institutions and Alternatives; 1988.

[7] Bogue J, Power K. Suicide in Scottish prisons, 1976-1993. Am J Forensic Psychiatry 1995; 6: 527-540.

[8] Spinellis CD, Themeli O. Suicide in Greek prisons: 1977 to 1996. Crisis 1997; 18:152–156.

[9] Tatarelli R, Mancinelli I, Taggi F, Polidori G. Suicide in Italian prisons in 1996 and 1997. J Offender Ther Comp Criminol 1999; 43: 438-447.

[10] Laishes S. Inmate suicides in the correctional service of Canada. Crisis 1997; 18: 157-162.

[11] Fruewald S, Frottier P, Eher R, Gutierrez, K, & Ritter, K. Prison suicides in Austria, 1975-1977. Suicide Life Threat Behav 2000; 30: 360-369.

[12] Lester D, Tartaro C. Suicide on death row. J Forensic Sci 2002; 47: 1108-1111.

[13] Haycock J. Double jeopardy. Suicide Life Threat Behav1993; 23: 130-138.

[14] Flaherty MG. The national incidence of juvenile suicide in adult jails and juvenile detention centers. Suicide Life Threat Behav 1983; 13: 85-94.

[15] Lester D, Danto B. Suicide behind bars. Philadelphia: Charles Press; 1993.

[16] Salive ME Smith GS, Brewer TF. Suicide mortality in the Maryland state prison system, 1979 through 1987. JAMA 1989; 262: 365-369.

[17] Shaw J, Baker D, Hunt IM, Moloney A, Appleby, L. Suicide by prisoners. Br J Psychiatry 2004; 184: 263-267.

[18] Winter MM. County jail suicides in a Midwestern state. Prison J, 2003; 83: 130-148.

[19] Blaauw E, Winkel FW, Kerkhof AJFM. Bullying and suicidal behavior in jails. Crim Justice Behav 2001; 28: 279-299.

[20] Eyland S, Corben S, Barton J. Suicide prevention in New South Wales correctional centres. Crisis 1997; 18: 158–164.

[21] Hayes LM. National study of jail suicides. Psychiatr Q 1989; 60: 7-29.

[22] White TW, Schimmel DJ. Suicide prevention in federal prisons. In L. M. Hayes (Ed.), Prison suicide. Washington, DC: US Department of Justice; 1995; pp. 48-59

[23] Inch H, Rowlands P, Soliman A. Deliberate self-harm in a young offenders' institution. J Forens Psychiatry Psychol 1995; 6: 161-171.

[24] Ingram A, Johnson G, Hayes I. Self-harm and suicide by detained persons. London, UK: Home Office Police Research Group; 1997.

[25] Hayes, LM. Special Issue: Preventing suicides through prompt intervention. Jail suicide/Mental health update, Volume 10, issue 3. Mansfield, MA: National Center on Institutions and Alternatives; 2001.

[26] McCleave NR, Latham D. Self-injurious behavior in police custody. J Clin Forensic Med 1998, 5: 13-26.

[27] Blaauw E, Kerkhof AJFM, Winkel FW, & Sheridan L. Identifying suicide risk in penal institutions in the Netherlands. Br J Forensic Practice 2001; 3: 22-28.

[28] NIJ Staff. Can screening be culturally sensitive? Corrections Today 2004; 66(3): 30-31.

[29] Dooley E. Prison suicide in England and Wales 1972-1987. Br J Psychiatry 1990; 156: 40-45.

[30] Joukamaa M. Prison suicide in Finland 1969-1992. Forensic Sci Int 1997; 89: 167-174.

[31] Hayes LM. Suicide in adult correctional facilities. Law Med Health Care 1999; 27: 260-269.

[32] Kennedy DB, Hormant R. Predicting custodial suicides. Justice Q 1988; 5: 441-456.

CHAPTER 8

The Impact of Unemployment on Suicide Rate in Hong Kong during the Period of Economic Recovery, 2003-2006

C.K. Law[1,2,*], Paul S.F. Yip[3,4] and Candi M.C. Leung[5]

[1]Hong Kong Institute of Asia-Pacific Studies, The Chinese University of Hong Kong; [2]Australian Institute for Suicide Research and Prevention, Griffith University; [3]HKJC Centre for Suicide Research and Prevention, The University of Hong Kong; [4]Department of Social Work and Social Administration, The University of Hong Kong and [5]Department of Psychology, The University of Hong Kong

Abstract: Literature has widely documented the positive association of unemployment with suicide. Since 1997, the transition of suicide rate has been in line with the unemployment rate in Hong Kong. We aim to examine the suicide risk ratio between the unemployed and the employed during the period of 2003-2006 by age and gender, and explore such unknown suicide-related socioeconomic factors as living arrangement and marital status among the unemployed. Descriptive analysis and Chi-square Test are employed. Results show that not every member in the community can benefit from economic recovery, for the unemployed individuals tend to face heightened risks of completing suicide in times of economic recovery. For developing an effective strategy for suicide prevention, the government should put more effort to empower unemployed individuals.

Keywords: Suicide, unemployment, Hong Kong, economic change, transition of suicide rate.

1. INTRODUCTION

Unemployment has been widely recognized as one of the most prominent factors that account for suicide and related self-inflicted injuries [1-5]. Ample evidence showed that unemployed individuals tended to face a higher suicide risk when compared to their employed counterparts [6, 7]. Over the decades, considerable research efforts have contributed to the conceptualization of this phenomenon. One major explanation came from Hamermesh and Soss's economic model [8], which asserted that the resultant additional economic distress from unemployment lowered gradually the remaining discounted lifetime utility of the unemployed to a level sufficiently below their benchmark, such that the unemployed were prompted to end their lives early. Alternative to this economic model, the economic goal blockage and loss resulting from unemployment might also put the unemployed persons at risks of suicide by affecting both their psychological and physiological risk factors for suicide [9, 10].

Although the positive association of unemployment with suicide has been well documented, existing knowledge on the basic profiles of unemployed deceased remains very limited. Previous epidemiological studies identified various profile variables, including gender, age, marital status, living arrangement and access to lethal means of self-destruction, as major risk factors for suicide [11-15]. Most of these studies were, however, confined to the basic profiles of general suicide population only [16-18]. To our best knowledge, there is only one local case-control psychological autopsy study on unemployed individuals [19]. More importantly, the findings of this study were significantly different from that of another similar local study on the general population [2]. While the association of suicide with marital status and living arrangement was insignificant among the unemployed in the former study [19], being never married and living alone were identified as significant suicide predictors for the general population in the latter study [2]. This suggests that the sub-populations' basic characteristics might be different from those of the general population because of their employment status.

With a view to developing effective suicide prevention strategies for the community, it is necessary to

***Address Correspondence to C.K. Law:** Hong Kong Institute of Asia-Pacific Studies, Room 507, Esther Lee Building, The Chinese University of Hong Kong, Shatin, Hong Kong, Republic of China; E-mail: lawckin1@gmail.com

Maurizio Pompili (Ed)

understand how unemployment affects the risk of suicide among different sub-groups and their transitions in relation to economic change. Following the economic recovery in late 2003, both a drop of the unemployment rate (from 7.9% to 4.8%) and the overall suicide rate (from 18.2 per 100,000 to 14.0 per 100,000) was witnessed for the period 2003-2006. Due to the socio-demographics of different sub-populations, it is hypothesized that the impact of employment on suicide risks of different groups will be different. However, whether these changes affected the transitions of suicide rates among the employment status groups during economic expansion remains unclear in the literature.

Therefore, the present study aims to fill the existing research voids in identifying transition trends of relative suicide risks and the associated factors among different employment status groups for people aged 20-59 during the economic recovery period from 2003 to 2006 in Hong Kong. This information is of great importance in developing specific suicide prevention strategies targeting different employment status groups in the future.

2. DATA AND METHODS

Information on completed suicides for the period of 2003-2006 was made available from the Coroner's Court of Hong Kong. Following the Tenth Edition of the International Classification of Diseases and Related Health Problems [ICD-10], all reportable deaths with an external cause code in the range from X60 to X84 were classified as suicide [20]. Since the present study targeted the working age population, information was only extracted from the case files of suicide deceased aged between 20 and 59. Profile variables collected include gender, age, employment status and other related factors encompassing marital status, living arrangement and suicide methods used by the suicide deceased.

Statistical Analysis

Basic profiles of suicide deceased for each employment status group (that is, the employed, unemployed and economically inactive groups) were reported. In assessing the changing risks of suicide among different employment status groups during the period of economic recovery, the age-, gender- and marital status-specific suicide rates for the three groups were compared. For all statistical analyses, Chi-square test was used to test the between- and within group differences at the 0.05 level of significance.

3. RESULTS

From 2003 to 2006, the suicide death toll for working population aged 20-59 had reached 2,826, comprising 66.1% of the total suicides in Hong Kong. Due to administrative delays, only 2,721 of the 2,826 case files were captured at the Coroner's Court, with 105 (3.7%) case files found to be missing. Overall, the mean age of suicide deceased was 40.2 (SD = 10.6) years with more males compared to females (Male: Female = 1.78). Among these 2,721 suicide deceased, nearly half of them were unemployed (48.3%), while 39.5% of them were employed and 12.2% were economically inactive.

Characteristics of Suicide Deceased by Employment Status

Table **1** shows the basic profiles of suicide deceased by gender and employment status over the study period of 2003-2006. When compared to the other two employment status groups, suicide deceased who had been unemployed were more likely to be male ($\chi^2 = 5.3$; $df = 1$; $p < 0.02$) and fall in younger age groups that were below 40 ($\chi^2 = 8.28$; $df = 3$; $p < 0.04$). Moreover, they tended to be never married ($\chi^2 = 101.9$; $df = 2$; $p < 0.001$) and live alone ($\chi^2 = 33.9$; $df = 1$; $p < 0.001$) prior to death. No significant difference was found in suicide method used across the three groups ($\chi^2 = 2.76$; $df = 3$; $p = 0.43$).

When taking gender into consideration, it was revealed that the age difference between the unemployed and the other two groups was significant only among the females ($\chi^2 = 9.9$; $df = 3$; p = 0.02) but not the males ($\chi^2 = 1.85$; $df = 3$; $p = 0.60$). In contrast, significant differences in the distribution of marital status and living arrangement between the unemployed and the others were observed in both sexes. It was worth noting, however, that males were more likely to be never married (53.0%) and live alone (32.7%) than females among the unemployed.

Table 1: Socio-demographic characteristics and death profile of suicide deceased by gender and whether unemployed, 2003-2006

	Male			**Female**			**All**		
	Unemployed (n=869) %	**Others [a] (n=872) %**	*p-value*	**Unemployed (n=445) %**	**Others [a] (n=535) %**	*p-value*	**Unemployed (n=1314) %**	**Others [a] (n=1407) %**	*p-value*
Age			0.603			0.020			0.041
20 - 29	19.4	19.6		20.6	20.3		19.7	19.8	
30 - 39	26.4	23.8		35.7	27.4		29.7	25.0	
40 - 49	29.2	31.2		27.0	30.3		28.4	31.0	
50 - 59	25.0	25.4		16.7	22.1		22.2	24.2	
Marital status			<.001			<.001			<.001
Never Married	53.0	36.3		40.5	26.9		48.6	32.7	
Married	34.4	53.2		39.4	58.6		36.2	55.3	
Ex-married [b]	12.6	10.5		20.1	14.5		15.2	12.0	
Living arrangement			<.001			<.001			<.001
Living alone	32.7	24.1		23.1	12.7		29.4	19.8	
Not living alone	67.3	75.9		76.9	87.3		70.6	80.2	
Means of self-destruction			0.465			0.428			0.430
Charcoal burning	32.1	34.2		25.3	26.5		29.9	31.3	
Hanging	16.9	17.4		10.4	13.5		14.8	15.8	
Jumping	45.3	41.7		55.8	51.8		48.7	45.6	
Others [c]	5.7	6.6		8.5	8.2		6.6	7.3	

[a] Others includes employed persons (those who were full-time employed, part-time employed and self-employed) and economically inactive persons (hose who were not in the labor force such as housewife, full-time students, disabled persons and retired workers).

[b] Ex-married persons included those who were widowed, divorced or legally separated.

[c] Others include poisoning, drowning, shooting, drug overdose, jumping into railway, cutting, burning, electrocution, suffocation and gassing.

Suicide Risk by Employment Status

As a well-established determinant of suicide, unemployment's contribution to the heighted suicide risk observed among the unemployed in Hong Kong was unquestionable (Table **2**). Over the study period, the suicide rate for the unemployed (164.5 per 100,000) was 19 times (*i.e.,* 19X) higher than those for the employed (8.5 per 100,000) and the economically inactive (8.7 per 100,000). In particular, unemployment seemed to exert greater influence on females (29.4X) than males (15.0X) in terms of risk ratios between the unemployed and the employed, despite the higher absolute suicidal risk of unemployed males at 169.2 per 100,000.

Throughout the study period, a significant upward trend in suicide risk ratio between the unemployed and the employed was noted (from 12.4 X in 2003 to 27.7X in 2006). This could be attributed to a reduced risk of suicide among the employed by 39.1% (from 11.5 per 100,000 in 2003 to 7.0 per 100,000 in 2006) and an increased risk among the unemployed by 35.9% (from 142.5 per 100,000 to 193.7 per 100,000) over the same period. Interestingly, the increasing suicide risk ratios between the unemployed and the employed was comparatively more prominent among the females (from 15.4X in 2003 to 47.9X in 2006) than the males (from 10.5X to 20.1X only), as a result of the more rapid increase in suicide rate (93.2%) among the unemployed females (from 106.6 per 100,000 to 206.0 per 100,000) than the unemployed males (from 161.4 per 100,000 to 186.9 per 100,000).

Table 2: Suicide rates (per 100,000) in Hong Kong by employment status and gender, 2003-2006

Employment status	Sex	Period of study				2003-2006
		2003	2004	2005	2006	
Employed[a]	Male	15.3	10.5	10.4	9.3	11.3
	Female	6.9	3.9	6.2	4.3	5.3
	Both sexes	11.5	7.4	8.5	7.0	8.5
Unemployed	Male	161.4	164.5	170.6	186.9	169.2
	Female	106.6	150.1	186.0	206.0	155.9
	Both sexes	142.5	159.2	176.1	193.7	164.5
Economically Inactive[b]	Male	17.5	9.1	14.3	13.3	13.5
	Female	10.3	7.0	6.7	6.1	7.5
	Both Sexes	11.8	7.3	8.3	7.4	8.7

[a] Employed persons included those who were full-time employed, part-time employed and self-employed.

[b] Economically inactive persons included those who were not in the labor force such as housewife, full-time students, disabled persons and retired workers.

Table 3: Suicide rates (per 100,000) in Hong Kong by employment status, marital status and gender, 2003 and 2006

Sex	Marital status	Employment status								
		Employed			Unemployed			Economically Inactive		
		2003	2006	% change	2003	2006	% change	2003	2006	% change
Male	Never married	17.2	10.5	-38.7	197.5	223.4	13.1	15.2	4.8	-68.0
	Married	13.1	7.5	-42.8	93.5	111.8	19.5	17.9	14.1	-21.3
	Ex-married[a]	43.7	36.8	-15.9	500.0	397.2	-20.6	54.1	27.4	-49.3
Female	Never married	6.7	3.9	-41.3	109.9	162.4	47.8	7.1	2.7	-61.1
	Married	5.6	3.7	-33.4	78.1	183.7	135.1	10.2	6.1	-40.3
	Ex-married[a]	19.8	10.0	-49.6	186.8	397.0	112.5	15.7	8.2	-48.0
Both Sexes	Never married	11.9	7.2	-39.9	167.7	201.2	20.0	11.3	3.8	-66.2
	Married	10.0	5.9	-40.9	88.6	134.4	51.7	11.1	7.1	-35.6
	Ex-married[a]	27.6	17.7	-35.8	318.5	397.1	24.7	20.1	10.9	-45.6

[a] Ex-married persons included those who were widowed, divorced or legally separated.

Further analysis on marital status showed notable differences in suicide risk transitions among the three employment status groups (Table **3**). Overall, suicide rate was the lowest among the married group and the highest among the ex-married group. The married group was, however, most affected by the widening gap of suicide risks between the employed and the unemployed, for its suicide risk ratio had jumped by more than 157% (from 8.9X to 22.8X) while that for the never married and ex-married groups had only increased by 98.3% (from 14.1X to 27.9X) and by 94.4% (from 11.5X to 22.4X) respectively. These transition differences in risk ratios were mainly contributed by the relatively rapid increase in suicide rate among the unemployed married group (51.7%) when compared to the never married (20.0%) and the ex-married groups (24.7%) .

When taking both sex and marital status into consideration, it was revealed that the ex-married females suffered the most during the period of economic recovery, for they experienced the greatest increase in the risk ratio between the unemployed and the employed that tripled from 9.4X in 2003 to 39.7X in 2006. The negative effect of economic recovery was the second highest among the married female group whose risk ratio had increased by 256% from 13.9X to 49.6X over the period. For the never married females, they tended to suffer less for their increase in risk ratio (153%) was relatively lower when compared to the females in ex-married and married groups.

4. DISCUSSION

This study examined how changes in unemployment correlated with the transition trends of suicide rates among different employment status groups in the time of economic recovery in Hong Kong. To a certain extent, the improvement in unemployment plays a crucial role in the recent reduction in suicide rate in Hong Kong. However, the findings of this study suggest that not everyone can benefit from economic recovery. Specifically, the suicide risk of the unemployed, particularly for married women, had been skyrocketing during the period of economic expansion. This indicates that the pressure of unemployment and its negative impact on psychological and mental well-being of the unemployed had indeed multiplied following the upswing of the economy. It is no surprise that the unemployed tended to suffer even more in terms of psychological distress and suicide risks in such a social environment [21].

The fact that the unemployed were selected into unemployment by the health selection process might help explain the rising trend of suicide risk among the unemployed at times of economic upswing. According to Bartley [22], under favorable economic circumstances, unemployment was highly selective and related to the accumulation of disadvantage and poor position in the labor market. Hence, during economic recovery in Hong Kong, people with prior poor mental and physical health might have been selected into the pool of unemployed [23, 24], which added further psychological distress to unemployed individuals and increased their likelihood of committing suicide.

Nonetheless, gender seemed to moderate the negative impact of economic recovery on unemployed individuals. Results showed that changes in unemployment during the economic recovery was the most detrimental to the unemployed females rather than their male counterparts in Hong Kong, which contradicted with the common belief and the findings of the two related Italian studies that unemployment affected males more than females [7, 25-27]. According to D'Zurilla and Nezu [28], this finding might be related to the unemployed females' less competent social problem-solving skills, the self-directed cognitive-behavioral process by which an individual attempted to identify or discover effective or adaptive ways of coping with problematic situations encountered in the course of everyday living. Indeed, previous local studies had consistently confirmed social problem solving skills as a significant protective factor of suicide [2, 19]. In such a service-orientated economy as Hong Kong, those females who are competent in social problem-solving skills are comparatively easier to find jobs than their male counterparts, so that unemployed females tend to be those who possess low social problem-solving skills. In line with Bartley's assertion that disadvantages and poor position in labor market of the unemployed accumulated during economic upswing [22], those females who remained unemployed tended to be selected into prolonged unemployment, resulting in prolonged psychological distress that made these unemployed females vulnerable to higher suicide risks than their male counterparts.

When taking marital status into consideration, those unemployed individuals who were married experienced the highest suicidal risk during the period of economic recovery in Hong Kong. This suggests that married individuals might suffer more from the harmful effects of unemployment due to their relatively higher financial commitment or needs to support their family [29]. It was noteworthy, however, that unemployed females who were married tended to suffer more than their male counterparts. With higher degree in responsibility to family among females than males [30], family might have become a burden for the married females who remained unemployed during economic recovery. Due to the stronger link between perceived stress and psychological symptoms among married females than males [31-34], those unemployed females who were married might thus experienced more intense psychological stress and become more vulnerable to suicide risks than their male counterparts.

Despite the findings of differentials in suicide risks and suicide rates transition trends between different sub-populations, this study had several major limitations. Due to insufficient information provided by our data, only a limited number of variables were included in this study. However, suicide is a multi-faceted phenomenon, with six factors significantly and independently contributing to suicide in Hong Kong [2]. To provide a complete picture on the relationship between unemployment and suicide during economic recovery, a more comprehensive surveillance and monitoring system on suicidal behaviors should be developed to include the remaining four factors, namely indebtedness, social support, psychiatric illness, and history of past attempt, for future analysis.

REFERENCES

[1] Blakely TA, Collings SCD, Atkinson J. Unemployment and suicide. Evidence for a causal association? J Epidemiol Community Health 2003; 57:594-600.

[2] Chen EYH, Chan WSC, Wong PWC, *et al.* Suicide in Hong Kong: A case-control psychological autopsy study. Psychol Med 2006; 36: 815-25.

[3] Chida F, Sakai A, Takayama Y, Otsuka K, Yoshida T. Social factors of suicide. Psychiatry 2006; 8: 352–8 (in Japanese).

[4] Johansson S-E, Sundquist J. Unemployment is an important risk factor for suicide in contemporary Sweden: An 11-year follow-up study of a cross-sectional sample of 37789 people. Public Health 1997; 111: 41-5.

[5] Yang B. The economy and suicide: A time series study of the U.S.A. AJES 1992; 51: 87–99.

[6] Agerbo E. Effect of psychiatric illness and labor market status on suicide: A health worker effect? J Epidemiol Community Health 2005; 59: 598-602.

[7] Platt S, Micciolo R, Tansella M. Suicide and unemployment in Italy: Description, analysis, and interpretation of recent trends. Soc Sci Med 1992; 34: 1191-201.

[8] Hamermesh DS, Soss NM. An economic theory of suicide. J Polit Econ 1974; 82: 83-98.

[9] Arnetz BB, Brenner SO, Levi L, *et al.* Neuroendocrine and immunologic effects of unemployment and job insecurity. Psychother Psychosom 1991; 55: 76–80.

[10] Ezzy D. Unemployment and mental health: A critical review. Soc Sci Med 1993; 37: 41–52.

[11] Masocco M, Pompili M, Vichi M, Vanacore N, Lester D, Tatarelli R. Suicide and marital status in Italy. Psychiatric Quarterly 2008; 79: 275-85.

[12] Stack S, Lester D. Body mass and suicide risk. Crisis 2007; 28: 46-7.

[13] Troister T, Links PS, Cutcliffe J. Review of predictors of suicide within 1 year of discharge from a psychiatric hospital. Curr Psychiatry Rep 2008; 10: 60-5.

[14] Yip PSF, Chi I, Yu KK. An epidemiological profile of elderly suicides in Hong Kong. Int J Geriatr Psychiatry 1998; 13: 631-7.

[15] Yip PSF, Thorburn J. Marital status and the risk of suicide: Experience from England and Wales, 1982-1996. Psychological Reports 2004; 94: 401-7.

[16] Khan MM, Mahmud S, Karim MS, Zaman M, Prince M. Case-control study of suicide in Karachi, Pakistan. The British Journal of Psychiatry 2008; 193: 402-5.

[17] Kposowa AJ. Marital status and suicide in the National Longitudinal Mortality Study. J Epidemiol Community Health 2000; 54: 254-61.

[18] Qin P, Agerbo E, Mortensen PB. Suicide risk in relation to socioeconomic, demographic, psychiatric, and familial factors: A national register-based study of all suicides in Denmark, 1981-1997. Am J Psych 2003; 160: 765-72.

[19] Chan WSC, Yip PSF, Wong PWC, Chen EYH. Suicide and unemployment: What are the missing links? Arch Suicide Res 2007; 11: 327-35.

[20] World Health Organization. The tenth revision of the International Classification of Diseases and related health problems. 10th ed. Geneva, Switzerland, WHO 1992.

[21] Warr PB, Jackson PR. Factors influencing the psychological impact of prolonged unemployment and re-employment. Psychol Med 1985; 15: 795-807.

[22] Bartley M. Unemployment and ill health: Understanding the relationship. J Epidemiol Community Health 1994; 48: 333-7.

[23] Halvorsen K. Impact of re-employment on psychological distress among long-term unemployed. Acta Sociol 1998; 41: 227-42.

[24] Mastekaasa A. Unemployment and health: Selection effects. J Community Appl Soc Psychol 1996; 6: 189-205.

[25] Artazcoz L, Benach J, Borrell C, Cortes I. Unemployment and mental health: Understanding the interactions among gender, family roles, and social class. Am J Publ Health 2004; 94: 82-8.

[26] Preti A, Miotto P. Suicide and unemployment in Italy, 1982-1994. J Epidemiol Community Health 1999; 53: 694-701.

[27] Theodossiou I. The effects of low-pay and unemployment on psychological well-being: A logistic regression approach. J Health Econ 1998; 17: 85-104.

[28] D'Zurilla TJ, Nezu A. Social problem solving in adults. In: P. C. Kendall PC, Ed. Advances in cognitive behavioral research and therapy (Vol. 1). New York, NY: Academic Press. 1982; pp.201-74.

[29] Kulik L. The impact of gender and marital status on attitudes and responses to unemployment. Socio Pract J Clin Appl Sociol 2001; 3: 19-36.

[30] Ellis JB, Lamis DA. Adaptive characteristics and suicidal behavior: A gender comparison of young adults. Death Stud 2007; 31: 845-54.

[31] Cleary PD, Mechanic D. Sex differences in psychological distress among married people. J Health Soc Behav 1983; 24: 111-21.

[32] Kandel DB, Davies M, Raveis VH. The stressfulness of daily social roles for women: Marital, occupational and household roles. J Health Soc Behav 1985; 26: 64-78.

[33] Parry G. Paid employment, life events, social support, and mental health in working-class mothers. J Health Soc Behav 1986; 27: 193-208.

[34] Stewart AJ, Salt P. Life stress, life-styles, depression, and illness in adult women. J Pers Soc Psychol 1981; 40: 1063-9.

CHAPTER 9

Psychopharmacology for Suicide Prevention

Ross J. Baldessarini[1,*] **and Leonardo Tondo**[1,2]

[1]*Department of Psychiatry, Harvard Medical School; Psychopharmacology Program, McLean Division of Massachusetts General Hospital Boston, Massachusetts, USA and* [2]*Faculty of Psychology, University of Cagliari, Italy*

> *"The medical treatment of the propensity to suicide, whether prophylactic or therapeutic, differs not from that which is applicable in cases of ordinary insanity."*
>
> George M. Burrows, M.D. (1828)

Reprinted by permission from: Suicide in psychiatric disorders, Tatarelli R, Pompili M, Girardi P, (eds.). Nova Science Publishers, Inc. New York, 2007, p 193-213, with updating in 2009-2011.

Abstract: Therapeutic research on suicide was virtually unknown a decade ago, but recently a great deal of clinically important information has emerged. A landmark event was approval by the US FDA of antisuicidal effects of clozapine in schizophrenia patients in 2003. Interest in effects of psychotropic drug treatments on suicidal behavior was strongly stimulated by recent regulatory warnings of increased risk of suicidal thoughts or behaviors in juveniles and young adults treated with modern antidepressants. This chapter reviews recent research findings pertaining to effects of psychoactive drugs on suicide risk. Antipsychotics other than clozapine are not known to reduce suicidal risk. Lithium has compelling evidence of long-term effectiveness in reducing risks of suicide and attempts by as much as 80% among patients with bipolar disorders, a mix of major affective disorders, and possibly also recurrent major depressive disorder. Its effects may be superior to those of some mood-stabilizing anticonvulsants. Several ecological studies, especially in the US and Nordic countries, find inverse associations between prescriptions for modern antidepressants and temporal or regional variance in suicide rates. However, suicide rates decreased in the same countries even before introduction of modern antidepressants, and other factors may be involved. Notably, lower regional suicide rates are associated with indices of greater access to clinical care. Many large cohort and case-control studies have found reduced suicidal risk with long-term antidepressant treatment; a minority found increased risk, which may be confounded by association of antidepressant treatment with more severe illness and selection of relatively nontoxic modern antidepressants for patients at increased suicidal risk. In many randomized, controlled trials in adults, antidepressants show reductions in suicidal ideation, along with other depressive symptoms, but without consistent effects on rates of suicidal acts. The FDA finds evidence of increased risk of suicidal thoughts and perhaps of attempts in juvenile and young adult patients treated with modern antidepressants *vs.* a placebo. It has long been recognized that some depressed patients experience increased agitation soon after exposure to antidepressants, and such reactions may increase suicidal risk. These effects usually can be anticipated and minimized by timely clinical interventions. The findings of beneficial effects of antidepressant treatment on suicidal ideation but not behavior, and of reduced risk of suicidal behaviors by lithium and clozapine, suggest differential pharmacologic effects on particular components of "suicidality," in that reduction of anger, aggression and impulsivity evidently can limit progression from suicidal ideation to acts. Effective suicide prevention requires focused assessment and supervision, especially early in clinical management of patients with major mood disorders, with appropriate pharmacological and psychosocial interventions.

Keywords: Psychopharmacology, suicide, prevention, mood disorders, schizophrenia.

1. INTRODUCTION

The world-wide annual suicide rate currently averages approximately 13/100,000 (0.013%/year), with

***Address correspondence to Ross J. Baldessarini:** Mailman Research Center, McLean Hospital, 115 Mill Street, Belmont, MA 02478-9106 USA; E-mail: rjb@mclean.org

higher average rates for men than women in all but a few countries, very low rates in children, and relatively high rates in elderly men [1-4]. Suicide rates vary markedly among world regions, countries, and locales, in part reflecting differences in case-identification and reporting procedures [2-5]. Notably, suicide rates are extraordinarily high in Eastern Europe and relatively low in Southern Europe and Latin America. In the US, annual suicide rates (per 100, 000 population) are far higher in Alaska (25.0), Montana (21.0), New Mexico (21.0), Nevada (20.2) and other areas in the Southwest and the Intermountain West than on the East or West Coasts, with lowest rates reported in Massachusetts and New York (6.5) and in the District of Columbia (6.0) [6]. Internationally, the overall average suicide rate has been rising gradually over the past half-century, with increases reported in about half of reporting nations, mainly among men, but moderate decreases found in another half, including in Northern Europe and North America. These improvements may reflect improved diagnosis and treatment of mood disorders in the same era [4, 7-9]. Paradoxically, the observed increases may in part reflect improved case-finding and reporting associated with overall improvements in national healthcare systems.

Estimated rates of suicide attempts are much less reliable than for completed suicides. Attempts average 20-30-times higher than rates of completed suicide in the general population, but at higher mortality raties probably under-reported, and range widely in seriousness of methods and intent [10, 11]. The ratio of attempts/suicides in clinical samples of mood-disorder patients is much lower, suggesting greater lethality of suicidal behaviors [12]. It is important to point out that most cases of suicide (81%-95%) in the general population involve psychiatric illnesses, nearly half of which (48.5%) are mood disorders [13].

In a study of men and women who attempted suicide and were evaluated in a medical emergency service (suggesting relatively serious attempts), later risk of completed suicide within five years was twice-higher among men than women (8.3% *vs.* 4.3%), as expected, and most likely to occur within a year of follow-up [14]. The ratio of attempts to later suicides (A/S) also was half as great in men as in women (12:1 *vs.* 23:1), consistent with greater lethality of suicide attempts in men. Risk of later suicide was higher in men below *versus* above the median age of 35 years (9.7% *vs.* 7.0%), but also in women older than this median (6.0% *vs.* 2.5%); accordingly, the relative risk among younger men was four-times higher than in younger women (9.7%/2.5%), whereas risks in older men and women scarcely differed (7.0%/6.0%), indicating that the lethality of suicidal behavior in women over age 35 approaches that of men of similar age.

Over the past decade, unprecedented interest has emerged in considering the excess mortality associated with major mental illnesses as an important and plausible therapeutic target [15]. Excessive mortality in mood, psychotic, and substance-use disorders includes risks (2-3-times above the general population) due to medical illnesses, particularly stress-sensitive disorders, sometimes worsened by the weight-gain and metabolic disorders associated with many modern psychotropic drug treatments, or with complications of comorbid substance-use disorders, or accidents [16-24]. Indeed, deaths associated with cardiovascular disorders probably account for the largest number of deaths among persons with mood disorders, as in the general population.

By far, however, the greatest source of a proportional excess of mortality is suicide, rates of which among patients with mood disorders can exceed those in the general population by 20-fold, particularly in bipolar disorders and in severe, recurrent major depression, with lesser rates in psychotic, anxiety, or primary substance-use disorders [10-25]. General risk factors for suicide include the presence of a major mood disorder with hopelessness, especially if complicated by comorbid abuse of alcohol or illicit drugs [2, 10, 13, 26]. Risk is especially high among young, impulsive-aggressive and older, unmarried men [2, 3]. Risk of suicide in bipolar disorder patients continues to be high, despite the introduction of a growing number of treatments with putative mood-stabilizing effects, reflecting the great difficulty in treating bipolar depressive and mixed manic-depressive states effectively. Indeed, approximately three-quarters of the surprisingly high proportion of unresolved morbidity among bipolar disorder patients (nearly 40% of weeks of long-term follow-up, even from illness-onset) is depressive [27-30]. This high level of residual depressive morbidity in treated bipolar disorder patients, no doubt, strongly encourages high rates of utilization of antidepressants in their treatment, even though such treatment is neither approved by regulatory bodies, nor well supported by available clinical research as either effective or safe in bipolar disorder patients [31, 32]. Moreover, antidepressant treatments are associated in some patients with dysphoric-mixed-agitated or psychotic states that can increase suicidal risk [33-35].

The unusually high risk of suicide among bipolar disorder patients was supported by our recent review of the medical records of nearly 3, 000 outpatients with major mood disorders evaluated at the Lucio Bini Mood Disorders Research Center in Cagliari, Sardinia. We found substantially greater suicide risks among bipolar disorder patients than in those with recurrent major depression [36]. The risk of suicides among 843 bipolar I and II disorder patients was 150/100, 000/year, or more than ten-times higher than in the general population of Sardinia, and three-times greater than among 1, 983 patients diagnosed with recurrent major depressive disorder. These rates suggest risk of dying by suicide among bipolar disorder patients of nearly 10%, considering potential risk-exposures of 60 years or more. The rate of suicide attempts was 1.26%/year among bipolar disorder patients, and 25% of these acts were violent, *versus* 0.48%/year among the unipolar cases and a rate of violent acts of only 12.5%, compared to approximate general population attempt rates of 0.2%-0.3%/year [10-13]. The ratio of attempts/suicides (A/S) as a proposed index of lethality of suicidal behavior [12], was 8.6:1 in bipolar disorder patients, and similar, at 9.6:1, in unipolar, recurrent major depression patients, compared to an estimated value of about 25:1 in the general population, indicating higher lethality among mood disorder patients. A particularly important observation was that more than one-third of all suicidal acts occurred within the first year from illness-onset, and more than half within the first five years of illness—indicating the need for early diagnosis and intervention in major mood disorders [36].

Effects of treatments on suicidal risk have been a topic of growing research interest in recent years. Evidence that most modern psychiatric treatments reduce long-term suicide risks is very limited, including methods as diverse as psychotherapy, rapid hospitalization, and even electroconvulsive treatment, which can be lifesaving in acute emergencies [2, 3, 37-39]. Suicide rates are surprisingly high among persons diagnosed with anxiety disorders [25-40] and severe anxiety may accompany suicidal behavior [41], but evidence that antianxiety medications alter suicidal risk in anxiety disorder patients is very limited [40]. The following sections summarize recent findings pertaining to effects of other psychotropic drug treatments on suicidal behavior and ideation, including antipsychotics, mood-stabilizers, and antidepressants, for which most evidence is available.

2. ANTIPSYCHOTIC DRUGS

The first US FDA-approved treatment with an antisuicide indication was clozapine for schizophrenia patients. This regulatory approval in 2003 was based largely on a single, remarkable randomized trial (InterSePT) comparing clozapine with olanzapine among not necessarily treatment-resistant schizophrenia patients at high suicidal risk [42], as well as other supportive evidence [43, 44]. The InterSePT trial supported a prolongation of time to interventions and reduced rates of suicide attempts, but not reduction of mortality. Other antipsychotic drugs have not been tested adequately for effects on suicidal behavior, but there is suggestive evidence that olanzapine may have beneficial effects on suicidal ideation when given in combination with a mood-stabilizing agent [45].

3. MOOD-STABILIZERS

Many studies support a suicide risk-reducing effect of long-term treatment of bipolar and other manic-depressive disorder patients with lithium [46-51]. We recently meta-analyzed data from nearly three-dozen studies of long-term lithium treatment in bipolar disorder or a mix of major mood disorder patients [12-52]. The findings support not only a marked reduction in risk of suicide attempts, but also of completed suicides (both by five-fold, or about 80%). We also found a more than two-fold higher proportion of attempts/suicides during treatment with lithium, suggesting reduced lethality of suicidal behavior. These findings include several randomized, controlled trials against either a placebo or alternative mood-stabilizing agents [12, 49, 52]. The strength of the evidence concerning antisuicidal effects of long-term treatment of lithium served as a basis for a recent citizen's petition to the US FDA seeking regulatory recognition of an antisuicide effect of all lithium products in bipolar I disorder patients [53].

In addition, in data compiled from eight studies by meta-analysis, we found a four-fold (76%) lower risk of suicide and attempts in patients diagnosed with recurrent major depressive disorder, treated with lithium compared to other alternatives (Risk Ratio [RR] = 4.2) (95% confidence interval; CI: 1.5-12.0) [54].

The evident beneficial effects of lithium in reducing mortality due to suicide are all the more remarkable for its potentially lethal toxicity in acute overdoses. Suicide attempts with lithium have been reported to be rare [55], and we found none among more than 700 patients with major mood disorders treated with lithium for several years at the Bini Mood Disorders Center in Sardinia [36]. Moreover, protection from lethal toxicity is afforded by vomiting often induced by acute overdoses of lithium as well as by the unique ability of dialysis methods to clear lithium from the circulation rapidly and efficiently [56, 57]. Recent national survey data from the US indicate that risk of fatalities following overdoses of lithium was similar to that of second-generation antipsychotic drugs and of antidepressants of the serotonin reuptake inhibitor (SRI) type [58].

There is little research that directly compares suicidal risks during treatment with other mood-stabilizers [39] but at least two studies found nearly three-fold average lower risks with lithium than with carbamazepine or divalproex among bipolar or schizoaffective disorder patients [59, 60]. Nevertheless, there are some indications that anticonvulsants, themselves, may have some beneficial effects on suicidal behavior [61, 62].

4. ANTIDEPRESSANTS

A highly controversial question is whether antidepressant treatment alters the risks of various aspects of "suicidality" among patients with major depressive disorders [63-69].

5. ECOLOGICAL STUDIES

Evidence that antidepressant treatment yields expected reductions in risk of suicides or attempts is mixed. It includes data from correlative or "ecological, " pharmacoepidemiological studies that compare suicide rates by regions or years with concurrent rates of prescriptions for antidepressant drugs [9]. In some Nordic countries and the US, modern, less-toxic antidepressants emerged in the 1990s to dominate current clinical practice, and their use was associated with moderate decreases in overall suicide rates, varying in sex and age groups [7-9, 70-75]. However, in the US, and some Nordic countries, at least, similar trends toward falling suicide rates were in evidence at least a decade before the introduction of the SRI fluoxetine, the first clinically successful modern antidepressant [9-75].

In our recent review of this body of research, only nine of 29 ecological studies found significant inverse correlations of increased use of modern antidepressants with diminishing national, regional, or temporal trends in suicide rates; another six found no relationships, and 14 found correlations in some sex or age subgroups that were inconsistent across studies. Moreover, our analysis of data from 78 reporting countries indicated that only about half (54%) experienced decreases in annual suicide rates between the 1950s (when antidepressants were not available) and the early 2000s (a decade after introduction of modern antidepressants), and that a similar proportion (46%) reported increases; the international distribution of decreases and increases between 1990 and the early 2000s was similar [4, 9, 76]. Moreover, both types of changes have been reported from similar world regions, including decreases and increases in Western and Eastern Europe, Latin America, and Asia. These outcomes suggest random, or at least highly complex phenomena likely to reflect the impact of many contributing factors.

As noted above, it is plausible to consider that improvements in public health, changes in legal, cultural, or social prohibitions against suicide, and improvements in identifying and reporting suicides might, paradoxically, associate higher suicide rates with increased access to modern psychopharmacologic agents in some countries. Additional socioeconomic factors may also contribute to the complex findings from the ecological studies in question. For example, in the US, we found strong correlations between state suicide rates and economic and demographic measures likely to be associated with access to clinical care in general, including population density, clinicians/100,000 population, per capita income, access to medical insurance, and public support of mental health services [6]. Such findings underscore the point that many factors, including access to clinical services or social supports, and not merely antidepressant prescription rates, are likely to be associated with regional and temporal variations in suicide rates. It is also important to emphasize that all such correlative studies suffer from a fundamental inability to relate medication exposure or other specific factors to suicidal behavior at the level of individuals [77]. At best, they may suggest hypotheses for further testing with less ambiguous methods, but they cannot prove a direct, causal relationship between antidepressant treatment and reduced suicidal risk at the level of individual persons.

6. COHORT AND CASE-CONTROL STUDIES

Other sources of data concerning antidepressants include large cohorts of depressed patients from general practice or health-maintenance organization data sources, and relatively large, case-control comparisons of subgroups varying in exposure to antidepressants. Such studies include over one-million, mainly clinically depressed, subjects in 17 reports [78-93]. These studies yield inconsistent findings; many (n=11) were designed to test for greater suicidal risks with SRI antidepressants compared to other agents or to nontreatment. The great majority of such studies (9/11) did not find evidence of greater suicidal risk in association with antidepressant treatment, and a majority of others addressing other related questions (4/6) found decreased or no difference in suicidal risk with more antidepressant treatment. Several of these studies encountered greater suicidal risk with more antidepressant treatment in general, or specifically with greater use of SRIs and other modern antidepressants, at least in some age-groups, including small increases among adolescents [89-92], larger increases in elderly patients [88], or inconsistently, fewer completed suicides but more attempts [93].

Interpretation of findings from such studies is severely compromised by their risk of "confounding by morbidity or by indication." That is, medical treatments, in general, are more likely to be sought and given to more severely ill patients at higher risk of suicide, and medicines with low risks of toxic effects on acute overdosing (such as the SRIs) are more likely to be selected clinically than more toxic agents (*e.g.*, tricyclic antidepressants) to treat patients considered to be at increased risk for suicide. The nonrandomized, clinically selected treatment in such studies can severely distort observed associations between greater suicidal risk and use of particular treatments.

7. RANDOMIZED, CONTROLLED TRIALS

Randomized, controlled trials (RCTs) should be the best source of data on effects of antidepressant treatment on suicidal risks, and hundreds of such trials support the licensing and clinical applications of modern and older antidepressants in major depressive and anxiety disorder patients. Individual trials are unlikely to include enough patients with identified suicidal acts to allow testing for treatment effects, especially since being acutely suicidal is usually a criterion for exclusion from such trials. However, pooling of data across many RCTs, such as by use of meta-analytic methods, may yield substantial numbers of suicide attempts and even completed suicides. Indeed, rates of suicide attempts and even of completed suicides, may be at least as high in controlled trials as in clinical samples of patients diagnosed with major depressive disorder. For example, suicide rates pooled across several recent large meta-analyses of modern and older antidepressants or placebo (given similar rates with all treatments) averaged 862/100, 000/year [94-96], or 66-times above average international general population rate of 13/100, 000/year [4]! In clinical samples of even relatively severely ill major depression patients, usually hospitalized at some time, the standardized mortality ratio (SMR) for suicide compared to the general population rarely exceeds 20-fold [25], and among less severely ill, ambulatory, depressed patients this risk ratio may be about three-times lower [97]. To considerable extent, such high observed rates of suicidal behaviors in RCTs reflect exaggeration arising from annualizing rates based on relatively brief exposure times (typically 8-12 weeks) encountered in most trials in acute depression and early in the course of treatment.

There have been several recent reports based on pooling data on rates of suicides and attempts from large numbers of RCTs and subjects involving modern antidepressants, older standard agents, and placebo [65, 94-96, 98-105].

Table 1: Summary of meta-analyses of randomized controlled trials of antidepressants *versus* placebo in major depression

	Suicides		*Attempts*	
Study	**Drugs**	**Placebo**	**Drugs**	**Placebo**
Khan *et al.*, 2000 [94]	32/16, 560	2/3079	115/16, 560	15/3079
Khan *et al.*, 2003 [95]	72/43, 382	5/4895	---	---
Fergusson *et al.*, 2005 [101]	---	---	80/14, 859	5/3273
Gunnell *et al.*, 2005 [102]	9/23, 804	7/17, 022	111/30, 814	61/21, 689
Acharya *et al.*, 2006 [96]	1/1812	1/1184	15/1812	5/1184
Laughren, 2006 [105]	5/30, 707	1/14, 873	61/30, 707	29/14, 873
Total	119/116, 265	16/41, 053	382/94, 752	115/44, 098
Crude Pooled Rates (%)	0.102%	0.039%	0.403%	0.261%

Note that the data analyzed probably overlap, and are uncorrected for exposure times, which may not be identical in drug and placebo arms of all trials. Nevertheless, the pooled data suggest moderately higher rates of suicide (2.62-fold) and attempts (1.54-fold) with antidepressants *versus* placebos. Estimated "lethality" (ratio of rates of attempt/suicides) for patients diagnosed with major depression was 4.16 (0.358/0.086); this ratio is much lower than ratios of 20-30 found in the general population, indicating greater lethality of suicidal acts among depressed patients, including in randomized treatment trials.

With the exception of one report finding a significant overall excess of suicidal acts during treatment with SRI antidepressants [101], other meta-analyses have found only minor differences in rates of suicidal behaviors between depressed patients treated with an SRI, other antidepressants, or a placebo, overall tending toward apparently greater risks with antidepressants, assuming that the trials analyzed were well-randomized and remained so, with well-balanced exposures in both drug and placebo arms throughout the duration of the trials. We have pooled the data reported from these previous meta-analyses to summarize the findings (Table **1**; Fig. **1**).

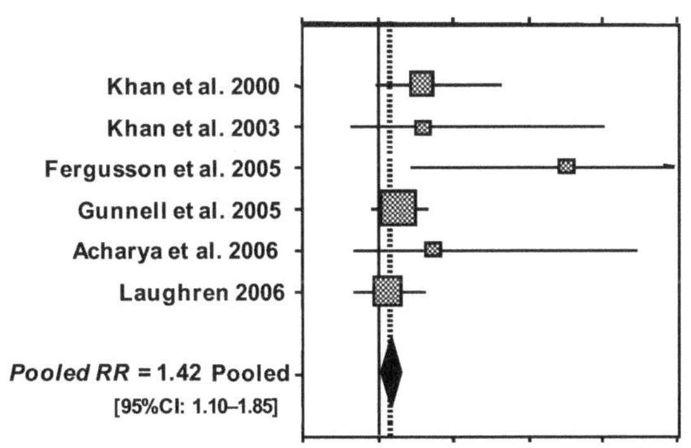

Figure 1: Forest plot of random-effect meta-analysis of reported summary findings from previous pooled analyses of data from randomized, placebo-controlled trials of antidepressants in adult major depression, based on the sum of *suicides and suicide attempts* (data in Table **1**). The overall, pooled Rate Ratio (RR) and its 95% confidence interval (CI) is 1.42 (CI: 1.10-1.85; z = 2.65, p = 0.008: black diamond and vertical dashed line; boxes are proportional to subjects numbers and variance measures), compared to the null value of RR = 1.0 (vertical solid line). One study (Fergusson *et al.* 2005) had relatively large RR (3.52 [CI; 1.43-8.69]). In addition, the computed, overall, pooled Risk Difference (RD) was 0.0015 (CI: 0.00032-0.0027), or 0.15% (CI: 0.03%-0.27%; z = 2.49, p = 0.013), indicating an estimated Number-Needed-to-Harm (NNH) of 667 (CI: 373-3135); without Fergusson *et al.* (2005): NNH = 1307 (CI: 636-infinity, z = 1.86, p=0.06). For completed *suicide*, RD = 0.022% (CI: 0.017%-0.060%; z = 1.11, p = 0.27), with an estimated NNH of 4651 (CI: 1675-infinity); for suicide *attempts* RD = 0.163% (CI: 0.014%-0.312%; z = 2.15, p =

0.03), with a correspondingly NNH = 613 (CI: 321-6993). These results suggest that more than 600 depressed patients would have to be exposed to an antidepressant for approximately two months (or about 100 treated for a year), early in the course of an episode of acute major depressive disorder, when spontaneous suicidal risk is particularly high, to yield one excess suicide attempt, and over 4500 to yield one excess suicide over the risk associated with untreated major depression itself.

One of the largest of these analyses was recently organized by the US FDA to review all available data from 386 controlled trials of modern antidepressant drugs involving 112, 875 patient-subjects with major depressive or other disorders [105]. By far, most of the identified suicidal events involved thinking considered to be suicidal, but of uncertain clinical significance. Reported instances of suicides (0.013%) and attempts (0.198%) may be low due to relatively brief exposure times averaging two months. Among adult patients diagnosed with major depressive disorder, the observed suicide rate, based on estimated exposure-times averaging eight weeks, was 77/100, 000/year (6/45, 580/0.17 year), or only six-times above the general population rate of 13/100, 000/year [4], compared to suicide rates of 862/100, 000/year found in similar controlled trials of modern antidepressants, as already noted [94-96]. There was no overall difference in risk of "suicidality" (mainly, suicidal ideation), even when previous data even when previous data from earlier analyses of data from RCTs of SRIs *versus* placebo used to treat juvenile depressed or anxious patients were included [100-103]. However, secondary analyses, based on stratifying by age-groups, suggested increased risk of broadly defined "suicidality" (mainly ideation) with modern antidepressants *versus* placebo at younger ages, and possible beneficial effects in older patients (Fig. **2**).

These provocative findings, pertaining almost entirely to increased observed risks of presumably new suicidal ideation with SRIs and other modern antidepressants over placebo, among children, adolescents, and young adults up to age 24 years, extend initial impressions of similar trends in meta-analyses carried out in RCTs involving children and adolescents by the UK drug regulatory agency [106] as well as the FDA [100-104]. In the initial FDA review of SRI trials data involving some 4400 depressed or anxious children and adolescents, there were no suicides, but there were a few self-injurious acts considered by independent experts to represent suicide attempts. For such acts, there was a suggestively greater meta-analytic relative risk during treatment with SRIs *versus* placebo (RR = 1.90; 95%CI: 1.00-3.63) [65-100].

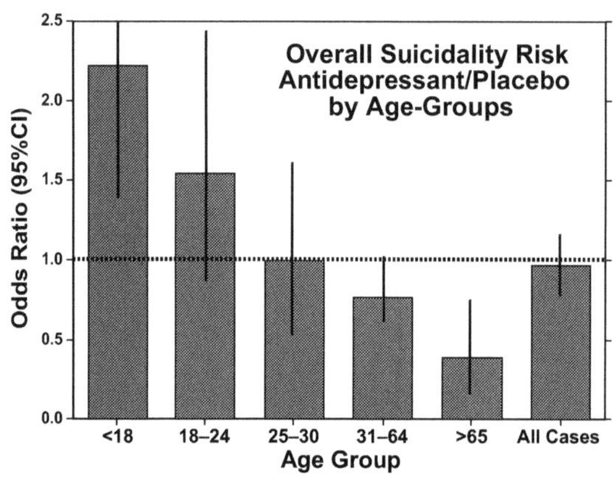

Figure 2: Overall suicidal risk in randomized, placebo-controlled trials of modern antidepressants, by age groups, as Odds Ratios (OR) for risk with drug *versus* placebo, with fixed-effect 95% confidence intervals (CI; vertical lines) compared to the null value of 1.0 (horizontal dashed line). Note that there is a slightly but statistically nonsignificantly lower overall risk of new suicidal ideation and suicidal acts with antidepressants *vs.* placebo (OR: 0.84, 95%CI: 0.69-1.02). Data are adapted from FDA analyses of spontaneous adverse-event reports from a total of 386 controlled trials involving 112, 875 adult and juvenile patient-subjects with major depressive or other disorders (Laughren 2006; Statistical Section, p 27). Most of the suicidal events pertain to ideation, whereas suicides and even attempts were rare. In addition, there was an age-associated decrease in risk of suicides and attempts (independent of treatment): <18 years (0.55%) > 18-24 (0.48%) > 25-30 (0.19%) > 31-64 (0.14%) > 65 (0.13%) (Laughren 2006; Statistical Section, pp 37), whereas risk of emerging suicidality (acts plus ideation) was similar among men (OR for antidepressant *vs.* placebo: 0.75, CI: 0.53-1.04) and women (OR: 0.89, CI: 0.70-1.13) (Laughren 2006; Statistical Section, p 40).

RCT data fail to support an expected overall reduction of risk of suicidal acts during treatment with antidepressants of all types, and even suggest that risk of suicide attempts and perhaps suicides may be greater during treatment with antidepressants of various types. However, many trials in adult depressive disorder patients have found substantially larger reductions in average ratings of suicidal ideation with antidepressants of various types than with placebo [96, 98, 107-109]. However, these findings are subjective, usually incidental, and based on post-hoc assessments of individual items on standard depression symptom-rating scales (Hamilton item 3 or Montgomery-Åsberg item 10), which may shift coincidentally with impressions of overall clinical improvement. Indeed, studies with antidepressants that explicitly consider suicidal ideation and behaviors as outcome measures remain to be carried out.

It should be noted that even RCTs have limitations that can lead to artifacts and uncertainties. These include potential unreliability of essentially incidental, passive reporting of suicidal thoughts or behaviors in most RCTs based on currently typical "adverse event reporting" systems, under conditions not designed explicitly to detect suicidal events. In addition, the relatively short duration of most trials of treatments for acute depression may not provide an adequate basis for evaluating the effects of treatment on rare suicidal behaviors, comparable to the long-term trials available for clozapine, lithium, and anticonvulsants already discussed. Moreover, much of what has been reported involves suicidal ideation of highly uncertain clinical significance and quantitatively very limited relationship to actual life-threatening behaviors. Another potential source of bias is that initial randomization in RCTs can break down during the conduct of trials. Premature, and potentially non-random, dropping out, owing usually to lack of perceived benefit, or emergence of intolerable side effects of treatment, is routinely encountered in most RCTs. More specifically, observed rates of "suicidal events" rarely are corrected for actual time of exposure of individual patient-subjects to specific treatments. Such correction to reported adverse event rates (events/persons/weeks) can be important if actual exposures are not closely matched across trial treatment arms, and particularly when rare events such as suicides and attempts are involved. For example, earlier dropping out of a trial arm involving ineffective placebo treatment can paradoxically limit observable suicidal risk with placebo, artifactually making active drug treatment seem "riskier" than placebo. The emergence of new suicidal behaviors among adults treated with antidepressants is very uncommon, involving perhaps 5/1000 patients within a year [110].

Recently, a meta-analytic review of large cohort and case-control studies of antidepressants found closely similar results as the FDA analyses. That is, younger patients experienced increased suicidal risks, whereas older adults had lower risks associated with antidepressant treatment [111]. These two post-hoc, meta-analyses show remarkably similar risks *versus* age [112] that require prospective and controlled assessment.

8. IMPLICATIONS OF CONTROLLED TRIALS OF ANTIDEPRESSANTS

The preceding findings led to FDA requirements for revision of drug manufacturer informational bulletins to include highlighted ("black box") warnings of the findings just summarized, pertaining to possible increases in risk of suicidal thinking and perhaps behaviors during treatment of juvenile and young adult patients with SRIs and other modern antidepressants. The warnings also carry implications that special care is appropriate in the early treatment of young depressed or other patients being given an antidepressant [100]. This recommendation is likely to further limit use of modern antidepressants in children, in addition to the fact that only fluoxetine is approved for juvenile major depression. The unique status of this agent is based on at least four controlled trials, some of which are large enough that their statistical power offsets the limited efficacy of SRIs and other antidepressants in children and adolescents [113], particularly one very large federally-funded trial with an unusually large separation of responses to the drug *versus* placebo [114]. In 12 large trials of SRIs in juvenile major depression the relative rate of responding to drug more than to placebo (RR) averaged 1.23 (95% CI: 1.14-1.33; $p<0.0001$) and in 14 much smaller trials of TCAs, the pooled RR of 1.15 (CI: 0.98-1.34; $p=0.098$) was of similarly modest magnitude but statistically nonsignificant [113].

The findings pertaining to possible worsening of suicidal risks in young antidepressant-treated patients suggest potential scientifically and clinically very important developmental differences in affective and behavioral responses to antidepressants that require further study, especially with respect to risks of actual suicidal behavior. We presented evidence recently that SRIs may carry an unusually high risk of inducing switching from depression into agitated, dysphoric, irritable states in children, specifically below age 14 years [63-115]. Such reactions are especially likely to arise among depressed juveniles previously not recognized as having bipolar disorders or other behavioral sensitivity to mood-elevating agents, but can arise also in adults [116, 117]. Such responses might contribute to the reported excess of suicidal ideation in young patients treated with modern antidepressants [104].

CONCLUSIONS

Our main conclusions arising from this overview of current knowledge of the relevance of psychopharmacological treatments to suicidal risk in patients with major psychiatric disorders are summarized in Table **2**. Since an initial case series reported soon after the introduction of fluoxetine [118], there have been repeated reports that a minority of depressed patients experience adverse behavioral and emotional responses to treatment with various types of mood-elevating medicines, and not only SRIs [66-116]. Typically, such responses arise early in treatment. Usually they can be identified clinically, and treatment appropriately modified, such as by removing antidepressant, adding sedating, antipsychotic, or mood-stabilizing treatments as well as providing additional individual support. The US FDA [100] has encouraged a re-examination of what appears to have become somewhat casual routine practices in the use of relatively safe modern antidepressants to treat depressed patients and others at risk for suicide, calling for close early clinical follow-up of newly depressed persons not well known to a treating clinician.

Finally, a new hypothesis is suggested by the findings reviewed above. That antidepressant treatment appears to reduce suicidal ideation in depressed adults, whereas only clozapine and lithium have secure evidence of reducing risk of suicide attempts or suicides, suggests that "suicidality" is not usefully considered as a unitary clinical phenomenon or therapeutic target. Instead, there may be a differential pharmacology of particular aspects of suicidality. These probably include a need to limit rage, aggression, and impulsivity in order to reduce risks of attempts and suicides [12]. Such properties are more to be expected of antipsychotic or mood-stabilizing agents than of antidepressants.

Table 2: Psychopharmacology and suicide: Summary of recent research findings

- Therapeutic research on suicide was virtually unknown a decade ago.
- Long-term treatment with lithium has strong evidence for up to five-fold reduced risks of suicide and attempts in bipolar and mixed samples of major affective disorders, and suggestive evidence of four-fold reduction of such risk in recurrent major depression.
- Long-term treatment with the anticonvulsant mood-stabilizers carbamazepine and divalproex appears to be less effective than lithium in reducing suicidal risk.
- Based on relatively limited data, clozapine has reduced risk of suicide attempts by nearly five-fold in schizophrenia patients and has unique FDA approval for this indication.
- A minority of ecological studies found minor decreases of suicide rates by region or time correlated with higher rates of prescribing modern antidepressants in the 1990s; such correlations are probably influenced by many factors associated with access to clinical care, and may have begun earlier.
- Most large clinical studies suggest decreased suicidal risk with antidepressant treatment, but some find increases at various ages; such studies risk confounding by associating antidepressant treatment with more severe depression, and so with greater suicidal risk; such risk may decline in older adults.
- Data pooled from relatively brief, randomized, controlled trials in acute major depression suggest increases in risk of suicide attempts, as well as increases in suicidal ideation in young patients, but decreases in older adults.
- Overall, antidepressants are not proved to have beneficial effects on risks of suicidal behaviors but may reduce suicidal ideation along with other symptoms of depression in adults.
- Differences between antidepressants and antipsychotic or mood-stabilizing agents may reflect differential benefits of the latter for irritability, anger, aggression, and impulsivity, which may worsen in some patients given antidepressants.
- Early depression requires particularly close clinical follow-up to identify emerging suicidal risks and treatable adverse behavioral reactions to treatment.

ACKNOWLEDGEMENTS

Based in part on lectures at the McLean Division of Massachusetts General Hospital (RJB) on 4 January 2007, and the Upjohn Center for Depression Research, University of Michigan at Ann Arbor, on 4 May 2007 (RJB). Supported, in part, by USPHS-NIH NIMH research grant MH-073779 (to LT and RJB), a research grant from Janssen Pharmaceuticals, Titusville, New Jersey (to LT and RJB), a grant from the Bruce J. Anderson Foundation and the McLean Private Donors Research Fund for Mood Disorders and Psychopharmacology Research (to RJB), and by the Centro Bini Private Donors Mood Disorders Research Fund (to LT). Some of the research results summarized arose from a task force that analyzed research on antidepressants and suicide, chaired by Mauricio Tohen, M.D., Dr.P.H. for the Eli Lilly Research Center in Indianapolis, Indiana.

DISCLOSURES

Dr. Baldessarini has been a consultant to, or has collaborated in research with the following corporations: Auritec, Biotrofix, IFI, Janssen, JDS, Eli Lilly, Merck, NeuroHealing, Novartis, and Solvay Corporations involved in the development and manufacture of a variety of psychotropic drugs. Dr. Tondo has received research support from Janssen Pharmaceuticals and Eli Lilly and Company. Neither author, nor any family member holds equity positions in biomedical or pharmaceutical corporations.

REFERENCES

[1] Goldsmith SK, Pellmar TC, Kleinman AM, Bunney WE (Eds). Reducing suicide. Washington, DC: Institute of Medicine of the US National Academies of Science; 2002.

[2] American Psychiatric Association (APA). Practice guideline for the assessment and treatment of patients with suicidal behaviors. Am J Psychiatry 2003;160 (11 Suppl.):1-60.

[3] Simon RI, Hales RE (Eds). Textbook of suicide assessment and management. Washington, DC: American Psychiatric Press; 2006.

[4] World Health Organization (WHO). International suicide rates. Available from: www.who.int/mental_health/prevention/suicide/ country_reports/en/index.html. Accessed 10 January 2007].

[5] Diekstra RFW. Epidemiology of suicide and parasuicide. Acta Psychiatr Scand 1993;371 (Suppl):9-20.

[6] Tondo L, Albert M, Baldessarini, RJ. Suicide rates in relation to health-care access in the United States. J Clin Psychiatry 2006;67:517-523.

[7] Isacsson G. Suicide prevention-a medical breakthrough? Acta Psychiatr Scand 2000;102:113-117.

[8] Grunebaum MF, Ellis SP, Li S, Oquendo MA, Mann JJ. Antidepressants and suicide risk in the United States, 1985-1999. J Clin Psychiatry 2004;65:1456-1462.

[9] Baldessarini RJ, Tondo L, Strombom I, *et al.* Analysis of ecological studies of relationships between antidepressant utilization and suicidal risk. Harv Rev Psychiatry 2007b:15:133-145.

[10] Tondo L, Isacsson G, Baldessarini RJ. Suicide in bipolar disorder: risk and prevention. CNS Drugs 2003;17:491-511.

[11] Kessler RC, Berglund P, Borges G, Nock M, Wang PS. Trends in suicide ideation, plans, gestures, and attempts in the United States, 1990-1992 to 2001-2003. JAMA 2005;293:2487-2495.

[12] Baldessarini RJ, Tondo L, Davis P, Pompili M, Goodwin FK, Hennen J. Decreased suicidal risk during long-term lithium treatment: meta-analysis. Bipolar Disord 2006b;8:625-639.

[13] Roy A. Suicide. In Sadock BJ, Sadock VA (Eds). Kaplan and Sadock's comprehensive textbook of psychiatry, seventh edition, vol 2 (pp 2031-2040). Philadelphia: Lippincott-Williams and Wilkins; 2000.

[14] Nordstrom P, Samuelsson M, Åsberg M. Survival analysis of suicide risk after attempted suicide. Acta Psychiatr Scand 1995;91:336-340.

[15] Baldessarini RJ, Jamison KR. Effects of medical interventions on suicidal behavior: Summary and conclusions. J Clin Psychiatry 1999;60 (Suppl. 2):117-122.

[16] Tsuang MT, Woolson RF. Mortality in patients with schizophrenia, mania, depression and surgical conditions: comparison with general population mortality. Br J Psychiatry 1977;130:162-166.

[17] Black DW, Winokur G, Nasrallah A. Is death from natural causes still excessive in psychiatric patients: follow-up of 1593 patients with major affective disorder? J Nerv Ment Dis 1987;175:674-680.

[18] Goodwin FK, Jamison KR. Manic-depressive illness, second edition. New York: Oxford University Press, 2007.

[19] Sharma R, Markar HR. Mortality in affective disorder. J Affect Disord 1994;31:91-96.

[20] Ahrens B, Müller-Oerlinghausen B, Schou M, *et al.* Excess cardiovascular and suicide mortality of affective disorders may be reduced by lithium prophylaxis. J Affect Disord 1995;33:67-75.

[21] Dening TR. Lithium and motor vehicle crashes: perhaps bipolar disorder is the risk, not its treatment. BMJ 2004;328:895-896.

[22] Evans DL, Charney DS, Lewis L, *et al.* Mood disorders in the medically ill: scientific review and recommendations. Biol Psychiatry 2005;58:175-189.

[23] Katon WJ, Rutter C, Simon G, *et al.* Association of comorbid depression with mortality in patients with type-2 diabetes. Diabetes Care 2005;28: 2668-2672.

[24] Khalsa HMK, Salvatore P, Hennen J, Tohen M, Baldessarini RJ. Suicidal events and accidents in 216 first-episode bipolar-I disorder patients: predictive factors. J Affect Disord 2008;106:179-184.

[25] Harris EC, Barraclough B. Excess mortality of mental disorder. Br J Psychiatry 1998;173:11-53.

[26] Tondo L, Baldessarini RJ, Hennen J, *et al.* Suicide attempts in major affective disorder patients with comorbid substance use disorders. J Clin Psychiatry 1999; 60 (Suppl 2):63-69.

[27] Judd LL, Akiskal HS, Schettler PJ, *et al.* Long-term natural history of the weekly symptomatic status of bipolar I disorder. Arch Gen Psychiatry 2002;59:530-537.

[28] Post RM, Denicoff KD, Leverich GS, *et al.* Morbidity in 258 bipolar outpatients followed for 1 year with daily prospective ratings on the NIMH life chart method. J Clin Psychiatry 2003;64,680-690.

[29] Baldessarini RJ, Salvatore P, Tohen M, *et al.* Morbidity from onset in first-episode bipolar I disorder patients: The International-300 study. Neuropsychopharmacology 2004;29 (Suppl 1):S88.

[30] Joffe RT, MacQueen GM, Marriott M, Trevor Young L. Prospective, longitudinal study of percentage of time spent ill in patients with bipolar I or bipolar II disorders. Bipolar Disord 2004;6:62-66.

[31] Ghaemi SN, Hsu DJ, Soldani F, Goodwin FK. Antidepressants in bipolar disorder: the case for caution. Bipolar Disord 2003;5:421-433.

[32] Baldessarini RJ, Leahy L, Arcona S, Gause D, Zhang W, Hennen, J. Prescribing patterns of psychotropic medicines in the United States for patients diagnosed with bipolar disorders. Psychiatr Serv 2007a;58:85-91.

[33] Koukopoulos A, Koukopoulos A. Agitated depression as a mixed state and the problem of melancholia. Psychiatr Clin North Am 1999;22:547-564.

[34] Akiskal HS, Benazzi F, Perugi G, Rihmer Z. Agitated "unipolar" depression re-conceptualized as a depressive mixed state: implications for the antidepressant-suicide controversy. J Affect Disord 2005;85:245-258.

[35] Maj M, Pirozzi R, Magliano L, Fiorillo A, Bartoli, L. Agitated "unipolar" major depression: prevalence, phenomenology, and outcome. J Clin Psychiatry 2006;67:712-719.

[36] Tondo L, Lepri B, Baldessarini RJ. Suicidal risks among 2826 major affective disorder patients. Acta Psychiatr Scand 2007;116:419-428.

[37] Rose RM, Burt RA, Clayton PJ. Consensus development conference statement: electroconvulsive therapy. JAMA 1985;254:2103-2108.

[38] Weinger RD (Ed). Practice of electroconvulsive therapy: recommendations for treatment, training, and privileging. task force report of the American Psychiatric Association, second edition. Washington, DC: American Psychiatric Press; 2000.

[39] Oquendo MA, Chaudhury SR, Mann JJ. Pharmacotherapy of suicidal behavior in bipolar disorder. Arch Suicide Res 2005;9:237-250.

[40] Khan A, Leventhal RM, Khan S, Brown WA. Suicide risk in patients with anxiety disorders: a meta-analysis of the FDA database. J Affect Disord 2002;68:183-190.

[41] Fawcett J. Treating impulsivity and anxiety in the suicidal patient. Ann NY Acad Sci 2001;932:94-105.

[42] Meltzer HY, Alphs L, Green AI, *et al.* Clozapine treatment for suicidality in schizophrenia: international suicide prevention trial (InterSePT). Arch Gen Psychiatry 2003;60:82-91.

[43] Hennen J, Baldessarini RJ. Suicidal risk during treatment with clozapine: meta-analysis. Schizophrenia Res 2005;73:139-145.

[44] Modestin J, DalPlan D, Agarwalla P. Clozapine diminished suicidal behavior: retrospective evaluation of clinical records. J Clin Psychiatry 2005;66:534-538.

[45] Houston JP, Ahl J, Meyers AL, Kaiser CJ, Tohen M, Baldessarini RJ. Reduced suicidal ideation in bipolar-I disorder mixed-episode patients in a placebo-controlled trial of olanzapine combined with lithium or divalproex. J Clin Psychiatry 2006;67:1246-1252.

[46] Ahrens B, Müller-Oerlinghausen B. Does lithium exert an independent antisuicidal effect? Pharmacopsychiatry 2001;34:132-136.

[47] Tondo L, Hennen J, Baldessarini RJ. Reduced suicide risk with long-term lithium treatment in major affective illness: meta-analysis. Acta Psychiatr Scand 2001;104:163-172.

[48] Angst J, Angst F, Gerber-Werder R, Gamma A. Suicide in 406 mood-disorder patients with and without long-term medication: 40-44 year follow-up. Arch Suicide Res 2005;9:279-300.

[49] Cipriani A, Pretty H, Hawton K, Geddes JR. Lithium in the prevention of suicidal behavior and all-cause mortality in patients with mood disorders: systematic review of randomized trials. Am J Psychiatry 2005;162:1805-1819.

[50] Kessing LV, Søndergard L, Kvist K, Andersen PK. Suicide risk in patients treated with lithium. Arch Gen Psychiatry 2005;62:860-866.

[51] Müller-Oerlinghausen B, Ahrens B, Felber W. Suicide-preventive and mortality-reducing effect of lithium. In Bauer M, Grof P, Müller-Oerlinghausen B (Eds), Lithium in neuropsychiatry (pp 179-192). London: Informa Healthcare; 2006.

[52] Baldessarini RJ, Tondo L. Lithium and suicidal risk. Bipolar Disord 2008;10:114-115.

[53] Baldessarini RJ, Goodwin FK. Antisuicidal efficacy of lithium products: Citizen's petition to the United States Food and Drug Administration, Washington, DC, (50pp), September, 2005. Available from: www.fda.gov/ohrms/dockets/dockets/05p0402/05p-0402-cp00001-001-vol1.pdf - 10-17-2005-Text Version. Accessed 20 May 2007].

[54] Guzzetta F, Tondo L, Centorrino F, Baldessarini RJ. Lithium treatment reduces suicidal risk in recurrent major depressive disorder. J Clin Psychiatry 2007;68:380-383.

[55] Waddington D, McKensie IP. Overdose rates in lithium-treated *vs.* antidepressant-treated outpatients. Acta Psychiatr Scand 1994;90:50-52.

[56] Baldessarini RJ, Tarazi FI. Drug therapy of depression and anxiety disorders, psychosis and mania. In Brunton LL, Lazo JS, Parker KL (Eds). Goodman and Gilman's the pharmacological basis of therapeutics (pp 429-500). New York: McGraw-Hill; 2005.

[57] Eyer F, Pfab R, Felgenhauer N, *et al.* Lithium poisoning: pharmacokinetics and clearance during different therapeutic measures. J Clin Psychopharmacol 2006;26:325-330.

[58] Watson WA, Litovitz TL, Klein-Schwartz W, *et al.* Annual report of the American Association of Poison Control Centers Toxic Exposure Surveillance System (2003). Am J Emerg Med 2004;22:335-404.

[59] Thies-Flechtner K, Müller-Oerlinghausen B, Seibert W, Walther A, Greil W. Effect of prophylactic treatment on suicide risk in patients with major affective disorders: data from a randomized prospective trial. Pharmacopsychiatry 1996;29:103-107.

[60] Goodwin FK, Fireman B, Simon GE, Hunkeler EM Lee, J, Revicki D. Suicide risk in bipolar disorder during treatment with lithium and divalproex. JAMA 2003;290:1467-1473.

[61] Yerevanian BI, Koek RJ, Mintz J. Lithium, anticonvulsants and suicidal behavior in bipolar disorder. J Affect Disord 2003;73:223-228.

[62] Baldessarini RJ, Tondo L. Meta-analytic comparison of antisuicidal effects of lithium *versus* anticonvulsants. Pharmacopsychiatry 2009;42:72-75.

[63] Baldessarini RJ, Faedda GL, Hennen J. Risk of mania with serotonin reuptake inhibitors *vs.* tricyclic antidepressants in children, adolescents and young adults. Arch Pediatr Adolesc Med 2005a;159:298-299.

[64] Baldessarini RJ, Pompili M, Tondo L, *et al.* Antidepressants and suicidal behavior: are we hurting or helping? Clin Neuropsychiatry 2005b;2:73-75.

[65] Baldessarini RJ, Pompili M, Tondo L. Suicidal risk in antidepressant trials. Arch Gen Psychiatry 2006a;63:246-248.

[66] Mann JJ, Emslie G, Baldessarini RJ, *et al.* ACNP task force report on SSRIs and suicidal behavior in youth. Neuropsychopharmacology 2006;31:473-492.

[67] Healy D. Did regulators fail over selective serotonin reuptake inhibitors? Br Med J 2006;333:92-95.

[68] Klein DF. FDA post-marketing safety decisions. J Clin Psychiatry 2006;67:1305-1306.

[69] Moller HJ. Evidence for beneficial effects of antidepressants on suicidality in depressive patients: systematic review. Eur Arch Psychiatry Clin Neurosci 2006;256:329-343.

[70] Helgason T, Tómasson H, Zoëga T. Antidepressants and public health in Iceland: time series analysis of national data. Br J Psychiatry 2004;184:157-162.

[71] Gibbons RD, Hur K, Bhaumik DK, Mann JJ. Relationship between antidepressant prescription rates and rate of early adolescent suicide. Am J Psychiatry 2006;163:1898-1904.

[72] Ludwig J, Marcotte DE. Antidepressants, suicide, and drug regulation. J Policy Anal Manag 2005;24:249-272.

[73] Henriksson S, Isacsson G. Increased antidepressant use and fewer suicides in Jamtland county, Sweden, after a primary-care educational program on the treatment of depression. Acta Psychiatr Scand 2006;114:159-167.

[74] Søndergård L, Kvist K, Lopez AG, Andersen PK, Kessing LV. Temporal changes in suicide rates for persons treated and not treated with antidepressants in Denmark during 1995-1999. Acta Psychiatr Scand 2006c;114:168-176.

[75] Reseland S, Bray I, Gunnell D. Relationship between antidepressant sales and secular trends in suicide rates in the Nordic countries. Br J Psychiatry 2006;188:354-358.

[76] Tondo L, Baldessarini RJ. Trends in suicide rates: an international perspective. Ital J Psychopathol 2006;12 (2 Suppl):202-203.

[77] Freedman DA. The ecological fallacy. Available from: http://www.stat.berkeley.edu/ ~census/ecofall.txt, 2002. Accessed 10 January, 2007].

[78] Jick SS, Dean AD, Jick H. Antidepressants and suicide. Br Med J 1995;310:215-218.

[79] Jick H, Kaye JA, Jick SS. Antidepressants and risk of suicidal behavior. JAMA 2004;292:338-343.

[80] Warshaw MG, Keller MB. Relationship between fluoxetine use and suicidal behavior in 654 subjects with anxiety disorders. J Clin Psychiatry 1996;57:158-166.

[81] Leon AC, Keller MB, Warshaw MG, *et al.* Prospective study of fluoxetine treatment and suicidal behavior in affectively ill subjects. Am J Psychiatry 1999;156:195-201.

[82] Oquendo MA, Kamali M, Ellis SP, *et al.* Adequacy of antidepressant treatment after discharge and the occurrence of suicidal acts in major depression: a prospective study. Am J Psychiatry 2002;159:1746-1751.

[83] Yerevanian BI, Koek RJ, Feusner JD, Hwang S, Mintz J. Antidepressants and suicidal behavior in unipolar depression. Acta Psychiatr Scand 2004;110:452-458.

[84] Barak Y, Olmer A, Aizenber, D. Antidepressants reduce the risk of suicide among elderly depressed patients. Neuropsychopharmacology 2005;31,178-181.

[85] Didham RC, McConnell DW, Blair HJ, Reith DM. Suicide and self-harm following prescription of SSRIs and other antidepressants: confounding by indication. Br J Clin Pharmacol 2005;60:519-525.

[86] Martinez C, Rietbrock S, Wise L, *et al.* Antidepressant treatment and the risk of fatal and non-fatal self harm in first episode depression: nested case-control study. Br Med J 2005;330:389-392.

[87] Bauer MS, Wisniewski, SR, Marangell LB, *et al.* Are antidepressants associated with new-onset suicidality in bipolar disorder? Prospective study of participants in the systematic treatment enhancement program for bipolar disorder (STEP-BP). J Clin Psychiatry 2006;67:48-55.

[88] Juurlink DN, Mamdani MM, Kopp A, Redelmeier DA. Risk of suicide with selective serotonin reuptake inhibitors in the elderly. Am J Psychiatry 2006;163:813-821.

[89] Olfson M, Marcus SC, Shaffer D. Antidepressant drug therapy and suicide in severely depressed children and adults: case-control study. Arch Gen Psychiatry 2006;63:865-872.

[90] Simon GE, Savarino J, Operskalski B, Wang PS. Suicide risk during antidepressant treatment. Am J Psychiatry 2006;163:41-47.

[91] Søndergård L, Kvist K, Andersen PK, Kessing, LV. Do antidepressants prevent suicide? Int Clin Psychopharmacol 2006a;21:211-218.

[92] Søndergård L, Kvist K, Andersen PK, Kessing LV. Do antidepressants precipitate youth suicide: a nationwide pharmacoepidemiological study? Eur Child Adolesc Psychiatry, 2006b;15:232-240.

[93] Tiihonen J, Lonnqvist J, Wahlbeck K, Klaukka T, Tanskanen A, Haukka J. Antidepressants and the risk of suicide, attempted suicide, and overall mortality in a nationwide cohort. Arch Gen Psychiatry 2006;3:1358-1367.

[94] Khan A, Warner HA, Brown WA. Symptom reduction and suicide risk in patients treated with placebo in antidepressant clinical trials: analysis of the FDA database. Arch Gen Psychiatry 2000;57:311-317.

[95] Khan A, Khan S, Kolts R, Brown WA. Suicide rates in clinical trials with SSRIs, other antidepressants, and placebo: analysis of FDA reports. Am J Psychiatry 2003;160:790-792.

[96] Acharya N, Rosen AS, Polzer JP, *et al.* Duloxetine: meta-analyses of suicidal behaviors and ideation in clinical trials for major depressive disorder. J Clin Psychopharmacol 2006;26:587-594.

[97] Bostwick JM, Pankratz *VS.* Affective disorders and suicide risk: a re-examination. Am J Psychiatry 2000;157:1925-1932.

[98] Tollefson GD, Rampey AH Jr, Beasley CM Jr, Enas GG, Potvin JH. Absence of a relationship between adverse events and suicidality during pharmacotherapy for depression. J Clin Psychopharmacol 1994;14:163-169.

[99] Storosum JG, Van Zwieten BJ, Van den Brink W, Gersons BP, Broekmans AW. Suicide risk in placebo-controlled studies of major depression. Am J Psychiatry 2001;158:1271-1275.

[100] FDA (US Food and Drug Administration). Antidepressant use in children, adolescents, and adults. Available from: http://www.fda.gov/cder/drug/antidepressants. Accessed 22 June 2006].

[101] Fergusson D, Doucette S, Glass KC, *et al.* Association between suicide attempts and selective serotonin reuptake inhibitors: systematic review of randomized controlled trials. Br Med J 2005;330:396-402.

[102] Gunnell D, Saperia J, Ashby D. Selective serotonin reuptake inhibitors (SSRIs) and suicide in adults: meta-analysis of drug company data from placebo controlled, randomized controlled trials submitted to the MHRA's safety review. Br Med J 2005;330:385-388.

[103] Hammad TA, Laughren TP, Racoosin, JA. Suicide rates in short-term randomized controlled trials of newer antidepressants. J Clin Psychopharmacol 2006a;26:203-207.

[104] Hammad TA, Laughren TP, Racoosin JA. Suicidality in pediatric patients treated with antidepressant drugs. Arch Gen Psychiatry 2006b;63:332-339.

[105] Laughren TP. Overview of a meeting of the psychopharmacology drug advisory committee (PDAC) concerning suicidal risk in trials of antidepressant drugs in juvenile and adult patients, (pp 27ff), 2006. Available from: http://www.fda.gov/ohrms/ dockets/ac/06/ briefing/2006-4272b1-index.htm. Accessed 26 December 2006.

- MHRA (UK Medicines and Health Regulatory Agency). Selective serotonin reuptake inhibitor (SSRI) antidepressants: committee on safety of medicines (CSM) working group findings. Available from: http://www.mhra.gov.uk/news/2004/2004.ht. Accessed 22 September 2005].

[106] Beasley CM Jr, Dornseif BE, Bosomworth JC, *et al.* Fluoxetine and suicide: meta-analysis of controlled trials of treatment for depression. Br Med J 1991;303:685-692.

[107] Filteau MJ, Lapierre YD, Bakish D, Blanchard A. Reduction in suicidal ideation with SSRIs: review of 459 depressed patients. J Psychiatr Neurol 1993;18:114-118.

[108] Pedersen AG. Escitalopram and suicidality in adult depression and anxiety. Int Clin Psychopharmacol 2005;20:139-143.

[109] Tondo L, Lepri B, Baldessarini RJ. Suicidal status during antidepressant treatment in 789 Sardinian patients with major affective disorder. Acta Psychiatr Scand 2008;118:106-115.

[110] Barbui C, Esposito E, Cipriani A. Selective serotonin reuptake inhibitors and risk of suicide: systematic review of observational studies. Can Med Assoc J 2009;180:291-297.

[111] Fawcett JA, Baldessarini RJ, Coryell WH, Silverman MM, Stein DJ. Defining and managing suicidal risk in patients taking psychotropic medications. J Clin Psychiatry 2009;70:782-789.

[112] Tsapakis E, Soldani F, Tondo L, Baldessarini RJ. Efficacy of antidepressants in depressed children and adolescents: meta-analysis. Br J Psychiatry 2008;193:10-17.

[113] March J, Silva S, Petrycki S, *et al.* Treatment for adolescents with depression study (TADS): fluoxetine, cognitive-behavioral therapy, and their combination for adolescents with depression. JAMA 2004;292:807-820.

[114] Faedda GL, Baldessarini RJ, Glovinsky IP, Austin NB. Treatment-emergent mania in pediatric bipolar disorder: retrospective case review. J Affect Disord 2004;82:149-158.

[115] Pompili M, Tondo L, Baldessarini RJ. Suicidal risk emerging during antidepressant treatment: recognition and intervention. Clin Neuropsychiatry 2005;2:66-72.

[116] Tondo L, Vázquez G, Baldessarini RJ. Mania associated with antidepressant-treatment: comprehensive meta-analysis. Acta Psychiatr Scand 2010.

[117] Teicher MH, Glod C, Cole JO. Emergence of intense suicidal preoccupation during fluoxetine treatment. Am J Psychiatry 1990;147:207-210.

[118] Burrows GM. Commentaries on the causes, forms, symptoms, treatment, moral and medical aspects of insanity. London: Underwood; 1828.

CHAPTER 10

Psychotherapy with Suicidal People: Some Common Factors with Attempters

Antoon A. Leenaars*

1500 Ouellette Avenue, Suite 203, Windsor, ON, Canada, N8X 1K7

Abstract: The villain for the would-be suicide attempter is pain; clinicians need something to fight that pain, an anodyne. Psychotherapy is such; yet, to assuage the pain, the clinician primarily needs to know what he/she is treating. This paper, thus, first offers an empirical, cross-cultural perspective on that 'what,' illustrated with the writings of William Styron. It is argued once one understands what we are treating, effective psychotherapy comes naturally. An outline of some common factors (or commonalities) in the field of psychotherapy with suicidal people is presented. The most essential common factor is the therapeutic relationship. What is effective and what is lethal are outlined, concluding that to treat the suicidal attempter effectively, the clinician has to be person-centred, not mental disorder centred. He/she has to know whom he/she is treating; this is quality care.

Keywords: Psychotherapy, suicide, prevention, psychological pain.

1. INTRODUCTION

A most insightful exegesis of the common factor in suicide, pain, much because of its literary style, is by William Styron in his book, Darkness Visible [1]. He calls the pain, "A veritable howling tempest of the brain" (p. 38). These are a few lines Styron wrote standing before the suicidal abyss, ready to attempt suicide. William Styron's book, which he painfully subtitles, "A memoir of madness", is a must read for any practicing and/or aspiring clinician wanting to treat a suicide attempter; for that matter, any suicidal person.

Styron is no stranger to writing; he is a most respected author. He authored the famed Sophie's Choice, and other scholarly books – books which themselves give expression to the desolation of melancholia and suicide. He has been awarded numerous awards including the Prix Mandial Cinco del Duca, which itself played a special significance in William Styron's malaise. It is his literary skill that makes Darkness Visible rich.

He writes:

> The pain is unrelenting, and what makes the condition intolerable is the foreknowledge that no remedy will come – not in a day, an hour, a month, or a minute. If there is mild relief, one knows that it is only temporary; more pain will follow. It is hopelessness even more than pain that crushes the soul. So the decision-making of daily life involves not, as in normal affairs, shifting from one annoying situation to another less annoying – or from discomfort to relative comfort, or from boredom to activity – but moving from pain to pain. One does not abandon, even briefly, one's bed of nails, but is attached to it wherever one goes (p. 62).

As a solution to the "tempest", William Styron planned his attempt:

> …during the next several days, as I went about stolidly preparing for extinction, I couldn't shake off a sense of melodrama – a melodrama in which I, the victim-to-be of self-murder, was both the solitary actor and lone member of the audience. I had not as yet chosen the mode of my departure, but I knew that that step would come next, and soon, as inescapable as nightfall (p. 64-65).

***Addresss correspondence to Antoon A. Leenaars:** 1500 Ouellette Avenue, Suite 203, Windsor, ON, Canada, N8X 1K7; Tel: 1-519-253-9377; Fax: 1-519-253-8486; E-mail: draalee@sympatico.ca

Maurizio Pompili (Ed)

He concludes, borrowing from the parting words of Cesare Pavese, another author who died by suicide, "No more words. An act. I'll never write again". Next, the act: an attempt to kill himself, but then something else fought the pain.

Styron's own memories are most revealing about what worked effectively. On a cold bitter night, "when I know that I could not possibly get myself through the following day", after his wife had gone to bed, William Styron planned to kill himself. Fortunately, however, he forced himself to watch a play of his. At one point in the play a piercing passage occurred from Brahms' Alto Rhapsody.

This sound resulted in a flood of recollections of his home: "The children who rushed through its rooms, the festivals, the love and work, the honestly earned slumber, the voices and the nimble commotion, the perennial tribe of cats and dogs and birds, 'laughter and ability and Sighing,/And Frocks and Curls'". It was this that he could not leave. It was anodynic. Styron also reveals, what another great scholar, a lead figure in the 20th century in suicidology, Edwin Shneidman calls a deeper anodyne: Attachments.

Styron needs to stop "the howling tempest of the brain". William Styron needs psychotherapy. Psychotherapy with suicidal people, whether they have made an attempt or not, is no different. They need to stop the "bed of nails". They need something to assuage the pain. They need an anodyne. Whether with William Styron, or whoever our patient is, the intent of the therapy is to reduce the person's psychological tempest. To quote Edwin Shneidman:

> If the villain is psychological pain then we need something that fights that pain. There is a word for that: anodyne. An anodyne is a substance that (or an agent or person who) assuages pain. Psychotherapy in general ought to be anodynic. But with a highly suicidal patient – with perturbation and, even more seriously, high lethality – the anodynic function of the therapist is vital [2].

Our method with our suicidal patient, whether he/she has attempted suicide or not, is to serve as an anodynic agent "to relieve the pain so that the patient's raison d'être for suicide is mollified and the need to end the inner suffering is no longer pressing" (p. 182). The tempest has to stop; the world has to shine at least somewhat. William Styron needs to not be a "walking casualty of war". The "pain of pain" needs to be no longer pressing [3-5]. Is there a manual or cookbook we can use to help William Styron, the suicide attempter? What works? An anodynic 'substance', with a long history, is psychotherapy [6, 7].

The purpose of this synopsis is to outline the research basis for an effective approach to psychotherapy with suicidal people [8]. The thesis is: Effective psychotherapy should be person-centred – or, if you prefer, patient-centred (or patient-oriented). Person-centred or person-oriented psychotherapy is derived from the focus on the individual – the individual in his/her entirety; *i.e.*, biological, psychological, sociological, and so on. This is why it is also sometimes called multicomponent or multimodal psychotherapy. This simply means that it is not only psychotherapy alone – cognitive, interpersonal, psychoanalytic, dialectical behavior, whatever – that is most useful, but it may be even more effective in some cases, like Styron, in combination with medication, hospitalization, and removing the gun from the house. The best anodyne is a multidimensional approach.

The question that is posed in this review is, "Is psychotherapy effective?" or more specifically, "Is psychotherapy effective with suicide attempters?" This, in fact, has been the question for millennia about an antidote for "the howling tempest". Before I present the answers from the research today, I will first briefly outline, what it is that we are treating: suicide and attempted suicide. This is to meet Shneidman's challenge: "We ought to know what we are treating".

2. SUICIDE

Almost a million people die by suicide every year around the world [9]. In addition, based on the WHO [9] estimates, there are probably at least 10 million attempters – and then there are the contemplators, and so on. What works effectively with people who have attempted suicide?

Suicide is a human malaise, a multi-dimensional event [10-13]. There are biological, psychological, intrapsychic, interpersonal, social, cultural, and philosophical elements in the suicidal event. Suicide is complex. Although space is limited, I here explicate an empirically, cross-culturally supported psychological theory of what it is that we are treating. This is very rare in suicidology [14]. Suicide, I believe, can be clinically understood from at least the following commonalities or patterns, both intrapsychic and interpersonal, within the context of a larger multi-dimensional ecological perspective [8, 9, 12].

3. INTRAPSYCHIC

1) Unbearable Psychological Pain

The common stimulus in suicide is unbearable psychological pain, the pain of pain [14, 15]. The suicidal person is in a heightened state of perturbation, an intense mental anguish. The person may feel any number of emotions such as boxed in, rejected, deprived, forlorn, distressed, and especially hopeless and helpless. The situation is unbearable and the person desperately wants a way out of it. The suicide, as Murray [16] noted, is functional because it abolishes painful tension for the individual. It provides escape.

2) Cognitive Constriction

The common cognitive state in suicide is mental constriction [13], *i.e.*, rigidity in thinking, narrowing of focus, tunnel vision, concreteness, *etc.* The person is figuratively "intoxicated" or "drugged" by the constriction; the intoxication can be seen in emotions, logic, and perception. This constriction is one of the most dangerous aspects of the suicidal mind.

3) Indirect Expressions

Ambivalence, complications, redirected aggression, unconscious implications, and related indirect expressions (or phenomena) are often evident in suicide. The suicidal person is ambivalent. Not only is it love and hate but it may also be a conflict between survival and unbearable pain. Yet, there is much more. What the person is conscious of is only a fragment of the suicidal mind [17, 18].

4) Inability to Adjust (Psychopathology)

People with all types of pains, problems, *etc.*, are at risk for suicide. Psychological autopsy studies, consistent with studies of suicide notes [11], suggest that 40 to 90% of people who kill themselves have some symptoms of psychopathology and/or problems in adjustment [10]. In those studies, up to 60% of the suicides appear to be related to mood disorders (although likely even lower, about 40%, in teens). Although the majority of suicidal people, as was the case with Styron, may, thus, fit best into mood nosological classifications, (*e.g.*, depressive disorders, bipolar disorders), other emotional/mental disorders have been identified. For example, anxiety disorders, schizophrenic disorders (especially paranoid type), panic disorders, borderline disorders, and antisocial disorders, have been related to suicides [11, 19, 20]. Suicidal people see themselves as in unendurable pain and unable to adjust. Having the belief that they are too weak to overcome difficulties, these people reject everything except death -- they do not survive life's difficulties.

5) Ego (Weakened Ego)

The ego with its enormous complexity [21] is an essential factor in the suicidal scenario. The Oxford English Dictionary (OED) defines ego as "the part of the mind that reacts to reality and has a sense of individuality". Ego strength is a protective factor against suicide. Suicidal people frequently exhibit a relative weakness in their capacity to develop constructive tendencies and to overcome their personal difficulties [22]. The person's ego has likely been weakened by a steady toll of traumatic life events (*e.g.*, loss, rejection, abuse, failure). A vulnerable ego, thus, correlates positively with suicide risk.

4. INTERPERSONAL

6) Interpersonal Relations

The suicidal person has problems in establishing or maintaining relationships (object relations). There are frequently disturbed, unbearable interpersonal situations. A positive development in those same disturbed relationships may have been seen as the only possible way to go on living, but such development was seen as not forthcoming. The person's psychological needs are frustrated [21]. Suicide appears to be related to an unsatisfied or frustrated attachment need, although other needs, often more intrapsychic, may be equally evident, *e.g.*, achievement, autonomy, dominance, honour.

7) Rejection-Aggression

Wilhelm Stekel first documented the rejection-aggression hypothesis in the famous 1910 meeting of the Psychoanalytic Society in Freud's home in Vienna [23]. Loss is central to suicide; it is, in fact, often an unbearable narcissistic injury. This injury/traumatic event leads to pain and in some, self-directed aggression and hate directed towards others [24]. Aggression is, in fact, a common emotional state in suicide.

8) Identification-Egression

Freud [16, 25, 26] hypothesized that intense identification with a lost or rejecting person or, as [22] showed, with any lost ideal (*e.g.*, health, employment, freedom) is crucial in understanding the suicidal person. Identification is defined as an attachment (bond), based upon an important emotional tie with another person (object) [25] or any ideal. If this emotional need is not met, the suicidal person experiences a deep pain (discomfort). There is an intense desperation and the person wants to egress. Suicide is escape.

In concluding, the theory outlined is an empirically supported point of view. It may be useful to not only meet Shneidman's challenge on "what we are treating", but also to develop complex implications for treatment. Often complex problems call for complex solutions – this is true with a suicidal "howling tempest". These common dimensions (or "sameness") are what suicide is. Not necessarily the universal, but certainly the most frequent or common characteristics provide us with a meaningful conceptualization of suicide. These are commonalities. There are few such empirically supported theories in suicidology and, indeed, one that has cross-cultural applicability [8, 10, 27]. Further, once we better empirically understand "what we are treating", whether in the United States or Russia or India or Italy or whatever country, the treatment, such as psychotherapy, comes naturally.

5. ATTEMPTED SUICIDE

A previous attempt is one of the best clues to future attempts [28]. However, not all previous attempters go on to attempt again [or kill themselves; about 15% do so *versus* 1.5% for the general population [29, 30]. Although it is obvious that one has to "attempt" suicide in order to commit it, it is equally clear that the event of "attempting suicide" does not always have death (cessation) as its objective. It is acknowledged that often the goal of "attempted suicide" (such as cutting oneself or ingesting harmful substances) is to change one's life (or to change the behavior of the "significant others" around one) rather than to end it. On some rare occasions death is actually intended and only luckily avoided. However, I wish to stress, as have others [31], that it is useful to think of the "attempter", and the "completer", as two sets of overlapping populations: (1) a group of those who attempt suicide, a few of whom go on to commit it, and (2) a group of those who commit suicide, many of whom previously attempted it. A great deal has to do with perturbation and lethality associated with the event.

Perturbation refers to how upset (disturbed, agitated, sane-insane) the individual is - rated as low-medium-high (or alternatively on a 1 to 9 scale) - and may be measured by various means (*e.g.*, self-reports, biological markers, psychological tests, observations). Lethality is roughly synonymous with the "deathfulness" of the act and is an important dimension in understanding any potentially suicidal patient. Lethality can be rated as low-moderate-high (or alternatively on a 1 to 9 scale). An example for measuring lethality is the following assessment item, derived from Shneidman [32]: "During the last 24 hours, I felt the chances of my actually killing myself (committing suicide and ending my life) were: absent, very low, low-medium, fifty-fifty, high medium, very high, extra high (came very close to actually killing myself)?" A critical distinction in suicide is that lethality - not perturbation - kills. All sorts of people are highly perturbed but are not suicidal. The ratio between suicide attempts and completions is about 4 to 1 to about 10 to 1 - one committed suicide for every four to ten attempts; however, in young people, some reports have the ratio at 50 to 1, even 100 to 1. The ratio, in fact, appears to vary a lot between nations and across risk groups, sex, age, and so on.

The "attempter" and the "completer" share some commonalities; however, they are, by and large, operationally quite different. There is a third group, the "contemplators", whose numbers are so vast that it is difficult to begin to highlight their commonalities, which are again quite different. A study -- a rare opportunity to actually compare attempters and completers -- actually found that there might be more psychological similarities than differences, however [29].

There is a need for studies of suicide that compare attempters to completers [33]. Are there common factors? Are there differences? There have been actually very few studies to answer these questions. Thus, we need to ask: Is our theory of suicide only applicable to completers? Alternatively, can we apply it to attempters – all, some or most? These are critical questions for prevention, and by implication, psychotherapy, with people who have attempted suicide or not. One avenue for such investigations is to compare the notes written by both groups, something generally neglected to date in the literature, except for the publication by Leenaars, Lester, Wenckstern, McMullin, Rudzinski, and Brevard [29]. The purpose of that study was to investigate suicide notes and notes from suicide attempters for the presence of the 8 clusters (and the individual items/protocol sentences in each cluster) that had been discussed earlier.

The sample of notes of the attempters consisted of letters written by individuals who attempted suicide. The notes of the attempters were obtained through the co-operation of a police department in a southwestern American town. There were regrettably no formal estimates of lethality of the attempts. This was not possible because police protocol would not allow for such a procedure, though the use of a lethality estimate would have been more desirable. Who were these attempters? Were they people of high lethality or low or moderate lethality? We know that the attempts were lethal enough to result in police involvement and the need for medical attention. Generally, based on consultation where possible, it is our impression that the attempts were of moderate to high lethality.

Each note of a person who attempted suicide was matched for age (+ 2 years) and sex with a suicide note written by an individual who killed himself/herself. Individuals were in adulthood (*i.e.*, 18 and/or above), with an age range from 18 to 70 for the notes of the attempters and an age range from 19 to 72 for the suicide notes.

The comparison on the eight clusters produced no significant differences. The suicide notes and attempter notes did not differ on the eight psychological common factors. Only one specific item or protocol difference (under Inability to Adjust) was found between the notes. The protocol item, namely that the individual considers himself/herself too weak to overcome his/her personal difficulties and therefore rejects everything to cope with the difficulties of life, was rated as more often true of attempter notes. It would appear - at least tentatively – that maybe attempters relatively more often see themselves as unable to adjust to life's difficulties, although they are not diagnosed as having a mental disorder more frequently. Maybe the attempt is a way to cope, sometimes chronically so, but also not always with a wish to die. Yet, from a statistical point of view, the sole finding could be one of chance. Even this observation would need replication.

The lone result is very limited, especially given the belief that attempters are different from completers; however, none of the clusters differed. Thus, maybe the psychological characteristics of suicide identified are as applicable to highly lethal attempters as they are to completers. There are, indeed, significant commonalities between attempters and completers [13]. Perhaps the ones identified here are some of those similarities, and thus, have application for psychotherapy, whether an attempter or not. It is likely, in fact, that there is a continuum of suicidal behavior, not merely a dichotomy of attempters and completers.

Suicide notes and notes from attempters may differ; yet, they may be more psychologically similar than different. Completers and attempters (at least the ones studied), based on their notes, appear not to differ in such characteristics as pain, aggression, cognitive constriction, hopelessness, psychopathology, and frustrated relationships. Our findings have clinical implications. Maybe we can treat attempters, as we should have the completers. Maybe completers let us know what we are treating, and thus, how to do psychotherapy effectively with suicide attempters and all suicidal people. Our theory, at least, appears to be as applicable to attempters as completers. Maybe completers, who have written last letters, have told us what to treat. Maybe the commonalities do provide an avenue to effective psychotherapy. After all, we need to know what we are treating, whether attempter or not.

6. PSYCHOTHERAPY

I hold to the tenet that understanding the person is the key to prediction and control. If we know the lethal "veritable howling tempest of the brain", we can better treat William Styron effectively. The next purpose of this synopsis is to outline some of the research-based facts in the field of psychotherapy with suicidal people. The core question is, "Is psychotherapy effective with patients who have attempted suicide?" Styron's question remains, 'What works?' The empirical answer to this question can be found in Michael Lambert's 5th edition [34] of Bergin and Garfield's classic in the field of research, Handbook of Psychotherapy and Behavior Change [35].

Saul Rosenzweig [36] is most famous in the field of psychotherapy for quoting Alice in Wonderland's Dodo bird, "Everybody has won, and all must have prizes". He writes,

> …it is justifiable to wonder (1) whether the factors alleged to be operating in a given therapy are identical with the factors that actually are operating, and (2) whether the factors that actually are operating in several different therapies may not have much more in common than have the factors alleged to be operating (p. 412).

He presented data that all psychotherapies were equally effective. Rosenzweig reframed the field [37] and asked the obvious question, "What do these therapies actually have in common that makes them equally successful?" He suggested that the therapist should be person-centred, focusing on what the individual needed.

There are many studies and reviews to date [34], but probably one of the best was by Luborsky, Singer and Luborsky [38]. They analyzed the studies comparing psychotherapies and suggested a verdict similar to the Dodo bird: "Everyone has won". The research on empirically based psychotherapy is more complex than empirically supported treatment – EST's (also called empirically-validated treatments, or EVT); yet, this issue needs a specific focus before I can proceed [39, 40].

There are too many researchers to cite on the topic of EST's; thus, I note the work of William Henry and Gerald Koocher. Henry [41] states that the EST's ignore the bulk of empirical research generated by decades of science, only to intrude an outmoded, paradigm of experimental design [42]. Koocher [43] addresses the issue, offering a solution, in a brief paper entitled, "Three Myths about Empirically Validated Therapies". Koocher provides a list of 3 Myths; they are as follows:

> Myth #1: EST's will save the field by proving to the world (at last) that we are true scientists.

Fact: There is no agreement what constitutes EST's (or EVT's). Are data only of randomized control trials acceptable? Published in refereed journals? Several papers? What?

Myth #2: Any practitioner not employing EST's is incompetent, unethical or both.

Fact: The truth is slavishly following a treatment manual would violate some ethical principles – it ignores the obligation to treat the person as an individual.

Myth #3: Psychotherapists must choose! You must be "for EST's" or "against EST's".

Fact: Therapists should keep up to date on all research.

I am, of course, not opposed to quantitative research; however, in its narrow-minded form, it is "a mess" (Wm. James), if not limiting [44]. There are others, including researchers sometimes associated to EST's that state the same, such as Aaron T. Beck [45]. Psychotherapy research must be more complex. The main task according to Henry [41] is the following: "We must not lose sight of the people in this people oriented endeavor" (p. 138). This is true with suicidal people who have made a lethal attempt.

7. COMMON FACTORS IN PSYCHOTHERAPY

Like clinicians, many researchers have come to the realization of the fact of equivalence and the empirically supported view of common factors; *i.e.,* commonalities or common factors [46]. The issue 'Is psychotherapy effective?' is like asking, 'Is surgery effective?' A better question would be Bruce Wampold's [47]: "Which treatments are most efficacious for which patients under which conditions?" (p. 21). This is true whether they have made an attempt or not – although often we are dealing with heightened lethality. Wampold offers a shift in paradigms; he writes:

> The case could be made that a discussion of the causal factors related to efficacy is irrelevant to the empirical validation of a treatment. That is, if treatment A is proven to be efficacious, then it is unimportant to identify exactly what characteristics of the treatment led to this conclusion. As appealing as this argument sounds, relatively few would adhere to it. First, treatment developers develop treatment operations to be consistent with theory and research and believe that the actions prescribed by the treatment lead to therapeutic change. Second, when that treatment is shown to be efficacious, the proponents believe that these specific operations were responsible for the positive outcomes and typically will argue to that end. Third, the very essence of looking for a set of empirically validated treatments supposes a belief that some treatments are not efficacious and consequently operations common to therapies cannot be responsible for treatment effects. Finally, knowledge of factors related to outcome leads to refining treatments and increased potency (pp. 24-25).

Many will have difficulty accepting that there is no evidence for treatment specificity. Yet, Wampold's and others' meta-analytic work clearly support common, not unique, factors. I earlier defined "common", under the discussion of Suicide; the definition is no different here. There are commonalities in suicide and suicide attempts. There are commonalities in psychotherapy. The wedding of these two will allow many of us to be more effective with suicidal people. Wampold [46] offers the following definition of commonalities: "The features that are shared by all these therapies…are designated as common features" (p. 25). Lambert, *et al.* [48] in the most recent update of the research study supports the common factors. They write:

> … research aimed at examining the in-session behavior of therapists across different theoretical orientations indicates that the distinctiveness of approaches is less pronounced in practice than it is at the abstract level of theory [49, 50]. Thus, theories of change are somewhat independent of therapists' actual activities which show a large degree of overlap across treatments – sometimes referred to as common factors (p. 7).

The common factors movement reflects an attempt to being open to research findings of any approach. The focus is consistent with fostering what works for treating patients. It fosters being person-centred [8, 51].

8. THERAPEUTIC RELATIONSHIPS

To return to Wampold's [47] common factor frame; he writes:

> ...the features that are shared by all therapies included in a single study are designated as common features. The most ubiquitous common feature of therapies is the therapeutic relationship and consequently, for all imaginable studies of psychotherapy, all treatments would involve the therapist and the patient forming a relationship, making this a common feature. Sensitive and empathic responding to patient-expressed pain could likely be a common feature (p.26).

The importance of the therapeutic relationship or therapeutic alliance, the collaborative bond between therapist and patient, has received the most attention [46]. Perhaps the most influential early study on the topic was a paper by Luborsky, McLellan, Woody, O'Brien and Auerbach (1985) entitled, "Therapist Success and Its Determinants". I will briefly outline this study and then proceed to the applications of the role of the therapeutic relationship with suicidal patients.

Lester Luborsky and his colleagues [52] begin with the obvious fact to most practitioners. There is wide variation in the effectiveness of individual therapists. They reported a study of the differential outcomes of patients seen by different therapists. The patients were "male, veteran, methadone hydrochloride – maintained, drug-dependent"; they were randomly assigned to well-trained therapists. Three modes of therapies were offered: concrete counseling, Karl Menninger's psychoanalytic therapy [14] and Aaron Beck's cognitive behavioral therapy [53]. The therapists were almost all M.D.'s or Ph.D.'s and supervised (Beck even participated). The therapist was trained to offer prescribed treatment. The study has been praised for its adherence to standards, common in contemporary research "in which the individual differences between therapists within a treatment are intentionally minimized" [48]. Measures of treatment outcome were multiple, ranging from Beck's Depression Inventory to measurement of psychotic symptoms. Despite these efforts, Luborsky *et al.* [52] concluded "profound differences were discerned in the therapists' success with the patients in their case load" (p. 602). Despite careful selection, training, supervision and so on, differences emerged, not between modes, but between therapists.

Luborsky and colleagues [52] carefully examined a variety of possible factors; patient qualities, therapeutic relationship, patient-therapist relationship qualities and therapist qualities. They found that effectiveness was associated with a number of interacting variables. Therapists had a profoundly different effect; therapist qualities, as judged by peers associated to this outcome, was labeled "interest in helping patients".

Luborsky's main conclusion was the now obvious: Patient therapist relationship is an important predictor of outcome for psychotherapy. Luborsky concluded:

> Our first finding of wide differences in therapist effectiveness by itself has potentially important implications for the study of psychotherapy. In particular, it is now widely accepted after decades of comparative studies that although most forms of psychotherapy are demonstrably effective, there have been little evidence for significant differences in outcomes among different psychotherapies [52].

The American Psychiatric Associations' practice guidelines for assessment and management of suicidal patients supported the view that the therapeutic relationship is central [54]. What are the qualities of an effective therapeutic alliance? Are there common factors with suicidal patients?

9. THERAPEUTIC RELATION WITH SUICIDAL PATIENTS

I, as stated, hold to the tenet that understanding is a key to prediction and control. If we know the lethal "howling tempest", we can treat it effectively; or the converse, if we do not, we cannot treat it effectively. This is consistent with Shneidman's challenge: "We ought to know what we are treating". To answer the question of the therapeutic relationship with suicidal people, let me begin with discussions, which took place in November 2001 in Edwin Shneidman's home [3-5, 13, 15]. I asked on that occasion whether he had any thoughts about psychotherapy with suicidal people. He offered:

> "Suicide prevention is about a person, a person wanting to be helped to stop their pain, what I call psychache".
>
> "In a sense, suicide prevention tries to mollify the whole person. Psychotherapy is concerned with what kind of person that individual is. What works is a view held by Sigmund Freud, William James, Erwin Stengel, not Pavlov or Skinner or any reductionist view" (I would, of course, add Shneidman to the list).
>
> "Our kind of treatment, psychotherapy and so on should address the person's story, his/her narrative, not the demographic, nosological category or this or that fact. It says, "Please tell me who you are…what hurts?" Not, "Please fill out this form…and give me samples of your body fluids".
>
> "Of course, the practical disadvantage of this approach is that it requires more than a few minutes per patient. Suicide prevention is not an efficiency operation. It is a human exchange".

Suicide prevention is based on a humanitarian approach to life. The psychotherapy, I believe, that works with people who have attempted suicide is a person-centred therapy, or if you prefer, a patient-centred therapy, not mental disorder centred therapy. The relationship should be what Martin Buber [55] called an "I-Thou", not "I-it". The relationship (attachment, bond) that the therapist develops is, in fact, central in effective psychotherapy with suicidal people. It is of note that the research cited shows that what works with suicidal people is, in fact, clearly associated to the helping relationship itself. I will go further. I believe that it is the relationship [8]. What we have known for a long time is that patients who persevere and benefit from psychotherapy are the ones that have developed a good working relationship or alliance [52, 56-59]. These patients can be saved. This is person-centred or person-oriented.

William Styron came to no different conclusion. After his survival of "the war" of life and death, William Styron advises those who suffer the pain: "Chin up". He quickly adds that although this is "tantamount to insult", that "one can nearly always be saved". In encouraging prose, he notes that when the pain is its "ghastliest" – and one is in a state of unbearable pain and unrealistic hopelessness – that others – family, friends, lovers, *etc.*, must "persuade the sufferer of life's worth". He reveals that it is the attachments to people (and/or other ideals) that are so critical in siding with life when one is facing one's final egression. William Styron also reveals a deeper relationship, his anodyne – attachments, which were not only relevant to one's choice of death but life – that his choice of life "may have been belated homage to my mother". She had sung to him, when he was young, the passage from the Alto Rhapsody. The relationship or alliance is the anodynic agent. Psychotherapy is no different.

> Styron wrote:
>
> This sound (Alto Rhapsody), which like all music – indeed, like all pleasure – I had been numbly unresponsive to for months, pierced my heart like a dagger, and in a flood of swift recollection I thought of all the joys the house had known: the children who had rushed through its rooms, the festivals, the love and work, the honestly earned slumber, the voices and the nimble commotion, the perennial tribe of cats and dogs and birds, "laughter and ability and Sighing,/And Frocks and Curls". All this I realized was more than I could ever abandon, even as what I had set out so deliberately to do was more than I could inflict on those memories, and upon those, so close to me, with whom the memories were bound. And just as powerfully I realized I could not commit this desecration on myself. I drew upon some last gleam of sanity to perceive the terrifying dimensions of the mortal predicament I had fallen into (p. 66-67) [1].

"Suicidal people", says Shneidman, "need a human exchange". Styron agrees, so do I. This is not armchair speculation, but evidence-based practice. A task force of the American Psychological Association (APA), Division of Psychotherapy, Division 29 [60] identified the following common elements of effective therapy relationships: therapeutic alliance (or rapport), therapist empathy and patient-therapist goal consensus and collaboration. This is consistent with the law of psychotherapy: We ought to know whom we are treating.

Lambert and Bergin [46] agree; they cite some of the core conditions in effective psychotherapy as empathy, worth and positive regard. The list may seem like ones from Carl Rogers [61], but behavior therapists too have embraced concepts such as warm, sensitive and the like [62] and so have cognitive-behavioral therapists [45, 63]. Freud [64] did. Lambert and Bergin [46] stress these ingredients as essential means to establish rapport. Luborsky, *et al.* [52] state the same; they use such descriptions as "supportive", "liked very much by the patients", "very persistent in trying to help". Styron, I am sure, as I read his book, would agree; his mother could be described so. Yet, they also highlight APA's Division of Psychotherapy finding on goal consensus and collaboration. Luborsky *et al.* found that those therapists whose sessions contained the highest adherence to the goal(s) of treatment showed better performance in the cases. They called it the purity of the therapy. They write:

> ...the high correlation between purity of technique and patient outcome suggests that once a helping alliance is formed, the therapists who do what they are supposed to do achieve their effectiveness in this way. However, an equally tenable, reverse-direction interpretation is that when a patient experiences a helping alliance, he enables the therapist to adhere to his intended technique (p. 610).

There should be goal consensus and collaboration, regardless of therapist's mode of psychotherapy or patient characteristics. The goal with suicide attempters is often obvious: Keep the person alive.

10. MULTI-MODAL OR MULTI-COMPONENT APPROACH

Some patients are difficult to treat; Styron was. Many suicidal patients, who have made an attempt, are difficult to treat effectively. The research suggests that with such patients, one must be multi-modal (or multi-component) [48, 27]. This simply implies that to treat a lethal suicidal person, like Styron, one may have to use adjuncts to psychotherapy. Psychotherapy with suicidal people often requires a multi-modal approach, not only counselling [65]. Medication, hospitalization and direct environmental control may be needed to be effective. This is not to say that active out-reach and use of community resources (*e.g.*, telephone - crisis lines) are not. These approaches are, in fact, integral to psychotherapy with almost all suicidal people. Psychotherapy with suicidal people should be a community approach. Communication, coordination and collaborative involvement of others, such as family members, nurses, social workers, and so on, are, in fact, strongly supported by the American Psychiatric Association [54]. It is a guideline to treating many suicidal people effectively; indeed, it was part of the guidelines at the very beginning of modern thoughts about effective treatment of suicidal people [24]. Medication, hospitalization and more direct environmental control may be equally protective factors and can be life saving. The research, according to the World Health Organization (WHO), shows, in fact, that these strategies may well be effective [66].

11. EFFECTIVENESS

Maybe it is appropriate to leave the question, "Is psychotherapy effective?" last. Psychotherapy is effective in helping people achieve their goal and overcome their psychopathology, even suicide risk [46]. It is anodynic. This is faster than natural healing, leaving the person alone, and the like. Of course, not every psychotherapy has been studied with every patient, never mind suicidal patients who have attempted. In fact, there is a lack. Be that as it may, the average psychotherapy patient is better off than 80% of untreated people [46].

The question of how much therapy is enough is important, both for practical and liability reasons. Some espouse 12 sessions, but research shows that most patients would be underserved [48]. It certainly did not stop William Styron's "howling tempest". Lambert and Ogles, in fact, write:

> Research suggests that a sizable portion of patients reliably improve after 10 sessions and that 75% of patients will meet more rigorous criteria for success after about 50 sessions of treatment. Limiting treatment sessions to less than 20 will mean that about 50% of patients will not achieve a substantial benefit from therapy (p. 156-157).

This fact is critical with suicidal patients; indeed, I would suggest that accepting a suicidal patient, who has attempted, for brief intervention is suicidogenic [67]. They often need long-term psychotherapy and more [8].

Are all patients helped by psychotherapy? Or are some patients not helped? Are there negative consequences? The literature is scant, and there is nothing on suicidal people in psychotherapy who do not benefit [46, 48]. Two variables that have been associated to negative outcomes in patients in psychotherapy are more severe problems at intake and significant interpersonal difficulties (both common in suicidal patients). The percentage of negative consequences may be as high as 5%, in fact [48], but then this is true with medication, hospitalization, or any treatment. Much greater research is needed; this, in fact, may well help in identifying those patients that benefit and those that do not.

What is lethal? Are there common problems in psychotherapy with suicidal patients? This may well be one of the most important questions, namely because they can – and have – resulted in deaths by suicide. There is only one, and most unique study on the question, the work of Hendin, Haas, Maltsberger, Koestner, and Szanto [68]. They examined the cases of patients who died by suicide while receiving psychotherapy (and most also medication and some hospitalisation too). Therapists of 36 patients were studied by multiple methods. Hendin and his group isolated six recurrent problems: poor communication between therapists, permitting patients and their relatives to control the therapy, avoidance of issues related to sexuality, ineffective or coercive actions resulting from the therapist's anxiety, not recognizing the meanings of patients' communications, and untreated or undertreated symptoms. It would be important that all therapists, regardless of orientation, pay very careful attention to these common problems, not only in psychotherapy with suicidal people.

One final point on effectiveness, change is multidimensional. Luborsky's work, for example, supports this fact [69]; they emphasize the multiple effects of psychotherapy. Bergin and Lambert [70] state:

> …divergent processes are occurring in therapeutic change; that people themselves embody divergent dimensions or phenomena; and that divergent methods of criterion measurement must be used to match the divergence in human beings and in the change processes that occur within them. This confirms the notion that any assumptions of uniformity in client characteristics or in changes thereof are simply mythical. [70-72].

Once more, we are in the realm of complexity; thus, effectiveness too must be measured in complex and individual ways. Effectiveness means being person-centred or person-oriented.

CONCLUDING THOUGHTS

Of greatest importance, we must understand that there are no universal formulations regarding suicide or attempted suicide. We can speak of understanding, but never as a single universal formulation. It follows that the search for a singular universal response is also a foolish and unrealistic fancy. There is no one implication for psychotherapy with people who have attempted suicide. The manual, the cookbook does not exist, although many wish it were so. The research strongly supports this opinion [48]. How do we then, effectively stop what Styron called the "veritable howling tempest in the brain" or "the bed of nails?" How do we treat Styron? The suicide attempter? The answer from the research: We have to be person-centred or person-oriented.

One should use all measures with highly lethal individuals, like Styron; and surely the person who has attempted suicide is lethal; many approaches are, in fact, effective [48]. Psychotherapy can be effective with suicidal people. This FACT is empirically supported/validated because there are common factors that make psychotherapy effective. The seeming uniqueness of a technique that some espouse, I believe, is simply semantic and stylistic. The common ("sameness") factors may be of overriding importance in effective psychotherapy. There are commonalities. With suicidal patients, this often implies that our treatment should also be multi-modal or multi-component. These measures may include support, cognitive-behavioral techniques, psychodynamic interpretation, medication, hospitalization (this was true for Styron), environmental control, and especially the involvement of others in the community, not only others to whom the patient was (or is) close to but also "social" agencies -teachers, priests, elders, doctors, social workers, *etc.* - all of which serve, directly or indirectly, to alleviate the pain [8, 13, 46, 54]. We need "The children who rushed through its rooms, the festivals, the love and work, the honestly earned slumber… " We need an anodyne. Treatment should often be multi-modal, but what this all entails with people who have attempted suicide needs greater study.

This snapshot of some common factors, of course, should be read as a prolegomena. Once we know some common factors or communalities of what we are treating and some commonalities of how to effectively treat, such as in psychotherapy, the same, then it follows that there are some commonalities in psychotherapy of whom we are treating. Each commonality of suicide has a common implication for psychotherapy, despite respect for the uniqueness of each person. One does not negate the other nor is this a cookbook approach. What this all entails is the topic of a whole volume, my own, Psychotherapy with Suicidal People [8]. It provides the full-length movie.

Of course, my book is not the only person-centred book. If I was asked, I would add the following 9 books (I do not include here the excellent specific books for specific age groups), the top 10 books on psychotherapy with suicidal patients: A. Berman, Suicide Prevention: Case consultations [73]; N. Farberow & E. Shneidman, The Cry for Help [74]; A. Freeman & M. Reinecke, Cognitive Therapy of Suicidal Behavior [75]; D. Jacobs, & H. Brown (Eds.) (1989) Suicide Understanding and Responding [76]; A. Leenaars, J. Maltsberger, & R. Neimeyer (Eds.) (1994), Treatment of Suicidal People [26]; M. Linehan (1993), Cognitive Behavioral Treatment of Borderline Personality Disorders [77]; J. Maltsberger, & M. Goldblatt (Eds.) (1996), Essential Papers on Suicide [78]; J. Richman (1986), Family Therapy for Suicidal People [79]; and M. Rudd, T. Joiner, & M. Rajab (2001), Treating Suicidal Behavior [80].

There is an anodyne for William Styron's pain. What works with suicide attempters, I believe, is quality care! This is as true in the therapy room as the operating room. There are common factors. Therefore, we can treat suicidal William Styron or the patient who has made a suicide attempt effectively.

And one final thought; to quote William Styron once more:

> If our lives had no other configuration but this, we should want, and perhaps deserve, to perish; if depression had no termination, then suicide would, indeed, be the only remedy. But one need not sound the false or inspirational note to stress the truth that depression is not the soul's annihilation; men and women who have recovered from the disease – and they are countless – bear witness to what is probably its only saving grace: it is conquerable.
>
> For those who have dwelt in depression's dark wood, and known its inexplicable agony, their return from the abyss is not unlike the ascent of the poet, trudging upward and upward out of hell's black depths and at last emerging into what he saw as "the shining world" (p.84).

Psychotherapy is an anodyne.

REFERENCES

[1] Styron W. Darkness visible. New York: Random House, 1990.

[2] Shneidman E. Anodyne therapy: Relieving the suicidal patient's psychache. In: Rosenthal H, Ed. Favorite counselling and therapy homework assignments. Philadelphia: Taylor & Francis. 2001; pp. 180-3

[3] Shneidman E. Psychotherapy with suicidal patients. Suicide Life Threat Behav 1981; 11:341-8.

[4] Shneidman E. Aphorisms of suicide and some implications for psychotherapy. A J Psychother 1984; 38:319-28.
[5] Leenaars A, Ed. Lives and deaths: Selections from the works of Edwin S. Shneidman. Philadelphia, PA: Brunner/Mazel, 1999 .
[6] Freedheim D, Ed. History of psychotherapy. Washington, DC: APA, 1992.
[7] May R. Foreword. In: Freedheim D. Ed. History of psychotherapy. Washington, DC: APA, 1992; pp. 20-6.
[8] Leenaars A. Psychotherapy with suicidal people: A person-centred approach. Chichester, UK: John Wiley & Sons. 2004.
[9] World Health Organization. World report on violence and health. Geneva: Author, 2002.
[10] Hawton, K, van Heeringen, C, Eds. The international handbook of suicide and attempted suicide. Chichester, UK: John Wiley & Sons, 2000.
[11] Leenaars A. Suicide notes. New York: Human Sciences Press, 1988.
[12] Leenaars A. Suicide: A multidimensional malaise. Suicide Life Threat Behav 1996; 26:221-36.
[13] Shneidman E. Definition of suicide. New York: Wiley, 1985.
[14] Menninger, K. Man against himself. New York: Harcourt, Brace & Co, 1938.
[15] Shneidman, E. Suicide as psychache. Northvale, NJ: Aronson, 1993.
[16] Murray, H. Dead to the world: The passions of Herman Melville. In: Shneidman E, Ed. Essays in self-destruction. New York: Science House. 1967; pp. 3-29
[17] Freud, S. Mourning and melancholia. In: J. Strachey, Ed. The standard edition of the complete psychological works of Sigmund Freud, London: Hogarth. 1974 (Original work published 1917a); Vol. XIV; pp. 239-60.
[18] Freud S. General theory of neurosis. In: Strachey J, Ed. The standard edition of the complete psychological works of Sigmund Freud. London: Hogarth Press. 1974 (Original work published 1917b); Vol. XVI; pp. 243-83
[19] Sullivan H. Schizophrenia as a human process, In: Perry H, Gorvell N, Gibbens M, Eds. The collected works of Harry Stack Sullivan. New York: WW Norton. 1962; Vol. II.
[20] Sullivan H. The fusion of psychiatry and social sciences. In: Perry H, Gorvell N, Gibbens M, Eds. The collected works of Harry Stack Sullivan. New York: WW Norton. 1964; Vol. II.
[21] Murray H. Explorations in personality. New York: Oxford University Press, 1938.
[22] Zilboorg G. Suicide among civilized and primitive races. Am J Psychiatry 1936; 92:1347-69.
[23] Friedman P, Ed. On suicide. New York: International Universities Press; 1967. (Original work published 1910)
[24] Shneidman E, Farberow N, Eds. Clues to suicide. New York: Harper & Row, 1957.
[25] Freud S. A case of homosexuality in a woman. In: Strachey J, Ed. The standard edition of the complete psychological works of Sigmund Freud. London: Hogarth Press. 1974 (Original work published 1920); Vol. XVIII; pp. 147-72.
[26] Freud S. Group psychology and the analysis of the ego. In: J. Strachey, Ed. The standard edition of the complete psychological works of Sigmund Freud. London: Hogarth Press. 1974 (Original work published 1921); Vol. XVIII; pp. 67-147.
[27] Leenaars A, Maltsberger J, Neimeyer R, Eds. Treatment of suicidal people. London: Taylor & Francis, 2007.
[28] Beck A, Kovacs M, Weissman A. Assessment of suicide intention: The scale of suicide ideation. J Consult Clin Psychol 1979; 47:343-52.
[29] Leenaars A, Lester D, Wenckstern S, McMullin C, Rudzinski D, Brevard A. A comparison of suicide notes and parasuicide notes. Death Stud 1992; 16:331-42.
[30] Leenaars A, Lester D. Assessment and prediction of suicide risk in adolescents. In: Zimmerman J, Annis G, Eds. Treatment approaches with suicidal adolescents. New York: Wiley. 1994; pp. 47-70
[31] Stengel E. Suicide and attempted suicide. Baltimore, MD: Penguin, 1964.
[32] Shneidman E. Sleep and self-destruction: a phenomenological approach. In: Shneidman E, Ed. Essays in self-destruction. New York: Science House. 1967; pp. 510-39.
[33] Smith K, Maris R. Suggested recommendations for the study of suicide and other life-threatening behaviors. Suicide Life Threat Behav 1986; 16:67-9.
[34] Lambert M, Bergin, A, Garfield, S. Introduction and historical overview. In: Lambert M, Ed. Bergin and Garfield's handbook of psychotherapy and behavior change. 5th ed. New York: John Wiley & Sons. 2004; pp. 3-15
[35] Garfield S, Bergin A, Eds. Handbook of psychotherapy and behavior change: An empirical analysis. 2nd ed. Chichester, UK: John Wiley & Sons, 1978.
[36] Rosenzweig S. Some implicit common factors in diverse methods of psychotherapy. Am J Orthopsychiatry 1936; 6:412-5.
[37] Kuhn T. The structure of scientific revolutions. Chicago: The University of Chicago Press, 1962.

[38] Luborsky L, Singer B, Luborsky L. Comparative studies of psychotherapies. Arch Gen Psychiatry 1975; 32: 995-1008.
[39] Lambert M, Ed. Bergin and Garfield's handbook of psychotherapy and behavior change. 5th ed. New York: John Wiley & Sons, 2004.
[40] Strupp H. On the limitations of therapy manuals. Clin Psychol Sci Prac 1997; 4:76-82.
[41] Henry W. Science, politics, and the politics of science: The use and misuse of empirically validated treatment research. Psychother Res 1998; 8: 126-40.
[42] Benjafield J. Research methods: A history of some important strands. Arch Suicide Res 2002; 6:5-14.
[43] Koocher G. Three myths about empirically validated therapies. Ont Psychol 2003; 35(3): 13.
[44] Marchel, C, Owens S. Qualitative research in psychology: Could William James get a job? Hist Psychol 2007; 10:301-24.
[45] Beck A, Freeman A, Eds. Cognitive therapy of personality disorders. New York: Guilford Press, 1990.
[46] Lambert M, Bergin A. Achievements and limitations of psychotherapy research. In: Freedheim D, Ed. History of psychotherapy. Washington, DC: American Psychological Association. 1992; pp. 360-90.
[47] Wampold B. Methodological problems in identifying efficacious psychotherapies. Psychotherapy 1997; 7: 21-43.
[48] Lambert M, Ogles B. The efficacy and effectiveness of psychotherapy. In: Lambert M, Ed. Bergin and Garfield's handbook of psychotherapy and behavior change. 5th ed. New York: John Wiley & Sons. 2004; pp. 139-93
[49] Ablan J, Jones E. Psychotherapy process in the National Institute of Mental Health Treatment of Depression Collaborative Research Program. J Consult Clin Psychol 1999; 67:64-74.
[50] Norcross J, Goldfried, M, Eds. Handbook of psychotherapy integration. New York: Basic Books. 1992.
[51] Leenaars A. Psychotherapy with suicidal people: The commonalities. Arch Suicide Res 2006; 10:305-22.
[52] Luborsky L, McLellan A, Woody G, O'Brien C, Auerbach A. Therapist success and its determinants. Arch Gen Psychiatry 1985; 42:602-11.
[53] Beck A. Cognitive therapy and emotional disorders. New York: International University Press, 1976.
[54] American Psychiatric Association.Practice guidelines for the assessment and treatment of patients with suicidal behavior. Am J Psychiatry 2003 (Supp): 160-11.
[55] Buber, MI & thou. In: W. Kaufman, Trans. New York: Charles Scribner's Sons, 1970.
[56] Donaldson, D, Spirito, A, & Overholser, J. Treatment of adolescent suicide attempters. In: Spirito A, Overholser J, Eds. Evaluating and treating adolescent suicide attempters: From research to practice. New York: Academic Press. 2003; pp. 295-321.
[57] Dyck R, Joyce A, Azim H. Treatment compliance as a function of therapist attributes and social support. Can J Psychol 1984; 29;212-6.
[58] Paulson, B, Everall, R. Suicidal adolescents: Helpful aspects of psychotherapy. Arch Suicide Res 2003; 7: 309-21.
[59] Treolar, A, Pinfold, T. Deliberate self-harm: An assessment of patients' attitudes to the care they receive. Crisis 1993; 14: 83-9.
[60] Task Force on Empirically Supported Therapy Relationships. Empirically supported therapy relationships: Conclusions and recommendations of Division 29 task force. Available from: http://academic.uofs.edu/faculty/NORCROSS/empir.htm, 2001.
[61] Rogers C. Client-centered therapy. Boston: Houghton Mifflin, 1951.
[62] Lazarus A. Behavior therapy & beyond. New York: McGraw-Hill, 1971.
[63] Meichenbaum D. 35 years of working with suicidal patients: Lessons learned. Can Psychol 2005; 46:64-72.
[64] Freud S. Analytic therapy. In: Strachey J, Ed. The standard edition of the complete psychological works of Sigmund Freud. London: Hogarth Press. 1974 (Original work published 1916); Vol. XVI; pp. 448-563.
[65] Thase M, Jindal R. Combining psychotherapy and psychopharmacology for treatment of mental disorders. In: Lambert M, Ed. Bergin and Garfield's handbook of psychotherapy and behavior change. 5th ed. New York: John Wiley & Sons. 2004; pp. 743-66.
[66] Bertolote J. Guidelines for the primary prevention of mental, neurological, and psychosocial disorders: Suicide. Geneva: World Health Organization, 1993.
[67] Leenaars A, Cantor C, Connolly J, EchoHawk M, Gailiene D. He Z, Kororina N, Lester D, Lopatin A, Rodriguez M, Schlebusch D, Takahashi Y, Vijayakumar L. Ethical & legal issues in suicidology: International perspectives. Arch Suicide Res 2002; 6:185-97.
[68] Hendin H, Haas A, Maltsberger J, Koestner B, Szanto, K. Problems in psychotherapy with suicidal patients. Am J Psychiatry 2006; 163:67-72.

[69] Strupp H, Hadley S. A tripartite model of mental health and therapeutic outcomes: With special reference to negative effects in psychotherapy. Am Psychol 1977; 32:187-96.

[70] Bergin A, Lambert M. The evaluation of therapeutic outcome. In: Garfield S, Bergin A, Eds. Handbook of psychotherapy and behavior change: An empirical analysis. 2nd ed. Chichester, UK: John Wiley & Sons. 1978; pp. 139-89.

[71] Kiesler D. A grid model for theory and research in the psychotherapies. In: Eron L, Ed. The relationship of theory and technique in psychotherapy. Chicago: Aldine. 1968; pp. 36-74.

[72] Kiesler D. Some myths of psychotherapy research and the search for a paradigm. Psychol Bull 1966; 65:110-36.

[73] Berman A, Ed. Suicide prevention: Case consultations. New York, Guilford, 1990.

[74] Farberow N, Shneidman E, Eds. The cry for help. New York, McGraw-Hill, 1961.

[75] Freeman A, Reinecke M. Cognitive therapy of suicidal behavior. New York: Springer, 1993.

[76] Jacobs D, Brown H, Eds. Suicide understanding and responding. Madison, Conn: International Universities Press, 1989.

[77] Linehan M. Cognitive behavioral treatment of borderline personality disorders. New York: Guilford, 1993.

[78] Maltsberger J, Goldblatt, M, Eds. Essential papers on suicide. New York: New York University Press, 1996.

[79] Richman J. Family therapy for suicidal people. New York: Springer, 1986.

[80] Rudd D, Joiner T, Rajab M. Treating suicidal behavior. New York: Guilford, 2001.

CHAPTER 11

Suicide in Europe

David Lester*

The Richard Stockton College of New Jersey, USA

Abstract: Suicide rates in Europe range from the very low to the highest in the world. For many years, Hungary had the highest suicide rate in the world but, in recent years, the newly independent Baltic States have risen to the top. Meanwhile, southern European nations, such as Greece and Spain, have very low suicide rates. The present chapter briefly reviews some of the intriguing trends and findings about suicide in Europe.

Keywords: Suicide, north-south, physiological factors, alcohol, antidepressants, miscounting suicides.

1. FROM THE NORTH TO THE SOUTH

In many nations of the world, Northerners and Southerners believe that they differ considerably from each other. The people in the north, typically a colder climate, are usually thought to be relatively calm emotionally, whereas people in the south are thought to be more expressive, an idea proposed by Montesquieu in 1748 [1].

To test whether this proposition has any validity, Pennebaker, *et al.* [2] surveyed more than 2,900 college students in 26 nations. Southerners were viewed as more emotionally expressive in 16 of the nations, significantly so in 12 of them. Lester [3] tested this proposition for suicide in Italy where the division between the northern and southern regions dates back to the 12th Century when German influence was strong in the north and Byzantine influence strong in the south. Lester found that the northern regions of Italy had higher suicide rates than the southern regions, and they differed in sociological variables too, with the northern regions having lower marriage, birth and unemployment rates but higher death rates.

For Europe as a whole, suicide rates can be found in the World Health Organization database, and recent suicide rates are shown in Table **1**.[1] It can be seen that the more southern European nations do, in general, have lower suicide rates, although there are, of course, exceptions.

Table 1: European suicide rates ranked from low to high by the male suicide rate

(From the WHO Database)			
Nation	**Date**	**Suicide Rate**	
		Males	**Females**
Azerbaijan	2002	1.8	0.5
Armenia	2003	3.2	0.3
Georgia	2001	3.4	1.1
Albania	2003	4.7	3.3
Greece	2006	5.9	1.2
Malta	2004	7.0	1.4
Macedonia	2003	9.5	4.0
UK	2005	10.4	3.2

***Address Correspondence to David Lester:** The Richard Stockton College of New Jersey, USA; E-mail: david.lester@stockton.edu

[1] www.who.int/mental_health/prevention/suicide_rates/en/print/htm accessed December 13, 2008 [4].

Maurizio Pompili (Ed)

Table 1: cont….

Italy	2003	11.0	3.4
Spain	2005	12.0	3.8
Netherlands	2004	12.7	6.0
Norway	2005	15.7	7.4
Ireland	2005	16.3	3.2
Portugal	2003	17.5	4.9
Luxembourg	2005	17.7	4.3
Denmark	2001	19.2	8.1
Sweden	2002	19.5	7.1
Bulgaria	2004	19.7	6.7
Germany	2004	19.7	6.6
Romania	2004	21.5	4.0
Slovakia	2005	22.3	3.4
Austria	2006	24.7	7.0
Switzerland	2005	24.7	10.5
Czech Rep.	2005	25.5	5.6
France	2005	26.4	9.2
Poland	2005	27.8	4.6
Serbia	2006	28.4	11.1
Croatia	2005	30.5	9.7
Finland	2006	31.1	9.6
Belgium	1997	31.2	11.4
Moldova	2006	31.5	5.1
Estonia	2005	35.5	7.3
Ukraine	2005	40.9	7.0
Latvia	2005	42.0	9.6
Slovenia	2006	42.1	11.1
Hungary	2005	42.3	11.2
Russia	2005	58.1	9.8
Belarus	2003	63.3	10.3
Lithuania	2005	68.1	12.9

National suicide rates are associated with many sociological indices, and so it is not necessarily the different climates that cause these national differences. In a broader study of nations of the world, Lester [5] found that suicide rates were higher in nations where the quality of life was higher, birth rates lower and the percentage of elderly higher, and where male and female participation in the labor force was higher, among other associations. It would be of great interest to carry out a similar study as that of Lester's but restricted to European nations.

Such a study was done in the 1960s by Sainsbury and his colleagues. Sainsbury, *et al.* [6] studied social correlates of suicide in European nations in 1962 and, in addition, how changes in those social variables were associated with changes in the suicide rate in the next ten years. Suicide rates in 1962 were associated with the proportion of young people, the divorce rate, illegitimate birth rates, female labor force participation, the murder rate and road accident mortality. Changes in the suicide rate in the next ten years were associated with the rates of unemployment and divorce and the proportion of young people in the population in 1962. Changes in the suicide rate were also associated with changes in most of the social variables studied. It would of great interest to replicate this study for a recent decade.

2. PHYSIOLOGICAL DIFFERENCES

As well as sociological variables and climate differences, there is some speculation that physiological differences may play a role in the differences in suicide rates in European nations.

Lester [7] estimated the proportion of people with the blood types A, B, AB and O in 17 industrialized nations, twelve of which were European, and found that the more type O people in a nation, the lower the suicide rate. He then checked the distribution of blood types in two nations not in this sample, but with the highest suicide rates in Europe at the time (Hungary and Czechoslovakia) and found that they had the lowest percentage of people with type O blood.

Kondrichin and Lester [8] explored whether the Finno-Ugrian gene (associated with Finns and Hungarians) is associated with suicide rates. For 30 European nations, they found that the proportion of Finno-Ugrians in the population and the national suicide rates correlated strongly ($r = 0.58$). Voracek, *et al.* [9] replicated this finding, showing that there is a J-shaped belt of high suicide rate countries spanning from central Europe (Austria, Hungary and Slovenia) to Northeastern Europe (Finland and the Baltic countries). Voracek, *et al.* noted that the countries in this belt differ greatly in culture, political system, and socioeconomic factors, but are similar in genetic communalities.

3. CHANGES OVER TIME

Lester and Yang [10] explored whether marriage and birth rates could predict suicide rates in nations from 1901 to 1988. Their data for European nations are shown in Table **2**. Although the signs of the birth and marriage rates as predictors of the suicide rate were not consistent, the amount of variance in the suicide rates accounted for by these two predictors (R2) was consistently high.[2] It would be of interest to explore why marriage and birth rates are protective factors in some European nations and risk factors in others.

Table 2: Predicting European suicide rates from 1901-1988

(From Lester & Yang, 1998 [10])				
Nation	**Constant**	**Birth**	**Marriage**	**R^2**
England & Wales	8.61	0.08	0.01	0.88
Finland	25.80	0.39*	-0.31*	0.93
Ireland	6.96	-0.16	0.05	0.87
Italy	6.01	0.08	-0.03	0.86
Netherlands	10.86	-0.21*	0.09	0.74
Norway	71.68	0.01	-0.31*	0.91
Scotland	10.02	-0.03	-0.03	0.89
Spain	7.45	-0.07	-0.03	0.71
Sweden	21.03	-0.03	-0.25	0.78
Switzerland	19.65	0.34	-0.18	0.73

* $p < .10$ or better.

Lester and Yang [10] also looked at predictors of national suicides rates for the period 1950 to 1985 (see Table **3**). For this set of nations, the divorce rate was added as a predictor, and the results for divorce were more consistent, with most of the regression coefficients positive[3]. These results raise two issues: (1) can

[2] Lester and Yang also ran these regressions separately for male and females suicide rates.

[3] Lester and Yang also ran these regressions separately for male and females suicide rates and, for nations which did not permit divorce, they ran the regressions again with just birth and marriage rates as predictors.

we explain the sign of the regression coefficients for the different nations (that is, why some are positive while others are negative), and (2) what would the results be for a more recent 35-year period?

Table 3: Predicting European suicide rates from 1950-1985

(From Lester & Yang, 1998 [10])					
Nation	**Constant**	**Marriage**	**Birth**	**Divorce**	**R^2**
Austria	11.79	-0.15	0.22	6.97*	0.81
Belgium	19.05	-0.87	-0.08	5.48*	0.95
Czechoslovakia	28.45	0.38	-0.33	-2.65	0.79
Denmark	23.83	-0.25	-0.36	3.41	0.84
England & Wales	8.43	-0.65	0.39	-0.04	0.95
Finland	19.64	-0.14	-0.08	3.49*	0.86
France	12.08	-1.07*	0.44*	4.87*	0.95
Hungary	49.46	-0.55	-0.21	3.20	0.96
Luxembourg	21.77	-1.11	-0.28	3.65	0.69
Netherlands	5.29	0.04	-0.02	2.71*	0.96
Northern Ireland	-1.60	0.35	0.37*	4.72*	0.65
Norway	0.24	-0.74*	0.46	6.32*	0.96
Portugal	8.42	-0.22	0.10	1.13	0.34
Scotland	6.65	-0.05	0.08	1.01	0.83
Sweden	12.08	-1.08	0.97*	0.34	0.58
Switzerland	15.41	0.92	-0.49	5.36	0.90
West German	26.76	-0.75*	-0.04	-0.36	0.80
Yugoslavia	32.11	-1.18*	-0.24*	-3.70*	0.93

* $p < 0.10$ or better

4. THE ROLE OF ALCOHOL

It has been argued that alcohol consumption plays a role in determining the time-series suicide rate, particularly in the European nations formerly under Communist rule in Eastern Europe. Earlier research indicated that alcohol plays more of a role in the suicide rate of northern European nations, such as Norway and Sweden where binge drinking is more common, than in the suicide rate of southern European nations, such as Italy and Spain where everyday-integrated drinking patterns are more common, and this was especially true for male suicide rates [11, 12]. Landberg [13] explored the role of alcohol consumption in the nations that were formerly part of Eastern Europe, and found a positive impact from alcohol consumption on post-war suicide rates, especially for those nations with "detrimental" drinking patterns (that is, a heavy consumption of spirits rather than wine and beer), such as Russia, Belarus and Poland. As with studies on Western European nations, the impact of alcohol on suicide rates was stronger for male suicide rates than for female suicide rates.

5. THE ROLE OF ANTIDEPRESSANTS

In recent years, the suicide rates of many European nations have been declining. Since these years have seen an increasing rate of prescribing antidepressants, particularly the selective serotonin re-uptake inhibitors (SSRIs), the decline has been attributed to the role of SSRIs. For example, Isacsson [14] studied Sweden for the period 1978-1996 and found that the declining suicide rate paralleled the rise in the prescribing of antidepressants. Similar results were found for Denmark, Finland and Norway. Isacsson found that trends in unemployment and alcohol consumption did not correlate as strongly with the suicide rate. However, Isacsson did not use regression analyses, but only a "naturalistic" analysis (comparing trends visually).

This hypothesis has not gone unchallenged [15]. For example, Oravecz *et al.* [16] did not find any association over time between suicide rates and antidepressant use in Slovenia. Similarly, Barbui, *et al.* [17] did not find a positive impact from SSRI use on suicide in Italy. However, much of this research has consisted of observing trends, without the use of regression analyses or controls for other sociological variables that might impact suicide rates. Nonetheless, if antidepressants do reduce depression, increasing the effectiveness of detecting depression in the population and increasing the prescribing of appropriate doses of appropriate medications should be expect to lower suicide rates. In the future, methodologically sound research is needed to test this possibility.

6. REGIONAL CORRELATES OF SUICIDE

Lester [18] reviewed his studies on the regional correlates of suicide within nations (see Table **4**). As can be seen, it proved difficult to get comparable data sets for the set of nations, and the correlations were not altogether consistent. The suicide rate was consistently associated in a positive way with the overall death rate and somewhat consistently with the divorce rate.

It would be interesting to compile comparable data sets for the same year (say the year 2000), with data on the same variables, for a large sample of European nations so that the consistent associations could be identified.

Table 4: Correlates of regional suicide rates within European nations

(From Lester, 1998-1999)								
Variable	**England**	**Finland**	**France**	**Hungary**	**Italy**	**Portugal**	**Sweden**	**Switzerland**
	1961	1986	1970	1985	1986	1980-2	1980	1990
	n=48	n=12	n=95	n=29	n=20	n=18	n=24	n=26
Births	-0.34*	-0.30	0.16	0.34	-0.68*	-0.70*	-0.04	0.16
Population	-0.31	-	-	-0.43	-0.25	0.31	0.28	
Pop density	0.03	-	-	-0.41	7-0.33	0.33		
Deaths	0.18	0.31	-	0.17	0.66*	0.40	0.21	0.29
Divorces	-	0.34	-0.23*	0.42*	-	-	0.32	
Unemployment	-	0.74*	-	-	-0.62*	-	-0.10	-0.12
Marriages	-	0.07	0.47*	0.27	-0.62*	-	0.11	
% Elderly	0.31*	-	-	-	0.49*	-	0.20	
Infant mortality	-0.23	0.20	-	0.51*	-	-	0.22	
% Children	-0.40*	-	-	-	-	-	-0.12	
Males/females	0.48*	0.25	-0.02					
Per capita income	-0.17	-	-	-	-	-		
Doctors/capita	0.21	-	-	-	-	-	-0.28	
Migration	-0.13	-	-	-				
% Born in region	-0.33*	-	-	-	-	-	-	
% Immigrants	0.26*	-	-	-	-	-	-	
Cirrhosis mortality	-0.60*	-						
Employment ratio	-0.01							
Illegitimate births	0.32							
%Roman Catholic	-0.30							
Median age	0.03							

* two-tailed p < .05.

7. MISCOUNTING SUICIDES

Differences in national suicide rates may be partly a result of differences in the accurate certification of suicides in some countries. For example, Lester [19] examined official suicide rates in regions in England with surveys carried out by suicidologists. There was a consistent under-count of suicides by about 40%. Lester argued that the official English suicide rate was, therefore, invalid.

In a study of 15 nations, 10 of which were European, Lester [20] found that adding some kinds of accidental deaths (those that could be hidden or disguised suicides) and undetermined deaths did change the absolute values of the suicide rates, but the relative ranking remained roughly the same. However, it remains possible that some nations do miscount (and under-report) the suicide rate, and this might be especially true in those nations where suicide is considered to be a sin, such as Roman Catholic nations.

The rise in suicide rates in some European nations toward the end of the 20th Century (such as Ireland and Norway) was suspected to be a result of more accurate counting of suicides. Cantor, *et al.* [21] examined whether this might be the case for Ireland where the official suicide rate began to rise in 1972. They concluded that the increase in the suicide rate from 1972 to 1978 was most likely a result of more accurate certification of the cause of death, and that the suicide rate prior to 1970 was probably twice the official suicide rate.

DISCUSSION

A number of factors have been identified that impact suicide rates in Europe, ranging from genetic variations in the populations (the Finno-Ugrian gene) to alcohol consumption, improvements in psychiatric treatment (the development of SSRIs), and sociological factors (such as divorce rates). Clearly much more research is needed to explore the role of these variables more thoroughly.

Incidentally, some factors have been ruled out as having an impact on suicide. For example, Mäkinen and Stickley [22] found that changes in agriculture in twenty European countries, in which small farmers have been displaced by larger companies, had no impact on suicide mortality. This research is important too since it enables us to reduce the number of variables that we have to take into account.

REFERENCES

[1] Montesquieu C de S. The spirit of the laws. New York: Cambridge University Press, 1989.
[2] Pennebaker JW, Rimé B, Blankeship VE. Stereotypes of emotional expressiveness of Northerners and Southerners. J Pers Soc Psychol 1996; 70: 372-80.
[3] Lester D. Suicide in Italy. I J Suicidol 1997; 7: 19-21.
[4] www.who.int/mental_health/prevention/suicide_rates/en/print/htm accessed December 13, 2008.
[5] Lester D. Patterns of suicide and homicide in the world. Commack, NY: Nova Science, 1996.
[6] Sainsbury P, Jenkins J, Levey A. The social correlates of suicide in Europe. In: Farmer R, Hirsch S, Eds.The suicide syndrome. London: Croom Helm. 1980; pp. 38-53.
[7] Lester D. National distribution of blood groups, personal violence (suicide and homicide), and national character. Pers Individ Dif 1987; 8: 575-6.
[8] Kondrichin SV, Lester D. Finno-Ugrians and suicide. Percept Mot Skills 1997; 85: 514.
[9] Voracek M, Fisher ML, Marusic A. The Finno-Ugrian suicide hypothesis. Percept Mot Skills 2003; 97: 401-406.
[10] Lester D, Yang B. Suicide and homicide in the 20th Century. Commack, NY: Nova Science, 1998.
[11] Norström T. Alcohol and suicide. Addiction 1995; 90: 1463-9.
[12] Skog PJ, Teixeira Z, Barrias J, Moreira R. Alcohol and suicide. Addiction 1995; 90: 1053-61.
[13] Landberg J. Alcohol and suicide in eastern Europe. Drug Alcohol Rev 2008; 27: 361-73.
[14] Isacsson G. Suicide prevention – a medical breakthrough? Acta Psychiatr Scand 2000; 102: 113-7.
[15] Zonda T. Depression and suicidal behavior. Crisis 2005; 26:34-5.
[16] Oravecz R, Czigler B, Leskosek F. Correlation between suicide rate and antidepressant use in Slovenia. Arch Suicide Res 2003; 7: 279-85.

[17] Barbui C, Campomori A, D'Avanzo B, Negri E, Garattini, S. Antidepressant drug use in Italy since the introduction of SSRIs. Soc Psychiatry Psychiatr Epidemiol 1999;34: 152-6.

[18] Lester D. Correlates of regional suicide rates. Omega 1998-1999; 38: 99-102.

[19] Lester D. The scientific study of suicide requires accurate data. Crisis 2002; 23: 133-4.

[20] Lester D. Miscounting suicides. Acta Psychiatr Scand 1992; 85: 15-6.

[21] Cantor CH, Leenaars AA, Lester D. Under-reporting of suicide in Ireland 1960-1989. Arch Suicide Res 1997; 3: 5-12.

[22] Mäkinen IH, Stickley A. Suicide mortality and agricultural rationalization in post-war Europe. Soc Psychiatry Psychiatr Epidemiol 2006; 41: 429-34.

CHAPTER 12

Suicide in Asia-I

David Lester*

The Richard Stockton College of New Jersey

Abstract: More than half of the world's population lives in Asia[1], and the region is diverse in ethnicity and religion, ranging from India where the major religion is Hinduism to Japan where the major religions are Buddhism and Shinto. The rates of suicide differ in the nations making up Asia, as do the methods used for suicide and trends in the suicide rates over the years. This chapter will briefly review some of the facts pertaining to suicide in Asia and identify similarities and differences from suicide elsewhere in the world.

Keywords: Suicide, Asia, India, Japan, China, Singapore, South Korea, Taiwan, Thailand, aborigines, reasons for suicide.

1. THE EPIDEMIOLOGY OF SUICIDE

The most recent suicide rates for Asia countries on the website of the World Health Organization (www.who.int) are shown in Table **1**.[2] The highest suicide rate was in Japan and the lowest in Singapore and Thailand. It is clear that many nations in Asia do not report mortality data to the WHO, and this is a gap that must be remedied. The study and prevention of suicide requires, first of all, good epidemiological data. There are, however, scholarly studies of suicide in Asian countries, and some of the information contained in these reports is presented below.

Table 1: The latest WHO data on suicide rates (per 100,000 per year)

Nation	Suicide rate		Years
	Males	Females	
Hong Kong	19.3	11.5	2006
Japan	34.8	13.2	2006
Singapore	12.9	7.7	2006
South Korea	29.6	14.1	2006
Thailand	12.0	3.8	2002
Macao	8.2	5.7	1994

2. HONG KONG

Hong Kong, after being under British rule since 1842, was returned to China in 1997. It is now a Special Administrative Region of the People's Republic of China. The suicide rate in Hong Kong remained stable through to the mid-1990s, after which it increased, rising to 18.6 in 2003 [1][3]. Although it is tempting to attribute this increase in the suicide rate to the change in administration, it should be noted that suicide rates

***Address Correspondence to David Lester:** The Richard Stockton College of New Jersey, USA; E-mail: david.lester@stockton.edu

[1] It should be remembered that the Asian continent begins in Istanbul which straddles Europe and Asia, but suicide in Middle Eastern countries is typically excluded from discussions of suicide in Asia. Furthermore, mortality statistics are more comprehensively collected in the "Far East," and research there is more common, theoretically based and methodologically sound.

[2] The latest data for Macao was for 1994.

[3] All suicide rates reported are per 100,000 per year.

Maurizio Pompili (Ed)

have risen during this period in other Asian countries, such as South Korea. For 2006, the WHO website gives the suicide rate in Hong Kong as 15.2: 19.3 for men and 11.5 for women, and a male/female ratio of 1.7.

Law and Yip [1] presented the basic epidemiology of suicide in Hong. Suicide rates rise with age, are lowest in the married, and are higher in those who are unemployed. One unique feature in Hong Kong, as compared to other Asian nations, is the increase in suicide using charcoal burning. Whereas in 1990, jumping was the most common method (56%) followed by hanging (28%), beginning in 1997 with one suicide, charcoal burning became the second most popular method for suicide in 2003 (25%) after jumping (46%). Chan, *et al.* [2] found that those using charcoal burning for suicide differed from those using other methods. For example, those using charcoal were more often employed and had financial or gambling problems, and they were less often psychiatrically disturbed. They engaged in more planning for the act, and so their suicides did not seem to be impulsive. This led Law and Yip to suggest that the rise in the popularity of this method for suicide had created suicides, and these individuals might not have killed themselves had charcoal burning not become a widely-publicized method for suicide in the media.

3. INDIA

The suicide rate in India rose from 7.2 in 1975 to 9.9 in 1994 [3]. The most common method throughout this period was the use of solids/liquids followed by hanging. Fire was also relatively common compared to other nations, and suicide by this method was primarily committed by women (69% of such acts). This is interesting given the practice of sati in which widows burn themselves on their husband's funeral pyre. Although banned in 1829 by the British, sati has continued, and several recent cases have attracted widespread publicity and debate in India.

In 1991, the suicides rates were 10.6 in men and 7.9 in women. In 1994, the suicide rates of the different Indian states varied from 1.7 in Manipur to 28.0 in Kerala, with a median of 8.6. Urban suicide rates were a little higher than rural suicide rates. Lester, *et al.* [3] correlated social indicators with the state suicide rates, and only population density was associated (positively) with the suicide rate. Percent urban, percent in poverty, per capita income and the murder rate were not significantly associated with the suicide rate. In a time-series study, the Indian suicide rate was higher in years when more females participated in the labor force and when the fertility rate was low [3].

More recently, Vijayakumar [4] reported a suicide rate in 2002 of 10.5, with a male/female ratio of 1.6 (12.8/8.2). The suicide rate showed an increasing trend from 1975 through to 2002. Because of the lack of good census data, suicide rates by age were unavailable, but the modal age of suicides was 30-44 years of age. The methods used for suicide were similar to those reported for the earlier period by Lester, *et al.* [3] but, of those using solids/liquids, Vijayakumar reported that 19% used pesticides. The use of pesticides is a growing problem in rural areas in developing nations, and much thought has gone into how to prevent these suicides, so far unsuccessfully [5].

In case-control psychological autopsy studies, Vijyakumar [4] reported that 88% of the suicides had a psychiatric disorder in one study (in Chennai) but only 43% in another study (in Bangalore). However, in both studies, affective disorders were not that common (present in only about a quarter of the suicides), and so depression does not seem to play as important a role in India as it does in Europe and North America. Alcohol seemed to play a more important role, with about 30%-50% of male suicides under the influence at the time of the suicide. The odds ratio for alcoholism predicting suicide was 9.3 in Chennai and 4.5 in Bangalore.

Vijyakumar noted that marital problems play a large role in the suicides of women in India, arising especially from disputes over dowries, and murders of wives (often camouflaged to look like suicides) are also common. Suicide pacts and family suicides (the latter often involving murder-suicides) are becoming more common in India. Pacts involving lovers and extramarital partners were more common than those involving spouses.

4. JAPAN

Takashi [6] noted that Japan has one of the highest suicide rates in Asia, reaching 23.1 in 2003, with a male/female ratio of 2.6. The rates rise with age in both men and women. The suicide rate has been rising in Japan since 1970.

The rates of suicide vary by prefecture in Japan, and Lester and Abe [7] found that the suicide rates of the 46 prefectures was associated positively with the percentage of elderly and negatively with per capita income and the birth rate, rather different from the associations for the United States. Over time from 1953 to 1982, Lester, Motohashi and Yang [8] found that the time-series suicide rate was associated with the unemployment rate and female participation in the labor force, similar to the associations found for the United States.

There has been good research evaluating the impact of suicide prevention tactics in Japan. Lester, Saito and Abe [9] found that the establishment of suicide prevention centers in Japan was associated with a reduction in the suicide rate above and beyond the impact of social and economic factors. Lester, Saito and Abe [10] studied the prefectures and found that the longer the centers had been open and the more there were, the less the increase in the suicide rate from 1970 to 1988.

Lester [5] conducted a number of studied in Japan with Kazuhiko Abe on the impact of restricting access to lethal methods for suicide. They found that detoxifying domestic gas, removing carbon monoxide from car exhaust, and limiting access to lethal medications such as barbiturates all led to a reduction in their use for suicide, and displacement to other methods of suicide when one was made less available did not always occur.

5. MAINLAND CHINA

Suicide in the People's Republic of China has received a great deal of attention in recent years since the reported suicide rate, based only on a small proportion of the total population, is higher in women than in men, the only nation for which this is true[4]. Phillips, Liu and Zhang [11] estimated that the suicide rate for the period 1990-1994 was 28.7, higher in women than in men and higher in rural areas than in urban areas. These differences have persisted through to 2001 [12], although the overall suicide rate appears to be declining. Suicide rates rise with age, as in other Asian countries, both for men and women.

In data from Shanghai for 1992-1996 [12], hanging was the most popular method for suicide in men (39%) followed by solids/liquids (30%). For women, solids/liquids was the most popular method (44%) followed by hanging (33%). The high female suicide rate in rural areas is primarily the result of the use of pesticides and other farming chemicals.

Although there has been much speculation about the reasons for the high female suicide rate in mainland China [13], there have been few studies that test any hypothesis of this difference. Most theories have focused on the availability of methods (pesticides in rural areas) and the low status of women, although Zhang [14] has speculated that hormonal levels may have relevance, with Chinese females having relatively higher levels of testosterone.

6. SINGAPORE

The suicide rate in Singapore has remained steady from 1993 to 2003, staying in a range of about 8 to 12 [15]. The male/female ratio is about 1.7, and jumping is the most common method for suicide. Suicide rates rise with age in both men and women, and have been very high in the past in elderly men, exceeding 60 in the 1960s (and even 80 in 1959-1961), but dropping to 30 by 2001-2003.

---

[4] There are occasion reports of this sex reversal in small subcultures within a nation.

There are two interesting features to suicide in Singapore. First, the most popular method for suicide is jumping. Lester [16] noted that the suicide rate by jumping from high-rise buildings rose from 1.4 in 1960 to 5.7 in 1976. The percentage of suicides using this method for suicide rose from 17% to 51% over this period. Lester showed that this rise paralleled the percentage of residents in Singapore living in high-rise buildings which rose from 9% in 1960 to 51% in 1981.

A second feature of suicide in Singapore is that the population is a mix of ethnicities, and the suicide rate varies by ethnicity. Lester [17] reported data from Murphy [18] on the suicide rate of the Chinese in Singapore by dialect: Hokkien 10.8, Teochui 11.4, Cantonese 15.7, Hailam 17.3, Hakka 14.4 and Hockchui 21.2. These rates are in the order of the proportion of the people speaking that dialect in the population, from highest to lowest, and so it can be seen that the smaller the percentage in the population, on the whole, the higher the suicide rate, a trend that fits with Lester's [19] social deviancy theory of suicide. Chia and Chia [15] noted that in recent years, the Chinese residents of Singapore have a higher suicide rate than the Indian residents who, in turn, have a higher rate that the Malay residents, both in men and women, a difference that is most pronounced in older residents.

7. SOUTH KOREA

Park and Lester [20] have described the epidemiology of suicide in South Korea which has seen a steady increase in the suicide rate over the years, from 6.8 in 1982 to 24.0 in 2003. In 2003, the male suicide rate was 33.2 and the female rate 14.9, giving a male/female ratio of 2.2.

The suicide rate increases with age, and the suicide rate in those aged 60-74 was 4.4 times higher than the suicide rate for those aged 15-29 in 2003, while the rate for those aged 75 and older was 10.6 times greater. Poisoning with solids/liquids is the most common method for suicide, followed by hanging.

Park and Lester examined the time-series correlates of the suicide rate for the period 1983-2003 and found that both the unemployment rate and the divorce rate predicted the male suicide rate, while only the divorce rate predicted the female suicide rate. Correcting for serial autocorrelation, marriage rates joined the predictors for both the male and the female suicide rates, but positively, meaning that the suicide rate was higher in years when the marriage rate was higher.

Two features of suicide in South Korea are of special interest. First, protest suicide has a long history in Korea. For example, several scholars committed suicide in 1905 to protest the colonial occupation of Korea by the Japanese. In the last thirty years of the 20th Century, nearly 100 people killed themselves in South Korea as a means of political protest, many by self-immolation. These fell mainly into two groups: (1) workers protesting the repression of workers and their unions by companies and by the government, and (2) students protesting the government's policies and its cooperation with the United States in the confrontation with North Korea. Park and Lester [21] found no differences in the suicide notes of these two groups. Park [22] noted that these suicides were not impulsive acts. Sometimes their suicide notes were written a few days before the act of suicide, and the protest suicides were mentioned in their diaries months earlier. Their decisions were reached after a great deal of reflection and soul-searching. They did not appear to be undertaken by people with psychiatric disorders, but rather were the product of mature reasoning. Their goal was to produce a change in the society and so may be classified as altruistic in Durkheim's [23] classification scheme. Park observed that the suicide notes typically involved a challenge or message to the suicide's own group, as well as a message to the powerful group against which they were struggling - a message that more should be done to overcome the wrongs and injustices.

Second, as in Hong Kong and Japan, the Internet has created the phenomenon of strangers who wish to commit suicide, contact each other *via* the Internet to meet up, and die together in a suicide pact [24]. It is estimated that this may account for almost one third of all suicides in South Korea [25].

8. TAIWAN

After the First-Sino Japanese War in 1895, Japan took over the control of Taiwan, then known as Formosa. After the Second World War, Taiwan was returned to China and, after the defeat of the Kuomintang by the

Communists on the mainland, the Nationalists retreated to the island and declared martial law which was not lifted until 1987. On February 27, 1947, there was civil unrest, and the mainlanders killed many thousands of Taiwanese (estimates range from 10,000 to 30,000). This has left to tension between the native Taiwanese and the mainlanders which is becoming more evident today.

The suicide rate in Taiwan has increased dramatically from 6.2 in 1993 to 19.3 in 2006 [26], more so in men than in women[5]. Residents of Taiwan are ethnically mixed, with some thirteen aboriginal groups (2%) and a Han Chinese majority consisting of native Taiwanese (Holo: 73%), Hakka (13%) and mainlanders (12%). Lester [17] reported old data [27] that showed that suicide rates were higher in the Holo (for whom the language is known as Hokkien) than in the Hakka from 1930 to 1950.

The sex ratio for suicide rates has increased from 1.52 in 1983 to 2.00 in 2003, when the male suicide rate was 18.7. Suicide rates rise with age in Taiwan, but the methods used have changed over time. In 1983, poisoning was most common followed by hanging, while in 2003 hanging was the most common method [26]. A noticeable change was in the 1990s when the use of carbon monoxide became increasingly common. By 2003, it was the third most popular method for suicide. Unlike Western nations where married individuals have a lower suicide rate than single individuals, the reverse is true in Taiwan. However, the widowed and divorced have the highest suicides as in the West [26].

Chao, *et al.* [26] noted a sharp increase in parent-child suicides in Taiwan, typically where the parent murders the child before committing suicide. Chao, *et al.* noted the growing trend for the child to be an adolescent and for the use of charcoal burning as the method for suicide.

Lester and Hu [28] found that the suicide rates of the regions (hsieh) of Taiwan were associated with the divorce, birth and crime rates positively and the population density, percentage of elderly and death rate negatively. This pattern of correlations was quite different from that found for the states of the United States. Lester [29] found that only the unemployment rate (and not the birth or divorce rates) predicted the time series suicide rate in Taiwan from 1959 to 1987.

As for suicide prevention, Huang and Lester [30] found that, as suicide prevention centers were established in Taiwan from 1965 on, they seem to have been associated with a declining suicide rate independent of changes in the marriage, divorce and birth rates.

9. THAILAND

There has been much less research on suicide in Thailand than in the other nations discussed in this chapter, but some data have been reported by Lotrakul [31]. The suicide rate in Thailand is much lower than in other Asian nations, declining from 8.6 in 1999 to 6.3 in 2005. The male/female suicide rate ratio has increased from 1.6 in 1988 to 3.6 in 2000. The distribution of suicide rates is bimodal. In 2005, those aged 70-74 had the highest suicide rate (10.3) followed b y those aged 25-29 (9.4), whereas in earlier years young adults had the highest suicide rate. Hanging is the most popular method for suicide in both men and women, and this has remained true from 1996 to 2005. The use of solids/liquids ranks second.

10. SUICIDE IN ABORIGINAL GROUPS

It must not be forgotten that each of the Asian nations has a diverse ethnic mix and, in particular, has aboriginal groups. For example, Cheng [32, 33] compared suicide in two aboriginal groups in Taiwan with suicide in the dominant Han group. The Atayal had a suicide rate of 68.2, the Ami 15.6 and the Han Chinese 18.0. The suicides in all three groups had a similarly high incidence of psychiatric disorder, and the high suicide rate in the Atayal was attributed to their high incidence of alcoholism and the earlier onset of

---

[5] The rate declined from 1983 to 1993.

major depressive disorders. This type of research has not been carried out yet for aboriginal groups in other Asian nations.

11. SUICIDE IN CHINESE POPULATIONS

More than any other ethnic group, the Chinese have migrated to and are found in many nations of the world, and this permits an examination and comparison of suicidal behavior among the Chinese in different nations. In this way, the influence of society and culture on suicide can be studied. Lester [17] collected data on suicide among the Chinese in Hong Kong, Singapore, Taiwan and the USA and identified common trends in the data. Lester found different suicide rates for the Chinese populations in 1984: 14.6 in Singapore Chinese, 10.9 in Taiwan and 9.2 in Hong Kong. The ratio of the male/female suicide rate in 1984 was, however, 1.4, 1.4 and 1.3 respectively. (In 1980, this ratio was 1.2 in Hong Kong, Taiwan, the Chinese in Singapore and the Chinese in the United States[6]). The most common methods for suicide were jumping in Singapore and Hong Kong, solids/liquids in Taiwan, and hanging in the Chinese in the United States. In all four nations, the suicide rates rose with age. Thus, Lester concluded that the male/female sex ratio and the age distribution were invariant over the nations, whereas the actual suicide rate and the methods used for suicide varied by nation.

12. SOCIOLOGICAL THEORIES

Durkheim's [23] theory of suicide continues to be the most important sociological theory and provides a basis for explaining and predicting the variation in the annual suicide rate. Durkheim proposed that two social characteristics determined the societal suicide rate: the degree of social integration (the extent to which people are bound together in social relationships) and the degree of social regulation (the extent to which the desires and aspirations of people are governed by social norms and rules). In particular, Durkheim hypothesized that marriage and children should increase the degree of social integration since they create new relationships, and they should result, therefore, in lower suicide rates. This hypothesis has been confirmed in time series studies of Western nations such as Canada and Yugoslavia [34, 35] Lester [35] tested this hypothesis for seven Pacific Rim nations: Australia, Hong Kong, Japan, New Zealand, Singapore, Taiwan and the United States over the time period 1969 to 1988. The results of his time-series regressions are shown in Table **2**.

Table 2: The association over time of marriage and birth rates with suicides rates, 1969-1988. (From Lester, 1994b)

	Constant	Marriage	Birth	R^2
Australia	46.73	-0.73	0.85*	0.70
USA	22.70*	-0.71*	-0.20*	0.56
New Zealand	22.52*	-1.42	-0.02	0.60
Japan	22.74*	0.27	-0.44	0.65
Taiwan	12.34*	0.10	-0.15	0.52
Singapore	12.59*	-0.62	0.24	0.09
Hong Kong	12.62	-0.26	0.06	0.04

* $p < 0.10$.

Although the two variables of marriage and birth rates accounted for a good proportion of the variance in the suicide rates for Japan and Taiwan (as they did for Australia, New Zealand and the United States) they did not do so for Singapore and Taiwan. Furthermore, whereas Durkheim's theory would predict negative regression coefficients for both marriage and birth rates, this was the case only for New Zealand and the United States.

---

[6] These rates have diverged more recently. Liu and Yip [12] report ratios of 1.9 for Japan and Taiwan, 1.5 for Singapore, and 1.3 for Hong Kong.

Lester and Abe [36] found that the predictors of the time-series suicide rate in Japan from 1970 to 1989 were different for the different methods of suicide. For example, only the suicide rate by hanging was positively associated with the divorce rate, as Durkheim's theory would predict. Suicide rates by other methods were not associated with the divorce rate.

Lester concluded that his results indicated that theories of suicide proposed by European scholars may not be applicable to non-Western nations and that scholars in Asia should endeavor to develop theories of suicide applicable to their own regions.

13. THE REASONS FOR SUICIDE

Two nations in Asia endeavor to classify the motives for each official suicide[7]. Lester and Saito [37] found that the most common reasons for suicide among Japanese men in 1995 were illness/ailments (34.3%), economic hardship (16.9%) and alcoholism/mental illness (15.1%). For women, the most common reasons were: illness/ailments (47.4%), alcoholism/mental illness (24.5%) and family problems (10.9%). Men were less likely than women to have family problems as a reason for suicide, illness/ailments and male/female relationships problems. Men were more likely to have economic hardship and school problems as reasons for suicide.

Over the period from 1978 to 1995, for men, the proportion of suicides motivated by illness/ailments, male/female relationship problems and school problems declined, whereas the proportion due to job stress increased. For women, the proportion of suicides motivated by family problems and male/female relationship problems declined during the period while the proportion due to alcoholism/mental illness increased.

Lester and Saito [37] then investigated whether socio-economic factors predicted these changes. For example, the unemployment rate during the period was positively associated with the proportion of suicides motivated by economic hardship, for both men and women. Lester and Saito [38] also found that the socioeconomic predictors of the suicide rate for each motive differed. Measures of domestic social integration predicted the suicide rate for interpersonal reasons, while the unemployment rate and the divorce rate predicted the suicide rate for work-related reasons.

The only other nation that attempts to classify motives for suicides is India, although many suicides have no motive identified by the government. Lester, Agarwal and Natarajan [3] reported that, in 1994, the most common motive for suicide in India was illness (13.5%), followed by marital problems (5.8%) and love (5.8%) and friction with parents (4.9%). Over the time period from 1975 to 1994, friction with parents became less common, as did suicide because of a serious illness or disease. Suicide in men was more often a result of failures in examinations, poverty, insanity, disputes over property, disease, unemployment, bankruptcy or sudden change in economic status, and a loss of social reputation. Suicide in women was more often a result of quarrels with in-laws and spouses, the death of someone, dowry disputes and illegitimate pregnancies.

14. DISCUSSION

In 1975, Normal Farberow edited a ground-breaking book on suicide in different cultures [39]. Of the fifteen chapters, three were on Asian countries, all written by the leaders of suicidology in those countries: Venkoba Rao for India, Hsien Rin for Taiwan and Mamoru Iga and Kichinosuke Tatai for Japan. Paul Yip's excellent edited book on suicide in Asia [40] shows the progress that has been in the thirty years since the publication of Farberow's book.

It is difficult to pick out one feature of suicide in Asia as the most striking, but perhaps the ratio of the male/female suicide rates is one. The majority of the ratios reported in this chapter have been in the range

---

[7] Interestingly, no European or North American nation has attempted to classify the motives for suicide for all the suicides each year.

of 1 to 2, and the ratio in mainland China is less than one. In contrast, the ratio for the United States is 4.0, Poland 5.0, Costa Rica 6.7, and Iceland 7.1 [41]. Suicide is a more egalitarian phenomenon for men and women in Asia. Since it is a general phenomenon, the explanation must lie outside of simple causes, such as the use of pesticides. There must be factors in Asian culture (such as religious values), psychology (such as having a Taoist orientation) or physiology that are responsible for the phenomenon.

The study of suicide in Asia has made great strides in the last thirty years. Let us hope that the next thirty years are similarly productive.

REFERENCES

[1] Law CK, Yip PSF. Hong Kong. In: Yip PSF, Ed. Suicide in Asia. Hong Kong: Hong Kong University Press. 2008; pp. 49-60.

[2] Chan KPM, Yip PSF, Au J, Lee DTS. Charcoal burning suicide in post-transition Hong Kong. Br J Psychiatry 2005; 186: 67-71.

[3] Lester D, Agarwal K, Natarajan M. Suicide in India. Arch Suicide Res 1999;5: 91-96.

[4] Vijayakumar L. India. In: Yip PS, Ed. Suicide in Asia. Hong Kong: Hong Kong University Press. 2008; pp. 121-31.

[5] Lester D. Preventing suicide: Closing the Exits revisited. Hauppauge, NY: Nova Science, 2009.

[6] Takahashi Y. Japan. In: Yip PSF, Ed. Suicide in Asia. Hong Kong: Hong Kong University Press. 2008; pp. 7-17.

[7] Lester D, Abe K. Social integration and suicide/homicide in Japan and the United States. Jpn J Psychiatry Neurol 1992; 46: 849-51.

[8] Lester D, Motohashi Y, Yang B. The impact of the economy on suicide and homicide rates in Japan and the United States. Int J Soc Psychiatry 1992; 38: 314-7.

[9] Lester D, Saito Y, Abe K. Have suicide prevention centers prevented suicide in Japan? Arch Suicide Res 1996; 2: 125-8.

[10] Lester D, Saito Y, Abe K. The effect of suicide prevention centers on suicide in Japan. Crisis 1997; 18: 48.

[11] Phillips MR, Liu H, Zhang Y. Suicide and social change in China. Cult Med Psychiatry 1999; 23: 25-50.

[12] Liu KY and Yip PSF. Mainland China. In: Yip PSF, Ed. Suicide in Asia. Hong Kong: Hong Kong University Press.2008; pp. 31-48.

[13] Pearson V and Liu M. Ling's death. Suicide Life Threat Behav 2002; 32: 347-58.

[14] Zhang J. Gender differences in athletic performance and their implications in gender ratios of suicide. Omega 2000; 41: 117-23.

[15] Chia BH, Chia A. Singapore. In: Yip PS, Ed. Suicide in Asia. Hong Kong: Hong Kong University Press. 2008; pp. 101-20.

[16] Lester D. Suicide by jumping in Singapore as a function of high-rise apartment availability. Percept Mot Skills 1994c; 79:74.

[17] Lester D. The epidemiology of suicide in Chinese populations in six regions of the world. Chinese Ment Health J 1994b; 7: 25-36.

[18] Murphy HBM. The mental health of Singapore. Med J Malaysia 1954; 9(1): 1-45.

[19] Lester D. Suicide from a sociological perspective. Springfield, IL: Charles Thomas, 1989.

[20] Park BCP, Lester D. South Korea. In: Yip PSF, Ed. Suicide in Asia. Hong Kong: Hong Kong University Press. 2008; pp. 19-30.

[21] Park BCP, Lester D. Protest suicide among Korean students and laborers. Psychol Rep 2009; 105: 917-20.

[22] Park BCP. Sociopolitical contexts of self-immolation in Vietnam and South Korea. Arch Suicide Res 2004; 8: 81-97.

[23] Durkheim E. Le suicide. Paris: FelixAlcan, 1897.

[24] Lester D. The use of the Internet for counseling the suicidal individual. Omega 2008-2009; 58: 233-50.

[25] Anon. Elusive, but not always unstoppable. The Economist 2007; 383(8534): 66-7.

[26] Chao A, Law CK, Li PC, Yip PSF. Taiwan. In: Yip PSF, Ed. Suicide in Asia. Hong Kong: Hong Kong University Press. 2008; pp. 61-79.

[27] Wolf M. Women and suicide in China. In: Wolf M and Witke R, Eds. Women in Chinese society. Palo Alto, CA: Stanford University Press. 1975; pp. 111-41.

[28] Lester D, Hu YH. The regional variation of suicide and homicide in the USA and Taiwan. Crisis 1993; 14: 126-8.

[29] Lester D. Domestic integration and the Taiwanese homicide and suicide rate. Chinese Ment Health J 1995; 8: 21-5.

[30] Huang WC, Lester D. Have suicide prevention centers prevented suicide? Chinese Ment Health J 1995; 8(3): 27-9.

[31] Lotrakul M. Thailand. In: Yip PSF, Ed. Suicide in Asia. Hong Kong: Hong Kong University Press. 2008; pp. 81-100.
[32] Cheng ATA. Mental illness and suicide. Arch Gen Psychiatry 1995; 52: 594-603.
[33] Cheng ATA. Personality disorder and suicide. Br J Psychiatry 1997; 170: 441-6.
[34] Lester D, Yang B. Suicide and homicide in the 20th Century. Commack, NY: Nova Science, 1998.
[35] Lester D. Domestic integration and suicide in Pacific Rim nations. Chinese Ment Health J 1994a; 7: 21-4.
[36] Lester D, Abe K. The suicide rate by each method in Japan. Arch Suicide Research 1998; 4: 281-5.
[37] Lester D, Saito Y. The reasons for suicide in Japan. Omega 1998-1999; 38: 65-8.
[38] Lester D, Saito Y. Predicting the time-series suicide rate in Japan by motive. Omega 2002; 45: 149-152.
[39] Farberow NL. Suicide in different cultures. Baltimore: University Park Press, 1975.
[40] Yip PSF, Ed. Suicide in Asia. Hong Kong: Hong Kong University Press, 2008.
[41] Canetto SS, Lester D. The epidemiology of women's suicidal behavior. In: Canetto SS, Lester D, Eds. Women and suicidal behavior. New York: Springer, 1995.

CHAPTER 13

Suicide in Asia-II

T. Maniam[*]

Department of Psychiatry, UKM Medical Centre, National University of Malaysia, Kuala Lumpur, Malaysia

Abstract: Asia accounts for more than half of all suicides in the world. Suicide rates in Asia vary vastly across the continent. Most suicides occur in China, India and Japan contributing more than 300,000 fatalities every year – about 40% of all suicides in the world. Countries in West Asia including the Middle East report very low rates, whereas countries such as Japan and Korea report much higher rates of suicide. These rates seem to have increased since the Asian Economic crisis that began in 1997 and has not abated since. A major problem with the study of suicide in Asia is, apart from a number of exceptions, the relative paucity of accurate suicide statistics. A few countries provide reliable data but the majority do not, and some provide none at all.

While hanging is the most popular method of committing suicide in most countries the use of pesticides is of particular concern in Asia, especially in rural areas. Suicide prevention programs are strongly supported by the government in a few countries and are non-existent in some others. Socio-cultural and political factors contribute to this state of affairs.

Keywords: Epidemiology, Asia, suicide, prevention.

Figure 1: Map of Asia. Source: [1]

1. INTRODUCTION

Asia, comprising 52 countries, is the most populous continent. It is home to more than 4 billion people, nearly two-thirds of the world population, and a myriad of cultures, tongues and tribal peoples. Six of the 10 most populous countries in the world are found in Asia. China and India, the Asian giants each with

*Address correspondence to T. Maniam: Department of Psychiatry, UKM Medical Centre, National University of Malaysia, Jalan Yaacob Latif, 56000 Kuala Lumpur, Malaysia; E-mail: tmaniam@yahoo.com

Maurizio Pompili (Ed)

more than a billion citizens, also figure prominently in terms of absolute suicide figures. It is estimated that most suicides in the world, up to 60%, occur in Asia [2].

2. CULTURAL ASPECTS

All the major religions of the world had their origins in Asia and exert much influence on the beliefs and behavior of Asians. Throughout much of human history religion has been an integrating factor in human society [3]. Hence its influence on suicidal behavior needs to be carefully considered. A brief outline of the views of the major Asian religions concerning suicide follows:

Buddhism

Suffering or *dukka* is part of life but suicide is not considered a positive way of dealing with such suffering. However, suicide is not condemned. Some Buddhist monks have committed suicide by self-immolation as a form of political protest.

Christianity

The Bible records 7 suicides, including that of Judas Iscariot, who betrayed Jesus. Christian theology holds that only God, who is the Author of life, has the right to take life. Therefore suicide is forbidden in the Christian faith. Christian theologians like Augustine of Hippo and Thomas Aquinas have elaborated on the wrongfulness of suicide, summarized by the 3 reasons Aquinas [4] gave for forbidding suicide: firstly, suicide is contrary to nature in that it is natural for every living thing to seek to preserve life; secondly, suicide violates man's social duty, in that killing oneself injures the whole human community; and thirdly, it is against religion since God alone ought to decide when one dies. In the past in some countries, normal church burials were denied to persons who had committed suicide. However this strict approach has softened in more recent times and there is a tendency to view people who commit suicide as being ill.

Hinduism

There are varying opinions among scholars as to the position of the Hindu scriptures regarding suicide. According to Adityanjee [5] there is an element of tolerance towards suicide in Hinduism – while some Hindu scriptures condemn suicide, others tacitly permit it, with one of them identifying 5 types of suicides as being justifiable. It might be acceptable in some schools of Hinduism to commit suicide if one has attained enlightenment, and that the ideal place for such suicides would be the confluence of two rivers. In Malaysia where about 6% of the population is Hindu there is certainly a higher risk of suicide among the Hindus compared to the Muslims and Christians [6]. In other words, the deterrence against suicide does not appear to be as strong in Hinduism. The Hindu practice of suttee (or sati) in which the widow was burnt when her husband's body was cremated has been declared illegal in India. However as a cultural practice it may not have completely died out, as described by Altekar [7], who in 1978, described the suicidal death of his own sister who would not be dissuaded by her family and who died on her husband's funeral pyre.

Islam

Suicide is strongly forbidden in Islam, hell being the destination of the person who dies by suicide. This has acted as a very strong deterrent to suicide among Muslim societies, though there may be indications that this deterrence may be weakening[1]. It might be that the consequences of industrialization and urbanization, with the resulting loosening of previously close societal ties and break-up of extended families, have weakened the deterrent effect of Islam. Nevertheless, most studies show that suicide rates are extremely low in Muslim societies.

---

[1] Murad Khan. Suicide in Pakistan: Is Islam not a deterrent anymore? Paper presented at the 24th Congress of the International Association for Suicide Prevention . Killarney, Ireland 2007

Jainism

Jainism appears to have a much more tolerant view of suicide. It is permitted to starve oneself to death. But death by violent means is forbidden because of strong insistence on non-violence.

Judaism

Suicide is sin and therefore is forbidden in Judaism. Its primary scripture, the Torah, portrays God as the creator, who alone determines the issues of life and death.

Shintoism

In this Japanese religion suicide does not carry much stigma. It might even be encouraged in the face of dishonour or as a means of protest. A samurai (warrior) might commit seppuku – the act of disembowelling oneself – rather than face defeat [8]. Suicide acts might be carried out in war, as the kamikaze pilots did during the Second World War, but that should perhaps be considered an act of war rather than as suicide.

Sikhism

Suicide is disapproved of in Sikhism because life is a gift of God. Even in the face of great suffering suicide is disapproved. In the purpose of God "suffering is medicine" [9].

Taoism

Taoism, which shares the belief in reincarnation with other religions such as Buddhism and Hinduism, disapproves of suicide though its opposition is not as stringent as that of the aforementioned Judeo-Christian religions [10].

3. EPIDEMIOLOGY OF SUICIDE IN ASIA

There are vast differences in the quality and reliability of suicide data available for Asia. The more developed societies of Asia, such as Japan and Singapore provide fairly accurate data, whereas many other countries do not provide any data at all. There are questions about the accuracy of the suicide statistics in many countries. For example, when trained interviewers investigated a large number of deaths in the southern Indian state of Tamil Nadu, they arrived at a suicide rate 10 times the reported rate [11].

Generally the East Asian countries, such as China, Japan and Korea, and south Asian countries such as India and Sri Lanka report higher suicide rates. Suicide rates for countries for which rates are available are provided in Table **1**.

Two notable features stand out from Table **1**: firstly, no data is available from most of the countries of West Asia, which are largely Muslim; secondly, where data is provided, as in the case of Iran, Syria and Jordan, these countries report extremely low rates.

Are the low levels reported by the latter a reflection of really low rates of suicide or are they due to incomplete reporting? The rates in Muslim countries might genuinely be low because of the strong prohibition against suicide in the religion of Islam. However there is some evidence that the rates, while low, may not be as low as reported.

Many factors influence the rate of reporting. The stigma of suicide prevents many from reporting the suicide of a loved one. In many countries deaths by suicide are generally required by law to undergo autopsy which is viewed with grave distaste in Muslim societies. Hence, many suicides may not be reported as such, but reported as accidental deaths instead. Furthermore, in many Asian countries a large proportion of deaths are not medically certified, and therefore the assignment of a cause for death is suspect. Even when the death certification is carried out by a medical practitioner, problems in data collection may account for a vast majority of suicides being misclassified. Maniam [14] has shown evidence that even the medically certified deaths are systematically misclassified in Malaysia, and has estimated that the actual suicide rate may be more than 10 times the reported rate. In some countries the reporting system is not efficient at all [15].

Table 1: Suicide rates in selected Asian Countries

Country	Suicide rate per 100,000	Year
Kazakhstan[a]	26.9	2007
South Korea[b]	26.1	2005
Japan[c]	25.2	2008
Sri Lanka[b]	23.9	1996
China[b]	23.2	1999
India[b]	17.4	1998
Hong Kong[b]	15.3	2006
Malaysia[b]	13.1	2000
Singapore[a]	10.3	2006
Kyrgyzstan[a]	9.2	2005
Turkmenistan[a]	8.6	1998
Thailand[a]	7.8	2002
Israel[a]	6.2	2003
Philippines[a]	2.1	1993
Pakistan[b]	2.9	2007
Kuwait[a]	2.0	2002
Armenia[a]	1.8	2003
Azerbaijan[a]	1.1	2002
Turkey[a]	1.8	1995
Iran[a]	0.2	1991
Syria[a]	0.1	1985
Jordan[a]	0.0	1979

[a]Reference [12].

[b]Reference [13].

[c]Calculated from: Takahashi Y, Yamamoto T, Kikuchi A, *et al.* Overview of Suicide and Suicide Prevention in Japan. Abstract of paper presented at The Second World Congress of Asian Psychiatry. Taipei, Nov 2009.

Other factors may also contribute to this state of affairs. An obvious example is the implications for insurance claims in the event of suicide. In the author's experience this misreporting happens not uncommonly in the uniformed services where the families of the deceased would miss out on insurance claims if the death is confirmed a suicide. These problems and the procedures employed in different Asian countries are discussed in detail in a recent WHO publication [13].

The high rates reported in Japan and Korea has been traced back to the economic difficulties faced by Asian countries as a result of the downturn in their economies in 1998. Japanese suicide rates jumped by about 30% following the economic turmoil, with especially high rates among men aged around 50 years or more[2]. Interestingly, even with the recovery of the economy since then the suicide rates in Japan have not returned to pre-1998 levels. Many factors have been cited for this and a major one being in the change in employment conditions in Japan following the Asian economic crisis. Whereas previously the Japanese worker was guaranteed a permanent job and the company looked after him for life, this security of tenure was shattered post-1998. In such a situation a middle-aged worker who has lost his job would become unemployable and face a bleak future.

---

[2] Takahashi Y. Suicide in Japan: How has the recent economic depression affected suicide? Paper presented at the 20th Congress of the International Association for Suicide Prevention, Athens, November 1999.

4. DIFFERENCES WITHIN COUNTRIES

There are not only vast differences in suicide rates between countries, but there may also be large differences between ethnic groups, gender and regions or provinces within each country.

Ethnic differences have been noted to be prominent in countries such as Malaysia, Fiji and the West Indies. The Indian Diaspora in these countries has consistently shown high suicide rates [16, 17, 18]. The reasons for these may be many: poverty, acculturation, alcoholism and the lack of a strong deterrent against suicide have been cited.

Suicide rates also vary across regions within the same country. In India the suicide rate varies very strikingly as one goes from north to south. The northern states generally have the lowest rates and as one traverses south the rate increases steadily with the southern most state of Kerala having the highest rate in India. Interestingly it is the southern states like Kerala, Tamil Nadu and Andhra Pradesh which have higher literacy, higher development and higher income, and yet which have higher suicide rates.

Urban-rural differences abound. In China the rural rates are much higher and this has been attributed to the use of pesticides by young women [19]. In a rural district in Malaysia, Maniam [20] demonstrated that the suicide rate among Indians was among the highest reported in the literature - again the use of pesticides and herbicides was the main method of suicide in this farming community.

5. METHODS OF SUICIDE

The choice of a method is determined by its availability, acceptability and socio-cultural meaning. Self-poisoning with pesticides is relatively common in the farming communities of Asia. In Singapore, where about 70% of the population lives in high-rise buildings, jumping off a building is the most popular method. In Sri Lanka, a very popular method is to ingest the poisonous seed of the yellow oleander which grows abundantly in rural areas [21]. Suicide by using firearms is relatively rare in most Asian countries because they are relatively inaccessible for most people. Many countries have very strict laws limiting ownership of guns.

In most Asian countries hanging is the most popular method followed by pesticide ingestion, jumping from heights and carbon monoxide (CO) poisoning. In some countries, especially Hong Kong, CO poisoning through charcoal burning has become increasingly popular, to the point that in Taiwan it has even been considered an epidemic[3]. In others, especially in Iran, Afghanistan and the Indian subcontinent self-immolation is not uncommon. In Herat, western Afghanistan, self-immolation appears to be the most popular method, and the incidence more than doubled between 2005 and 2006 [22].

Pesticides ingestion is such a major means of suicide in Asia that it warrants special mention.

Within Asia's large farming communities, the use of pesticides is widespread and access to it is relatively easy. In many farms agricultural biocides (pesticides such as organophosphates and herbicides such as paraquat) are generally stored in unsecured areas. Distressed persons have easy access to highly lethal substances. Agricultural communities often do not have quick access to medical facilities. It is not uncommon that persons, who are acting impulsively, in anger or protest, ingest agricultural poisons and die before adequate treatment can be administered. Many of these suicides are not suicides *per se*, but people who engage in deliberate self-harm with no intention of dying but end up dead because of the highly lethal means they used. An example of a case seen by the author illustrates this:

---

[3] Chang S, Gunnell D, Wheeler B, Yip P, Sterne JAC. The Evolution of the Epidemic of Charcoal-Burning Suicide in Taiwan: A Spatial and Temporal Analysis. Poster presented at 2nd World Congress of Asian Psychiatry. Taipei November 2009.

> A young Malaysian man, who felt humiliated because of false accusations about a broken love relationship, ingested a small amount of weedicide. While in hospital, he pleaded with the doctors to save him because he had no intention of dying. He died.

Unplanned impulsive acts in ingesting pesticides are therefore a major problem contributing to suicides in Asia. In a Chinese study Li *et al.* [23] have shown that more than a third of those who were hospitalized for serious but non-fatal suicide attempts had merely thought about the attempt for 10 minutes or less.

Gunnel and Eddleston [24] have suggested a number of approaches to prevent suicides by self-poisoning using pesticides. Reducing the availability of pesticides would obviously be a major step, which includes safer storage such that distressed people do not have quick and easy access to these lethal substances. Other approaches include developing safer pesticides, adding stenching agents and emetics to the pesticides in order to discourage their use, public education about safe storage and proper usage. A further approach is providing better immediate management of pesticide poisoning in rural areas, which are usually far from specialised medical centres.

6. SUICIDE PACTS

This rather uncommon phenomenon is being reported increasingly with the advent of the internet. Among Asian countries it is probably Japan and Hong Kong that have reported the most number of cases [25]. These involve usually young people who make contact *via* the internet chat rooms and then meet together to kill themselves. In many cases the method chosen is charcoal burning.

> The author managed the case of a depressed young man who had searched the internet for suicide sites and who was led to a chat room through which he came into contact with four other men with whom he made a pact to commit suicide together in the near future. After a course of electroconvulsive treatment the young man recovered and his suicidal wish disappeared. He, together with the author, tried to contact the erstwhile friends but was unable to because the site, which had been hosted in Australia, had been closed down because of a new law in that country banning the promotion of suicide through websites.

7. RISK FACTORS FOR SUICIDE AND PSYCHOLOGICAL AUTOPSY STUDIES IN ASIA

A number of psychological autopsy studies have been conducted in Asia. Teoh's [26] study conducted in Kuala Lumpur Malaysia in the pre-DSM-III era, utilised an unstructured clinical interview and found only about 40% of suicides had a psychiatric diagnosis, whereas subsequent studies by others elsewhere have used structured interview schedules and found higher rates of mental disorder. Cheng *et al.* [27] study in Taiwan showed 97 to 100% of completed suicides having one form or other of a mental disorder, indicating similarities with western studies. Vijayakumar and Rajkumar [28] studied Indian suicides in Tamil Nadu and again found high rates of mental disorder leading them to conclude that their findings "suggest that risk factors for completed suicide are universal across countries and cultures." Such similarities have also been noted by Phillips *et al.* [29].

However, in Asia the situation with regard to psychiatric illness in suicides is not a straightforward one. Phillips[4] has argued that most suicides among women in rural China do not have a psychiatric diagnosis because in rural China pesticide poisoning is often an impulsive act of people facing crises, who are not psychiatrically ill and who do not have a definite intention to die and, but the subjects end up dead because they had chosen this particularly lethal method. A similar hypothesis was postulated by Maniams[5] to account for the very high suicide rates revealed in a community survey among young women in the farming

---

[4] Phillips MR Symposium on Women and Suicide. Presented at the 21st Congress of the International Association for Suicide Prevention, Chennai, India. November 2001.

[5] Maniam T. 1985. Suicide and Parasuicide in Cameron Highlands – Demographic Aspects of Cases from October 1973 and September 1984. Dissertation for Partial Fulfillment of Master of Psychological Medicine Degree, University of Malaya, Kuala Lumpur, 1985.

district of Cameron Highlands in Malaysia where agricultural biocides were the major means of committing suicide.

It is not an uncommon practice in many South Asian cultures for marriages to be arranged by the family. This often causes unhappiness to young people. Anita Raj *et al.* [22] have documented cases of self-immolation in Afghanistan precipitated by arranged marriages. In Indian societies caste differences between lovers often result in parental refusal for marriage and this not uncommonly leads to a suicide attempt or suicide [20].

Suicide as a means of protest is not uncommon in some Asian countries. It is the ultimate means of registering one's powerlessness against perceived or real injustices and has been reported in Asia. An illustrative case from Hong Kong is reported by Sing Lee[6] of an actress whose alleged affair was widely reported in the local media, who committed suicide by inhaling charcoal gas.

8. SUICIDE PREVENTION PROGRAMS

Many Asian governments are increasingly recognizing the seriousness of suicide as a public health problem. Some countries have launched national suicide prevention programs but in many others either there are no such programs or, if there are, competing priorities and limited resources have prevented these programs from being pursued with vigour. One of the things that ail prevention programs is the lack of political will [7]. The authorities often do not view the statistics and graphs as researchers do and often these data have to be translated into forms that would persuade them to commit public funds.

In the absence of full government participation in these programs in many countries, it has been left to nongovernmental organizations (NGO) to undertake suicide prevention activities. NGOs, like SNEHA in India and Befrienders in Malaysia, similar to the Samaritans in the United Kingdom, have played major roles in providing crisis counselling to distressed and suicidal individuals. In some cities in Malaysia the Befrienders provide counselling services in four languages – Chinese, English, Malay and Tamil to cater to the many sectors of the population – a testament to the complexities of providing such services in culturally diverse societies.

There can be no one model of suicide prevention for the diversity of problems faced by the vulnerable peoples of Asia. It is commonsensical that the approaches to reduce the high suicide rates among young women facing gender issues in rural China, Malaysia or Afghanistan should be different from that of reducing suicide among Japanese men in their 50s who commit suicide after losing their jobs.

Japan has a developed suicide prevention program driven by the rise in suicide rates since the Asian economic crisis of 1997. Japan has also tested a public awareness program that has been shown to reduce suicides [30].

Recognizing the role of sensational reporting in the media in contributing to suicide contagion, some Asian countries (*e.g.,* Korea and Malaysia) have launched national guidelines on media reporting.

Since pesticide suicides are a massive problem in Asia (an estimated 3 million cases of pesticides poisoning occur each year in developing countries of which between 200 000 to 300 000 end in death [31]), attempts are being made to limit the access that vulnerable people have to this lethal means of suicide. One such method is secure access to pesticides by using locked boxes to store pesticides where the key is held by two senior members of the family such that a distressed family member cannot resort to self-poisoning in an

---

[6] Lee S. Suicide as moral resistance. Paper presented at Collegium Internationale Neuropsychopharmacologicum (CINP) Regional Meeting, Kuala Lumpur, March 2000.

[7] Maniam T. Suicide Prevention in Malaysia. Paper presented at Symposium on Suicide Prevention: Crossnational perspective. Paper presented at 2nd World Congress of Asian Psychiatry. Taipei November 2009.

impulsive manner. This idea has had preliminary testing in Sri Lanka and is now in the process of being more fully tested [31].

Training of mental health personnel and primary care doctors in early recognition and treatment of depressed persons is a major undertaking. Some countries in Asia have embarked on this but often it is not in a systematic way. Both public sector agencies and NGOs have contributed to training. However evaluation of these efforts as to their effectiveness in reducing suicides has not been fully studied.

Other preventive efforts and assistance for survivors have been more fully documented in a WHO publication [32].

REFERENCES

[1] Available from: http: //projectvisa.com/regions/Asia. Accessed 15/2/2010.

[2] Beautrais AL and Mishara BL. Editorial: World Suicide Prevention Day: Think Globally, Plan Nationally, Act Locally. Crisis 2008; 29: 59-63.

[3] Berger PL, Berger B and Kellner H. The homeless mind: Modernization and consciousness New York: Random House; 1973.

[4] Aquinas T: Aquinas' Summa Theologica. Notre Dame Indiana: Ave Maria Press; 1989.

[5] Adityanjee DR. Suicide Attempts and Suicides in India: Cross-Cultural Aspects. Int J Soc Psychiatr 1986; 32: 64-73.

[6] Morris P and Maniam T. Ethnicity and Suicidal Behavior in Malaysia: A review of the literature. Transcultural Psychiatry 2001; 38: 51-63.

[7] Altekar AS. The Position of Women in Hindu Civilization. Delhi: Moti Lal Banarsi Das; 1978.

[8] http: //urantiabook.org/archive/readers/601_shinto.htm. Accessed 15/3/2010.

[9] Available from: http: //www.sikhwomen.com/antiviolence/suicide.htm. Accessed 15/3/2010.

[10] http: //simple.wikipedia.org/wiki/Suicide#Dharmic_and_Taoist. Accessed 15/3/2010.

[11] Gajalakshmi V and Peto R. Suicide rates in rural Tamil Nadu,South India: Verbal Autopsy of 39000 deaths in 1997-98. Int J Epidemiol 2007; 36: 203-7.

[12] http: //en.wikipedia.org/wiki/list_of_countries_by-suicide_rate. Accessed 15/2/2010.

[13] Hendin H, Vijayakumar L, Bertolote JM, Wang H, Phillips MR and Pirkis J. Epidemiology of Suicide in Asia. In: Hendin H, Phillips MR, Vijayakumar L, *et al.* Eds. Suicide and Suicide Prevention in Asia. Geneva, World Health Organization. 2008; pp. 7-18.

[14] Maniam T. Suicide and undetermined violent deaths in Malaysia, 1966-1990: Evidence for the misclassification of suicide statistics. Asia Pac J Publ Health 1995; 8: 181-5.

[15] Bose A, Konradsen F, John J, Suganthy P, Muliyil J and Abraham S. Mortality rate and years of life lost from unintentional injury and suicide in South India. Trop Med Int Health 2006; 11: 1553-6.

[16] Maniam T. Why do Malaysia Asian Indians have high suicide rates? In: Vijayakumar, L. Ed. Suicide Prevention: Meeting the Challenge Together. Chennai: Orient Longman Limited. 2003; pp. 198-213.

[17] Haynes RH. Suicide in Fiji: a preliminary study. Br J Psychiatry 1984; 145: 433-8.

[18] McCandless FD. Suicide and the Communication of Rage: A Cross-cultural case study. Am J Psychiat 1968; 125: 197-205.

[19] Phillips MR, Li X and Zhang Y. Suicide rates in China, 1995-99. Lancet 359: 835-40.

[20] Maniam T. Suicide and Parasuicide at a hill resort in Malaysia. Br J Psychiatry, 1988; 153: 222-5.

[21] Eddleston M, Gunnell D, Karunaratne A, *et al* Epidemiology of intentional self-poisoning in rural Sri Lanka. Br J Psychiatry 2005; 187: 583-4.

[22] Raj A, Gomez C and Jay Silverman JG. Driven to a Fiery Death — The Tragedy of Self-Immolation in Afghanistan. New Engl J Med 2008; 358: 2201-3.

[23] Li XY, Xu YC, Wang YP, Zhang C and Ji HY. Characteristics of serious suicide attempts treated in a general hospital. Chin J Ment Health 2002; 16: 681-4.

[24] Gunnell D, Eddleston M. Suicide by intentional ingestion of pesticides: a continuing tragedy in developing countries. Int J Epidemiol 2003; 32: 902–9.

[25] Lee DTS, Chan KPM and Yip PSF. Charcoal burning is also popular for suicide pacts made on the internet. BMJ 2005; 330: 602.

[26] Teoh JI. An analysis of completed suicides by psychological postmortem. Ann Acad Med Singapore. 1974; 3: 117–24.

[27] Cheng ATA, Chen THH, Chen CC and Jenkins R. Psychosocial and psychiatric risk factors for suicide: Case-control psychological autopsy study. Br J Psychiatry, 2000; 177: 360-5.

[28] Vijayakumar L and Rajkumar S. Are risk factors for suicide universal? A case-control study in India. Acta Psychiat Scand 1999; 99: 407–11.

[29] Phillips MR, Yang G, Zhang Y, Wang L, Ji H and Zhou M. Risk factors for suicide in China: a national case-control psychological autopsy study. Lancet 2002; 360: 1728 – 36.

[30] Motohashi Y, Kaneko Y, Sasaki H and Yamaji M. A decrease in suicide rates in Japanese rural towns after community-based intervention by the public health promotion approach. Suicide Life-Threat 2007; 37: 593-9.

[31] Mishara BL. Report on the International Workshop on Secure Access to Pesticides in Conjunction with the Annual Congress of the International Association for Suicide Prevention, Durban. September 12, 2005. Available from: http: //www.iasp.info/pdf/papers/Mishara.pdf . Accessed 4 April 2010.

[32] Hendin H, Xiao S, Li X, Huong TT, Wang H, Hegerl U and Phillips MR. Suicide Prevention in Asia: Future Directions. In: Hendin H, Phillips MR, Vijayakumar L, *et al.* Eds. Suicide and Suicide Prevention in Asia. Geneva, World Health Organization. 2008; pp. 97-108.

CHAPTER 14

Suicide and Suicidal Behavior in Australia

Karolina Krysinska[1,*] and David Lester[2]

[1]*Faculty of Psychology and Educational Sciences, KU Leuven, University of Leuven, Belgium and* [2]*The Richard Stockton College of New Jersey, USA*

Abstract: The present chapter reviews epidemiological research on suicidal behavior in Australia, in the population as a whole and in Indigenous Australians and immigrants. Australia has proposed a National Suicide Prevention Strategy, and this is briefly described.

Keywords: Suicide, attempted suicide, australia, indigenous australians, immigrants.

1. INTRODUCTION

Compared to other countries, over the last decade Australia has had moderate suicide rates, ranging from 14.7 per 100,000 in 1997 to 10.3 in 2005 [1, 2]. Since mid-1960s, there have been significant fluctuations in suicide rates in Australia, especially among young males, a pattern which has also been found in other Western countries [3], and the National Suicide Prevention Strategy might have contributed to the reduction in suicide among young Australian males [4]. This chapter reviews the epidemiology of suicide in Australia and, based on national surveys and hospitalization records, presents information on suicidal attempts and ideation among Australian adults. Suicide in two special Australian subpopulations – Indigenous Australians and immigrants - is discussed as well as the sociological studies of suicide in Australia. Finally, the chapter outlines the National Suicide Prevention Strategy which has been implemented in Australia since 1995 [5].

2. SUICIDE IN AUSTRALIA

According to the most recent available data[1], in 2007, 1,881 people died by suicide in Australia which resulted in an overall suicide rate of 8.9 (13.9 for males and 4.0 for females) [6]. Although the median age for deaths from all causes in Australia was 77.5 years for males and 83.5 years for females, for suicides the median age was 41.7 years for males and 44.5 years for females. In 2007 the highest age-specific suicide rate (23) was observed among males older than 85 years of age. High age-specific suicide rates were also reported among middle-aged males: 20.8 in the 35-44 year age group and 18.7 in the 45-54 year age group. Although the age-specific suicide rate was the lowest among young males aged 15-24 years (12.5), suicide in this age group comprised 20% of all deaths. Among females, in 2007, the highest age-specific suicide rate of 5.7 was reported both in the 45-54 year age group and the 55-64 year age group, while elderly females aged between 75 and 84 years of age had the lowest age-specific suicide rate (3.3) [6].

Hanging was the most frequently used method of suicide in Australia in 2007 and accounted for 54% of all self-inflicted deaths. Two other frequent methods were poisoning by drugs and poisoning by other methods, including motor vehicle exhaust (12% of suicide deaths each), while firearms were responsible for 9% of suicide deaths. The remaining self-inflicted deaths resulted from drowning, jumping from a high place, and other methods [6]. Important (and continuing) changes in numbers of suicides by firearms and hanging

---

***Address correspondence to Karolina Krysinska:** Faculty of Psychology and Educational Sciences, KU Leuven, University of Leuven, Tiensestraat 102 - bus 3720, 3000 Leuven, Belgium, E-mail: karolina.krysinska@ppw.kuleuven.be

[1] The Australian Bureau of Statistics (ABS) calls for caution when viewing the mortality data in regard to coroner-certified deaths registered after 1 January 2007. These data will be subject to a revision process, and it is expected that the number of deaths attributed to suicide for 2007 will increase [6].

Maurizio Pompili (Ed)

have been observed in Australia between 1997 and 2004 [7-9]. Introduction of strict firearms legislation in late 1990s as well as increasingly negative societal perception of this method seems to have contributed to a decline in firearm suicides from 12.1% in 1997 to 8.1% in 2004. Over the same period, suicide by hanging has increased from 36.3% to 47.6%. These partly overlapping trends have raised serious concerns over method substitution and the problem of preventing suicide by hanging, a method which seems "unpreventable" at the societal level due to its almost unlimited availability, high lethality and increasing social acceptability [10, 11].

Differences in the geographical distribution of suicide across Australia which is comprised of six states (New South Wales, Queensland, South Australia, Tasmania, Victoria, Western Australia) and two major mainland territories (Australian Capital Territory and Northern Territory) have been reported [1]. The relatively small number of suicides in some states/territories, low general population numbers (especially in the Northern Territory) and differences in coroner procedures across the country call for caution in analysing the data, although combining data from several years allows for more reliable comparisons [1]. Over the period 2001-2005, Northern Territory had the highest rate of suicide in Australia (24.0), which was approximately twice as high as the national rate (11.2). Tasmania reported the second highest suicide rate in the country (15.6), followed by Queensland and South Australia (both 12.8). Suicide rates in the Australian Capital Territory, New South Wales and Victoria were lower than the national average [1].

Over the last five decades Australia has witnessed significant changes in the prevalence of suicide. Between 1964 and 1997 the rate of suicide among young Australian males under the age of 35 increased significantly, which included more than doubling of suicide rates among males aged 15-24 [12]. A similar trend had been observed in a number of countries, such as New Zealand, the United States, Canada and some Western European countries, including Belgium and England and Wales [3]. In the same period, suicide rates among both males and females over the age of 35 declined and suicide rates among young females (15-24 years old) remained relatively unchanged.

Since mid-1990s, there has been a gradual decline in the overall suicide rate in Australia from the peak of 14.7 in 1997 to 10.3 in 2005 [1]. Although the reduction in suicide rates could be observed in most age groups, the decline has been particularly evident among the young males aged 15-24; in this group the suicide rates have declined from 31.0 in 1997 to 16.2 in 2005. Suicide rates among females have remained relatively low and steady over this period [1]. The reduction in suicide rates among young males has been attributed to the effectiveness of the National Suicide Prevention Strategy [4, 8, 13]. However, problems related to the accuracy of national suicide mortality data call for caution in considering the strategy's impact [15, 16].

3. SUICIDE ATTEMPTS AND SUICIDAL IDEATION

The two Australian National Surveys of Mental Health and Wellbeing (NSMHWB) conducted in 1997 [17] and in 2007 [18] have provided data on the prevalence of suicidal attempts and ideation among Australian adults. The 1997 NSMHWB involved 10, 641 adults (with a 78% response rate) and yielded data on the 12-month and lifetime prevalence of suicidal ideation and attempts [17]. The data showed that, over their lifetime, 16% of respondents had thought about suicide and 3.6% had made a suicide attempt. Over the last 12 months, 3.4% of respondents had suicidal thoughts and 0.4% had attempted suicide. The respective numbers were higher for females than for males (Table **1**). The predictors of suicidal attempts and ideation in the last 12 months included affective, anxiety and substance abuse disorders and single marital status. In other words, in the last 12 months approximately one in 34 adult Australians had thought about suicide and about one in 307 had attempted suicide.

The 2007 NSMHWB included 8, 841 respondents aged 16-85 (with a 60% response rate) [18]. In total, in their lifetime, 13.3% of respondents had thought about suicide, 4% had made a suicide plan and 3.2% had made an attempt. In regards to the 12-months prevalence, 2.3% of respondents had suicidal thoughts, 0.6% made a plan and 0.4% made a suicide attempt. Extrapolating these data to the 2007 Australian adult population, during their lifetime more than 2.1 million Australians seriously considered suicide, more than 600, 000 made a suicide plan and more than 500, 000 attempted suicide.

Table 1: Lifetime and 12-month prevalence of suicidal ideation and attempts in the general population in Australia based on community survey data

	1997 Australian National Survey of Mental Health and Wellbeing (Pirkis, *et al.*, 2000)		**2007 Australian National Survey of Mental Health and Wellbeing (Johnston, *et al.*, 2009)**		**2007 WHO Suicide Prevention-Multisite Intervention Study on Suicide (Bertolote, *et al.*, 2005§)**	
	Lifetime	12-month	Lifetime	12-month	Lifetime	12-month
Males						
Suicidal ideation	13.2%	2.7%	11.5%	1.8%	-	-
Suicide plan	-	-	2.9%	0.4%	-	-
Suicide attempt	2.5%	0.3%	2.1%	0.3%	-	-
Females						
Suicidal ideation	18.2%	4.0%	15.0%	2.7%	-	-
Suicide plan	-	-	4.9%	0.7%	-	-
Suicide attempt	4.5%	0.5%	4.4%	0.5%	-	-
Total						
Suicidal ideation	16%	3.4%	13.3%	2.3%	11.0%	-
Suicide plan	-	-	4.0%	0.6%	10.6%	-
Suicide attempt	3.6%	0.4%	3.2%	0.4%	4.2%	-

§ Data for Brisbane, Queensland, only.

Based upon available data, Johnston, *et al.* [18] presented a more detailed picture of the 12-month prevalence of suicidality in the Australian adult population. Suicidal ideation and behavior were more frequent among females males than among males (Table **1**), and were more prevalent among people outside the labor force, people with mental disorders, and younger people. A lower prevalence was observed in people who were married or stayed in a *de facto* relationship, and among people with a moderate level of education. There were differences observed between males and females in different age groups. For men the highest prevalence of suicidal ideation, plans and attempts was observed in the 35-44 age group while for females the risk was the highest in 16-24 age group and gradually decreased with increasing age.

In summary, there were only small differences observed between the 1997 and 2007 samples in regard to the prevalence of suicidal ideation and attempts. However, differences between the two NSMHWB survey instruments, including differences in the screening questions, make comparisons between the two sets of results difficult [18]. In comparison with recent international surveys, Australians reported higher levels of lifetime suicidal ideation and attempts than participants of the World Health Organization World Mental Health (WHOWMH) Survey conducted in 17 countries world-wide [19] and the European Study on the Epidemiology of Mental Disorders (ESEMED) carried out in six European countries [20]. The estimated lifetime prevalence of suicidal ideation, plans and attempts in the WHOWMH cross-national sample was 9.2%, 3.1% and 2.7%, respectively [19] and 7.8% for suicidal ideation and 1.3% for suicidal attempts in the ESEMED sample [20]. In the Australian 2007 NSMHWB survey, 13.3% of adult Australians reported lifetime suicidal ideation, 4.0% suicide planning and 3.2% suicide attempt [18]. Again, differences in methodologies used in the surveys call for caution when comparing their results.

Another Australian study, conducted as a component of the international World Health Organisation Suicide Prevention-Multisite Intervention Study on Suicide (WHO/SUPREMISS) provided data on the prevalence of suicidal ideation and behavior in Brisbane, Queensland [21]. The survey was administered in 2002-2004 to 13, 810 community participants over the age of 17 (with a response rate of 61%). The results were similar to results obtained in the national surveys described above. In total, during their lifetime 11%

of Brisbane respondents had seriously thought about suicide, 10.6% made a suicide plan and 4.2% made a suicide attempt. In comparison to other sites of the WHO/SUPREMISS study, Brisbane (along with Karaj in Pakistan) had the highest rate of lifetime suicide attempts (4.2%), and medium rates of lifetime thoughts and plans. (For both, the highest rates were found in Durban in South Africa, 25.4% and 15.6%, respectively.)

There is limited information available in Australia on the rates of suicide attempts which lead to hospitalisation [22]. Data available for the period 1995-1996 to 2005-2006 showed that, apart from the initial decrease early in the mid-1990s, the crude total hospitalization rate was stable at approximately 115 per 100, 000 until 1998-1999. Over the next two years it increased to 162 and has remained relatively stable since then. The age-standardized total rate has been similar. In the early period, the suicide attempt hospitalization rate was around 135 with an increase to approximately 195 in the later period. The female to male hospitalized suicide attempt rate ratio of 1.5 to 1 has remained stable over the period of 1996-1996 to 2005-2006 [22].

4. SUICIDE AMONG INDIGENOUS AUSTRALIANS

Indigenous Australians, that is, the Aboriginal people, Torres Strait Islanders and people identifying as both Aboriginal and Torres Strait Islanders, comprise 2.5% of the total Australian population, and 517, 200 Indigenous Australians lived in the country in 2006 [23]. Still experiencing the tragic consequences of centuries-long history of colonization and discrimination, Indigenous Australians do not have the same level of access to many health services, including mental health services, as do other Australians, and there is a 17-year gap between life expectancy at birth for Indigenous and non-Indigenous males and females (59 *vs.* 77 years and 65 *vs.* 82 years; respectively) [23, 24].

Despite obvious and significant cultural, socio-economic and historical differences between Indigenous Australians and Indigenous populations in New Zealand, Canada and the United States, there are certain patterns in suicidal behavior and risk which are shared by these populations [25, 26]. These include the high incidence of suicide among young Indigenous males, a lower age of Indigenous suicide deaths, clustering of suicides, and a significant role of alcohol in suicidal behavior. Still, the situation of Indigenous Australians looks grim even by comparison to other Indigenous populations worldwide [27], and not much has changed since 1995 when Ring observed that "expectations for life for Indian populations in Canada and the United States, and for the Maoris in New Zealand are at least 10 years more than for Australian Aborigines, an enormous difference" [28].

Although problems with quality and availability of mortality and morbidity data in regard to Indigenous Australians call for caution in analysing the numbers [14], over the period of 2001-2005, external causes of mortality, such as accidents, suicide and assaults represented 16% of all deaths among Indigenous Australians (compared with 6% of deaths in the non-Indigenous population) [23]. In 2001-2005, suicide was the leading cause of death from external causes for Indigenous Australian males, comprising 35% of such deaths, and the second leading external cause of death for Indigenous Australian females (18% of deaths). For males, the overall Indigenous suicide rate was almost three times higher than that suicide rate for non-Indigenous males, with the biggest differences in the younger age groups of 0-24 and 25-34 years. The suicide rate among Indigenous Australian females aged 0-24 was five times the rate of non-Indigenous females and, in age groups 45-54 and over, the suicide rates were similar or lower than the rates for non-Indigenous females.

Regarding non-fatal self-harm, Queensland Health hospital separation data for 2002-2003 and 2003-2004 show that Aboriginal and Torres Strait Islanders were almost twice as likely to be admitted to a hospital following an episode of self-harm than non-Indigenous people (2.5 per 1000 *vs.* 1.5 per 1, 000) [29].

Hanging has been the most common method of Indigenous suicide and attempted suicide in Australia since the mid-1980s [30, 31]. For example, in Queensland in 2003-2004, suicide by hanging accounted for 92% of Indigenous suicides (compared to 67% of suicides due to hanging in the general population of the state)

[11]. Indigenous suicides by hanging are of special concern due to the easy availability and high lethality of the method and acquired deep political and cultural meaning linked to the Report of the Royal Commission into Aboriginal Deaths in Custody[2] [32]. A pattern of high risk has been observed among impulsive young Indigenous males who, under the pressure of interpersonal problems and under the influence of alcohol, choose this common, popular and culturally and politically meaningful method with a fatal or a non-fatal result [33].

Among the particular features of Indigenous Australian suicide is the temporal clustering of deaths in certain geographical areas and communities, an increasing number of suicides among Indigenous children and adolescents, and a high suicide risk in Indigenous inmates. Clusters of Indigenous suicide have been reported in at least two parts of Australia: Queensland [33] and the Northern Territory [34, 35]. For example, in the late 1990s, Hunter and his colleagues [33] examined the distribution of suicide through time in one of the Northern Queensland communities and found aggregations of suicide deaths, with gaps of several years between the aggregates. The possible first cluster of three suicides in the span of as many months occurred in 1986-1987, and a more significant and extensive cluster of 17 suicides lasted between June of 1991 and November of 1996.

Of special concern is the high incidence of suicide, suicide attempts and suicidal ideation among Indigenous Australian children and adolescents. The Western Australian Aboriginal Child Health Survey [36] showed that 9% of Aboriginal girls and 4% of Aboriginal boys aged 12-17 had made a suicide attempt in the 12 months prior to the study. Suicidal ideation was almost twice as prevalent among young females as among young males (20% *vs.* 12%) and, overall, 16% of young people had thoughts about ending their own life in the previous 12 months. In Queensland, in 2008-2009, Aboriginal and Torres Strait Islander children and adolescents (10-17 years of age) accounted for approximately a half of the young suicides despite comprising only 6.6% of the state youth population [37]. In 2008-2009, the rate of suicide among Indigenous Queensland children was thirteen times greater than for non-Indigenous children (23.8 per 100, 000 and 1.8 per 100, 000; respectively).

High suicide risk among Indigenous people in contact with the correctional system warrants special attention, especially in the aftermath of the Royal Commission into Aboriginal Deaths in Custody [32] which had a significant social and political impact on the way Aboriginal suicide is perceived in Aboriginal communities and in the mainstream culture [38, 39]. The proportion of Indigenous Australians in the prison population is very high[3]. In 2009, Indigenous prisoners comprised a quarter of the prison population in Australia (25%) [41]. The overall mortality and suicide rates among both Aboriginal and non-Aboriginal inmates are high [42], and suicide has been reported as a leading cause of death in prisoners after release from jail, especially among Indigenous and non-Indigenous males [43]. Aboriginal adolescents in custody are as likely as their non-Aboriginal fellows to attempt suicide and, given their over-representation among people in custody, they comprise a high-risk group requiring special attention [44].

5. SUICIDE IN IMMIGRANTS

Australia is a country that has welcomed immigrants, and this permits an examination of the suicide rate of immigrants in Australia with the suicide rates in their home nations. In the United States in 1959, Sainsbury and Barraclough [45] found a strong association between the suicide rates of eleven immigrant groups and the suicide rates in their home nations, although the suicide rates of the immigrants groups were higher than

---

[2] The Royal Commission into Aboriginal Deaths in Custody [32] investigated the causes of deaths of Indigenous people held in custody after being arrested or convicted. The Royal Commission analysed cases of suicide, deaths due to natural causes, medical conditions and injuries caused by police.

[3] There are multiple reasons for the overrepresentation of Aboriginal Australians in the inmate population, such as systemic bias in policing and judicial systems, social and economic disadvantage, high rates of crime in the communities, early contact with juvenile justice system and high rates of re-offending [40].

that in their home nations. Lester [46] and Sainsbury [47] replicated this result using immigrants to Australia.[4]

Burvill, *et al.* [49] noted that the methods used for suicide by immigrants changed after arrival in Australia. Rather than using the most common methods in the countries from which they emigrated, they switched to the methods used in Australia. This suggests that the availability of methods for suicide and the publicity about suicides in the media shape the behavior of suicidal individuals planning to commit suicide. Burvill, *et al.* [50] confirmed this result and showed, in addition, that the suicide rates of the immigrants converged to the suicide rate in Australia.

In recent years, the immigrants to Australia have come from a more diverse set of countries, and the old results of Burvill need to be modified. McDonald and Steel [51] documented significant differences in the methods of suicide used by immigrants from Asia, for example, from those used by native-born Australians. However, it will be interesting to see whether the methods used by these recent immigrants converge to the Australian methods with time spent in Australia.

6. THE SOCIOLOGICAL STUDY OF SUICIDE IN AUSTRALIA

In the United States, it has been proposed that there is a violent subculture in the southern states. Murder and assault rates are very high, and there is widespread ownership of guns and their use in both murder and suicide. Lester [52] found a similar phenomenon in Australia. For the six states, Lester found strong correlations between gun ownership per capita, the overall suicide rate, the suicide rate by gun, the percentage of suicides using guns and the percentage of murders committed with guns. The results for Australia matched the results calculated for these correlations over the nine major regions of the United States.

Lester and Yang [53] found very different correlates of the time-series suicide rate in Australia and the United States for the period 1946-1984. The Australia suicide rate was predicted by female labor force participation (positively) and the divorce/marriage ratio (negatively), whereas the signs of these predictors were reversed for the United States. The results for Australia were opposite to those predicted on the basis of Durkheim's [54] theory.

Lester [55] studied the time-series suicide rate for the period 1950-1985 and found no associations between the suicide rate and marriage, divorce and birth rates, and the same lack of associations was found for New Zealand. Thus, again, predictions based on Durkheim's theory of suicide were not supported. Lester concluded that the Australian suicide rate did not conform to standard sociological theories of suicide and that new theories were needed to explain the results of these studies. Hassan and Tan [56] found that the male/female suicide rate ratio for 1901-1985 was positively associated with an index of modernization and with unemployment, and negatively with time (but was not associated with the occurrence of war).

Lester [57] explored the role of alcohol consumption in predicting the Australian time-series suicide rate. For the period 1966-1985, the suicide rate was negatively associated with alcohol consumption, the opposite of what was expected. Furthermore, higher unemployment rates predicted lower female suicide rates (but had no association with male suicide rates).

Ecological studies of small regions have been more supportive of classic sociological theories. For example, Burnley [58, 59] for that suicide rates of the districts of Sydney were higher the lower the proportion of married people. Suicide rates of the districts were positively associated with population density, education, unemployment, low income, one-person households and indices of social isolation. In Queensland, Cantor, *et al.* [60] found that suicide rates were higher in districts that were more disadvantaged (low income, low education and high unemployment) and that fewer economic resources.

[4] A meta-analysis of 33 studies from seven countries by Voracek and Loibl [48] confirmed the validity of this result.

It has been argued that only a limited proportion of individuals in any birth cohort have the propensity for suicide. Thus, if a cohort has a high suicide rate at one point in its life-span, it will have a low suicide rate at other points. Lester [61] explored this hypothesis using data for Australia and found that the hypothesis was supported for Australian females but not for Australian males, a result that was consistent with results from a study in the United States.

7. THE NATIONAL SUICIDE PREVENTION STRATEGY IN AUSTRALIA

Australia was one of the first countries to introduce a national strategy for the prevention of suicide. The initial National Youth Suicide Prevention Strategy was implemented over the period of 1995-1999 and was followed by the National Suicide Prevention Strategy targeting all age groups [5, 62]. The strategy was based on the Living is For Everyone (LIFE) Framework which provided the overall structure and conceptual guidance for national and local initiatives and programs [63]. The framework's aims were to prevent suicide and to promote resilience and mental health in the Australian population across all age groups, with a special focus on the youth and young adults. Over a period of seven years, 22 national and 156 state/territory projects were funded under the strategy [64, 65]. The majority of the projects were universal and selective suicide prevention initiatives implemented in community-based settings, and the three major target groups for interventions were the youth, Indigenous Australians and people living in rural and remote areas [64].

In early 2006, the Commonwealth Government Department of Health and Ageing recommended a review of the effectiveness, relevance and appropriateness of the LIFE Framework and consequently a new model - Living is For Everyone (LIFE) Framework - has been developed and implemented in 2008[5] [63]. The framework is based upon a vision that "suicide prevention activities will reduce suicide attempts and the loss of life through suicide by providing individuals, families and communities with access to support so that no-one in crisis or experiencing personal adversity sees suicide as their only option" [63]. The framework is guided by three fundamental principles: doing no harm, client-centered service delivery, and community ownership and responsibility for action. Table **2** presents the Framework's six action areas.

Table 2: The six action areas of the LIFE Framework [63]

Action Area 1: Improving the evidence base and understanding of suicide prevention.
Action Area 2: Building individual resilience and the capacity for self-help.
Action Area 3: Improving community strength, resilience and capacity in suicide prevention.
Action Area 4: Taking a coordinated approach to suicide prevention.
Action Area 5: Providing targeted suicide prevention activities.
Action Area 6: Implementing standards and quality in suicide prevention.

The suggested evaluation measures for programs, projects and other activities implemented under the LIFE Framework include reduction in suicide attempts and/or suicidal thinking, reductions in suicide risk factors and vulnerabilities (including mental illness and hopelessness), improvements in individual protective or resiliency factors (*e.g.*, coping skills and help-seeking behaviors), increase in awareness of suicide prevention, changes in behaviors and response to suicide prevention strategies, and improvements in service models and practices.

Besides the national strategy, the health authorities in each state and territory of Australia have their own policies or programs in regards to prevention of suicide, and some of the states have developed and implemented strategies. These include the Queensland Government Suicide Prevention Strategy 2003-2008 [66] and the Western Australian Suicide Prevention Strategy 2009-2013 [67].

---

[5] Available online from: http://www.livingisforeveryone.com.au

CONCLUSIONS

Despite the acknowledged problems with the official suicide and other mortality statistics in Australia, it can be concluded that the national suicide rate have been declining or at least (to err on the side of caution) have been staying relatively stable over the last decade. The decline in suicide, especially among young males, has been attributed to the effectiveness of the National Youth Suicide Prevention Strategy. However, the question remains which components of the strategy have contributed to the decline. Goldney [8] and Martin [13] have pointed out several factors, including improved community awareness of suicide prevention programs, provision of accessible mental health services, implementation of well-designed mental health promotion programs, and better recognition and treatment of depression. Also, a number of socio-cultural changes in the broad Australian society could have contributed to the reduction in numbers of suicides, especially limiting access to firearms and increased mobile phone ownership which can be linked to better social connectedness. In summary, a complex mix of factors seems to have contributed to the observed changes, and in the words of Martin [13], "what is important is that the overall mix, over the last 10 years, has worked as a whole to reduce suicides. However, my personal view is that we need to keep as much of the whole program as we can working - at the level of the population with education and awareness programs, for professionals with regular updates about evidence-based practice and how to maintain pathways to care, for journalists to maintain the cautions in reporting, but most importantly in the area of continuing to build resilience, connectedness and capacity for mental wellness, in our population of young people" (p. 12).

REFERENCES

[1] Australian Bureau of Statistics 2007. Suicides 2005 (3309.0). Canberra: Australian Bureau of Statistics, 2007.

[2] Bertolote J, Fleischmann A. A global perspective on the magnitude of suicide mortality. In: Wasserman D, Wasserman C, Eds. Oxford textbook of suicidology and suicide prevention: A global perspective. Oxford: Oxford University Press. 2009; pp. 91-8.

[3] De Leo D, Evans R. International suicide rates and prevention strategies. Göttingen: Hogrefe and Huber, 2004.

[4] Morrell S, Page AN, Taylor R. The decline in Australian young male suicide. Soc Sci Med 2007; 64: 747-54.

[5] Commonwealth Department of Health and Aged Care 2000. Areas for Action, LIFE: A framework for prevention of suicide and self-harm in Australia. Canberra: Commonwealth Department of Health and Aged Care, 2000.

[6] Australian Bureau of Statistics. Causes of death 2007 (3303.0). Canberra: Australian Bureau of Statistics, 2009a.

[7] Australian Bureau of Statistics. Suicides 1994-2004 (3309.0). Canberra: Australian Bureau of Statistics, 2006.

[8] Goldney R. Suicide in Australia: Some good news. Med J Aust 2006; 185-304.

[9] Klieve H, Barnes M, De Leo D. Controlling firearms use in Australia: Has the 1996 gun law reform produced the decrease in rates of suicide with this method? Soc Psychiatry Psychiatr Epidemiol 2009; 44: 285-92.

[10] De Leo D, Dwyer J, Firman D, Neulinger K. Trends in hanging and firearm suicide rates in Australia: Substitution of method? Suicide Life Threat Behav 2003; 33: 151-64.

[11] Tait G, Carpenter B. Firearm suicide in Queensland. J Sociol 2009; 46: 83-98.

[12] Cantor CH, Neulinger K, De Leo D. Australian suicide trends 1964-1997: Youth and beyond. Med J Aust 1999; 171: 137-41.

[13] Martin G. [Editorial] Success! The Australian national youth suicide prevention strategy (1995–2000) worked. But what exactly made the difference? Aust E J Adv Mental Health 2007; 6-3.

[14] Moller J. Understanding national injury data regarding Aboriginal and Torres Strait Islander peoples. Australian Injury Prevention Bulletin, 14. Adelaide: National Injury Surveillance Unit, 1996.

[15] De Leo D. Suicide mortality data need revision. Med J Aust 2007; 186-257.

[16] Elnour AA, Harrison J. Suicide decline in Australia: Where did the cases go? Aust N Z J Public Health 2009; 33: 67-9.

[17] Pirkis J, Burges P, Dunt D. Suicidal ideation and suicide attempts among Australian adults. Crisis 2000; 21: 16-25.

[18] Johnston AK, Pirkis JE, Burgess PM. Suicidal thoughts and behaviors among Australian adults: findings from the 2007 National Survey of Mental Health and Wellbeing. Aust N Z J Psychiatry 2009; 43: 635-43.

[19] Nock MK, Borges G, Bromet EJ, *et al.* Cross-national prevalence and risk factors for suicidal ideation, plans and attempts. Br J Psychiatry 2008; 192: 98-105.

[20] Bernal M, Haro JM, Bernet S, *et al.* Risk factors for suicidality in Europe: Results from the ESEMED Study. J Affect Disord 2007; 101: 27-34.

[21] Bertolote JM, Fleischmann A, De Leo D, *et al.* Suicide attempts, plans, and ideation in culturally diverse sites: The WHO SUPRE-MISS community survey. Psychol Med 2005; 35: 1457–65.

[22] Pirkis J, Beautrais A and Durkee T. Suicide attempts in New Zealand and Australia. In: Wasserman D, Wasserman C, Eds. Oxford textbook of suicidology and suicide prevention: A global perspective. Oxford: Oxford University Press. 2009; pp. 127-131.

[23] Australian Bureau of Statistics and Australian Institute of Health and Welfare. Health and welfare of Australia's Aboriginal and Torres Strait Islander Peoples 2008. Canberra: AIHW and ABS, 2008.

[24] Krysinska K, Martin G, Sheehan N. Identity, Voice, Place: A Framework for Social and Emotional Wellbeing and Suicide Prevention in Indigenous Australians. Unpublished Manuscript. Brisbane: University of Queensland, 2009.

[25] Krysinska, K., Martin, G., Sheehan, N. Identity, Voice, Place - Suicide prevention for Indigenous Australians - a social and emotional wellbeing approach. Brisbane: University of Queesland, 2009.

[26] Kirmayer LJ, Brass GM, Holton TL, Paul K, Simpson C, Tait C. Suicide among Aboriginal Peoples in Canada. Ottawa: Aboriginal Healing Foundation, 2007.

[27] Freemantle J, Officer K, McAullay D, Anderson I. Australian Indigenous health - Within an international context. Darwin: Cooperative Research Center for Aboriginal Health, 2007.

[28] Ring I. An open letter to the President of the Public Health Association. Aust J Public Health 1995; 19: 228-30.

[29] Partnerships Queensland. Baseline Report: Future directions framework for Aboriginal and Torres Strait Islander policy in Queensland 2005-2010. Brisbane: Department of Communities, Office for Aboriginal and Torres Strait Islander Partnerships, 2006.

[30] Davidson JA. Presentation of near-hanging to an emergency department in the Northern Territory. Emerg Med 2003; 15: 28-31.

[31] Kosky RJ, Dundas P. Death by hanging: Implications for prevention of an important method of youth suicide. Aust N Z J Psychiatry 2000; 34: 836-41.

[32] Royal Commission into Aboriginal Deaths in Custody. Final Report. Canberra: Australian Government Publishing Service, 1991.

[33] Hunter E, Reser J, Baird M, *et al.* An analysis of suicide in Indigenous communities of North Queensland: The historical, cultural and symbolic landscape. Canberra: Mental Health/Health Services Development Branch, Commonwealth Department of Health and Aged Care, 1999.

[34] Hanssens L, Hanssens P. Research into clustering effect of suicide within Indigenous Communities, Northern Territory, Australia. Aborig Isl Health Work J; 2007: 31: 6-11.

[35] Parker R, Ben-Tovim DI. A study of factors affecting suicide in Aboriginal and 'other' populations in the Top End of the Northern Territory through an audit of coronial records. Aust N Z J Psychiatry 2002; 36: 404-10.

[36] Zubrick S, Silburn S, Lawrence D, *et al.* Western Australian Aboriginal Child Health Survey: The social and emotional wellbeing of Aboriginal children and young people. Perth: Curtin University of Technology and Telethon Institute for Child Health Research, 2005.

[37] Commission for Children and Young People and Child Guardian Queensland. Annual Report: Deaths of children and young people, Queensland, 2008–09. Brisbane: Commission for Children and Young People and Child Guardian Queensland, 2009.

[38] Hunter EM. Commissions and omissions: The wider context of Aboriginal suicides in custody. Med J Aust 1989; 151: 218-23.

[39] Reser JP. Australian Aboriginal suicide deaths in custody: Cultural context and cluster evidence. Aust Psychol 1989; 24: 325-34.

[40] Krieg AS. Aboriginal incarceration: Health and social impacts. Med J Aust 2006; 184: 534-6.

[41] Australian Bureau of Statistics. Prisoners in Australia (4517.0). Canberra: ABS, 2009b.

[42] Dalton V. Death and dying in prison in Australia: National overview, 1980-1998. J Law Med Ethics 1999; 27: 269-74.

[43] Stewart LM, Henderson CJ, Hobbs MST, Ridout SC, Knuiman MW. Risk of death in prisoners after release from jail. Aust N Z J Public Health 2004; 28: 32-6.

[44] Lawlor D, Kosky R. Serous suicide attempts among adolescents in custody. Aust N Z J Psychiatry 1992; 26: 474-8.

[45] Sainsbury P, Barraclough BM. Differences between suicide rates. Nature 1968; 220:1252.

[46] Lester D. Migration and suicide. Med J Aust 1972; 1: 941-2.

[47] Sainsbury P. Suicide. Proc R Soc Med 1973; 66: 579-87.

[48] Voracek M, Loibl LM. Consistency of immigrant and country-of-birth suicide rates. Acta Psychiatr Scand 2008; 118: 259-71.

[49] Burvill P, McCall M, Reid T, Stenhouse N. Methods of suicide of English and Welsh immigrants in Australia. Br J Psychiatry 1973; 123: 285-94.

[50] Burvill P, McCall M, Woodings T, Stenhouse N. Comparison of suicide rates and methods in English, Scots and Irish immigrants in Australia. Soc Sci Med 1983; 17: 705-8.

[51] McDonald B, Steel Z. Immigrants and mental health: An epidemiological analysis. Sydney, Australia: Transcultural Mental Health Center, 1997.

[52] Lester D. Restricting the availability of guns as a strategy for preventing suicide. Biol Soc 1988a; 5: 127-9.

[53] Lester D, Yang B. The relationship between divorce, unemployment and female labor force participation and suicide rates in Australia and America. Aust N Z J Psychiatry 1991; 25: 519-23.

[54] Durkheim E. Le suicide. Paris: Felix Alcan, 1897.

[55] Lester D. Exploration of a Durkheimian theory of suicide and homicide in Australia and New Zealand. Med Sci Law 1998; 38: 170-2.

[56] Hassan R, Tan G. Women's emancipation and suicide in Australia. Aust N Z J Sociol 1993; 28: 89-104.

[57] Lester D. Alcohol consumption and rates of personal violence in Australia. Drug Alcohol Depend 1992; 31: 15-7.

[58] Burnley IH. Differential and spatial aspects of suicide mortality in NSW and Sydney, 1980 to 1991. Aust J Public Health 1994; 18: 293-304.

[59] Burnley IH. Socioeconomic and spatial differentials in mortality and means of committing suicide in New South Wales, Australia, 1985-91. Soc Sci Med 1995; 41: 687-98.

[60] Cantor CH, Slater PJ, Najman JM. Socioeconomic indices and suicide rate in Queensland. Aust J Public Health 1995; 19: 417-20.

[61] Lester D. Suicide rates in birth cohorts in Australia. Psychol Rep 1988b; 62: 922.

[62] De Leo D, Krysinska K. Suicide prevention in Australia. In: Wasserman D, Wasserman C, Eds. Oxford textbook of suicidology and suicide prevention: A global perspective. Oxford: Oxford University Press. 2009; pp. 783-4.

[63] Commonwealth of Australia 2008. Living Is For Everyone (LIFE) Framework: A Framework for Prevention of Suicide in Australia. Canberra: Australian Government Department of Health and Ageing, 2008.

[64] Headey A, Pirkis J, Merner B, *et al.* A review of 156 local projects funded under Australia's National Suicide Prevention Strategy: Overview and lessons learned. Aust E J Adv Mental Health 2006; 5-3.

[65] Robinson J, McGorry P, Harris MG, *et al.* Australia's National Suicide Prevention Strategy: The next chapter. Aust Health Rev 2006; 30 (3): 271-6.

[66] Queensland Health 2003. Reducing Suicide: Queensland Government Suicide Prevention Strategy 2003–2008. Brisbane: Queensland Government, 2003.

[67] Government of Western Australia 2009. Western Australian Suicide Prevention Strategy 2009-2013. Perth: Government of Western Australia, Department of Health, 2009.

CHAPTER 15

Suicide in North America

David Lester*

The Richard Stockton College of New Jersey, USA

Abstract: The epidemiology of completed suicide in Canada and the United States is described, and the differences in the results between the two countries are noted. For the United States, suicidal behavior in the various immigrants and native groups is explored while, for Canada, the efforts to develop a uniquely Canadian suicidology are discussed.

Keywords: Suicide, Canada, the United States, immigrants, Native-Americans, first peoples, slaves.

1. THE UNITED STATES

A cursory glance at recent suicide statistics in America reveals that the suicide rate has remained remarkably constant over the last 20 years – mostly around 12 per 100,000 per year. Indeed, since 1945 the rate has ranged only from 9.8 to 13.3. In contrast, other nations of the world have witnessed dramatic increases in their suicide rate during this period (nations such as Norway, from 6.5 to 16.8) or decreased (such as England and Wales, from 12.1 to 7.4).

In recent years, the suicide rate has declined in many European countries, perhaps as result of the increasing prescribing of antidepressants [1]. This declining trend has not been noted in the United States, perhaps because antidepressants have been found to be ineffective for those with mild depressions [2]. This suggests that changing socioeconomic conditions may be responsible for trends in national suicide rates rather than the provision of improved mental health treatment.

If we look more closely at the American suicide rate, we do find differences by gender, with male suicide rates increasing in recent years and female suicide rates decreasing, and we also can find differences by age. The latest year for which suicide rates are available is 2006 (www.suicidology.org). The overall suicide rate was 11.1 (and since 1996 had ranged from 10.7 to 11.6); 17.8 for men and 4.6 for women; 12.4 for whites and 5.5 for non-whites (including 4.9 for African Americans). The suicide rate varies geographically, increasing in general toward the west. In 2004, the lowest suicide rate was in New York (6.0) and the highest in Alaska (23.6).

In 2005, the suicide rates were 16.1 in men aged 15-24 and 37.8 in those over the age of 75 (www.who.int). For women, these rates were 3.5 and 4.0, respectively. For men, suicide rates rose with increasing age, whereas for women suicide rates peaked in middle age (8.0 for women aged 45-54).

The United States is a nation of relatively recent immigrants and the descendants of immigrants – and the patterns of suicidal behavior in the different ethnic groups differ greatly and raise some interesting issues.

2. SUICIDE IN IMMIGRANT GROUPS

Many years ago, Sainsbury and Barraclough [3] correlated the suicide rates of 11 nations in 1959 with the suicide rates of immigrants from those nations to America and found a strong association, despite the fact that the suicide rates for the immigrant groups were on the whole higher than the suicide rates of those who remained in their home nations. Immigration is perhaps stressful (or perhaps the more suicidal people decide to emigrate) but, for example, the Irish had one of the lowest suicide rates of the nations studied in

***Address Correspondence to David Lester:** The Richard Stockton College of New Jersey, USA; E-mail: david.lester@stockton.edu

Maurizio Pompili (Ed)

1959 and Irish immigrants were one of the groups with the lowest suicide rates among the immigrant groups [4]. This general rule has been replicated in Australia [5-8], Canada [9], and America as a whole [7], as well as in Chicago in the 1920s [10][1]. Immigrants come from a particular culture and bring their culture with them when they emigrate, a culture that involves language, dress, codes of behavior, and perhaps the risk of suicidal behavior. Interestingly, however, Burvill, *et al.* [11, 12] noted that British immigrants to Australia quickly changed their methods for committing suicide once they arrived in Australia, suggesting that the availability of methods for suicide may be important in this choice [13].

Suicidal behavior may be quite differently determined and have different meanings in different cultures. The classic study demonstrating this was Hendin's [14] study of suicide in Scandinavia. In Denmark, Danish mothers created strong dependency in their sons which led to depression and suicidality after adult experiences of loss or separation. In Sweden, there was a strong emphasis on performance and success by parents, resulting in ambitious children for whom work was central to their lives. Suicide typically followed failure in performance that had damaged the men's self-esteem. In Norway, where the suicide rate was lower, there was strong dependency of the sons on their mothers, but Norwegian children were less passive and more aggressive than Danish children. Alcohol abuse was more common, and Norwegian men were more open about their feelings – able to laugh at themselves and cry more openly. These national patterns will probably continue to have influence on the immigrants from these nations in America.

Lester [15] proposed a social deviancy theory of suicide in which groups that found themselves deviant from the community in social characteristics would experience more stress and, as a result, exhibit more psychiatric disorder and suicidal behavior. Consistent with this theory, Lester found that, the smaller the size of an immigrant group in Australia, the higher the suicide rate of that group, but he failed to replicate this finding in Canada [15-17]. However, for the United States, states with a greater proportion of African Americans had lower suicide rates for African Americans [18]. It would be of great interest to repeat this analysis for immigrants to the United States from particular regions of the world.

This is the general pattern for immigrants, but let us look at one immigrant group to American in particular, Chinese Americans, a group of interest because the Chinese are native to many nations (such as the People's Republic of China and Hong Kong) and have emigrated in large numbers to nations such as America.

3. SUICIDE IN CHINESE

The suicide rates of Asian Americans are relatively low compared to Whites in America. For example, in 1980 in America, the suicide rates were 13.3 per 100,000 per year for Native Americans, 13.2 for white Americans, 9.1 for Japanese Americans, 8.3 for Chinese Americans, 6.1 for African Americans, and 3.5 for Filipino Americans [19].

Lester noted that the patterns of suicide also differed for these ethnic groups. The ratio of male to female suicide rates was much larger for Whites and African Americans than for Asian Americans, and whereas suicide rates increased with age for Asian Americans, the suicide rates peaked in young adulthood for African Americans and Native Americans. Asian Americans used hanging for suicide much more often than Whites and African Americans, and used firearms relatively less often.

Lester concluded that the epidemiology of Asian Americans in America showed similarities to the results of epidemiological studies of Asian Americans in their home nations, indicating that cultural factors have an important influence on the circumstances of suicidal behavior.

---

[1] Incidentally, these results provide evidence for the relative reliability and validity of national suicide rates despite the differences among nations in the methods for certifying the cause of death.

4. SUICIDE IN AFRICAN AMERICAN SLAVES

Of course, not all immigrant Americans came here freely as a result of their own decisions. Many were brought here as slaves. At the National Civil Rights Museum in Memphis, Tennessee, the exhibit for 1619 mentions that slaves fought against their bondage by stealing, escape, arson, and as a last resort, suicide. Lester [18] has explored suicide in the enslaved in greater depth.

Suicide was very common among the slaves when they were captured, while they were being transported to America, and immediately upon arrival [20]. The myth was widespread in Africa that Whites cooked and ate the captured Africans, and the slave traders helped perpetuate the myth – the English traders claiming that the Portuguese traders did eat their victims and *vice versa*. Slaves watching Whites drink red wine often thought that they were drinking blood [21]. Slaves already in America, helping to deal with the newly arrived slaves, also teased the newcomers with these stories. As a result, some slaves did commit suicide to escape being eaten, and mass suicides were not uncommon. Snelgrave [22] reported groups of more than 20 slaves hanging themselves in the West Indies. Nobility, older slaves, and male slaves seemed to fare worse, and Ibo slaves from Nigeria were noted for the high rate of suicide. Many African tribes believed that the soul returned home after death, and so suicide was seen by some as a means of returning to their homeland.

Ellenberger [23], in writing of the voluntary commitment of psychiatric patients and of wild animals captured in zoos, noted that the trauma of captivity can be severe, leading to two syndromes: anxiety and self-mutilation or depression and stupor – and Piersen [20] noted that the slaves often showed these syndromes while on the slave ships and after arrival.

Commentators disagree how common suicide was among those born in slavery, but statistical data are lacking for the early years. However, Lester [18] located mortality data for 1850 and calculated the suicide rates for Whites as 2.12 per 100,000 per year, for Black slaves 0.72, and for free Black slaves 1.15. The rates followed the same pattern for both males and females. Although, of course, these statistics may be quite unreliable, for even contemporary suicide statistics are criticized for inaccuracies, it is interesting to note that the ethnic difference here is found currently in America, where Whites have higher suicide rates than African America [19], and in African nations such as Zimbabwe and South Africa [24, 25].

The possible phenomenon of high suicide rates during capture and transportation combined with lower suicide rates later has modern parallels. Kwiet [26] noted that the suicide rate was high among Jews in Austria during the period of rounding up by the Nazis and transportation to the concentration camps, but lower later in the camps. The uncertainty about the future may later be replaced by clear external agents to blame for one's misery, and perhaps anger develops to compete with anxiety and depression, a situation that Henry and Short [27] in their theory of suicide and homicide viewed as decreasing the risk of suicide.

Under what circumstances did the enslaved commit suicide? Lester found examples of suicide in slaves after severe punishment, after unsuccessful rebellion, and when threatened with separation from a spouse and children as a result of being sold to another slave owner.

Why was suicide not more common among the enslaved? Initially, the slave owners tried to deter suicide by mutilating the corpses, hoping that the slaves would be deterred from committing suicide (in order to return to their homeland) if their bodies were dismembered. As the slaves adopted the Christian religion, suicides were branded as criminal and denied Christian burial. Today, the African American church is strongly opposed to suicide [28], and the view of suicide as acceptable only as a very last resort in the face of extreme stress is consistent with modern Afrocentric optimal psychology [29].

5. SUICIDE IN NATIVE AMERICANS

When the immigrants, voluntary and forced, arrived in America, they found, of course, an earlier group of immigrants, who perhaps migrated from Asia across from what is now Russia into Alaska and down through the Americas some 12 to 15 thousand years ago - Native Americans. Much has been written in recent years about suicidal behavior in Native Americans, but only two issues are addressed here: first, is the high rate of suicide sometimes found in groups of Native Americans a new phenomenon or have these groups always had high suicide rates, and second, what is the role of the clash of cultures in precipitating suicide in Native Americans?

Jilek-Aal [30] noted that suicide was present in traditional Native Americans societies, among the elderly and infirm, to prevent capture in warfare, or as atonement. Suicides in the past were often honored. Youths today learn this from the stories told by their elders, and perhaps today's youth hope for attention and acceptance in their own suicides.

It is interesting to track down reports of suicidal behavior in Native American tribes from previous centuries to see whether suicidal behavior occurred and under what circumstances. For example, Wallace [31] has reprinted accounts by a visitor to the Iroquois in the 1600s.

> "Some Savages", reported LeMercier of the Huron, "told us that one of the principal reasons why they showed so much indulgence toward their children, was that when the children saw themselves treated by their parents with some severity, they usually resorted to extreme measures and hanged themselves, or ate of a certain root they call Audachienrra, which is a very quick poison" ... while suicides by frustrated children were not actually frequent, there are nevertheless a number of recorded cases of suicide where parental interference was the avowed cause (p. 38-39).

Le Clercq [32] reported on the Micmac for the period 1675 to 1686.

> The Gaspesians, however, are so sensitive to affronts which are offered them that they sometimes abandon themselves to despair, and even make attempts on their own lives, in the belief that the insult which has been done them tarnishes the honour and the reputation which they have acquired, whether in war or in hunting (p. 247).

Le Clercq gave the account of a boy who, having been inadvertently hit by a servant, went out and hung himself from a tree, only to be rescued by his sister, who was passing by. His brother had earlier hung himself because he was refused by a girl whom he loved and whom he wanted to marry. The women and girls tended to commit suicide more often as a result of grief after the death of their relatives and friends, typically by hanging also.

Writing of the Delaware, Hackewelder [33] noted that they saw suicide as a result of mental disorder.

> Between the years 1771 and 1780, four Indians on my acquaintance took the root of may-apple, which is commonly used on such occasions, in order to poison themselves, in which they all succeeded, except one. Two of them were young men, who had been disappointed in love, the girls on whom they had fixed their choice, and to whom they were engaged, having changed their minds and married other lovers (p. 251).

One of the remaining cases was married man whose wife took a lover, and he was depressed at the thought of having to leave her and his children. He had hoped that the lover would not follow them when they went to their sugar camp, but he came home from work one day to find the lover with his wife. He left the camp and killed himself by eating a poisonous root.

Zeisberger [34], writing about the Delaware in the period of 1767 to 1780, also reported that suicide was not uncommon among the men if they discovered their wives to have been unfaithful.

> Many a one takes her unfaithfulness so to heart that in the height of his despair he swallows a poisonous root, which generally causes death in two hours, unless an antidote be administered to good time; this is often done, the Indians knowing that the properties of certain herbs counteract

each other and being able to judge from the effects what poison has been taken. Women, also, have been known to destroy themselves on account of a husband's unfaithfulness (p. 83).

Of course, we do not have many of these accounts, and we cannot estimate suicide rates from the reports. But the accounts are of interest because they come from an era when the clash of the two cultures was in its early stages. A more detailed analysis of the effects of cultural clashes is provided in Chapter 2.

Today, there are frequent reports of extremely high rates of suicide on some Native American reservations. For example, in the 1960s, the Papago and the Blackfoot had suicide rates of 100 per 100,000 per year or higher, as did the Shoshone in the 1950s and the Kwakiutl in the 1970s [35]. However, rates for Native Americans as a whole in the United States are not excessively high. Lester [35] found estimates of 14.6 in 1959-1961, 23.1 in the late 1960s, and 19.2 in 1976, an apparent increasing trend. However, Hisnanick (1994) noted a declining trend through to 1988 of about 2.7% per year.

Bachman [36] examined the correlates of the suicide rate in 120 counties in America that are partially or totally located on Reservation land and found that economic deprivation, rather than acculturation, seemed to be the strongest correlate of Native American suicide rates.

Supportive results for the influence of acculturation on suicide in Native Americans comes from Van Winkle and May [37], who examined suicide rates in three groups of Native Americans in New Mexico (the Apache, Navajo, and Pueblo) and attempted to account for the differences in terms of the degree of acculturation. Overall, the crude suicide rates were 43.3 per 100,000 for the Apache, 17.8 for the Pueblo, and 12.0 for the Navajo. As noted in Chapter 2, acculturation rather than social integration predicted the rank ordering of the suicide rates of these three groups.

6. A COMPARISON OF CANADA AND THE UNITED STATES

Lester and Leenaars [38] have conducted a number of studies comparing suicide in Canada and the United States, and some of their findings will be reviewed in this section.

It is often assumed that the features of suicidal behavior are identical in both Canada and the United States, but there are large cultural differences, particularly in recognition of authority, patterns of deviance, achievement motivation and patterns of association and marriage [39], which may impact suicidal behavior. Leenaars and Lester [40] compared suicide in both countries for the period 1960-1988 and noted that, after 1977, the Canadian suicide rate rose above that for the United States. Although suicide rates rose for adolescents and young adults in both countries, the rise was more dramatic in Canada so that young adult men in Canada had the highest suicide rates by 1988. Whereas elderly male suicide rates declined during this period in the United States, there was no change in the suicide rate of this group in Canada.

There are also differences between the two countries in other areas. For example, Leenaars and Lester [41] looked at time series correlates of suicide rates in Canada and the United States for the period 1950-1985. The correlations between the suicide rate and the birth rate and the unemployment rate (negative) and the divorce rate (positive) were similar in both countries, but the marriage rate was significantly associated with the suicide rates only in the United States (positively). Lester and Leenaars [42] noted differences in the methods used for suicide, with Americans using guns relatively more and Canadians using hanging and overdoses relatively more

In other areas, there are similarities. For example, Leenaars and Lester [43] found no differences in the belief in myths about suicide in Canadian and American college students. From 1969 to 1987, the size of the cohorts aged 20-34 were positively associated with the suicide rates of these cohorts in both countries, in line with Easterlin's [44] hypothesis that a greater cohort size will lead to greater competition for resources and, therefore, greater stress [45].

Despite the differences between suicide in Canada and the United States, Cantor *et al.* [46], comparing suicide in eight predominantly English-speaking countries, found that the phenomena of suicide in these two countries were much more similar with each other than with the phenomena in the Australia and New Zealand and those in the Old-World countries (England and Wales, Northern Ireland, Scotland and Ireland).

7. DISCUSSION

In 1998, Leenaars and his colleagues edited a book on suicide in Canada [42]. The chapters, written by Canadians interested in suicide and suicide prevention, reviewed research and programs carried out in Canada. It is interesting to note that a similar book ("Suicide in the United States") would be unlikely to appear, since American suicidologists tend to assume that research carried out in the United States has generality worldwide. Indeed, the majority of research into suicidal behavior is carried out in the United States, and so the majority of citations in a book, such as the comprehensive textbook of suicidology edited by Maris, *et al.* [47], relate to research carried out in the United States.

The two leading scholarly journals of suicidology (Archives of Suicide Research and Suicide & Life-Threatening Behavior) are both currently published in the United States with American editors. Only Crisis is published outside with United States (in Germany) and has a non-American editor. The two leading thanatology journals (Death Studies and Omega) are also based in the United States with American editors.

Suicidologists know that the epidemiology of suicide varies greatly from country to country. As Lester has noted in Chapter 2 in this book, it should not be assumed that the results of psychiatric, psychological and sociological research into suicidal behavior are applicable to every country and to every culture. The recent textbook by Wasserman and Wasserman [48] made an effort to recruit contributors from around the world and included thirty chapters (out of 134) on suicide in particular regions and countries.

It is important that advancements in suicide research and prevention remain central goals for governments. Leenaars [49] has commented that this no longer seems to be the case for Canada, where several Canadian suicidologists have either emigrated or changed the topics that they research and where government funding for suicidology has been minimal. It is to be hoped that this situation changes in the near future.

REFERENCES

[1] Isacsson G. Suicide prevention: a medical breakthrough? Acta Psychiatr Scand 2000; 102: 113-7.

[2] Fournier JC, Derubeis RJ, Hollon SD, *et al.* Antidepressants effects and depression severity. JAMA 2010; 303: 47-53.

[3] Sainsbury P, Barraclough B. M. Differences between suicide rates. Nature 1968; 220: 1252.

[4] Dublin LI. Suicide. New York: Ronald Press, 1963.

[5] Burvill P, Woodings T, Stenhouse N, McCall. Suicide during 1961-1970 in migrants in Australia. Psychol Med 1982; 12: 295-308.

[6] Lester D. Migration and suicide. M J Aust 1972; 1: 941-2.

[7] Lester D. The validity of national suicide rates. Br J Psychiatry 1980; 136: 107-8.

[8] Sainsbury P. Suicide. Proc R Soc Med 1973; 66: 579-87.

[9] Kliewer EV, Ward RH. Convergence of immigrant suicide rates to those in the destination country. Am J Epidemiol 1988; 127: 640-53.

[10] Lester D. Suicide rates in immigrant groups and their countries of origin. Psychol Rep 1989; 65: 818.

[11] Burvill P, McCall M, Reid T, Woodings T, Stenhouse N. Comparison of suicide rates and methods in English, Scots and Irish immigrants in Australia. Soc Sci Med 1983; 17: 705-8.

[12] Burvill P, McCall M, Reid T, Stenhouse N. Methods of suicide of English and Welsh immigrants in Australia. Br J Psychiatry 1973; 123: 285-94.

[13] Clarke RV, Lester D. Suicide Closing the exits. New York: Springer-Verlag, 1989.

[14] Hendin H. Suicide and Scandinavia. New York: Grune & Stratton, 1964.

[15] Lester D. Social deviancy and suicide. J Soc Psychol 1987; 127: 339-40.

[16] Lester D. Suicide rates in immigrants to Australia. Med J Aust 1986; 144: 280.

[17] Lester D. Suicide in immigrant groups as a function of their proportion to the country. Percept Mot Skills 1994; 79: 994.

[18] Lester D. Suicide in African Americans. Commack, NY: Nova Science, 1998.
[19] Lester D. Differences in the epidemiology of suicide in Asian Americans by nation of origin. Omega 1994; 29: 89-93.
[20] Piersen WD. White cannibals, black martyrs. J Negro Hist 1977; 62: 147-59.
[21] DuPratz LP. The history of Louisiana. London. Becket and PA deHondt, 1764.
[22] Snelgrave DJ A new account of some parts of Guinea and the slave trade. London, UK: Knapton J & P, 1734.
[23] Ellenberger E. Zoological garden and mental hospital. Can Psychiatr Assoc J; 1960: 5: 136-49.
[24] Lester D. Personal violence (suicide and homicide) in South Africa. Acta Psychiatr Scand 1989; 79: 235-7.
[25] Lester D, Wilson, C. Suicide in Zimbabwe. Cent Afr J Med 1988; 34: 147-9.
[26] Kwiet K. The ultimate refuge. Leo Baeck Institute Yearbook 1984; 29: 135-67.
[27] Henry AF, Short JF. Suicide and homicide. Glencoe, IL: Free Press, 1954.
[28] Early KE. Religion and suicide in the African-American community. Westport, Ct: Greenwood, 1992.
[29] Myers LJ. Understanding an Afrocentric world view. Dubuque, IA: Kendall Hunt, 1993.
[30] Jilek-Aall L. Suicidal behavior among youth. Transcult Psychiatr Res Rev 1988; 29: 87-105.
[31] Wallace AFC. The death and rebirth of the Seneca. New York: Vintage, 1972.
[32] Le Clercq C. New relations of Gaspesia. Toronto: Champlain Society, 1910.
[33] Heckewelder J. An account of the history, manners and customs of the Indian nations who once inhabited Pennsylvania and neighboring states. Transactions of the Historical and Literary Committee of the American Philosophical Society 1819; 1: 1-348.
[34] Zeisberger D. David Zeisberger's history of the North American Indians. In: Hulbert AB, Schwarz WN, Eds. Ohio Archaeological and Historical Publications. 1910; 19. pp. 1-189.
[35] Lester D. Suicide in American Indians. Commack, NY: Nova Science, 1997.
[36] Bachman R. Death and violence on the reservation. New York: Auburn House, 1992.
[37] Van Winkle NW, May PA. Native American suicide in New Mexico, 1959-1979. Human Organizations 1986; 45: 296-309.
[38] Lester D, Leenaars AA. Suicide in Canada and the United States. In: Leenaars AA, Wenckstern S, Sakinofsky A, Dyck RJ, Kral MJ, Bland RC, Eds. Suicide in Canada. Toronto: University of Toronto. 1998; pp. 108-21.
[39] Spencer M. Foundations of modern sociology. Scarborough, Ontario: Prentice-Hall, Canada, 1985.
[40] Leenaars AA, Lester D. Comparison of rates and patterns of suicide in Canada and the United States, 1960-1988. Death Stud 1992; 16: 417-30.
[41] Leenaars AA, Lester D. Domestic and economic correlates of personal violence in Canada and the United States. Italian J Suicidol 1994; 4: 7-12.
[42] Leenaars AA, Wenckstern S, Sakinofsky I, Dyck RJ, Kral MJ, Bland RC, Eds. Suicide in Canada. Toronto: University of Toronto Press, 1998.
[43] Leenaars AA, Lester D. Facts and myths of suicide in Canada and the United States. J Soc Psychol 1992;132: 787-9.
[44] Easterlin R. Birth and fortune. New York: Basic Books, 1980.
[45] Leenaars AA, Lester D. Testing the cohort size hypothesis of suicide and homicide rates in Canada and the United States. Arch Sui Res 1996; 2: 43-54.
[46] Cantor C H, Leenaars AA, Lester D, Slater PJ, Wolanowski AM, O'Toole B. Suicide trends in eight predominantly English- speaking countries 1960-1989. Soc Psychiatry Psychiatr Epidemiol 1996; 31: 364-73.
[47] Maris RW, Berman A L, Silverman MM. Comprehensive textbook of suicidology. New York: Guilford, 2000.
[48] Wasserman D, Wasserman C, Eds. Oxford textbook of suicidology and suicide prevention. Oxford, UK: Oxford University Press, 2009.
[49] Leenaars AA. The death of suicidology in Canada. CASP News 2008;17: 2.

CHAPTER 16

Suicide in Latin America

Jorge Tellez-Vargas[1,*] and Jorge Forero Vargas[2]

[1]Universidad El Bosque, IASP Colombia National Representative, Associate Secretary Treasurer World Federation of Societies of Biological Psychiatry, Bogota, Colombia and [2]Universidad El Bosque, Coordinator Suicide Prevention Presidential's Program, Latin American Psychiatry Association (Apal) Bogota, Colombia

Abstract: Suicide rates in Latin America are lower than in other regions of the world. The suicide behaviour is known starting with the pre Colombian culture and right now it is associated with specific factors such as poverty, violence and displacement.

The suicide rates are increasing in countries such Brazil, Chile, Costa Rica, Ecuador, México, Nicaragua, Paraguay y Uruguay as especially among teenagers and old people.

With the exception of Mexico, suicides are more frequent in men and the well known method is the mechanical asphyxia.

The few epidemiological studies have identified as factors of risk in family background, the presence of depressive and anxiety disorders, the abuse of psychoactive substances and alcohol, family dysfunction and school abuse (buying).

In some countries in Latin América there are programs of suicide prevention than consist in the epidemiological surveillance early detection of mental pathologies, psycho education and family attendance, nevertheless in countries with higher signs of poverty, suicide is not considered as a public health problem.

Keywords: Suicide, latin america, teenagers, elderly, risk factors, prevention.

1. INTRODUCTION

Latin America is one of the world regions with the lowest suicide rates, even though suicide was a frequent practice within pre-Columbian cultures.

Suicide rates among Latin America young people (6.8 deaths per 100.000) are higher than those found in Africa (1.3) and Europe (6.7), and significantly lower than those existing in Asia (9.6), North America (10.1) and Oceania (12.2). These data contrast with this homicide high rates in Latin America, which are two-fold higher than those in Africa, three-fold higher than those of North America and significantly higher than those in Europe [1].

In the Latin America continent, there exist, at present time, some psychological factors that make several countries more prone to aggression and suicide. Among such factors, the following should be highlighted: the high levels of: poverty, especially among indigenous people in Guatemala, Mexico, Peru, Bolivia and Paraguay; malnutrition conditions which are higher among Guatemala indigenous groups; the high number of family supported by single mothers in Costa Rica and El Salvador. These factors cause chronic deficiencies, unmet daily acute survival needs, and feelings of desperation and hopeless, all such conditions are responsible for the triggering of suicide behaviour [2].

The suicidal phenomenon is gradually increasing in several Latin American countries; however, this

***Address correspondence to Jorge Tellez-Vargas:** Universidad El Bosque. IASP Colombia National Representative. Associate Secretary Treasurer World Federation of Societies of Biological Psychiatry. Bogota, Colombia; E-mail: tellezjorge@hotmail.com

Maurizio Pompili (Ed)

situation is not considered to be a public health priority by the local governments, such as Nicaragua, Honduras, and Guatemala, which prefer to assign their scarce economic resources to HIV early detection programs, to the treatment of dengue and malaria, and to achieve full vaccination coverage of the infant population.

The main objective of this chapter is the following: to review and analyze the historical and socio-demographic issues associated with suicidal behaviour during the current decade in several Latin America countries.

2. SUICIDE PRACTICE IN PRE-COLUMBIAN CULTURES

The Suicide in Maya Culture

The settlement of Maya civilization began 3000-years ago in the territory currently comprised by Mexico, Guatemala and Belize. It is considered that between 300 and 900 B.C. there were 2 million Maya people living in 40 cities [3].

According to maya culture, the universe operated in a logic and reliable manner and human beings were able to exploit universe cyclic nature if they could become adapted to those cycles. They also believed that priests and warriors who died in the battle, the women dying during delivery, and those individuals immolated to the gods went up to the paradise to share a site in the paradise with some gods as: Kin (the sun), Uh (the moon), Xaman Ek (the pole star), and Noh Ek (Venus planet) [3, 4].

For maya people, suicide was linked to human nature and customs. Suicide was considered as an honourable death.

This people worshiped Ixtab, the goddess of death, suicide and gibbet. This goddess was represented as a partially rotten corpse with closed eyes, hanging down from a tree. Her duty was to protect the people which commit suicide, accompanying and guiding them toward an especial paradise. The goddess duty was to guide the souls, and such role was named by mayas as "psicopompo" (Fig. **1**).

Figure 1: The maya suicide and death goddess, called Ixtab. Source: www.aztlanvirtual.com

The goddess is represented suspended in the air, after the suicidal act as if she was down on her knees; her hands and face traits suggesting some type of religious ritual, which is the result of belief of the search of happiness. Her face appearance and hands and feet posture are suggestive that Ixtab is in a static meditation posture, before coming into the paradise [4].

Ixtab was a well-known and benevolent goddess. Some historical documents suggest that the worship to Ixtab impelled mayas to commit suicide rather than suffering the domain of spanish conquerors, when suffering from any disease condition of falling from favor, creating a spate of suicides among high-class people, similar to seppuku in the japanese tradition [4].

During Spanish Conquest, a vast number of collective suicides took place, the most famous being that staged by Cholultecas, who, after being conquered, climbed up to Quetzalcoatl pyramid and jumping from the top [5, 6].

Suicide made part of maya's ritual human sacrifices. When an important personage of the tribe died, his wife and some family members committed suicide to accompany the deceased during the travel to paradise

Mayas used several different methods to commit suicide: for instance they flung themselves into a deep lake or from any precipice or any temple, such as Quezalcoalt pyramid, as aforementioned.

Suicide in Inca Culture

Inca culture was contemporary to maya culture and was settled in the territory currently comprised by Peru, Bolivia and Ecuador. This culture reached significant architectural development, as evidenced in Machu Pichu, the sacred city of such culture.

In 2008 spanish archaeologist Martín-Rubio discovered the tomb of Paullo, the son of Huayna Capac, the last Inca Emperor. Paullo cooperated with spanish conquerors to force Inca empire to be submitted to them, and for such reason Paullo received some significant favors and gifts from spanish crown such as an monetary income, several farms, Colcampata palace belonging to the Panaca or descendant of Manco Capac (the first Inca) and the authorization of be buried under his ancestors tradition and rite [7].

When his tomb was discovered Inca emperor's skeleton was found, and that of his preferred concubine (named ñusta by Inca people) who apparently was 13 or 14 years old and the skeleton of other two women and two children and a dog's head.

This finding allowed for confirming that suicide was a common practice among incas as religious right. They believed that after death, there exists other life similar to that in the earth, and therefore, when the emperor or any important personage died, when starting the way towards the life beyond the grave, they needed for their wives and concubines and other women to accompany them in the life after death. In order to be able to accompany them, the women had to commit suicide. The children were narcotized and buried near to the emperor for them to purify Inca entrance in the other world. And the dog's head placed in the tomb to act as the guardian of the Inca buried [7].

The Suicide in Guane Culture

Guane culture settled in Colombian central region and even though it failed to reach the progress of maya or Inca cultures, it is known due to its excellent weaving and goldsmith works. Guane community succumbed to the wiping out by the spanish conquerors although many tribes preferred rather commit collective suicide of warriors, children and women preferred to the humiliation and attacks they were subject to by conquerors [8].

The native tribes settled in Velez province, preferred the death impaled in the caves dying of hunger with their wives and children, while Tausa or Guican inhabitants used such methods as jumping from the so called "precipices of death" [8].

Arhuacos tribe inhabiting Santa Marta Sierra Nevada, northern Colombia located near the Caribbean Sea, practiced suicide when they were suffering from any incurable disease, or severe physical troubles and their property passed to Cacique, the political head of the tribe [9].

3. SUICIDE RATES IN LATIN AMERICA: AN UP-DATE

Dominican Republic is the Latin American country showing the lowest suicide rate: 1.6 deaths per 100.000 in 2004. This data remain stable from 1990, following a slight increase in 1975 (3.3/100,000) [8] (Fig. **2**).

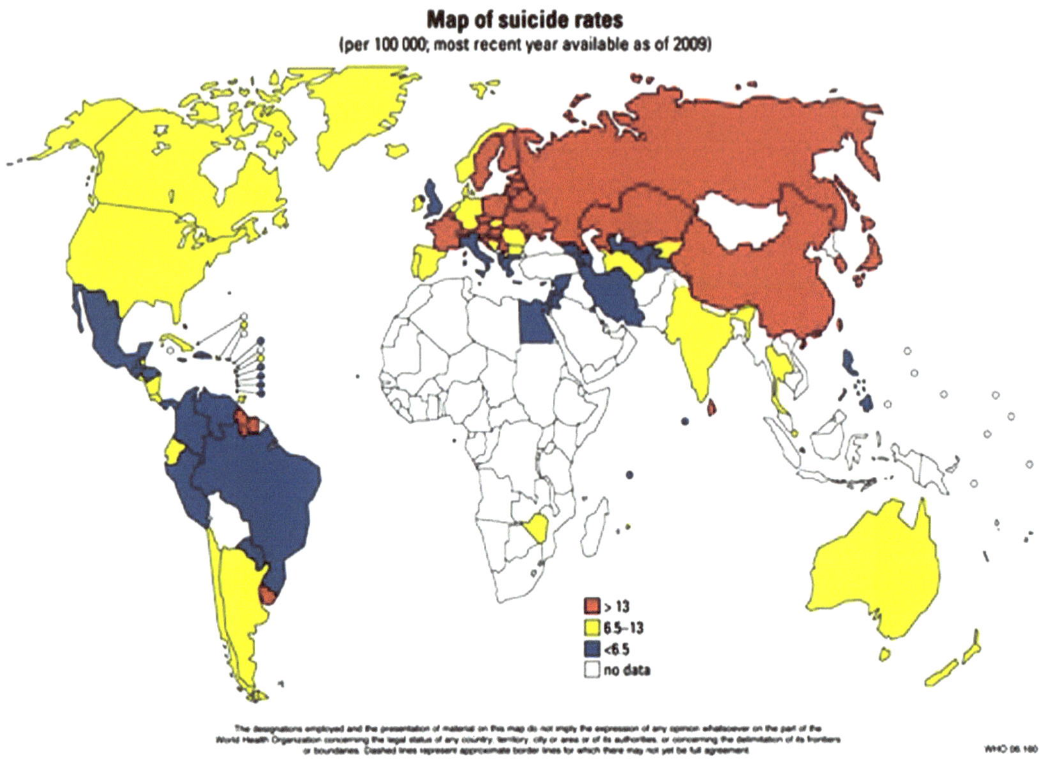

Figure 2: Suicide rates in Latina America. Source: World Health Organization, Geneva, 2009

Suicide is more frequently committed by males than females between 25 and 34 years of age and by senior citizens, males and females, who are over 65 years of age (7.5/100,000). The major prevalence of suicide committed by females was found in the group which age between 25 and 34 years old [10] (Table **1**).

Table 1: Suicides rates Bnin Latin América 2005

Country	Rate per 100,000
Uruguay **	15.8
Cuba *	12.3
Chile	10.3
Brazil	8.0
Costa Rica *	8.0
Argentina	7.9
Puerto Rico	7.4
Nicaragua	7.2
Ecuador *	6.8
El Salvador *	6.8
Panama *	5.7
Colombia	4.9
Paraguay	4.1
Paraguay **	4.1
Mexico *	4.0

Table 1: cont….

Venezuela	3.8
Guatemala *	2.3
Dominican Republic	1.6

* 2006, ** 2004.

For several decades, Cuba presented the highest suicide rates in Latin America, but as from 1992 (21.3/100,000) a gradual declining has been observed until reaching the rate of 12.3 in 2006. The 2006 results show a dramatic increase in the suicide rate in males and females in the 45-year-old group until reaching a rate of 88.6/100,000 in the group of males who are over 75 years of age [10] (Table **2**).

Table 2: Suicide Rate trends in Latin America (2000-2006)

Increase	Stable	Decrease
Brasil	Colombia	Argentina
Chile	Guatemala	Cuba
Costa Rica	Panama	El Salvador
Ecuador	Peru	Puerto Rico
Mexico	Dominican Republic	Venezuela
Nicaragua		
Paraguay		
Uruguay		

Mexico and Central America

In Mexico, the more populated country in this region, suicide is the fifth leading cause of mental disorder after depression, psychoactive substances abuse, eating disorders, and anxiety disorders [11].

The data show a gradual increase of suicide rates as from 1985 (1.9/100,000) up to 2006 when reaching a rate of 4.0/100,000. Suicide trend is more frequent in males who are over 24 years old and even more prevalent in senior citizen who are over 75 years old (13.2 per 100,000) [10].

In a recent paper published in the web site of Mexico Secretariat of Health, it is stated that in 2007 in Mexico occurred 2800 suicides (1600 women, 1200 men), This data show, for the first time, that suicide is more frequently committed by females, such phenomenon which is unusual in Latin America [11].

In Costa Rica, the politically and economically more stable country in Central America, has been observed a gradual increase of suicidal phenomenon as from 1970 (2.3/100,000) up to 2006 when reached 8.9/100,000. In 2006 the highest frequency of suicides, in both genders, has been observed in people between 35 and 65 years of age, and in the people over 75 years old [10].

In El Salvador after the suicide rate increase in 1970-1980 span period, when reaching 11.4/100,000. Recently, a gradual decline of suicide rate has been observed until reaching 6.8/100,000 in 2006 [10]. Suicide frequency is higher in males, especially in people between 25 and 34 years old (20.7/100,000) and in those over 65 years of age (15.5 per 100,000).

In Guatemala suicide rates have remained stable as from 1960 (2.7/100,000) until 2006 (2.3/100,000) showing a slight increase in 1970 (3.2/100,000). The suicide rate is higher among males between 15 and 54 years of age (6.3 per 100,000) and reach a higher prevalence in males over 75 year old (10.6/100,000). In females, significant variation is observed although the lowest prevalence (0.3/100,000) occurs in people between 55 and 64 years of age [10].

In Nicaragua a gradual increasing of the number of suicides has been observed until reaching the rate of 7.2/100,00 in 2005. The 2005 results show a higher suicidal prevalence among the teenagers and among the people over 75 years old [10].

The increase of suicide rate among teenagers has been so dramatic and actually, Nicaragua is the Latin American country with the highest rate of suicide in this age-group (Table **3**).

Table 3: Suicide in young people (15- to 24 years old) in Latin America

Country	Rate x 100.000
Nicaragua	14.8
Uruguay	14.6
El Salvador	12.9
Ecuador	12.2
Argentina	12.1
Chile	11.7
Costa Rica	9.3
Colombia	9.2
Paraguay	7.8
Panama	7.2
México	6.2
Venezuela	5.6
Puerto Rico	5.4
Brazil	4.7
Cuba	4.3
Guatemala	4.2
Dominican Republic	1.3
Peru *	1.8
Haiti	0.1

(*) year 2000.
Source: World Health Organization, Geneva, 2006

Suicide rates in Panama has been stable as from 1965 (5.5/100,000) up to 2006 (5.7/100,000) with a decline in 1980 (2.1/100,000). Males commit suicide more frequently than females (6:1) mainly the males over 75 years old (30.6/100,000), such rate is the highest in Latin America whiten this group [10].

Honduras has not suicide records as from 1955, when suicide rate was 3.1 per 100,000 with predominance among males (2.5:1) [10].

South America

In Argentina suicide rate shows a declining rate, going from 9.4/100,000 (1996) deep to 7.9/100,000 in 2005, with predominant frequency among males (3:1) in all age groups. The 2005 results show that suicide is more frequent, in both genders, in young people which their age is between 15 and 24 years old and those over 75 years of age [10].

Statistic data shows an increased rate of suicide among adolescents. Some authors consider that the threats of violence by classmate peers (bullying) triggers suicidal behaviour in this etary group (bullycide) [12].

In Brazil, the most Latin America populated country, suicide rate remained near to 3.2/100,000 during 1980-1995 period, and as from that date, a slight and gradual increase has been observed until reaching 4.5 out 100,000 in 2005. The 2005 results show that suicide is more frequent committed by males (3.5:1) within all etary groups and the rate has been gradually rising from the males which age is over the 45 years old and reaching the highest level in the individuals which are over 75 years of age [10].

Suicide behaviour is increasing in some population segments, such as young male people, indigenous individuals, farmers, young women and pregnant women which living in the rural area [13]. Additionally, Porto Alegre is the city with the higher suicide rates (16 per 100,000) [13].

In Chile, suicide rates remained stable during 1950's (4.2/100,000) and has been increase during 1965-1975 time period reaching 6.7/100,000 rate, coinciding with Chilean military dictatorship. As from such year, suicide rates show a declining tendency, until 2000, when suicide rate went up to 9.6/100,000 and reaching the highest level in 2005 (10.3/100,000). The 2005 results show that suicide behaviour is more prevalent in males [10].

In Ecuador suicide rates have been increasing as from 1985 (4.2 per 100,000) until reaching 6.8 in 2008. Actually, suicide is the 14th leading mortality cause in the general population, with 73.5/100,000 rate [13]. Males committed suicide more frequently than females (2:1) but in the people between 15 and 24 years old a gender difference is not observed [10].

According to data from Quito Suicide Observatory, suicide rate in Quito, the capital city of Ecuador, is 8.0/100,000, the highest suicidal rate in the country, and suicide episodes occur in any time of the year [14]. The provinces suffering from the highest number of suicide events during the aforementioned period are Guayas, Pichincha, Manabí, Azuay and Tungurahua [15].

In 2006 on any difference in suicide frequency was observed whiten the several etary groups. Sanitary authorities and local press, however, have been alarmed because of the increased suicide occurrence among teenagers during the last few years, mainly in Cuenca city, the third more important city of the country [16].

The same behaviour is observed in Paraguay, where the suicide rates has been rising from 1955 (1.1/100,000) up to 2004 (4.1/100,000) with more frequent suicide events among teenagers (7.8/100,000) [10].

In Uruguay suicide rate has been gradually rising from 10.4/100,000 in 1971 up to 15.8 in 2004, with a significative increase of suicide episodes among males which their age is over 55 years old, reaching a rate of 40.7/100,000 within the group of those which age is over 75 year of age [10]. This is the highest suicidal rate in Latin America for those are over 65 years of age.

In Uruguay two daily suicides occur, with the higher prevalence occurring in the city of Sarandi del Yi (41.5/100,000) [17].

Between 1960 and 2005 it is observed in Venezuela a declining suicide rate going from 6.6/100,000 down to 3.6/100,000, with prevalence in males (3.1) and more frequent in those are over 65 years old [10].

Suicide records in Peru are not updated as yet. A declining tendency of suicide rate was observed going from 2.2/100,000 in 1970 down to 0.9 in 2000, predominant in men (2:1). Suicide is more frequent whiten the people over 75 years of age [10].

In Colombia has been observed a decreasing suicide rate that going from 4.9/100,000 in 2000 down to 3.9/100,000 in 2005, with a slight increase in 2008 [18] (Fig. **3**).

The results of the National Mental Survey conducted by the Ministry of the Social Protection in 2004 show that suicidal ideation in the last year (4.0%), suicide planning in the last year (1.3%) and suicidal attempts in the last year (1.7%) are more frequent in males, while whiten the female group show higher frequency of suicidal ideation in lifetime (12.5%), and suicide planning in lifetime (4.3%). Suicidal attempt in lifetime show similar tendency in both genders (4.9%) [19] (Table **4**).

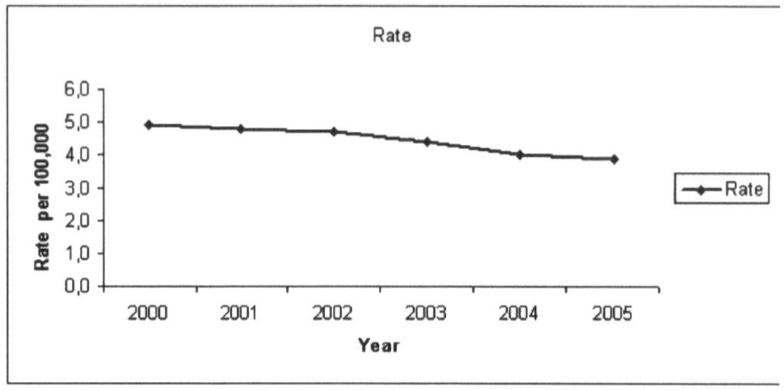

	2000	2001	2002	2003	2004	2005
Rate	4,9	4,8	4,7	4,4	4,0	3,9

Figure 3: Suicide rates in Colombia 2000-2005.
Source: SIAVAC - DRIP. Instituto de Medicina Legal y Ciencias Forenses. Bogotá, 2006

Table 4: Suicide behaviour in Colombia

Suicide behaviour	Males %	Females %
Suicide ideation lifetime	12.1	12.5
Suicide planning lifetime	3.8	4.3
Suicide attempt lifetime	4.9	4.9
Suicide ideation past 12 months	4.0	3.1
Suicide planning past 12 months	1.3	0.8
Suicide attempt past 12 months	1.7	0.9

Source: Mental Health National Survey. Ministerio de Protección Social, 2004.

A predominant trend in males is observed (3:1). The higher suicide frequency occurs in both genders in individual between 18 and 34 years old [1-18]. The higher number of suicide occurs inside the home and is more frequent among students, housekeepers, farmers, and unemployed people [1-18].

Caribbean Region

There is not availability of data because most of the countries, excepting Cuba, Dominican Republic, and Puerto Rico, fail to keep a reliable record of suicides, and their reports are not regularly registered and made available.

In Puerto Rico, the most populated country of the region, a declining suicide rate is observed going from 11.2/100,000 in 1955 down to 7.4/100,000 in 2005 and an increase in 1990 (10.5/100,000). Suicides were more frequently committed by senior citizens over 65 years of age [10].

Cuba and Dominican Republic suicide data were early commented.

4. RISK FACTORS

Suicide risk factors are individualized (any serious risk factor to any individual could be negligible for any other subject), generational factors (different in the infancy, adulthood, and elderly ages), generic (different for male and female), cultural and own for the specific historical time [20].

According to data compiled by health institutions at national level, suicide risk factors are similar in such countries as Argentina, Mexico, Colombia, Brazil and Ecuador.

In Mexico, a cross-sectional prevalence survey, based on data from a representative sample including 22.966 subjects of the national population, between 12 to 65 years old, during 2008 found 8.70%

prevalence of any suicidal ideation (with 4.3 and 6.2 variances, depending on the question used), 1.22% for suicide plan and 0.79% for suicidal attempts in the last 12 months. Females, single women or free union marital status, those of lower educational level groups in the younger subjects, and under-employees, showed the higher rate of suicidal behaviour [21].

A family history of suicide or attempted suicide, the presence of depressive disorders, anxiety disorders, psychotropic substances abuse, alcohol abuse, family disruptions, intra-family violence and school abuse by the own peers (buying) [11, 13, 14, 18] ,have been identified as suicide risk factors

Affective disruptions, economic problems, and academic failures have been considered as suicide triggering events [13, 14, 18]. In teenagers and people under 25-years old, the disruption of any affective relationship, the receipt by teachers, and the academic failure were identified as determinant factors of suicidal behaviour [11].

In a case and control study, conducted in Medellin, Colombia, including 108 suicides (cases) and 108 deaths for other reasons (controls) it was found that the rupture with the affective partners, unemployment, and economic pressure are adverse events independently associated to suicide behaviour [22].

In Quito, Ecuador, it was found the higher suicide events to occur during the second fortnight of December, and the first fortnight of January, on occasion of Christmas and New Year holidays [14].

In Colombia, especially in Bogotá, the capital city, suicides more frequently occur during the first quarter year and weekends, although no any appropriate explanations of this phenomenon has been found to explain such occurrence [18].

5. METHODS USED

During the last few years, the methods used by suicide victims have changed, and even though firearms continue to be the most used means, it has been observed that mechanical suffocation (hanging), has been the most used method in Colombia, Ecuador, and Uruguay [14, 17, 18].

Ingestion of toxic substances (poisoning) or over dosage of medications, becomes the third method used by suicide victims, and used specially by women [18].

6. SUICIDE AMONG TEENAGERS

Suicide is not considered to be one of the leading cause of death among the adult population; however, it is now the second leading cause of death among those people who are between 15 and 34 years of age [23].

Teenager suicide rates have been rising in almost all Latin American countries, mainly in Nicaragua, Uruguay, El Salvador and Argentina (Table **3**).

In Argentina, the clinical profile of teenager suicide corresponding to a boy who is between 12 and 15 years old, lives in an urban area, and belongs to the middle-class level, and has frequently been the victim of bullying [24].

According to data derived from the Observatorio de la Convivencia Escolar in Mendoza, Argentina, one out of four students, between 10 and 18 years old, and one out of three, aged 12 to 15, claim that they are afraid of some classmates, and 6% of them feel permanently excluded by their peers [24].

Suicide is the second leading cause of death among Mexican young people, after automobile crashes. During the last three years, the rate of suicide among teenager under the age of 15, raised from 8.3/100,000 up to 11/100,000 among boys and up from 12.1/100,000 to 16.5/100,000 among girls [25]. Tabasco,

Yucatán and Campeche are the cities with the highest teenager suicide incidence. Fifty-five percent (55%) of suicide victims are lonely children, catholic, and their suicide events occurs usually in their homes [22].

In Bogotá, Colombia, adolescent suicide episodes represented 40% of the total suicides in the period 2004-2007, and during the year 2008 a percent decline was observed (34%). Suicides occurred more frequently among boys, and the most widely used method was that of mechanical suffocation (55%) [26].

In Chile, a recent study found suicidal events occur more frequently among teenagers with low self-esteem, high impulsivity, family disruptions, and poor social support [27].

A study conducted by Serfaty [28] in a sample of teenagers in Buenos Aires, Argentina, found adolescents from mothers with depressive conditions or use of alcohol by their father, or use of psychoactive drugs by a sibling, to be more prone to suicidal ideation, compared to the group lacking such family history.

The following suicide risk factors have been identified in adolescents [29]:

- Family or personal history of suicidal attempts.
- Intra-family violence.
- Physical and sexual abuse.
- Poor communication between family members.
- Frequent moves of the family nucleus (migration, displacement).
- Rigid family environment, and difficulty to exchange criteria with younger people.
- Authoritarianism, loss of authority between the parents, or mutual and permanent denial of parental authority.
- Identification and idealization of figures (icons) or adolescents have who committed suicide.
- Crowding and living together in small and closed space affecting intimacy of family members.
- As triggering factors the following have been identified: [29].
- Divorce of parents.
- Death of loving persons.
- Improper relationships with parents, physical ill-treatment, negligence, emotional abuse, sexual abuse.
- Academic problems: learning or disciplinary problems.
- Drawing attention in an improper manner by parents, tutors, teachers, or any authority figure, in public or private setting.

In the survey conducted by Secretariat of Education in Bogotá, Colombia, in 2001, using a sample including 1132 students, it was found 11.4% students had made suicide attempts in the last year, such behaviour associated to the existence of depressive symptoms, family problems, and hopeless feelings [30]. The application of risk-suicide scale to this sub-group evidenced that 12.8% subjects were in suicide high risk. All interviewed subjects with suicide ideation were living with their primary family group, and only a small percent (5.7%) had sought psychological aid [30].

Freitas & cols. identified as risk factors to suicidal attempts in female pregnant teenagers the frequent changes of residence during the last year before the pregnancy (OR=6,3), the attempted sexual or physical abuse (OR=5,4), the death of parents during childhood (OR=4.4), family history of suicide (OR=2.2), the existence of suicide ideation (OR=2,8) and tobacco abuse (OR=1,9) [31].

In spite that teenagers suicide means a serious health problem increasingly growing, unfortunately, usually parents refuse for their children attempting to commit suicide seeking for psychological help or to take part in clinical research studies [32].

7. SUICIDE AMONG ELDERLY

Rate suicide among the elderly is increasing, especially in Cuba (27.3 per 100,000), Uruguay (21.7), Chile (12.9), Puerto Rico (12.6), and Argentina (12.3) (Table **5**).

Table 5: Suicide rates in elderly (65 to 74 years old) in Latin America

Country	Rate x 100.000
Cuba	27.3
Uruguay	21.7
Chile	12.9
Puerto Rico	12.6
Argentina	12.3
El Salvador	8.2
Panama	8.1
Venezuela	7.7
Nicaragua	7.5
Colombia	7.5
Brazil	7.4
Costa Rica	7.2
Ecuador	7.0
Paraguay	6.6
México	5.2
Dominican Republic	3.7
Guatemala	2.8
Peru *	1.0
Haiti	0.0

Source: World Health Organization, Geneva, 2005.

Suicide among the elderly seems to be the result of several psychological phenomena: the increase in life expectation that allows some elderly individuals in Latin America and in the developing countries, to live longer without adequate; seeing their children became old and/or die, and emigration and displacement phenomena which make the senior citizen more dependent, isolated, and discriminated whiten the family setting [33]. To the above-mentioned factors it is necessary to add some medical factors, such as terminal states diseases, Alzheimer´s disease in its initial stages, affective disorders, and alcohol abuse [34].

The Ministry of Health of Uruguay has identified the following social factors which are related to suicide among elderly, which increase as the individual grow older [33]:

- Prejudice against the elderly.
- Loneliness and estrangement.
- Social isolation.
- Income reduction accompanied by economic situation changes.
- Obligatory retirement.
- Loss of social roles.
- Humiliating events as a result of social prejudices.
- In the same document those family factors that involve potential suicidal behaviours in the elderly are highlighted.
- Widowhood, especially during the first year of mourning.
- Suicide family history.
- Physical, patrimonial and psychological neglect or negligence.
- Sexual abuse.
- Seclusion in a nursing home.
- Overprotection, which gives rise to the loss of autonomy.
- Loss of privacy.

8. SUICIDE ATTEMPTS

Suicide attempts are not easy to count because many are not treated in a hospital or may not be recorded as self-inflicted injuries.

In Bogotá, the capital city of Colombia, it has been observed suicide attempts to be more frequent in females (2:1) and show 7:1 ratio with the completed suicides. Suicide attempts are more in both genders within 15-19 age groups, 73.1% of which have used intoxication as the method to attempt suicide [35].

Eighty five percent (85%) attempted suicides occur in the house or home of the subject intending to commit suicide and 80% of the episodes occur during daytime [34].

Secretariat of Education in Bogotá, Colombia, has designed a program to lower suicide rate from 3.1 per 100,000 (2007) down to 3,0 per 100,000 in 2012, by the study and evaluation of suicide attempts, which shall be compulsorily reported by emergency and primary care units.

The number of suicide attempts reported is increasingly growing during the last three years (2074 cases in 2008) making intervention in 61% of the events. Draw the attention that 332 subjects (16%) rejected psychological assistance. The difficulties precluding development of program make reference to the (public or private) assistance model, uncompleted information, healthcare personnel turnover, and delay to notice the event [36] (Fig. **4**).

In a survey conducted in Medellín, Colombia, including 140 patients diagnosed with major depressive condition and occurrence of at least one suicide attempt, if was found that individuals using more lethal methods to commit suicide usually were living alone, had history of suicide attempt or nicotine and psychoactive substances abuse but no alcohol abuse. Multivariate analysis determined that living alone and using psychoactive substances is independently associated to suicide attempts with high and extreme lethal method [37].

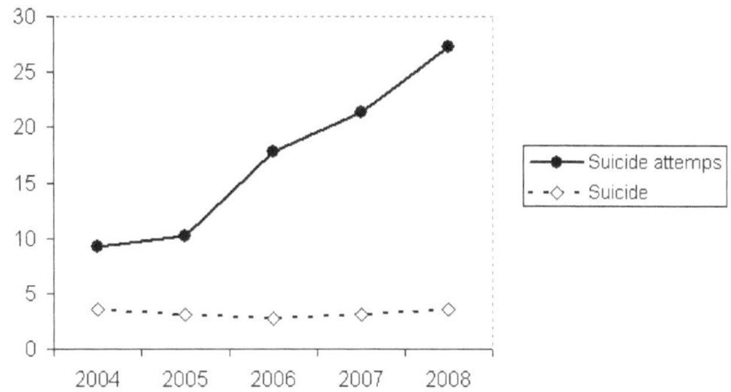

	2004	2005	2006	2007	2008
Suicide attemps	9,3	10,2	17,8	21,4	27,3
Suicide	3,5	3,1	2,7	3,1	3,6

Figure 4: Rates completed and attempted suicide in Bogota, Colombia 2004-2008.
Source: Bogota Health Secretary, Colombia

9. SUICIDE AND VIOLENCE

Latin America is a continent that. since the last century suffers from many violence elements: armed conflicts, dictatorships, violation of human rights, drug trafficking, human being traffic, gangs, displacement of people, extreme poverty, such circumstances overcame by some countries, but are dramatic conditions in some variable extent in other Latin America countries.

As aforementioned, such conditions result in chronic failures, acute unmet needs and desperation feelings becoming risk factors and triggering suicide behaviour [2].

On the other hand, it is accepted, as a paradigm, that during war situation, suicide events decrease, although the Latin American behaviour of suicide rates seems to deny such assertion. An increased suicide rate is found in Chile, Uruguay and Costa Rica, the countries with a stable economy and in the way to overcome internal political and social conflicts In Colombia and Guatemala, both countries with a high number of displaced people and internal social conflict, suicide rates are intermediate and almost reaching stability.

Unfortunately, no studies have been made with proper statistic validity and enough samples to assess connection between violence and suicide in Latin America.

A cross-sectional analytical study completed in Pucallpa, A Peruvian city, including 530 adolescents (12 to 19 years old), concluded that 31.3% of them stated their passive desire to die; 21.1% suicidal ideation, more often females subjects and 18.1% had made at least one attempt to commit suicide, more often by females, specially in 15- to19 years old group. The tendency to violence was expressed by their thought in 51-7% and violent conduct in 18.7% of sample, mainly in males ($p<0.001$). Multivariate analysis found association between suicide ideation and violent conduct (OR=4.9 IC95% 1.4-17.5), not just with hetero-aggressive ideas (OR=2.1 IC95% 0.9-4.9) [38].

Some studies conducted with small samples suggest that intra-family violence and school bullying are closely related to suicide conduct as risk factors and triggering factors [17-28]. In Sarandí del Yí, the

Uruguay city showing the higher suicide rate, "domestic violence problems are observed, mainly in those families disrupted and then discussing about patria potestas of under age children. Denounces of offences and menaces are received" [17].

In some Latin America Countries, such as Colombia, Mexico, Venezuela and Argentina, homicide increased rates are observed, but no studies have been made to evaluate the association to suicide. Basile has noted that suicide and homicide rates in Argentina, show similar tendency [28].

10. NATIONAL PREVENTION PROGRAMS

Mexico, Colombia, Uruguay and Chile have designed epidemiologic vigilance programs to improve successful and attempted suicide records.

In Mexico, Community Psychiatric Program is aimed at early detecting depressive disorders in the elementary schools and high-schools toward the application of screening tests [11].

The program for telephone attention to individuals under suicide risk has been poorly implemented. Few are the Latin America cities where this service has been implemented, like as Guanajuato (the city with the highest teenager suicide rate in Mexico) [11] and Bogotá and Medellin in Colombia.

It is necessary to implement primary care physicians training in evaluation of suicide risk and early detection and the opportune treatment of depressive, disorders, to remove suicide conduct risk factors. This strategy has been adopted by Health Regional Secretariats in Colombia, Mexico [39] and Uruguay.

In Bogotá (Colombia) and Guanajuato (México) pragmatic workshops are organized addressed to 13-19 aged young people aimed at reinforcing protection factors, mainly relate to life decisions, for the purposes to promote cooperation of the same classmate peers to detect the first symptoms of suicidal behaviour [39, 40].

Brazil and Uruguay have released in web site of the respective Ministries of Health the directives related to suicide prevention, unfortunately there are no programs in place for suicide prevention, supported by the same Ministry of Health in El Salvador, Guatemala and Nicaragua.

En Brazil in 2006 a national suicide prevention plan was drafted and implemented the project "Comviver" (Living together) for suicide prevention and to make available information and accompaniment to the families [41].

The Secretariat of Health of Bogotá, Colombia has designed a program to reduce suicide rate to 3,0 per 100,000 in 2012, by the study and evaluation of suicide attempts, the implementation of psychiatric programs to prevent suicide behaviour in the public official medium educational schools and the training of health care personnel for early detection and the proper treatment of suicide behaviour.

The Latin American Psychiatric Association (Apal) has designed a specific program addressed to the investigation and prevention of suicide behaviour and promotion of the most effective continued education activities and professional training on mental health. Encouraging the release of psychological education of community and the production of a specialist directory about suicide issues in Latin America [42].

11. SUICIDE IN LATIN AMERICA

Suicide in Latin America, in spite of showing rates considered as low, involves a health problem which has not been properly addressed as yet by most governments of Latin American countries.

Violence situations and poverty, so intimately rooted in Latin America countries, are associated to suicidal behaviour, and especially in teenager and elder adult groups, where a gradual suicide rates increase is observed.

It is mandatory to address the study, prevention and analysis of suicidal behaviour in a holistic manner. The contributions offered by the several different research groups are of critical significance if they are analyzed in a comprehensive manner, and may point out the true ways allowing for declining suicidal rates and enhancing the quality of life of Latin American people.

ACKNOWLEDGEMENTS

We would like to acknowledge professors Emma Saad (Ecuador), Pilar Cardona (Colombia), Hector Basile (Argentina) and Sergio Perez (Cuba), because their valuable comments and contributions and the assignment of statistic data from their respective countries.

REFERENCES

[1] Tellez J, Taborda LC. El suicidio en cifras. En: Suicidio: Neurobiología, factores de riesgo y prevención. Asociación Colombiana de Psiquiatría Biológica, Bogotá, 2006; pp. 24-41.

[2] Ruiz P, Prólogo. En: Suicidio una realidad en Latinoamérica. Martinez JC, Saad E, Forero J, Eds. Asociación Psiquiátrica de América Latina (Apal). Quito, Ecuador, 2009; pp. 17-26

[3] Aimi A. Mesoamérica. Olmecas, mayas, aztecas: las grandes civilizaciones del Nuevo Mundo. Editorial Electa. Barcelona, 2003.

[4] Morley SG, Brainerd GW, Sharer RJ. The ancient Maya. 5th Edition. Stanford University, 2005.

[5] Available from: http://www.aztlanvirtual.com/aztlan/nueva_aztlan/noticias/2005/07/el-suicidio-era-una-practica-tolerada.htlm. Access January 10th, 2010.

[6] Villaseñor SJ, Rubio EL. Hermenéutica del suicidio. En: Suicidio una realidad en Latinoamerica. Martinez JC, Saad E, Forero J, Eds. Asociación Psiquiátrica de America Latina (Apal). Quito, Ecuador, 2009; pp. 17-26.

[7] De Betanzos J, Martín-Rubio MC. Suma y narración de los Incas: seguida del Discurso sobre la descendencia y gobierno de los Incas Madrid: Polifemo, 2004.

[8] Fray Pedro Simon. Noticias historiales de las conquistas de Tierra Firme en las Indias Occidentales. Biblioteca Luis Angel Arango. Banco de la República, Bogotá, 1992.

[9] Sistema Nacional de información cultural. Ministerio de Cultura de Colombia. Available from: http://www.sinic.gov.co/SINIC/ColombiaCultural/ColCulturalBusca.aspx?AREID=3&SECID=8&IdDep=47&COLTEM=211

[10] World Health Organization. Geneve 2010. Available from: http://www.who.int/mental_health/prevention/suicide/charts/en/ index.html. Access January 10th, 2010.

[11] México Sano. 2008 sep; 1(4):11.http://portal.salud.gob.mex. Access January 10th, 2010.

[12] Diario La Nueva, Noviembre 26 2008. Available from: http://lanueva.com/edicion_impresa/nota/26/11/2008/8bq099.html.

[13] Portal Da Saude. Available from: www.saude.gov.br. Access January 10th, 2010.

[14] Instituto Nacional de Estadística y Censos del Ecuador 2008. Available from: www.inec.gov.ec. Access January 10th, 2010.

[15] Available from: http://www.telegrafo.com.ec/policiales/noticia/archive/policiales/2009/08/12/Suicidios-ya-no-se-dan-por-temporadas.aspx. Access January 10th, 2010.

[16] Available from: www.hoy.com.ec/.ecuador/cuenca-mas-intentos-de-suicidio-278182-278182.html. Access January 10th, 2010.

[17] Available from: http://www.elpais.com.uy. Access January 10th, 2010.

[18] SIAVAC - DRIP. Instituto Nacional de Medicina y Ciencias Forenses, 2005.

[19] Ministerio de Protección Social. Encuesta Nacional de Salud Mental. Bogotá, 2004.

[20] Belfort E. Introducción. En: Suicidio una realidad en Latinoamérica. Martínez JC, Saad E, Forero J, Eds. Asociación Psiquiátrica de América Latina (Apal). Quito, Ecuador, 2009; pp. 11-3.

[21] Borges G, Medina M, Orozco R, Villatoro J, Bautista C.Distribución y determinantes sociodemográficos de la conducta suicida en México. Salud Mental 2009; 32(5):413-25.

[22] García J, Palacio CA, Diago J, *et al.* Eventos vitales adversos y suicidio: un estudio de autopsia psicológica en Medellín, Colombia. Revista Colombiana de Psiquiatria 2008; 37(1):11-28.

[23] Aldrich RS, Cerel J. The development of Effective Message Content for Suicide Intervention. Crisis 2009, 30(4):174-9.

[24] Encuesta Observatorio de Convivencia Escolar Universidad Católica Argentina. 2008. Available from: http://www.uca.edu.ar. Access January 10th, 2010.

[25] Available from: www.cronica.com.mx/nota.php?id_nota=140424. Access January 10th, 2010.

[26] Instituto Nacional de Medicina Legal y Ciencias Forenses, Bogotá, 2008.

[27] Salvo L, Melipilla R. Predictores de suicidalidad en adolescentes. Revista Chilena de Neuropsiquiatría 2008, 46(2):115-23.

[28] Serfaty E. Suicidio en la adolescencia. Adolescencia Latinoamericana. 1998, 1: 105-10.

[29] Basile H. Suicidio: Concepto Generales con especial referencia al suicidio adolescente. En: Suicidio una realidad en Latinoamérica. Martinez JC, Saad E, Forero J, Eds. Asociación Psiquiátrica de América Latina (Apal). Quito, Ecuador, 2009. pp. 17-26.

[30] Alcaldía Mayor de Bogota. Secretaría de Gobierno. Caracterización del comportamiento suicida en el Distrito Capital. Aportes a su explicación y prevención. Bogotá, 2001.

[31] Freitas G. Comportamento suicida em adolescents grávidas: Um estudo de caso-controle. Campinas 2007. Available from: www.projetocomviver.org.br. Access January 10th, 2010.

[32] Campo G, Roa JA, Pérez A, *et al.* Intento de suicidio en niños menores de 14 años atendidos en el Hospital Universitario del Valle, Cali. Colombia Médica 2003; 34(1):9-16.

[33] Ministerio de Salud Pública de la República Oriental del Uruguay. Programa Nacional de Salud Mental. Guías de Prevención y detección de factores de riesgo de conductas suicidas. Montevideo, 2006.

[34] Rodríguez M, Boris D, Rodríguez O. Algunos aspectos clínico epidemiológicos de la depresión en la ancianidad. Medisan 2009; 13(5):15-23.

[35] Alejo H. Comportamiento del intento de suicidio en el año 2005. Secretaria de salud de Bogotá, Colombia, 2006.

[36] Cardona GP.Intentos de suicidio en la ciudad de Bogotá DC, primer semestre 2006-2007. Boletín Epidemiológico Cuatrimestral DRIP. Subdirección de servicios forenses. División de referencia de información pericial. Volumen 1. No. 1, Abril de 2007.

[37] Aristizabal A, Gonzalez A, Palacio C, Garcia J, Lopez C. Factores asociados a letalidad de intentos de suicidio en sujetos con trastorno depresivo mayor. Revista Colombiana de Psiquìatria 2009; 38(3):446-63.

[38] Cano P, Gutiérrez C, Bizama M. Tendencia a la violencia e ideación suicida en adolescentes escolares en una ciudad de la amazonía peruana. Revista Peruana de Medicina Experimental y Salud Pública 2009; 26(2):175-81.

[39] Mexico Sano. 2009 mar; 2(7):21. http://portal.salud.gob.mex. Access January 10th, 2010.

[40] Chavez AM, Medina MC, Macías LF. Modelo psicoeducativo para la prevención del suicidio en jóvenes. Salud Mental 2008; 31(3):197-203.

[41] Projeto Comviver. Available from: www.projetocomviver.org.br. Access January 10th, 2010.

[42] Asociación Psiquiátrica de America Latina, Apal. Available from: www.apalweb.org

CHAPTER 17

Suicide in Austria

Elmar Etzersdorfer[1], Nestor D. Kapusta[2], Ingo W. Nader[3], Thomas Niederkrotenthaler[4,5], Kristina Ritter[6], Thomas Stompe[6], Martin Voracek[3,*], and Gernot Sonneck[5,7]

[1]Furtbach Hospital, Furtbachstraße 6, D-70178 Stuttgart, Germany; [2]Department of Psychoanalysis and Psychotherapy, Medical University of Vienna, Währinger Gürtel 18-20, A-1090 Vienna, Austria; [3]Department of Basic Psychological Research and Research Methods, School of Psychology, University of Vienna, Liebiggasse 5, A-1010 Vienna, Austria; [4]Department of General Practice and Family Medicine, Center for Public Health, Medical University of Vienna, Währingerstraße 13a, A-1090 Vienna, Austria; [5]Department of Medical Psychology, Center for Public Health, Medical University of Vienna, Severingasse 9, A-1090 Vienna, Austria; [6]Department of Psychiatry and Psychotherapy, Medical University of Vienna, Währinger Gürtel 18-20, A-1090 Vienna, Austria and [7]Ludwig Boltzmann Institute for Social Psychiatry, Lazarettgasse 14A-912, A-1090 Vienna, Austria

Abstract: Austria ranked among the countries with highest suicide rates for decades. The suicide rate increased until 1986, but decreased continuously since then. At present, Austria's suicide rate is about the European average. The most common method for both sexes is hanging, followed by shooting (for men) or jumping from heights (for women). This chapter presents epidemiological data as well as a study concerning the acceptance of suicide motives. Furthermore, the Austrian National Suicide Prevention Plan is outlined. It comprises activities to increase awareness of suicide risk, support and treatment after suicide attempts, treatment of mental illness, education of health care staff, restriction of access to means of suicide, and responsible media reporting. Although the plan has not yet been approved by the Austrian parliament, many of the activities have already been implemented on a regional level.

Keywords: Epidemiology, suicide, prevention, Austria.

1. INTRODUCTION

For decades, Austria ranked among countries with the highest suicide rates in the world [1]. As in many other western countries, the overall Austrian suicide rate increased until 1986 and decreased since then continuously [2, 3]. Since the enlargement of the European Union, with Eastern European member states joining in 2004 and 2007, the Austrian ranking has changed considerably from one of the highest to the European average (Fig. **1**).

2. EPIDEMIOLOGY OF SUICIDE IN AUSTRIA

Data Quality of Official Austrian Mortality Statistics

In Austria, a death certificate has to be filled in for every deceased person who did not consult a physician within in the 10 days prior to death by a physician authorized by the local health authority. Consent of relatives is not required for autopsies. Hence, the rate of autopsies in Austria is rather high in international comparison: 34% of all deaths in Austria in 1983, and even 51 to 53% in the capital, Vienna, between 1983 and 1987 [4]. A more recent work reports an average autopsy rate of 29% between 1991-2000 for persons who died aged 50 years or above [5]. However, more recent analyses suggest a further decrease of autopsy rates in Austria [6], which corresponds to the worldwide decrease of autopsies [7] and which may have an impact on the accuracy of suicide numbers. An autopsy is performed if any uncertainty about the cause of death is revealed. If the cause of death is unclear, there is also a further investigation by the official

***Address correspondence to Martin Voracek:** Department of Basic Psychological Research and Research Methods, Faculty of Psychology, University of Vienna; Liebiggasse 5, A-1010 Vienna, Austria E-mails: martin.voracek@univie.ac.at and wienerwerkstaette@suizidforschung.at

Maurizio Pompili (Ed)

bureau of statistics (Statistics Austria). It tends to count deaths as suicide if it is the most probable cause of death, even without evidence in a legal sense. Thus the strategy is more clinically than legally oriented and therefore broader than in countries like the UK. Since 1970, the electronic classification of suicides is based on the International Classification of Diseases.

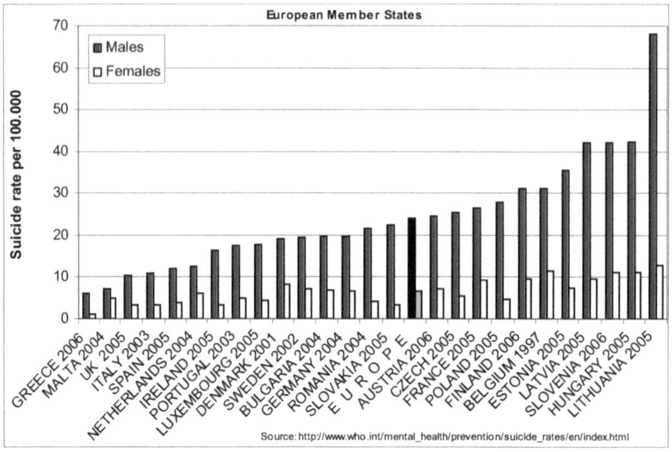

Figure 1: Ranking of the Austrian suicide rate, most recent available year.

Age Groups

The decrease of the overall suicide rate between 1986 and the most recent available year (2008) was from 28.3 to 15.2 per 100,000 population per year (*i.e.*, a reduction of 46%). This decrease can be found among all age groups, except for men aged 85 years or above [8, 9]. Suicide rates increase with age, and more intensely so among men than among women (Fig. **2**). Whereas suicide rates were 14 (men) and 5 (women) per 100,000 among the age group 20-24, corresponding rates were 108 and 22 per 100,000 among those aged 85 and over in 2008 [9].

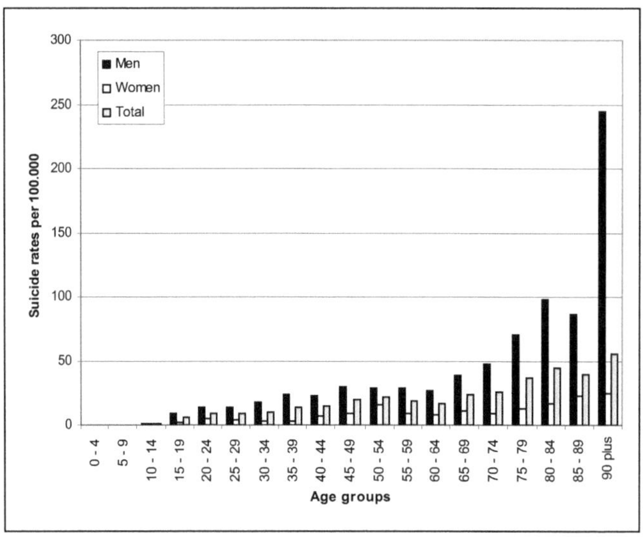

Figure 2: Suicide rates among age groups in Austria 2008.

Suicide Methods

For both sexes, the most common suicide method in Austria is hanging. During the last decade (1999-2008), men have chosen hanging in 50%, followed by shooting in 21% of all suicides. Among women, hanging (35%) is now followed by jumping from heights (19%), which has replaced poisonings (18%).

Poisonings were the second-most common method prior to the last decade, but decreased considerably over the last 30 years. The decrease of the overall suicide rate is based on a decrease of hangings and poisonings, as well as of firearm suicides (see Fig. **3**).

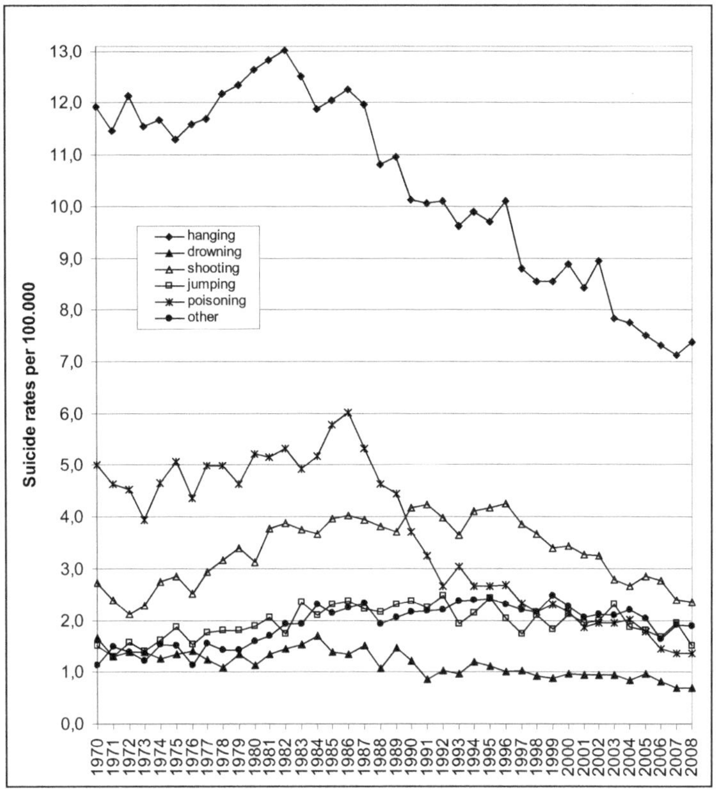

Figure 3: Time trend of suicide methods in Austria.

Epidemiological Research

Several studies have examined the decrease of suicide rates in the light of societal changes and prevention efforts in Austria and have suggested a multicausal explanation. Following research, the implementation of media guidelines for suicide reporting in 1987 had a considerable impact on suicide rates [10]. Similarly, the decrease of suicide rates after 1987 coincides with an increased prescription of antidepressant compounds and an increase of the density of psychotherapists, thus suggesting improved mental health care reduced suicide incidence [11]. In addition, the strengthening of the Austrian firearm law in 1997, resulting in restricted access to licensed firearms, led to a decrease of firearm licensees and of firearm suicide and homicide rates [12]. A cross-sectional study showed firearm suicide rates to correlate with firearm licence density across Austrian federal states [13]. Both studies support the preventive potential of stronger firearm laws in Austria. Interestingly, among the youth, firearm suicides increased during the media debate on firearm law strengthening, but this effect was temporary and the usage of this method decreased thereafter (and still is decreasing) among youth, in line with the decrease seen in youth suicide rates [14, 15].

3. ACCEPTABILITY OF SUICIDE MOTIVES IN AUSTRIA

National suicide rates are relatively stable, but differ considerably across nations [16]. In contrast, with the exception of China, studies evaluating the global suicide risk found a relatively constant increase in the ratios of male and female suicide rates even over longer periods of time: 3.2 to 1 in 1950 and 3.6 to 1 in 1995 [17]. In 2006, the sex ratio for completed suicides was very similar in Austria (3.5 to 1). Another stable, almost cross-cultural universal is the association between increasing age and increasing suicide rate (Fig. **2**).

Numerous studies have analyzed health and socio-economic factors possibly accounting for the sex differences in suicidal behavior [18]. In both sexes, mental illness was the most important predictor associated with suicidal behavior. Unemployment, retirement, and being single increases the risk for lethal suicide acts in men, whereas for women no significant risk factors other than mental illness have been identified. Moreover, in European countries men have a higher risk than women for using firearms and hanging, and a lower risk of poisoning by drugs, drowning, and jumping [19].

There are also numerous factors in the life of elderly subjects, like particular losses, loneliness, social isolation, higher rates of depression, and chronic medical illness, that are held responsible for the increased risk of suicidal behavior found in most cultures [20]. Consequentially, suicide notes of elderly often reflect the wish to escape from suffering [21].

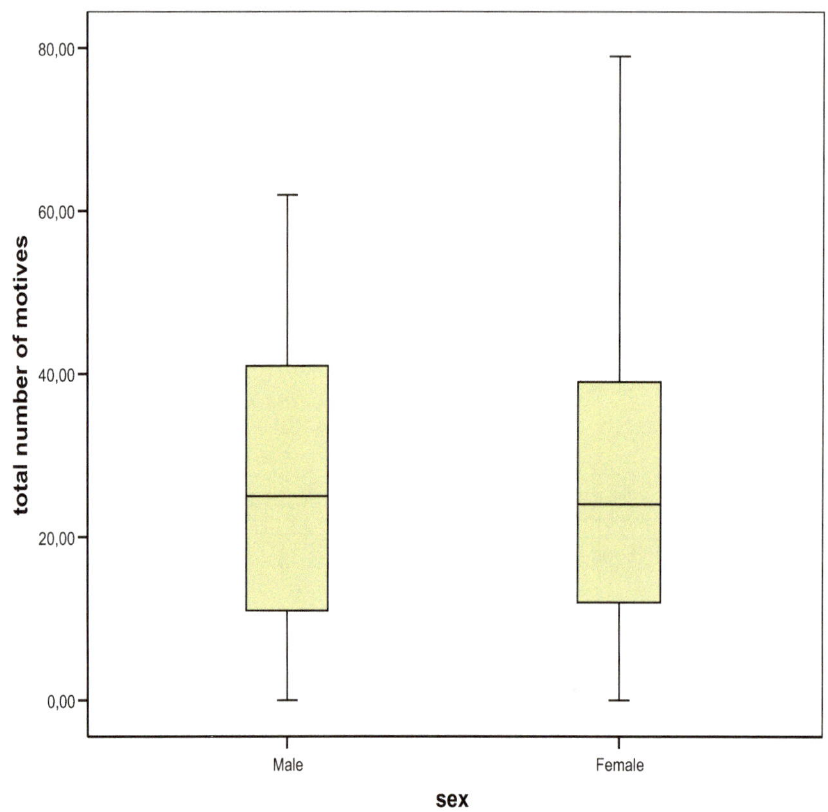

Figure 4: Sex and the acceptance of suicide motives in Austria ($N_f = 86$, $N_m = 67$).

In 2006, we have started a multi-center survey on this research question, with the aim to explore possible relations between the acceptance of suicide motives in the healthy population and national suicide rates. We included 610 healthy subjects from Georgia, Lithuania, Nigeria, Austria, Pakistan, and Poland. After giving informed consent, all subjects completed a 46-item questionnaire on attitudes towards and assessment of suicide motives (0 = no reason for suicide; 1 = under certain circumstances; 2 = yes) [22, 23]. Our main hypothesis was that a high acceptance of a broad range of different suicide motives in certain cultures could perhaps lower the threshold for suicidal behavior in critical life situations. Compared to the subjects from the five other countries, Austrians showed the highest tolerance towards very different suicide motives, such as severe illness, pain, hurt, loss, and feelings of guilt or shame [23]. In the meantime, we have expanded the study with interviewees from China, Japan, Turkey, Mexico, and Iran.

Comparisons of total scores for the acceptance of suicide motives between men and women yielded no statistically significant sex differences in the Austrian sample (Fig. **4**).

This is not really surprising, bearing in mind that women have a considerably higher prevalence of attempted suicide than men [24]. However, we found no association between age and the acceptance of suicide motives (Fig. **5**).

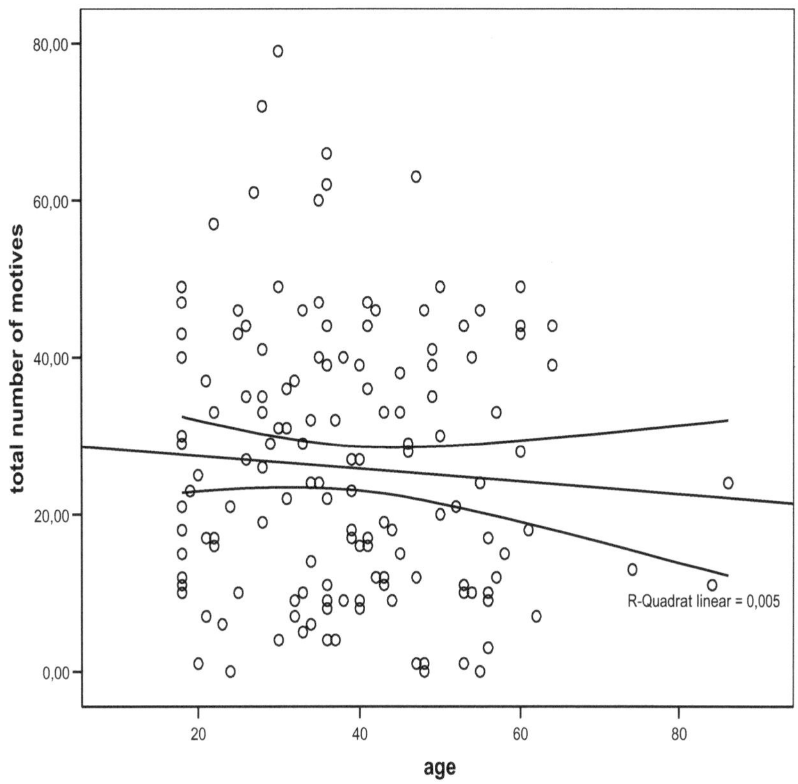

Figure 5: Age and the acceptance of suicide motives in Austria (N = 153, lines are the regression line (predicted mean by age) and the 75% confidenceinterval).

Several reasons might be responsible for this finding. First, the Austrian sample included only a few persons older than 60 years. Second, we have only investigated physically and mentally healthy subjects. However, suicidal behavior might be the result of the interaction between the (premorbid) value system and critical life situations – the latter being more prevalent in older than in younger individuals. Third, elder subjects tend to be more religious than younger ones. Therefore, the issue of suicide is widely tabooed in the older generation. Keeping these limitations in mind, we plan to enlarge our sample and place emphasis on healthy people older than 70 years, but also on subjects with mental disorders.

4. THE AUSTRIAN SUICIDE PREVENTION PLAN

Suicide prevention in Austria has a long tradition [25]. Already back in 1909, a treatment service for people after suicide attempts was provided in Vienna. Due to the aftermath of World War II, continuous suicide preventive activities have been available not earlier than 1946. In 1971, Austria became probably one of the first countries in Europe where suicide prevention was mentioned as a declared aim in a government program. At this time, suicide prevention was already a topic within the World Health Organization (WHO). In 1980, the need for suicide preventive activities in the WHO European region was made explicit for the first time in the initiative "Health for All in the Year 2000". Specifications to this initiative have been made, among others, in 1999 in Health 21 [26]. Also, in 1999, the first Austrian National Suicide Prevention Plan (SPA) was elaborated and presented to the public [27]. It was based on guidelines from the United Nations (UNO) [28] and on the experiences from other countries which already had implemented national programs. From 2001 onwards, the WHO/EURO Network on Suicide Research and Prevention has further developed and coordinated these international efforts. In 2005, the implementation of national suicide prevention programs was recommended by the WHO European Region Assembly. This recommendation was endorsed by the European Council of Ministers in 2007 [29]. In its latest edition from 2008 [25], the SPA includes the following prevention strategies: restriction of access to means of suicide, treatment of mental illness, support and treatment after suicide attempts, responsible media reporting, and education of health care staff. As of this writing, a national suicide prevention plan (SUPRA) is now forthcoming, but is still awaiting approval by the Austrian parliament [30, 31].

General and Specific Preventive Activities

There are many causes and triggers that may result in suicidal constriction, and, on the other side, equally many measures that may prevent suicide. General preventive activities, including psychological, medical, educational, and social measures, all aim at improving the capabilities of the population to deal with difficulties in the life course. Equally important, specific prevention programs provide either direct support to suicide-prone people or serve their needs more indirectly, by identifying and offering service and treatment to risk groups (*e.g.*, substance abusers, individuals with mental illness, people in psychosocial crisis, or grown lonely elderly).

Action Plan

There are 10 different working areas in the current SPA. Each working area targets at different stakeholders and population groups and applies different methods:

1. Increase of awareness
2. Support and treatment
3. Children and adolescents
4. Adults
5. Elderly
6. Risk groups
7. Education and development
8. Access to means of suicide
9. National collaboration
10. Legislation change

4.1. ACTIVITIES TO INCREASE AWARENESS

Awareness campaigns aim at promoting the idea that suicide risk is not a irrevocable destiny, but rather that suicide prevention is possible. In this area, education on the current state of the art in suicide prevention and specifications of strategies to meet future challenges are of utmost importance. Apart from the distribution of tailor-made information and guidelines for the problem of suicide and for the ways of how to prevent it for different stakeholders, evaluations of such campaigns and the development of a documentation on how to provide information on the issue of suicide is necessary, in order to reach a preventive effect and to avoid copycat effects. Appropriate ways of information and discussion in the media should be encouraged.

4.2. SUPPORT AND TREATMENT

Psychological, medical and social support, and treatment for suicide-prone people in various settings (*e.g.*, in crisis intervention centers, crisis hotlines, hospitals, and in outpatient treatment) have to be made available to those in need. This aim requires several measures:

Crisis Management

The main aims in this area are to offer education and training in crisis intervention and conflict management strategies, to provide individual and institutional support of people after personal loss and/or disasters; and to foster an early detection of suicidality and mental illness, including appropriate support and treatment.

Health Services

It is a major aim of effective suicide prevention to provide adequate diagnostic screening and treatment to every patient who enters health service facilities and is suicidal. Knowledge on risk groups, suicidal development, the pre-suicidal syndrome in stakeholders working in health-care settings and other institutions are key aspects to provide adequate support and treatment.

- Development of quality criteria for psycho-social and medical treatment of suicidal persons in inpatient and outpatient facilities.
- Implementation of suicide prevention teams to provide expert knowledge and supervision (psychological and psychotherapeutic treatment in hospitals).
- Special focus on the needs of patients; effective treatment and suicide prevention in patients with depressive psychoses, schizophrenia, substance abuse, and personality disorders.
- Continuous education of health care staff on suicide prevention.
- Development of adequate means to reach out to suicidal people and to enable continuity in treatment and support, particularly in transition from in- to outpatient treatment.
- Support of families with a history of suicide and support of bereaved.

4.3. TARGET GROUP CHILDREN AND ADOLESCENTS

Education

The incorporation of learning strategies on topics such as how to cope with crises and mental illness into curricula is an important aim in this target group. Risk signs, including *e.g.,* the announcement (sometimes misunderstood as "threats") of suicide plans, suicide attempts, frequent truanting from school, apparent fatigue, aggression, isolation, substance abuse, fits of rage, and dissocial behavior need to be identified and understood. The staff of education services such as kindergartens and schools, children groups and youth clubs, and communities of interest are important stakeholders in these activities. The increased risk of suicide after a suicide or suicide attempt in the child's or adolescent's environment needs to be considered.

Health Services, Social Work

The availability of help services needs to be low-threshold, anonymous, and quick.

- Specific consideration of risk factors in the family environment of adolescents and children (broken home, violence, abuse, unemployment, poverty) and of behavioral changes that may indicate difficult family situations.
- Increased support of families with a history of suicide or suicide attempt and/or other self-destructive tendencies, alcoholism or other substance abuse, mental illness, violence and inadequate emotional reactions. Specific consideration of problems of lone mothers and fathers and migrants.

4.4. TARGET GROUP ADULTS

Crises in relationships, divorce and psycho-social stress in the working environment, as well as unemployment are periods of increased vulnerability to mental illness and suicide.

Crises in Relationships

Adequate information on how to build up and arrange partnerships, and on how to deal with relationship problems or divorce is of high importance, particularly in this age group. This includes support of persons who are in relationship crises or who experience isolation, loss of job, depression, and suicidal behavior.

Companies and Workplace

Structural problems at the workplace can lead to anxiety in staff which may result in suicidality in sensitive persons. Suicide preventive activities include:

- Conversation possibilities (individual and in groups) focusing on acute working problems, *e.g.*, reorganisation, economisation, or close-downs.
- Consideration of stressors in the working environment that may lead to isolation and may be reflected in substance abuse, mental illness, mobbing and bullying, and sexual harassment.
- Specific focus on staff with recent experiences of loss and/or disasters, early recognition and treatment of suicidality in the workplace environment, recognition of mental illness, and knowledge of treatment possibilities in companies.
- Specific focus on the problems of migrants and minorities; diversity management.

4.5. TARGET GROUP ELDERLY

Retirement, illness, depression, and loss due to death are major stressors that frequently affect this age group and that may result in crisis reactions.

Social and Relationship Problems

Suicide-preventive measures comprise:

- Facilitations for elderly people to use their intellectual, emotional, and social resources (*e.g.*, part-time work and gliding retirement).
- Destigmatization of marriage problems and sexuality at an older age.
- Knowledge about crisis reactions, depression, dementia, and suicidality at an older age.
- Increased cooperation between organizations to enable smooth transitions between the various forms of elderly care.
- Development and implementation of psycho-social and medical services that provide support, treatment, and care to people in the phase of dying, including appropriate palliative care.

4.6. RISK GROUPS

Education of stakeholders on social skills necessary to deal with people who suffer from alcoholism, substance abuse, with HIV-positive people and people suffering from Aids, with those suffering from mental illness, with victims of violence or self-injury including suicide attempts, migrants, detainees, are necessary.

Healthcare and Social Work

Group-adequate, active ways of reaching out to specific risk groups that contribute to a better understanding of the specific problems and needs in these groups and enable self-help are warranted to prevent suicide in risk groups. The expansion of organisations which deal specifically with risk groups is a major aim.

4.7. EDUCATION

Methods and material for educating various groups of stakeholders have to be developed. Stakeholders comprise, among others, teachers, social workers, health care staff, psychologists, psychotherapists, clergymen, the police force, rescue, armed forces, and security officers.

4.8. RESTRICTED ACCESS TO MEANS OF SUICIDE

Traffic

The development of alco blocks, initiatives to reduce of carbon monoxide in exhaust gases and development of devices that stop the engine idling if a certain concentration of carbon monoxide is in the air, airbags as a standard in all cars, protection and public telephones in locations with high suicide frequencies (hot spots), and measures to prevent train and subway suicides are some important suicide preventive measures with focus on traffic.

Firearms and Weapons

A restrictive policy on possession of firearms and weapons is warranted.

Medical Prescription Practice

The development of less toxic medication and the availability and prescription of small sized packages in case of potentially toxic medication are important requirements in this working area. Also frequent surveillance of the compliance with medication regimes contribute to suicide prevention.

4.9. NATIONAL COLLABORATION

The establishment and expansion of centers for suicide research and prevention, coordinating various suicide preventive initiatives and providing effective epidemiological monitoring, is of high priority.

Databases

The expansion of a database providing anonymized case data on suicides and suicide attempts in Austria and in neighbouring countries is crucial for research on the bio-psycho-socio-cultural determinants of suicidal behavior. Furthermore, a database of completed and ongoing projects on suicide and suicide prevention, including relevant literature that is easily accessible for those providing educative services, is warranted.

Quality Assurance

In order to further increase the quality of research output, the definition of priority areas for research on mental illness is needed. The establishment of a Center for Suicide Research and Prevention with the following objectives would support this idea in several ways:

- Development and updating of media recommendations for reporting on suicide, with a focus on different media types [32, 33]. Current recommendations are available at www.suizidforschung.at.

- Planning and conduction of studies on risk and protective factors for suicidal behavior.

- Development of methods and guidelines for how to implement specific suicide-preventive measures.

- Development of evaluation tools measuring the effects of interventions aimed at preventing mental illness and suicide.
- Increased networking across disciplines in the fields of suicide research and in practical prevention.
- Public mental health promotion: Professional information for specific target groups, *e.g.*, the public, political stakeholders, and health professionals.

4.10. LEGISLATION

In many areas, improved suicide prevention necessitates changes or specifications in legislation. A major aim is therefore to develop legislative proposals that enable and support educational measures in schools, equality, human resources development, gliding retirement, and interventions focusing on restricted access to means of suicide.

Translation of the SPA

This program has been adopted by the Austrian Society for Suicide Prevention (ÖGS) and is translated in collaboration with Pro Mente Austria. Many of the listed activities have already been implemented on a regional level. The Austrian federal states Styria and Upper Austria have developed regional suicide prevention plans, and there are various suicide preventive activities across the country. For instance, several initiatives in Salzburg and Tyrol focus on suicide prevention in schools, the European Alliance Against Depression (EAAD, www.eaad.net) fosters health promotion in risk groups, the public, and stakeholders in Carinthia, Lower Austria, Styria, Tyrol, and Vienna.

Several public health initiatives have been evaluated and shown to be associated with a decrease in suicidal behavior:

In 1997, a directive of the European Council to harmonize firearm legislation across the member states has been translated into Austrian legislation [12]. After implementation, there was a clear reduction of firearm licences in the population, and a corresponding decrease of firearm suicides (40%) and firearm homicides (60%) which was not compensated for by a switch to other methods [12]. In children and adolescents, a short-term increase of firearm suicides was observed during the change of legislation, which may have been attributable to sensationalist media reporting on firearm legislation during that time [14]. In the long run, the changed legislation also seems to have contributed to a decrease in child and adolescent suicide rates [14].

The national implementation of media guidelines for the reporting of suicide has been shown to be associated with improvements in the quality of reporting and with a decrease in Viennese subway suicides and of national suicide rates [13]. The decrease of suicide rates was most pronounced in regions with strong collaboration with the media [13]. Several characteristics of media reporting on suicidal behavior are still widely divergent from suicidal behavior in the population [34], but only a limited fraction of suicide articles seems to be followed by copycat effects [35]. It could be shown that celebrity status increased the risk of copycat suicides, whereas criminality of the reported suicide victim decreased the risk of post-report increases of suicides. Some media reporting may even have a protective effect: Reports on individuals in adverse circumstances who adopted constructive ways of coping in crisis were found to be less sensationalist and associated with decreases of suicides (Papageno effect) [36]. These reports may turn out to be particularly useful for suicide prevention. The continuous assistance of journalists and editors who report on suicide is an important target in this working area of the SPA.

Research on regional variations in suicide rates is [37] information and education campaigns have been repeatedly provided to stakeholders, in order to increase awareness and to reduce the stigma surrounding suicide. All of these initiatives are typical bottom-up projects and fostered by pioneering spirit, idealism, and social responsibility. In contrast to countries such as Finland, Denmark, Sweden, Germany, and the

USA, the program has not yet been approved by the Austrian parliament. The fact that suicide prevention is a declared aim in the current government program (2008-2013) may turn out as an important first step in this direction.

For further information on the SPA, please contact gernot.sonneck@meduniwien.ac.at and thomas.niederkrotenthaler@meduniwien.ac.at

REFERENCES

[1] Liu KY. Suicide rates in the world: 1950-2004. Suicide Life Threat Behav 2009; 39: 204-13.

[2] Etzersdorfer E, Fischer P, Sonneck G. The epidemiology of suicide in Austria 1980-1990. Wien Klin Wochenschr 1992; 104: 564-99.

[3] Etzersdorfer E, Voracek M, Kapusta N, Sonneck G. Epidemiology of suicide in Austria 1990-2000: general decrease but increased suicide risk for old men. Wien Klin Wochenschr 2005; 117: 31-5.

[4] Sakr L, Bibus B, Dutz W, *et al.* Zur hohen Autopsierate in Wien [Concerning the high rate of autopsies in Vienna]. Wien Klin Wochenschr 1989; 101: 511-4.

[5] Waldhoer T, Berzlanovich A, Vutuc C, Haidinger G. Rates of postmortem examination in Austria: the effect of distance between location of death and site of examination. J Clin Epidemiol 2003; 56: 891-5.

[6] Kapusta ND, Tran US, Rockett IR, De Leo D, Naylor CP, Niederkrotenthaler T, Voracek M, Etzersdorfer E, Sonneck G. Declining autopsy rates and suicide misclassification: a cross-national analysis of 35 countries. Arch Gen Psychiatry 2011;68:1050-7

[7] Kapusta ND, Etzersdorfer E, Sonneck G. Trends in suicide rates among the elderly in Austria 1970-2004: An analysis of changes by age group, suicide method and gender. Int J Geriatr Psychiatry 2007; 22: 438-44.

[8] Kapusta ND. Current data, facts and numbers of suicides in Austria 2007. Suicidology Online 2009; 1: 2-4.

[9] Niederkrotenthaler T, Sonneck G. Assessing the impact of media guidelines for reporting on suicides in Austria: interrupted time series analysis. Aust N Z J Psychiatry 2007; 41: 419-28.

[10] Kapusta ND, Niederkrotenthaler T, Etzersdorfer E, *et al.* Influence of psychotherapist density and antidepressant sales on suicide rates. Acta Psychiatr Scandin 2009; 119: 236-42.

[11] Kapusta ND, Etzersdorfer E, Krall G, Sonneck G. Firearm legislation reform in the European Union: impact on firearm availability, firearm suicide and homicide rates in Austria. Br J Psychiatry 2007; 191:253-7.

[12] Etzersdorfer E, Kapusta ND, Sonneck G. Suicide by shooting is correlated to rate of gun licenses in Austrian counties. Wien Klin Wochenschr 2006; 118: 464-8.

[13] Niederkrotenthaler T, Till B, Herberth A, *et al.* Can media effects counteract legislation reforms? The case of adolescent firearm suicides in the wake of the Austrian firearm legislation. J Adolesc Health 2009; 44: 90-3.

[14] Dervic K, Friedrich E, Oquendo MA, Voracek M, Friedrich MH, Sonneck G. Suicide in Austrian children and young adolescents aged 14 and younger. Eur Child Adolesc Psychiatry 2006; 15: 427-34.

[15] Lester D. Suicide and culture. World Cult Psychiatry Res Rev 2008; 3: 51-68.

[16] Stompe T. Suicide in a global perspective. World Cult Psychiatry Res Rev 2008; 3: 48-50.

[17] Qin P, Agerbo E, Westergård-Nielsen N, Eriksson T, Mortensen PB. Gender differences in risk factors for suicide in Denmark. Br J Psychiatry 2000; 177: 546-50.

[18] Värnik A, Kõlves K, van der Feltz-Cornelis CM, *et al.* Suicide methods in Europe: a gender-specific analysis of countries participating in the "European Alliance Against Depression". J Epidemiol Community Health 2008; 62: 545-51.

[19] Lester D. Suicide among elderly in the world. In: De Leo D, Ed. Suicide and euthanasia in older adults: a transcultural journey. Göttingen, Hogrefe & Huber Publishers. 2001; pp. 1-20.

[20] Farberow NL, Shneidman ES. Suicide and age. In: Shneidman ES, Farberow NL, Eds. Clues to suicide. New York, McGraw-Hill. 1957; pp. 41-9.

[21] Ritter K, Stompe T. Die Akzeptanz von Suizidmotiven: ein Schlüssel zu den Unterschieden nationaler Suizidraten? [Acceptancy of suicide motives: a key to understanding differences in national suicide rates?] Neuropsychiatry 2008; 22: 1-8.

[22] Ritter K, Chaudhry HR, Idemudia E, *et al.* Suicide motives and culture: degree of modernisation, response behavior and acceptance. World Cult Psychiatry Res Rev 2008; 3: 69-76.

[23] Mościcki EK, O'Carroll P, Rae DS, Locke BZ, Roy A, Regier DA. Suicide attempts in the Epidemiologic Catchment Area Study. Yale J Biol Med 1988; 61: 259-68.

[24] Sonneck G, Niederkrotenthaler T. Zum österreichischen nationalen Suizidpräventionsplan. [The Austrian National Suicide Prevention Plan]. Spectrum Psychiatrie 2008; 2: 20-3.

[25] World Health Organization. Health 21. The health for all policy framework for the WHO European region. WHO Europe: Copenhagen; 1999. Available from: http://www.euro.who.int/document/health21/wa540ga199heeng.pdf

[26] Sonneck G. Krisenintervention und Suizidverhütung [Crisis intervention and suicide prevention]. Wien: Facultas, 2001.

[27] World Health Organization. Prevention of suicide: guidelines for the formulation and implementation of national strategies. Geneva: World Health Organization, 1996.

[28] WHO European Ministerial Conference on Mental Health. Facing the challenges, building solutions. Copenhagen: WHO Europe, 2005. Available from: http://www.euro.who.int/document/mnh/edoc07.pdf

[29] World Health Organization. Suicide prevention in Europe. The WHO European monitoring survey on national suicide prevention programmes and strategies. Copenhagen: WHO Regional Office for Europe, 2002.

[30] Mittendorfer Rutz E, Wasserman D. The WHO European monitoring surveys on national suicide preventive programmes and strategies. Suicidologi 2004; 9: 23-5.

[31] Stein C, Tomandl G, Sonneck G. Medienleitfaden. [Media guidelines for the reporting on suicides]. Vienna: Kriseninterventionszentrum Wien, 2005. Available from: http://www.suizidforschung.at/leitfaden.pdf.

[32] World Health Organization. [homepage on the Internet]. Geneve: The Organization, c2008 [cited Feb 10, 2009]. Preventing suicide. A resource for media professionals. Available from: http://www.who.int/mental_health/prevention/suicide/resource_media.pdf

[33] Niederkrotenthaler T, Till B, Herberth A, *et al.* The gap between suicide characteristics in the print media and in the population. Eur J Public Health 2009; 19: 361-4.

[34] Niederkrotenthaler T, Till B, Voracek M, Dervic K, Kapusta ND, Sonneck G. Copycat effects after media reports on suicide: A population-based study. Soc Sci Med 2009; 69: 1085-90.

[35] Niederkrotenthaler T, Voracek M, Herberth A, Till B, Strauss M, Etzersdorfer E, Eisenwort B, Sonneck G. The role of media reports in completed and prevented suicide – Werther versus Papageno effects. British Journal of Psychiatry 2010; 197: 234-243.

[36] Watzka C. Sozialstruktur und Suizid in Österreich. [Social structure and suicide in Austria]. Wiesbaden: VS Verlag für Sozialwissenschaften, 2008.

CHAPTER 18

Active Sport Participation, Sport Spectatorship and Suicidal Behavior

Karolina Krysinska[1,*], Karl Andriessen[2], David Lester[3], Michele Battuello[4] and Maurizio Pompili[4,5]

[1]*Faculty of Psychology and Educational Sciences, KU Leuven, University of Leuven, Belgium;* [2]*Parenting and Special Education, Faculty of Psychology and Educational Sciences, University of Leuven, Belgium;* [3]*The Richard Stockton College of New Jersey, USA;* [4]*Department of Neurosciences, Mental Health and Organs Functions, Suicide Prevention Center, Sant'Andrea Hospital, Sapienza University of Rome, Italy and* [5]*McLean Hospital - Harvard Medical School, USA*

Abstract: The present chapter reviews the existing evidence regarding the link between physical activity, active and passive involvement in sports, and suicidal behavior, and presents possible explanations regarding this relationship as well as their application for suicide prevention.

Keywords: Sport, athletes, physical activity, spectators, suicide, body mass index, exercise.

1. INTRODUCTION

Engagement in sport and physical activity, either actively as an athlete or in a passive way as a spectator, is of great importance in many people's lives, across countries and throughout history [1-3]. Many studies have shown that a strong link exists between health status and physical activity, sports activities and level of fitness [4-6], and the perception that involvement in physical activity and sports is a protective factor against stress, depression and other behaviors (notably risk taking and drug use) is spreading among health professionals and policy makers [7, 8]. Participation in physical activity has been associated with positive mood, greater self-esteem and greater physical and psychological well-being. Therefore, physical activity has been suggested as a potential protective agent that may reduce the prevalence of mental health disorders and suicidal behaviors among adults and adolescents [9, 10], and this has led some professionals to build prevention programs based on the promotion of sport activities [7, 11, 12].

Several mechanisms have been hypothesized to account for this link. Biochemical mechanisms, involving the release of endorphins and increased serotonin and norepinephrine synthesis, have been suggested. Another hypothesis is that exercise reduces emotional strain and serves as a buffer against stressful events. In addition, participation in regular physical exercise programs may convey a sense of mastery and increased self-esteem. Participation in sport and exercise group may also provide social interaction and promote social support [13]. However, in recent years, studies have focused also on the possibility that physical activity may be not only a protective factor for mental disorder and suicide risk, but also that it could be a risk factor. In fact, elevated physical activity is characteristic for bipolar patients who carry a high risk of suicide [14, 15].

There has also been research on the impact of sport events on spectators, that is, individuals who witness a sports event in person or *via* the media [16]. Attending sports events or watching them on television can impact individual functioning on many levels, including interpersonal behavior (*e.g.*, violence) and physical and mental health. Sports-related violence usually refers to aggression and riots by sports fans, and includes soccer hooliganism [16], but watching sports events might also increase the risk of domestic violence against women by legitimizing and reinforcing violent behavior [17]. Some major sports events, such as international championships and Olympic Games have been found to change patterns of mortality from coronary heart disease and stroke [18] and to have an impact on the number of presentations to Accident

***Address correspondence to Karolina Krysinska:** Faculty of Psychology and Educational Sciences, University of Leuven, Tiensestraat 102 - bus 3720, 3000 Leuven, Belgium; E-mail: karolina.krysinska@ppw.kuleuven.be

Maurizio Pompili (Ed)

and Emergency Departments [19, 20]. However, this relationship cannot be generalised to all sports events and all groups of spectators [21, 22].

In regard to mental health and well-being, watching games might increase a sense of belonging, allow for release of tension, induce positive mood [23] and reduce the number of psychiatric presentations [24]. However, the defeat of the favored team may lead to high psychological distress, in some cases reaching clinically significant levels similar to the impact of traumatic events, such as physical threats and natural disasters [25].

The present chapter reviews the existing evidence regarding the link between physical activity, active and passive involvement in sports, and suicidal behavior, and presents possible explanations regarding this relationship as well as their application for suicide prevention.

2. METHOD

This review is based on two MedLine and PsycINFO searches, one from 1980 to 2009, the second from the respective starting years of the databases to 2009. Selection of papers suitable for this review allowed the inclusion only of articles published in English-language peer-reviewed journals and studies that added an original contribution to the literature. The searches were conducted in two steps. In the first step, four search terms (*i.e.*, "sport", "physical activity", suicide* and "mental health") were used to identify studies on active sports engagement and suicidality and each category was cross-referenced with the others using the MeSH method (Medical Subjects Headings).

In the second step, twelve search terms (*i.e.*, "sport*", "mass sport*", "sport event*", "football", "basketball", "soccer", "rugby", "hockey", and "Olympics" in combination with "suicide*", "attempted suicide" and "suicidal behavior*") were applied to search for publications regarding spectatorship involvement and suicidal behavior. The lists of references of the retrieved articles were searched to identify further material.

3. PARTICIPATION IN SPORTS ACTIVITIES AND SUICIDALITY

3.1. The American Youth Risk Behavior Surveys

Many authors have studied the association of physical activity and sports participation in the United States, using the Youth Risk Behavior Surveys (YRBS). These results are summarised in Table **1**.

Table 1: Studies on the association between physical activity, sports participation and suicidality based on the Youth Risk Behavior Survey in the US [4, 26-31]

Author	Year	N°	Activity	M	F
Unger	*1997*	*10.506*	*1 or plus per week* *6/7 per week*	*Low SI* *High AS (PA+Team)*	*High SI* *Low AS*
Page	*1998*	*10.506*	*Team*	*Low AS*	*Low AS*
Pate	*2000*	*14.221*	*Team*	*Low SI* *High IS (African American)*	*Low SI+AS (only white females)*
Sabo	*2002, 2005*	*14.221*	*Team*	*Low SI*	*Low SI*
Brown	*2002*	*10.530*	*PA+Team*	*Low SI*	*Low AS*
Taliaferro	*2008*	*13.857*	*6/7 per week* *½ per week*	*Low SI+AS*	*Not signif* *Increase H*

Notes: Team: Team Sports Participation; SI: suicidal ideation; AS: suicide attempt; PA: physical activity; H: hopelessness.

It can be seen that the protective impact of physical activity and sports participation is more consistent for boys than for girls, and the associations are more often statistically significant for suicidal ideation than for attempted suicide. There appear to be differences by ethnicity (the protective impact may be absent for

African American youths), and the use of multiple regression analysis to control for other variables typically eliminates the statistical significance.

3.2. Other Research

Worldwide, many other studies, found similar results to the ones conducted using the YRBS data. These are shown in Table **2**.

Table 2: Other studies on the association between physical activity, sports participation and suicidality [7, 10, 32-37]

Author	Year	Country	N°	Activity	M	F
Adams	*2007*	*US*	*47.755*	*6/7 per week*	-	*Low SI*
Brosnahan	*2004*	*Texas (US)*	*1.870*	*6/7 per week*	*Low SI*	*Low SI*
Oler	*1994*	*Kentucky (US)*	*10.530*	*Team*	*Low SI*	*Low SI+AS*
Ferron	*1999*	*Switzerland*	*9.628*	*2 or plus per week*	*Low AS*	*Low AS*
Taylor	*2007*	*Australia*	*5.037*	*PA*	*Low SI*	*Low SI*
Tao	*2007*	*China*	*5.433*	*1 or less per week*	*High SI*	*High SI*
Tomori	*2000*	*Slovenia*	*4.504*	*PA + Team*	*Low AS*	*Low AS*
Baumert	*1998*	*Georgia (US)*	*7.179*	*PA*	*Low H*	*Low H*

Notes: Team: Team Sports Participation; SI: suicidal ideation; AS: suicide attempt; PA: physical activity; H: hopelessness.

The majority of these studies indicate that participation in physical activity and sports is associated with lower suicidality. In contrast to the results of most of the research reviewed above, Choquet *et al.* [38] surveyed adolescents aged 15-18 in France and in Quebec, Canada, and found no link between suicidal ideation (in the prior year in France and in the prior week in Quebec) and engaging in sports activities.

3.3. Studies of Adults

Simon *et al.* [39] studied individuals, aged 13 to 34, who made a nearly lethal suicide attempt in Houston (Texas), comparing them with random controls from the same area. Making a suicide attempt was associated with being male, 13-18 years of age, Hispanic, and depressed, hopeless, alcoholic and medically ill. Engaging in physical activity in the past month was negatively associated with making a nearly lethal suicide attempt, but the intensity of the physical activity or frequency did not play a significant role. In this sample, body mass index (BMI) was not associated with attempting suicide. The fact that this study used normal controls in the community, rather than depressed but non-suicidal individuals as controls introduces depression as a confounding variable.

Brown and Blanton [30] analysed data from the 1995 National College Health Risk Behavior Survey of 4, 838 college students. The frequency of suicidality (ideation, planning and attempts) in the past year was similar in men and women, less common in those over the age of 25, in white students, those who never smoked, those who did not engage in heavy alcohol use in the past 30 days, those who had never used drugs in their lifetime, and those with lower BMI and perceived weight. For men, suicidality was least in those with low physical activity (*versus* none or heavy physical activity). For women, suicidality was less in those who did not engage in physical activity. However, both men and women who participated in sports had less suicidality than those who did not participate.

Paffenbarger *et al.* [40] studied 21, 569 male alumni from Harvard University, followed-up for 23-27 years. The found no association between regular physical activity during adulthood (including how far walked daily, number of stairs climbed daily, and types and frequencies of sports or recreational participation in hours per week) and their rate of completed suicide. Rates of depression were, however, lower in those who were physically active or sports players. In an earlier study, however, Paffenbarger and Asnes [41] followed up 40, 000 former male students at Harvard University and found that those who subsequently completed suicide as adults (at least at Harvard University) were less often varsity athletes than randomly chosen control students. This was especially so for those who killed themselves before the age of 35. The suicides did not differ in choice of sport or amount of participation.

3.4. Body Mass Index

Since body mass index (BMI) is associated with engaging in physical activity [42], research relating BMI to suicidality is relevant here. Mukamal *et al.* [43] follow-up 46, 735 male health professional (doctors, dentists, *etc.*) from 1986 on and found that those who died from suicide had lower BMI scores than those who did not die from suicide. Those with BMI scores less than 21 had a suicide rate of 52 per 100, 000 person-years as compared to a rate of 21 for those with BMI scores of 30 of higher. Height and physical activity were not associated with the risk of dying from suicide.

On the other hand, Stack and Lester [44] examined mortality data for 18, 733 American adults over the age of 25. Comparing death from suicide with accidental deaths from motor vehicle accidents, they found no differences in BMI scores after controlling for ethnicity and other covariates (such as living alone and alcohol abuse).

Eaton *et al.* [45] looked at data from the 2001 YRBS. They found that perceiving oneself as very overweight and the BMI were both associated with suicidal ideation and with attempting suicide in the prior year. The associations with attempting suicide were significant for white youths, African American youths and, for being overweight, for Hispanic youths. Interestingly perceiving oneself as very underweight was also associated with prior suicidal ideation and attempting suicide. In multiple regressions, perceived weight was more important in predicting suicidality than was the BMI.

Brunner *et al.* [46] examined the association of high cholesterol, triglycerides and body-mass index in a community sample of German adults. A history of attempted suicide in the past year in depressed adults was associated with these three indices after controls for age and sex.

4. SPECTATORS' INVOLVEMENT IN SPORTS AND SUICIDE

A systematic review of the literature published in English in peer-reviewed journals on the impact of sport events on suicidal behavior [1] identified nine studies published between 1986 and 2009 on the relationship between sports events and suicidal behavior. Four of these studies focused on suicide and homicide as an outcome [47-50], three on completed suicide [51-53], and two on suicide attempts [54, 55]. The sports events were related to American football (the Superbowl), baseball, soccer, hockey, and basketball. A study on the impact of geographical relocation of teams [48] and a study on strikes of professional teams [49] were also included in the review. Details of the studies and the results are presented in Table **3**.

In summary, the current evidence, based on data on national or local suicide rates, shows that sport events can have an impact on suicide mortality and morbidity. This relationship seems to be mediated by age, gender, marital status and alcohol consumption, as well as the process and outcome of the game, such as victory *versus* defeat of the favoured team. The possible explanations regarding the relationship between sports spectatorship and fatal and non-fatal suicidal behavior are presented in the next part of the chapter.

Table 3: Sports events and fatal and non-fatal suicidal behavior [47-60]

Study	Country	Sport Event	Time Range	Background Theory	Type of Study	Outcome Focus	Results
Curtis, Loy & Karnilowicz (1986)	US	Super Bowl Sunday (football) and last game of World Series (baseball)	1972-1978	Theory of social integration (Durkheim, 1897) and theory of religion and ceremonies (Durkheim, 1912/1965)	Quasi-experimental comparison of observed *versus* expected suicide frequencies around sports events	Suicide	No significant decrease in suicide

Table 3: cont….

Lester (1988)	US	Super Bowl Sunday (football) and last game of World Series (baseball)	1972-1984	Not specified	Comparison of observed *versus* expected suicide frequencies around sports events	Suicide (and homicide)	No significant decrease in suicide (and homicide)
Masterton & Strachan (1987)	Scotland (UK)	World Cup Soccer	1974, 1978, 1982, 1986	Not specified	Comparison of number of hospital admissions for deliberate self-harm before, during and after sport events and during control years	Non-fatal suicidal behavior	Significant reduction in deliberate self-harm hospital admissions
Steels (1994)	England (UK)	Soccer Cup Final	1991, 1992	Sudden disappointment, otherwise not specified	Comparison of number of hospital admissions for deliberate self-harm before, during and after sport events	Non-fatal suicidal behavior	Significant increase in deliberate self-harm hospital admissions after team defeat in 1991 and a non-significant increase after a less important team defeat in 1992
Trovato (1998)	Canada (Quebec)	Hockey Stanley Cup	1951-1992	Theory of social integration (Durkheim, 1897) and routine activities theory (Cohen & Felson, 1979)	Time trends analysis and comparison of incidence of suicide before and after a playoff game	Suicide	No significant impact of sport events on overall suicide rates and mixed findings regarding incidence of suicide in different age, gender and marital status groups during the sport event
Fernquist (2000)	US (30 metropolitan areas)	Baseball, basketball, football, and hockey	1971-1990	Broken promise effect (Gabennesch, 1988), anomie (Durkheim, 1897), and theory of religion and ceremonies (Durkheim, 1912/1965)	Comparison of suicide and homicide rates when sports teams reach playoffs and win championship	Suicide (and homicide)	Significant inverse relation between championship status and suicide rates, and inverse relation between suicide (and homicide) rates and playoff status
Fernquist (2001)	US (3 areas)	Baseball, and football	1957, 1995-1996 and 1997-1998	Broken promise effect (Gabennesch, 1988) and anomie (Durkheim, 1897),	Comparison of suicide and homicide rates before, during, and after geographical relocation of sports teams	Suicide (and homicide)	A significant impact of geographical relocation of teams on suicide rates (no impact on homicide rates)

Table 3: cont….

Fernquist (2002)	US	Baseball and hockey	1993-1996	Broken promise effect (Gabennesch, 1988) and theory of religion and ceremonies (Durkheim, 1912/1965)	Comparison of suicide and homicide rates before, during and after strikes of professional sports teams	Suicide (and homicide)	No significant impact of professional teams strikes on suicide rates (and significant impact on homicide rates)
Joiner, Hollar & Van Orden (2006)	US	College football (Study 1), Olympic hockey "Miracle on ice" (22 February 1980; Study 2) and Super Bowl Sunday (football; Study 3)	1990-2000 (Study 1), 1972-1989 (Study 2) and 1984-1994 (Study 3)	Interpersonal-psychological theory of suicide (Joiner, 2005)	Comparison of ranking of county college teams and county suicide rates (Study 1), comparison of number of suicides on 22 February 1980 and any other February 22 between 1972 and1989 (Study 2) and comparison of number of suicides on Super Bowl Sundays and other Sundays (Study 3)	Suicide	Significant correlation between college team ranking and county suicide rates (Study 1), significantly reduction in suicide on 22 February 1980 (Study 2), and significant reduction in suicide on Super Bowl Sundays (Study 3)

5. POSSIBLE LINKS BETWEEN PARTICIPATION IN SPORTS ACTIVITIES AND SUICIDALITY

5.1. Depression and Hopelessness

As Ferron *et al.* [7] and other researchers have pointed out, all of these studies were correlational in nature and, therefore, do not show cause and effect. It may be that participation in physical activity and sports results in a reduction of depression and suicidality. However, it may be that depressed and suicidal youths are less likely to become involved in physical activity and sports. No studies were found which employed an experimental design to distinguish between these alternatives.

Huang *et al.* [61] did assign 657 American adolescents randomly to a one-year behavioral program that targeted physical activity, sendentary behavior and dietary behaviors. Although the researchers did not study the impact on suicidality, they found no impact of the program on self-esteem or body dissatisfaction. This is type of study that is required for studying the impact on physical activity on suicidality.

Similarly, although they did not study suicidality, Sagatun *et al.* [13] studied 3,811 Norwegian 10th graders for the association between weekly hours of physical activity and general mental health. They followed-up these same students two years later. This type of study could be used to focus on changes in physical activity over time and changes in suicidality.

Most of the studies reviewed above failed to control for depression. Brown *et al.* [30] in their study noted that the association of suicidality with physical activity and participation in sports with was no longer significant for girls after controlling for feeling sad or hopeless, while the association remained statistically significant for boys.

A study by Simantov *et al.* [62] of 5,513 American youths suggests other important mediating factors. Although they did not study suicidality, Simantov *et al.* found that smoking and drinking among adolescents aged 10 to 17 was associated with a history of physical and sexual abuse, family violence and stressful live events. Although this study was correlational in nature, it suggests the hypothesis that abusive and stressful childhoods may increase the probability of later depression and suicidality and, perhaps less involvement in sports and physical activity (which are often social in nature).

Chioqueta and Stiles [63] compared Norwegian military conscripts who engaged in sports and those who did not. Those who engaged in sports had significantly lower hopelessness scores on the Beck Hopelessness Scale, but not on dysfunctional attitudes, automatic thoughts associated with depression or depression scale scores. In a two-way analysis, a lack of engagement in sports and a high score of the automatic thoughts questionnaire resulted in the highest hopelessness scores. Since hopelessness is one of the strongest correlates and predictors of suicidality, this study suggests that hopelessness and irrational thinking may be mediating variables in the association between sports participation and suicidality.

5.2. Weight and BMI

Engaging in sports and physical activities has an impact on weight. Indeed, one of the major life style changes recommended to help people lose weight is to engage in physical activity. Physical activity will, therefore, lead to reduced weight (and BMI) and associated changes such as a lower cholesterol level which has been found to be associated with suicidality [64]. Lester [64] noted that one possible mediating pathway between cholesterol level and suicidality is that serum cholesterol levels are associated with central nervous system cholesterol levels which have been thought to affect the serotonergic system [65]. Others have suggested that cholesterol levels impact the level of depression which in turn impacts suicidality [66].

Brunner *et al.* [46] suggested that maladaptive nutritional behavior may lead to a high BMI and high levels of cholesterol and triglycerides. This could result in weight gain, and obesity itself has been linked to suicidality [67]. At the other extreme, those with eating disorders such as anorexia and bulimia have a high rate of suicide [67] and also have inadequate nutritional intake. The role of weight and the appearance of the body may have a large impact simply through the effect on body-image, self-esteem and depression levels. It may also help individuals cope with stress. Future research on the association between physical activity and suicidality should control for the role of depression, self-esteem, and other variables discussed here.

5.3. Social Interaction

There is a great difference between engaging in physical activity *per se*, and engaging in team sports. Team sports involve social interaction with other team members, and team athletes often engage in maladaptive behaviors such as excessive alcohol use and other risky behaviors such as sexual activity. Indeed, Page *et al.* [27], reviewed above, found an increase in sex without condoms in those participating in team sports. Running, which is often a solitary activity, may have a different impact on depression and suicidality than working out in gym where others are present. On the positive side, engaging in team sports provides a social network and a culturally-determined script (or role) which should increase the level of social integration and social regulation, important protective factors according to Durkheim's [56] theory of suicide.

Sabo *et al.* [29] also noted that sports participation provides status gains in the community and greater educational and labor market success as an adult. These impacts may, however, differ by class, gender and race/ethnicity. Among African Americans, for example, sports participation was sometimes viewed as an alternative to achievements in the educational and business world.

6. POSSIBLE LINKS BETWEEN SPORTS SPECTATORSHIP AND SUICIDAL BEHAVIOR

6.1. Social Rituals, Integration and Anomie

Certain links between sports events and suicidal behavior have been suggested by Durkheim's theories of suicide, rituals, ceremonies and religion [56, 57, 68, 69]. Fernquist [48] applied the notion of anomie associated with sudden changes in social environment to the sport-suicide relationship in the context of the geographical relocation of professional sports teams. He suggested that such a change can lead to anomie and heightened risk of suicide among fans deeply identified with the team who are bereaved by the relocation and no longer can support the team in their area. His study of suicide rates in geographical areas affected by such moves supported this hypothesis [48].

Studies of suicide rates around major social events and ceremonies, such as presidential elections, national holidays, and religious holidays showed a so-called "death dip", *i.e.*, lower suicide and overall mortality rates in these periods [70-72]. Such drops have also been found in regard to rates of attempted suicide [73, 74]. Surprisingly, such "death dips" have not been found consistently around major sports events: Curtis *et al.* [51] and Lester [50] did not find significant drops in suicide numbers on sport-related occasions, albeit in the former study the death dip was observed around national holidays (July 4th and Thanksgiving Day). The absence of a death dip around sport events, in contrast to other social ceremonies, such as national holidays, could be explained in several ways. It is possible that sports event have smaller integrative effects than national holidays, either in the intensity of social integration or in its scope (*i.e.*, the actual numbers of people who participate in the event), and thus have less impact on suicide [51]. Also, public holidays involve people in a direct and physical manner, including parties and gift-giving, while involvement in sports events often has a vicarious character. Events are watched on television or followed *via* other mass media. Public holidays involve face-to-face interpersonal interaction usually concentrated on one particular day, while sports spectatorship is more impersonal (focused on the game), and its impact may be smaller if it involves a series of games spread across time. In addition, public holidays are observed by practically everyone, while sports events usually engage only certain groups, such as young males. Consequently, sports events could have an impact on suicide only in certain subpopulations. Although the aggregated data that Curtis *et al.* [51] used in their study of suicide rates around the last day of the American baseball World Series, the American football Superbowl Sunday, July 4th and Thanksgiving Day did not allow testing this hypothesis, the results of Trovato's [53] study on suicide during the Stanley Cup for Hockey in Quebec seem to support this assumption.

6.2. The Broken Promise Effect

Failures of teams, particularly if repeated and in relation to important outcomes (*e.g.*, not winning a championship *versus* not making the playoffs), might constitute a "broken promise" [59] leading to dysphoric and suicidal moods in individuals deeply identifying with the teams. According to the original formulation of the broken promise effect, "an event which generally induces positive anticipation may itself cause the suicidal individual's outlook to worsen by virtue of the unfavorable contrast between raised expectancy and stubborn reality (...). A dysphoric mood is the result of the negative discrepancy between how one feels and how one expects (hopes) to feel" [59] (p. 138).

An analysis of suicide (and homicide) rates after strikes in sports [49] and geographical relocation of professional teams [48] showed a complex picture of the broken promise effect in sports. Apparently, the source of the disappointment should be taken into consideration. If external, such as cancellation of the game related to a strike, it might result in negative emotions, including anger, being turned outward and leading to externalized aggression (*i.e.*, homicide) instead of suicide. In contrast, loss of the team due to its geographical relocation, might lead to feelings of loss and grief in faithful fans, and thus be seen as a "broken promise" and increase suicidality.

6.3. Routine Activities Theory

According to the routine activities theory, people who share similar social backgrounds tend to share interests and lifestyles and participate together in social activities [53, 58]. Watching sports on television with friends and significant others might discourage or impede people from considering suicide and prevent them from taking action. Also, the proximity of others increases the chances of being found and rescued in case of a suicide attempt. An early defeat of the favored team might result in "an earlier than usual disbandment of the socially integrative context (p. 119)" [53] and thus in increased risk of suicidality. Results of Trovato's [53] study supported this hypothesis. Early elimination of the local hockey team from the Stanley Cup was associated with increased suicide rates among young single males.

6.4. The Interpersonal-Psychological Theory of Suicide

The interpersonal-psychological theory of serious suicidal behavior identifies the need to belong as one of the core human needs [60]. The fulfilment of the need to belong is a powerful protective factor against suicide. However, its frustration caused by lack of meaningful social relationships, social isolation or a lack of connectedness, might increase the risk of suicide. Being a sports fan creates camaraderie, gives a sense of belongingness and a feeling of being cared for, and such sports-related "pulling together" might protect against suicide. Sports events also bring people together and, especially under condition of success of the favored team, increase positive interpersonal interactions, including positive face-to-face social contact, and all this may lower the individual risk of suicide and decrease suicide rates on local and national levels [60]. Results of Joiner *et al.*'s [52] studies presented earlier in this chapter support this theory.

6.5. Other Possible Links

Media reports of suicide cases are linked to "copycat" (imitative) suicides [75], and it has been hypothesised that major sport events shift the media focus to sport outcomes and related news instead of reporting negative events, such as suicides, and thus lead to a decreased incidence of "copycat" suicides [51]. Watching sports events can provide distraction from personal problems and decrease the levels of negative interpersonal interactions, for example, in couples living together, thus preventing conflicts leading to suicidal ideation and behavior. According to Masterton and Strachan [54], the media have suggested that the decreased level of interpersonal contact in couples and disruption of family life might increase the risk of suicide among female partners of sport fans (the so-called "football widows"), but the results of their study did not support this suggestion. Losing at gambling on sports could also be a risk factor for suicide, but it is not certain whether this could cause a measurable and significant effect [51].

In addition, referring to the soccer "tartan army", Masterton and Stachan [54] suggested that the climate of "patriotism as during war" (p. 368) could have a preventive effect against suicide. However, this suggestion necessitates some caution as recent literature on the effect of war on suicide rates presents a mixed picture and, specifically in Scotland, the suicide rate of young males increased dramatically during the 2nd World War [76].

7. SPORT AND SUICIDE PREVENTION

Adams *et al.* [32] noted that exercise is relatively inexpensive and has few bad side-effects, unlike some pharmacological treatment for depression and other psychiatric disorders. In addition, exercise has positive effects on medical health such as improved coronary functioning and reducing obesity. Encouragement of active engagement in sports has already become a component of some suicide prevention programs for adolescents and young adults [77], prisoners [78] and Indigenous communities in Australia with a high risk of suicide [11]. For example, the "Sports Challenge" program for "at risk" children and adolescents showing signs of low self-esteem and a low sense of basic trust has been operating in Australia since 1992 and in Singapore since 1996 [77]. The program is addressed to children and young people in community groups, schools and detention centers and aims to improve their self-esteem and reduce the risk of engaging in harmful behaviors by teaching them preparation-for-life skills such as stress management and realistic goal setting through engagement in sports (*e.g.*, basketball).

Interest in sports as a spectator can also become a vehicle for mental health promotion and suicide prevention programs. One of such programs is a "It's a Goal!", a community-based project in the UK run in collaboration between local health authorities and the soccer team Macclesfield Town [12]. This program aims to help men to address issues related to self-esteem, depression and inclusion through group interventions and using football as a metaphor. The program's initial evaluation shows that "the power of football as a both motive and method for engaging this group (*i.e.*, young males) is evident even in these early stages of the project, and it may well be that the experience at Macclesfield Town can be developed not only by other football clubs but also by other sports such as rugby and cricket where young men make up a large proportion of the attendance (p. 238)" [12].

Similar initiatives have been developed in other counties. In Scotland, the National Strategy and Action Plan to Prevent Suicide [79] issued a special suicide prevention postcard. The front side of the card shows a discarded football shirt with the slogan "There is no substitute for life" while its back contains information on suicide warning signs, helpline telephone numbers and basic advice on how to help a person in a crisis. In Belgium, the Flemish Working Group on Suicide Survivors [80] established the Sports Division which supports an indoor soccer team and participates in sports events aiming to increase public awareness of suicide prevention and support for people bereaved by suicide.

DISCUSSION AND CONCLUSIONS

Despite some inconsistencies in the results both in regards to physical activity and active sports engagement and sport spectatorship, this review has indicated that physical activity and sports participation as well as sports spectatorship may have a beneficial impact on suicidality, at least in certain age and gender groups (especially boys and young men) and in some ethnic groups. In regards to sport spectatorship, characteristics of the sport event and its outcome, as well as excessive use of alcohol during or after the game should be taken into consideration as mediating factors for suicidal behavior.

It is not clear; however, whether physical activity acts directly on suicidality or through a mediating variable such as depression or self-esteem. The majority of the studies reviewed here were of adolescents and young adults. It would of interest in future research to explore whether the same associations are found for older adults and the elderly. It would also be of interest in future research to distinguish between physical activity that is engaged alone and that which is carried out in groups. Playing soccer is very different with regard to social interaction with others than jogging or running by oneself. Is it the social interaction in sports or the physical activity itself which may be beneficial for alleviating depression and suicidality? There has also been no research of whether all team sports have a similar impact on mental health and suicidal behavior or on which kinds of physical activity has the most impact. Are there differences, for example, between participation in soccer *versus* track and field, jogging *versus* weight-training, or anaerobic exercise *versus* strength-toning?

In regards to sports spectatorship, the studies reviewed focused on the impact of sports event at the societal level and analysed data regarding national or local suicide rates. Although practically all the authors hypothesised how involvement in sports may affect individuals, particularly Joiner *et al.* [52], there is a lack of studies using individual, case-based data regarding the relationship between sport spectatorship and suicide risk on individual level. Consequently, it is practically impossible to show that suicides or suicide attempts recorded at the time of sport events were related to the games and their results, and whether the victims were interested or even aware of the events. Studies in sport psychology show that sport spectators are not a homogenous group, and there are significant differences in levels of sport involvement [81], types of motivation for attendance at sport events [82], identification with the sport team [83, 84] and other psychological factors which could mediate the relationship between interest in sport, mental well-being and suicide risk. It is also possible that even die-hard fans suffering from depression and in suicidal crisis lose their interest in sports as much as in other aspects of their lives [85] and are not affected by successes and failures of "their teams." Our current knowledge in this area is quite limited, or even non-existent, and may lead to the ecological fallacy [86], that is, a logical error in the interpretation of statistical data in which conclusions about an individual are based upon aggregate statistics obtained from the group to which this individual belongs.

Integration of ecological studies, individual case studies, psychological studies and psychological autopsies might increase our knowledge regarding causal relationships sensitive for gender and age, thus providing clues for prevention. In addition, multi-center studies on epidemiology of attempted suicide and psychological studies of individuals who engage in non-fatal suicidal behavior could provide information regarding non-fatal suicidal behavior among sports fans and spectators.

REFERENCES

[1] Andriessen K, Krysinska K. Can sport events affect suicidal behavior? A review of the literature and implications for prevention. Crisis 2009; 30: 144-52.

[2] Lester D, Battuello M, Innamorati M, *et al.* Partecipation in sport activities and suicide prevention. Int J Sport Psychol; 2010; 41: 58-72.

[3] Weber E. Gymnastics and sports in fin-de-siècle France: Opium for the classes? Am Hist Rev 1971; 76: 70-98.

[4] Pate RR, Trost SG, Levin S, Dowda M. Sports participation and health-related behaviors among US youth. Arch Pediatr Adolesc Med 2000; 154: 904-11.

[5] Steptoe A, Butler N. Sports participation and emotional wellbeing in adolescents. Lancet 1996; 347:1789 –92.

[6] Warburton DER, Nicol CW, Bredin SSD. Health benefits of physical activity: The evidence. Can Med Assoc J 2006; 174: 801–9.

[7] Ferron C, Narring F, Cauderay M, Michaud PA. Sport activity in adolescence: Associations with health perceptions and experimental behaviors. Health Educ Res 1999; 14: 225-33.

[8] Street G, James R, Cutt H. The relationship between organised physical recreation and mental health. Health Promot J Austr 2007; 18: 236-9.

[9] Babiss LA, Gangwisch JE. Sports participation as a protective factor against depression and suicidal ideation in adolescents as mediated by self-esteem and social support. J Dev Behav Pediatr 2009; 30: 376-84.

[10] Brosnahan J, Steffen LM, Lytle L, Patterson J, Boostrom A. The relation between physical activity and mental health among Hispanic and non-Hispanic white adolescents. Arch Pediatr Adolesc Med 2004; 158: 818-23.

[11] Cunningham J, Beneforti M. Investigating indicators for measuring the health and social impact of sport and recreation programs in Australian Indigenous communities. Int Rev Sociol Sport 2005; 40: 89-8.

[12] Pringle A, Sayers P. It's a Goal!: Basing a community psychiatric nursing service in a local football stadium. J R Soc Promot Health 2004; 124: 234-8.

[13] Sagatun A, Sogaard A J, Bjertness E, Selmer R, Heyerdahl S. The association between weekly hours of physical activity and mental health: A three-year follow-up study of 15-16-year-old students in the city of Oslo, Norway. BMC Public Health 2007; 7: 155.

[14] Pompili M, Rihmer Z, Innamorati M, Lester D, Girardi P, Tatarelli R. Assessment and treatment of suicide risk in bipolar disorders. Expert Rev Neurother 2009; 9: 109-36.

[15] Rihmer Z. Prediction and prevention of suicide In bipolar disorders. Clin Neuropsychiatry 2005; 2: 48-54.

[16] Wann DL, Melnick MJ, Russell GW, Pease DG. Sport fans: The psychology and social impact of spectators. New York: Routlegde, 2001.

[17] White GF, Katz J, Scarborough KE. The impact of professional football games upon violent assaults on women. Violence Vict 1992; 7: 157-71.

[18] Witte DR, Bots ML, Hoes AW, Grobbee DE. Cardiovascular mortality in Dutch men during 1996 European football championship: Longitudinal population study. Br Med J 2000; 321: 1552-4.

[19] Jorm LR, Thackway SV, Churches TR, Hills MW. Watching the games: Public health surveyance for the Sydney 2000 Olympic Games. J Epidemiol Community Health 2003; 57: 102-8.

[20] Moody WE, Hendry RG, Muscatello D. Were attendances to accident and emergency departments in England and Australia influenced by the Rugby World Cup Final 2003? Eur J Emerg Med 2007; 14: 68-71.

[21] O'Donnell JJ. The Football World Cup 2002: Analysis of related attendances to an Irish Emergency Department. Ir Med J 2003; 96: 90-1.

[22] Toubiana L, Hanslik T, Letrilliart L. French cardiovascular mortality did not increase during 1996 European football championship. Br Med J 2001; 322: 1306.

[23] Pringle A. Can watching football be a component of developing a state of mental health for men? J R Soc Promot Health 2004; 124: 122-8.

[24] Masterton G, Mander AJ. Psychiatric emergencies and the World Cup Finals. Br J Psychiatry 1990; 156: 475-8.

[25] Banyard P, Shevlin M. Responses of football fans to relegation of their team from the English Premier League: PTS? Ir J Psychol Med 2001; 18: 66-7.

[26] Unger JB. Physical activity, participation in team sports, and risk of suicidal behavior in adolescents. Am J Health Promot 1997; 12: 90-3.

[27] Page RM, Hammermeister J, Scanlan A and Gilbert L. Is school sports participation a protective factor against adolescent health risk behaviors? J Health Educ 1998; 29: 186-92.

[28] Sabo D, Miller KE, Melnick MJ, Farrell MP, Barnes GM. Athletic participation and the health risks of adolescent males. Int J Men Health 2002; 1: 173-94.

[29] Sabo D, Miller KE, Melnick MJ, Farrell MP, Barnes GM. High school athlete participation and adolescent suicide. Int Rev Sociol Sport 2005; 40: 5-23.

[30] Brown DR, Blanton C J. Physical activity, sports participation, and suicidal behavior among college students. Med Sci Sports Exerc 2002; 34: 1087-96.

[31] Taliaferro LA, Rienzo BA, Miller MD, Pigg RM Jr, Dodd V J. High school youth and suicide risk: exploring protection afforded through physical activity and sport participation. J Sch Health 2008; 78: 545-53.

[32] Adams TB, Moore MT, Dye J. The relationship between physical activity and mental health in a national sample of college females. Women Health 2007; 45: 69-85.

[33] Oler MJ, Mainous AG 3rd, Martin CA, Richardson E, Haney A, Wilson D. Depression, suicidal ideation, and substance use among adolescents. Are athletes at less risk? Arch Fam Med 1994; 3: 781-5.

[34] Taylor A, Dal Grande E, Gill T, Fisher L, Goldney R. Detecting determinants of suicidal ideation: South Australian surveillance system results. Int J Public Health 2007; 52: 142-52.

[35] Tao FB, Xu ML, Kim SD, Sun Y, Su PY, Huang K. Physical activity might not be the protective factor for health risk behaviors and psychopathological symptoms in adolescents. J Paediatr Child Health 2007; 43: 762-7.

[36] Tomori M and Zalar B. Sport and physical activity as possible protective factors in relation to adolescent suicide attempts. Int J Sport Psychol 2000; 31(3): 405-13.

[37] Baumert PW Jr, Henderson JM, Thompson NJ. Health risk behaviors of adolescent participants in organized sports. J Adolesc Health 1998; 22: 460-5.

[38] Choquet M, Kovess V, Poutignat N. Suicidal thoughts among adolescents: an intercultural approach. Adolescence 1993; 28(111): 649-59.

[39] Simon TR, Powell KE, Swann AC. Involvement in physical activity and risk for nearly lethal suicide attempts. Am J Prev Med 2004; 27(4): 310-15.

[40] Paffenbarger RS Jr, Lee IM, Leung R. Physical activity and personal characteristics associated with depression and suicide in American college men. Acta Psychiatr Scand 1994; 377: 16-22.

[41] Paffenbarger RS, Jr, Asnes DP. Chronic disease in former college students. 3. Precursors of suicide in early and middle life. Am J Public Health Nations Health 1966; 56: 1026-36.

[42] Levin S, Lowry R, Brown DR, Dietz WH. Physical activity and body mass index among US adolescents: youth risk behavior survey 1999. Arch Pediatr Adolesc Med 2003; 157: 816-20.

[43] Mukamal KJ, Kawachi I, Miller M, Rimm EB. Body mass index and risk of suicide among men. Arch Intern Med 2007; 167: 468-75.

[44] Stack S, Lester D. Body mass and suicide risk. Crisis 2007; 28: 46-7.

[45] Eaton DK, Lowry R, Brener ND, Galuska DA, Crosby AE. Associations of body mass index and perceived weight with suicide ideation and suicide attempts among US high school students. Arch Pediatr Adolesc Med 2005; 159: 513-9.

[46] Brunner J, Bronisch T, Pfister H, Jacobi F, Hofler M, Wittchen HU. High cholesterol, triglycerides, and body-mass index in suicide attempters. Arch Suicide Res 2006; 10: 1-9.

[47] Fernquist RM. An aggregate analysis of professional sports, suicide and homicide rates: 30 U.S. metropolitan areas. Aggress Violent Behav 2000; 5: 329-41.

[48] Fernquist RM. Geographical relocation, suicide and homicide: An exploratory analysis of the geographic relocation of professional sports teams in three U.S. areas and the impact on suicide and homicide rates. Soc Sport Online, 2001, 4. Retrieved November 21, 2009. Available from: http://physed.otago.ac.nz/sosol/v4i2/v4i2Fernquist.htm.

[49] Fernquist RM. The 1994-1995 baseball and hockey strikes and their impact on suicide and homicide rates in the United States. Arch Suicide Res 2002; 6: 103-10.

[50] Lester D. Suicide and homicide during major sports events 1972-1984: Comment on Curtis, Loy, and Karnilowicz. Sociol Sport J 1988; 5: 285.

[51] Curtis J, Loy J, Karnilowicz W. A comparison of suicide –dip effects of major sport events and civil holidays. Sociol Sport J 1986; 3: 1-14.

[52] Joiner TE, Hollar D, van Orden K. On Buckeyes, Gators, Super Bowl Sunday, and the Miracle on Ice: "Pulling together" is associated with lower suicide rates. J Soc Clin Psychol 2006; 25: 179-95.

[53] Trovato F. The Stanley Cup of Hockey and suicide in Quebec, 1951-1992. Soc Forces 1998; 77: 105-27.

[54] Masterton G, Strachan JA. Parasuicide, Scotland, and the World Cup. Br Med J 1987; 295: 368.

[55] Steels MD. Deliberate self-poisoning: Nottingham Forest Football Club and F.A. Cup defeat. Ir J Psychol Med 1994; 11: 76-8.

[56] Durkheim É. Le Suicide. Étude de Sociologie. Paris: Presses Universitaires de France, 1897.

[57] Durkheim É. The Elementary Forms of the Religious Life [Transl. by J.W. Swain. Orig.: Les Formes Élémentaires de la vie religieuse: Le système totémique en Australie. Paris, 1912]. New York: Free Press, 1965.

[58] Cohen LE, Felson M. Social change and crime rate trends: A routine activity approach. Am Sociol Rev 1979; 44: 588-608.

[59] Gabennesch H. When promises fail: A theory of temporal fluctuations in suicide. Soc Forces 1988; 67: 129-45.

[60] Joiner T. Why people die by suicide? Cambridge: Harvard University Press, 2005.

[61] Huang JS, Norman GJ, Zabinski MF, Calfas K, Patrick K. Body image and self-esteem among adolescents undergoing an intervention targeting dietary and physical activity behaviors. J Adolesc Health 2007; 40: 245-51.

[62] Simantov E, Schoen C, Klein JD. Health-compromising behaviors: why do adolescents smoke or drink?: identifying underlying risk and protective factors. Arch Pediatr Adolesc Med 2000; 154(10): 1025-33.

[63] Chioqueta AP, Stiles TC. Cognitive factors, engagement in sport, and suicide risk. Arch Suicide Res 2007; 11(4): 375-90.

[64] Lester D. Serum cholesterol levels and suicide: a meta-analysis. Suicide Life Threat Behav 2002; 32: 333-46.

[65] Conroy RM. Low cholesterol and violent death: The evidence, the gaps, the theory and the practical implications. Ir J Psychol Med 1993; 10: 67-70.

[66] Manfredini R, Caracciolo S, Salmi R, Boari B, Tomelli A, Gallerani M. The association of low serum cholesterol with depression and suicidal behaviors: New hypotheses for the missing link. J Int Med Res 2000; 28: 247-57.

[67] Pompili M, Lester D, Grispini A, Calandro F, de Pisa E, Innamorati M. Suicide and attempted suicide in anorexia nervosa, bulimia nervosa, obesity and weight-image concern. In: Tatarelli R, Pompili M and Girardi P, Eds. Suicide in psychiatric disorders. Hauppauge: Nova Science. 2007; pp. 153-79.

[68] Birrell S. Sport as ritual: Interpretations from Durkheim to Goffman. Soc Forces 1981; 60: 354-76.

[69] Pope W, Durkheim E. In: Stones R, Ed. Key sociological thinkers. New York: Palgrave Macmillan. 2008; 76-89.

[70] Boor M. Effects of United States presidential elections on suicide and other causes of death. Am Sociol Rev 1981; 46: 616-8.

[71] Masterton G, Platt S. Parasuicide and general elections. Br Med J 1989; 298: 803-4.

[72] Phillips DP, Feldman KA. A dip in deaths before ceremonial occasions: Some new relationships between social integration and mortality. Am Sociol Rev 1973; 38: 678-96.

[73] Bergen H, Hawton K. Variation in deliberate self-harm around Christmas and New Year. Soc Sci Med 2007; 65: 855-67.

[74] Jessen G, Jensen BF, Arensman E, *et al.* Attempted suicide and major public holidays in Europe: Findings from the WHO/EURO Multicenter Study on Parasuicide. Acta Psychiatr Scand 1999; 99: 412-8.

[75] Westerlund M, Schaller S, Schmidtke A. The role of mass media in suicide prevention. In: Wasserman D, Wasserman C, Eds. Oxford textbook of suicidology and suicide prevention. A global perspective. Oxford: Oxford University Press. 2009; pp. 515-23.

[76] Henderson R, Stark C, Humphry RW, Selvaraj S. Changes in Scottish suicide rates during the Second World War. BMC Public Health 2006; 6: 167.

[77] Tester GJ, Watkins GG, Rouse I. The Sports Challenge International programme for identified "at risk" children and adolescents: A Singapore study. Asia Pac J Public Health 1999; 11: 34-8.

[78] Cooper C, Berwick S. Factors affecting psychological well-being of three groups of suicide-prone prisoners. Curr Psychol 2001; 20: 169-82.

[79] Scottish Government. Choose Life: A National Strategy and Action Plan to Prevent Suicide in Scotland, 2002. Retrieved November 21, 2009. Available from: http://www.chooselife.net/web/FILES/Choose_Life.pdf.

[80] De fauw N, Andriessen K. Networking to support suicide survivors. Crisis 2003; 24: 29-31.

[81] Shank MD, Beasley FM. Fan or fanatic: Refining a measure of sports involvement. J Sport Behav 1998; 21: 435-43.

[82] Bernthal MJ, Graham PJ. The effect of sport setting on fan attendance motivation: The case of minor league *vs.* collegiate baseball. J Sport Behav 2003; 26: 223-39.

[83] Wann DL. Understanding the positive social psychological benefits of sport team identification: The team identification-social psychological health model. Group Dyn 2006a; 10: 272-96.

[84] Wann DL. Examining the potential causal relationship between sport team identification and psychological well-being. J Sport Behav 2006b; 29: 79-95.

[85] Shneidman E. Suicide as Psychache: A clinical approach to self-destructive behavior. Northvale, NJ: Jason Aronson, 1993.

[86] Robinson WS. Ecological correlations and the behavior of individuals. Am Sociol Rev 1950; 15: 351–7.

CHAPTER 19

Cancer and Suicide

Michele Raja*

Private Practice, Via Prisciano 26, 00136 – Rome, Italy

Abstract: The review explores the association between completed suicide and neoplasms. Several studies demonstrated that the risk of suicide in cancer patients is higher than that for the general population. The risk of suicide increases with disease severity; the severity of the cancer increases the suicide risk. The risk is highest shortly after the diagnosis has been made, but for some cancer types, the risk remains increased for more than 5 years after diagnosis. Men have a higher suicide risk than women. Mood disorders, pain, and poor physical functioning are important clinical correlates. Screens for depression and suicide in people with cancer should be done after diagnosis and redone during the first 6 months regularly, particularly in the primary-care setting. More attention to cancer patients' psychological and care situation and public education are needed to decrease the stigma associated with having a cancer diagnosis. Assessment and treatment of depression could improve the prognosis for cancer patients who suffer from unrecognized depressions and in turn reduce their risk of suicide.

Keywords: Suicide, cancer, pain.

1. INTRODUCTION

Suicide is a major public health problem and one of the leading causes of death among adults in the general population. Several suicidal risk factors have been confirmed repeatedly, the most noteworthy being mental disorders and previous suicide attempts. There is a well-established relationship between suicide and mood disorders, and it has been estimated that 50-80% of completed suicides are associated with mood disorders. A range of other clinical and socio-demographic factors have also been associated with both ideation and attempts, including male gender [1], old age [1, 2], Caucasian ethnicity [3, 4], being single, separated, widow or widower [1, 2, 5-8], unemployment [2, 8-10], low socio-economic status [11-14], adverse life events [15, 16], and disability [2, 17].

2. SUICIDE AND MEDICAL ILLNESS

The association between suicide and medical disorders has not received as much attention as the association between suicide and psychiatric disorders. Recently, the relationship between suicidal behaviour and specific illnesses has become the focus of research studies and an increased risk of death from suicide has been observed in several medical illnesses, including cancer, stroke, myocardial infarction, and many neurological illnesses. It is not yet clear whether these illnesses are related with an increased suicide risk *per se* or indirectly through and increased risk of mood disorders. Actually, consistent evidence shows that although medical illness cannot be considered a sole determinant of a so complex and multi-determined event such suicide, it may be regarded as a predominant factor [18].

The present review explores the association between completed suicide and neoplasms.

3. SUICIDE AND NEOPLASMS

Prolonged survival of patients affected by cancer after treatment mandates better insight into issues of cancer survivorship and patients' quality of life. Although many neoplasms are completely curable nowadays, the specter of dismal prognosis is still associated with the diagnosis of cancer. Unfortunately,

***Address correspondence to Michele Raja:** Private Practice, *Via* Prisciano 26, 00136 – Rome, Italy; E-mails: michele.raja@libero.it and michele.raja@fastwebnet.it

Maurizio Pompili (Ed)

too many neoplastic diseases remain inexorable infirmities leading to short term death. Therefore, receiving such a diagnosis often induces devastating effects on patients, including suicidal ideation and behaviour.

Several studies demonstrated that the risk of suicide in cancer patients is higher than that for the general population. However, estimates vary, with some stating that the risk is two- to four-fold increased and others stating that it only slightly exceeds that of the general population. Differences between studies in patient populations, methods, and areas of focus contribute to variations in finding. The key methodological problem of such studies is collecting representative samples of suicide and cancer from good-quality registers of large populations, and combining them.

4. MAIN STUDIES ON THE SUICIDAL RISK IN CANCER PATIENTS

In a study [19] on the 28,857 cancer cases registered by the Finnish Cancer Registry in 1955, 1960 and 1965 (63 suicides by the end of 1970), the suicide rate among males was 1.3 times higher ($p<0.01$) and among females 1.9 times higher ($p<0.05$) than the rate in the general population. The highest suicide risk [Relative Risk (RR) 2.5, $p<0.001$] was associated with gastrointestinal cancer. Patients with a non-localized tumor at diagnosis had a two-fold risk of suicide and the rate was higher among patients undergoing no treatment, or treatment with chemotherapy or hormones only. It was estimated that 23% of all suicides among male cancer patients and 46% among female cancer patients was associated with the patients having cancer.

In a study [20] based on the Connecticut Tumor Registry from 1940-1973 (144,530 patients; 192 suicides), Standardized Mortality Ratio (SMR) for males was significantly elevated (2.3; $P<0.005$), but not for females. In men, but not in women, SMR was higher soon after the diagnosis than in later years since diagnosis.

In a cohort study based on the Swedish Cancer-Environment Register [21], the overall SMR in suicide was 1.9 [95% confidence interval (CI): 1.8-2.1] for males and 1.6 (CI: 1.5-1.8) for females. There were no substantial differences in suicide rate between different sites of tumor, although higher suicide rates were observed in patients of both genders with cancer in the lungs and upper airways and in men with gastro-intestinal tumors.

Suicides and suicide attempts in cancer patients were analyzed by following all patients treated for cancer in Stockholm County from 1975 to 1985 [22]. Among 59,845 patients, 144 suicides and 196 suicide attempts occurred during the follow-up, which represents a more than two-fold excess mortality from suicide and a moderately increased rate of suicide attempts.

Levi *et al.* [23] used data collected by the Cancer Registry of the Canton of Vaud in Switzerland to estimate the risk of suicide for patients diagnosed with cancer. Among 24,166 cases of invasive neoplasms other than non-melanomatous skin cancer reported between 1976 and 1987 and followed through integrated active follow-up to the end of 1987, for a total of 57,164 person years at risk, there were 55 registered suicides *vs.* 21.3 expected (SMR = 2.6; 95% Cl: 2.0-3.4). The ratio was slightly, but not significantly higher for men (SMR = 2.8) than for women (SMR = 2.2) and comparable across subsequent age groups.

Linking the National Cancer Registry and mortality files, Storm *et al.* [24] found 568 suicides among 296,331 patients with cancer in Denmark from 1971 to 1986. The RR of suicide was significantly increased in the first 2 years after a cancer diagnosis, independent of age at cancer diagnosis. A lower suicide risk was seen after diagnosis of localized cancer (RR = 1.3; 95% CI: 1.1-1.4), compared with that seen after a non-localized cancer (RR = 1.9; 95% CI: 1.5-2.4). High risks for suicide were observed for patients of each sex after diagnoses of tumors of the nervous system and with cancer of the lung, stomach, rectum, and kidney. High risks were found among male patients only after a diagnosis of lymphoma or pancreatic cancer.

In a population-based cohort study [25] of 27,123 cancer patients resident in central Italy where the general suicide rate is low, a high suicide mortality risk was observed. Forty-one suicides occurred (SMR = 2.36) which were only 0.2% of all deaths. However, the highest risk (SMR = 27.7) during the first 6 months after diagnosis, represents a greater contrast with the general population than has been observed in other studies.

In an Estonian cohort of 65,419 persons diagnosed with cancer in 1983-1998, during 192,078 person-years of follow-up between 1983 and 2000, 197 suicides occurred [26]. SMR calculated using the suicide rates of the population of Estonia as a reference found an increased suicide risk for men (SMR=1.73; 95% CI: 1.45-2.01), but not for women (SMR=0.50; 95% CI: 0.37-0.66). Men had the highest risk 90-179 days following their diagnosis (SMR=4.27; 95% CI: 2.81-6.21). During this time interval, among men, the risk was more pronounced for cancers of the esophagus (SMR=35.63; 95% CI: 9.71-91.22) and pancreas (SMR=14.53; 95% CI: 1.76-52.50).

In a cohort study [27] of all cancer patients registered in the Cancer Registry of Norway 1960 to 1997 (N = 490,245 patients with 520,823 cancer diagnoses), during the period 1960-1999, 589 cancer patients (407 males and 182 females) committed suicide. The RR was elevated for males and females, with SMRs of 1.55 (95% CI: 1.41-1.71) and 1.35 (95% CI: 1.17-1.56), respectively. Risk was highest in the first months after diagnosis. For both sexes, the relative suicide risk was higher for those who were divorced or separated and unmarried (P< .001). The risk was not elevated for widowed or married women. For both men and women, there was a significant decrease in suicide risk over decades (P = .02 for both sexes). The same pattern was observed for 5-year follow-up, with the relative suicide risk being higher in the 1960s (2.81 and 2.73 for men and women, respectively) and lower in the 1990s (1.69 and 1.39 for men and women, respectively). The risk was markedly increased among male patients with cancer of respiratory organs (SMR, 4.08; 95% CI: 2.96-5.47). Otherwise, the SMRs varied from 0.76 to 3.67 across cancer types. The number of deaths by suicide was very low compared with other causes of death in cancer patients.

In a register study [28], cancer patients run a higher risk of suicide than the general population. The suicide rate ratio between male cancer patients and the general population was about 2.5 in 1965-74, which thereafter reduced to about 1.5 in 1985-94. The suicide rate among female cancer patients was in excess of 2.9 in 1965-74 and 2.3 in 1985-94. In fact, a slightly higher rate for women was observed for 1985-94 than for 1975-84. There was also a strong negative association between survival rates and suicide rates, *i.e.,* suicide rates were higher for severe cancer sites with low survival rates.

In a Danish study [29], patients registered in the Danish cancer registry, with a first cancer diagnosed between 1971 and 1999 in Denmark, were followed-up for completed suicide through 1999. Excluding non-melanoma skin cancer, 564,508 cancer patients were included and 1241 suicides observed. The overall SMR was increased to 1.7 (95% CI: 1.6-1.9) for men and 1.4 (95% CI: 1.3-1.5) for women. Following the cancer diagnosis, the suicide risk was highest in the first 3 months for men and between months 3 and 12 for women. The risk was higher for non-localized cancer and for cancers with perceived poor prognosis. Breast cancer patients had a higher risk than other cancer patients with similar good prognosis. The suicide rates among cancer patients decreased with calendar time, but less so than the rates in the general population.

A retrospective cohort study [30] compared suicide rates in persons with cancer identified in a network of population-based incident tumor registries from the United States (US) with the general US population and examined patient and disease characteristics associated with higher suicide rates. Among 3,594,750 SEER registry patients observed for 18,604,308 person-years, 5,838 suicides were identified, for an age-, sex-, and race-adjusted rate of 31.4/100,000 person-years. In contrast, the suicide rate in the general US population was 16.7/100,000 person-years. This gave a SMR of 1.88 (95% CI: 1.83-1.93). Higher suicide rates were associated with male sex, white race, and older age at diagnosis. The highest suicide risks were observed in patients with cancers of the lung and bronchus (SMR = 5.74; 95% CI: 5.30-6.22), stomach (SMR = 4.68; 95% CI: 3.81-5.70), oral cavity and pharynx (SMR = 3.66; 95% CI: 3.16-4.22), and larynx (SMR = 2.83; 95% CI: 2.31-3.44). Characteristics associated with suicide in the cancer population, such as older age and male sex, were similar to those in the general population.

A retrospective cohort study [31] of 121,533 patients diagnosed with cancer in Western Australia identified 129 suicides in this group (108 in men). The SMR for suicide in cancer patients was 1.61 (95% CI: 1.36-1.92). An initial period of peak risk was seen in the first 3 months after cancer diagnosis (SMR, 5.75; 95% CI: 3.89-8.51), mainly in patients with a poor prognosis. A second peak period of risk was found to occur

12-14 months after diagnosis (SMR, 2.33; 95% CI: 1.11-4.89) in those with a good or moderate prognosis, possibly due to cancer recurrence or treatment failure.

A study [32] calculated SMRs for suicide in 206,129 men and 211,443 women diagnosed with cancer in South East England between 1996 and 2005, relative to suicide rates in the general population and found a significantly increased risk of suicide in men (SMR 1.45, 95% CI: 1.20-1.73) and a moderately increased risk in women (SMR 1.19, 95% CI: 0.88-1.57). In both sexes, RR of suicide was greatest in the first year after cancer diagnosis (SMR for men 2.42, 95% CI: 1.84-3.13; SMR for women 1.44, 95% CI: 0.82-2.33), and was also greater in individuals diagnosed with types of cancer with high fatality (SMR for men 2.67, 95% CI: 1.71-3.97; SMR for women 2.17, 95% CI: 0.80-4.73).

A recent review of the literature [33] reported incidence of completed suicide in cancer patients ranged from SMR of 1 to 11. The reported percentages of suicidal ideation in non-psychiatric populations of cancer patients ranged from 0.8 to 71.4%, compared to a reported prevalence of suicidal ideation in the general population, of between 1.1 and 19.8%. Despite the prevalence of suicidal ideation in the cancer population was comparable to the general population, the prevalence of completed suicide was elevated.

5. SPECIFIC NEOPLASTIC DISEASES

Several studies have observed that cancers at certain anatomic sites are associated with particularly increased suicide rates. However, the sites associated with the greatest risk vary depending on the report [19, 21-24, 27-29]. Specifically, three Scandinavian studies were large enough to compare suicide rates by anatomic cancer site, with inconsistent results among the studies. Particularly high rates were seen in patients with respiratory and breast cancers in Denmark [29], respiratory and oropharyngeal cancers in Norway [27], and esophageal, pancreatic, and respiratory cancers in Sweden [28].

The studies have shown similarly elevated suicide rates in patients with lung cancer, but have not been unanimous in identifying high rates of suicide among those with stomach and head and neck cancers [21-27-29].

6. BREAST CANCER

Women with breast cancer account for one in five of all cancer survivors in the US, numbering approximately 2 million in 2001 [34]. Given the current 10-year relative survival of 78% [35], most patients with breast cancer can expect to live for many years. A diagnosis of breast cancer has been associated with excess risks of suicide of 30%–50% in Scandinavia [21, 24, 27, 29] and Canada [36], albeit based on small studies. A large population-based investigation [37] quantified suicide risk among 723,810 1-year breast cancer survivors diagnosed between 1953 and 2001, and reported to 16 population-based cancer registries in the US and Scandinavia. Among breast cancer survivors, SMRs and excess absolute risks (EARs) compared with the general population, and the probability of suicide were calculated. In total 836 breast cancer patients committed suicide (SMR = 1.37, 95% CI: 1.28-1.47; EAR = 4.1 per 100,000 person-years). Risk was elevated throughout follow-up, including for 25 or more years after diagnosis (SMR = 1.35, 95% CI: = 0.82-2.12), and was highest among black women (SMR = 2.88, 95% CI: 1.44-5.17). Risk increased with increasing stage of breast cancer and remained elevated among women diagnosed between 1990 and 2001 (SMR = 1.36, 95% CI: 1.18-1.57). The cumulative probability of suicide was 0.20% 30 years after breast cancer diagnosis. Although most patients with breast cancer appear to adapt well, a minority suffer from significant psychosocial distress [38]. Estimates of the prevalence of clinical depression or depressive symptoms in patients with breast cancer vary greatly, ranging from 1.5% to 46% [39]. Importantly, psychosocial factors (including depression) and use of antidepressant medications do not appear to be risk factors for the development of breast cancer [40, 41].

The increased long-term risk of suicide after a breast cancer diagnosis is surprising. Actually, suicide risk for most cancers decreases to expected levels several years after diagnosis [24]. This difference may reflect the unique chronic and indolent nature of breast cancer with recurrences possible many years after diagnosis. Breast cancer might be believed by patients to be more life threatening than it is [29].

7. PROSTATE CANCER

A population-based, retrospective cohort review [42] of men age 65 and older, residing in South Florida found an average annual incidence of suicide for men was 55.32 per 100,000 persons, and 274.7 per 100,000 for men with prostate cancer. The risk of suicide in men with prostate cancer was 4.24 times that of an age- and gender-specific cohort. The clinical correlates included depression (70%), cancer diagnosis within 6 months of suicide (80%), physician visit within 1 month of suicide (60%), and being foreign-born (70%).

In a study on men newly diagnosed with prostate cancer [43], a total of 136 (0.08%) prostate cancer patients committed suicide within 1 year after cancer diagnosis. The risk for suicide was more than doubled among prostate cancer patients compared to the cancer-free men (RR 2.6). The excess risk was highest during the first week after diagnosis (RR 8.4) and decreased with time since diagnosis, but was still clearly significant by the end of the first year (RR 1.9). The RR for suicide after diagnosis was 4.6 among men 54 y or younger, approximately twice that of older age groups. The risk of suicide remained more than doubled throughout the entire study period and was not modified by educational level, marital status, or prior psychiatric hospitalization. The risk of suicide remained elevated beyond the first year of follow-up (RR 1.8; 95% CI: 1.6–2.0) during the entire study period. The excess risks were highest during the first week after diagnosis, suggesting that the stress of diagnosis itself rather than subsequent factors such as hormonal treatment or operations plays a role.

8. HEAD AND NECK CANCER

In a total of 1.3 million cancer cases, a total of 265 female and 1307 male suicides were enumerated, reflecting 0.04% and 0.19% from each gender, and providing an overall hazard ratio for male suicide of 6.2 (95% CI: 5.4-7.1) [44]. Females with colorectal ($P = 0.01$) and cervical ($P < 0.0001$) cancers showed decreased suicide rates. Males with head and neck cancers ($P < 0.0001$) and myeloma ($P = 0.02$) had increased rates, whereas rates were decreased in males with lung cancer ($P = 0.01$), liver ($P = 0.01$), brain tumors ($P = 0.04$), and leukemia ($P = 0.007$). The hazard ratio associated for male suicide with distant metastasis was 2.84 (95% CI: 2.49-3.24); for married status, 0.46 (95% CI: 0.39-0.54); and for African-American ancestry, 0.24 (95% CI: 0.17-0.34). Comparable ratios were seen here for female suicides. In head and neck cancers, with both genders analyzed together, the suicide hazard was increased if surgery was contraindicated (3.0, 95% CI: 1.3-6.8), but not if refused.

The reasons for particular types of cancers to be associated with increased suicide rates are unknown. However, there has been considerable speculation over why some patients with certain cancer types seem to carry a higher suicide risk than others. For example, it has been suggested that certain cancer types may have more profound effects on quality of life and induce stronger degrees of anxiety or fear because of symbolic values, cognitive functions, change in body image, or difficulties of speech, breathing, or eating [21, 45, 46]. Cancers in respiratory organs among men seem to be of particular concern. Patients with lung cancer may struggle with their grave prognoses. One study found a 25% prevalence of depression among patients with lung cancer [47], and other work has suggested that lower quality of life in patients with lung cancer is related to emotional distress [48]. Examination of psychological reactions in newly diagnosed patients with gastric cancer showed high levels of psychological distress [49]. Patients with head and neck cancers have a high prevalence of depression as well [50]. Head and neck cancers could have a particularly devastating effect on quality of life through their impact on appearance and essential functions such as speech, swallowing, and breathing [51]. It should also be considered the potential confounding role of comorbid medical and psychiatric conditions, including characteristics that could bear on the incidence of cancer (such as tobacco and alcohol use) that may also be associated with an increased risk of suicide. Tobacco [52, 53] and alcohol use [54, 55] have been associated with increased suicide risk, although the strengths of these associations vary widely (ranging from RR of 1.4 to 4.3) depending on the study. Because tobacco and alcohol use can be common in patients with lung and head and neck cancer, this may account for some of the increased suicide rates in these groups of patients. For example, Hem *et al.* [27] found that bronchus, trachea, and lung cancers carried the highest suicide risks among men, whereas cancers in the buccal cavity and pharynx carried the highest risk among women. These cancer types are associated with smoking and, in part, alcohol abuse. These factors are interrelated with depressive disorders. That is, people who smoke often also consume alcohol and *vice versa*, and those who are depressed have higher rates of both alcohol misuse and smoking, as well as greater difficulty in quitting [46, 56, 57]. The relation of smoking and alcohol abuse to suicidal behaviour may, in part, confound the linkage of these lifestyle-associated cancers to high suicide risk. Hence, the high relative suicide risk in some cancer sites may indicate a confounding effect.

9. THE IMPACT OF MOOD DISORDERS

The suicide of a person suffering from cancer may be regarded as a rational alternative to the prolonged physical and mental distress caused by the disease. However, remarkably few cancer patients commit suicide, even at the terminal stage [58]. In an Italian study, only 0.22% of all deaths of cancer patients were a result of suicide [25]. At the same time, most patients with cancer do not develop major depression, suggesting that cancer is a risk factor, not a mandate, for depression [59].

Mood disorders are commonly associated with suicide, and depressive symptoms are prevalent among cancer patients. Improved treatment of mood disorders could reduce the suicide rate in the cancer patients. Improved treatment and increased focus on depressive symptoms among cancer patients may also explain the decreasing suicide risk [60]. The reported decline in suicide risk during the last decades [27, 29] may also reflect improvements in treatment, including less-mutilating surgical interventions, improved medical outcomes, and psychosocial support [61]. However, significantly increased risk of suicide in more recent years has also been reported [24].

Depressive symptoms have been found to be equally common among cancer suicides and other suicides [58]. However, few data explain why some cancer patients suffering from major depression have suicidal ideation, whereas others do not. Some findings suggest that severe depression, pain, and poor physical functioning are important indicators of suicidal ideation among cancer patients [62, 63]. Cancer is the most prevalent diagnosis for patients who request physician-assisted suicide and euthanasia [64, 65] and depression rates among terminally ill patients requesting physician-assisted suicide and euthanasia are particularly high [66].

Pain, dyspnea, incontinence, regurgitation, delirium associated with cancer or drug treatment can disrupt sleep patterns, determine sleep deprivation, and induce mood alterations.

10. SUICIDE RISK AND TIME SINCE DIAGNOSIS

The results of the studies are inconsistent concerning the duration of increased risk after diagnosis. A review of Stenager *et al.* [67] suggested that the suicide risk is greatest during the first year after diagnosis of the disease. In the study of Hem *et al.* [27], the risk was highest in the first months after diagnosis. In the study of Levi *et al.* [23], the risk of suicide was high during the first year after notification (SMR = 3.9) and decreased to 2.2 between 1 and 5 years and to 1.5 over 5 years. In the study of Fall *et al.* [43] the risk was highest during the first week after prostate cancer diagnosis. Possible mechanisms remain unknown but the emotional shock caused by the diagnosis, anxiety for the pending choice of treatment, together with emotional isolation, may explain the impulsive action.

In most studies, the suicide risk tends to decline as time since diagnosis increases. This may be explained by the natural course of the cancer disease and the gradual adaptation to having or having had a life-threatening disease. The number of patients with the poorest prognosis for survival will be highest in the first years after diagnosis, and these patients may also be the most vulnerable to suicide. Eventually, surviving patients will be cured, and 5 years after diagnosis, the risk should be about the same as for the general population [21]. However, because cancer is often a chronic disease, clinicians' alertness to depressive symptoms and suicidality should not be restricted to only the first months after diagnosis. This is of special relevance for breast cancer, which has an unpredictable course. In the cohort study of Allebeck *et al.* [21], where the overall SMR in suicide was 1.9 (95% CI: 1.8-2.1) for males and 1.6 (95% CI: 1.5-1.8) for females, the suicide rate was highest during the first year after cancer diagnosis, with an SMR of 16.0 (95% CI: 13.5-18.9) in males and 15.4 (95% CI: 11.2-20.6) in females. However, an excess risk was observed up to 7 years after diagnosis [21].

In the cohort study of Misono *et al.* [30], the relative increase in suicide risk among persons with cancer was highest in the first 5 years after diagnosis with cancer and declined gradually thereafter, but remained elevated compared with that of the general US population 15 years after diagnosis. The highest relative suicide risks persisted over time in patients with cancers of the lung and bronchus, oral cavity and pharynx, larynx, nervous system, prostate, and cervix. This is similar to the elevation in suicide risk seen in breast cancer survivors in the SEER program, some of whom were included in this study, which lasted more than 25 years after diagnosis even after definitive treatment of their cancers [37]. Interpretation of results from patients who survived 15 or more years after their cancer diagnosis was limited by small numbers of suicides associated with some cancer sites. However, in addition to lung and head and neck cancers, cancers of the nervous system, prostate, and cervix seemed to be associated with long-term increases in suicide risk.

11. GENDER DIFFERENCES

The results from the best studies indicate an increased risk among men (SMR, 1.9 to 2.8), but they are inconsistent as to whether women have an increased risk (SMR, 0.9 to 1.9) [68, 69].

12. SUICIDES IN CANCER PATIENTS *VERSUS* SUICIDES IN PATIENTS WITH OTHER ILLNESSES

A case-control study [70] of the suicide risk associated with medical illness among 1,408 New Jersey residents age 65 years or older found 128 cases of suicide. Control patients (n = 1,280) were frequency-matched to patient cases on age and sex. In adjusted analyses, the only medical condition that remained associated with suicide was cancer (OR, 2.3; 95% CI: 1.1-4.8). The risk of suicide in older adults was higher among patients with cancer than among patients with other medical illnesses, even after psychiatric illness and the risk of dying within a year were accounted for. Suicide also remained associated with a diagnosis of affective disorder (OR, 2.3; 95% CI: 1.3-4.2), anxiety/personality disorder (OR, 2.2; 95% CI: 1.3-3.6), treatment with antidepressants (OR, 2.0; 95% CI: 1.2-3.2), and treatment with opioid analgesics (OR, 1.6; 95% CI: 1.0-2.5).

CONCLUSIONS

Risk factors identified for completed suicide in cancer patients include mental health, socio-demographic and illness factors. Some of these risk factors extend to the general population; however, some are specific to cancer such as cancer site, physical functioning and prognosis.

Consistent findings in the literature are that: 1) cancer is a risk factor for suicide; 2) the risk increases with disease severity; the severity of the cancer increases the suicide risk; 3) the risk is highest shortly after the diagnosis has been made, but for some cancer types, the risk remains increased for more than 5 years after diagnosis; 4) men have a higher suicide risk than women; 5) depression, pain, and poor physical functioning are important clinical correlates.

The increased suicide rate among cancer patients indicates a need for further attention to social and psychological aspects of the care and treatment of cancer patients. Screens for depression and suicide in people with cancer should be done after diagnosis and redone during the first 6 months regularly, particularly in the primary-care setting. More attention to cancer patients' psychological and care situation and public education are needed to decrease the stigma associated with having a cancer diagnosis.

Assessment and treatment of depression could improve the prognosis for cancer patients who suffer from unrecognized depressions and in turn reduce their risk of suicide. Frank discussion of suicidal ideation with cancer patients is important. Although clinicians often fear such discussion, there is no evidence that talking about suicide encourages people to attempt suicide. Identifying and treating depression among cancer patients has been shown to decrease morbidity and mortality [71]. It is particularly important to evaluate the presence of hopelessness, which may be a stronger predictor of suicidal risk than depression itself [72]. Patients' existential suffering may be a difficult topic to address [73, 74]. The ability of physicians to communicate openly and clearly with their patients about these difficult issues should be a part of the physician's toolbox.

Although the absolute number of deaths from suicide in cancer patients is low, the increased risk highlights the problems of coping with severe illness and the need for psychological and social support in the management of patients with cancer care.

REFERENCES

[1] Bland RC, Newman SC, Dyck RJ. The epidemiology of parasuicide in Edmonton. Can J Psychiatry 1994; 39: 391-6.
[2] Arensman E, Kerkhof AJ, Hengeveld MW, Mulder J D. Medically treated suicide attempts: A four-year monitoring study of the epidemiology in The Netherlands. J Epidemiol Community Health 1995; 49: 285-9.
[3] Roberts RE, Chen YR, Roberts CR. Ethnocultural differences in prevalence of adolescent suicidal behaviours. Suicide Life Threat Behav 1997; 27: 208-17.
[4] Roberts RE, Chen YW. Depressive symptoms and suicidal ideation among Mexican-origin and Anglo adolescents. J Am Acad Child Adolesc Psychiatry 1995; 34: 81-90.
[5] Petronis KR, Samuels JF, Moscicki EK, Anthony JC. An epidemiologic investigation of potential risk factors for suicide attempts. Soc Psychiatry Psychiatr Epidemiol 1990; 25: 193-9.
[6] Stack S, Wasserman IM. Marital status, alcohol abuse and attempted suicide. A logit model. J Affect Disord 1995; 14: 43-51.
[7] Pirkis J, Burgess P, Dunt D. Suicidal ideation and suicide attempts among Australian adults. Crisis 2000; 21: 16-25.
[8] Kjøller M, Helweg-Larsen M. Suicidal ideation and suicide attempts among adults Danes. Scand J Public Health 2000; 28: 54-61.
[9] Roy A, Draper R. Suicide among psychiatric hospital in-patients. Psychol Med 1995; 25: 199-202.
[10] Morgan HG, Stanton R. Suicide among psychiatric in-patients in a changing clinical scene. Br J Psychiatry 1997; 171: 561-3.
[11] Beautrais L, Joyce PR, Mulder RT. Youth suicide attempts : A social and demographic profile. Aust N Z J Psychiatry 1988; 32: 349-57.
[12] Beautrais L, Joyce PR, Mulder RT. Risk factors for serious suicide attempts among youths aged 13 through 24 years. J Am Acad Child Adolesc Psychiatry 1996; 35: 1174-82.
[13] Fergusson DM, Lynskey MT. Childhood circumstances, adolescent adjustment, and suicide attempts in a New Zealand birth cohort. J Am Acad Child Adolesc Psychiatry 1995; 34: 612-22.
[14] Schmidtke A, Bille Brahe U, DeLeo D, Kerkhof A. Attempted suicide in Europe: Rates, trends and socio-demographic characteristics of suicide attempters during the period 1989-1992. Results of the WHO/EURO Multicentre Study on Parasuicide. Acta Psychiatr Scand 1996; 93: 327-38.
[15] Vijayakumar L, Rajkumar S. Are risk factors for suicide universal? A case-control study in India. Acta Psychiatr Scand 1999; 99: 407-11.
[16] Cavanagh JTO, Owens DGC, Johnstone EC. Life events in suicide and undetermined death in south-east Scotland: a case-control study using the method of psychological autopsy. Soc Psychiatry Psychiatr Epidemiol 1999; 34: 645-50.
[17] Forsell Y, Jorm AF, Winblad B. Suicidal thoughts and associated factors in an elderly population. Acta Psychiatr Scand 1997; 95: 108-11.
[18] Hughes D, Kleespies P. Suicide in the medically ill. Suicide Life Threat Behav 2001; 31(suppl): 48-59.
[19] Louhivuori KA, Hakama M. Risk of suicide among cancer patients. Am J Epidemiol 1979; 109: 59-65.
[20] Fox BH, Stanek EJ 3rd, Boyd SC, Flannery JT. Suicide rates among cancer patients in Connecticut. J Chronic Dis 1982; 35: 89-100.
[21] Allebeck P, Bolund C, Ringback G. Increased suicide rate in cancer patients. A cohort study based on the Swedish cancer-environment register. J Clin Epidemiol 1989; 42: 611–16.
[22] Allebeck P, Bolund C. Suicides and suicide attempts in cancer patients. Psychol Med 1991; 21: 979-84.

[23] Levi F, Bulliard JL, La Vecchia C. Suicide risk among incident cases of cancer in the Swiss Canton of Vaud. Oncology 1991; 48: 44-7.

[24] Storm HH, Christensen N, Jensen OM. Suicides among Danish patients with cancer: 1971–1986. Cancer 1992; 69: 1507–12.

[25] Crocetti E, Arniani S, Acciai S, Barchielli A, Buiatti E. High suicide mortality soon after diagnosis among cancer patients in central Italy. Br J Cancer 1998; 77: 1194-6.

[26] Innos K, Rahu K, Rahu M, Baburin A. Suicides among cancer patients in Estonia: a population-based study. Eur J Cancer 2003; 39: 2223-8.

[27] Hem E, Loge JH, Haldorsen T, Ekeberg Ø. Suicide risk in cancer patients from 1960 to 1999. J Clin Oncol 2004; 22: 4209-16.

[28] Björkenstam C, Edberg A, Ayoubi S, Rosén M. Are cancer patients at higher suicide risk than the general population? Scand J Public Health 2005; 33: 208-14.

[29] Yousaf U, Christensen M-LM, Engholm G, Storm HH. Suicides among Danish cancer patients 1971–1999. Br J Cancer 2005; 92: 995–1000.

[30] Misono S, Weiss NS, Fann JR, Redman M, Yueh B. Incidence of Suicide in Persons With Cancer. J Clin Oncol 2008; 26: 4731–8.

[31] Dormer NR, McCaul KA, Kristjanson LJ. Risk of suicide in cancer patients in Western Australia, 1981-2002. Med J Aust 2008; 188: 140-3.

[32] Robinson D, Renshaw C, Okello C, Møller H, Davies EA. Suicide in cancer patients in South East England from 1996 to 2005: a population-based study. Br J Cancer 2009; 101: 198-201.

[33] Robson A, Scrutton F, Wilkinson L, Macleod F. The risk of suicide in cancer patients: a review of the literature. Psycho-oncology 2010;19(12):1250-8

[34] Rowland J, Mariotto A, Aziz N, *et al.* Cancer survivorship—United States, 1971–2001. MMWR Morbidity and Mortality Weekly Report 2004; 53: 526–9.

[35] Ries LAG, Eisner MP, Kosary CL, *et al.* SEER cancer statistics review, 1975–2002. Bethesda (MD): National Cancer Institute, 2004. Available from: http://seer.cancer.gov/csr/1975_2002. Accessed on September 22, 2005.

[36] Juurlink DN, Herrmann N, Szalai JP, Kopp A, Redelmeier DA. Medical illness and the risk of suicide in the elderly. Arch Intern Med 2004; 164: 1179–84.

[37] Schairer C, Morris Brown L, Chen BE, *et al.* Suicide After Breast Cancer: an International Population-Based Study of 723810 Women . J Natl Cancer Inst 2006; 98: 1416-9.

[38] Hewitt M, Greenfield S, Stovall E. From cancer patient to cancer survivor: lost in transition. The National Academies Press. Washington (DC), 2006.

[39] Massie MJ. Prevalence of depression in patients with cancer. J Natl Cancer Inst Monographies 2004; 32: 57–71.

[40] Butow PN, Hiller JE, Price MA, Thackway SV, Kricker A, Tennant CC. Epidemiologic evidence for a relationship between life events, coping style, and personality factors in the development of breast cancer. J Psychosom Res 2000; 49: 169–81.

[41] Bahl S, Cotterchio M, Kreiger N. Use of antidepressant medications and the possible associations with breast cancer risk. Psychother Psychosom 2003; 72: 185–94.

[42] Llorente MD, Burke M, Gregory GR, *et al.* Prostate cancer: a significant risk factor for late-life suicide Am J Geriatr Psychiatry 2005; 13: 195-201.

[43] Fall K, Fang F, Mucci LA, *et al.* Immediate risk for cardiovascular events and suicide following a prostate cancer diagnosis: prospective cohort study. PLoS Med 2009; 6(12):e1000197.

[44] Kendal WS. Suicide and cancer: a gender-comparative study. Ann Oncol 2007; 18: 381-7.

[45] Hammerlid E, Ahlner-Elmqvist M, Bjordal K, *et al.* A prospective multicentre study in Sweden and Norway of mental distress and psychiatric morbidity in head and neck cancer patients. Br J Cancer 1999; 80: 766-74.

[46] Duffy SA, Terrell JE, Valenstein M, Ronis DL, Copeland LA, Connors M. Effect of smoking, alcohol, and depression on the quality of life of head and neck cancer patients. Gen Hosp Psychiatry 2002; 24: 140-7.

[47] Carlsen K, Jensen AB, Jacobsen E, Krasnik M, Johansen C. Psychosocial aspects of lung cancer. Lung Cancer 2005; 47: 293-300.

[48] Sarna L, Padilla G, Holmes C, Tashkin D, Brecht M, Evangelista L. Quality of life of long-term survivors of non–small-cell lung cancer. J Clin Oncol 2002; 20: 2920-9.

[49] Nordin K, Glimelius B: Psychological reactions in newly diagnosed gastrointestinal cancer patients. Acta Oncol 1997; 36: 803-10.

[50] Duffy SA, Ronis DL, Valenstein M, *et al.* Depressive symptoms, smoking, drinking, and quality of life among head and neck cancer patients. Psychosomatics 2007; 48: 142-8.

[51] Semple CJ, Sullivan K, Dunwoody L, Kernohan WG. Psychosocial interventions for patients with head and neck cancer: Past, present, and future. Cancer Nurs 2004; 27: 434-41.

[52] Miller M, Hemenway D, Bell NS, Yore M, Amoroso P. Cigarette smoking and suicide: A prospective study of 300,000 male active-duty Army soldiers. Am J Epidemiol, 2000a; 151: 1060-3.

[53] Miller M, Hemenway D, Rimm E. Cigarettes and suicide: A prospective study of 50,000 men. Am J Public Health 2000b; 90: 768-73.

[54] Pirkola SP, Suominen K, Isometsa ET. Suicide in alcohol-dependent individuals: Epidemiology and management. CNS Drugs 2004; 18: 423-36.

[55] Wilcox HC, Conner KR, Caine ED. Association of alcohol and drug use disorders and completed suicide: An empirical review of cohort studies. Drug Alcohol Depend 2004; 76(suppl): S11-S19.

[56] Tanskanen A, Tuomilehto J, Viinamäki H, Vartiainen E, Lehtonen J, Puska P. Joint heavy use of alcohol, cigarettes and coffee and the risk of suicide. Addiction 2000; 95: 1699-1704.

[57] Malone KM, Waternaux C, Haas GL, Cooper TB,Li S, Mann JJ. Cigarette smoking, suicidal behaviour, and serotonin function in major psychiatric disorders. Am J Psychiatry 2003; 160: 773-9.

[58] Henriksson MM, Isometsä ET, Hietanen PS, Aro HM, Lonnqvist JK: Mental disorders in cancer suicides. J Affect Disord 1995; 36: 11-20.

[59] Raison CL, Miller AH. Depression in cancer: New developments regarding diagnosis and treatment. Biol Psychiatry 2003; 54:283-94.

[60] Greer S, Moorey S, Baruch JD, *et al.* Adjuvant psychological therapy for patients with cancer: A prospective randomized trial. Br Med J 1992; 304: 675-80.

[61] Spiegel D, Giese-Davis J. Depression and cancer: Mechanisms and disease progression. Biol Psychiatry 2003; 54: 269-82.

[62] Akechi T, Okamura H, Yamawaki S, Uchitomi Y. Why do some cancer patients with depression desire an early death and others do not? Psychosomatics 2001; 42: 141-5.

[63] Akechi T, Okamura H, Nishiwaki Y, Uchitomi Y. Predictive factors for suicidal ideation in patients with unresectable lung carcinoma. Cancer 2002; 95: 1085-93.

[64] Hedberg K, Hopkins D, Southwick K. Legalized physician-assisted suicide in Oregon, 2001. N Eng J Med 2002; 346: 450-2.

[65] van der Maas PJ, van der Wal G, Haverkate I, de Graaff, *et al.* Euthanasia, physician-assisted suicide, and other medical practices involving the end of life in the Netherlands, 1990-1995. N Eng J Medicine 1996; 335: 1699-705.

[66] Chochinov HM, Wilson KG, Enns M, *et al.* Desire for death in the terminally ill. Am J Psychiatry 1995; 152: 1185-91.

[67] Stenager EN, Bille-Brahe U, Jensen K. Cancer and suicide. Review of the literature. Ugeskr Laeger 1991; 153: 764-8.

[68] Stenager EN, Stenager E. Physical illness and suicidal behaviour. In: Hawton K, Van Heeringen K, Eds. The International Handbook of Suicide and Attempted Suicide. Chichester, United Kingdom; John Wiley. 2000; pp. 405-20.

[69] Maris RW, Berman AL, Silverman MM, *et al.* Physical illness and suicide. In: Maris RW, Berman AL, Silverman MM, Eds. Comprehensive Textbook of Suicidology. New York, NY: Guilford Press. 2000; pp. 342-56.

[70] Miller M, Mogun H, Azrael D, Hempstead K and Solomon DH. Cancer and the risk of suicide in older Am J Clin Oncol 2008; 26: 4720-4.

[71] Massie MJ, Chertkov L, Roth AJ. Psychological issues. In: DeVita VT Jr, Hellman S, Rosenberg SA, Eds. Cancer: Principles and Practice of Oncology (ed 6). Philadelphia, PA; Lippincott Williams & Wilkins. 2001; pp. 3058-65.

[72] Holland JC, Gooen-Piels J. Psycho-oncology. In: Kufe DW, Holland JF, Frei E, Eds. Holland-Frei Cancer Medicine (ed 6). Ontario, Canada: Hamilton, Decker. 2003; pp. 1047-54.

[73] Kohlwes RJ, Koepsell TD, Rhodes LA, Pearlman RA. Physicians' responses to patients' requests for physician-assisted suicide. Arch Intern Med 2001; 161: 657-63.

[74] Back AL, Starks H, Hsu C, Gordon JR, Bharucha A, Pearlman RA. Clinician-patient interactions about requests for physician-assisted suicide: A patient and family view. Arch Intern Med 2002; 162: 1257-65.

CHAPTER 20

Suicide and Self-Mutilation

Sara Martino and David Lester*

The Richard Stockton College of New Jersey, USA

Abstract: Lester [1] introduced self-mutilation into mainstream psychology with a review of relevant research in a leading journal of the American Psychological Association (Psychological Bulletin) and discusses the relationship between self-mutilation and suicidal behavior. The present chapter compares our current understanding of self-mutilation with that of attempted suicide to explore similarities and differences.

Keywords: Self-mutilation, cutting, attempted suicide trichotillomania.

1. SELF-MUTILATION

The following is an example of self-injury (from the International Child and Youth Care Network):

> After having an awful day at work and an even worse time fighting traffic to come home, Joan wanted nothing more than to sit down on her couch, turn on the television, order out for pizza and relax for the rest of the evening. But when Joan walked into the kitchen, what she saw indicated that this would not be the evening of her dreams. Standing in front of the sink was her fourteen-year-old daughter, Maggie. Maggie's arms were covered with blood, long slashes on her forearms dripping fresh blood into the running water of the kitchen sink. A single edged razor blade sat on the counter along with several once-white towels, now stained crimson by Maggie's own blood. Joan dropped her briefcase and stood before her daughter in silent shock, unable to believe what she saw [2].

This dramatic account of a teen experiencing self-mutilation is an example of this serious problem. Self-mutilation has in the past been linked with serious mental illness, including borderline personality disorder [3, 4]. Research suggests two goals of self-mutilation: anxiety reduction and hostility [5], while other research points to past sexual abuse, substance abuse, suicidal behavior, and attachment issues as relevant factors [6-8]. Regardless of its relationship to mental illness, self-mutilation is a growing concern in our society.

Self-injurious behaviors, or self-mutilation, are defined as, "deliberately destroying body tissue, at times to change a way of feeling" [9]. It has been further defined by Favazza as follows:

> Self-mutilation (SM) refers to the deliberate direct destruction or alteration of body tissue without conscious suicidal intent. The work deliberately distinguishes it from an accidental act; self-mutilators who accidentally cut or burn themselves feel as much pain and discomfort as anyone else. It is direct as opposed to indirect methods of affecting body issues such as starvation, chronic alcohol ingestion, and or terminating dialysis. Overdoses and swallowing objects are also excluded from the category of SM. Cutting one's hand and trimming one's nails are technically forms of SM but, except when these behaviors are extreme, are of no clinical significance [10].

It is important to note that self-mutilation is a coping mechanism for many who exhibit the behavior. Some of the "benefits" of cutting behaviors include a means of grounding for people who dissociate (shut out certain events or memories), a way to calm down during troubling times, and allowing for a release of emotions.

***Address Correspondence to David Lester:** The Richard Stockton College of New Jersey, USA; E-mail: david.lester@stockton.edu

Maurizio Pompili (Ed)

Self-mutilation has become more prevalent in our culture, especially among adolescents [9]. Examples of self-mutilating behaviors include cutting, burning, self-hitting, interference with wound healing, hair pulling (trichotillomania) and bone breaking [10]. However, there are more specific classifications of self-mutilation.

2. TYPES OF SELF-MUTILATION

Favazza [10] has classified self-mutilation into three distinct categories: stereotypic, major, and superficial/moderate.

1. Stereotypic: Examples of stereotypic self-mutilation include head-banging and hitting, arm hitting, throat and eye gouging, tooth extraction, and self-biting. These types of self-mutilation are most prevalent in inpatient settings and, specifically, with individuals diagnosed with mental retardation [10]. The meaning of these repetitive behaviors is difficult to understand. It is also difficult to define what affect or feeling is associated with the behaviors. This category of self-injury is similar to the stereotypic motor behavior that is seen in patients with schizophrenia. Repeatedly making the same movements, or in this case the same method of self-injury, seems to be some type of coping mechanism in clients who exhibit the behaviors.

2. Major self-mutilation: This is the rarest form of self-mutilation and usually involves massive tissue damage. Examples of major self-mutilation are amputation of genitals, eye gouging, and limb amputation [10]. These behaviors are sometimes identified as being part of religious beliefs, perhaps aiming for religious purification. This type of cutting is not related to any specific diagnosis but is common during episodes of psychosis.

3. Superficial/moderate: This type of self-mutilation is the most common form and is often associated with borderline personality disorder (BPD) and other psychiatric disorders. This is the type of self-mutilation that most people think of when they hear about self-harm behaviors. There are three subtypes of the superficial/moderate category: compulsive, episodic, and repetitive.

i. The compulsive subtype involves nail biting and hair pulling. The most common form of compulsive subtype is trichotillomania. Trichotillomania is a form of impulse control disorder that involves compulsions to pull hair either from the head, the face (*e.g.,* eyebrows, eyelashes) or the genitals. This is followed by extreme relief or pleasure after the pulling occurs. This disorder is commonly mistaken for obsessive-compulsive disorder, but is defined by the uncontrollable impulse to pull out hair.

ii. Episodic is the most common subtype, involves cutting or burning of skin, and is common in BPD.

iii. The repetitive subtype involves using more than one method of self-mutilation in response to stress.

3. WHO EXHIBITS SELF-MUTILATION?

Recent statistics in the United States indicate that between 1%-2% of the population currently engages in self-injurious behaviors, such as cutting [9]. It is more common in females than males, and the majority of those who self-injure are between the ages of 11 and 25 years old [11]. It has been on the rise among adolescents, although the behaviors tend to decrease when people reach their 20's. We also know that there are certain factors associated with risk for cutting behaviors and they are [8]:

1. Being a female.
2. Being Caucasian.
3. Having a history of sexual abuse.

4. Having poor impulse control.

Self-mutilation is unique in that it is a violent and risk-taking event that is mainly exhibited by females. Herpetz, Sass, and Favazza [12] have found a link between self-mutilation and impulsive personality traits which may explain this atypical gender presentation. Impulsive women are engaging in behavior that is somewhat less than typical. Men usually engage in more risk-taking behaviors than women (*e.g.*, driving fast, drinking, substance abuse, and sexual promiscuity) [13]. It is interesting to note that women who self-mutilate are more likely to be susceptible to other risk-taking behaviors as well, such as substance abuse and sexual promiscuity, perhaps a result of their more impulsive nature. Self-mutilation in young women is often associated with self-punishment [10], something that has not been linked with risk-taking behaviors in men. For women, there appears to be an internal process (turning their emotional pain onto themselves) that makes it a unique risk-taking behavior. Men typically engage in risk-taking to externalize or avoid dealing with emotional content.

Self-mutilating behaviors typically take place during adolescence. The behaviors are seen as a coping mechanism for stress, and many adolescents experience stress during puberty. Some statistics indicate that as many as 14% of adolescents engage in self-cutting behaviors [8]. Typically, a young woman who begins self-mutilation during adolescence will increase her pattern of cutting behaviors until her twenties [11].

4. WHY WOMEN?

Why do women exhibit this risky behavior, and why is it uncommon in men? There may be a link to coping mechanisms that contribute to this problem. There are two main types of coping during periods of stress: emotion-focused coping and problem-focused coping [14].

Emotion-Focused Coping

Although everyone uses both of these coping styles in times of stress, men may be more likely to display emotion-focused coping in initial reactions to stressors. We socialize men to avoid emotional content in order to appear strong. Individuals who use this type of coping will try to divert their attention to other things, deny their feelings, use drugs, or drink alcohol in order to keep the emotions in check. "I'll deal with it later" may be a common mentality for a person who is using this style of coping. The problem with denial is that is does not address the underlying problem [15]. It serves simply as a diversion from confronting the problem or the emotion.

Problem-Focused Coping

Women may be more likely to engage in problem-focused coping. This type of coping style involves confronting the emotions, talking about them with others, and trying to handle the emotional reaction internally. The benefit to this style of coping is that the stressor is confronted directly, but confronting the stressor may include some aggressive behaviors [15].

Women talk about their emotions and so they are generally more aware of them. They may be psychologically healthier because they are not in denial. However, the downside of this style of coping is rumination. Rumination involves thinking repetitively about feelings of distress and personal concerns in an effort to cope with them [16]. Women tend to ruminate, or continually dwell on experiences over and over again, more so than do men. Rumination can lead to anxiety, depressed mood, and self-harm behaviors such as cutting. Therefore, it may be that women are socialized to be more susceptible to cutting behaviors than men. It is important to understand how the socialization of men and women may have contributed to women being susceptible to self-mutilation. It is also important to understand what self-mutilation is not by examining some of the myths.

5. MYTHS ABOUT SELF-MUTILATION

Attention-Seeking

While some may believe that young women exhibit these behaviors in order to to get more attention, it is actually a way for the person to experience emotional release. This is typically done in private and not where other people can see the behaviors. Typically a person who self-mutilates will also wear clothing to hide any visible cuts or scars. "Self-mutilation by mentally ill persons is a private, solitary act that often temporarily alleviates pathological symptoms" [17]. In addition, cutting behaviors have been described in clinical populations as a way to cope with feelings of disconnect or fragmentation [18].

Viewing self-mutilation as an attention-seeking behavior takes away from the serious nature of the problem. It makes it seem trivial and does not allow for people to feel comfortable sharing how they are feeling or trying to cope. However, there is some evidence that some cutting behaviors are about attention-seeking.

There is some evidence of a cluster or contagion effect in self-mutilation [19]. Cluster effects refer to an increase in the incidence of a behavior (such as attempted suicide) after the observation of a peer or simply after a person who exhibiting the behavior is reported in the mass media. Research from the Suicide and Mental Health Association International indicates that contagion or cluster suicides account for 1%-5% of teen suicides. Approximately 100 to 200 young people in our country die every year from cluster suicides [20].

While most reports of self-mutilation behaviors are in those diagnosed with mental illness, self-mutilation can occur among adolescents not diagnosed with mental illness. One such example in a school setting was reported in which several females were involved in cutting behaviors initiated by one young woman who was described as "hard core" and had been diagnosed with mental illness [19].

Dangerousness to Others

Another myth concerns the level of lethality or danger to others associated with self-mutilation. There is little reason to believe that a person who self-mutilates is harmful to others. The main target of the pain or frustration in self-mutilation is the self. It should also be clear there is not a high degree of lethality for the person who self-mutilates as this is behavior turned inward. Self-harm is a coping mechanism for difficult emotions.

6. DISORDERS ASSOCIATED WITH SELF-MUTILATION

There is a wide-range of disorders now recognized in relationship to self-mutilation, including BPD, psychosis, mental retardation, and eating disorders.

Self-Mutilation and BPD

Psychoanalysts were the first to identify BPD, describing it as a person on the "border" between neurosis and psychosis. This means that people with this disorder, again usually women, struggle between basic anxiety or fear and more destructive behaviors that indicate a break from reality, such as dissociation. Dissociation is a detachment of the mind from an emotional experience. For people who struggle with BPD, their experience of dissociation may look very similar to psychosis. The symptoms of BPD, according to the American Psychiatric Association [21] are at least five of the following:

1. Efforts to prevent real or imagined abandonment.
2. A pattern of unstable relationships characterized by idealization and devaluation (also associated with splitting).
3. An unstable sense of self.
4. Recurrent suicidal behavior, and threats or thoughts of self-mutilating behaviours.
5. Impulsivity in at least two risky behaviors (*e.g.*, shopping, sexual promiscuity, substance abuse, reckless driving and binge eating). Note: self-mutilation behaviors are not counted in this criterion.
6. Emotional instability due to reactive moods.
7. Chronic feelings of emptiness.
8. Inappropriate anger and difficulty controlling anger.

9. Stress-related ideation or dissociative symptoms.

As a result of the emotional problems that a person with BPD experiences (*e.g.*, anxiety, anger, impulse control), cutting allows them to experience a sense of calm or relief from their emotional experience.

Anxiety Disorders and Self-Mutilation

Self-mutilation has been associated with several anxiety disorders, including posttraumatic stress disorder (PTSD), dissociative disorder, and obsessive-compulsive disorder (OCD). Both PTSD and dissociative disorder are linked to one of the risk factors for self-mutilation - a history of sexual abuse. Both disorders tend to occur after significant trauma such as abuse. Dissociative disorder involves an emotional cutoff of experience, which may result in temporary amnesia or a depersonalization in which the person experiences a disconnection between their experiences and feelings. PTSD involves more complex symptoms of nightmares, hyper vigilance and a reliving of the experience or trauma that triggered the disorder.

One disorder that has not been linked to childhood abuse is OCD. OCD involves the presence of either obsessions or compulsions (or both) [21]. Obsessions are described as:

1. Intrusive and repetitive thoughts that are considered distressing.

2. The thoughts (or images associated with the thoughts) are not part of "normal" worries or anxieties.

3. The person attempts to ignore or suppress the thoughts or divert the thoughts to another thought or action.

4. The person recognizes that the thoughts come from their own mind (as opposed to an episode of psychosis).

Compulsions are defined as:

1. Repetitive behaviors or mental acts that a person feels compelled to perform as a result of an obsession or according to rules that must be executed rigidly.

2. The behaviors or mental acts are aimed at reducing anxiety or preventing some perceived threat.

In addition, a person with OCD must recognize that these thoughts or actions are not normal and experience marked distress from them. The thoughts or actions must be time-consuming (at least one hour per day) and are not caused by any other disorder or general medical condition.

The person who exhibits self-mutilation is sometimes thought to be experiencing a compulsion to cut themselves. They feel that the cutting behavior, or other self-mutilation, will calm anxiety or prevent some perceived threat. In addition, they may be experiencing obsessive thoughts that lead to the compulsion to self-mutilate.

Bipolar Disorder and Self-Mutilation

Bipolar disorder is a mood disorder that is characterized by periods of mania and depression. According to the DSM-IV, a person diagnosed with bipolar disorder must meet the criteria for at least one manic episode, which entails at least three of the following symptoms that persist for more than one week:

1. Inflated self-esteem or grandiosity.

2. Decreased need for sleep (*e.g.*, feels rested after only 3 hours of sleep).

3. More talkative than usual or pressure to keep talking.

4. Flight of ideas or subjective experience that thoughts are racing.

5. Distractibility (*e.g.*, attention too easily drawn to unimportant or irrelevant external stimuli).

6. Increase in goal-directed activity (either socially, at work or school, or sexually) or psychomotor agitation.

7. Excessive involvement in pleasurable activities that have a high potential for painful consequences (*e.g.*, engaging in unrestrained buying sprees, sexual indiscretions, or foolish business investments).

Criterion seven involves "excessive involvement in pleasurable activities that have a high potential for painful consequences". One of those impulsive and risk-taking behaviors may take the shape of self-mutilation. Also, during periods of depression, people may exhibit self-mutilation as a way to express their emotions when they are experiencing an emotional numbness or lack of emotion.

Dissociative Disorders and Self-Mutilation

Cutting behavior has been described in clinical populations as a way of coping with feelings of disconnect or fragmentation [18]. It has been associated in this manner with dissociation, or feeling disconnected from your life and experiences. When a person dissociates, there is typically an interruption of the person's consciousness, such as forgetting of experiences. The type of dissociative disorder that may be associated with self-mutilation is depersonalization disorder. According to the DSM [21], there are several criteria for this disorder. These include:

1. A lasting or recurring feeling of being detached from one's own body.

2. Throughout the experience, the patient knows this is not really the case. Their sense of reality is intact, but there is a surreal experience of detachment.

3. The feeling of detachment causes significant distress or impairs work, social or personal functioning.

4. This problem is not better explained by another illness or by the influence of drugs.

The purpose of mentioning dissociative disorders in particular is that the person who self-mutilates due to dissociation is focused on a different goal than other self-mutilators. By cutting, the person is able to feel alive again and typically is able to overcome the dissociation.

7. SUICIDE AND SELF-MUTILATION

A critical question is to what extent self-mutilation resembles attempted suicide. Martino [22] argued that it does not. She noted that the most common type of self-mutilation that teenagers exhibit is the superficial/moderate type. This is mostly likely to be nail biting, hair pulling or cutting or burning skin in response to stress. Since it involves the most "superficial" type of self-harm, it is better understand as an emotional release rather than a suicide attempt. Walsh and Rosen [23] have also taken this position.

Researchers in the field of suicidology have long confronted the problem that many individuals who make what has traditionally been called a "suicide attempt" do not intend to die. It has been documented that people may calculate what a less-than-lethal dose of a medication is and then ingest that amount [24]. Others may swallow a handful of aspirin or acetominophen tablets (known as Tylenol in the United States and paracetamol in Europe), often in front of bystanders. Dorpat and Boswell [25] classified suicide attempts as gestures, ambivalent attempts (ambivalent as to whether death was sought or not), and serious attempts. Kreitman, Philip, Greer and Bagley [26] suggested calling non-lethal suicide attempts parasuicide to get away from the notion that attempted suicides are trying to kill themselves, but this term has been dropped in recent years. Researchers now prefer terms such as self-poisoning or self-injury, removing the word "suicide" completely from the label.

However, even if many acts of self-injury and self-mutilation are not engaged in with any intent to die, those who self-mutilate are at higher risk for subsequent suicide [7, 27]. For example, Jones [28] found that prisoners who self-mutilate attempted suicide in prison more often than did non-mutilators. Walsh and Rosen [23] noted that estimates of self-mutilators with suicidal ideation range from 28% to 40%. In their study of adolescent self-mutilators, they found that 13% had suicidal thoughts at the time when they self-mutilated and 31% had previously attempted suicide. The suicide attempters and those who did not do so did not differ in the characteristics of their self-mutilating behavior.

Lester [29] analyzed data from a study by Bongar, [30] on self-mutilation in patients with BPD and found that recent self-mutilation was associated with a history of attempted suicide. In a sample of adolescent psychiatric inpatients, Zlotnick, Donaldson, Spirito and Pearlstein [31] found that those who had attempted suicide had more often self-mutilated in the prior year. Soloff, Liss, Kelly, Cornelius and Ulrich [27] also found that patients with BPD who self-mutilated were more likely to attempt suicide and have more serious suicidal ideation, although they were not more depressed. The suicidal behavior of those who self-mutilated was more manipulative but did not differ in lethality.

However, self-mutilators and attempted suicides do differ in personal characteristics. Sonneburn and Vanstraelen [32] compared attempted suicides and self-mutilators, all of whom used burning. The attempters more often used inflammable liquids and set fire to their clothes; the self-mutilators used matches and lighters more and made direct burns on their skin. The two groups did not differ in past psychiatric history or previous suicide attempts, but the attempted suicides were more likely to receive a diagnosis of affective disorder while the self-mutilators were more likely to receive a diagnosis of BPD.

Stanley, Gameroff, Machalsen and Mann [33] noted that previous researchers had estimated that between 55%-85% of self-mutilators have made at least one suicide attempt and, therefore, their suicidal behavior should be assumed to be genuinely suicidal. They studied 53 psychiatric patients who had attempted suicide, 30 of whom were also self-mutilators. Most were female (79%), Caucasian (89%) and single (70%). The two groups did not differ in age, sex, ethnicity, marital status, religious affiliation, education or employment. The two groups also did not differ in having first-degree relatives who had attempted or completed suicide, the number of psychiatric hospitalizations or being in psychotherapy. Differences did emerge in their history of punishment, with the self-mutilators being physically punished more often, but they did not differ in the frequency of sexual abuse or the severity of the physical abuse. The two groups also differed in personality. The self-mutilators had higher scores on measures of lifetime aggression, as well as on measures of hopelessness and depression (and overall psychopathology as assessed by the Brief Psychiatric Rating Scale). Although all the patients had a personality disorder (all but three had BPD), the self-mutilators had more severe borderline pathology.

Regarding their suicidal behavior, although the majority of self-mutilators used cutting to self-mutilate, both groups used pills to attempt suicide (77% of the self-mutilators and 74% of the non-mutilators). The impulsivity *versus* planning of the attempts was similar in both groups. The two groups did not differ in the number of lifetime suicide attempts, the time since the last attempt, or their suicidal intent and suicidal ideation. The self-mutilators had longer periods of suicidal ideation and more frequent suicidal ideation. The self-mutilators were less likely to believe that their equally lethal attempts would result in death, believed more that they would be rescued, and were more likely to view death as similar to sleep and involving a reunion with their ancestors.

Stanley, *et al.,* [33] concluded that the attempted suicides who also self-mutilated were more psychiatrically disturbed and at greater risk for suicide. They were more depressed and hopeless and had more aggressive and severe borderline pathology. They also underestimated the lethality of their suicidal acts and viewed death with less finality. Stanley, *et al.*, warned that clinicians should never discount the suicide attempts of patients with a history of self-mutilation.

DISCUSSION

It is clear that researchers and clinicians view self-mutilation and suicide attempts as different behaviors despite that fact that the two behaviors are often associated. However, suicidal individuals are more likely to engage in self-mutilation, and self-mutilators are more likely to have suicidal ideation and attempt suicide. The fact that self-mutilation is often associated with suicidal ideation puts them at risk for suicidal behavior and, thus, links the two behaviors.

Both non-lethal suicide attempts and acts of self-mutilation may be classified as counterintentioned suicidal acts, to use Shneidman's [34] term, in which self-destruction is threatened but not carried out[1]. Kessel [24] argued that the self-poisoner tries to effect a temporary escape from a situation that is intolerable and also tries to manipulate the situation and the people involved by means of the act. Clearly, the secondary gain and manipulative aspects of the suicide attempt are similar (although not identical) to the secondary gain and manipulative aspects of acts of self-mutilation. Individuals who engage in self-mutilation often report that this is an escape from their problems and that they cannot deal with their emotional life without cutting [22].

In addition to these similarities, there are some parallels in the research findings for suicidal behavior and self-mutilating behaviour:

1. In suicidal behavior, men tend to use more violent methods than women, methods such as firearms and hanging. In self-mutilating behavior, delicate wrist-cutting[2] and hair pulling are more common in women, whereas head banging and genital mutilation are more common in men.

2. The role of parental deprivation seems to be important in both kinds of acts. For suicidal behavior, researchers have found antecedent childhood experiences of complete parental deprivation through divorce or death to be common whereas, for self-mutilation, clinical data indicate partial loss through emotional distancing and inconsistent maternal warmth to be common.

3. The role of anger and difficulties in expressing aggression has been noted in both groups. Suicide is often conceptualized as anger turned inward onto the self. When anger can be acknowledged and expressed outwardly, the depression in the suicidal individual frequently lifts, and the suicidal preoccupation is reduced. The inability of self-mutilators to express anger and the overly composed appearance that they often present have been frequently noted. Their anger is turned inward and difficult for others to see unless noticed by family or friends [22].

Menninger [36], a psychoanalyst who accepted the existence of a death instinct, saw many behaviors as motivated by self-destructive and suicidal urges. He labeled individuals such as alcoholics and drug abusers as chronic suicides, since they were slowly committing suicide by behaving in ways that shortened their lives. Focal suicide referred to acts that damaged a part of the body, but left the individual still living. For Menninger, self-mutilation was an act of focal suicide in which the suicidal impulse is concentrated on a part of the self as a substitute for the whole. When describing the suicidal impulse, Menninger noted three components: the desire to hurt others, the desire to be punished and the desire to die. In self-mutilation, the first two components are

---

[1] Shneidman's other types of suicidal behavior are *intentioned*, *subintentioned*, and *unintentioned* [34].

[2] Researchers often distinguish between delicate and coarse wrist-cutting [35], the latter being more life-threatening (often involving deep cuts and tendon and ligament damage).

often apparent. The patient is often angry at some person and desires to hurt that person. He or she also feels the need to be punished for some actual or imagined crime or sin. The act of self-mutilation makes the significant other distressed and causes pain to the self. Thus, it satisfies two motives.

It is clear from the research in this area that self-mutilation and suicide are related behaviors. Depending on the researcher, however, it is less clear whether the two behaviors are the same and if the personalities of those who engage in self-mutilation and attempt suicide are similar. Since self-mutilation is most often diagnosed as a part of another disorder at risk for suicide, such as BPD or bipolar disorder, we may never know the full extent of their relationship. What is apparent from the research of these two concepts is that clinicians and researchers alike should be aware of both behaviors when they find the presence of one in an individual. Future research should explore the two behaviors further to determine the extent of the relationship between them.

REFERENCES

[1] Lester D. Self-mutilating behavior. Psychol Bull 1972; 78: 119-28.

[2] Alderman T. Self-Inflicted Violence: Helping those who hurt themselves. The International Child and Youth Care Network, 2006. Last accessed 5/30/08. Available from: Available from: http://www.cyc-net.org/reference/refs-self-mutilation-alderman1. html.

[3] Levy KN. The implications of attachment theory and research for understanding borderline personality disorder. Dev Psychopathol 2005; 17: 959-86.

[4] Segal-Trivitz Y, Bloch Y, Goldburt Y, Sobol-Havia D, Levkovitch Y, Ratzoni, G. Comparison of symptoms and treatments of adults and adolescents with borderline personality disorder. Int J Adolesc Med Health 2006; 18: 215-20.

[5] Ross S, Heath NL. Two models of adolescent self-mutilation. Suicide Life Threat Behav 2003; 33: 277-87.

[6] Zila L, Kiselica MS. Understanding and counseling self-mutilation in female adolescents and young adults. J Couns Dev 2001; 79: 46-52.

[7] Krysinksa K, Heller TS, De Leo D. Suicide and deliberate self-harm in personality disorders. Curr Opin Psychiatry 2006; 19(1): 95-101.

[8] Brown LK, Houck CD, Hadley WS, Lescano CM. Self-cutting and sexual risk among adolescents in intensive psychiatric treatment. Psychiatric Services 2005; 216-8.

[9] American Academy of Child and Adolescent Psychiatry. (AACAP). Self-Injury in Adolescents 2006. Retrieved on 5/30/08 Available from: http://www.aacap.org/publications/factsfam/73.htm.

[10] Favazza AR. The coming of age of self-mutilation. J Nerv Ment Dis 1998; 186: 259-68.

[11] Self Harm. Mental Health Foundation, 2006. Retrieved 10/3/07. Available from: http://www.mentalhealth.org.uk/information/mental-health-a-z/self-harm/.

[12] Herpertz S, Sass H, Favazza A. Impulsivity in self-mutilative behavior: psychometric and biological findings. J Psychiatry Res 1997;31: 451-65.

[13] Wagner M. Behavioral characteristics related to substance abuse and risk-taking, sensation- seeking, anxiety sensitivity and self-reinforcement. Addict Behav 2001;26: 115-20.

[14] Nevid J, Rathus S, Greene B. Abnormal Psychology in a Changing World. 6th Edition. New York: Prentice Hall, 2005.

[15] Folkman S, Lazarus R, Gruen R, DeLongis A. Appraisal, coping, health status, and psychological symptoms. J Pers Soc Psychol 1986; 50: 571-9.

[16] Nolen-Hoeksema S, Corte C. Gender and self-regulation. In: Baumeister RF, Vohs KD, Eds. Handbook of self-regulation: Research, theory, and applications. New York: Guilford. 2004; pp. 441-521.

[17] Favazza AR. Bodies under siege: Self-mutilation in culture and psychiatry. Baltimore, MD: John Hopkins University Press, 1987.

[18] Shapiro S. Affect integration in psychoanalysis: a clinical approach to self-destructive behavior. Bull Menninger Clin 1991; 55: 363-74.

[19] Fenning S, Carlson G, Fenning S. Contagious self-mutilation. J Am Acad Child Adolesc Psychiatry 1995; 37: 211-7.

[20] Gould M. Suicide contagion. The Suicide and Mental Health Association International (SMHAI), 2004. Last accessed on 5/30/08. http://suicideandmentalhealthassociationinternational.org/suiconclust.html.

[21] American Psychiatric Association. Diagnostic and statistical manual of mental disorders, (4th ed., text revision). Washington, DC: American Psychiatric Association, 2000.

[22] Martino S. Scars: Creative approaches to understanding and coping with self-mutilation. Baltimore, MD: Apprentice House, 2009.
[23] Walsh BW, Rosen PM. Self-mutilation. New York: Guilford, 1988.
[24] Kessel N. The respectability of self-poisoning , and the fashion of survival. J Psychos Res 1966; 10: 29-36.
[25] Dorpat TL, Boswell JW. An evaluation of suicidal intent in suicide attempts. Compreh Psychiatry 1963; 4: 117-25.
[26] Kreitman N, Philip AE, Greer S, Bagley C. Parasuicide. Br J Psychiatry 1969; 115: 747-8.
[27] Soloff P, Lis J, Kelly T, Cornelius J, Ulrich R. Self-mutilation and suicidal behavior in borderline personality disorder. J Pers Disord 1994; 8: 257-67.
[28] Jones A. Self-mutilation in prison. Crim Justice Behav 1986; 13: 286-96.
[29] Lester D. Boderline personality disorder. Psychol Rep 1993; 73: 394.
[30] Bongar B, Peterson L, Golann S, Hardiman J. Self-mutilation and the chronically suicidal patient. Ann Clin Psychiatry 1990; 2: 217-22.
[31] Zlotnick C, Donaldson D, Spirito A and Pearlstein T. Affect regulation and suicide attempts in adolescent inpatients. J Am Acad Child Adolesc Psychiatry 1997; 36: 793-8.
[32] Sonneburn CK, Vanstraelen PM. A retrospective study of self-inflicted burns. Gen Hosp Psychiatry 1992; 14: 404-7.
[33] Stanley B, Gameroff MJ, Michalsen V, Mann JJ. Are suicide attempters who self-mutilate a unique population? Am J Psychiatry 2001;158: 427-32.
[34] Shneidman ES. Suicide, sleep, and death. J Consult Psychol 1964; 28: 95-106.
[35] Pao P. The syndrome of delicate self-cutting. Br J Med Psychol 1969; 42: 195-206.
[36] Menninger K. Man against himself. New York: Harcourt, Brace and World, 1938.

CHAPTER 21

Hypothalamic Pituitary Adrenal Axis and Prolactin Abnormalities in Suicidal Behavior

Gianluca Serafini[1,*], Paolo Girardi[1], Denise Erbuto[1], David Lester[2] and Maurizio Pompili[1,3]

[1]*Department of Neurosciences, Mental Health and Organs Functions, Suicide Prevention Center, Sant'Andrea Hospital, Sapienza University of Rome, Italy;* [2]*The Richard Stockton College of New Jersey, USA and* [3]*McLean Hospital – Harvard Medical School, USA*

Abstract: Hypothalamic Pituitary Adrenal (HPA) axis hyperactivity measured with the dexamethasonesuppression test and the dexamethesone/CRH test may be found to have some predictive power for suicidal behavior in mood disorders. Increased prolactin (PRL) levels may be related both to physiological and pathological conditions. HPA axis abnormalities and increased levels of PRL may coexist and common neuroendocrine changes may activate both HPA axis and PRL release. HPA axis hyperactivity is presumably present in a large subpopulation of depressed subjects. Suicidal behavior is considered to be a form of inward directed aggression and aggressive behavior has been connected to high androgen levels. However, lower plasma total testosterone levels have also been reported in subjects with depression and higher suicidality. Lipid/immune dysregulations, the increased ratio of blood fatty acids and increased PRL levels may be associated with the increased production of pro-inflammatory cytokines, which were reported both in major depression and suicidal behavior. Although no studies have been done to determine whether antemortem physical stress may be detected by raised post-mortem PRL, this would be of great interest for physicians.

Keywords: Suicidal behavior, stress, prolactin, HPA axis.

1. INTRODUCTION: INCIDENCE AND DEMOGRAPHICS

Suicide has taken lives around the world and across the centuries, and it accounts for about one million deaths annually, with devastating socioeconomic costs and consequences [1]. It is one of the world's largest public health problems and has multiple causes in which, according to a stress-diathesis model, both genetic make up and acquired susceptibility contribute to a person's predisposition to suicidal acts in stressful situations [1, 2].

Suicide results from various factors, including psychiatric, biological and environmental factors which may be considered as risk factors in determining suicidal behavior. In particular, biological dysregulations may increase suicide risk regardless of psychiatric disorders as well as that may lead to vulnerability for developing a psychiatric disorder. Prospective studies suggest that dysfunctions in the HPA axis have some predictive power for suicide in mood disorders [3-5].

HPA axis hyperactivity may be considered a relevant risk factor for suicide both in people with and without mood disorders [6, 7]. Disturbances in the HPA system may be measured with the Dexamethasone Suppression Test (DST) and Dexamethasone/CRH test. Also, PRL dysregulations may be associated with physiological increased suicidal risk [8, 9]. Elevated PRL secretion may be associated both to physiological and pathological conditions. HPA axis abnormalities and increased levels of PRL may be associated, although not directly, to a common stimulus like stress which may determine both of these conditions.

The aim of this chapter is to shed light upon some biological dysregulations underlying suicidality with particular regard to hyperprolactinemia, HPA axis abnormalities and their relationship. One of the most relevant issues concerns whether PRL and cortisol levels as possible stress indicators may serve as a useful element to identify a possible neurobiological risk profile as predictor of suicidal behavior.

***Address correspondence to Gianluca Serafini:** Department of Neurosciences, Mental Health and Organs Functions, Suicide Prevention Center, Sant'Andrea Hospital, Sapienza University of Rome, Italy; E-mail: gianluca.serafini@uniroma1.it

2. HYPERPROLACTINEMIA: DEFINITION AND ETIOLOGY

Hyperprolactinemia (increased plasmatic PRL levels) is a hormonal abnormality that may interfere with the functioning of reproductive, endocrine, and metabolic systems [10].

Hyperprolactinemia determines both short- and long-term consequences that may seriously affect the quality of life: menstrual disturbances, galactorrhea, sexual dysfunction, gynecomastia, infertility, decreased bone mineral density, and breast cancer [10].

Increased PRL levels may be related to physiological conditions such as pregnancy and lactation, breast feeding, nipple and breast stimulation, sleep, and exercise or emotional stress [11, 12] and to several pathological conditions. Pathological causes include pituitary and hypothalamic diseases like prolactinomas, excess thyrotropin-releasing hormone (TRH), primary hypothyroidism, myocardial infarction and epilepsy and also iatrogenic causes such as the side effects of many anti-psychotics, tricyclic antidepressants, cimetidine, verapamil, methyldopa, oestrogens, opiates medications side effects oestrogens and opiates [13].

Vilar *et al.* [14] investigating clinical and laboratory features of 1234 patients with different etiologies of hyperprolactinemia found that prolactinomas, drug induced hyperprolactinemia, and macroprolactinemia were the three most common causes of hyperprolactinemia and that the highest PRL levels were observed in patients with prolactinomas. Clinical manifestations were similar irrespective of the etiology of the hyperprolactinemia.

3. HPA AXIS ACTIVITY AND SUICIDE

The HPA axis is the neuroendocrine system that regulates the body's response to stress. CRH and vasopressin are released from neurosecretory nerve terminals at the median eminence and act synergistically to stimulate the secretion of stored ACTH from corticotroph cells. Both CRH and AVP are required for a normal pituitary and adrenal response to some acute stressful stimuli. ACTH is transported to the adrenal cortex of the adrenal gland, where it rapidly stimulates biosynthesis of corticosteroids such as cortisol from cholesterol. Corticosteroids produce several behavioral changes [15].

Prospective biological studies suggest that dysfunctions in the HPA axis have some predictive power for suicide in mood disorders [3-5, 16]. Several studies have reported that HPA axis hyperactivity may be a relevant risk factor for suicide both in patients with major depressive disorder and in patients without a clear psychiatric diagnosis [6, 7].

Considerable evidence suggests that hypercortisolemia is a frequent finding in depressed patients and persists between episodes [17-20]. Also, HPA axis hyperactivity is associated with both non-fatal suicidal behavior and completed suicide. Virkkunen [21] have found that habitually violent offenders with an antisocial personality disorder had a significantly lower excretion rate of urinary free cortisol than did all the other groups of offenders or the control subjects.

Roy *et al.* [22] and Norman *et al.* [23] found that violent suicide attempters had higher cortisol levels than those who made non-violent suicide attempts. Also, post-mortem studies have found evidence of chronic axis activation in completed suicides, such as adrenal hyperplasia, increased CRH content in the CSF [24], down-regulated the CRF1 receptors by CRH and induced the CRF1 expression in hippocampal and cortical regions of the immature rat brain [25].

There are also some reports of a significant association between HPA axis hyperactivity and completed suicide in mood disorder [23, 26, 27]. Two other studies found the relationship to be confined to depressed patients who had attempted or seriously contemplated suicide [4, 28].

In a sample of borderline personality disorder (BPD) patients with minimal exposure to treatment, Jovev *et al.* [29] found that parasuicidal behavior might be associated with greater activation of the HPA axis.

Increased pituitary gland volume, a measure of HPA axis activation, is associated (in animal studies) with increased levels of CRH, circulating cortisol levels and a subsequent increase in the size and the number of pituitary corticotrophs (ACTH-producing cells) [30].

However, studies of high-risk patients with a major depressive disorder have shown that abnormalities in HPA axis function exist prior to the onset of the clinical symptoms and it has been hypothesized that these abnormalities may merely precipitate depressive episodes [31].

4. THE DEXAMETHASONE SUPPRESSION TEST

Disturbances in the HPA system measured with the DST and the DEX/CRH test have been associated in prospective studies with increased risk of suicide in depressed patients [27, 32, 33].

Higher cortisol levels after a dexamethasone test (DST: a clinical measure of HPA axis hyperactivity) indicate an increased risk of suicide by as much as 14-fold [26], and an elevated cortisol response to the DEX/CRH test is associated with a 4- to 6-fold higher risk for depressive relapse [34]. The DST non-suppressor rate is significantly higher in suicide attempters compared to non-attempters [4].

In prospective follow-up study of inpatients with major or schizoaffective depressive disorders, patients who had an abnormal DST result were significantly more likely to complete suicide [35]. Additionally, a recent meta-analysis of seven studies concluded that DST nonsuppression increases the risk of suicide by a factor of 4.6 [36]. DST non-suppression distinguished with higher specificity and predictive value between suicide attempters and non-attempters in young depressed inpatients. Also, Jokinen and Nordstrom [37] found that elderly mood disorder inpatients who fail to suppress cortisol in the DST have a higher risk of suicide.

However, DST non-suppression may not be a useful predictor of subsequent completed suicide for mood disorder outpatients or for those without a clinical history of a suicide attempt [28].

Aging increases the cortisol response to a pharmacological challenge with CRH, and increasing insensitivity of the HPA axis to the feedback of cortisol may be another factor involved in the activation of the HPA axis during aging [37]. In a recent meta-analysis of 45 studies, including both pharmacological challenges and non-pharmacological challenges (*e.g.*, psychosocial stress), and both challenge and suppression procedures, there was an increased cortisol response to challenge in the older compared to younger patients, as well as a threefold stronger effect of aging on cortisol responses to challenge in women as compared with men [38].

5. HPA AXIS ABNORMALITIES AND PRL LEVELS IN SUICIDAL BEHAVIOR

PRL have also been measured as it is known to be stress responsive [39]. Increased PRL may be found both in psychiatric patients who had attempted suicide as possible indicator of stress [8] and in males with severe or moderate traumatic brain injury [40]. But what is the relationship between increased PRL levels and HPA axis abnormalities in determining suicidal behavior?

The HPA axis has complex interactions with brain serotonergic, noradrenergic, and dopaminergic systems. Hood *et al.* [41] hypothesised that tryptophan depletion increased the psychological (increase in subjective anxiety measures), neuroendocrine (*e.g.*, cortisol and PRL increases) and autonomic responses to single breath 35%CO_2 in normal volunteers. They stated that tryptophan depletion may act as a stressor, as measured by plasma cortisol (and to a lesser extent PRL) increases and tryptophan depletion may produce an aversive state that is perceived as stressful and indirectly results in increased cortisol levels.

It's also possible that reduced central 5-HT *via* tryptophan depletion may be relevant in modulating the HPA axis activity. Serotonin is known to influence the HPA axis through direct actions at the HPA axis levels [42] with serotonergic systems having both facilitatory and inhibitory actions on the axis (Lowry *et al.*, 2005).

Further, these systems may also act through the hippocampal negative feedback regulation of the HPA axis causing disinhibition of the axis and a rise in cortisol levels [43]. However, it is not clear why tryptophan depletion produced a neuroendocrine stress response in volunteers in the absence of a psychological stress response. In some diseases, such as chronic fatigue syndrome, circadian rhythms and HPA axis impairment may be associated with higher levels of PRL [44], and acute peripheral enhancement of IL-1beta may induce neuroendocrine changes in the hypothalamus that activates both HPA axis and PRL release [45].

However, although often co-occurring, the different dimensions of the stress response (increased PRL levels axis hyperactivity) do not necessarily need to appear together; so assessing the stress response in all possible domains is crucial.

6. ANDROGEN LEVELS, PRL CONCENTRATION AND SUICIDALITY

Some studies have addressed the role of androgen levels in attempted suicide. Suicidal behavior is considered to be a form of inward-directed aggression, and aggressive behavior has been connected to high androgen levels [46].

However, lower plasma total testosterone levels have been reported in patients with depression and higher suicidality and in those who used violent suicidal methods [47] and in the cerebrospinal fluid of suicide attempters. Markianos *et al.* [8] found that lower testosterone levels were not related to increased cortisol and PRL levels in suicidal attempters.

The stress response is expected to influence testosterone levels, since both mental and acute metabolic stress can lower plasma testosterone levels [48] and increase the cortisol levels in violent suicide attempters more than non-violent attempters [49]. The observed low testosterone and the increased cortisol levels could be due both to the severe medical condition and to the suicide attempt.

However, in acute serious medical conditions, a suppression of the reproductive axis may occur [50], so the low testosterone levels could be due to the severe medical conditions rather than to the suicide attempt. It is also possible that testosterone exerts an inhibitory action on the HPA axis response to stress in males; in fact, testosterone administration in rats, may reverse the increased ACTH and corticosterone responses to acute stress after gonadectomy [51, 52].What is the relationship between lower plasma testosterone and increased PRL levels, and how might they affect suicidality?

Increased PRL concentrations seem not to be accompanied by any change in testosterone, LH, or FSH [8], and similar findings have been found in patients with traumatic brain injury [40].

However, the increased PRL plasma levels observed during immobilization stress and hemorrhage could have a negative effect on testosterone levels [53]. This needs to be confirmed in future prospective studies where the levels of sex hormones, especially testosterone, LH and PRL, may be monitored as possible predictive factors of violent suicide attempts. As Jokinen *et al.* [59] have noted, there is a need for biological data that may be used as suicide predictors to enhance the detection of patients at high risk for suicide.

7. PRL AND CYTOKINES IN THE ASSOCIATION BETWEEN LEPTIN DYSREGULATION AND SUICIDALITY

Lower levels of serum cholesterol, leptin and fatty acids have been found in suicidal individuals [54]. Leptin is an adipose-derived hormone involved in the maintenance of neuroendocrine homeostasis. Actually, an explanation for how altered lipid metabolism in the peripheral circulation could affect behavior and elevate the risk of suicide is lacking.

Leptin receptor, fatty acid desaturase, phosphoinositide-3-kinase and stearoyl-CoA desaturase were found consistently down-regulated in the frontal cortex of depressed suicides compared to non-suicidal comparison subjects [55].

Friedman and Halaas [56] hypothesized that reduced leptin concentrations, generally associated with low cholesterol levels, may serve as a "starvation signal" resulting in less leptin entering the brain and binding to its receptors to exert its numerous effects including signaling pathways that affect mood and behavior.

It has been demonstrated that leptin exerts antidepressant effects in rats, increasing neuronal activation in the hippocampus [57]; reduced serum levels of leptin had been found in suicide attempters [58, 59] and depressed patients [60]. But what is the role of stress hormones?

Increased ratios of blood omega-6/omega-3 fatty acids are associated with increased stress [61] (Logan, 2003), presumably through the increased PRL levels that might lead to increased production of pro-inflammatory cytokines, linked both to depression and suicidal behavior. Lalovic *et al.* [55] have suggested that the link between alterations in lipid metabolism/immune response gene expression and major depression and suicidal behavior may be mediated by cytokines.

However, higher levels of leptin are found to be significantly correlated with higher PRL levels in pituitary adenomas tissues with no statistically significant differences for TNF-alpha and IL-6 [62].

Finally, leptin dysregulation is presumably related to mood disorders and suicide through the activation of the stress system related to PRL levels and cytokines. However, the nature of this correlation remain unclear and not well documented.

8. POST-MORTEM PRL AS ANTE-MORTEM STRESS

No post-mortem study of suicides has demonstrated whether ante-mortem psychological stress before self-harm is associated with increased plasma PRL at necropsy.

Additionally, no study has determined whether the level of post-mortem PRL is correlated with a history of ante-mortem physical stress. Jones and Hallworth [63] suggested that PRL in all cases of trauma was in the normal range (up to 500 mU/l), whereas, in cases of sudden unexpected death, the mean concentration was 533 mU/l.

Postoperative deaths or cases with chronic disease had a mean value of 1027 mU/l, while suicides had a mean value of 1398 mU/l. In suicide cases, females had a mean value of 2072 mU/l compared with 692 mU/l of males.

The same authors suggested that it is possible to detect PRL in post-mortem venous blood samples and to identify hyperprolactinaemia, finding that the level of PRL was roughly comparable with the duration of antemortem physical stress. However, the levels found were higher than previously reported [13].

9. PITUITARY ABNORMALITIES

Pituitary microadenomas and adrenal enlargement, clinical as well as subclinical, are relatively frequent in completed suicides [31, 64-67].

In a retrospective study, Furgal-Borzych *et al.* [64] found pituitary microadenomas were found in 47.7% of completed suicides as compared to only 18.3% of the non-suicidal group. Logistic regression analysis in a model controlling for age and sex showed that microadenomas constituted a unique risk factor. The immunohistochemical phenotyping revealed a higher percentage of immunopositive (secreting) microadenomas in the nonsuicidal group as compared to the suicidal group (80.0% *vs.* 59.4%) and a predominance of growth hormone-secreting microadenomas in both groups.

Some post-mortem changes, such as the the precursor molecule for ACTH (POMC), were found in the pituitaries of the completed suicides, both as mRNA and peptide content, as an indication of chronic axis activation of the HPA axis.

CONCLUSIONS

HPA axis hyperactivity measured with the DST and the DEX/CRH test may be found and has some predictive power for suicidal behavior in mood disorders.

Increased PRL levels may be related both to physiological and pathological (dysmetabolic) conditions and hyperprolactinemia is a complex phenomenon which may have implications for suicidal behavior.

Both hyperactivity of the HPA axis (which is also present in patientss with mood disorders in whom it may precipitate depressive episodes) and increased PRL levels may be found in suicidal individuals.

It is not well documented how the stress response influences plasma testosterone levels and whether testosterone directly exerts an inhibitory action on the HPA axis response to stress.

Additionally, there are conflicting data about the relationship between increased PRL concentrations and androgen levels.

Also, pro-inflammatory cytokines, such as TNF-alpha and IL-6, might play a relevant role in suicidal behavior presumably by mediating the alterations of both the lipid metabolism/immune system (*e.g.*, leptin dysregulation and the concentration of blood fatty acids) and the activation of the stress system.

Finally it seems possible to detect PRL in post-mortem venous blood samples of people who die by suicide as indicators of ante-mortem stress, and PRL values at necropsy differ according to the cause of death; in cases of deaths by suicide, this might exert relevant implications for researchers in identifying some possible ante-mortem predictor of future suicide.

REFERENCES

[1] Mann JJ. Neurobiology of suicidal behavior. Nat rev 2003; 4(10): 819-28.

[2] Wasserman D. Suicide - an unnecessary death. London: Martin Dunitz Publishers, 2001.

[3] Claes SJ. CRH, stress, and major depression: a psychobiological interplay. Vitam Horm 2004; 69: 117-50.

[4] Jokinen J, Nordstrom P. HPA axis hyperactivity as suicide predictor in elderly mood disorder inpatients. Psychoneuroendocrinology 2008; 33: 1387–93.

[5] Pariante CM. Depression, stress and the adrenal axis. J Neuroendocrinol 2003; 15(8): 811-2.

[6] Nemeroff CB, Owens MJ, Bissette G, Andorn AC, Stanley M. Reduced corticotropin releasing factor binding sites in the frontal cortex of suicide victims. Arch Gen Psychiatry 1988; 45(6): 577-9.

[7] Rao VP, Krishnan KR, Goli V, *et al.* Neuroanatomical changes and hypothalamo-pituitary-adrenal axis abnormalities. Biol Psychiatry 1989; 26(7): 729-32.

[8] Markianos M, Tripodianakis J, Istikoglou C, *et al.* Suicide attempt by jumping: a study of gonadal axis hormones in male suicide attempters *versus* men who fell by accident. Psychiatry Res 2009; 170(1): 82-5.

[9] van Heeringen K. The neurobiology of suicide and suicidality. Can J Psychiatry 2003; 48(5): 292-300.

[10] Bostwick JR, Guthrie SK, Ellingrod VL. Antipsychotic-induced hyperprolactinemia. Pharmacother 2009; 29(1): 64-73.

[11] Molitch ME. Pathologic hyperprolactinemia. Endocrinol Metab Clin North Am 1992; 21(4): 877-901.

[12] Sonino N, Navarrini C, Ruini C, Fallo F, Boscaro M, Fava GA. Life events in the pathogenesis of hyperprolactinemia. Eur J Endocrinol 2004; 151(1): 61-5.

[13] Zis AP, Haskett RF, Albala AA, Carroll BJ. Morphine inhibits cortisol and stimulates prolactin secretion in man. Psychoneuroendocrinol 1984; 9(4): 423-7.

[14] Vilar L, Freitas MC, Naves LA, *et al.* Diagnosis and management of hyperprolactinemia: results of a Brazilian multicenter study with 1234 patients. J Endocrinol Invest 2008; 31(5): 436-44.

[15] Chrousos GP, Gold PW. The concepts of stress and stress system disorders. Overview of physical and behavioral homeostasis. JAMA 1992; 267: 1244–52.

[16] Paykel ES. Stress and affective disorders in humans. Semin Clin Neuropsychiatry 2001; 6(1): 4-11.

[17] Goodyer IM, Herbert J, Tamplin A, Altham PM. Recent life events, cortisol, dehydroepiandrosterone and the onset of major depression in high-risk adolescents. Br J Psychiatry 2000; 177: 499–504.

[18] Harris TO, Borsanyi S, Messari S, *et al.* Morning cortisol as a risk factor for subsequent major depressive disorder in adult women. Br J Psychiatry 2000; 177: 505–10.

[19] Ribeiro SC, Tandon R, Grunhaus L, Greden JF. The DST as a predictor of outcome in depression: a meta-analysis. Am J Psychiatry 1993; 150: 1618–29.

[20] Young EA, Aggen SH, Prescott CA, Kendler KS. Similarity in saliva cortisol measures in monozygotic twins and the influence of past major depression. Biol Psychiatry 2000; 48: 70–4.

[21] Virkkunen M. Urinary free cortisol secretion in habitually violent offenders. Acta Psychiatr Scand 1985; 72: 40–4.

[22] Roy A, Lamparski D, De Jong J, *et al.* Cerebrospinal fluid monoamine metabolites in alcoholic patients who attempt suicide. Acta Psychiatr Scand 1990; 81: 58–61.

[23] Norman WH, Brown WA, Miller IW, Keitner GI, Overholser J. The dexamethasone suppression test and completed suicide. Acta Psychiatr Scand 1990; 81: 120–5.

[24] Arato M, Rihmer Z, Szadoczky E Seasonal influence on the dexamethasone suppression test results in unipolar depression. Arch Gen Psychiatry 1986; 43: 813.

[25] Brunson KL, Grigoriadis DE, Lorang MT, Baram TZ. Corticotropin-releasing hormone (CRH) downregulates the function of its receptor (CRF1) and induces CRF1 expression in hippocampal and cortical regions of the immature rat brain. Exp Neurol 2002; 176: 75–86.

[26] Coryell W, Schlesser M. The dexamethasone suppression test and suicide prediction. Am J Psychiatry 2001; 158: 748–53.

[27] Coryell W, Schlesser M. Combined biological tests for suicide prediction. Psychiatry Res 2007; 150: 187–91.

[28] Coryell W, Young E, Carroll B. Hyperactivity of the hypothalamic-pituitary-adrenal axis and mortality in major depressive disorder. Psychiatry Res 2006; 142: 99–104.

[29] Jovev M, Garner B, Phillips L, *et al.* An MRI study of pituitary volume and parasuicidal behavior in teenagers with first-presentation borderline personality disorder. Psychiatry Res 2008; 162: 273–7.

[30] Gertz BJ, Contreras LN, McComb DJ, Kovacs K, Tyrrell JB, Dallman MF. Chronic administration of corticotropin-releasing factor increases pituitary corticotroph number. Endocrinology 1987; 120(1): 381-8.

[31] Holsboer F. The corticosteroid receptor hypothesis of depression. Neuropsychopharmacology 2000; 23(5): 477-501.

[32] Lester D. The dexamethasone suppression test as an indicator of suicide: a meta-analysis. Pharmacopsychiatry 1992; 25(6): 265-70.

[33] Yerevanian BI, Feusner JD, Koek RJ, Mintz J. The dexamethasone suppression test as a predictor of suicidal behavior in unipolar depression. J Affect Disord 2004; 83(2-3): 103-8.

[34] Zobel AW, Nickel T, Sonntag A, Uhr M, Holsboer F, Ising M. Cortisol response in the combined dexamethasone/CRH test as predictor of relapse in patients with remitted depression. a prospective study. J Psychiatr Res 2001; 35(2): 83-94.

[35] Coryell W, Schlesser MA. Suicide and the dexamethasone suppression test in unipolar depression. Am J Psychiatry 1981; 138(8): 1120-1.

[36] Mann JJ, Brent DA, Arango V. The neurobiology and genetics of suicide and attempted suicide: a focus on the serotonergic system. Neuropsychopharmacol 2001; 24(5): 467-77.

[37] Jokinen J, Nordström P. HPA axis hyperactivity and attempted suicide in young adult mood disorder inpatients. J Affect Disord 2009; 116(1-2): 117-20.

[38] Otte C, Hart S, Neylan TC, Marmar CR, Yaffe K, Mohr DC.A meta-analysis of cortisol response to challenge in human aging: importance of gender. Psychoneuroendocrinol 2005; 30(1): 80-91.

[39] Freeman ME, Kanyicska B, Lerant A. Nagy G. Prolactin: structure, function, and regulation of secretion. Physiol Rev 2000; 80: 1523–631.

[40] Agha A, Rogers B, Mylotte D, *et al.* Neuroendocrine dysfunction in the acute phase of traumatic brain injury. Clin Endocrinol (Oxf) 2004; 60(5): 584-91.

[41] Hood SD, Hince DA, Robinson H, Cirillo M, Christmas D, Kaye JM. Serotonin regulation of the human stress response. Psychoneuroendocrinol 2006; 31(9): 1087-97.

[42] Chaouloff F. Serotonin, stress and corticoids. J Psychopharmacol 2000; 14: 139–151.

[43] Lowry CA. Functional subsets of serotonergic neurones: implications for control of the hypothalamic–pituitary–adrenal axis. J Neuroendocrinol 2002; 14: 911–23.

[44] Racciatti D, Guagnano MT, Vecchiet J, *et al.*Chronic fatigue syndrome: circadian rhythm and hypothalamic-pituitary-adrenal (HPA) axis impairment. Int J Immunopathol Pharmacol 2001; 14(1): 11-5.

[45] Skurlova M, Stofkova A, Jurcovicova J. Exogenous IL-1beta induces its own expression, but not that of IL-6 in the hypothalamus and activates HPA axis and prolactin release. Endocr Regul 2006; 40(4): 125-8.

[46] Archer J. The influence of testosterone on human aggression. Br J Psychol 1991; 82 (Pt 1): 1-28.

[47] Tripodianakis J, Markianos M, Rouvali O, Istikoglou C. Gonadal axis hormones in psychiatric male patients after a suicide attempt. Eur Arch Psychiatry Clin Neurosci 2007; 257(3): 135-9.

[48] Zitzmann M, Nieschlag E. Testosterone levels in healthy men and the relation to behavioral and physical characteristics: facts and constructs. Eur J Endocrinol 2001; 144(3): 183-97.

[49] Roy A. Hypothalamic-pituitary-adrenal axis function and suicidal behavior in depression. Biol Psychiatry 1992; 32(9): 812-6.

[50] Spratt DI, Longcope C, Cox PM, Bigos ST, Wilbur-Welling C. Differential changes in serum concentrations of androgens and estrogens (in relation with cortisol) in postmenopausal women with acute illness. J Clin Endocrinol Metab 1993; 76(6): 1542-7.

[51] Handa RJ, Burgess LH, Kerr JE, O'Keefe JA. Gonadal steroid hormone receptors and sex differences in the hypothalamo-pituitary-adrenal axis. Horm Behav 1994; 28(4): 464-76.

[52] Viau V, Meaney MJ. The inhibitory effect of testosterone on hypothalamic-pituitary-adrenal responses to stress is mediated by the medial preoptic area. J Neurosci 1996; 16(5): 1866-76.

[53] Jurcovicová J, Kvetnansky R, Dobrakovová M, Jezová D, Kiss A, Makara GB. Prolactin response to immobilization stress and hemorrhage: the effect of hypothalamic deafferentations and posterior pituitary denervation. Endocrinology 1990; 126(5): 2527-33.

[54] Westling S, Ahrén B, Träskman-Bendz L, Westrin A. Low CSF leptin in female suicide attempters with major depression. J Affect Disord 2004; 81(1): 41-8.

[55] Lalovic A, Klempan T, Sequeira A, Luheshi G, Turecki G. Altered expression of lipid metabolism and immune response genes in the frontal cortex of suicide completers. J Affect Disord 2010; 120(1-3): 24-31.

[56] Friedman JM, Halaas JL. Leptin and the regulation of body weight in mammals. Nature 1998; 395(6704): 763-70.

[57] Lu XY, Kim CS, Frazer A, Zhang W. Leptin: a potential novel antidepressant. Proc Natl Acad Sci USA 2006; 103: 1593–8.

[58] Atmaca M, Kuloglu M, Tezcan E, Ustundag B. Serum leptin and cholesterol levels in schizophrenic patients with and without suicide attempts. Acta Psychiatr Scand 2003; 108: 208–14.

[59] Atmaca M, Kuloglu M, Tezcan E, Ustundag B, Gecici O, Firidin B. Serum leptin and cholesterol values in suicide attempters. Neuropsychobiology 2002; 45: 124–7.

[60] Jow GM, Yang TT, Chen CL. Leptin and cholesterol levels are low in major depressive disorder, but high in schizophrenia. J Affect Disord 2006; 90: 21–7.

[61] Logan AC. Neurobehavioral aspects of omega-3 fatty acids: possible mechanisms and therapeutic value in major depression. Altern Med Rev 2003; 8: 410–25.

[62] Balci H, Akgun-Dar K, Gazioglu N, Kapucu A, Bolayirli M, Oz B. The relationship between prolactin (PRL), leptin, nitric oxide (NO), and cytokines in patients with hyperprolactinemia. Pituitary 2009; 12(3): 170-6.

[63] Jones TJ, Hallworth MJ. Postmortem prolactin as a marker of antemortem stress. J Clin Pathol 1999; 52(10): 749-51.

[64] Furgal-Borzych A, Lis GJ, Litwin JA, Rzepecka-Wozniak E, Trela F, Cichocki T. Increased incidence of pituitary microadenomas in suicide victims. Neuropsychobiology 2007; 55(3-4), 163-6.

[65] Maes M, Lin A, Bonaccorso S, *et al.* Increased 24-hour urinary cortisol excretion in patients with post-traumatic stress disorder and patients with major depression, but not in patients with fibromyalgia. Acta Psychiatr Scand 1998; 98(4): 328-35.

[66] Modell S, Yassouridis A, Huber J, Holsboer F. Corticosteroid receptor function is decreased in depressed patients. Neuroendocrinology 1997; 65(3): 216-22.

[67] Scott LV, Dinan TG. Vasopressin and the regulation of hypothalamic-pituitary-adrenal axis function: implications for the pathophysiology of depression. Life Sciences 1998; 62(22): 1985-98.

CHAPTER 22

Homicide - Suicide

Paolo Roma, Antonella Spacca and Stefano Ferracuti*

Department of Neurosciences, Mental Health and Organs Functions, Suicide Prevention Center, Sant'Andrea Hospital, Sapienza University of Rome, Italy

Abstract: Murder - suicide is an event where a person kills another and then suicide. Murder - suicide is more rare than other forms of violent deaths, but it is certainly mostly tragic and usually more shocking than homicide or suicide when taken individually, especially when the event involves a mass murder.

This chapter will present an overview of the main types of murder-suicide, outlining the most common features of the crime and providing some guidelines on prevention. Thematic context of homicide followed by suicide, including victim - perpetrator relationship, age, sex, race, ethnicity, and occupation in addition to precipitating factors, motivation, type of fatal injury, and location of event, is discussed.

For each different category of crime the incidence of the phenomenon in the Italian context is given. The Italian data were collected in a span of 24 years (from 1 January 1985 to December 31, 2008), using the information disclosed by the state press agency and the four national newspapers of greater circulation.

Keywords: Homicide – suicide, murder – suicide, spousal murder – suicides, filicide – suicide, extra familial murder suicide, mass murder – suicide.

1. INTRODUCTION

> "Between the admirable sacrifice of the honest person, who spontaneously kills himself, and murder of the delinquent, even when driven by passion, there are other ways in which the internal storm of the soul is released and manifested; ways by which the passage from homicide to suicide is made clear. In other words, while some take their lives and leave their lover, cause of their fatal resolution, free to live....others – who are more selfish, attempt to persuade their lover to die with them, and finally take their lover's life before taking their own" [1].

Homicide-suicide is a relatively rare event, yet it has always caught the attention of the press and of scholars due to the impact it holds within the community. Homicide-suicide is a criminal manifestation in which the subject decides to kill himself, after having killed the victim; the reasons for suicide are complex, resulting from a large number of factors that are not always related only to the tolerance of frustration and to an impulsive tendency.

The relation between homicide and suicide, due to the common element of aggressiveness, has been known for a long time; Menninger [2] wrote that suicide is equally motivated by the desire to die, the desire to be killed, and the desire to kill. In order to explain the different appearance of the two phenomena, Lombroso [3] wrote that the barbarous man prefers to sacrifice other people's lives, in case of adversity in his own life; the civilized man, instead, prefers to commit suicide because he needs to reinforce his moral sense, which is based on respect for others. Also Sighele [1] supported the idea of a civilization process, asserting that the honest and civil man prefers suicide to homicide.

Many authors, starting from Guerry [4] in the first half of the 19th century, tried to explain the statistic relation between the two phenomena. Some, such as Ferri [5] observed inverse trends; others like Tarde [6] noticed parallel trends; some others like Henry and Short [7] believed that individuals who are conditioned by external containers are more inclined to having a hetero-aggressive reaction, while those who are free

***Address correspondence to Stefano Ferracuti:** Department of Neurosciences, Mental Health and Organs Functions, Suicide Prevention Center, Sant'Andrea Hospital, Sapienza University of Rome, Italy; E mail: stefano.ferracuti@uniroma1.it

from family or social ties are more likely to respond with a self-harm reaction.

Homicide and suicide are generally considered to be two opposite behaviors. Suicide appears as the most personal action an individual can do, representing a rebellion to the world around him.

Homicide, instead, is the most slanderous action one can think of against man and humankind, with few exceptions, which will be later analyzed.

Suicide has always been surrounded by a mystic halo and by a dichotomy between the idea of it being a brave action and the conviction that it is actually cowardice. In some ancient societies, suicide was praised. Among the Maya "The Lady of the rope" (Ixtab) – a divinity that was depicted as hanging on a noose – was the goddess of suicides who had their own paradise, because they were considered sacred.

In the Egypt of pharaohs, high rank criminals were allowed to commit suicide in order to escape an ignominious death. Queen Cleopatra, for example, escaped Ottaviano's prison by committing a ritual suicide through a sacred snakebite, which made her a divine figure.

Although the ancient Greeks rejected suicide, dissertations on the matter treat it with calm and balance; they considered it a free choice that should not offend the Gods. For this reason, the impulse of death had to be noble and glorious. Under this prospective, if a citizen was able to justify his choice to die he was granted permission to do so. The problem of suicide changed views: it was not a question of whether to perform suicides or not, it was a question of how to do it with the greatest amount of dignity. This is the concept of suicide handed down to the Romans, who emphasized the emotional content of suicide: there were no taboo related to voluntary death, this instead became a test bed for courage and for latin "virtus".

In the Japanese culture, the concept of *seppuku* was born from an identical ideological matrix, many years before Christ. In the New Testament is reported that reports Judas' suicide, which can be seen as a catharsis in the search of ransom for a homicidal act: the betrayal of Jesus. Only after the IV century, will the Church condemn suicide as a reaction to the those who performed the act in search of martyrdom. Saint Augustine stigmatized suicide as a crime itself, because it was in contrast to the divine killing ban. In fact, those who kill themselves are double murderers as they take away their own life, and deny the gift of life God gave them at the same time.

In 533 a.C. the synod of Orleans decided to deny funeral rites to suicides under trial; the synod of Prague extended this to all suicides, in 562 a.C. while in 693 a.C, in Toledo it was decided that suicides could not be buried in consecrated soil. Also, the Church decided that those who killed themselves or attempted to take their life would be excommunicated.

Homicide is an extreme act of violence and abuse that does not know any historical or cultural limits; in fact, it characterizes every historical age, in every part of the earth.

Even though under different points of view, all cultures incriminate homicide; however, when motivated by defensive, moral, and spiritual reasons, homicide can be raised to a honourable, moral, and spiritual action. This is the case of wars, euthanasia, and religious disputes.

When both homicide and suicide are perpetrated, we can observe an extreme levels of aggressive drive, which can be referred to the death-like experience at the base of the two actions, according to Freud [8]. Since 1800, the study of homicide-suicide has been under the attention of philosophers and researchers, even though the occurrence of such events was not frequent. Scientists aimed at comprehending the mechanisms in this particular form of aggressiveness. To follow, we will try to retrace the evolution of thought regarding such a phenomenon, with focus on the most recent theories.

Historical Reconstruction of the Homicide-Suicide Phenomenon

In the last twenty years of the 800s, in his essays on delinquents and political crime, Lombroso described homicides-suicides committed by *passion delinquents* who killed their lover to then kill themselves, or by *political delinquents* who perpetrated homicide-suicide. Not long after, Enrico Ferri [9] also called people's attention to the need for a careful study of the different cases of homicide –suicide. He underlined the idea that both crimes are the consequence either of moral insensitivity related to the *"born" delinquent,* who does not care about his own life ("he killed himself with a cold soul", Ferri 1907, p. 131), or the consequence of an emotional overflow that characterizes the *"crazy" delinquent,* who immediately repents after having killed someone and takes his own life as well, for "the moral rebound, momentarily stifled by passion or madness" [9].

Following one of Morselli's [10] theories, Ferri asserted that both homicide and suicide are alternative responses to a common cause, and that they vary inversely. In Spain [11] proposed a study on the consenting couple, distinguishing *simple homicide-suicide* (one of the two killed the other and then killed himself) from *complex homicide-suicide* (both killed themselves at the same time)

In Germany, in his discussion on homicide-suicide, Emile Durkheim [12], initially asserted that a high rate of homicide gives a sort of immunity towards suicide. Later on, the author modified his statement, considering that there were a few exceptions to the idea that homicide- suicide are related. For example, he observed that in most countries women had low rates of homicide as well as suicide. Durkehim [12] gave a number of typologies and theories on homicides and suicides, explaining suicide as a part of the concept of homicide-suicide: starting from the idea that there is a connection between suicide and social condition, he proposed different categories of suicide, namely the egoistic, altruistic, anomic and fatalistic suicide. The egoistic and altruistic types represent two opposite situations, regarding the level of integration and cohesion of the group or society in which the individual lives. Egoistic suicide is described in terms of excessive withdrawal in oneself (for instance, in case of isolation or separation due to the sudden loss of a loved one). Altruistic suicide suggests the opposite, that is the excessive identification of the individual with their social group or organization (for instance, in the case of old or invalid people committing suicide as a duty to their society). Anomic and fatalistic suicide represent opposites, regarding social regulation. Durkehim discusses the consequences of social disorganization in connection with the anomic suicide, especially in times of rapid social changes, when traditional rules and bonds are broken, making people act under their impulses. Durkheim [12] did not fully develop a theory the construction of fatalistic homicide, and it appears only as a note in his work. However, as a hypothesis, he stated that fatalistic suicide comes from an excess of rules and oppressive discipline; such is the case of a slave or a prisoner, when "a future individual is pitilessly blocked and his passion is violently stifled" (p. 276).

Other scholars widened the fatalistic suicide construct [13, 14]. Cavan [13] alludes to fatalism in his description of homicide-suicide cases, in the following passage:

> The person interprets his difficulty as sufficient to prohibit adjustment; he has, he believes, reached the end of the way, and suicide is a means of solution for him. However, his happiness has been ruined or prevented by some person. Before he kills himself he kills that person in anger, in revenge, or in jealousy and to prevent another from succeeding where he has failed (p. 228).

Cavan [13] stated that homicide-suicide, both *planned* and *impulsive*, is the result of an emotional outburst, without the natural sense of remorse between the two acts.

Freud [8] agreed with Durkheim (without ever quoting or mentioning him) in the idea that both homicide and suicide are alternative responses to a common cause. Both conducts are expressions of aggressiveness, with suicide representing the impulse to kill someone else referred towards oneself. Freud asserted that suicide has two origins: Thanatos, or death instinct, and sexual frustration. In his essay, *Beyond the principle of pleasure*, Freud [8] stated that the will of killing oneself is mainly connected to the desire of eliminating the tension that life brings. As an alternative, the instinct of life (Eros) can contrast Thanatos, turning self-destructive impulses towards the outside (for example, homicide). Suicide can also result from the frustration that comes with the desire to commit a homicide. The bond between homicide and suicide is underlined by Freud even more explicitly in *Mourning and Melancholia: "we have long known that no* neurotic *harbours thoughts of* suicide *which he has not turned back upon himself from* murderous impulses *against others".*

Freud's prospective suggested a series of other theories, particularly the hypothesis of frustration-aggressiveness developed in 1939 by Dollard [15]. According to this theory, frustration brings different types of responses among which there is aggressiveness. One of the best examples of the hypothesis of frustration – aggressiveness, applied to the comprehension of homicide-suicide, was given by Henry and Short [7], although their approach included sociological and economic aspects. Their theory asserted that homicide and suicide have the same cause, namely frustration as a consequence of social, economic or derivation factors. Particularly important is the thesis regarding cases of homicide followed by suicide, which suggested the idea that those who deprive themselves of a "primary source of gratification/frustration" by committing homicide can commit suicide because of this loss. Suicide, therefore, reflects the attachment to the victim of the perpetrator, who then commits suicide. Although this hypothesis is hard to test, some researchers [16-18] found support to the thesis according to which the stronger the attachment is between the murderer and his victim, the higher the possibility for suicide; this is presumably due to the great sense of guilt that comes from murder. As Wolfgang [18] stated, it may be that:

> "Following his killing of another person, the individual may suffer such a threat to his self-esteem that he feels the only way to demonstrate the hatred society should inflict upon him is to kill himself"

Continuing the work of Henry and Short [7], West [19] based his study on a specimen of 148 homicide-suicide cases in England and Wales between 1954 and 1961. He concluded that a suicide that occurs within 30 days of a homicide is an extension of the murder, deeply rooted in the killer's need for self-destruction.

Gamna and Fornari [20], following psychoanalytical and phenomenological interpretations, recall freudian and kleinian hypotheses, regarding the symbolic representation of death in ritual sacrifices, to explain why homicide –suicide is extended to the people dearest to the perpetrator; it is also related to the oral phase of libidic development, in which there is a mixture of love and hate. According to Ganma and Fornari, there is an inability to see the difference between oneself and the other, and to respect the autonomy of the other in his will, his rights, and, most importantly, his right to live. The two authors define this type of crime with the expression "enlarged suicide".

Ponti, Cerretti e Merzagora [21] believed that, in some cases, the contiguity between the two instincts is such that it makes the two acts almost interchangeable.

Few researchers have produced classifications for homicide-suicide types. Among them, Alison and Wallace [22] propose three types of homicide-suicide: Conflict, the most common one, related to cases of domestic violence; Altruism, regarding cases that involve old people or ill people; Mental Abnormality, which includes cases in which murderers had previous diagnoses of mental illnesses. Later on, Marzuk [23] proposed five subtypes of homicide-suicide: *Spousal murder-suicides with amorous jealousy,* the most common type, which usually involves men who kill their intimate partner; *spousal murder-suicides with declining health*, which involves couples, often old and ill, that are no longer able to face life problems; *filicide-suicides*, which typically involves depressed mothers with psychotic characteristics; *familicide-suicides*, often perpetrated by depressed men, with paranoid features, who consume drugs; *extrafamilial-murder-suicides* committed by paranoid, unhappy individuals who feel that they have been wronged in some way.

Stack [17] proposed a classification of 5 typologies of suicide-homicide that are based on measures of positive attachment or responsibility between the killer and the victim (or victims). The five types are named according to the relationship between the victim and the murderer: son/daughter; present spouse or lover; past spouse or lover; present fiancé; friends. Stacks states that the probability of suicide is higher in the first three cases. According to Stacks [17]:

> "The probability of suicide following homicide increases when the offender has close ties to the victim and/or society" (p. 46).

On the basis of the results recovered from the most recent researches on the phenomenon of homicide-suicide, it is possible to outline a few prevalent characteristics of this crime.

However, it should be stated beforehand that there is still no commonly accepted operational definition of homicide-suicide, making conceptualization, estimation of occurrences, validation of classification schemes, and comparison of research results difficult. For example, the amount of time that lapses between the homicides and suicides in these studies ranges from 24 hours to 30 days. The lack of specific rules in the collection of data makes results of homicide-suicide studies less homogeneous and not completely comparable. In the next paragraphs, following and integrating the classification by Marzuk [23] the most common characteristics of homicide-suicide crimes will be outlined and some guidelines on prevention will be given.

Spousal Murder-Suicides with Amorous Jealousy

The most frequent type of homicide- suicide is the one between intimate lovers or ex-lovers [18, 24-26]. Felthous and Hempel [27] name this particular kind of homicide-suicide "possessive", underlining the presence of a "symbiotic" relationship [28], with reciprocal and pathological dependence [29], a dominant/dominated functioning type and fusion model [30], and perhaps even characterized by repeated abuse and mistreatment [31, 32]. In this type of crime, the rates of which have increased since the 60s, the perpetrator is typically the man, and the woman is guilty of having rejected him or having attempted to make a few steps towards separation [33-38]. The man appears unable to accept the idea of losing his love object when the relationship with his partner is socially withdrawn and based on exclusiveness and authoritarianism [39]; in these situations men find themselves completely devoid of any point of reference after the separation: the loss of the object coincides with the end of themselves [40]. The crime, therefore, would arise from the fear of abandonment and/or betrayal (cheating), which invades the perpetrator's thoughts and in some cases becomes an actual jealousy delusion [23, 24, 41], with the paranoid conviction of infidelity on behalf of their partner, on both an emotional and sexual level [42]. The natural jealousy that characterizes love relationships, therefore, becomes deviant. Jealous individuals needs to have constant control over their partners because of the tormenting fear of being abandoned; this is a selfish need and, in extreme cases, the partner can become an object of possession. When a jealous individual kills, they continue to love their victim and the crime produces a terrible sense of remorse in the perpetrator, to the point where it pushes him to commit suicide (which is often planned before the homicide took place). Di Girolami and Nesci [43] explain that, in these cases, husbands did not at all kill out of love, but only to confirm their absolute possession and power over their love object. According to Palermo and Ferracuti [44]:

> "The aggressor has profound needs of dependence towards their partner […] suicide is motivated by feelings of despair, guilt, and loss, by the delusional belief that they will be reunited with their loved one after death […] a symbiotic relationship between two people of the same sex or of different sexes – spouses, lovers, or couples – can sometimes develop into a severely neurotic behavior and, in particular circumstances, may generate an intense ambivalence and hostility, followed by a destructive type of behavior. A romantic relationship, in which the main character reveals a self-centred, narcissistic attitude and unrealistic expectations, may at times represent a fertile ground for the love-hate pattern".

In some cases, the separation has already occurred and there is a need to recontact the individual's loved one, which can turn into a spasmodic, frantic search for the other with phone calls, letters, or notes, performing small or big acts of revenge (such as making a scene in public, spreading rumors or secrets), and following or stalking them [45]. The motivation that drives the individual to activate persecutory strategies is the desire to be present in the life of their partner or ex-lover, to not be forgotten by them, and to receive recognition. Gamna and Fornari [20] explain that in crimes of passion, the inability to distinguish oneself from the other is very clear, as is the inability to respect the other's autonomy, their will, their rights, including the right to life, not tolerating that they could live independent of one another and maybe even separated.

In accordance with the concepts developed so far, individuals who committed homicide-suicide acts were often found to be in a state of depression. Rosenbaum [46], for example, conducted a study on a small group of couples, comparing 12 cases of homicide-suicide of passion to 24 cases of homicide, in which he ascertained that the majority of individuals who committed homicide-suicide were depressed with a high level of jealousy, while almost all of those who only committed homicide did not suffer from mood disorders: half of these were women. This data shows that the number of men who commit suicide after killing their partner is undeniably higher than that of women.

Marzuk [23] found a 19-26 % of suicide among men who commit uxoricide, against a percentage of 0-3 for women. Among the possible explanations for this is the different crime genesis of female and male uxoricide: wives tend to kill after having been harassed and oppressed and they sometimes kill to defend themselves or their children from their husband's mistreatment [47]; motivations like these make it understandable that a suicide would less probably follow. In agreement with these findings, many authors make sociological speculations on how various societies view women as a possession of man [24]. Others [48], on the other hand, suggest that social and legislative changes that occurred in the United States from the 70s to present (order of protection, arrest policies for violent partners, more resources for female victims of domestic violence), allow mistreated women the possibility to flee from a violent partner without being forced to find themselves in a situation where they feel they have no other way out but to kill their husband.

The preliminary results of our study on the occurrence of homicide-suicide in Italy between 1985 and 2008 (Table **1**), refer to a sample made up of 662 cases, 560 of which were men and 102 were women. Twenty-four percent of these cases (156) can be attributed to amorous jealousy. 26% of these (144) is committed by men and 12% (12) is committed by women.

Table 1: Homicide Suicide in Italy from 1985 to 2008

Apparent Motivation	Male Author		Female Author		Total	
Amorous jealousy	144	25.7%	12	11.7%	156	24%
Mercy killing (because of declining health of victim or offender)	59	10.3%	13	12.7%	72	10.8%
Altruistic or extended suicides (includes salvation fantasies of rescue and escape from problems)	57	10.3%	15	14.8%	72	10.8%
Family financial or social Stressors	92	16.4%	21	20.6%	113	17%
Retaliation	48	8.7%	6	5.9%	54	8.1%
Other	50	8.9%	14	13.7%	64	9.6%
Unspecified	110	19.7%	21	20.6%	131	19.7%
Totale	560	100%	102	100%	662	100%

Spousal Murder – Suicides in Older Persons with or without Declining Health

This type of homicide-suicide refers to elderly couples who are no longer able to face their daily life problems. Usually the executer, who has an intense attachment with the victim, perceives some event as a threat to the integrity of their relationship [30]. The threat can consist of a health problem relating to one of the two, whether real or imaginary, or a psychosocial problem, such as poverty, moving to a new home, family disputes, increasing social isolation, death of a son or daughter [49]. These events generate depression, conflict, the sense of powerlessness or failure, and an excessive amount of stress; all elements which, added to the apparent impossibility of emerging from the negative situation, drive the person to perpetrate homicide. The majority of researches on the matter [23, 50, 51] concur that the fundamental elements that can be found in homicide-suicide cases among the elderly are: a) white, male perpetrator with a dominant personality [52]; b) presence of a strong attachment and "sense of responsibility" towards their partner; c) real or imaginary separation from the other; d) weapon possession; e) sense of shame and embarrassment regarding a family event that has occurred recently or in the past; f) presence of depression in the aggressor [53].

According to Cohen [50], this sort of crime can be divided into three subtypes: the first is called *protective dependence*. In these circumstances, the agent of the murder is usually the husband who has to take care of his chronically ill wife, who's disease typically can not be cured clinically. These homicide-suicides are not impulsive acts; the men who commit these crimes have long premeditated this "dyadic death" and, generally, the longer and more serious the illness, the more the death is premeditated. A recently defined variant of this subtype is the "keeper-dependent" homicide-suicide, where depression and isolation, together with various elements of stress, produce a sense of powerlessness in the man caring for his wife, which sets off the urge for the act of homicide. In the majority of cases, it is the husband who have to attend to their wives, however it is not clear whether the motivation for suicide is associated to the fact that they refuse to live with a handicap, with the chronic pain or stress of having to take care of another person, or rather to feeling of pity towards their suffering loved one [54]. After all, in these cases there is a significant increase of responsibility for the person taking care (care-giver) of their partner, leading to depression or dysthymia [55]. Often in these situations, the victim is unwilling or even unaware of their spouse's intentions and often they are killed in their sleep [56, 57].

The second subtype is that of *aggressive/domestic violence*, in which there is usually a history of physical and verbal violence and abuse on behalf of one of the spouses. In this scenario, the element that triggers the homicide-suicide is related to long-standing issues, which even other relatives are aware of. Also in this case, the victim is unaware of their spouse's intentions.

The last subtype is called *symbiotic* and relates to a situation in which both partners are ill and depend deeply on one-another; there isn't always an actual agreement regarding suicide [23, 51], but often acquaintances and friends refer that the couple often spoke of their desire to die together and they fantasized about being better off once they died. Within this group, many "*incomplete homicide-suicides*" were identified, in which the victim usually is found dead and the performer of the murder is injured.

From a strictly quantitative point of view, Cohen *et al.* [50] found that homicide-suicide instances among the elderly represent: around 20% of all homicide-suicides in Florida; around 3% of all suicides in the elderly population; circa 12% of all homicides in the elderly population. In the United States, it is estimated that around 200 homicide-suicides occur among people that are over 55 years of age [58].

In Italy (Table **1**), these crimes represent, according to the data relating to our sample, 10,8% (72) of all crimes. Of these 12,7% (13 cases) is committed by women, while 10,3% (59) is committed by men.

Filicide – Suicides

A woman who kills her child, according to Lombroso [3] is an evil trick of nature. The idea of striking an innocent and defenceless being is in itself unacceptable according to our society; when the person performing the act of violence is the infant's parent, therefore the person who by definition is supposed to care for the child, it is all the more difficult to understand the situation. In this type of felony, the following categories can be distinguished: *neonaticide*, when the crime takes place on the same day in which the child is born; *infanticide* when the victim is less than a year old; *pedicide* if the minor's age is between 1 and 16. Generally there is a greater number of mothers that murder their children than fathers [25, 59, 60] but men more often commit suicide after the murder [23, 27, 28, 51, 61-67]. This may also be due to the fact that the rate of suicide is higher for men than for women.

The majority of mothers who commit suicide after having killed one or more of their children (*MFS - Murder Filicide Suicide*), are considered "perfect mothers" [68] even though the majority of cases were reported to have psychopathologies. For example, studies conducted in the past 20 years show that over 70% of mothers and fathers who commit suicide (or attempt to) after committing filicide, have undergone a psychotherapy in the year previous to the crime [59, 68-72].

Depression seems to be the main cause of the fatal act [27, 28, 51, 59, 64, 73, 74].

Feelings of inadequacy, self-devaluation, difficulty in the ability to cover their role as a mother, problems with their partner, rumination in suicide ideation, prior anomalous behaviors towards the children, pessimistic and anxious beliefs regarding the child's physical or mental future, often accompanied by obsessive thoughts of the possibility of hurting the child or children may often be a cause; previous suicide attempts may also be present [75], as well as a symbiotic and over protective relationship with the child [64, 68-70] and mental disorders [25, 59, 60, 74, 76-82].

The main content of the mother's ideation consists in the belief that her son or daughter will lead an unhappy life (at times because they are ill) and they feel they have the duty to "save" them from it. In some sporadic cases, parents were found to have motivations of revenge towards their partner or they were driven by a feeling of guilt for having abused their child or for not having wanted them enough [64].

Usually the act is carefully planned and performed deliberately, not impulsively. The murder is usually carried out using methods such as gas or drowning.

Two researches [71, 72] noticed a typical configuration of personality characteristics and psychopathological symptoms in MFS, called *Melancholic Personality Structure*. These characteristics are related to performance anxiety, the fear of not being able to meet social standards, excessive sense of responsibility, conscientiousness and perfectionism with hypersensitivity to criticism, social rejection or disapproval. Okumura and Kraus [72] state that mothers of small children with a Melancholic Personality tend to view and treat their children as a prolongation of themselves and find it difficult to think of their children as separate individuals. The negative attitude towards the possibility of changing their future and that of their children leads the mother to having a pathological feeling of guilt, which can be even more intense when the child is suffering from some form of disability. This process becomes a sort of vicious cycle, which can lead MFS. This process is also well described by the psychological theory on suicide by Baumeister [83]. According to this theory, at the basis of the person's sufferance are both the disappointment of not being able to meet certain standards, which they value as primary and essential, and reaching the image of their ideal self; among the most common motivations for the lethal act are the pain due to an illness or other unmodifiable situations, deteriorated relationships with their spouse, solitude, romantic disappointments; less frequent are financial difficulties, humiliation, remorse, and revenge. The defence mechanism mostly used by these women appears to be fantasy, especially among individuals with avoidant personality disorder, in which sensitivity and fear of social rejection are the key psychopathologic symptoms [84].

Analysing the phenomenon from a strictly quantitative view point, the literature regarding the issue reports that every homicide committed towards a son or daughter involves the risk of a subsequent suicide [26, 59, 60, 73, 74, 77, 79, 85-87]. In Canada, between 1993 and 2003, at least 60% of homicides performed on children between 12 and 17 years of age are followed by the suicide of the parent who committed the crime [88]; in a Swedish study, 43 out of 63 filicides were filicide-suicides [74].

Our study (Table **1**) encompass this typology inside the label of altruistic or extended suicide representing the 10,8% of the cases (72). Among these the 14,8% (15) is performed by woman.

Extrafamilial Murder-Suicides and Mass Murder-Suicide

This type of homicide refers to the killing of one or more people that are in some way related to the perpetrator and/or belonging to their same group or community, who find themselves involved in the act, which is committed with the intention of punishing a representative of a private or public institution. In this sense, the target of the murder can be a specific victim (for example the head of an office or company), or even the people who frequent an environment for opportunistic or casual reasons (for example other employees). The perpetrator's intensions are always motivated by personal matters of revenge or ransom.

Various studies [89] suggest the possibility of tracing certain rather constant characteristics in the perpetrators: male, unemployed, less than 40 years of age, in possession of fire arms, socially isolated, highly susceptible and sensitive to criticism, with persecutory ideation, and a high sense of justice and rights. Also, the perpetrator often has a history of victimization and isolation as a child, with antisocial and criminal behavior in adolescents, substance abuse, contacts with mental health services, also due to homicidal intentions. They appear, therefore, to have rigid and obsessive traits, internal anger, emotional vulnerability, and difficulty in controlling their impulses, which renders them quick to turn their thoughts into actions when faced with stressful events.

Regarding criminal dynamics, [89] report that the majority of executors initially kill someone they have specific feelings of resentment towards, while the following victims are struck casually. Once the killer begins running amok, he does not cease until he has completed his *mission*: annihilating all the "enemies".

In contemporary history, the concept of mass-murder – suicide was strongly reintroduced during World War II, when the Japanese troops founded the Special Attack Unit, which had the purpose of committing attacks on the enemy through suicide, by crashing their aircraft against the enemy's vehicles. The name Kamikaze was given to these volunteers of death, in honour of the storm (the divine wind) that, in the middle ages, killed a Chinese army that was attempting to invade Japan. From an ideological point of view, the Kamikaze gave their lives up to serve Japan and its emperor. Just like in honour suicides (named Harakiri) death during war became a means to join the spirits of one's anscestors.

Once the war ended, the concept of kamikaze attacks was applied to a much larger variety of mass murders with suicides, often confusing war targets (against which kamikazes would crash their planes) with civil targets, which can be better defined as terrorism. The Japanese press, the only one that actually carefully differentiates the two, defines these mass murder suicides with the expression "self-exploding terrorists". In these cases, the victims, although strangers to the killer, may belong to a specific group of individuals that the executer chooses as a target, being the object of anger for his beliefs. These convictions may have implicitly induced by the individual's culture or society. This appears to be typical of groups with a strong internal cohesion, with strong charismatic leaders (Zealots, Hashishianins, Tamil Tigers) and ceremonial rituals that seal the individual's affiliation to the group. Up until recently, it was believed that those who committed mass suicide suffered from some form of psychosis. More recent studies, however, find that most mass murderers do not appear to have schizofrenia or active psychotic symptoms in the moment of the murder [27]. Their personalities present traits of grandeur, narcissism, with possible dissociative behaviors present [27, 89]. This is found also in the criminal dynamics, as the massacres and attempted mass murders are usually extensively planned. According to an article written on Science [90], regarding the genesis of suicide terrorism, there is no apparent psychopathology, and the fundamental mistake that psychiatrists make is to regard the phenomenon as an individual event, while instead it is an expression of the pressure on behalf of a particular social group. If anything it is a group psychopathology. The classic criteria for psychopathologies that are applied to the logic of suicide terrorists (in terms of thought functioning, the form and content of thought, the personal suffering) are scarce or absent for a correct correlation to a formal mental disorder. Could it be a delusion? It's a very delicate matter, which concerns the comparison between the normal conviction "my life is useful and I have to preserve it" and the exceptional belief "my death is useful if it causes the death of others and benefits me and my country". "The spirit of this department will keep disaster far from our country".

A Possible Prevention

The social impact of homicide-suicide as phenomenon is larger than that of homicide and suicide cases taken into consideration individually. As mentioned earlier, homicide-suicides have not increased in such a way that one can consider it an "epidemic"- like phenomenon. However, we call for the process of civilization to lead to less and less violence and we find it even more scandalous when violence occurs in environments, such as family, in which an individual expects to be protected and loved.

Despite the fact that various categories of homicide-suicide have been defined, not many attempts to prevent this crime have been made compared to the high risk it represents, unlike suicide, for which many preventative measures have been taken.

Regardless of the nature of the phenomenon, the difference between the patriarchal families of the past and the nuclear structure of today's families could be a key element in the understanding of family violence. One of the possible explanations lies in the fact that today's nuclear-type families are isolated, which does not allow the intervention of external elements or institutions. In patriarchal and matriarchal families of the past, the larger number of its components guaranteed a certain amount of control on their behaviors, and therefore on the violence exerted by and towards the family's members. Today's mononuclear structure lost this possibility of control, as well as the possibility to count on the advice of the elderly members.

Many times, in family homicide-suicides, there is a scarce reaction on behalf of the institutions to the families who request support. In this case, the more appropriate answer could be to improve social-assistance services who provide an effective response to the needs of nuclear families. Economic difficulties, unemployment, and underemployment are factors that are often associated to family homicides, and therefore assistance aimed at improving these conditions could limit the implementation of crime. Unlike what occurred in the past, economic malaise can appear in the form of "relative deprivation", or rather, not so much actual poverty, as much as a discrepancy between the economic conditions of families that live within the same context. In this sense, the ostensive display and public glorification of external symbols of well-being makes the comparison even more mortifying. The sufferance, therefore, lies in the comparison that the individual makes between his own economic condition and that of neighboring families, which often turns into an existential malaise, with feelings of failure and related auto and hetero aggressive conduct. It's not a coincidence, in fact, that the most brutal and perturbing among recent cases of homicide-suicide in Italy occurred in environments that were not at all poor and at least socially "normal".

Prevention, furthermore, should be put into effects also by improving the social networks that allow the isolation and abandonment of families in distress to be avoided. For example, in those cases in which the victim was affected by an age-old medical illness that the perpetrator of the crime had to face alone, support from institutions is fundamental in contrasting the risk of conducts that are motivated by exasperation.

An ulterior method of prevention, both in intra-familiar an extra-familiar homicide-suicide, is through a greater amount of awareness towards mental ailment and particularly depressive symptoms, both often underestimated by social and public operators. In numerous case, in fact, the presence of irritability, depression, of changes in habits, eccentricity, of bizarre emotions and behaviors, erroneously attributed to fatigue or stressful situations, are precursors of an unbalance that precedes the performance of an uncontrolled act. In the specific case of depression, a study conducted by Rout and Rout [91] reported the "blindness" that medical specialists have towards medical psychiatric-psychological matters. The authors assert that doctors, in England, not only rely exclusively on their personal experience as an empirical source of information, but also disregard the criteria that are recognized in the diagnosis of depression and tend to use non pharmacological therapies.

Regarding depression, the "World Health Organization" reports that over half of the cases of depression are not diagnosed as such, despite the fact that, according to the same source, at least 400,000 people commit suicide in the world each year. This estimate may not even be expressed literally due to cultural reasons and to the stigma connected to the disorder [92]. A correct education, without alarmism, perhaps through courses or workshops for experts and even a campaign to make people more aware of the problem, to promote a "psychiatric alphabetization" for citizens, may be an effective means of prevention.

Finally, particular attention, in terms of prevention, should be given to homicide-suicide cases among the elderly, as they represent a high percentage within the different types of crime, that we have taken into consideration. The majority of researches on the matter [23, 50, 51] concur that the fundamental elements that can be found in homicide-suicide cases among the elderly are: a) white, male perpetrator with a dominant personality [52]; b) presence of a strong attachment and "sense of responsibility" towards their partner; c) real or imaginary separation from the other; d) weapon possession; e) sense of shame and embarrassment regarding a family event that has occurred recently or in the past; f) presence of depression in the aggressor.

Therefore, the fact that many studies have confirmed the presence of recurrent and constant factors in homicide-suicide cases among the elderly, regarding the perpetrator's tendency to premeditate the act, allows for a guide line for prevention to be outlined.

Doctors should evaluate the risk of homicide-suicide for all elderly patients that present the following factors: 1) the patient has been married for a long period of time and one or both of the spouses have health problems; 2) when adversarial relationships, violence, separation or divorce are present; 3) presence of suicidal, homicidal, or violent ideation.

Furthermore, it is very important that the operators in health centers be aware that individuals are at high risk of homicide-suicide when their spouse has been hospitalized for a large amount of time, when there is a chance they will be put in a retirement home, or when the individual is a terminal patient and is forced to stay in bed for a long period of time, *etc.*

Therefore, it may be a useful means of prevention to speak with the patient, their spouse, and/or other family members. In some cases, the perpetrators had often referred their "intention" to one or more of their adult sons or daughters, but often they did not believe their parent enough to refer this to others or did not accept the idea of it.

In conclusion, accurate descriptions of epidemiologic models and risk factors associated to homicide-suicide are the first step towards the development of prevention strategies and intervention. It is important to replicate the methods in literature that proved to be effective, through prospective, long-term studies, which are necessary to verify the hypotheses regarding prevention. Performing research, with the help of psychological "autopsies", is essential to clarify the role of psychopathologies, as well as the intentionality and the variety of motivations.

Although depression, schizophrenia, and other diseases are strongly implicated in cases of homicide-suicide, these violent crimes are related to cultural, psychological, and environmental factors. Homicide-suicides, therefore, are the results of multiple elements, including culture and bio-psycho-social stress factors. Future research should explain the interaction between these factors to aid the understanding of what underlies the risk of homicide-suicide, as opposed to homicide and/or suicide.

REFERENCES

[1] Sighele S. La coppia criminale. Archivio di psichiatria, scienze penali ed antropologia criminale. 1882;13:505-42.
[2] Menninger K. Man against Himself. New York: Harcourt, Brace & World, 1938.
[3] Lombroso C. L'uomo delinquente. Torino: Fratelli Bocca, 1878.
[4] Guerry M. Statistique comparée de l'état de l'instruction et du nambre de crimes. Paris: Everat, 1832.
[5] Ferri E. L'omicida. Torino: UTET, 1925.
[6] Tarde G. L'opinion et la foule, 1901. Tr It: Conforti R, Ed. L'opinione e la folla. La Città del Sole, 2005.
[7] Henry A, Short JF. Homicide and suicide. New York: Free Press, 1954.
[8] Freud S. Lutto e melanconia; 1917. Tr It: Opere VIII. Torino: Boringhieri, 1976.
[9] Ferri E. Criminal Sociology. Boston: Little, Brown, 1917.
[10] Morselli E. Il metodo clinico nella diagnosi della pazzia. I. Esame anamnestico degli alienate. Milano: Vallardi, 1882.
[11] Cortes D. Caregiver Stress Risk of Homicide-Suicide. Geriatric Times 2000;1 (4).
[12] Durkheim E. Le Suicide. 1897. Tr It: Il suicidio. Studio di sociologia. Milano: Rizzoli, 1987.
[13] Cavan RS. Suicide. University of Chicago Press, 1928.
[14] Hendin H. Suicide. J Nerv Ment Dis 1963;136:236-44.
[15] Dollard J, Miller NE, Doob Leonard W, *et al.* Frustration and Aggression; 1939. Tr It: Frustrazione e Aggressività. Firenze: Giunti, 1967.
[16] Gillspie M, Hearn V, Silverman RA. Suicide following homicide in Canada. Homicide Stud 1998; 2: 46-63.
[17] Stack S. Homicide followed by suicide: an analysis of Chicago data. Criminol 1997; 35: 435-53
[18] Wolfgang M. An analysis of homicide-suicide. J Clin Exp Psych Quarterly Rev Psychiatry Neurol 1958; 19: 208-21.
[19] West D. Murder followed by suicide. Cambridge MA: Harvard University Press, 1966.
[20] Gamna G, Fornari U. Contributo allo studio clinico e criminologico del suicidio allargato. Annali di Freniatria e Scienze Affini 1965;78 (2):171–200.
[21] Ponti G, Ceretti A, Merzagora - Betsos I. Il viaggio dall'auto all'eteroaggressività nell'omicidio del depresso. In: Sanna MN, Lorettu L, Eds. La Depressione – Aspetti Clinici e Forensi, Atti del II Convegno Sardo di Psichiatria Clinica e Psicopatologia Forense. Italy 3–5 Giugno, 1990.
[22] Wallace A. Homicide: The Social Reality. New South Wales, Australia: New South Wales Bureau of Crime Statistics and Research, 1986.
[23] Marzuk PM, Tardiff K, Hirsch CS. The epidemiology of murder-suicide. J Am Med Assoc 1992; 267 (23): 3179-83.
[24] Eastel P. Homicide-Suicides between adult sexual intimates: an Australian study. Suicide Life Threat Behav 1995; 24 (2): 140-51.

[25] West D. J Murder Followed by Suicide. London: Heinemann, 1965.

[26] West D. Malattie Mentali, Imputabilità e Pericolosità Sociali. In: Ferracuti F, Ed. Trattato di Criminologia, Medicina Criminologia e Psichiatria Forense. Milano: Giuffrè. 1990; 13: 207.

[27] Felthous AR, Hempel A. Combined homicide-suicide: a review. J Forensic Sci 1995; 40: 846-57.

[28] Palermo GB, Smith MB, Jentzen JM, *et al.* Murder-suicide of the jealous paranoia type: a multicenter statistical pilot study. Am J Forensic Med Pathol 1997; 18: 374-83.

[29] Berman AL. Dyadic death: homicide-suicide. Suicide Life Threat Behav 1979; 26 (4): 342-50.

[30] Merzagora - Betsos I, Pleuteri L. Odia il prossimo tuo come te stesso - L'omicidio-suicidio a Milano e Provincia. Milano: Franco Angeli, 2005.

[31] Palmer S, Humprey JA. Offender-victim relationship in criminal homicide followed by offender's suicide, North Carolina, 1972-1977. Suicide Life Threat Behav 1980; 10: 106-18.

[32] Allen NH. Homicide followed by Suicide. Suicide and Life - Threat Behav 1983; 13: 155 –63.

[33] Giusti G, Bifano M. L'omicidio in famiglia a Roma dal 1990 al 1995 attraverso le sentenze delle Corti di Assise e la cronaca de "Il Messaggero". Rivista Italiana di Medicina Legale, 1996.

[34] Celesti R, Ferretti G. L'omicidio volontario nell'ambito della famiglia. Casistica del settorato medico legale genovese nel quindicennio 1968-1982. Rassegna di Criminologia 1983; 15: 257-80.

[35] Eurispes. Secondo rapporto sugli omicidi in famiglia. Primo semestre 1994, Roma.

[36] Eures. L'omicidio volontario in Italia. Rapporto 2003, Roma, 2004.

[37] Campbell J. "If I Can't Have You, no One Can": Power and Control in Homicide of Female Partners. In: Radford J, Russell D, Eds. Femicide. The politics of women killing. New York: Twaye. 1992; pp. 99-113.

[38] Daly M, Wilson M. Sex, Evolution and Behavior. Boston: Willard Grant Press, 1983.

[39] Borasio V. Omicidio e rapporto di coppia. Rassegna di Criminologia 1982; 13(1): 21–5.

[40] Andreoli V, Ed. Il lato oscuro, 2002.

[41] Milroy CM. Reason for homicide and suicide in episodes of dyadic death in Yorkshire and Humberside. Med Sci Law 1995; 35: 213–7.

[42] Pancheri P. Trattato italiano di psichiatria. Milano: Masson, 1992.

[43] Di Girolami F, Nesci DA. L'uxoricidio in Italia. Rassegna Penitenziaria e Criminologica 1981; 1(2): 481 –503.

[44] Palermo GB, Ferracuti S. Alcune considerazioni sull'omicidio – suicidio. Quaderni di Psichiatria Forense 1993; 2(2): 255–72.

[45] Edlund JE, Heider JD, Scherer CR, *et al.* Sex Differences in Jealousy in Response to Actual Infidelity. Evolutionary Psychol 2006; 4: 462-70.

[46] Rosenbaum M. The role of depression in couples involved in murder-suicide and homicide. Am J Psychiatry 1990; 147:1036–39.

[47] Merzagora Betsos I. Mi uccido e ti porto con me, ti uccido ma vengo con te. Cattedra di Criminologia- Istituto di Medicina Legale dell'Università di Milano, 2005.

[48] Dugan L, Nagin DS, Rosenfeld R. Expoure Reduction or Relation? The Effects of Domestic Violence Resources on Intimate - Partner Homicide. Low and Society Rev 2003; 371: 169-99.

[49] Hannah SG, Turf E, Fierro MF. Murder-Suicide in Central Virginia. J Forensic Med Pathol 1998; 19: 275-83.

[50] Cohen D, Llorente M, Eisdorfer C. Homicide-suicide in older person. Am J Psychiatry 1998; 155 (3): 390-6.

[51] Hanzlick R, Koponen M. Murder-suicide in Fulton County, Georgia, 1988-1991. Comparison with a recent report and proposed typology. Am J Forensic Med Pathol 1994; 15 (2): 168-73.

[52] Malphurs J, Eisdorfer C, Cohen D. A comparison of antecedents of Homicide-suicide and suicide in older married men. Am J Geriatr Psychiatry 2001;9(1):49-57.

[53] Berman AL. Dyadic death: murder-suicide. Suicide Life Threat Behav 1979; 9 (1): 15-93.

[54] McIntosh JL, Santos JF, Hubberd RW. Elder Suicide: Research, Theory and Treatment. Washington, DC: Am Psychol Assoc, 1995.

[55] Malphrus JE, Cohen D. A newspaper Surveillance Study of Homicide – Suicide in the United States. Am J Forensic Med Pathol 2002; 32 (2): 142 -8.

[56] Cohen D. Homicide-suicide in older people. Psychiatric Times 2000; 17(1): 49-52.

[57] Cohen D, Eisdorfer C. Characteristics of perpetrators of homicide-suicide in older couples. Session 5-07-1. Presented at the 9th Congress of the International Psychogeriatric Association. Vancouver, British Columbia, 1990.

[58] Malphurs JE, Cohen D. A Statewide Case-Control Study of Spousal Homicide-Suicide in Older Person. Am J Geriatr Psychiatry; ProQuest Psychol J 2005; 3: 13.

[59] Bourget D, Cagné P. Maternal filicide in Quebec. J Am Acad Psychiatry Law 2002; 30: 345-51.

[60] Harder T. The psychopathology of infanticide. Acta Psychiatr Scand 1967; 43:196-245.
[61] Crittenden P, Graig S. Developmental trends in the nature of child homicide. J Interpers Viol 1990; 5: 202-16.
[62] Marks MN, Kumar R. Infanticida in Scotland. Med Sci Law 1996; 36:299-305.
[63] Daly M, Wilson M. Homicide. New York: Aldine de Gruyter, 1988.
[64] Friedman SH, Hrouda DR, Golden CE, *et al.* Filicide-Suicide: Common Factors in Parents Who Kill Their Children and Themselves. J Am Acad Psychiatry Law 2005; 33 (4): 496-504.
[65] Marleau JD, Poulin B, Webanck T, *et al.* Paternal filicide: a study of 10 men. Can J Psychiatry 1999; 44:57-63.
[66] Cooper M, Eaves D. Suicide following homicide in the family. Violence Victims 1996; 11: 99-112.
[67] Collins PL, Shaughnessy MF, Bradley L, *et al.* Filicide-suicide: in search of meaning. N Am J Psychol 2001; 3: 277-92.
[68] Haapasalo J, Petaejae S. Mothers who killed or attempted to kill their child: Life circumstances, childhood abuse, and types of killing. Violence Vict 1999; 14(3): 219-39.
[69] Alder CM, Baker J. Maternal Filicide: more than one story to be told. Women and Criminal Justice 1997; 15-39.
[70] Alder C, Polk K. Child victims of homicide. Cambridge: Cambridge University Press, 2001.
[71] Meszaros K, Fischer-Danzinger D. Extended suicide attempt: Psychopathology, personality and risk factors. Psychopathol 2000; 33: 5–10.
[72] Okumura Y, Kraus A. 12 patients with extended suicide - psychology, personality, motivation, previous history and psychosocial conflict environment. Fortschritte Neurol Psychiatr 1996; 64 (5): 184-91.
[73] Bourget D, Gagné P. Paternal filicide in Québec. J Am Acad Psychiatry Law 2005; 33: 354-60.
[74] Sommander LK, Rammer LM. Intra - and extra - familial child homicide in Sweden 1971-1980. Child Abuse Neglect 1991;15:45-55.
[75] Bourget D, Grace J and Whitehurst L. A Review of Maternal and Paternal Filicide. J Am Acad Psychiatry Law 2007; 35(1): 74-82.
[76] Resnick PJ. Child murder by parents: a psychiatric review of filicide. Am J Psychiatry 1969; 126:73-82.
[77] Rodenburg M. Child murder by depressed parents. Can Psychiat Assoc J 1971; 16:41-8.
[78] Bourget B, Bradford JMW. Homicidal parents. Can J Psychiatry 1990; 35: 233-8.
[79] Myers SA. Maternal filicide. Am J Dis Child 1970; 120: 534-6.
[80] Adelson L. Slaughter of the innocents: a study of forty-six homicides in which the victims were children. N Engl J Med 1961; 264:1345-9.
[81] Campion JF, Cravens JM, Covan F. A study of filicidal men. Am J Psychiatry 1988; 145:1141-4.
[82] McKee GR, Shea SJ. Maternal filicide: a cross-national comparison. J Clin Psychol 1998; 54:679-87.
[83] Baumeister RF. Suicide as escape from self. Psychol Rev 1990; 97(1): 90-113.
[84] Millon T, Davis RD. Disorders of Personality: DSM-IV and Beyond. New York, NY: John Wiley & Sons, Inc, 1996.
[85] Tuteur W, Gloptzer J. Murdering mothers. Am J Psychiatry 1959; 116: 447-52.
[86] McKnight CK, Mohr JW, Quinsey RE, *et al.* Mental illness and homicide. Can Psychiatry Assoc J 1966; 11:91-8.
[87] McGrath P. Maternal filicide in Broadmoor Hospital. J Forensic Psychiatry 1992; 3:271-97.
[88] Gannon M. Family homicide, in Family Violence in Canada: A Statistical Profile. In: Johnson H, Aucoin K, Eds. Canadian Centre for Justice Statistics. Ottawa: Statistics Canada. 2004; pp. 35-52.
[89] Klott J, Jongsma AE. The Suicide and Homicide Risk Assesment and Prevention Treatment Planner. New York: John Wiley & Sons, 2005.
[90] Atran S. Genesis of Suicide Terrorism. Science 2003; 299:1534-9.
[91] Rout U, Rout J. Diagnosis and treatment of depression by general practitioners in England. Psychol Rep 1996; 78 (2): 516–8.
[92] Scocco P, De Leo D. Patologia psichiatrica e comportamenti suicidari. Giornale italiano di suicidologia 1995; 5: 107-26.

CHAPTER 23

Suicide Among the Elderly

Mario Amore[1,*], Stefano Baratta[1], Cristina Di Vittorio[1], Marco Innamorati[1,2] and David Lester[3]

[1]Department of Neurosciences, Division of Psychiatry, University of Parma – Italy, Str. Del Quartiere, 2, IT-43100 Parma, Italy; [2]Department of Neurosciences, Mental Health and Sensory Functions, Suicide Prevention Center, Sant'Andrea Hospital, Sapienza University of Rome, Italy and [3]The Richard Stockton College of New Jersey, Pomona, NJ, USA

Abstract: Suicide among older adults is a critical public health problem. International statistics indicate an average of one suicide in the world every 90 minutes among those 65 years of age and older. The assessment of suicide risk in older people should include the assessment of risk factors such as the presence of physical illness, functional limitations, the severity of depression and hopelessness, a lack of reasons for living, social isolation and the occurrence of stressful life events. In addition, greater emphasis should be placed in medical education on the recognition and effective treatment of depressive disorders and suicidal states in older people.

Keywords: Suicide, elderly, risk factors, prevention.

1. INTRODUCTION

Suicide among older adults is a critical public health problem. International statistics indicate an average of one suicide in the world every 90 minutes among those 65 years of age and older [1]. In a recent cross-national study of 62 developing and developed countries, Shah reported an increase in suicide rates with age in males and females in 25 and 27 countries, respectively. The suicide rate for the elderly in many countries is higher than that of any other age group, with the rates among people aged 75 and older roughly three times that of adolescents, although suicide is only the 13th leading cause of death in this age group [2]. Rates of completed suicide in elderly people may vary locally as well as between countries.

Pooled international data published by the World Health Organization (WHO) show a rise in the rate of completed suicide with age. For men, the rate increases from 19.2 per 100,000 inhabitants per year in the 15-24 year-old age group to 55.7 in those over 75. For women, the respective rates are 5.6 and 18.8. The male to female ratio for completed suicide in the elderly ranges between 3:1 and 4:1, similar to that of other age groups.

In the US, each year approximately 32,000 deaths result from suicide, of which more than 5,000 (14%) are among people older than 65 years. The dramatically increase of suicide rates at 65 years of age is widely attributable to a steep rise in the suicide rate among older white men who account for 80% of the suicides in the 65 years and over age groups. Furthermore, white men aged 85 years and older have the highest suicide rate for all age, sex and racial groups (48.7), more than 2.5 times the rate for men of all ages and races (18.0) and more than four times the nation's overall age-adjusted rate of 11.1 [3, 4]. Black men show a bimodal distribution, with peaks in younger adulthood and older age. Rates among women are generally lower.

The latest statistics available for Canada are those for 2005. In that year, elderly people had suicide rates ranging between 7.6 (in people over the age of 90) and 13.1 (in people aged 75 to 79). For Canadian males, elderly suicide rates ranged from 17.0 in those aged 70 to 74 to 22.7 in those aged 75 to 79. For Canadian females, elderly suicide rates ranged from 2.9 those aged 70 to 74 to 5.5 in those aged 75 to 79. The suicide rates of the general population was 11.6 (17.9 for men and 5.4 for women) [5].

***Address correspondence to Mario Amore:** Institute of Psychiatry, Department of Neurosciences, University of Parma, Piazza Matteotti 9, 43100 Parma, Italy; E-mail: mario.amore@unipr.it

Recently, we investigated suicide rates in the European Union between 1980 and 2006, analyzing differences between new members (countries that were admitted between 2004 and 2007) and countries admitted earlier [6]. Our research indicated that age-standardized suicide rates in the elderly were 22.90 (SD= 3.79) for the early EU members and 31.30 (SD= 4.74) for the new EU members. Suicide rates in elderly males were 39.13 (SD= 5.33) and 54.52 (SD= 6.23), respectively, for the early EU members and the new EU members, while suicide rates in elderly females were 13.20 (SD= 3.29) and 17.27 (SD= 3.92), respectively, for the early EU members and the new EU members. Over the years studied, elderly suicide rates of the early EU members decreased from 26.52 in 1980 to 17.67 in 2006, with an Average Annual Percentage Change (AAPC) of -2.0% ($p<0.05$). Analyzing suicide rates for men and women separately, both male and female elderly age-adjusted suicide rates decreased during the time period. For females, suicide rates changed from 16.80 in 1980 to 8.64 in 2006, with an AAPC of -3.1% ($p<0.05$). For males, suicide rates changed from 43.22 in 1980 to 31.25 in 2006, with an AAPC of -3.1% ($p<0.05$).

Elderly suicide rates in the new EU members decreased from 37.01 in 1980 to 23.17 in 2006, with an AAPC of -1.9% ($p<0.05$). Both male and female age-adjusted elderly suicide rates decreased in the index period of time. For females, suicide rates changed from 21.82 in 1980 to 10.73 in 2006, with an AAPC of 2.9% ($p<0.05$) and, for males, suicide rates decreased from 61.78 in the 1980 to 43.72 in 2006, with an AAPC of -1.4% ($p<0.05$). Our results indicated that suicide rates in elderly members of the EU are decreasing significantly, both in early and in new members with a comparable speed, in line with a general trend for the whole EU population. Furthermore, small but significant differences exist in suicide rates among older individuals according to their residence in new *versus* early EU countries. This could mean that, over time, we will see a smaller inequality in general suicide rates, but a greater gap between older men and women, especially in the new EU members.

In most countries, male older adults are more likely to die by suicide than their female pairs [6, 7]. This was not true in some Asian countries. For example, in rural China, the suicide rates for men and women are comparable, with rates rising to more than 100 in the oldest age groups of both genders. In 1995-1999, the estimated suicide rate for women (25.9) exceeded that of men overall (20.7). However, men aged 60 to 84 years had a higher suicide rate (72.0) than did older women (64.3) [8].

2. RESEARCH METHODOLOGIES

Despite the dramatic association between gender, increasing age and elevated suicide rates, and the proposition that nearly all of these deaths are premature and preventable, research on late-life suicide still remains limited [9].

The psychological autopsy approach to studying suicide is becoming a common research method. The purpose of the psychological autopsy method is to reconstruct *a posteriori* the life history of suicides (their experiences, emotions, possible presence of psychiatric symptoms, behavior, and life circumstances during the previous weeks and months) in order to understand the reasons for their choice of suicide. In applying the psychological autopsy method, multiple sources of information are used, including evidence presented at the inquest, hospital records if they were in psychiatric care shortly before or at the time of death, and information from general practitioners. The most important source, however, comes from interviews of relatives and other informants, such as parents, partners, friends and other relatives, when available.

The psychological autopsy has considerable methodological and practical limitations, particularly for the elderly. Indeed, identification of a reliable informant can be extremely difficult, especially if the subject lived in isolation or if the individual and the family were not known to a general practitioner [10, 11].

Three other main types of study of suicidal behavior in the elderly are reported (in addition to the psychological autopsy): epidemiological approaches, clinical follow-up studies and studies of suicide attempters. Epidemiological studies of suicidal behaviors report the prevalence and incidence of suicide attempts or suicide rates based on national mortality data. They are used in analytic approaches in order to define and compare potential risk factors. Clinical follow-up studies permit obtaining data on potential risk factors for suicide (in later life), particularly with regard to mental illness. The study of suicide attempters throws light on the state of mind prior to suicide, and this approach typically is not subject to the retrospective biases of the psychological autopsy. Nevertheless, this method has rarely been used to examine suicides among older persons [9].

Characteristics of Suicidal Behavior in Late-Life

Suicidal behavior occurs in a spectrum ranging from thoughts of hopelessness through indirect self-destructive behavior and deliberate self-harm to completed suicide. Trivial acts of self-harm occurring in older people can be indicators of high suicidal intent and serious psychiatric disorder [12].

Suicidal Ideation

Suicidal ideas are not an inevitable consequence of aging, disability or depression. Duberstein and colleagues found that suicidal ideation is rooted in "longstanding patterns of behaving, thinking, and feeling" [13]. Feelings of hopelessness are common in older persons. Hopelessness, defined as a system of negative beliefs and expectancies concerning oneself and one's future [14], is an important risk factor for both suicide ideation and completed suicide in elderly depressed people.

Reasons for living are beliefs or expectancies that are thought to mitigate the risk for suicide, and include survival and coping beliefs, responsibilities to family and relatives, fear of suicide, fear of social disapproval and moral objections to suicide [15]. Reasons for living may also weaken the association between hopelessness and suicidal ideation. Individuals who believe they have more reasons for living may be better prepared to endure the negative effects of hopelessness. Just as optimism and attitudes toward suicide have been demonstrated to moderate the relation between hopelessness and suicide ideation [16, 17], so may reasons for living [18].

Although most people who kill themselves give direct or indirect warnings, older persons are less likely to directly communicate their intent to die, or the warnings are less likely to be heard [19]. Elderly suicides are more likely to avoid intervention, take precautions against discovery, and are less likely to communicate their intent to others. This is confirmed by the fact that older people who commit suicide have higher intent on the Suicide Intent Scale [20].

Ladwig *et al.* [21] sought to determine sex- and age-related suicidal ideation point prevalence rates (for a two-week period) in the general population. The data stem from a population-based survey of 3,154 subjects, 35 to 84 years, living in the city of Augsburg (Bavaria, Germany) and from surrounding districts. Among the study population, a total of 170 subjects (5.4%; 95% CI 4.6–6.2) reported some form of suicidal ideation within the prior 2 weeks. The suicidal ideation prevalence increased with increasing age ($p<0.001$). For both sexes, the prevalence was highest in the oldest age group (75–84 years) where the difference between sexes was marginal (9.9% in the males and 11.0% in the females). In those aged 65 to 74, the years elderly, the prevalence rates were 4.0% in males and 7.0% in females.

Sirey *et al.* [22] using a community based participatory research partnership, implemented a routine screening for depressive symptoms and suicidal ideation among older recipients of Westchester County's (USA) home meal program. In this sample of 403 meal recipients, 13.4% of older adults reported suicidal thoughts in the last two weeks.

Recently, Neufeld and O'Rourke [23] examined impulsivity, hopelessness, depressive symptomatology, and sociodemographic factors vis-à-vis suicide-related ideation among 117 Canadian older adults (age range 50 to 92) at risk of self-harm. Participants were recruited with multiple methods (people who previously participated to a web-based mental health research, those who responded to newspaper advertisements, referrals from health care practitioners). Older adults were selected either if they had scores within the clinical range on the Center for Epidemiologic Studies—Depression Scale (CES-D) (for those recruited through the Internet), espoused feelings of hopelessness, pronounced sadness, or worthlessness (for those recruited through newspaper advertisements), or for those referred from health care practitioners

any of the following criteria: suspected or manifest suicide-related ideation, pronounced depressive symptomatology, a previous suicide attempt, and (or) a combination of affective disorder(s) and physical health problems (for example, chronic pain). 57 participants provided CES-D Scale responses suggestive of clinically significant levels of depressive symptomatology. Depression levels did not significantly differ between older men (mean 17.00, SD 13.83) and women (mean 16.78, SD 12.42; $t = 0.09$, $df = 115$, $P = 0.93$), but men reported significantly higher levels of suicide-related ideation (mean 33.78, SD 25.22) than did women (mean 23.41, SD 20.52; $t = 2.40$, $df = 115$, $P < 0.05$). Furthermore, the groups reported a mean BHS (Beck Hopelessness Scale) of 20.32 (SD=13.43) denoting higher levels of hopelessness. The single strongest predictor of suicide-related ideation was hopelessness.

Britton *et al.* [18] tested the hypothesis that reasons for living (RFL) are inversely related to suicide ideation in 125 adults 50 years or older receiving treatment for a mood disorder recruited from the clinical services of three teaching hospitals in Rochester, NY. 58% of the participants reported suicidal ideation, and this was more common among patients with higher scores on the Hamilton Rating Scale for Depression and on the BHS, while the survival and coping beliefs, fear of suicide, and moral objections subscales of the RFL scale were negatively associated with the presence of suicidal ideation. Multivariate analyses revealed that patients with higher levels of fear of suicide were less likely to report suicide ideation. The interaction of responsibilities to family and hopelessness was also significant but, unexpectedly, responsibilities to family strengthened rather than attenuated the association between hopelessness and suicide ideation.

Indirect Self-Destructive Behavior

Farberow [24] was the first to use the term "sub-intentional suicide", referring to indirect self-destructive behaviors (ISDB), in which noncompliance with the treatment regimen was not a result of cognitive impairment. There are subtle behaviors, especially in elderly, with conscious or unconscious intent to die, such as refusal to eat or drink with the aim of starving oneself, not taking prescribed medication or extreme self-neglect, behaviors which, although not directly suicidal, still increase the chance of dying [25]. These self-destructive behaviors, which often lead to premature death, may be particularly common in certain settings such as institutional settings, and may be a substitute for overt suicidal acts in physically-ill and non-autonomous individuals. Indirect self-destructive behaviors are particularly frequent amongst women and the very old [26].

Deliberate Self-Harm and Attempted Suicide

Although older people are at higher risk for completed suicide than younger segments of the population, epidemiological studies and community samples demonstrate that they are less likely to have made a suicide attempt during their lifetimes [27, 28]. As a result, the ratio of attempted to completed suicides decreases dramatically with age from as high as 200:1 in young adulthood to 4:1 in the elderly [29]. This greater lethality of suicidal acts among older people has been explained by a variety of factors. Older people have fewer physical reserves and are, therefore, less likely to survive self-damaging acts. Social and physical factors contribute to make them more isolated and thus less likely to be rescued after inflicting self-harm than are younger individuals. Moreover, the suicidal acts of older people are more planned and less impulsive. They give fewer warnings to others of their suicidal intent and use more violent and immediately lethal methods than do younger people. The result is that older persons more easily than younger adults achieve the goal of death. Regarding demographic characteristics, 60% of those elders who complete suicide are men, while about 75% of those who attempt suicide are women. While those who complete suicide use more lethal means such as guns or hanging, those who attempt suicide commonly overdose on medications or cut themselves [30, 31].

Brådvik and Berglund [32] investigated the reduced incidence for initial, repeated, or severe suicide attempts with age in suicide victims and controls by gender. The authors reported that the incidences of initial suicide attempt were reduced with age for female suicide victims and controls, and for male controls but not for the male suicide group. The rates of repetition were only reduced in the female control group when compared with female suicide victims. This difference for reduced rates of repeated suicide attempt by age was not found in the male group. The rate of severe suicide attempts was reduced in older age in the female suicide group, and not in the female control group. In contrast, the incidence of severe attempts was significantly more reduced in male controls as compared with male suicide victims.

Completed Suicide

Although rates of completed suicide in elderly people vary between countries, as well as locally, pooled international data published by the World Health Organization show a rise in the rate of completed suicide with age. For men, the rate increases from 19.2 per 100.000 inhabitants per year in the 15-24-year-old age group to 55.7 in those over the age of 75. For women, the respective rates are 5.6 and 18.8. The male to female ratio for completed suicide in the elderly ranges between 3:1 and 4:1, similar to that of other age groups. The methods used for suicide are often more lethal than in young. There are sex differences in methods of suicide, with men more often using shooting, hanging and other violent methods and women more often using drug overdoses [33, 34].

Shields, Hunsaker, and Hunsaker [35] presented a 10-year (1993–2002) retrospective review of 348 Kentucky elderly suicides (out of 940 individuals aged 65 years or older who completed suicide in Kentucky between 1993 and 2002) using files from the Medical Examiner. The majority of the suicides were Caucasian (98.9%) and male (86.8%), while in this jurisdiction and age bands Caucasian females represented only 55.9% of the total population of that age group and sex, and Caucasian males only 38.4%. In this study, 80.7% of the suicides used firearms. Gunshot wounds of the head accounted for 75.8% of the firearm fatalities and 61.2% of the total suicides. The second and third leading methods among men were hanging followed by carbon monoxide poisoning, and among women overdose followed by hanging. Post-mortem toxicological analyses were negative in 43.2% of the suicides. Only 11.5% of the suicides were positive for antidepressant medications. Furthermore, only 2.9% of the subjects had a documented previous suicide attempt.

Risk Factors for Suicide in Older People

Psychiatric Illness and other Psychological Factors

During the past decade, a number of studies have demonstrated a clear relationship between suicide and psychiatric illness. A diagnosable psychiatric illness is present in 90% or more of individuals who complete suicide. Those with a diagnosis of depression may be at particularly high risk. Major Depressive Disorders are more common among older people who commit suicide than among their younger counterparts [37].

Conwell *et al.* [2] conducted a psychological autopsy study on elderly suicides and found that from 71-95% of them fulfilled criteria for at least one DSM-IV axis I diagnosis at the time of death, and that major depressive disorder was the most common psychiatric disorder in the older suicides. In contrast, primary psychotic disorders (such as schizophrenia, schizoaffective disorder and delusional disorder), anxiety disorders and personality disorders accounted for only a small percentage of the elderly suicides.

In a case-control study, Waern and colleagues [36] found that single-episode unipolar major depression was associated with approximately a ninefold higher risk of suicide. In addition, they found that recurrent major depressive disorder was the psychiatric disorder most strongly associated with suicide in older people, and that elevated risk was present also in those with minor depressive disorders and with dysthymic disorders. In Denmark, during the period 1990 to 2000, Erlangsen and colleagues [37] examined psychiatric inpatients who were 60 years or older at the date of discharge from a psychiatric hospital and confirmed that the risk of suicide was significantly associated with late onset of affective disorders. The seriousness of depressive symptoms is the stronger predictive factor of suicide. Patients with the most serious depressive symptomatology are 23 times more likely to die by suicide than those who have no symptoms [38].

The co-occurrence of depression and alcohol use disorders increases suicide risk, although Conwell *et al.* found that the role of alcohol and other substance use disorders seem to be more pronounced among younger age groups than their older counterparts [39]. Most studies that have evaluated the role of alcohol in elderly suicide have focused on older adults who met DSM criteria for abuse and/or dependence. Nevertheless, most of elderly who are experiencing problems related to their alcohol use do not meet alcohol abuse/dependence DSM criteria. However, the role of at-risk and problem alcohol use in geriatric suicide may be underestimated. The relationship between alcohol use and later-life suicide is complex and currently ill defined. It is more likely that alcohol use increases suicide risk through interactions with other factors that are more frequent in this age group, such as physical illness, depressive symptoms, negatively perceived health status, and poor social support [40].

Suicide risk increases if major depression is associated with poverty in cognitive function and other psychological factors, such as the presence of an anankastic personality, and high levels of neuroticism and hopelessness [41-43]. Hopelessness represents the main risk factor in the long term (2-10 years), and suicidal behavior is associated with hopelessness more strongly than with the severity of depressive disorder [44].

In conclusion, affective disorder is a powerful independent risk factor for suicide in the elderly. However, despite this, mood disorders may be under-diagnosed in older adults [45]. Although personality disorders are present in a small proportion of completed suicides among older individuals, there is an association between specific personality traits and suicidal behavior in the elderly. Few studies, however, have attempted to diagnose personality disorders in elderly subjects perhaps because the applicability of Axis II criteria sets to older people has not been established clearly [46]. Personality traits associated with suicide in later life include timidity, shyness and seclusiveness [47], and hypochondriasis, hostility and a rigid independent style [48]. Only two personality traits, anankastic (obsessional) traits and anxious traits, have been found to be predictors of suicide in a case-control study [49].

Duberstein and colleagues [50] have showed a link between suicide in old age and a lower score on the Openness to Experience (OTE), in addition to higher levels of Neuroticism. They found that suicides over the age of 50 years were best characterized by the NEO Personality Inventory [51] as methodical, anhedonic, and emotionally constricted. Compared with matched controls and younger suicides, older suicides had lower scores on the "openness to experience" factor. Individuals with low OTE have muted affective and hedonic responses, a constricted range of interests, and comfort with the familiar. Perhaps the link between low levels of OTE and increased risk of suicide is located in their restricted adaptability to the challenges of aging, and their distress may be more difficult for others to detect [2].

Psychology of Aging and Mood

Aging, with its various aspects, provides a continuous process of modification of human existence - the changing social role, the addition of new experiences, having to cope with various life events, the onset of physical illness, and changes in the cognitive sphere. Understanding the psychology of the elderly means a comparison with their earlier life and an evaluation of their social context and the biological changes associated with the aging process [52]. Important limitations relate to muscle efficiency, the perceptive faculties (hearing, sight and smell), and memory ability [53], along with the resulting progressive isolation of the elderly and inevitable painful feelings of exclusion. The somatic changes go hand-in-hand with psychological crises, and sometimes this culminates in a general feeling of negative transformation in the attempt to restructure the existential situation [54, 55]. In the elderly, the perception of time can change too. The future is missing, the present passes slowly, and boredom can take over so that life becomes a burden [56]. In fact it can be said, with Ajuraguerra, that "people age as people live." Only those who accept ageing are able to age in the right way, without succumbing to despair and denying the imminent end.

Life Events and Social Factors

Older persons who have experienced a large number of negative life events and social problems in the previous year have a wide range of depressive symptoms [57]. The specific types of life events most pertinent to suicide in later life differ from those of younger victims [58-60]. Interpersonal discord, financial and job problems, and legal difficulties are more typical of suicide in young and middle adulthood, whereas physical illness and other losses are most common stressors in elderly suicides [2]. In a descriptive and case-control study, conducted in five English counties, Harwood *et al.* [61] found that the three most frequent life problems associated with suicide in the elderly were physical illness, interpersonal problems and bereavement. They suggested that financial, accommodation and retirement problems may also be risk factors.

Rubenowitz and colleagues [62] investigated the occurrence of stressful life events among elderly suicide cases and population controls, in a cases-control study conducted in the southwestern part of Sweden from 1994 to 1996. They found a significant association between suicide and family discord, financial trouble and somatic illness. Almost half of the suicides had experienced family discord during the last 24 months.

Duberstein *et al.* [63] examined the contribution of stressors to suicide risk, comparing 86 suicides and 86 controls over the age of 50 years. Based on prior research [64], they examined eight categories of events: death of first-degree relatives; serious or terminal illness, or need for in-home assistance due to a medical condition; terminal illness in first-degree relative; family discord; separation/divorce; financial trouble; employment change; and legal difficulties. Elderly suicides were more likely to have lived alone, been unmarried, been unemployed or on disability, and more likely to have had an active mental disorder. 23% developed a first-time mental disorder in the last year of life. Furthermore, they were less likely to engage in religious practice or community activities, and they had lower levels of social interaction. A trimmed logistic regression model showed that marital status, social interaction and religious involvement were all associated with suicide, even after statistical adjusting for the effects of affective disorder and employment status. Adding substance abuse to the model eliminated the effects of religious involvement. Therefore, the association between family and social/community indicators of poor social integration and suicide was robust and largely independent of the presence of mental disorders [65].

Erlangsen and colleagues [66] investigated specifically the role of loss of partner in increasing the risk of suicide among the elderly. Although the majority of older persons who commit suicide are widowed, only a small proportion has experienced the bereavement recently. However, the first year after bereavement is clearly associated with a significant increase in the risk of suicide. In absolute terms, the oldest elderly men experience the highest increase in their suicide risk after the loss of a partner, and the oldest elderly men are more prone to commit suicide after the loss than are women. In addition, it takes a longer time for men in this age group to recover from the death of the spouse. Apparently, becoming widowed offers more obstacles to overcome for very elderly men than it does for women. Men may be less able to manage on their own after a long marriage and, after a loss, men are more likely to become dependent on the help of others (*e.g.*, for household work) than are married men [67].

Social factors are associated with suicide in controlled studies of older adults, although less is known about these risk factors. Social factors associated with suicidal ideation in older adults include a limited social network (encompassing family, friends, helpful others, confidants and living arrangements), few contacts with friends or relatives, few close friends and relatives, lack of a confidante, and a perceived lack of social support. Pompili and colleagues [68], in a psychological autopsy study conducted in a northern Italy region in the period from 1994 to 2004, found that the ninety-nine suicides aged 65 years and older were nine times more likely to live alone. Cases for psychological autopsy interviews were suicide victims aged 65 years or older (the age range was 65–96) who died between 1994 and 2004, and who were resident in the Provinces of Parma and Piacenza. Comparison subjects were suicide victims aged less than 65 years old (age range: 15–64). Younger victims were subdivided in two more homogeneous groups: young adults (age < 36 years) and adults (age: 36–64 years). Ninety-nine elderly suicide victims (77 men and 22 women) and 134 younger comparison victims (115 men and 19 women) were selected for the final samples. Bivariate analyses identified 11 significant differences out of 17 between the three age groups; however, after adjustment for the presence of other variables, only five effects resulted in independent predictors of age differences among suicide victims in a multinomial logistic regression analysis and only three effects concurred to discriminate elderly victims from the adult comparisons. Elderly victims were nine times more likely to live alone than younger suicides adult victims ($p = 0.025$), whereas younger victims ($p = 0.001$) were less likely to live alone than adult victims. As expected, older adults were 26 times more likely to be retired than adult victims ($p = 0.001$). Elderly victims were also 14 times more likely to have attended school for no more than 5 years than adult victims (p = 0.003). Furthermore older victims visited their family physicians in the few months before suicide more often than their younger comparisons: 48% of elderly visited their family physicians in the last 6 months before suicide *versus* 30% of the adult victims and only 7% of the young adult victims. In this sample suicide victims were characterized by low levels of education, frequent symptoms of severe mental illness, and several life stressors, such as medical comorbidity, loss of job status, and poor social support. Despite this situation, they were seldom treated for psychiatric symptoms. The last feature of the suicide among elderly was the high lethality of the methods chosen for suicide. More than 90% of the older suicides died by violent methods *versus* around 70% of the younger suicides considered as a whole. Further, only one in three older suicides left a suicide note.

In a sample of 552 subjects aged 65 years and older, Rowe and colleagues [69] investigated social support factors in relation to well-known clinical risk factors for suicidal ideation in a high-risk population of elderly requiring home health care, and the associations between suicidal ideation and objective and subjective measures of social support. Lower social interaction patterns and lower perceived social support were significantly associated with suicidal ideation but, after adjusting for potential confounders, only lower perceived support remained significantly associated with suicidal ideation. In post hoc analyses of the social support scale items, satisfaction with one's relationships and feeling useful to family and friends were significantly associated with a lower likelihood of suicidal ideation in the final multivariate logistic regression model after controlling for possible confounding variables. It is important to note that subjective social support is a potentially modifiable risk factor for suicide in later life.

Physical Illness

The presence of serious physical diseases, especially those that result in functional limitations, such as malignant neoplasms, severe pain, visual impairment and neurological disorders, has been associated with high suicide risk among the elderly, especially in the first year after diagnosis [61]. The coexistence of multiple illnesses increases the risk of suicide. For example, patients with three illnesses are three times more risk of suicide than patients with no identified illness, and patients with five illnesses have about a fivefold increase in risk [68].

Most of the association between medical illness and suicide are inferred from uncontrolled case studies, and there have been few rigorous studies [36, 50, 62, 70]. Juurlink *et al.* [71] identified a large cohort of elderly patients (1354) who died of suicide and, in these suicides, congestive heart failure, chronic obstructive lung disease, seizures, and moderate and severe pain were independently associated with an increased risk for suicide.

Particular attention should be paid to patients with severe pain and inadequate analgesia. In these subjects suicide can be viewed as a means of escape from suffering, especially in those with terminal illness [72]. However, the role that terminal illness plays in suicide is controversial. Suicide may result from an associated poor prognosis for the physical illness, concerns over debility, the loss of independence or the fear of posing a burden to loved ones. However, several investigators have found that terminal illness is rare in elderly suicides. Conwell and Caine found that only one person among 85 completed suicides had a terminal illness, but this sample was not restricted to the elderly [73].

The link between physical illness, functional impairment and suicide, may be mediated *via* depression and hopelessness. Taking in account the well known relation existing on the one hand between mood disorders and suicide and on the other hand between physical illness and depression, it is possible to suppose that affective disorders can play a role in the correlation (act as a link) between increased suicidal risk and organic diseases: subjects developing a clinical depressive disorder in response to organic disease seem to have higher chance of suicide.

Dementia alone does not appear to increase the risk of suicide, but comorbid depression and dementia conferred the greatest risk for suicide in elderly men in one large study [2, 36, 37]. In case-controlled studies, depressed elderly with mild cognitive impairment were more vulnerable to unplanned and impulsive suicide attempts than older adults with depression alone [72, 73]. Those with a genotypic risk factor for Alzheimer's disease (ε4 allele of the apolipoprotein E) may also have higher rates of attempted suicide [74]. Taken together, these studies suggest that dementia and cognitive impairment may play a role in late-life suicide [75].

Suicide Prevention in Later Life

Suicide is a complex and multi-determined phenomenon and preventive interventions for suicide in the geriatric population are still very rare. Considering the magnitude of the phenomenon, it is important to plan preventive strategies at multiple levels.

The assessment of suicide risk in older people should include the assessment of other risk factors such as the presence of physical illness, functional limitations, the severity of depression and hopelessness, a lack of reasons for living, social isolation and the occurrence of stressful life events [25].

Preventive strategies include universal, selective, and indicated interventions. Universal preventive interventions target the general population and should provide educational programs concerning normal aging, ageism, stigma regarding mental illness, and depression and suicidal behaviors. Selective preventive interventions target asymptomatic or presymptomatic subjects, subgroups who have distal risk factors for suicide, and those who have a higher-than-average risk for developing mental disorders or other more proximal risk factors. Selective prevention focuses on preventing suicide-related morbidity and mortality through addressing the specific characteristics that place the elderly at risk. Selective interventions include: promoting community programs to contact and support isolated elders for those experiencing social isolation; focusing medical and social services on reducing disability and enhancing independent functioning; increasing access to home care and rehabilitation services; improving access to pain management and palliative care services; providing gatekeeper training and linking outreach and gatekeeper services to comprehensive evaluation and health management services in a continuum of care; and implementing strategies to provide more accessible, acceptable, and affordable mental health care to elders. Selective prevention tries to prevent the development of depressive disorders and the expression of suicidal behavior through the treatment of individuals who have precursors and symptoms related to suicide [76]. Retrospective studies have shown that over 70% of older people who commit suicide have had a contact with their primary care physician within the month of their death, and about one third in the preceding week [77-81]. General practitioners should be trained to recognize and treat affective disorders in the elderly, and they should use screening instruments for depression that are sensitive and easy to use.

Lastly, indicated interventions should be targeted to subjects who have detectable symptoms of mental illness or other proximal risk factors for suicide. Even if depression is the most common psychopathology associated with suicide in late life, and the most prevalent mental disorder seen among older patients in primary care settings, many studies in medical and psychiatric literature have demonstrated that primary care practitioners have difficulties recognizing treatable depression in their patients. Two recommendations follow from these observations: self-administered screening tools for depression have been validated for use in elderly primary care patients (Geriatric Depression Scale [82] and the Center for Epidemiological Studies-Depression Scale [83]). Such measures should be used routinely in primary care offices.

In addition, greater emphasis should be placed in undergraduate, graduate and continuing medical education on recognition and effective treatment of depressive disorders and suicidal states in older people. Since older people rarely utilize mental health services, active collaborations between psychiatry and primary care in medical settings may yeld optimal outcomes [84].

Finally, concerning mental health outreach initiatives, in Italy De Leo and colleagues [85] indicated that a telephone distress and support program may reduce late-life suicide risk. They examined the prevalence of suicides among 18,641 users of TeleHelp-TeleCheck who were aged 65 years and over. Physicians typically refer older patients to this social support service outfitting at-risk individuals with personal alarm buttons linked to a response network (TeleHelp) that provides telephonic support calls twice weekly and (or) as needed (TeleCheck). TeleHelp-TeleCheck users had significantly fewer deaths by suicide than expected overall. Significant risk reduction was observed for female service users but not for male service users. Again, caution is warranted, as observed suicides were compared with estimates based on regional suicide rates, rather than with control subjects [86].

REFERENCES

[1] World Health Organization. Figures and facts about suicide. Geneve: WHO; 1999. Report No: WHO/MNH/MBD/99.1 Contract No.: Document Number|.

[2] Conwell Y, Duberstein PR, Caine ED. Risk factors for suicide in later life. Biol Psychiatry 2002; 52: 193-204

[3] Centers for Disease Control and Prevention. Web-Based Injury Statistics Query and Reporting System (WISQARS). 2009 [updated 2009; cited 2009 January3rd].Available from: http://www.cdc.gov/ ncipc/dvp/ Suicide/suicide_data_sheet.pdf.

[4] National Center for Injury Prevention and Control. WISQARS Injury Mortality Reports, 1999-2007. Atlanta, GA: Centers for Disease Control and Prevention; 2010 [updated 2010 06/01/10; cited 2010 December, 28]. http://webappa.cdc.gov/sasweb/ncipc/mortrate10_sy.html

[5] Statistics Canada. Suicides and suicide rate, by sex and by age group. Ottawa: Statistics Canada; 2010 [updated 2010 2010-11-16; cited 2010 December, 28].

[6] Innamorati M, Tamburello A, Lester D, *et al.* Inequalities in suicide rates in the European Union's elderly: trends and impact of macro-socioeconomic factors between 1980 and 2006. Can J Psychiatry 2010; 55: 229-38.

[7] Canetto SS. Gender and suicide in the elderly. Suicide Life Threat Behav 1992; 22: 80-97.

[8] Phillips MR, Li X, Zhang Y. Suicide rates in China, 1995-99. Lancet 2002; 359: 835-40.

[9] Pearson JL, Caine ED, Lindesay J, Conwell Y, Clark DC. Studies of suicide in later life: methodologic considerations and research directions. Am J Geriatr Psychiatry 1999; 7: 203-10.

[10] Hawton K, Appleby L, Platt S, *et al.* The psychological autopsy approach to studying suicide: a review of methodological issues. J Affect Disord 1998; 50: 269-76.

[11] Beskow J, Runeson B, Asgard U. Psychological autopsies: methods and ethics. Suicide Life Threat Behav 1990; 20: 307-23.

[12] Jacoby R, Oppenheimer C, Dening T, Thomas A. Oxford textbook of old age psychiatry. Oxford: Oxford University Press; 2008.

[13] Duberstein PR, Conwell Y, Seidlitz L, Denning DG, Cox C, Caine ED. Personality traits and suicidal behavior and ideation in depressed inpatients 50 years of age and older. J Gerontol B Psychol Sci Soc Sci 2000; 55: 18-26

[14] Stotland ET. The psychology of hope. San Francisco: Jossey-Bass; 1969.

[15] Linehan MM, Goodstein JL, Nielsen SL, Chiles JA. Reasons for staying alive when you are thinking of killing yourself: the reasons for living inventory. J Consult Clin Psychol 1983; 51: 276-86.

[16] Hirsch JK, Conner KR. Dispositional and explanatory style optimism as potential moderators of the relationship between hopelessness and suicidal ideation. Suicide Life Threat Behav 2006; 36: 661-9.

[17] Gibb BE, Andover MS, Beach SR. Suicidal ideation and attitudes toward suicide. Suicide Life Threat Behav 2006; 36: 12-8.

[18] Britton PC, Duberstein PR, Conner KR, Heisel MJ, Hirsch JK, Conwell Y. Reasons for living, hopelessness, and suicide ideation among depressed adults 50 years or older. Am J Geriatr Psychiatry 2008; 16: 736-41.

[19] Conwell Y, Duberstein PR, Cox C, Herrmann J, Forbes N, Caine ED. Age differences in behaviors leading to completed suicide. Am J Geriatr Psychiatry 1998; 6: 122-6.

[20] Beck AT, Schuyler D, Herman I. Development of suicidal intent scales. In: Beck AT, Resnik HLP, Lettieri D, editors. The prediction of suicide. Bowie: Charles Press. 1974; pp. 45–56.

[21] Ladwig KH, Klupsch D, Ruf E, *et al.* Sex- and age-related increase in prevalence rates of death wishes and suicidal ideation in the community: results from the KORA-F3 Augsburg Study with 3,154 men and women, 35 to 84 years of age. Psychiatry Res 2008; 161: 248-52.

[22] Sirey JA, Bruce ML, Carpenter M, *et al.* Depressive symptoms and suicidal ideation among older adults receiving home delivered meals. Int J Geriatr Psychiatry 2008; 23: 1306-11.

[23] Neufeld E, O'Rourke N. Impulsivity and hopelessness as predictors of suicide-related ideation among older adults. Can J Psychiatry 2009; 54: 684-92.

[24] Farberow NL. Indirect self-destructive behavior: classification and characteristics. In: Farberow NL, editor. The many faces of suicide: indirect self-destructive behavior. New York: McGraw-Hill. 1980; pp. 15-27.

[25] Szanto K, Gildengers A, Mulsant BH, Brown G, Alexopoulos GS, Reynolds CF, 3rd. Identification of suicidal ideation and prevention of suicidal behavior in the elderly. Drugs Aging 2002; 19: 11-24.

[26] Osgood NJ, Brant BA, Lipman A. Suicide among the elderly in long-term care facilities. New York: Greenwood Press; 1991.

[27] Moscicki EK, O'Carroll P, Rae DS, Locke BZ, Roy A, Regier DA. Suicide attempts in the Epidemiologic Catchment Area Study. Yale J Biol Med 1988; 61: 259-68.

[28] Schmidtke A, Bille-Brahe U, DeLeo D, *et al.* Attempted suicide in Europe: rates, trends and sociodemographic characteristics of suicide attempters during the period 1989-1992. Results of the WHO/EURO Multicentre Study on Parasuicide. Acta Psychiatr Scand 1996; 93: 327-38.

[29] Parkin D, Stengel E. Incidence of suicidal attempts in an urban community. Br Med J 1965; 2: 133-8.

[30] Conwell Y. Suicide in elderly patients. In: Schneider LS, Reynolds III CF, Lebowitz B, Friedhoff AJ, editors. Diagnosis and treatment of depression in late life. Washington, DC: American Psychiatric Press. 1994; pp. 397-418.

[31] McIntosh JL, Santos JF. Methods of suicide by age: sex and race differences among the young and old. Int J Aging Hum Dev 1985; 22: 123-39.

[32] Bradvik L, Berglund M. Repetition and severity of suicide attempts across the life cycle: a comparison by age group between suicide victims and controls with severe depression. BMC Psychiatry 2009; 9: 62.

[33] Harwood DM, Hawton K, Hope T, Jacoby R. Suicide in older people: mode of death, demographic factors, and medical contact before death. Int J Geriatr Psychiatry 2000; 15: 736-43.

[34] Kelly S, Bunting J. Trends in suicide in England and Wales, 1982-96. Popul Trends 1998: 29-41

[35] Shields LB, Hunsaker DM, Hunsaker JC, 3rd. Suicide: a ten-year retrospective review of Kentucky medical examiner cases. J Forensic Sci 2005; 50: 613-7.

[36] Waern M, Runeson BS, Allebeck P, *et al.* Mental disorder in elderly suicides: a case-control study. Am J Psychiatry 2002; 159: 450-5.

[37] Erlangsen A, Zarit SH, Tu X, Conwell Y. Suicide among older psychiatric inpatients: an evidence-based study of a high-risk group. Am J Geriatr Psychiatry 2006; 14: 734-41.

[38] Ross RK, Bernstein L, Trent L, Henderson BE, Paganini-Hill A. A prospective study of risk factors for traumatic deaths in a retirement community. Prev Med 1990; 19: 323-34.

[39] Conwell Y, Duberstein PR, Cox C, Herrmann JH, Forbes NT, Caine ED. Relationships of age and axis I diagnoses in victims of completed suicide: a psychological autopsy study. Am J Psychiatry 1996; 153: 1001-8.

[40] Blow FC, Brockmann LM, Barry KL. Role of alcohol in late-life suicide. Alcohol Clin Exp Res 2004; 28: 48S-56S.

[41] Dombrovski AY, Butters MA, Reynolds CF 3rd, *et al.* Cognitive Performance in Suicidal Depressed Elderly: Preliminary Report. Am J Geriatr Psychiatry 2008; 16: 109-15.

[42] Heisel MJ, Links PS, Conn D, van Reekum R, Flett GL. Narcissistic personality and vulnerability to late-life suicidality. Am J Geriatr Psychiatry 2007; 15: 734-41.

[43] Baud P. Personality traits as intermediary phenotypes in suicidal behavior: genetic issues. Am J Med Genet C Semin Med Genet 2005; 133: 34-42.

[44] Beck AT, Steer RA, Beck JS, Newman CF. Hopelessness, depression, suicidal ideation, and clinical diagnosis of depression. Suicide Life Threat Behav 1993; 23: 139-45.

[45] Suominen K, Isometsa E, Lonnqvist J. Elderly suicide attempters with depression are often diagnosed only after the attempt. Int J Geriatr Psychiatry 2004; 19: 35-40.

[46] Henriksson MM, Marttunen MJ, Isometsa ET, *et al.* Mental disorders in elderly suicide. Int Psychogeriatr 1995; 7: 275-86.

[47] Batchelor IRC, Napier MB. Attempted suicide in old age. Br Med J 1953; 2: 1186-90.

[48] Clark DC. Narcissistic crises of aging and suicidal despair. Suicide Life Threat Behav 1993; 23: 21-6.

[49] Harwood D, Hawton K, Hope T, Jacoby R. Psychiatric disorder and personality factors associated with suicide in older people: a descriptive and case-control study. Int J Geriatr Psychiatry 2001; 16: 155-65.

[50] Duberstein PR, Conwell Y, Caine ED. Age differences in the personality characteristics of suicide completers: preliminary findings from a psychological autopsy study. Psychiatry 1994; 57: 213-24.

[51] Costa PT, McCrae RR. Revised NEO Personality Inventory and NEO Five Factor Inventory: professional manual. Odessa, FL: PAR; 1992.

[52] Amore M. La depressione nell'anziano. Clinica e Terapia. Torino: UTET; 2001.

[53] Lowenthal MF, Berkman PL. Aging and mental disorders in San Francisco. San Francisco: Jossey-Bass; 1967.

[54] Fasullo S. Valutazione degli aspetti psicosociali in geriatria. Psichiatria e Medicina 1990; 4: 30-8.

[55] Berlincioni V, Bezoari M. Il delirio nell'anziano. In: Petrella F, editor. Psicoterapia dell'anziano. Torino: Centro Scientifico Torinese, 1986.

[56] Agresti E. Quadro psicologico. Trattato di Psicogeriatria. Firenze: USES Edizioni Scientifiche; 1990.

[57] Hays JC, Landerman LR, George LK, *et al.* Social correlates of the dimensions of depression in the elderly. J Gerontol B Psychol Sci Soc Sci 1998; 53: P31-9.

[58] Carney SS, Rich CL, Burke PA, Fowler RC. Suicide over 60: the San Diego study. J Am Geriatr Soc 1994; 42: 174-80-

[59] Conwell Y, Rotenberg M, Caine ED. Completed suicide at age 50 and over. J Am Geriatr Soc 1990; 38: 640-4.

[60] Heikkinen ME, Lonnqvist JK. Recent life events in elderly suicide: a nationwide study in Finland. Int Psychogeriatr 1995; 7: 287-300.

[61] Harwood DM, Hawton K, Hope T, Harriss L, Jacoby R. Life problems and physical illness as risk factors for suicide in older people: a descriptive and case-control study. Psychol Med 2006; 36: 1265-74.

[62] Rubenowitz E, Waern M, Wilhelmson K, Allebeck P. Life events and psychosocial factors in elderly suicides--a case-control study. Psychol Med 2001; 31: 1193-202.

[63] Duberstein PR, Conwell Y, Conner KR, Eberly S, Caine ED. Suicide at 50 years of age and older: perceived physical illness, family discord and financial strain. Psychol Med 2004; 34: 137-46.

[64] Kraaij V, Arensman E, Spinhoven P. Negative life events and depression in elderly persons: a meta-analysis. J Gerontol B Psychol Sci Soc Sci 2002; 57: P87-94.

[65] Duberstein PR, Conwell Y, Conner KR, Eberly S, Evinger JS, Caine ED. Poor social integration and suicide: fact or artifact? A case-control study. Psychol Med 2004; 34: 1331-7.

[66] Erlangsen A, Jeune B, Bille-Brahe U, Vaupel JW. Loss of partner and suicide risks among oldest old: a population-based register study. Age Ageing 2004; 33: 378-83.

[67] van Grootheest DS, Beekman AT, Broese van Groenou MI, Deeg DJ. Sex differences in depression after widowhood. Do men suffer more? Soc Psychiatry Psychiatr Epidemiol 1999; 34: 391-8.

[68] Pompili M, Innamorati M, Masotti V, *et al.* Suicide in the elderly: a psychological autopsy study in a north Italy area (1994-2004). Am J Geriatr Psychiatry 2008; 16: 727-35.

[69] Rowe JL, Conwell Y, Schulberg HC, Bruce ML. Social support and suicidal ideation in older adults using home healthcare services. Am J Geriatr Psychiatry 2006; 14: 758-66.

[70] Beautrais AL. A case control study of suicide and attempted suicide in older adults. Suicide Life Threat Behav 2002; 32: 1-9.

[71] Juurlink DN, Herrmann N, Szalai JP, Kopp A, Redelmeier DA. Medical illness and the risk of suicide in the elderly. Arch Intern Med 2004; 164: 1179-84.

[72] Upadhyaya AK, Conwell Y, Duberstein PR, Denning D, Cox C. Attempted suicide in older depressed patients: effect of cognitive functioning. Am J Geriatr Psychiatry 1999; 7: 317-20.

[73] Conner KR, Duberstein PR, Beckman A, *et al.* Planning of suicide attempts among depressed inpatients ages 50 and over. J Affect Disord 2007; 97: 123-8.

[74] Hwang JP, Yang CH, Hong CJ, Lirng JF, Yang YM, Tsai SJ. Association of APOE genetic polymorphism with cognitive function and suicide history in geriatric depression. Dement Geriatr Cogn Disord 2006; 22: 334-8.

[75] Schmutte T, O'Connell M, Weiland M, Lawless S, Davidson L. Stemming the tide of suicide in older white men: a call to action. Am J Mens Health 2009; 3: 189-200.

[76] Conwell Y, Thompson C. Suicidal behavior in elders. Psychiatr Clin North Am 2008; 31: 333-56.

[77] Conwell Y, Olsen K, Caine ED, Flannery C. Suicide in later life: psychological autopsy findings. Int Psychogeriatr 1991; 3: 59-66.

[78] Diekstra RF, van Egmond M. Suicide and attempted suicide in general practice, 1979-1986. Acta Psychiatr Scand 1989; 79: 268-75.

[79] Frierson RL. Suicide attempts by the old and the very old. Arch Intern Med 1991; 151: 141-4

[80] Miller M. Geriatric suicide: the Arizona study. Gerontologist 1978; 18: 488-95.

[81] Murphy GE. The physician's responsibility for suicide. II. Errors of omission. Ann Intern Med 1975; 82: 305-9.

[82] Yesavage JA, Brink TL, Rose TL, *et al.* Development and validation of a geriatric depression screening scale: a preliminary report. J Psychiatr Res 1982; 17: 37-49,

[83] Radloff LS, Teri L. Use of the Center for Epidemiological Studies-Depression Scale with Older Adults. Clinical Gerontologist 1986; 5: 119-36.

[84] Conwell Y. Suicide in later life: a review and recommendations for prevention. Suicide Life Threat Behav 2001; 31 Suppl: 32-47.

[85] De Leo D, Carollo G, Dello Buono M. Lower suicide rates associated with a Tele-Help/Tele-Check service for the elderly at home. Am J Psychiatry 1995; 152: 632-4.

[86] Heisel MJ. Suicide and its prevention among older adults. Can J Psychiatry 2006; 51: 143-54.

INDEX

A

B

C

D

E

Maurizio Pompili (Ed)

www.ingramcontent.com/pod-product-compliance
Lightning Source LLC
LaVergne TN
LVHW070947210926
848482LV00002B/130